P9-DUA-601

Benching Jim Crow

SPORT AND SOCIETY

Series Editors
Benjamin G. Rader
Randy Roberts

*A list of books in the series
appears at the end of this book.*

To Cheryl and Jeff,
my favorite sports fans

Contents

Acknowledgments

When I began research for this study, I envisioned a modest volume that would examine the racial integration of college sports during the 1960s and 1970s in the state of Texas and maybe the Southeastern Conference. Little did I know that I would later decide, perhaps unwisely, to expand my geographical focus to include the entire South and to extend the time period of my study back into the late nineteenth century. As a result, the years spent researching and writing this manuscript have vastly exceeded my original projections, and I sometimes wondered if the project would ever end. Throughout this seemingly interminable journey, my wife and fellow historian, Cheryl English Martin, has suffered through far more conversations about famous teams, outstanding athletes, controversial coaches, racial confrontations, Confederate flags, and sporting traditions than any spouse should ever have to endure. Amazingly, she also repeatedly read and critiqued the manuscript with only a few complaints, improving it with numerous recommendations. For all of this, I shall be eternally grateful. Two other scholars who specialize in the social and cultural history of college sports, Patrick Miller and Andy Doyle, repeatedly offered me words of encouragement over the years. Both interrupted their own schedules to share their research findings with me and to comment on selected chapters, saving me from several factual errors and various lapses in judgment.

The anonymous readers of the book manuscript and of several earlier article manuscripts at times questioned my approach and my preliminary interpretations, pushing me to think more deeply about my subject. Peter Wallenstein, Jim Hodges, Randy Roberts, David Wiggins, Neil McMillen, Alton Bryant, Willie Ray Parish, Charles Wilson, and Charles Eagles were more than willing to exchange ideas with me about social change and southern sports, as did many other friends and colleagues, especially members of the North American Society for Sport History. Some of them will be almost as delighted as me to see the project end. Joan Paul long ago encouraged me to pursue the topic and shared survey data that she had collected about racial pioneers in the Southeastern Conference. John Coski called my attention to a remarkable editorial from the *Richmond Times-Dispatch* that offered a priceless defense of athletic segregation. In the final stages of manuscript preparation, Charles Ambler and Michael Lomax each offered a forum at which I could present my revised conclusions and receive one final round of suggestions. Richard Wentworth originally contacted me on behalf of the University of Illinois Press. His successor, Bill Regier, enthusiastically supported the project from our first conversation at a banquet in Lake Placid, New York, and politely nudged me toward its completion.

Several archivists went well beyond the call of duty to assist me in identifying materials in their collections. A special thanks for such help goes to Terry Birdwhistell of the University of Kentucky, Leon J. Stout of Pennsylvania State University, Diane Windham Shaw of Lafayette College, Gilbert Head of the University of Georgia, Dwayne Cox of Auburn University, and Rebecca Abromitis of the University of Pittsburgh. A very long list of additional university archivists and members of sports information (now often media relations) offices provided me with copies of personal correspondence, newspaper clippings, press releases, oral history transcripts, and miscellaneous materials. Since in this book I write in detail about athletic teams at nearly forty colleges and make some references to about sixty more, I obviously could not have completed this project without their help. My deepest thanks goes out to those kind folks at the following institutions: Arizona State University, Baylor University (Institute of Oral History), Beloit College, Boston College, Boston University, Butler University, Clemson University, Cornell University, Dartmouth College, DePauw College, Drake University, Duke University, Florida State University, Georgia Tech University, Harvard University, Indiana University, Iowa State University, Kansas State University, Louisiana State University, Loyola Marymount University, and Michigan State University.

Additional assistance came from archivists and sports information specialists at North Carolina State University, Northern Arizona University, Northwestern University, Ohio State University, Rice University, St. Mary's College of Texas, San Jose State University, Southern Methodist University, Syracuse University, Texas A&M University, Texas Christian University, Texas Tech University (Southwestern Collection), Tulane University, United States Naval Academy, University of Alabama, University of Arizona, University of California–Santa Barbara, University of Cincinnati, University of Houston, University of Iowa, University of Louisville, University of Maryland, University of Miami, University of Michigan, University of Mississippi, University of Missouri, University of Nebraska, University of North Carolina, University of Notre Dame, University of Oregon, University of Pennsylvania, University of South Carolina, University of Southern California, University of Tennessee, University of Texas at Arlington, University of Texas at Austin (Barker Texas History Center), University of Texas at El Paso, University of Texas–Pan American, University of Virginia, Vanderbilt University, Wabash College, and Wake Forest University.

Tim Peeler and Gerald Walton helped at the last minute with locating several key photographs for the book. Fred Woodward, David Perry, and John Fahey volunteered professional and technical advice. A grant from the National Endowment for the Humanities and a travel grant from UTEP's University Research Institute helped support my research. Finally, I owe an enormous debt to the coaches, administrators, fans, and especially the players who kindly agreed to be interviewed by me in person, over the telephone, or by written communication. Their names are listed in the essay on sources. This is their story, and I hope that they are not too disappointed by what they read.

Introduction

The Strange Athletic Career of Jim Crow

The problem of the Twentieth Century
is the problem of the color-line.

—W. E. B. Du Bois, 1903

Think of what a rich recruiting field the South would offer
if its own schools started seeking out good Negro athletes,
instead of losing them by default to the rest of the country.

—*Louisville Courier-Journal,* March 1963

In the first week of April 1989, Wade Houston left Louisville, Kentucky, and traveled to Knoxville, Tennessee, where he formally accepted the position of head basketball coach at the University of Tennessee (UT). Such coaching changes are a regular feature of the collegiate athletic scene, but Houston's hiring was anything but routine. In fact, it represented a historic racial milestone for the university, the Southeastern Conference, and the American South. In assuming his new job Houston became not only the first African American head coach at Tennessee but also the first black coach in any major sport during the fifty-five-year history of the SEC, the Deep South's premier athletic conference. This unprecedented development seemingly confirmed the continuing racial revolution in higher education in the South, once the country's most rigidly segregated region. It further suggested that racial concerns were now rapidly disappearing in the modern world of southern college sports. Subsequent events, however, soon disrupted this progressive narrative of unimpeded racial progress and briefly highlighted the continued presence of racial discrimination in the region.

Houston's personal journey epitomized the sweeping social transformation of the South since the mid-1960s. A Tennessee native, Houston had grown up in the industrial town of Alcoa some fifteen miles south of Knoxville and had rooted for the Volunteer athletic teams during his youth. The young basketball star graduated from Alcoa's all-black Hall High School in May 1962, at a time when no student from the school had ever attended the nearby University of Tennessee. In fact, the university had accepted its first three black undergraduates just one year earlier, and all of its athletic teams remained exclusively white. Ignored by UT coaches, Houston subsequently left the state to accept a basketball scholarship from the University of Louisville (UL), where he and two other recruits became that school's first African American basketball players.

In the spring of 1989, some twenty-seven years later, social conditions in Tennessee appeared to have changed dramatically. During Houston's absence from the state, the University of Tennessee had become a more diverse institution, and its athletic teams now included numerous African American players. Moreover, African American students, staff, and faculty constituted a noticeable though not large presence on campus. Houston's hiring rekindled excitement among Volunteer basketball fans and attracted positive comments across the wider community. The *Nashville Banner* even suggested in a somewhat apologetic headline that "Houston's UT welcome is 27 years late." Within a week, though, charges of continuing racism shattered this harmony. On April 5 a local newspaper reported that the prestigious Cherokee Country Club had refused to accept Houston as a member, even though the university subsidized several memberships at the facility for its senior athletic staff. Forced to confront an unpleasant reality that they had previously ignored, embarrassed school officials canceled all of their memberships at the Cherokee Country Club and transferred them to another local club that did not practice racial discrimination.[1]

The brief tempest over Houston's country club membership aptly captured the contradictions that marked southern college sports near the end of the twentieth century. From the 1890s into the 1960s southern universities, especially those that were located in the Deep South and belonged to the Southeastern Conference, had consistently maintained a policy of racial exclusion in the classroom. When the federal government finally forced these institutions to desegregate in the early 1960s, this historic breakthrough created the possibility that their intercollegiate athletic teams might voluntarily seek out black players. Influenced by continuing white hostility toward desegregation, most coaches did not immediately pursue this option. Eventually, though, between 1966 and 1973, SEC members gradually dropped their internal color lines and integrated their athletic teams. During the 1970s and 1980s these universities hired a small but expanding number of black assistant coaches. Now, in 1989, Tennessee and Wade Houston had shattered the glass ceiling that had blocked African Americans from advancing to head coaching positions. Yet in the midst of this celebration of color blindness in southern sports, the controversy over the Cherokee Country Club's restrictive membership policy temporarily derailed this triumphalist narrative of uninterrupted racial progress and demonstrated that racial discrimination, though greatly diminished, still remained an unresolved issue in the South, even within the supposedly enlightened world of higher education.

Since the early twentieth century college athletics had mattered enormously to southern white males, whether they were enrolled students, alumni, or sports fans who had never set foot inside a college classroom. University administrators eventually realized that their school teams constituted the best-known public symbols of their institutions and had become, in the words of one historian, "the ultimate public relations weapon." Football especially came to inspire such fanatical passion across Dixie that it constituted what Andrei S. Markovits termed a "hegemonic team sport," one that unites masses of citizens from a region or nation in a collective emotional embrace of triumph or defeat. This southern obsession with team sports dated from the late nineteenth century, when southerners first embraced competitive athletics. Football, an Americanized version of rugby, initially developed at male prep schools and men's colleges in the northeastern United States and then spread rapidly across the South in the 1890s through a process of cultural diffusion. Despite some initial opposition from administrators and faculty, as well as religious leaders, virtually every major southern university had established an official football team by 1900. Some of these institutions excluded women from enrollment, and at the others male students greatly outnumber their female classmates. In such a robust masculine environment young white men welcomed such a manly new sport with great enthusiasm and soon established competitive rivalries with neighboring institutions.[2]

By the end of the first decade of the new century southern universities had started to look beyond their region in search of enhanced competition and national recognition. Through intersectional contests against the more prestigious northern teams like Harvard, Yale, and Michigan, they sought not only to display their athletic skills but also to claim cultural recognition from their more esteemed counterparts in higher education. Southern teams consciously carried a deep sense of sectional pride and much more with them when they crossed the Mason-Dixon line to challenge Yankee teams. Intersectional games provided them with the opportunity to erase the stigma of an allegedly backward and defeated region by demonstrating the good health, robust manliness, technical skills, and cultural modernity of southern men. Most of these contests proved uneventful, but in a few cases heated confrontations over the color line did erupt. At the time there were only a tiny number of African American students at predominantly white northern universities. In fact, some northern colleges did not have even one black student enrolled. If African American males were present at a university, though, they sought to join their school's athletic teams just like their white counterparts. Thus, whenever a southern college scheduled a game against a northern opponent, there existed the possibility of a conflict over racial policy.[3]

Intersectional contests in the early 1900s developed at a time when a new, harsher system of white supremacy had tightened its grip on the South. The widespread political disfranchisement of African American voters, the prevalence of lynchings and other forms of racial violence, and the increasing adoption of state laws and municipal ordinances separating black and white residents in public accommodations marked the "nadir" of African American rights in the postemancipation era. Segregation, and the color line that delineated its boundaries, restricted public spaces by reserving certain zones only for whites and excluding African Americans. Railroads, streetcars, public schools, restaurants, and movie theaters were just some of the public sites helping construct what Grace Elizabeth Hale has termed "the culture of segregation." Athletic arenas offered additional racialized spaces where a new emphasis on "whiteness" could be performed for white spectators, free from any participation by African Americans. During the latter half of the nineteenth century limited athletic competition between black and white southerners had been tolerated, primarily in boxing, but this practice disappeared by the start of the new century, as whites tightened the color line. The *Richmond Times* summed up the new status quo in January 1900 when it pronounced, "God Almighty drew the color line, and it cannot be obliterated. The negro must stay on his side of the line, and the white man must stay on his side."[4]

White southerners automatically applied these new, more rigid racial values to the world of college athletics. However, their beliefs clashed with the egalitarian ethos of the amateur code of competition developed by New England schools. When playing northern colleges white southerners insisted that the color line must always be drawn, regardless of a specific game's geographical location. To them, athletic contests should be understood primarily as a social activity. If a southern team were to compete on the football field or on the basketball court against an African American, such an encounter would represent "social equality," thereby violating the protected white space that segregation had created and upsetting the "natural" racial hierarchy of the region. Moreover, the white players involved would have dishonored themselves and the South by their association, brief though it might have been, with a member of an inferior race. The *Richmond Times-Dispatch* captured this ideology in a spirited 1923 editorial that appeared after Washington and Lee College of Virginia had refused to take the field for a football game in Pennsylvania, because the home team included one black player: "Social equality has not been extended the negro here. . . . There would not be the slightest difference in playing football with him and in sitting down with him at a formal dinner or meeting him for a game of golf on the country club links. College sports are purely social. And social distinctions necessarily are arbitrary."[5]

At the same time, the social and cultural values accompanying the development of football in the northeastern United States formulated an egalitarian athletic creed. This ideology assumed equal access to a level playing field, required "fair play" from all participants, and insisted that character, not raw talent or social status, would ultimately prevail in athletic contests. Such values were not always honored in practice, of course, as gamesmanship often trumped sportsmanship in the heat of competition. Moreover, racial discrimination in sports existed not just in the South but all over the nation. In the early 1900s some northern colleges did not permit African Americans to enroll, others refused to allow them to participate in athletics, and a mixture of these schools would not permit their teams to play against African Americans. In 1903 and again in 1904, for example, Wabash College of Indiana had several football games canceled by its opponents because the Wabash squad included one African American each year. The most persistent case of northern bias came from the Big Ten Conference. Although league members had long permitted African Americans to participate in football, these same schools totally excluded black players from varsity basketball until 1944 and did not make serious efforts to recruit black high school stars until the early 1950s. Nonetheless, the ideology of college sports insisted, at least in theory if not always in practice, that what truly mattered in athletic competition was individual character and merit, not outside social considerations. The *New York Times* reaffirmed this idealized view of athletic competition in 1959, when the newspaper called for eliminating the color line in athletics at southern schools: "Sport . . . puts no artificial barriers as race or religion in the way of performance. What counts and what matters is what the given individual can do."[6]

The conflict between the southern white policy of racial exclusion and the American athletic creed of equality on the playing fields shaped both intersectional competition and internal policy at southern universities for the first seven decades of the twentieth century. The ebb and flow of this protracted struggle to control racial policy for southern and American college athletics can be divided into four somewhat distinct chronological stages. In the first era, lasting roughly from 1890 through the early 1930s, white southerners were able to dictate national policy concerning intersectional games. As southern teams commenced intersectional competition in the early 1900s, they often lacked specific information about their northern opponents and experienced a few unexpected confrontations over black participation. In order to avoid any racial surprises on game day, these schools developed the so-called gentleman's agreement. According to this informal but widely understood policy, nonsouthern colleges would automatically bench any black player on their roster when playing a southern team, regardless of the game's location, in deference to the southerners' sensitivity concerning interracial contact. Since southern schools did not possess the athletic or cultural clout within higher education to impose this policy unilaterally, the practice of racial exclusion required northern complicity for its implementation. Until the 1940s many northern universities were quite willing to make this concession in order to gain the "gate receipts and glory" that they received from high-profile intersectional games. Such a concession to expediency also exposed the marginal status of African American students on northern campuses.[7]

In the second period of the athletic color line's history, which lasted from the early 1930s through about 1950, northern schools increasingly challenged the use of the gentleman's agreement for games staged in the North. Beginning in 1936 a few southern teams opportunistically abandoned racial exclusion for football contests held outside the South, in order to seek a higher national ranking, receive a generous paycheck, or audition for a coveted invitation to the Rose Bowl. After the end of World War II the gentleman's agreement increasingly came under ideological attack as a denial of the basic democratic values for which the recent war had been fought. By the early 1950s liberal students and administrators, sometimes led by World War II veterans, had won the fight for "democracy on the playing fields" in the North.

The third era of contested racial policy, for athletic events staged within the South, lasted from the late 1940s through the mid-1960s. Northern universities now turned the tables on southern schools and demanded that they agree to drop all racial restrictions on northern teams for games held in the South or forfeit the profits and prestige that accompanied these contests. Most southern universities gradually yielded to such pressure, although teams from Alabama and Mississippi resisted for a while longer, due to political pressures from segregationist politicians. Regardless of their position on intersectional contests, almost all major southern colleges continued to field all-white teams through at least the mid-1960s, if not later. The initial enrollment of a few African Americans as undergraduate students during this period, often through federal pressure, did not immediately alter this policy. Thus, the protected white space of the football field and the basketball court continued to remain relatively safe from the intrusion of African Americans for up to a decade after the initial desegregation of southern universities.

In the fourth era, from the mid-1960s through 1974, southern teams at last recruited their first African American players. Athletic integration often represented the final racial frontier in the transition from the token desegregation of college classrooms to the full integration of all campus activities. The delay in recruiting African American athletes particularly upset black students, who felt that participation on school football and basketball teams was essential if they were ever to be regarded as full-fledged members of the university community. Inquiries from the United States Office of Education concerning discrimination by institutions that received federal funds also helped motivate administrators to abandon racial restrictions in athletics. By 1980 a substantial number of African Americans were wearing their school colors on the gridiron and especially on the basketball court, and black stars now helped lead their teams to victory in front of tens of thousands of cheering white fans. Full athletic integration had been achieved, and Jim Crow had been banished to the sidelines and permanently benched.

The main purpose of this book is to describe and analyze the shifting racial policies and practices of athletic programs at historically white southern universities, from 1890 through 1980. I have used the phrase *historically white* because it conveniently parallels the commonly used term *historically black colleges and universities,* or HBCUs. Technically, though, as Peter Wallenstein has emphasized, these white schools might more accurately be labeled "nonblack colleges," since Native Americans, Asian Americans, and Mexican Americans were legally permitted to enroll there and normally allowed to participate in athletics. Only African Americans were singled out for complete exclusion. Thus, for example, Art Matsu, a Japanese American, could not only enroll at the College of William and Mary in the mid-1920s but also play quarterback and punt for the "Indians." Tackle Joe Guyon, a Chippewa who spent two years on the Carlisle Indian School team, won All-American honors as an offensive tackle for Georgia Tech in 1918. Several southern white colleges including Mississippi State University (MSU) also scheduled football contests against the Native American teams from Carlisle and Haskell Institute. Ironically, then, it was permissible for southern white males to play football on a Saturday afternoon against eleven American Indians without endangering their whiteness, their masculinity, or their honor, but not against one solitary African American! Despite the possible linguistic imprecision, I have continued to use *historically white* or simply *white* because these are the terms that are most commonly understood by the general public and by scholars.[8]

In researching the Jim Crow policies of southern universities, I have attempted to evaluate the significant role that college athletics played in reinforcing the traditional social structure and racial hierarchy of the South through the 1960s. I have also tried to document the important contributions that sports eventually made to dismantling this racial hierarchy and transforming southern universities and the larger region, from the mid-1960s to 1980. Prior to the sixties southern universities did not enjoy an isolated ivory-tower existence within Dixie. Instead, they mostly remained in "cultural captivity" and fully supported the region's white supremacist values concerning black exclusion from such white spaces as the classroom, the gridiron, and the basketball court. For a brief period in the early 1950s, however, it appeared that southern white schools were leading a modest liberalizing trend in race relations by accepting an expanding number of integrated intersectional games, even at home. However, this fragile racial moderation was immediately overwhelmed by the white backlash that followed the United States Supreme Court's *Brown v. Board of Education* ruling in 1954, which declared public school segregation to be unconstitutional. Following the *Brown* decision, southern colleges returned to their passive role and rarely moved ahead of mainstream white public opinion in their respective states. As segregationists lost strength in the 1960s, though, southern colleges rejoined the national sporting community by resuming intersectional games and eventually recruiting African Americans for their own teams.

A secondary goal of this book is to explain the social and cultural meaning that athletic integration provided to southern colleges and their surrounding communities and states. Many black liberals and sports fans had long hoped that sports integration would serve as an inspirational model for racial progress beyond the athletic arena. As a writer in *The Crisis* hopefully declared in 1938, "Fair play in sports leads to fair play in life." Historian Patrick B. Miller has labeled this concept "muscular assimilationism," while other scholars have used the phrase "liberal integrationism." As of 1980 it seemed that racial integration in college sports had indeed fostered a more tolerant attitude in the South. By the 1990s, though, racial liberals began to make fewer claims for sports' ability to significantly influence the existing social structure. The continuation of such traditional problems as excessive commercialization, academic dishonesty, and academic underperformance also helped modify optimism about the lessons that sports taught to the general community. On the other hand, integrated teams led by black stars did provide rallying points for black and white southerners seeking racial reconciliation and created shared symbols that could unite a previously divided population. Overall, the impact of athletic integration on racial practices off campus was less than racial liberals had hoped for. This disappointment, as well as despair about the prospects for social and economic equality in the United States, has caused many scholars to unnecessarily denigrate the positive achievements of athletic integration. Nevertheless, this historic shift from rigid segregation to full inclusion represents an important but sometimes overlooked accomplishment of the civil rights era.[9]

This volume's narrative starts with the formation of organized football programs around 1890 and continues through the emergence of fully integrated football and basketball teams featuring black stars by 1980. I have focused primarily on the athletic contests themselves, specific efforts to exclude African American players, the actual integration of individual southern teams, and the campus and public discourse over racial policy for athletics. University archives and student newspapers have therefore provided essential material for my research. Of course, the integration of college athletic programs cannot be separated from the larger issue of university desegregation in the South. Somewhat surprisingly, no scholar has yet produced a comprehensive monograph that documents integration across the entire region. However, Melissa Kean has recently published an important comparative study of desegregation at five prominent private universities, while Amilcar Shabazz has authored an important book on the African American struggle for educational equality at public universities in Texas. To the extent possible, I have tried to place my account of athletic integration within the context of each university's geographical location, social setting, and political environment.[10]

This book is the first comprehensive monograph to describe the process of athletic integration at the South's historically white colleges and universities and to analyze the larger role that college athletics played in the eventual racial transformation of the region.[11] As such, the study weaves together both sport history and southern history. It is also relevant to the history of higher education and to African American history. Southern college sports offer a particularly valuable window through which to observe the evolution of racial practices and their intellectual rationalizations over a ninety-year period. Until the expansion of professional sports in the 1960s, college athletics represented the pinnacle of athletic achievement in the region and attracted disproportionate public attention. Hence, college basketball and especially football spectacles provided an important public display of southern whiteness and masculinity, reinforcing as "natural" the existing racial structure and the exclusion of African Americans. The public discourse over these racial practices likewise provides a rich cultural text through which one can attempt to interpret the clash of fundamental values between white supremacy, national commercialized sporting culture, the competitive desire to win games, and the amateur creed of equal competition on a level playing field. The tenacity with which white southerners resisted integrated competition prior to the 1950s and the recruitment of black athletes after the initial desegregation of southern universities demonstrates that college sports played an important role in the maintenance of racialized space and the public culture of segregation.

In telling this story, I have investigated the actual experiences of athletic teams and the university policies that governed them at nearly forty colleges, including member institutions from the three major conferences of the 1960s and 1970s (the Atlantic Coast Conference [ACC], the now defunct Southwest Conference [SWC], and the Southeastern Conference), the most important southern independents, and their frequent northern opponents. I have focused on these elite teams because they represented the most influential universities in the region, because the media and sports fans followed their games extensively, and because they frequently served as models for public policy and cultural representation within the region. In other words, these elite institutions and their teams dominated public discourse concerning racial policy in college athletics across Dixie. Consequently, I have not included much information about racial policies at smaller institutions and junior colleges (JCs). The relatively unexplored racial struggles at such institutions were important to their communities, but their influence on broader regional policy was modest. Whenever possible, I have also attempted to highlight the experiences of those pioneering African American athletes who found themselves at the center of controversies over the color line. This has not always been an easy task, since the mainstream press generally slighted or ignored their experiences. Fortunately, black newspapers and oral history interviews have proved extremely fruitful in identifying such individuals and in re-creating at least some of their experiences. Their stories reveal the personal side and the emotional cost of athletic integration. I have also devoted some attention to the heated campus debates that athletic integration unleashed over the use of such traditional southern symbols as the Confederate battle flag and the song "Dixie" at athletic events, especially football games.[12]

Because of space restrictions, I have not attempted to tell the full story of athletics at historically black colleges and universities in the South. African American students at these schools embraced football and basketball with the same enthusiasm as their white counterparts, eventually developing a separate and parallel sporting culture while adding their own cultural flourishes. For the most part, I have included their experiences only when they illuminate particular aspects of the broader structure and practices of American college sports. Their history is important, but that is a story for other authors to tell.[13] I have also not attempted to produce a history of competitive sports for southern college women. This is because women's physical and sporting activities existed in their own separate sphere and followed a different trajectory from that of the highly commercialized, mass-spectacle form of men's athletics, at least into the 1980s. The famous Title IX amendment of the Educational Amendments Act of 1972 proved to be a watershed for women's sports, but the competitive athletic programs for women that were subsequently established in the South followed the new male model of integrated competition already in place by 1975. Furthermore, the Southeastern Conference did not even hold its first championship in a women's sport until 1976, after the color line had collapsed. The National Collegiate Athletic Association (NCAA) waited even longer, sponsoring its first Division I national championships in women's basketball, volleyball, and other sports during the 1981–82 school year.[14]

In exploring the racial politics of big-time southern college sports, this book seeks to provide a balanced and nuanced account that avoids both the perils of celebratory history as well as those of excessive cynicism. In order to make my story as coherent as possible, I have provided in the first three chapters a chronological narrative of the rise and fall of the gentleman's agreement in college sports, from the late nineteenth century through the mid-1960s. Beginning with chapter 4, I shift to a conference-by-conference approach in order to describe in detail the process of athletic integration on specific campuses and the reasons behind institutional and subregional variations. Chapter 1 specifically covers the period from 1890 to 1929. It explains how, after initial conflict with northern teams over the use of African American players, southern schools established racial exclusion as the norm for intersectional competition and developed the so-called gentleman's agreement to cloak and implement this white supremacist policy. Chapter 2 examines the period from 1929 to 1945, during which the gentleman's agreement still dominated intersectional competition. In the latter half of the 1930s, though, a few southern schools opportunistically abandoned racial exclusion for games held in the North, and the special circumstances of World War II encouraged further toleration of interracial athletic activities.

Chapter 3 describes the widespread northern opposition to racial exclusion that emerged after World War II, the growing acceptance of integrated games by southern colleges if played outside the South, and the so-called massive-resistance backlash after the *Brown v. Board of Education* ruling in 1954. By the mid-1960s, though, all major southern universities had enrolled black students, setting off a debate over whether African Americans would be permitted to participate in the protected white space of college athletics. Chapter 4 offers a case study of Texas Western College (TWC) in El Paso, which was the first major white university in an ex-Confederate state to recruit African Americans extensively in basketball and football. By opportunistically utilizing black players to strengthen its athletic teams, Texas Western (now the University of Texas at El Paso [UTEP]) gained regional and national recognition, especially after winning the NCAA basketball championship in 1966.

Chapters 5 and 6 examine the racial patterns found in the Atlantic Coast Conference, the first of the three major southern conferences to integrate its football and basketball programs. More extensive interaction with northern schools, especially in basketball, and a desire to compete nationally against the best teams regardless of their racial composition were the keys to the ACC's flexibility. Chapter 7 examines the Southwest Conference, which after 1925 consisted of teams from the states of Texas and Arkansas. Although segregation did not exercise quite as strong a grip on this area as it did elsewhere in the Lower South, athletic officials at most SWC schools hesitated to break the color line, reflecting a southern rather than a western identity for their athletic culture. Chapters 8 and 9 examine basketball and football in the Southeastern Conference, which represented the "final citadel of segregation" in college athletics. These two chapters recount the vigorous opposition to integration of both sports found at several conference schools, especially those located in the state of Mississippi, and the final collapse of this resistance.

The final chapter offers a series of conclusions about the accomplishments and limitations of athletic integration. It critiques the historical memory of many white southern sports fans and college administrators that "sports integration has been the single greatest contributor to racial progress and development in the South" and contrasts this view with the more pessimistic conclusion of Patrick Miller that "the principal sites of racial change lay beyond the playing fields." It also cautions that the triumph of liberal integrationism by 1980 did not eliminate all racial problems within southern college athletics and that numerous issues continue to challenge big-time sports. In short, the football field and the basketball court remained contested terrain even after the demise of their protected white space, providing cultural sites in which black and white southerners could find a variety of meanings concerning racial values in their society.[15]

Benching Jim Crow

1

White Supremacy and American College Sports

The Rise of the Gentleman's Agreement, 1890–1929

God Almighty drew the color line, and it cannot be obliterated. The negro must stay on his side of the line, and the white man must stay on his side.

—*Richmond Times,* January 12, 1900

Having been born and educated in the South, to me it is unthinkable that such a typically southern school as Georgia would condescend to enter into any athletic contest against a team on which a negro plays.

—A white southerner, November 1929

During the second half of the nineteenth century, male students at American colleges unleashed a great passion for competitive sports. Once derided as weak, effete, upper-class dilettantes, these young men now embraced physical culture with a vengeance, eventually even rivaling students at British private schools in their enthusiasm for "manly" pursuits. Individually and collectively, American students participated in a wide variety of athletic activities, including cricket, baseball, boxing, wrestling, several forms of football, track and field, sailing, crew, bowling, and ice skating. At first, competition remained mostly of an intramural nature, but enthusiastic students soon formed school teams in order to compete against neighboring institutions. Regional play in turn led to national competition, as successful squads sought out more challenging matches against top teams from other parts of the country.

As limited intersectional competition between southern and northern colleges developed in the 1890s, the participating schools sometimes disagreed over rules and policies, including the racial composition of the Yankee teams. By tradition and law, higher education was segregated in the South, and state legislatures there were in the process of constructing an elaborate Jim Crow code that separated whites and blacks in most areas of public life. Teams from white universities thus rejected any competition against black players. After a period of conflict that lasted until World War I, white southerners forced northern schools to accept "southern rules" for intersectional play, thus barring African American athletes from such competition. The so-called gentleman's agreement, whereby northern schools agreed to withhold automatically any black player on their rosters from a match against a southern white squad, enforced this policy of racial exclusion. This unwritten agreement reigned supreme in intersectional competition until the end of the 1920s, when a few northern students and sportswriters challenged the policy. Such potential conflict lay far in the future, though, when students in the northeastern United States first discovered the joy of sports in the mid-nineteenth century.

The Rise of Intercollegiate Sports

College faculty and administrators initially refused to bestow official recognition upon school athletic teams, fearing that such activities would distract participants from their studies. Persistent student pressure eventually forced them to back down and sanction such competition. The first organized sport to receive institutional support and attract wide public interest was crew, which students imported from England. During the 1850s the famous Harvard–Yale race and larger collegiate regattas sometimes drew twenty thousand spectators or more. A decade later baseball suddenly exploded across college campuses after the end of the Civil War. By the mid-1870s official school teams could be formed in five approved sports: crew, baseball, football, cricket, and track and field. In the early 1900s the sport of basketball, invented in 1891 by physical educator James A. Naismith, gradually gained popularity in urban areas and on northeastern campuses.[1]

Faced with the growing enthusiasm for sports, college administrators eventually reversed their previous skepticism and encouraged student participation in athletics. Some of them hoped that football would contradict the popular stereotype that male college students "were sissified, effeminate souls who shunned physical challenges and cowered behind their books." Presidents and professors also acknowledged the genuine need for recreational outlets and hoped that team sports would represent an improvement over the individual mischief and general mayhem often displayed by rowdy students in the late 1700s and early 1800s. As one college president warned, "There should be some virile game for American lads to play in the autumn months in our colleges, or else their youth and energy [will] flow in directions less good." Supporters of the new physical culture touted its many benefits, including healthy exercise for the body and the development of what Theodore Roosevelt termed "the more virile virtues." For example, President Edwin Alderman of Tulane University stated that he would "rather see a boy of mine on the rush line, fighting for his team, than on the sideline, smoking a cigarette," while President John Franklin Crowell of Trinity College (now Duke University) asserted that football would attract male undergraduates away from "sensual indulgence, mollycoddling, and gambling, to say nothing about drinking and carousing." Furthermore, football provided a practical education in those character traits necessary for success in an increasingly commercialized society. As Yale coach Walter Camp, the "father" of American football, contended, the sport performed a great service in teaching college men "those attributes which business desires and demands." Team sports also provided a social focus for the campus and united the entire university community behind a shared manly enterprise. Finally, on a more basic level, the violent nature of football clearly aroused the passions of players, students, and spectators alike. As one exuberant South Carolina fan candidly confessed in 1892, "It beats baseball all to pieces for excitement."[2]

Elite private men's colleges in the northeastern United States, especially the "big three" of Harvard, Yale, and Princeton, pioneered in the construction of this new athletic culture. Through a process of cultural diffusion, southern and midwestern students eventually embraced the northeastern model of intercollegiate athletics. Initially, football spread from campus to campus without institutional assistance, as enthusiastic young men spontaneously formed their own teams and managed their own affairs. As a result, the rules and regulations for the game varied widely. Most of these differences fell into two basic categories concerning fundamental principles. The first pattern of play was modeled after English football or soccer, which emphasized use of the feet and prohibited handling the ball. The second variation mostly followed the rules for rugby and permitted participants to pick up the ball and carry it forward. It was this Americanized version of English rugby that eventually triumphed on campus and came to be known simply as "football." In November 1869 Rutgers and Princeton played the first intercollegiate football game, apparently under soccer-style regulations, with Rutgers claiming a 6–4 victory. In the fall of 1875 Harvard defeated Yale in the first formal intercollegiate match held under the new Americanized rules. The new style of play quickly captured the hearts of male students, and within only a few years the new sport had spread to virtually every northeastern college.[3]

College Football Invades Dixie

White college students in Dixie began experimenting with the new athletic fad in the late 1870s and early 1880s. Football arrived first in the Upper South because of the area's social and cultural interaction with the North, then expanded into the Southeast and eventually on to the more sparsely populated Southwest. As early as 1877, Washington and Lee College students and Virginia Military Institute cadets had informally played against each other in an early version of the evolving game. Responding in 1888 to continued student pressure, four southern colleges—the University of North Carolina (UNC), Wake Forest College, Trinity College, and the University of Virginia (UVa)—became the first institutions in the region to authorize intercollegiate football teams. What was apparently the first officially sanctioned college football game played in the ex-Confederate South took place on October 18, 1888, at Raleigh, North Carolina, when an uncertain Wake Forest squad defeated an equally confused University of North Carolina team by a score of 6–4. Football fever quickly spread to other schools in the Upper South. By 1892 Washington and Lee, Randolph-Macon, Virginia Military Institute, the University of Maryland (UM), North Carolina State, the University of the South (Sewanee), as well as several public colleges in Kentucky were all fielding intercollegiate teams. In the Lower South, the University of Georgia (UGA) and Mercer College staged the first official game in January 1892. Also fielding their first teams that year were the University of Alabama (UA), Georgia Tech, and Auburn.[4]

Despite male students' enthusiasm for football, the sport's rapid advance was not completely uncontested. The remarkable popularity that football later enjoyed in Dixie has obliterated any popular memory of the persistent doubts voiced by earlier critics. Cultural nationalists as well as many evangelical southern ministers initially greeted the new game with suspicion and reproach. As Andrew Doyle has pointed out, members of both groups "interpreted the arrival of football in the South as one more chapter in the long surrender of southern values after Appomattox." Cultural conservatives disliked the sport's Yankee roots and modernist values, while southern evangelicals condemned most "worldly amusements" including sports. Evangelicals believed that football, like boxing, appealed to the "lower" instincts in human beings and created a carnival atmosphere at the games. As one southern religious magazine declared, "No other form of athletics stirs the animal spirit as does football. There is an excitement about it that carries away both players and spectators." This fear over the morality and safety of college students was succinctly captured in a resolution adopted by the North Carolina Methodist Conference, which denounced football as "dangerous to the health, life, and morals of our young men." Throughout the 1890s, and for two decades thereafter, southern evangelical leaders continued their crusade against the corrupting influence of football.[5]

As football gained greater popularity and wider cultural acceptance off campus, administrators, faculty, students, and even alumni all engaged in a prolonged power struggle to control and regulate the sport. At first students enjoyed considerable autonomy, but administrators eventually enforced their institutional authority. College alumni also exerted some influence over athletic policy, especially as universities turned to them for financial assistance. Since each college set its own standards, the issue of player eligibility proved to be particularly contentious, since some teams recruited nonstudents in order to win games. One angry University of Georgia fan sarcastically described the rival 1893 team from Georgia Tech as a "heterogeneous collection of Atlanta residents, a United States Army surgeon, a medical student, a lawyer, and an insurance agent among them, with here and there a student of Georgia's School of Technology thrown in to give the mixture a Technological flavor." In order to standardize rules and procedures, universities formed regional athletic conferences. In December 1894 the two Georgia colleges, Alabama, and the University of the South joined with Johns Hopkins, Vanderbilt, and the University of North Carolina to form the Southern Intercollegiate Athletic Association, the first sports conference in Dixie. More than a dozen additional colleges soon joined the new organization. Through the use of sanctions the SIAA eliminated a few of the more egregious practices of the era. For example, the organization required Tulane University to sit out the 1897 football season because of its widespread use of ineligible players. Nonetheless, rule violations remained endemic to the game.[6]

During the course of the 1890s football's mounting injury toll inspired additional opposition to the game. The growing use of mass running plays, especially the flying wedge, created larger pileups and increased the number of serious injuries. Public concern over this alarming trend strengthened religious objections to the sport, an important influence in a region where nearly one-half of all colleges were church related. One Baptist journalist in Mississippi denounced football as a "murderous" activity, "more brutal that a bull-fight, more reprehensible than a prize-fight, and more deadly than modern warfare." During the decade at least six major southern colleges, including the University of North Carolina and the University of Alabama, discontinued football for at least one season. Wake Forest, a Baptist institution, and Trinity College, a Methodist school, took even more vigorous action. In October 1895 the Wake Forest faculty voted to abolish football permanently, a policy that lasted for twelve years. Not to be outdone by the Baptists, North Carolina Methodists drove off the pro-football president of Trinity and prohibited the sport from 1895 until 1920. As the school's new anti-football president, John Kilgo, explained, the brutal game was "unfit to be played by young men at college, especially at a Christian college."[7]

Although these scattered challenges to football slowed the sport's growing ascendancy, three major crises during the period from 1897 to 1909 presented an even greater threat to the game's future. The regional outcry over the shocking death of a southern player in 1897, the larger national crisis of 1905–6 over violent play, and the death of another southern player in 1909 forced virtually every southern university to rethink its institutional commitment to football.

During an October 1897 contest in Atlanta against the University of Virginia, Georgia linebacker Richard Von Gammon attempted to stop a massed running play and received a serious head injury in the ensuing pileup. Von Gammon died the next day, and his death inspired numerous calls across the Southeast for eliminating the sport. In Athens, the home of the University of Georgia, the local newspaper warned that no longer could "this modern-day dangerous, brutal, and savage football contest be justified or excused." Responding to the incidents, the Georgia legislature overwhelmingly approved a bill outlawing football at state-supported colleges. But Georgia professor Charles H. Herty convinced Von Gammon's mother to write a touching letter to Governor W. Y. Atkinson, urging him not to let her son's tragic death discredit such a manly sport. Heeding her plea, Atkinson vetoed the bill, and the movement to ban football gradually lost its momentum. Nonetheless, the narrowness of the sport's political victory demonstrated that football had not yet fully established its cultural hegemony over the southern public.[8]

In 1905 progressive journalists published several exposés illuminating football's darker side and unexpectedly thrusting the sport into the national spotlight. These accounts focused on continued violent play and widespread ethical improprieties, including improper financial aid to athletes, secret slush funds, academic fraud, and use of ineligible players. During the fall of 1905 eighteen high school and college players reportedly suffered fatal injuries, touching off a public crisis and inspiring intervention by President Theodore Roosevelt. Roosevelt and other football supporters worried that staunch opponents of the game, such as President Nicholas Murray Butler of Columbia University, would exploit the wave of injuries in order to eliminate the sport. Their fears were well justified. Butler soon abolished football at his school, and several nonsouthern colleges, including Northwestern, Stanford, and the University of California, joined Columbia in dropping the game. In the South several colleges discontinued football. In 1906 the Board of Trustees at Baylor University, a Baptist institution, accepted the recommendation of President Samuel Palmer Brooks and also voted to abolish football. In response, disappointed students staged a mock funeral on the school's main quadrangle, burying an actual football and erecting a gravestone over it which read:

> Long may his ashes rest;
> He died by vote of the trustees,
> And not by our request.[9]

Proponents of football responded to the crisis with passionate reaffirmations of its cultural value and specific suggestions to improve the game's safety. From the White House, President Roosevelt personally pressured educators to save the character-building game by making it both safe and honest. In a

series of meetings held in late 1905 and early 1906, reformers took several significant steps. First they established the sport's first national governing body,
the Intercollegiate Athletic Association, which later changed its name to the
National Collegiate Athletic Association. Next they pressured two separate rules
committees into joint discussions, which eventually led to several key changes
reducing violent play. The most important new rules included legalizing the
forward pass, creating a neutral zone between the teams at the line of scrimmage, requiring ten yards instead of five for a first down, and expanding the
officiating crew to four persons.[10]

Although these changes came too late to head off defections by such prominent
schools as Columbia and Stanford, the reforms were sufficient to reassure the
general public that the sport was now safe. Students at several southern colleges
immediately renewed their campaign to win back official sanction for football. In
June 1907 trustees at Baylor University, noting that "many objectionable features
of the game have been eliminated," approved a request by the school's president
to reestablish football. In an even more significant reversal, Wake Forest trustees
voted in May 1908 to resume football competition after a twelve-year absence.
Still, the strength of the initial attack on the sport illustrated the continuing
public resistance to full acceptance of big-time football in Dixie. Football had
been badly bloodied by the crisis, but its future now looked secure.[11]

The untimely deaths of three more young men in the fall of 1909 provoked
yet another national debate over the sport. In November 1909 Virginia halfback
Archer Christian suffered a fatal concussion in a game against Georgetown
University. Players at the U.S. Naval Academy and the U.S. Military Academy
also died from injuries suffered that fall. These three incidents inspired renewed attacks on football. Immediately following Archer Christian's death,
the Georgetown faculty and administration voted to discontinue the sport. In
Virginia several religious leaders called for the sport's abolition, prompting one
legislator to introduce a bill to outlaw the game. At the University of Virginia,
President Edwin Alderman, who passionately believed that football promoted
manly virtues, countered by organizing a group of southern college presidents
to lobby for further rule changes. Outmaneuvering conservatives who desired
only token concessions and radicals who wanted to eliminate the sport entirely,
Alderman and other reform-minded educators again pressured the NCAA rules
committee into action.[12]

In May 1910 the committee approved several additional rule changes in order
to further reduce dangerous play. These included requiring seven men on the
line of scrimmage, prohibiting teammates from pushing the ball carrier forward, and reducing the penalty for an incomplete forward pass. Even more
so than in 1906, these popular reforms undercut football's fiercest opponents
and once again reassured the general public that the sport was under control.

Religious conservatives would continue to issue their jeremiads against the evils of organized sports for another decade, but not even evangelical Protestantism could now derail the triumphal march of football across Dixie. Over the following years the sport further expanded its cultural dominance, as college administrators discovered that successful teams excited thousands of fans who lacked any previous ties to higher education and could transform them into loyal supporters of individual universities. Big-time football thus helped southern colleges develop large off-campus constituencies and proved to be "the ultimate public relations weapon."[13]

African Americans and Football

The passion for football displayed by white students at southern colleges was soon replicated at many of the region's black institutions. During the 1890s the more established black colleges began fielding their own school teams. African American young men proved to be just as enthusiastic about football as their white counterparts, demonstrating both the sport's universal appeal and its spreading cultural hegemony. The first formal intercollegiate game played between black colleges took place in December 1892 at Salisbury, North Carolina, where Biddle University (now Johnson C. Smith College) defeated Livingstone College by a score of 4–0. Other black colleges soon imitated these pioneers. As part of Emancipation Day activities on January 1, 1894, Atlanta University and Tuskegee Institute began an annual football series that continued for the next three decades. Later that same year, Howard University and Lincoln University held the inaugural match in their hotly contested series, which soon became the most widely followed black college rivalry. By 1901 black college football had spread west to the state of Texas, where Wiley College in Marshall boasted that "athletic sports are not only allowed, but encouraged."[14]

Football fulfilled the same social needs for African American students as it did for whites, and the sport also produced many of the same institutional problems and abuses. In the early years of black college football, there were numerous arguments over ineligible players, violent play, and neglect of academics, as well as persistent problems within adequate funding. As more and more schools fielded teams after 1900, African American institutions increasingly saw the need for an organization that would help standardize and regulate their athletic competition. Since the NCAA excluded them from membership, a group of black colleges, mostly in the Upper South, joined together in 1912 to form the Colored Intercollegiate Athletic Association, the first African American sports conference. Several similar regional conferences were eventually formed in other sections of the South. The ensuing intercollegiate competition produced popular teams, respected coaches, and star players. The Saturday football game quickly became the center of social life during the fall semester, and the "big game" against one's archrival on Thanksgiving Day was as crucial to black students as it was to whites. Although relatively unknown to most whites, black college stars became heroic figures to fans and positive symbols of black masculinity on campus and in the larger African American community. Floyd "Terrible" Terry of Alabama's Talladega College, a rugged two-way player, was one of the first such legendary figures in the early twentieth century.[15]

Some African Americans hoped to gain more than mere entertainment and excitement from football. These ambitious educators and race champions envisioned participation in national sporting culture as a crucial vehicle for promoting racial advancement. Through the "universal language" of sports, one Howard University student explained in the 1920s, "we hope to foster a better and more fraternal spirit between the races in America and so to destroy prejudices." But this desire to earn full inclusion into the mainstream of American life through competitive athletics, a process that Patrick Miller has termed "muscular assimilation," remained only a dream for African Americans during the first half of the twentieth century. The racial color line that white southerners had successfully constructed literally divided higher education, including competitive sports, into separate worlds for blacks and whites. No interaction between the two was permitted; little progress toward "a universal brotherhood" was possible. Instead, black athletes at northern colleges were the ones who eventually took the first tentative steps in a long journey toward the mainstream of college sports.[16]

In the later part of the nineteenth century a few remarkable African American students appeared on athletic fields in the North representing their almost totally white schools. These pioneering athletes were an exceptional group, of course, since the total number of black students enrolled in northern colleges remained extremely small and the number of aspiring athletes even smaller. Still, their occasional appearance proudly wearing their school's colors delivered an important symbolic message to northern campuses. Probably the first black athlete in any intercollegiate team sport at a white northern college was Moses Fleetwood Walker, who enrolled at Oberlin College in 1878 and starred on the school's first varsity baseball team in 1881. Weldy Walker, his brother, enrolled at Oberlin in 1881 and also joined the baseball squad. Both brothers later transferred to the University of Michigan. The first African Americans known to have played football on a northern white squad were William H. Lewis and William T. S. Jackson at Amherst College and Thomas Fisher at Beloit College, all in 1889. Lewis, who went on to graduate from Harvard Law School, was a talented athlete whose stellar performances earned him a spot on Walter Camp's All-America team in 1892 and 1893. One year after the first appearance of this trio, George Jeweth at Michigan and William Arthur Johnson at the Massachusetts Institute of Technology became the next African Americans to participate in northern college football. Following them were George A. Flippin at Nebraska and F. D. Patterson at Ohio State in 1891 and Preston Eagleson at Indiana in 1893.[17]

Despite the acceptance of these talented athletes, racism remained widespread on northern campuses. A few colleges still refused to accept African Americans as students, while others barred them from many extracurricular activities, including athletics. Although information is sketchy for the period before 1920, it is safe to assume that a few aspiring black athletes were turned away from their college teams and quietly accepted their fate, leaving no public record of their private humiliation. Such exclusion initially occurred most commonly in football, but it eventually became identified with the developing sport of basketball, for reasons that are not completely clear. Football contained far more violent physical contact than basketball, but resistance to black participation gradually disappeared in the North. Perhaps the more intimate physical contact between sweating players wearing only limited clothing during a basketball game offended many whites' sensitivity. Obvious talent was no guarantee against racial exclusion; even outstanding black athletes sometimes faced resistance when they tried out for their school's team. The legendary Paul Robeson, despite a brilliant high school career, had to fight his way onto the Rutgers eleven in 1915 because of initial hostility from several veteran players. Even as late as 1931 Michigan coach Harry Kipke encountered opposition from alumni and senior administrators when recruiting Willis Ward, a Detroit high school football and track star with excellent grades.[18]

In addition to rejecting African Americans for their own teams, some northern colleges also tried to avoid competition against integrated opponents. Thus, the athletic color line, usually identified with the South, could also be found within the North, especially before 1920. Many northern whites saw competition against African Americans as "lowering" one's status by competing against social inferiors. In the mid-1890s, when the University of Chicago baseball team played several games against local amateur black teams, President William Rainey Harper privately commented that the series "has brought disgrace upon us." Occasional incidents also took place in New England. In December 1904 a black newspaper reported that an unnamed Massachusetts college had been fined by its conference for refusing to allow a black basketball player from a rival school to play on its campus. This sporadic resistance to integrated games reflected the marginal status of African American students on northern campuses and the widespread racism of the era.[19]

Several incidents involving black football players at Wabash, Dartmouth, and Brown demonstrated the difficulties that African Americans initially faced on the gridiron in the North. A controversy in 1903 between two Indiana football teams unintentionally publicized racial exclusion in the Midwest. During the first half of the fall season, several opposing schools protested the appearance of Samuel S. Gordon in the Wabash College lineup. After the first of several such incidents, Wabash students staged a rally in support of Gordon, at which Coach "Tug" Wilson delivered a powerful speech "placing the Negro in a very favorable light and showing the latent hopes and ambitions of the colored race." In late November, Wilson planned to use Gordon in Wabash's showdown with traditional rival DePauw College. But when the visitors arrived in Crawfordsville, they refused to take the field because of Gordon's presence. Only after several prominent Methodist leaders confronted the players and begged them "not to disgrace a Christian college by drawing the color line" did the DePauw squad agree to play the game. Having won the argument over Wabash's right to determine its own roster, Coach Wilson subsequently withheld Gordon from the match, perhaps for his personal safety. In 1904 Gordon did not return to school, but another African American, tackle William M. Cantrell, joined the Wabash squad. Unlike Gordon, Cantrell did not encounter any resistance from opposing teams during the season. Yet administrators at Wabash and DePauw worried about the possible response of DePauw students to him and reluctantly canceled their end-of-the-season contest. When Cantrell did not attend Wabash in 1905, the two colleges resumed the series.[20]

After several incidents in the early 1900s Princeton College acquired a reputation for hostility to black athletes. The institution did not accept African Americans until the 1940s and enrolled more white southerners than any other Ivy League school. In October 1903 the Tigers hosted Dartmouth and its African American end Matthew Bullock. Because the Princeton Inn refused to house an integrated group, the Dartmouth men stayed at a New York City hotel. In the subsequent game Bullock suffered a broken collarbone in a violent collision during the first minute of play and was lost for the season. A Princeton player promptly punched his replacement and told him, "We'll teach you to bring colored men down here. You must take us for a gang of servants." Afterward, Dartmouth players privately accused Princeton of deliberately injuring Bullock because of his race, but the college decided not to complain publicly. One Princeton player later defended the Tigers against the charges of racial bias, offering the dubious excuse that his teammates had deliberately roughed up Bullock, not because of his race but instead because he was "the most dangerous man on the opposing team."[21] In 1908 another black Dartmouth football player encountered problems with Princeton. Leslie Pollard, an outstanding freshman halfback from Chicago, turned in several fine performances during the season. However, Dartmouth did not even list Pollard on the travel squad for its November 7 game against Princeton at the Polo Grounds in New York City. Instead, he apparently remained on campus in Hanover, New Hampshire. The Dartmouth student newspaper published no explanation for Pollard's absence. Whether the college withheld him as a concession to Princeton's racial bias or in order to protect him from possible violence cannot be determined conclusively.[22]

Conditions had improved somewhat when Fritz Pollard, Leslie's younger brother, played for Brown University in 1915 and 1916. The younger Pollard earned numerous accolades, and Walter Camp even selected him for his 1916 All-America squad. Pollard's flashy running style so impressed Camp that he once described the elusive halfback as "a veritable will-o'-the-wisp that no one can lay hands on." Yet when the father of Pollard's teammate Wallace Wade, a native of Tennessee, learned about the presence of an African American on the squad, he angrily threatened to withdraw his son from school. Brown officials eventually persuaded the disgruntled parent to allow the young southerner and future coach at Alabama and Duke to remain on the team. None of Brown's opponents apparently demanded that Pollard be benched, suggesting that by 1915 most northeastern colleges no longer objected to playing against African Americans in football. Nonetheless, rival schools subjected the speedy halfback to racial taunts and dirty play on several occasions. During the 1915 Yale–Brown encounter in New Haven, for instance, several Yale fans yelled "Catch that nigger!" and "Kill that nigger!" After the contest Jim Sheldon, a burly Yale lineman from Georgia, walked up to Pollard, stuck out his hand, and bluntly exclaimed, "You're a nigger, but you're the best goddamn football player I ever saw." The following year during the Yale–Brown match, New Haven fans serenaded Pollard with the song "Bye, Bye, Blackbird."[23]

The gradual acceptance of African Americans on northern college teams ran counter to the prevailing racial trends within American society. Between 1890 and 1910 American race relations dipped to a new low, one that historian Rayford Logan labeled the "nadir" of the post-Reconstruction black experience. By the mid-1890s the Republican Party had virtually abandoned southern blacks, who would soon be legally disfranchised by conservative Democrats in every southern state. In its infamous 1896 ruling in the case of *Plessy v. Ferguson,* the United States Supreme Court gave its seal of approval to the legal fiction of "separate but equal" public accommodations, thereby providing a firm legal foundation for an expanding Jim Crow system. Growing fears that inferior immigrants from southern and eastern Europe might overwhelm and outbreed older-stock Americans meshed with traditional southern white racism to strengthen popular ideologies of racial hierarchies and racial subordination. Even some upper-class white reformers in the North seemed to be retreating from a paternalistic interest in African Americans. As memories of the Civil War faded, many northerners voiced a desire for closer ties with the former Confederate states. Since the racial component of the ensuing "sectional reconciliation" was implemented on southern terms, African Americans, especially in Dixie, found their dreams of equality sacrificed on the altar of national unity.

Reflecting this growing northern retreat from equal rights and racial democracy, most professional sports moved to purge black competitors from those integrated athletic activities in which they had previously participated. During the late nineteenth century African Americans had competed successfully in horse racing and in cycling races, but by the early 1900s they found themselves excluded from both sports. The same progression occurred in professional baseball. Moses Fleetwood Walker was the best-known African American to compete in what were considered the major leagues of that era. However, his Toledo team released him after the 1884 season, ending blacks' presence in the big leagues until Jackie Robinson's arrival in 1947. Other African Americans continued to play in integrated minor leagues until 1898, when owners conspired to eliminate them completely. Although African American boxers mostly fought against members of their own race, a few talented black fighters occasionally took on whites, and several even won national titles. After 1900, however, they found it much more difficult to find white pugilists who would fight them. This trend toward racial exclusion in professional sports meant that the elite sport of college football was the last remaining athletic activity pretending to practice democratic values, at least for games held in the North.[24]

In the South after the Civil War professional sports had usually required racial separation, except in New Orleans. From 1865 to about 1890 in the Crescent City, "sports brought Negro and white athletes together in friendly rivalry." Black and white baseball teams competed against each other well into the mid-1880s, boxing clubs occasionally staged prizefights between black and white fighters, and members of both races mingled with each other at horse races and bicycling events. But after 1885 conditions changed rapidly. In 1892 black boxing champion George Dixon successfully defended his featherweight title against a white challenger, provoking numerous complaints from influential local whites that his victory sent a dangerous message to the African American community. The *New Orleans Times-Democrat* declared that it had been "a mistake to match a negro and a white man, a mistake to bring the races together on any terms of equality, even in the prize ring." Subsequently, boxing promoters and clubs eliminated interracial matches, while baseball, horse racing, and cycling increasingly drew the color line at their activities. As Dale Somers concluded in his study of New Orleans sports, "By the turn of the century, interracial sporting events had virtually disappeared." These athletic developments were clearly influenced by such concurrent southern trends as racial violence, an expanding Jim Crow system, and black disfranchisement.[25]

It was during this period of hardening racial attitudes that the foundations of southern college football were established. To white southerners, athletic competition between blacks and whites was unthinkable, because it would violate the fundamental principles of white supremacy and racial subordination.

Racial mixing on the playing fields would lower the high status that whiteness conferred and bring dishonor to the participating players. Equal competition between blacks and whites in athletic events also posed the unacceptable possibility of white defeat and the resulting blow to southern masculinity. As "a loyal Southerner" angrily exclaimed in 1897 after personally halting one of the last interracial prizefights in Louisiana, "The idea of niggers fighting white men! Why, if that darned scoundrel would beat that white boy the niggers would never stop gloating over it, and, as it is, we have enough trouble with them." The application of this intensifying white racism to athletics guaranteed that black college sports would remain ensconced in a separate world, sealed off from the larger national sporting community. On the other hand, white colleges and their athletic teams suffered no such disability and eagerly sought to participate fully in national sporting culture, especially as their teams acquired more experience and sophisticated skills.[26]

The Rise of Intersectional Competition

Intersectional games between southern and northern football squads began as early as 1890 and were from their inception packed with special meaning for white southerners. As they crossed the Mason-Dixon line heading north, southern football teams carried with them the hopes and insecurities of their region. Far more than northerners, southerners saw such contests as a rematch of the Civil War and the Lost Cause. Thus, a good showing, or better yet a victory over the ancient foe, could help reassert regional pride and overcome memories of "causes lost." At intersectional matches the use of such regional symbols as rebel yells, the Confederate battle flag, and the song "Dixie" added a distinctive southern spirit to these public spectacles. Defeat of a northern rival could also affirm the superiority of such southern traditions as honor and chivalry. Furthermore, gridiron success in a scientific and manly sport like football could help shatter the image of the South as a backward and primitive area populated by mental and physical defectives. Athletic victories would also resolve any lingering questions about southern masculinity. According to one southern educator, football's popularity proved that southern young men were "still strong, virile, and manly." Football competition also drew on the southern military tradition. One Atlanta newspaper exuberantly declared that the University of Alabama's upset win in the 1926 Rose Bowl represented "the greatest victory for the South since the first battle of Bull Run." Sportswriters north and south would further embellish the stereotype of southern athletes as Confederate soldiers refighting the Civil War, but the sectional pride that southern teams embodied was indeed genuine.[27]

Intersectional games also offered southern universities the opportunity to upgrade their rather lowly national status in higher education and overcome feelings of cultural inferiority. Since elite private universities in the Northeast, especially the "big three" of Harvard, Yale, and Princeton, dominated college sports, meeting such opponents on the gridiron as equals would bring increased cultural recognition and respect to southern institutions. Football games, not academic achievement, would thus establish a southern university as a full-fledged member of academe. Midwestern and West Coast colleges also went through this same process in the early twentieth century as part of the nationalization and democratization of college football. According to Robin Lester, the University of Chicago–Princeton series of 1921–22 demonstrated the arrival of midwestern cultural parity with the East. Chicago's 9–0 upset win over the Tigers in the initial match of the series represented the first victory ever for a midwestern squad over one of the big-three teams, and Princeton's 1922 visit to Chicago was the first time that a big-three school had deigned to go west for a football game. Intersectional matches offered the same promises and rewards to southern institutions.[28]

Although the difficulties of travel initially limited their frequency, intersectional games soon became part of the annual college football scene. In fact, by the mid-1920s these highly publicized contests became an essential element in the game's tremendous popularity. Intersectional battles began in the early 1890s, usually matching a squad from the Upper South against a Yankee team. After the turn of the century, such encounters became more common, with Lower South teams increasingly participating. Almost all of these early intersectional contests took place in the North, reflecting the superior prestige, scheduling clout, and larger stadia of the established northern teams. This one-way travel was less pronounced in baseball, still the number-two sport on most southern campuses, because of weather conditions. Northern baseball teams sometimes came south in the early spring in order to take advantage of Dixie's warmer climate for early-season games. Regardless of the game's location, southern football teams did not fare well in the early interregional competition. The University of Virginia eleven learned just how rudimentary its skills were in 1890 when Princeton inflicted a humiliating 115–0 defeat on the southerners. As the number of these North-South matches expanded, southern squads improved their performances, but an unexpected source of conflict occasionally complicated their scheduling.

During the early years of intersectional competition, southern football and baseball teams were shocked on a few occasions to discover an African American player on their northern opponents' rosters. At this time the "South" of college sports, as constructed by racial custom, included not only the eleven states of the Old Confederacy but also the border states of Missouri, Kentucky, Maryland, and West Virginia, as well as the District of Columbia. These border states maintained segregated public schools and universities by law, just like their neighbors to the south. Athletic teams from these areas were almost as strongly committed to white supremacy as were their Deep South brethren. Because southern teams in the 1890s and early 1900s rarely knew anything about the composition of their northern opponents' rosters, they unexpectedly encountered integrated squads from time to time. Lacking any prior agreements or established precedents, southern teams could either agree to compete against an African American or stand on principle and sacrifice a chance to play an important rival, probably suffering a financial penalty and personal inconvenience as well. Although relatively few in number, such confrontations represented a potential barrier to the expansion of interregional competition.

Around the turn of the century a series of incidents involving such universities as Missouri, Harvard, and Rutgers dramatized this problem and inspired southern colleges to develop a uniform policy for such situations. The development of racial policy at the University of Missouri illustrates how southern colleges, as well as schools in border states who played by southern rules, gradually shifted from grudging acceptance of occasional interracial competition to firm insistence on total racial exclusion. Located in a former slave state, the University of Missouri was forced by geographical convenience to interplay rather extensively with nonsouthern teams. A football series with the University of Nebraska created a serious problem in 1892, when Missouri officials discovered that the visiting Cornhusker squad featured star halfback George A. Flippin, an African American. Upon discovering Flippin's race, Missouri administrators requested that Nebraska leave him behind for the game. When their demand was rejected, Missouri then forfeited the contest. Because of the game's cancellation, the Western University Interstate Athletic Association adopted a new rule that imposed a fifty-dollar fine on any team forfeiting a scheduled match. As a result, the Missouri squad reluctantly played against Flippin in 1893 and 1894, but did so in Kansas City, rather than in Columbia.[29]

Two years later, however, Missouri experienced yet another racial confrontation, this time over a home contest against the University of Iowa Hawkeyes. The Iowa team that arrived in Columbia in November 1896 included black halfback Frank "Kinney" Holbrook, the university's first African American player. Inside the visitors' hotel, several Columbia residents loudly voiced their hope that the local squad would "kill the Negro." After Missouri officials unsuccessfully demanded that Holbrook be benched, they reluctantly allowed the contest to proceed, perhaps fearing possible sanctions from the conference. The resulting game quickly turned into an emotional and physical battle. Fans yelled vicious abuse at the Iowa halfback throughout the match, shouting

"Kill the nigger!" and other racial epithets. At halftime two agitated Missouri gridders apparently slugged the referee. Early in the second half, with Iowa leading 12–0, the entire home team walked off the field to protest the referee's decisions. As a result, Iowa temporarily dropped Missouri from its schedule, and Missouri officials apparently resolved never to permit such an integrated contest again. The two schools resumed their rivalry on an annual basis in 1902, but a familiar problem resurfaced in 1910 when the Hawkeye squad included another African American, halfback Archie A. Alexander. This time Missouri administrators refused to allow Alexander to participate in the game and intimidated the Iowa coaches into accepting their decision. In response, Iowa officials not only canceled the 1911 match in protest but this time permanently terminated the annual series.[30]

Several other incidents around the turn of the century further demonstrated the inconsistency of racial policies in college athletics. Harvard University and its baseball team emerged at the center of these disputes. Like other northern colleges, Harvard scheduled several early-season baseball games in the South because of the milder spring weather. However, the presence of four-year starter William Clarence Matthews on the Crimson squad created controversy when the team headed south. In 1902 Harvard yielded to its opponents' demands and benched Matthews for road games held in Washington, D.C., against Virginia and the United States Naval Academy. The following year, though, Harvard refused a similar request from Georgetown University and forced the D.C. school to play against him. As a result, the Hoyas' starting catcher, like Matthews a native of Selma, Alabama, personally boycotted the game. In 1904 Georgetown apparently succeeded in barring Matthews from the annual contest. As a result, Harvard removed Georgetown, the U.S. Naval Academy, and Trinity College from its tentative 1905 schedule when these schools all insisted that Matthews be banned. Another example of North-South conflict came in June 1907 when the touring University of Alabama baseball team arrived in Burlington, Vermont, for two games against the state university. Upon learning that the host squad included two African American starters, Alabama coach John H. Pollard, a graduate of Dartmouth College, indignantly argued that the two must be benched for the series. When Vermont declined to do so, Pollard refused to play the games, incurring a three hundred–dollar cancellation fee.[31]

Nine years later, Rutgers College displayed typical northern ambivalence when confronted with southern demands to bench the school's first African American player. The college's shabby treatment of Paul Robeson, an exceptional all-round athlete, revealed just how weak the egalitarian spirit could be north of the Mason-Dixon line. A Phi Beta Kappa scholar and eventual winner of fifteen varsity letters in four sports, Robeson starred on Rutgers's football squad from 1916 to 1918. In naming Robeson to his 1918 All-America team, Walter

Camp described the gifted player as "the greatest end to ever trod the gridiron." But in October 1916, when Rutgers hosted Washington and Lee College from Virginia, the college president personally ordered Robeson withheld from the game. Respect for the feelings of white southerners undoubtedly influenced his decision. More important, though, Rutgers was also in the midst of a major fund-raising drive, which made school officials particularly sensitive to alumni concerns over Robeson's participation. Coach G. Foster Sanford disagreed with the decision but loyally accepted it. Later in the season the coach of the West Virginia University team wrote Sanford to request that Robeson be withheld from their upcoming game, bluntly stating, "We've got a lot of southern boys on this team, and they don't want to play against your man Robeson." Left alone by the school administration this time, Sanford rejected the demand, and Robeson suited up. Despite enduring brutal punishment throughout the game, Robeson played brilliantly as Rutgers tied the favored Mountaineers 0–0. In a remarkable gesture after the final whistle, every member of the West Virginia team lined up and shook Robeson's hand. Nonetheless, West Virginia's concession to Rutgers was a major exception to the emerging national trend toward black exclusion from intersectional contests.[32]

The Triumph of the Gentleman's Agreement

A new, unofficial national policy governing intersectional competition, eventually known as the gentleman's agreement, resolved the conflict over African American participation. In the first two decades of the twentieth century, southern universities took an intransigent position on racial exclusion for games held in Dixie and pressed hard for a similar concession for contests staged in the North. Since many athletic activities had already excluded black participants, these demands for a rigid color line in intersectional football competition did not seem unreasonable within the national sporting context. By about 1920 it had become clear that virtually every participant in intersectional competition had accepted the new consensus. This informal governing policy was never publicly announced; rather, it represented a widely shared private understanding among (white) gentlemen. According to this policy, African Americans would be automatically barred from intersectional matches against southern teams, regardless of the game's location. Even on a northern campus the home team would still be expected to voluntarily withhold any black players on its roster, as a courtesy to southern sensibilities. In accepting the gentleman's agreement, northern schools thus agreed to a form of "sectional reconciliation" in athletics based exclusively on southern terms, sacrificing African Americans on the altar of national harmony.

The heyday of the gentleman's agreement coincided with a surge in popularity for college football. During "the prosperity decade," football's audience expanded in total numbers and in geography, making the game truly a nationwide sport. As Benjamin Rader has noted, "During the 1920s, attendance at college games doubled and gate receipts tripled." Such widespread support solidified college football's position as the country's number-two team sport. Newspapers often featured popular sportswriters like Grantland Rice who provided vivid accounts of major sporting events. The new medium of radio further contributed to this growing obsession with sports. The 1920s were also the age of such legendary sports stars as baseball's Babe Ruth, boxing champion Jack Dempsey, golfer Bobby Jones, and tennis king William "Big Bill" Tilden. In college sports fans across the country idolized heroes like Harold "Red" Grange of Illinois, immortalized as the "galloping ghost," and the famed "four horsemen" of the Notre Dame backfield. Successful coaches like Knute Rockne of Notre Dame and Glenn S. "Pop" Warner of Pittsburgh and Stanford became household names to millions of sports fans.[33]

The increased interest in college football inspired an explosion of stadium construction on university campuses. Harvard Stadium and the Yale Bowl, long the spiritual centers for the game, served as models for newer universities. During the decade several ambitious midwestern universities built huge stadia that surpassed in size the Harvard and Yale facilities. New stadia became the benchmark of progress, and, as Robin Lester has observed, these towering structures "dominated the horizons of the campuses as completely as the medieval cathedrals had their world." Such projects were expensive, of course, so colleges needed to keep these new facilities packed with fans in order to pay off construction costs, thereby creating a financial spiral that remains alive today. Southern universities likewise embraced the stadium-construction trend, hoping to demonstrate to the rest of the country that "the South had acquired 'big league' status." In 1926 Southern Methodist University (SMU), only eleven years old at the time, completed construction of Ownby Stadium in Dallas, financing the fifteen thousand–seat facility through a $175,000 bond issue. Three years later the University of Georgia completed work on Sanford Stadium, which seated thirty thousand and cost $360,000.[34]

High-profile intersectional football games between top-rated teams played an important role in the exploding popularity of college football during the 1920s. These events produced national publicity and usually attracted huge crowds, thereby generating considerable revenue. As Georgia Tech coach William A. Alexander bluntly stated, "If you've got to lose, lose before a crowd of people and bring a lot of money home." Notre Dame's football program exemplified the trend. Under Coach Knute Rockne, teams from the previously obscure Indiana school traveled so widely for interregional matches that the team's informal nickname became the Ramblers. Promoters in New York City and other large metropolitan areas staged major football contests in professional baseball stadia like Yankee Stadium, drawing on "subway alumni" to pack the stands. The ballyhoo increasingly surrounding college football reflected the growing commercialization of the sport. With more money at risk, college officials understandably wanted to avoid any disagreements that might interfere with the marketing of their product. In an age of racial complacency, the gentleman's agreement served their interests quite well.[35]

In addition to modern stadia, victories on the gridiron were necessary before southern universities could earn competitive respect and social recognition from football's traditional leaders. This was not easy, because the more prestigious northern teams insisted that intersectional games be played north of the Mason-Dixon line. Through occasional upsets of northern opponents and several good showings in the Rose Bowl, southern teams gradually earned national respect. In the first prominent North-South match, Virginia had suffered an ignominious 115–0 loss to Princeton in 1890, but in 1915 the Cavaliers regained some honor by upsetting Yale 10–0 in New Haven. Tiny Centre College from Danville, Kentucky, produced the most spectacular upset of the era. In October 1921 the Praying Colonels journeyed to Boston and handed mighty Harvard its first defeat in intersectional play in forty years. A few southern squads even competed for national honors. In 1917 the Georgia Tech squad went 9-0 under Coach John Heisman and claimed to have won the mythical national championship.[36]

Impressive performances by Alabama and Georgia Tech in the Rose Bowl during the late 1920s earned southern football new respect. Participation in the prestigious annual event offered an exciting trip to exotic Southern California and a generous financial reward. In 1926 the University of Alabama became the first southern team to play in the contest. Led by halfback Johnny Mack Brown, whom one excited journalist described as "slicker than an eel in a sea of stewed okra," the underdog Crimson Tide upset the University of Washington 20–19. Both Alabama's glorious 1926 victory and its 7–7 tie the following year against a favored Stanford squad boosted regional pride among white southerners who were tired of "lost causes" on the gridiron and helped "put southern football on the map." Two years later the Georgia Tech Yellow Jackets defeated the University of California 8–7 in the 1929 Rose Bowl. In the aftermath of the Georgia Tech victory, Richard H. Edmonds, publisher of the *Manufacturers Record,* proudly announced, "The Georgia Tech team has therefore rendered an invaluable service to the South . . . by showing to all sections the superb physical and mental stamina and alertness of the people of the South." To many southerners, these Rose Bowl triumphs refuted negative images of a benighted South and demonstrated the vigorous manliness of the region's young men.[37]

While southern white teams gained increased national recognition during the 1920s, black athletes remained on the periphery of big-time college football.

Almost none of them gained national recognition, because most African American students and athletes at the time were enrolled at historically black colleges and universities. As of 1927, for example, about 90 percent of the approximately fifteen thousand African Americans taking postsecondary courses attended predominantly black institutions. Within the separate world of black college sports, African American males could validate their manliness and display their athletic skills, earning the respect of fellow students and black sports fans. Several achieved near-legendary status. Probably the most heralded football player at a black university in the twenties and thirties was halfback Benjamin F. Stevenson of Tuskegee Institute. Exploiting the absence of a rule limiting players to four years of competition, Stevenson scored numerous touchdowns and reportedly made "forty-two runs of fifty or more yards" during his unique eight-year career at Tuskegee. The dazzling open-field running of Lincoln University's Franz Alfred "Jazz" Byrd earned him the nickname of "the Black Red Grange." John "Big Train" Moody of Morris Brown College repeatedly shredded opposing teams' defenses during the late 1930s and scored a total of thirty-nine touchdowns for his school. Nonetheless, the national white press ignored these outstanding performances. Instead, it was the tiny contingent of African American athletes at white colleges who received the opportunity to earn recognition for themselves and their race through the "universal language" of sports.[38]

The challenges facing African American athletes at northern colleges were not limited to the playing fields. Both they and their fellow black students faced considerable discrimination on campus and in surrounding neighborhoods. Dormitories, dining halls, swimming pools, and campus clubs often remained closed to minority students. Even the football team at some integrated colleges was not automatically open to black students, and some coaches quietly refused to recruit black high school stars. On the other hand, the racial policy of Big Ten basketball coaches was neither subtle nor ambiguous during the 1920s and 1930s; they simply excluded all African Americans from their teams. Even when black athletes made it onto the football field, they could be subjected to verbal abuse and foul play. Walter Gordon, a powerful defensive end in 1917 and 1918 for the University of California Golden Bears, sometimes encountered "not only rough and dirty play, but also vituperation and insult" during games. Rival coaches often issued the simple pregame instruction of "Get Gordon." These incidents took place on the West Coast, where racism in athletics remained less intense than in the Midwest and where after graduation Gordon could be hired by his alma mater as an assistant coach.[39]

The tragic death of Jack Trice, Iowa State's first black football player, in 1923 demonstrated the ultimate danger to African American gridders. In the second game of the season, the Cyclones took on the University of Minnesota in Minneapolis. The match was a rough one, and the Minnesota offense aimed much of its attack at Trice, a fearless lineman and the heart of the Iowa State defense. After one massive pileup in the second half, Trice had to be helped from the field and was then rushed to a hospital. Two days later he died from internal bleeding. After his death, friends found in his clothes a note that he had composed the night before the game: "The honor of race, family, and self are at stake. Everyone is expecting me to do big things. I will. My whole body and soul are to be thrown recklessly about the field tomorrow." Trice was not the only football player to die that fall; at least eight others, all white, suffered a similar fate. Nor were serious injuries restricted to games between white college teams. Howard University's Haywood "Speed" Johnson died one year later, in October 1924, from injuries received in a game against Greensboro A&T College. Nonetheless, Trice's death and the touching reflections contained in his private note highlighted the special pressures, and dangers, that black athletes sometimes endured at white colleges.[40]

During the 1920s a few more African Americans gradually suited up at historically white colleges in the North. Although none earned the tremendous recognition given Paul Robeson of Rutgers and Brown's Fritz Pollard in the previous decade, several enjoyed excellent careers. In 1921 Duke Slater of Iowa, a powerful tackle, earned second-team All-American honors from Walter Camp and first-team honors in several other polls. Quarterback Charles West of Washington and Jefferson became the second African American to play in the Rose Bowl in 1922 when his team tied the California Golden Bears 0–0 on a muddy, rain-soaked field. Possibly the most talented black player at a predominantly white university in the 1920s was Brice Taylor, a lineman for the University of Southern California (USC) from 1924 to 1926. Although a birth defect left him with only one hand, Taylor was an excellent all-round athlete who earned a spot on two All-America teams in 1925, despite playing in relative obscurity on the West Coast. The prominence of these stars and the absence of southern teams on their colleges' schedules protected them from racial exclusion. Other less well-known black players were not so lucky.[41]

During the 1920s the gentleman's agreement was quietly used on at least a dozen or more occasions to bench African American players in intersectional matches. Documenting such racial exclusion is difficult, because white newspapers often refused to report such incidents, and the athletes involved rarely complained publicly. The lack of public outrage concerning these benchings illustrated the complacency about racial discrimination that existed on northern campuses. The actual number of incidents can never be fully established. Some African American students at white schools were discouraged from trying out for their own teams. Those who were substitutes, even if they saw action in most games, could quietly be left on the bench for a particular game without raising undue suspicion. Even a black player who usually started might be "accidentally" kept on the sidelines because of his coach's strategy in handling the strict substitution rules of the era.

Several cases of racial exclusion in athletics during the 1920s can be identified, despite the limited sources available. These incidents normally involved midwestern squads, since New England colleges were more resistant to the gentleman's agreement. In 1925 Butler University in Indianapolis left football player John Southern at home when his team traveled to Shreveport, Louisiana, to play Centenary College. Three years later Butler officials apparently withheld another African American player, Alonzo Watford, from a 1928 match against Washington University in St. Louis. Colgate's Raymond Vaughn earned the unfortunate distinction of being benched four times during his career, the most of any African American during the decade. In 1926 Colgate left Vaughn, a sophomore, behind when the team went south to play the U.S. Naval Academy in Maryland. Later that season, Vaughn sat out a road game at the University of Pittsburgh. Responding to complaints from black fans who had come to see Vaughn, a Pennsylvania native, play, Colgate officials later released a terse statement declaring that he "was not used because he was not needed." During his senior year Colgate again benched Vaughn for a home game against Virginia Polytech and a road contest at Vanderbilt. These two actions prompted one white New York sportswriter to criticize Colgate for its "cold-blooded discrimination." Such a stand by a white journalist was unusual, however. At Duquesne College, tackle Raymond Kemp received some support for All-America honors during his senior year of 1930. However, one year earlier Duquesne officials had withheld Kemp from a road game at West Virginia University. All of these incidents reveal that northern schools were quite willing to surrender to southern racism in order to schedule intersectional games.[42]

Challenges to the Gentleman's Agreement

The silence of the national press about the gentleman's agreement was shattered only once during the first eight years of the 1920s. On October 6, 1923, Washington and Jefferson College in Washington, Pennsylvania, hosted Washington and Lee College from Lexington, Virginia, in a gridiron confrontation between the Presidents and the Generals. When the southerners arrived at the field, they were surprised to discover that black quarterback Charles West was in uniform and immediately demanded that he be benched. Apparently, Washington and Lee coaches had assumed that the home team would automatically honor the gentleman's agreement and had not bothered to inquire about West's status. Washington and Jefferson officials vigorously defended West's right to play during a heated discussion with the visitors. Uncertain how to proceed, the Washington and Lee coaches telephoned school officials back in Virginia, who ordered them not to play against West. The W&L team then packed up its bags and drove away shortly before the scheduled kickoff time, forfeiting the game.[43]

In the days that followed Washington and Lee spokesmen justified the school's action by insisting that they were honoring a worthy tradition of never having competed against a black player. The fault for the game's cancellation thus lay with the home team, which had failed to be a gracious host and exclude West. The *Richmond Times-Dispatch* agreed, suggesting that there must have been a "tacit agreement" for West to be absent, since "Washington and Jefferson must have known that no southern team would meet a negro in sport." The newspaper emphasized that athletic contests were social events and that competition against African Americans represented social equality, which white southerners would never accept. "Social equality has not been extended the negro here. The Negro understands that perfectly and appreciates the reason for it. There would not be the slightest difference in playing football with him and in sitting down with him at a formal dinner or meeting him for a game of golf on the country club links. College sports are purely social. And social distinctions necessarily are arbitrary. . . . The question of sportsmanship is not involved, nor is that of political rights."[44]

On the other hand, Washington and Jefferson maintained that it too had a proud tradition to protect—one of never making a distinction in sports based on race or color. President S. V. Baker defended West as "an honor to the school as a student and as an athlete, adding to its prestige by his gentlemanly conduct and his efforts as an athlete." Irate local residents derided the Virginians as "yellow" and "crackers." The *New York World* temporarily broke the silence of the mainstream press on racial exclusion, denouncing Washington and Lee for maintaining "a shabby tradition" and for being afraid to risk losing to a person whom they regarded as a social inferior. Predictably, the black press condemned the Virginians' behavior and applauded the home team. The *Pittsburgh Courier* praised Coach Heisman as "truly a big man" and described West as "a credit to the game and an example of the highest type of manhood of the Negro race." These sentiments reflected the older philosophy of equality between gentlemen athletes on the playing fields, an approach that many northern schools had abandoned by 1920. Instead, the gentleman's agreement embodied the new modus vivendi of intersectional sports, reflecting the "southernization" of intersectional competition.[45]

The only integrated football game played by a major southern team that can be documented for the 1920s took place on the West Coast. Not only was such a contest highly unusual, but it also took place by accident. In 1924 several civic groups in Los Angeles sponsored a special Christmas Day charity game. This match, sometimes confused with the Rose Bowl game in Pasadena on January 1, pitted the University of Southern California against the University of Missouri. The 1924 USC squad contained two African Americans, fullback John Riddle and tackle Brice Taylor. Missouri officials apparently learned about the presence of the two African Americans on the USC roster only after arriving in California. Having crossed the country for a special contest, they grudgingly compromised their principles and agreed to play the game. With Riddle and Taylor both seeing action, the Trojans ultimately prevailed 20–7 before forty thousand fans. Because the match was held on the West Coast, most eastern newspapers provided scant coverage and ignored the game's racial dimension.[46]

In the fall of 1929 a controversial game between the University of Georgia and New York University in New York City thrust the gentleman's agreement into the national spotlight. Coach Chick Meehan of NYU had developed the Violets into a national power through skillful coaching, physical tactics (the team was sometimes called "the Violents"), and flashy showmanship, thereby drawing large crowds to games at Yankee Stadium and the Polo Grounds. As part of their strategy, NYU officials regularly scheduled "big-name" opponents from around the country. But the presence of two African Americans on the NYU squad complicated the scheduled November 9 game in Yankee Stadium, especially when eastern sportswriters reported that the gentleman's agreement would be implemented for the match. Like NYU, Georgia sought national prominence for its football program. The ambitious university had dedicated its large new stadium the previous month at a game against Yale, which had never previously deigned to visit the Deep South. Four weeks later the Georgia squad headed north, hoping to gain additional prestige and profits through its contest with NYU.[47]

The approach of the Georgia–NYU game ignited a controversy in the national media over whether NYU would voluntarily bench its two African American players, David Myers and William O'Shields. Because O'Shields rarely played, attention focused on his more talented teammate. Earlier that season NYU had secretly honored the gentleman's agreement by withholding David Myers from an October 5 home game against West Virginia Wesleyan, claiming that he was suffering from a cold. Circumstances were quite different for the Georgia game, however, after several New York newspapers reported that NYU had agreed to bench Myers. Several white sportswriters, including Ed Sullivan of the *New York Evening Graphic* and Heywood Broun of the Scripps-Howard chain, condemned NYU's decision. Sullivan praised Myers as "a fine type of colored boy" and urged the NYU administration not to allow "the Mason-Dixon line to be erected in the center of its playing field." In the future, he recommended, NYU should avoid such problems "by banning intersectional games with southern schools, rather than by banning the Negro player." Heywood Broun ridiculed Chick Meehan as "the gutless coach of a gutless university," while the National Association for the Advancement of Colored People denounced Meehan for a "cowardly capitulation to color prejudice." New York congressman Emmanuel Celler, the NAACP, several African American leaders, and black newspapers also sent protests to NYU president Elmer E. Brown.[48]

The widening protest in New York alarmed Georgia alumni, as well as southern sports fans. Several whites sent letters to President Charles M. Snelling and the student newspaper, the *Red and Black*, urging Georgia to uphold the gentleman's agreement or cancel the game. One Washington, D.C., resident wrote that "it is unthinkable that such a typically Southern school as Georgia would condescend to enter into any athletic contest against a team on which a negro plays." Another writer reminded President Snelling that the principles of white supremacy and racial purity were far more important "than the doubtful honor of winning a foot ball game." These reports did not alarm Snelling, who assured one correspondent that "the colored boy will not be in the game." His prediction proved accurate. Five days before the game NYU officials announced that Myers had reinjured a shoulder in the previous Saturday's game against Georgetown and would be physically unable to participate in the upcoming match. With the Myers issue resolved, Georgia and NYU finally squared off in Yankee Stadium on Saturday, November 9, with NYU claiming a 27–19 victory before more than forty thousand fans. Although Georgia lost the actual game, the university had won the larger struggle to maintain the color line for intersectional competition.[49]

White critics and African Americans expressed disappointment that the gentleman's agreement had been upheld and condemned both universities for their decisions. The *Pittsburgh Courier* lashed out at NYU by suggesting that "some of the Violet authorities have yellow streaks." Even David Myers himself came under attack. The *Pittsburgh Courier* contended that if school officials had told him that he could not play, then Myers should turn in his uniform, "if he has the manhood and self-respect to quit the team." Iconoclastic columnist George S. Schuyler praised white sportswriter Heywood Broun for his "manly stand on the matter" but characterized Myers's silence as reflecting a lack of "manly spirit." The NAACP monthly magazine, *The Crisis*, declared that it felt "nothing but contempt" for the NYU player when he subsequently rejoined the team. Ironically, then, Myers ended up excluded by the Georgians, abandoned by his own university, and shunned by fellow African Americans who questioned his masculinity.[50]

The University of Georgia–NYU game dramatically exposed the widespread acceptance of the gentleman's agreement in big-time college sports at the end of the Roaring Twenties. At the same time, opponents of the policy took some comfort from the fact that they had finally forced the sporting public to acknowledge the agreement's existence and the discrimination that it embodied. Moreover, they had mobilized the first organized public opposition to its implementation. During the following decade a growing number of northern sportswriters, students, and fans would increasingly challenge the color line's hegemony over college sports. For the moment, though, the gentleman's agreement still reigned supreme over intersectional competition.

2

"Fair Play" versus White Supremacy

The Gentleman's Agreement under Attack, 1929–45

Public sentiment in the southeastern states simply demands
that no team in this section play against a Negro athlete.
—Georgia Tech coach William A. Alexander,
January 1934

The University of North Carolina is still standing, and none
of the young men representing it on the gridiron appears to
be any worse off for having spent an afternoon competing
against a Negro player. . . . No white North Carolinian's
daughter will marry a Negro as a result of Saturday's play.
—Roy Wilkins, October 1936

As the 1930s began, white supremacy and racial exclusion continued
to regulate intersectional competition between southern and northern college
teams. Despite the public exposure that the gentleman's agreement had received
during the 1929 Georgia–New York University football controversy, northern
schools continued to honor the policy during the first half of the ensuing decade. Professional sports likewise practiced widespread racial discrimination
throughout the Depression years. Major League Baseball, the number-one team
sport, and its affiliated minor leagues maintained their long tradition of excluding black players. The racial status quo declined even further in 1934 when the
National Football League (NFL) initiated an eleven-year ban on African Americans players. On northern university campuses black athletes did not always
receive the same treatment as their white teammates, and white sportswriters
sometimes neglected them when passing out postseason honors. Conditions
in the developing sport of college basketball were even worse than in football.
In the most egregious example, basketball coaches in the Big Ten Conference
continued to exclude black athletes from their teams until the 1940s.[1]

In the middle of the Depression decade, however, a growing number of students and administrators at nonsouthern universities, influenced in part by the political radicalism of the era, directly challenged the legitimacy of the gentleman's agreement. The exclusion of the University of Michigan's Willis Ward from that school's intersectional football game against Georgia in 1934 provoked the largest public protest since the 1929 Georgia–NYU contest and proved to be the harbinger of increasing opposition to racial exclusion. In the seven years that followed this confrontation at least eight white southern universities broke with tradition and voluntarily competed against integrated teams outside the South. Despite these hopeful signs, several ambitious northern teams, including Boston College (BC) and NYU, continued to honor the traditional policy by benching their black players for contests against southern teams. As of 1941 the gentleman's agreement remained a major factor in intersectional college athletics, although it no longer exercised total control. During the wartime years most colleges reduced or temporarily suspended their athletic activities. At the same time, military bases often formed sports teams, and through them some limited interracial competition took place. Because of the exceptional wartime conditions, these violations of Jim Crow were rarely documented and quickly forgotten. By 1945, though, the growing emphasis on democratic rights that the war inspired seemed to bode ill for racial restrictions in college sports.

Racial Exclusion in the Early 1930s

Several incidents in the early and middle 1930s confirmed the hegemony of the gentleman's agreement. Most of the cases that can be documented involved football games, because of the wide coverage afforded the sport by the popular press. Undoubtedly, there were similar examples in basketball, baseball, track, and even lacrosse, but because of the limited newspaper coverage of these sports only a few can be clearly identified. A variety of colleges, including such prominent Big Ten members as Minnesota, Ohio State, and Michigan, willingly abandoned their African American players during the Depression decade. The University of Minnesota was quite shameless about benching its black players for home games against southern colleges. In 1931 athletic officials withheld three-year letterman Ellsworth H. Harpole from a game against Oklahoma State University (OSU), and in 1932 they again benched him again, this time against Ole Miss. In 1935 Minnesota coaches kept sophomore Dwight Reed on the bench throughout the Gophers' 20–0 victory over Tulane. The following year Minnesota honored the gentleman's agreement for a fourth time when it withheld both Reed and sophomore Horace Bell from a match against the University of Texas (UT). Although the Gophers easily defeated the Longhorns 47–19, the two black players sat quietly on the sidelines for the entire contest.[2]

Ohio State University (OSU) attracted more extensive publicity and criticism than Minnesota for its surrender to southern racism. The athlete at the center of the controversy was William Bell, the school's first African American football player and an All–Big Ten tackle. Early in the fall of 1930, Bell's junior season, rumors circulated in Columbus that Ohio State would leave Bell behind for a November 8 road game in Baltimore against the U.S. Naval Academy. Upon learning about this possibility, Walter White of the NAACP hurriedly wired President George W. Rightmire, urging him not to "yield to racial prejudice" and "violate canons of good sportsmanship." President Rightmire responded by denying that Ohio State planned to discriminate against Bell. Instead, he cleverly argued that the university actually planned to protect "him from [the] unpleasant experience of probable race discrimination manifested in a southern city." This transparent excuse would be utilized in similar circumstances by other college administrators over the next thirty years. Although Ohio State easily defeated Navy 27–0, Bell's exclusion irritated some Buckeye fans and sportswriters. The *Cleveland Press* accused OSU of surrendering to race prejudice, while the *Akron Times-Press* published a critical editorial titled "Bell Should Have Played." On the other hand, a black student organization defended Coach Sam Willaman and expressed confidence in his decision not to play the junior tackle.[3]

The start of the 1931 season inspired renewed debate about Ohio State's commitment to the gentleman's agreement, since the Buckeye schedule included home games against Vanderbilt and the Naval Academy. In the first game of the season Coach Willaman did not start Bell but sent him into the game as the first substitute. But the following week, when Ohio State hosted Vanderbilt, Bell remained on the bench throughout the match, despite complaints from the crowd. Meanwhile, the Vanderbilt offense shredded the Buckeye defense en route to a 26–21 victory. Afterward, one disgusted sportswriter reported that "rabid Buckeye fans . . . think that Bell was shelved for the Rebels; that Ohio has joined the Confederacy." Three years later Ohio State athletic director L. W. St. John privately admitted in a letter that in fact the university had always intended to withhold Bell. Willaman's use of him as a substitute in the season opener merely represented a clever scheme to disguise his plans for the Vanderbilt game. Several weeks after the Vanderbilt contest, attention shifted to the Naval Academy's November 7 visit to Columbus. This time Willaman started Bell, and the senior tackle played brilliantly against the Middies, leading the Buckeyes to a 20–0 victory. His performance was so outstanding that several Navy players even shook hands with him after the match. Bell's participation against a "southern" team represented an important shift in racial policy at Ohio State and also signaled a partial change for the Naval Academy, which had previously refused to compete against African Americans in football at any venue. More significantly, though, the academy did not change its policy of racial exclusion for home games in Maryland.[4]

Ohio State and Minnesota were not the only major midwestern universities who honored the gentleman's agreement. From 1932 through 1937 at least five other teams—Iowa, Indiana, Michigan State, Cincinnati, and Michigan—withheld African American players from football games against opponents from southern or border colleges. One of these incidents happened in the nation's capital in 1932, when the University of Iowa visited George Washington University. The Hawkeye team included two African Americans who normally saw action as substitutes, but they remained on the sidelines for the entire game. Also in 1932 Indiana kept Fitzhugh Lyons on the bench when the Hoosiers hosted Mississippi State. Michigan State, a rising football power that would eventually earn membership in the Big Ten in the late 1940s, had suited up several black players before 1930. Nonetheless, in December 1934 the university left halfback James McCrary and end Albert Baker at home when the team traveled to Texas to challenge the Texas A&M Aggies. The University of Cincinnati likewise demonstrated that ambitious scheduling could trump loyalty to one's own players, if those players had dark skin. Cincinnati officials achieved a major scheduling coup when they convinced the highly popular Vanderbilt football team to visit Ohio for a 1934 game, but they had to agree to withhold London Gant, the school's lone African American player, from the contest. Because none of the black athletes involved in these incidents were prominent players, the mainstream press mostly ignored their exclusion.[5]

In contrast, the University of Michigan attracted considerable public attention in October 1934 when the school sold out the Wolverines' only African American player in order to host a widely followed intersectional game against Georgia Tech. This controversial game exposed the continuing strength of the gentleman's agreement but also inspired greater resistance by northern students. The controversy centered on Willis Ward, an outstanding end and track star for the Wolverines. Coach Harry Kipke had aggressively recruited Ward, an honor student at his Detroit high school, despite strong opposition from many white alumni and athletic director Fielding H. Yost, the son of a Confederate soldier. Ward's accomplishments in both football and track guaranteed that any discrimination against him would not go unnoticed. But when Georgia Tech officials had discussed the possible contest with Michigan earlier in 1934, they made it clear that they would not venture north unless guaranteed that Ward would remain on the sidelines. As Coach William A. Alexander bluntly explained, "Public sentiment in the southeastern states simply demands that no team in this section play against a Negro athlete." Soon after the fall semester began at Michigan, word leaked out that Michigan had promised to withhold Ward from the game. Liberal and leftist students, the student newspaper, the NAACP, and black newspapers responded by launching a protest movement defending Ward's right to play against the southerners. Ward himself initially voiced disappointment over his benching, but as the game drew near he became silent.[6]

Public pressure and the threat of a student boycott of the game forced Michigan representatives to huddle with Georgia Tech coaches immediately after the southern team arrived in Ann Arbor. After a heated discussion officials from the two universities agreed to a bizarre compromise whereby Michigan would withhold Willis Ward from the game, and in return Tech would bench star end Hoot Gibson. This highly unusual arrangement permitted Tech to maintain its racial principles without placing Michigan at a competitive disadvantage. In the actual game, a rather dull affair, Michigan escaped with a 9–2 victory. Yet in a larger sense Georgia Tech actually won the more important battle, because the Yellow Jackets had forced Michigan to honor the gentleman's agreement.[7]

The racial trade-off that permitted the Michigan–Georgia Tech game to be held disappointed fans from both universities and prompted some southern colleges to rethink their strategy for intersectional contests. *The Crisis,* the NAACP monthly magazine, scolded Michigan for not defending Ward's right to play and Georgia Tech for falsely assuming that its players were superior to Ward. *The Crisis* ridiculed the Yellow Jackets as "superior sons of the South who got that way by never going into a situation where a black boy might have an equal chance, under common rules, to show them up." As for Willis Ward, the young athlete was emotionally scarred by his benching. Many years later he told an interviewer, "That Georgia Tech game knocked me right square in the gut. It was wrong. . . . [I]t killed my desire to excel." The game's controversy also prompted some observers to suggest that intersectional games be eliminated. Concerned about the threat to the gentleman's agreement, Ralph McGill of the *Atlanta Constitution* argued that "until this time-honored custom is honored more in the breach than the observance, it might be well for southern and northern teams to avoid scheduling games when there is any possibility of racial friction." Yet most major southern universities were unwilling to give up the profits and prestige of such events, especially during a depression. Instead, they began obtaining advance information about the racial composition of potential opponents and, more important, to insert formal "No Negroes" clauses into game contracts, no longer relying exclusively on the informal protocols of the gentleman's agreement.[8]

The First Southern Defections from Jim Crow

Beginning in 1936 three prominent universities from the Southern Conference and three more from the Southwest Conference unexpectedly reversed their historical positions and agreed to play against integrated teams in the North and

West. This limited departure from southern tradition did not immediately inaugurate a broad regional trend. However, it did indicate that the pursuit of national prominence by southern colleges and the accompanying need to generate revenue for football programs during an economic depression could result in a victory for racial inclusion on the gridiron. However, since the South's Jim Crow system remained securely entrenched and the violations of the gentleman's agreement took place outside Dixie, conservative politicians and racial ideologues saw no immediate need to launch a counterattack to enforce total conformity.

The University of North Carolina became the first major southern university to participate in an integrated football game when it challenged NYU in 1936 at the Polo Grounds. Administrators from the two schools apparently did not discuss the possibility of an integrated game when they scheduled the contest, and North Carolina neglected to insert a "No Negroes" clause into the formal contract. Nonetheless, the NYU team included one African American, sophomore halfback Ed Williams, who played a prominent role in the Violets' offense. As game day approached, newspapers reported that Williams was one of several injured players who might not see action that weekend. This news inspired speculation that NYU officials were secretly planning another surrender to southern racism, just as they had done in the David Myers case in 1929. In reality, though, the president of UNC, Dr. Frank P. Graham, had no intention of demanding Williams's exclusion. A strong supporter of civil liberties, improved race relations, and other progressive causes, Graham had also recently served as a national sponsor of the Committee on Fair Play in Sports, which criticized the German handling of the Olympic Games in Berlin. Sensing an opportunity to stand up for racial justice and good sportsmanship, Graham sent a telegram to NYU chancellor Harry W. Chase requesting that Coach Mal Stevens be informed that the Tar Heels would "play the team he puts on the field."[9]

The North Carolina–NYU game took place without incident before a modest crowd of ten thousand fans, with the visitors claiming a narrow 14–13 triumph. Although Ed Williams did not start the game, he entered the field late in the first quarter and played competently until he was replaced during the fourth quarter. Afterward, Stevens personally thanked the Carolina coaching staff for their team's excellent sportsmanship, for treating Williams just like any other player, and for not "giving expression to any other unfair attitudes." Writing in the *New York Amsterdam News,* Roy Wilkins of the NAACP confirmed the good sportsmanship of the Carolina players and reported that he had not heard any racial slurs or jeers from Tar Heel fans during the contest. Ridiculing the fears of white segregationists, Wilkins cleverly noted that "the University of North Carolina is still standing, and none of the young men representing it on the gridiron appears to be any worse off for having spent an afternoon competing against a Negro player." Wilkins went on to predict "that no white North Carolinian's daughter will marry a Negro as a result of Saturday's play, much to the chagrin of the peddlers of the bugaboo of social equality." Despite the game's lack of controversy, though, it was not clear if the integrated contest was a onetime event or the harbinger of a new trend for southern universities.[10]

Although President Graham apparently did receive some minor criticism over the game, it did not prevent him from arranging two subsequent matches against NYU. Both were also scheduled for New York City, though, as not even Graham was prepared to challenge the color line inside North Carolina. In the 1937 rematch the Tar Heels emerged victorious by a score of 19–6. According to one newspaper account, Ed Williams "played a whale of a game." The following year sportswriters picked NYU to win the annual meeting, but the Tar Heels pulled off a surprising 7–0 upset. The student newspaper at Chapel Hill acknowledged Williams's outstanding performances in both games and described him as "a hard, hell-bent plunger." Commenting on the 1938 game, the ever-hopeful *Pittsburgh Courier* argued that since three consecutive games between the two universities had been played without racial incidents, the series provided an "excellent precedent" for the future. The newspaper made fun of segregationists' fears over such violations of the color line by noting that "the sky didn't fall!" Of course, intersectional matches were not completely lacking in symbolic importance or emotion to white North Carolinians. As one sportswriter in the *Daily Tar Heel* reminded readers, "Any time a southern team plays one from the North, it fights the Civil War all over again and starts protecting home and hearth against the damnyankees."[11]

President Frank Graham and the university escaped significant public criticism over the NYU series, perhaps because the three games were played in New York City. Yet at least one extreme segregationist became alarmed over the repeated violations of the color line. J. W. Cantrell, a Florida resident, wrote Graham several times to condemn North Carolina's action as a betrayal of white supremacy. In his letters Cantrell summed up the classic racist argument against integrated athletic events. Carolina's willingness to play against Williams constituted a serious error in judgment, Cantrell argued. The spirit of fair play could never justify competition against a black player, he insisted, because of the "hideous consequences" that might result from such permissiveness. Consequently, Cantrell argued that UNC should demand "a no Negro stipulation" in all its athletic contracts, so as to prevent any possible misunderstandings. Alerting Graham to the dangers that lurked in the future, he warned ominously, "If Negro players continue to be admitted against you, in a few years someone will say that you cannot have your rights except by having Negro players of your own." Finally, Cantrell fell back on a eugenicist interpretation of black inferiority and white supremacy, urging Graham not to assist in the destruction of "the most valuable accumulation of chromosomes on earth."[12]

Despite the fears of racists like Cantrell, two additional members of the old Southern Conference—the University of Maryland and Duke—followed North Carolina's lead and abandoned the gentleman's agreement in 1938 for games against Syracuse University. Maryland's conversion proved especially dramatic, since the university had imposed a policy of racial exclusion on Syracuse the previous year in Baltimore. Leading the 1937 Orangemen squad was an outstanding quarterback with the unlikely name of Wilmeth Sidat-Singh. A Cornell football coach had discovered Sidat-Singh, an African American who had been legally adopted by his East Indian father, a New York City physician, during an intramural football game. Since the junior quarterback had not played during the 1936 season, eastern sportswriters and fans knew nothing about him. As a publicity gimmick, school officials tricked several national newspapers into identifying the relatively light-complexioned student as "the only Hindu football player in the country." This deception fell apart shortly after the Syracuse squad arrived for their October 23 match against the Terrapins. The afternoon before the game Maryland administrators learned that a local black newspaper would expose the visiting quarterback as an African American in its Saturday edition. Understandably stunned by this news, these officials hastily informed the Syracuse staff that, because of his race, Sidat-Singh would not be allowed to play. Several of his teammates indignantly protested the ban, but school officials felt obligated to accept their host's policy. Consequently, Sidat-Singh remained at the hotel the next day while his teammates fell to Maryland by a score of 13–0. But the following year, when the Terrapin squad traveled to Syracuse for the return leg of their series, Maryland officials reversed their position and accepted Sidat-Singh's participation. Even if they had demanded his benching, Syracuse probably would have refused to do so. In a game that undoubtedly proved quite satisfying to the quarterback, Sidat-Singh led the powerful Orangemen to a 53–0 trouncing of the Terrapins.[13]

Duke University also scheduled Syracuse for a road contest in 1938, thereby creating another test of the gentleman's agreement. During the 1930s Coach Wallace Wade developed the Blue Devil squad into a formidable power with a growing national reputation. A native southerner, Wade had played at Brown with Fritz Pollard and had twice coached his University of Alabama teams to the Rose Bowl in the 1920s. The Duke coach enjoyed wide respect from fellow coaches. In fact, *Time* once honored him by placing his photograph on its cover. Wade's outstanding 1938 team, known as the "Iron Dukes" for its tenacious defense, aspired to win the conference championship and earn an invitation to the Rose Bowl. For the Blue Devils, the road to Pasadena ran through Syracuse, New York. Wade fully understood the politics of college football and realized that a public controversy over excluding Sidat-Singh might derail the school's bowl dreams. Although Duke had prudently inserted a "No Negroes" clause into the original game contract, Wade opportunistically decided that it would be in the Blue Devils' self-interest to waive the stipulation. He also believed that his team could defeat the Orangemen even with Sidat-Singh in the lineup. On the other hand, to claim victory over a weakened Syracuse eleven while its star quarterback sat on the bench would depreciate the value of the win and taint the Blue Devils. Thus, Wade candidly warned Duke administrators that if Sidat-Singh did not play, "no matter what the score is, we'll get no credit for winning," and the university expediently waived the exclusion clause. Some students and especially alumni were reportedly "up in arms" over the announcement, but the school administration did not back down. Wade told his players that anyone who personally disagreed with the decision could sit out the match, but he instructed them not to treat the rival quarterback any differently from his teammates. On the field Sidat-Singh showed flashes of brilliance, but the "Iron Duke" defense controlled the contest and ground out a 21–0 win. At the end of the season, the Durham squad remained undefeated, untied, unscored upon, and, according to one skeptical journalist, "uninteresting." Nonetheless, the team received its highly coveted invitation to the Rose Bowl, vindicating Wade's strategy.[14]

Several African American spokesmen expressed hope that Duke's decision to play against Sidat-Singh represented a growing trend against racial discrimination in big-time sports. In its November 1938 issue, *The Crisis* placed a photograph of Sidat-Singh on its cover, demonstrating the symbolic power of college football and the NAACP's belief that interracial cooperation through sports would provide a model for other areas of American society. North Carolina's leading black newspaper, the *Carolina Times* of Durham, praised Duke for abandoning its opposition to interracial play. Many black fans, the newspaper reported, had anticipated that the Blue Devils would "resort to ungentlemanly conduct on the field, because a Negro was playing on the Syracuse team," but in reality the Duke players had treated Sidat-Singh just "as any other player." The newspaper speculated that it might not be long before Duke and North Carolina would even play integrated teams in the South. Finally, the *Carolina Times* even prophesied that sports integration would eventually undermine segregation in the classroom. "Some day, and that day is not far away," the newspaper optimistically predicted, " Duke University and the University of North Carolina too, will admit Negroes to their graduate schools."[15]

Disloyalty to the Gentleman's Agreement in the Southwest

In the state of Texas loyalty to Jim Crow in college sports was somewhat less entrenched than at universities elsewhere in the Deep South. During the late 1930s financial incentives for Texas college teams to accept integrated games in California partially undermined the gentleman's agreement. The first known white college from the Lone Star State to compete against an African American player was Texas Technological University, a small and relatively unknown institution located in Lubbock on the high plains of West Texas. The college held its first classes on September 15, 1925, two weeks *after* its new football team had started practicing. Officials at Texas Tech sought to overcome their school's status as an obscure regional institution by developing a high-profile football program and utilizing intersectional games to gain national recognition. In October 1934 the Red Raiders played Loyola College in Los Angeles in the school's first major intersectional match. Loyola's star tackle Al Duval, an African American, started the game and played almost the entire contest, helping the home team gain a 12–6 victory. Afterward, Duval praised the Texans for their clean play and good sportsmanship. Because Texas Tech was not a well-known school and the game took place on the West Coast, most newspapers failed to report this racial milestone. Thus, Tech's pioneering action did not have any influence on the more prestigious colleges in the region.[16]

The desire to earn additional revenue and high national rankings motivated three leading Southwest Conference teams to abandon the athletic color line during the late 1930s. Southern Methodist University, Texas Christian University (TCU), and Texas A&M all fielded strong teams during that period, and each school abandoned Jim Crow for high-profile games on the West Coast in hopes of winning a national championship and earning a coveted invitation to the Rose Bowl. Financial concerns strongly motivated all three universities, while one coach, SMU's Matty Bell, also voiced an idealistic belief in equal opportunity on the gridiron. Because all of these important games were held in the Los Angeles metropolitan area, they received less coverage in the eastern press than did the integrated matches played by Duke, North Carolina, and Maryland in the Northeast. SMU became the first Southwest Conference member to compete against an integrated team. Intercollegiate athletics enjoyed a central role at the Dallas school, which had formed its first football team immediately after opening its doors in 1915. The university upgraded its athletic program in 1926 by constructing a modern facility, Ownby Stadium, at a cost of $175,000. The bond issue that financed this construction was scheduled to be retired over a ten-year period, with a balloon payment at the end. However, the Great Depression seriously weakened the college's financial status and created large deficits in its athletic budget. As part of a general retrenchment campaign, SMU trustees slashed faculty salaries, reduced the president's pay from $10,000 to $7,500, but maintained the football coach's salary at $12,000. Since the bulk of the bond issue—approximately $85,000—fell due in 1936, Mustang athletics faced an uncertain future.[17]

Coach Matty Bell and the 1935 SMU football team rescued the athletic department from this looming financial disaster. A former professional player who had competed alongside such black stars as Fritz Pollard and Paul Robeson, Bell became the school's new head coach in 1935. Bell quickly confirmed the wisdom of his hiring by directing the Mustangs to their best season ever. In November the undefeated Mustangs traveled to Los Angeles to meet UCLA in an unofficial tryout for the Rose Bowl. SMU passed this test with flying colors, inflicting a 21–0 defeat on the Bruins. Three weeks later the Mustangs defeated archrival TCU and star quarterback Sammy Baugh 20–14 in a dramatic game dubbed the conference's "game of the century," thereby clinching the league title. Sportswriters subsequently selected the undefeated Mustangs as the regular-season national champions. More important, SMU's outstanding record also earned the team a prized invitation to the Rose Bowl, the first bid ever extended to a Texas team. Although West Coast champion Stanford upset the Mustangs 7–0 on January 1, SMU received a generous paycheck of nearly $90,000 for its participation. The university used this huge sum to resolve the athletic department's financial crisis by paying off the outstanding debt on Ownby Stadium. This financial windfall impressed other conference members and made them eager to duplicate SMU's good fortune.[18]

Southern Methodist jumped at the opportunity to return to Los Angeles in 1937 and 1940 to play UCLA and again audition for the Rose Bowl. But the racial composition of the UCLA teams had changed significantly, because the 1937 and 1940 squads included several talented African Americans. In 1937 halfback Kenny Washington and end Woody Strode were the main offensive weapons for the Bruins. Since UCLA officials believed that the matchup with SMU would attract a large crowd and create a financial bonanza for both schools, they callously offered to bench Washington and Strode if SMU insisted. Matty Bell personally favored allowing Washington and Strode to participate but consulted his players, who voted unanimously to play against the two Bruin stars. From the players' perspective, a victory over a depleted Bruin squad "would be a hollow triumph" lacking in honor. As one Mustang explained, "We figured we wouldn't get much credit for beating UCLA without Washington and Strode. They are the best men they have, so we voted unanimously that they be permitted to play in the game." The matchup between these two "dark boys," as the SMU student newspaper described them, and a team of white southerners also heightened spectator interest in the match.[19]

The November 20 contest between the two colleges proved to be "a typical display of razzle-dazzle football," as the Mustangs rallied from a two-touchdown deficit to defeat the Bruins 26–13. UCLA's Kenny Washington turned in one of his best career performances. As he left the field in the fourth quarter, the large crowd, including the SMU section, gave him a tremendous ovation. Newspaper accounts, especially those in the African American press, praised SMU for playing "fair and hard" and depicted the game as a sign that "the sun is breaking through." The following year Wendell Smith, the most influential black sportswriter of that era, gained an interview with the Mustang coach, who told him, "I don't believe in drawing the color line in sports." Bell went further and even predicted that sometime in the future southern white schools would recruit black players. In 1940, when SMU returned to California, the Bruin squad featured two African American stars, versatile halfback Jackie Robinson and end Ray Bartlett. Despite a sensational eighty-eight-yard touchdown run by Robinson, SMU defeated their hosts 9–6. Afterward, "Coach Matty Bell and the entire SMU team showed their real sportsmanship down on the field by congratulating Robinson and Ray Bartlett."[20]

In September 1939 Texas Christian University made the long trip out to the West Coast to challenge UCLA. The Fort Worth college, affiliated with the Disciples of Christ denomination, had won the unofficial national championship the previous year behind gifted quarterback Davey O'Brien, the Heisman trophy winner. TCU officials naturally hoped to impress Rose Bowl sponsors and duplicate the financial success achieved by SMU. They were to be disappointed, however. Before sixty-five thousand fans in the Los Angeles Coliseum, Kenny Washington, Woody Strode, Jackie Robinson, and Ray Bartlett led the Bruins to a 6–2 upset of the Horned Frogs, ending the visitors' fourteen-game winning streak. There were no complaints after the contest about violent play, and the black press reported that both teams displayed "excellent sportsmanship." Furthermore, TCU coach "Dutch" Meyers publicly praised Washington and Robinson for their outstanding performances.[21]

In the fall of 1940 Texas A&M University became the third Southwest Conference team to abandon the gentleman's agreement for high-profile games outside the South. Located in College Station in East Texas, the all-male institution required two years of military training and embodied social conservatism and hypermasculinity. An emerging national power, the Aggies won or shared three consecutive conference championships from 1939 to 1941, and the undefeated 1939 team won the mythical national championship. On October 12, 1940, before sixty thousand spectators in the Coliseum, Texas A&M defeated the Bruins 7–0 behind All-American fullback John Kimbrough. After the game angry UCLA fans accused the Aggies of dirty play by using "back-alley tactics" to knock Jackie Robinson and several other Bruin players out of the game. One sportswriter pointedly contrasted the brutal behavior of these "southern gentlemen" with the good sportsmanship displayed by SMU and TCU. The following year Texas A&M arranged another major intersectional game, this time in New York City against NYU and fullback Leonard Bates. Aggie officials apparently made no effort to bar Bates from the contest, which they won by a lopsided 49–7 score. Despite Texas A&M's conservative campus culture, opportunistic school officials had again refused to allow a racial issue to distract their football team from the pursuit of profits and prominence.[22]

In addition to the three Southwest Conference schools, one additional Texas college team waived the policy of racial exclusion for away games during the late 1930s. The Texas College of Mines, known later as Texas Western College and today as the University of Texas at El Paso, was located in the border city in far West Texas. Although El Paso was the westernmost city in the ex-Confederate states, local ordinances and state laws enforced a Jim Crow system, and the college traditionally did not compete against integrated teams. Because of its distance from other Texas universities, the College of Mines belonged to the Border Conference, which included such regional rivals as New Mexico A&M, the University of New Mexico, and the University of Arizona. In November 1937 the Miners abandoned the gentleman's agreement when they played Arizona State College (ASC) in Tempe. Included on the Arizona State roster was Emerson Harvey, one of the first two black college players in the state. (Harvey played most of the game in a 19–0 loss to the Texans.) Apparently, some of the Miners singled out Harvey for rough treatment. According to the Tempe squad's graduate manager, one Miner player admitted several years later that "we just beat the hell out of him." Since Arizona State was also a Border Conference member, the Miners had little choice but to accept integrated matches there unless they wished to endanger their good standing in the league. The following year, however, when Arizona State traveled to El Paso for a rematch, ASC coach Dixie Howell left Harvey behind in Tempe, in deference to the Texans' racial policies. Later in 1937 the College of Mines also hosted Northern Arizona College, whose squad included Augustus Shaw Jr., apparently the first black athlete at the school. Because of the Miners' racial code, Northern Arizona left Shaw behind in Flagstaff. Since the College of Mines and other Texas members of the Border Conference refused to host integrated games, the New Mexico and Arizona schools eventually worked out an informal compromise whereby they could use their black players at home but not when competing inside Texas.[23]

In 1938 the College of Mines unexpectedly encountered a direct challenge to its Jim Crow policies from Santa Barbara State College. Several weeks before the scheduled October 29, 1938, contest in El Paso, College of Mines officials learned that the visiting squad would include two new players, starting end Larry Pickens and second-string tackle Melvin Dennis, both African Americans. The College of Mines athletic council promptly ruled that Pickens and Dennis were ineligible to compete in El Paso because of their race. In response, Santa Barbara officials threatened to scrub the game. However, they did make a counteroffer to either move the contest to Los Angeles and give the Miners the home-team share of the game revenue or meet the Miners at a neutral site. Rejecting these proposals, College of Mines officials canceled the game and severed all athletic relations with the California college.[24] Their decision proved to be popular in Texas. Coach Mack Saxon commented that he "wouldn't draw the color line if the game was at Santa Barbara," out of respect for that school's traditions, but that the Californians were being unreasonable in demanding the right to use Pickens and Dennis in El Paso. "As far as I know, no college team in Texas [has] ever played another team using Negro players in a Texas city," he declared. The campus newspaper strongly endorsed the game's cancellation, explaining that "our southern custom has been recognized for everybody concerned. We were again' it." In Austin supportive University of Texas students circulated a petition warning that interracial games would be "a step towards destruction of the honest man-to-man relationship the southern white man and southern Negro have labored for two generations to rebuild." Hoping to avoid such controversies in the future, College of Mines officials later announced that thenceforth all school contracts for home games would include a "No Negroes" clause.[25] All of these decisions by Texas universities in the 1930s to participate in integrated football games away from home suggest that the state's athletic culture was becoming slightly more flexible than that found in the lower southern states with which Texas had historically been grouped.

Defections in the Border States

Several universities in the border states that traditionally had followed "southern" policies in athletics also modified their commitment to the gentleman's agreement in the latter part of the decade. In October 1939 football teams from the University of Missouri and the University of Oklahoma left Jim Crow behind when they traveled north to challenge Big Ten opponents. On October 7, one week after the TCU–UCLA game in Los Angeles, Missouri met an integrated Ohio State team in Columbus. The Buckeyes' black halfback Charles Anderson not only played in the game but even scored a touchdown in OSU's 19–0 victory. That same afternoon in Evanston, Illinois, the Oklahoma Sooners shut out Northwestern University 23–0 in another intersectional contest. In the second half Wildcat James Smith entered the game as a substitute, provoking a loud wave of boos and catcalls from the Sooner fans. This crude display so upset the Oklahoma student newspaper that it suggested no future games be scheduled against integrated northern squads unless civilized behavior from its fans could be ensured. Reflecting on the significance of the two games, columnist Fay Young of the *Chicago Defender* praised the two Big Ten colleges for standing "by their guns and using varsity players regardless of color against southern football elevens." Young and other black spokesmen optimistically viewed the absence of the color line in these two games, as well as the earlier actions by

North Carolina, Maryland, and Duke, as indications of a rising tide of racial tolerance in athletics. *The Crisis* likewise agreed that racial change in college sports was now at hand. The NAACP magazine firmly believed that athletics could serve as a valuable model of racial tolerance and equal opportunity for other areas of American life. "Fair play in sports leads the way to fair play in life," one magazine editorial declared. "May the honor roll increase!"[26]

Northern students increasingly challenged racial exclusion in college sports in the late 1930s. In the spring of 1939 a small controversy over a track meet at the University of Missouri demonstrated this growing assertiveness. The University of Missouri had scheduled a triangular meet with the University of Wisconsin (UW) and Notre Dame for April 15 in Columbia. When Missouri officials discovered that the Wisconsin squad included black hurdler Ed Smith, they quietly informed Badger coaches that he would not be allowed to compete. In response, students at the Madison campus staged a series of protest rallies, the student newspaper urged the university to withdraw from the competition, and a faculty resolution recommended against any future participation in segregated athletic contests. Wisconsin officials subsequently canceled the team's trip by "mutual agreement" with Missouri. Next, a small group of liberal Missouri students circulated a petition urging Notre Dame to follow Wisconsin's example. Subsequently, Notre Dame officials announced that their runners would also stay home, forcing the meet's cancellation. The surprising success of this student pressure seemed to forecast further problems for the gentleman's agreement on northern campuses.[27]

Small colleges also participated in the conflicts over the gentleman's agreement, but news of their activities rarely received coverage in the large metropolitan dailies. As a result, the full range of incidents involving black players on their teams will never be known. One incident that has been recorded involved Trenton State Teachers College from New Jersey and Wilson Teachers College from the District of Columbia. The two small colleges had scheduled their first home-and-home series in basketball for the 1934–35 season. The Trenton State basketball team that year included junior Lloyd Williams, the "flashy Trenton Negro." When the New Jersey squad arrived in Washington for the first game in the series in January 1935, Wilson College officials refused to allow Williams to take the court. Trenton coaches yielded to the demand and suffered a lopsided 39–13 loss. The following month, one week before the Wilson team was due to visit New Jersey for the return match, school newspaper editor Samuel A. Alito penned a blistering editorial describing Williams's benching as "an embarrassing affair involving the worst in racial animosity and sectionalism." Alito condemned Trenton State officials for surrendering to "race prejudice of a past era" and insisted that they should sever athletic relations with any school that made similar demands in the future. When the two colleges met again on

February 15, Williams was in the starting lineup, and the home team pulled out a narrow 29–26 victory. The following year, when Williams served as team captain, Trenton State dropped Wilson Teachers College from its schedule.[28]

Several other sporting events involving small colleges hinted at growing tolerance for interracial competition during the late 1930s. Football and basketball contests between predominantly white northern colleges and southern black universities represented a new development. Apparently, the first such contest took place in January 1938, when Brooklyn College hosted Hampton Institute of Virginia in a basketball game. Although the event was ignored by the large New York newspapers, it received favorable coverage from the *Daily Worker*, the newspaper of the Communist Party of the United States. Under sports editor Lester Rodney, the communist newspaper regularly joined with black spokesmen to campaign for an end to discrimination in American sports, especially in Major League Baseball and college football. In December 1940 the Brooklyn basketball team hosted another southern black school, Virginia Union College, in a game held in a Harlem arena with a racially mixed officiating crew. Long Island University and St. Francis College also played basketball games against African American college teams at that time. In October 1941 a small northern white college actually visited the border South to play a black university. In possibly the first event of its kind in college football, tiny Rio Grande College of Ohio played a road game at West Virginia State University. Later in the month, Rio Grande College also hosted another contest against a southern black college.[29]

Continued Loyalty to the Gentleman's Agreement in the North

The guarded optimism that greeted the abandonment of the gentleman's agreement by such southern universities as North Carolina and SMU was offset at the end of the 1930s by the continued racial exclusion practiced by several major northern and western colleges. Boston College, NYU, UCLA, and the University of California all tarnished their reputations by refusing to defend their African American players. Boston College's flagrant mistreatment of halfback Lou Montgomery on six occasions when playing southern teams was especially egregious, as the school withheld him "from more games than any other football player in the annals of the sport." An outstanding multisport athlete at Brockton High School, Montgomery joined a group of other local stars who decided as a group to compete for Boston College. The first black football player at the school, Montgomery started on the 1937 freshman team but saw only limited action in his first varsity season the following year. In 1939 new coach Frank Leahy, a former pupil of the legendary Knute Rockne at Notre Dame, installed a new wide-open offense, the Notre Dame box, which was perfectly suited to exploit the talents of the 5'7", 150-pound Montgomery and passing quarterback Charlie O'Rourke.[30]

Boston College hired Leahy to oversee its drive to achieve big-time status in college football. As part of this campaign, the college sought to upgrade its schedule by adding games against prominent opponents. In anticipation of larger crowds, the university moved important matches from the school's small Alumni Field complex to the more spacious Fenway Park, home of the Boston Red Sox. But when the elite eastern squads declined to play the upstarts from Chestnut Hill, BC turned to southern teams, many of which were eager for national exposure. The implications of this decision for Lou Montgomery did not become apparent until the third game of the 1939 season. Fully aware of Montgomery's presence on the Eagles' roster, University of Florida (UF) officials demanded that he be benched or they would refuse to play, citing a clause in the game contract allowing the Gators to cancel the match without financial penalty in order to avoid competing against an African American. After Boston College officials failed to convince Florida to change its position, they told Montgomery that he could not play. Several of his teammates threatened to sit out the game, but Montgomery, acting as a loyal team member and a "good Negro," urged them to carry on. Perhaps because of the furor, the heavily favored Eagles played sluggishly, and Florida pulled off a 7–0 upset. Montgomery briefly considered quitting because of the incident, but since no one "imagined this was going to be a regular thing," he decided to remain on the team. In response to local criticism over their actions, college officials announced that they would not sign any new racially restrictive game contracts. However, they cleverly neglected to mention whether they had previously signed any other such agreements.[31]

Three weeks later the duplicity of Boston College administrators became obvious when the powerful Auburn University squad arrived in town for a November 4 contest. Local newspapers soon reported that the southerners' game contract also included a provision that barred BC from using black players. Once more embarrassed by the exposure of a secret agreement and fearful of the financial consequences of a game cancellation, BC representatives begged Auburn officials to allow the Tiger football players to vote on whether to waive the clause, but Auburn refused to do so. Consequently, the Eagle squad once more took the field without Montgomery, but this time Boston College ground out a 13–7 win. Gaining confidence each week, BC ripped through the rest of its schedule and finished with a 9-1 record. Montgomery played extensively in these contests but never returned to the starting lineup, despite making several long touchdown runs and compiling a phenomenal rushing average of almost ten yards per carry. In recognition of Boston College's new status, the Cotton Bowl extended to the school an invitation to play in its January 1, 1940, classic against Clemson in Dallas. This honor constituted a major milestone for BC, since it marked the first time that the Eagles had ever been invited to a postseason game.[32]

Since the Cotton Bowl did not permit African Americans to compete in its game, Lou Montgomery was banished to the sidelines for the third time that season. As Curtis Sanford, the founder of the postseason contest, bluntly explained, "In view of the general attitude towards Negroes in Texas, it was deemed advisable that Montgomery refrain from playing." Boston College officials never considered declining the Cotton Bowl invitation because of Montgomery's exclusion. As a result, Boston sportswriters and black critics again condemned BC for displaying "out-and-out cowardice." One newspaper lamented that the college had been influenced more by "dollars and cents, rather than the democratic ideals for which the institution is supposed to stand." Montgomery remained in Boston and eventually released a public letter in which he expressed the hope that future intersectional games would be contested "under northern standards." Montgomery's absence failed to remove all sectional overtones from the contest. At the ceremonial coin toss before the game, one Boston College captain allegedly joked to his Clemson counterparts, "Let's not have any North-South bitterness. Remember, when your grandfathers were fighting Yankees, our grandfathers were in Poland and Czechoslovakia." After Clemson won the game by a narrow 6–3 margin, BC coaches and players sent their missing teammate a telegram reading, "We missed you, Lou."[33]

The 1940 season brought even greater public glory and private shame to Boston College football. The Eagles enjoyed their best season ever, overwhelming all ten of their opponents while packing the stands at Fenway Park. After Montgomery scored a touchdown in the season-opening win over Centre College, his chances of becoming a starter looked good. Unfortunately, two subsequent games against Deep South teams revealed that school administrators would continue to sacrifice him to expediency. In the second week of the season BC traveled to New Orleans and handily defeated the Tulane Green Wave 27–7. School officials viewed the game as an audition for the Sugar Bowl, and the Eagles clearly impressed their hosts. Montgomery accompanied the team to New Orleans and actually sat in the press box during the game. But because of segregated housing he stayed separately from his teammates with the head coach at Xavier University, a black Catholic institution. This one case of exclusion in the Deep South did not overly worry Montgomery, since school officials had previously assured him that he would play in all home games. A few weeks later, however, Auburn returned to Boston for a rematch, and again the Alabama team insisted that Montgomery be benched. Boston College officials privately suggested to Auburn coach Jack Meagher the possibility of each team withholding one player from the game. Meagher seriously considered the unusual compromise but ultimately rejected it. Consequently, Montgomery watched from the sidelines as the Eagles soundly whipped the Tigers 33–7. Since BC officials had known Auburn's position concerning Montgomery for more than a year, their decision not to renegotiate the exclusion clause or drop Auburn from the schedule indicated that they were determined to achieve national prominence in football, regardless of the cost.[34]

Boston College's undefeated season earned the school a second straight post-season bid, this time to the 1941 Sugar Bowl in New Orleans. The invitation did not include Lou Montgomery, of course. Although he missed the two games against Tulane and Auburn, the talented halfback still had scored six touchdowns and passed for a seventh in the other eight games. Yet his excellent performance proved irrelevant to postseason action. "By that time I was really fed up," Montgomery later recalled, and he again made plans to stay home. But school officials persuaded him to accompany the team to New Orleans, in the name of team harmony. As Montgomery watched from the press box, Boston College drove the length of the field late in the game to score the winning touchdown and claim an exciting 19–13 victory over previously undefeated Tennessee. Like other black players involved in similar situations, Montgomery had swallowed his pride and acted as a "good sport," thereby helping Boston College partially conceal its callous sacrifice of principle, a decision he later came to regret. Sympathetic African Americans viewed Montgomery as a heroic victim and a symbolic representative of their race. As one journalist explained, when "he suffered, the entire Negro race suffered. For when he was barred, the entire race was barred." On the other hand, Wendell Smith of the *Pittsburgh Courier* took a more critical position, chastised Montgomery for passively accepting his benching, rather than challenging such discrimination, and for remaining enrolled at the college that had treated him so shabbily.[35]

Like the Lou Montgomery case, the Leonard Bates controversy at New York University during 1940–41 further exposed continued northern complicity in maintaining the gentleman's agreement. At the same time, NYU students responded by developing the largest campus movement to that date against racial exclusion in college sports. The controversy began when the university deferred to the University of Missouri and left Bates, NYU's starting fullback, at home for their November 1940 game in Columbia. Although Missouri had by 1940 abandoned demands for racial exclusion when playing outside the state, the school still refused to compete against African Americans at home. The Bates case immediately evoked memories of the 1929 controversy over the NYU–Georgia game in New York, when university officials had honored the gentleman's agreement and withheld David Myers. This time, however, unprecedented numbers of NYU students loudly protested Bates's exclusion and demanded that the principle of racial equality be observed.

Several New York newspapers touched off the Bates crisis when they reported in October 1940 that NYU would leave the starting fullback behind for the intersectional match, "because Missouri considers herself a southern school." Indignant NYU students responded by holding several rallies at the university's Washington Square campus, one of which reportedly drew a crowd of nearly two thousand. The protesters demanded that either "Bates must play" or the university should cancel the game. Eventually, some thirty student organizations, the student council, and ten fraternities endorsed this position. A few radicals even called for severing all athletic relations with universities that excluded African Americans from enrolling. One handout aptly summed up the protesters' position by stating that "no football team is worth the sacrifice of the ideals of liberty and freedom."[36]

NYU officials denied that any discrimination was involved and claimed that Bates himself was not interested in participating in the Missouri contest. To prove this point the school released without permission a private letter by Bates in which he stated that he had been informed about the game when he first joined the football squad and had not objected at the time to the arrangement. In reality, though, the junior fullback did want to play against the Tigers, but he was reluctant to say so publicly because he might endanger his scholarship. Behind the scenes, though, Bates quietly supported the student movement. Nonetheless, his refusal to speak out publicly upset several black sportswriters, who accused him of lacking courage and displaying a plantation mentality. One African American journalist even wrote, "Folks don't want him up North if he hasn't any manhood." Despite widespread student support for the "Bates must play" movement, the administration held firm. On October 31 the NYU players, minus their fullback, boarded the train for Missouri, where they absorbed a 33–0 loss. Reflecting on administrators' submission to Missouri's demands, two journalists sarcastically commented that the university should change its school colors from violet to yellow, given their lack of courage to defend Bates.[37]

Over the following months the "fair-play movement" continued to be active on NYU's two campuses and added new recruits at several other New York colleges. When additional examples of apparent racial discrimination involving the NYU basketball and track teams eventually surfaced, these activists became even more outspoken. In December 1940 students learned that Jim Coward, the basketball team's lone black player, had been dropped from the squad and would therefore miss a January trip to the University of North Carolina and Georgetown University. NYU officials claimed that Coward had been removed from the squad because of unsatisfactory grades and not because of any racial demands from the two colleges. The unexpected statement of North Carolina coach Bill Lange that his players were willing to compete "against NYU at its full strength" gave the student movement some slight hope. But NYU chancellor Harry W. Chase, who had previously served as the president of UNC, made his position quite clear when he stated, "The time has not arrived when we can ask southern schools to play against Negro players on southern campuses." Subsequently Coward remained in New York and off the team.[38]

In February 1941 the fair-play movement became even more aggressive when students learned that NYU had agreed to leave behind three black runners when the track team traveled to Washington, D.C., in March for a meet at Catholic University. Once again students staged rallies and circulated petitions denouncing school officials. When protest leaders refused to call off their campaign or repudiate a flyer accusing the administration of racial discrimination, the university began disciplinary proceedings against several of them, eventually expelling the so-called student seven. Meanwhile, the fair-play movement spread to several other northeastern universities, including Harvard. Eleanor Roosevelt even addressed a crowd of nine hundred students at a Manhattan rally in behalf of the seven, although she gently chided them for using overly aggressive tactics. Despite all these efforts, including a sit-in protest by more than one hundred students at a disciplinary hearing, a university appeals committee eventually upheld the seven expulsions. Worse yet, NYU officials refused to withdraw their team from the track meet at Catholic University. Despite these setbacks, student activists had nonetheless succeeded in mobilizing much of the NYU student body, in spreading the fair-play campaign to several additional universities, and in expanding student and public awareness of racial discrimination in college athletics. Although these activists failed to force a formal change in the school's policy concerning away games against southern teams, their efforts probably guaranteed that in the future NYU would never again bench an African American player for a home game. Some sixty years later, in May 2001, the "student seven" belatedly received vindication when NYU officially honored them for their courageous stand in support of racial justice.[39]

The 1941 NYU football season confirmed that university officials would no longer honor the gentleman's agreement for home games. At the start of the fall, though, it was not known if the three southern and border teams on the schedule—Texas A&M, Tulane, and Missouri—had agreed to compete against Leonard Bates. The senior fullback began the season in the starting backfield for the Violet squad, which was greatly weakened by the unexpected enlistment of six players in the armed forces. Against Texas A&M on October 11 at Yankee Stadium, Bates played well, running back one kickoff fifty-seven yards in a lopsided 49–7 loss to the Aggies. In the fifth game of the season, however, Bates suffered a serious shoulder injury that threatened to end his season prematurely. A week later Coach Mal Stevens announced that he would withhold Bates and two other injured starters from the upcoming Missouri and Tulane games, in order to allow their injuries to heal properly before the season finale against Fordham. Apparently, Stevens had planned to use Bates against the two southern teams but genuinely withheld him because of his injury. Still not at full strength, the senior fullback briefly returned to action against Fordham but proved unable to help the Violets avoid their seventh straight loss. Although NYU stood behind Bates in 1941, the behavior of college officials during the previous school year had exposed the continued reluctance of some northern college officials to challenge racial exclusion for athletic contests played in the South.[40]

On the West Coast several major California universities began to seek out football games against eastern and southern teams in the late 1930s in order to raise their national profile, but the issue of the color line complicated scheduling. The University of California, Berkeley, placed expediency over idealism in the fall of 1940 when the Golden Bears traveled to Atlanta to meet Georgia Tech. Left behind for that contest was Walter Gordon, the son of an assistant coach and former Cal player. The following year the Berkeley team was scheduled to host Georgia Tech in a December rematch. As the season wound down, liberal California sportswriter Art Cohn contacted officials from both schools concerning Gordon's status and subsequently reported that Cal had apparently agreed to bench Gordon for the upcoming game. However, in the wake of the Japanese attack on Pearl Harbor on December 7, the contest was canceled, so one can only surmise that California probably would have withheld Gordon. That same month UCLA made a cross-country trip to Jacksonville for a special end-of-the-season game against the University of Florida. In order to placate their hosts, the Bruins left halfback Clarence Mackey at home. These callous decisions by UCLA and Cal, previously unreported by scholars, reveal that West Coast colleges were not above selling out their black players in order to schedule games against southern teams in major intersectional games.[41]

The District of Columbia and Maryland Go Separate Ways

Toward the end of the 1930s several universities in the border state of Maryland and in the District of Columbia began to waiver slightly in their commitment to Jim Crow. These regions had never been part of the Confederacy, and they interacted extensively with neighboring states to the north. In October 1938 the Butler University football team from Indianapolis traveled to heavily segregated Washington, D.C., for a game against George Washington University. When GW officials discovered that Butler's star halfback Tom Harding was African American, they threatened to cancel the contest unless he was left at home. Harding apparently was a respected figure on the Butler campus, since the student newspaper praised him as "a coach's dream; a player who is well acquainted with all phases of the game, exhibits coordination, and has the correct mental attitude." Coach Tony Hinkle discussed the situation with Harding and supposedly offered to cancel the trip. But the junior halfback, following the unofficial script expected of black athletes in such situations, declined the gesture and graciously urged the team to make the trip anyway, provided that GW agreed to a return match the following year in Indianapolis. The following year George Washington indeed honored its promise to play Butler without any racial restrictions. Led by Harding's inspired performance, Butler upset the favored visitors 13–6. Harding scored all of his team's thirteen points, his second touchdown coming on an electrifying seventy-two-yard run. However, the conduct of some GW players drew criticism from the student newspaper at Butler, which charged that Harding was on the receiving end of what it termed "most of the illegal playing" by the Colonials. One year later another college from the District of Columbia followed George Washington's example. In October 1940 Georgetown University ventured north to New York City, where the Hoyas played against NYU and fullback Leonard Bates, one week before Bates was left at home for NYU's controversial game at Missouri. Despite these concessions, George Washington, Georgetown, and Catholic University all still refused to allow black athletes to compete in any sporting events held within the District of Columbia. This position reflected the continued hold that southern culture and racial etiquette had on Washington, D.C.[42]

Colleges in Maryland generally shared the prejudices of their neighbors in the District of Columbia, but at the start of the 1940s several Maryland schools reluctantly accepted integrated games within the state. A principled stand by several northern universities, aided by calls for increased patriotism and national unity produced by the war in Europe, combined to make racial exclusion in sports seem undemocratic. Although Maryland was technically a border state where most aspects of public life remained tightly segregated, extensive interaction with adjacent northern states and the lack of a Confederate heritage may have permitted college sports to take the first small steps away from total segregation. In the spring of 1941 the Harvard University lacrosse team visited the area for games against the University of Maryland and the Naval Academy. Playing against a Harvard squad in any sport still carried considerable prestige, but when the host institutions discovered that the visiting team had included on the travel roster Lucien Alexis, an African American student from New Orleans, they became upset. Harvard representatives apparently talked Maryland into permitting Alexis to participate in their match at College Park, after the Terrapin players voted to play against him. This racial milestone was apparently the first integrated college game held in the state in the twentieth century, and racial liberals naturally hoped that it would serve as an opening wedge for additional interracial competition.[43]

The U.S. Naval Academy ignored Maryland's example and barred Alexis from its home lacrosse match against Harvard. Just six months earlier Navy had required the Drake University football team to withhold two African American players when it visited Annapolis. Academy officials saw no reason to make an exception for a mere lacrosse team, even one from mighty Harvard, although they briefly did discuss withholding one of their own players as compensation. The superintendent of the Academy, Rear Adm. Russell Willson, forcefully complained about Alexis's unannounced presence to Harvard athletic director William J. Bingham, who reluctantly agreed to withhold Alexis. Bingham's action represented a step backward for Harvard, which back in 1916 had canceled a dual track meet in Annapolis because Navy refused to allow star long jumper Edward "Ned" Gourdin to participate. Many Harvard students, faculty, and alumni were outraged at news of Bingham's decision. Influenced by the fairplay movement spreading across the Northeast, angry students demanded a firm policy statement from the university supporting democracy in sports. One African American at Harvard Law School summed up student opinion when he asserted, "If southern schools wish to meet the northern universities in athletics, they should accept the standards of the North." These complaints soon brought results. Two weeks after the incident the Harvard Corporation publicly announced a new guideline that explicitly stated that the university would not tolerate any racial discrimination involving its athletic teams. This stand by one of the most prestigious athletic programs in the United States indicated the growing strength of the movement for "fair play and democracy" in intersectional sports and provided inspiration for further attacks on Jim Crow.[44]

Five months later the Naval Academy unexpectedly yielded to the growing pressure and abandoned the color line for athletic events at home. In October 1941 the Middies were scheduled to host Cornell in a football game at Baltimore. This intersectional match represented an important milestone for the university, because it was the first time that Cornell had played south of the Mason-Dixon line. Several weeks before the game Maryland newspapers identified sophomore end Samuel Pierce Jr. as a member of the Cornell squad. Since Coach Carl Snavely regularly used Pierce as one of his first substitutes off the bench, he would normally see action against the Middies. Several Cornell alumni living in Maryland telephoned the school's acting athletic director, Robert J. Kane, and other university officials, urging them to bench Pierce out of respect for Navy's traditions. Kane and Snavely conferred and resolved not to let an opposing team dictate who could play for Cornell. Perhaps because of the repercussions from the previous spring's conflict with Harvard over Lucien Alexis and the potential public relations embarrassment of discriminating against a black player during a national military buildup, Navy officials unexpectedly changed their position.

Several days before the match Rear Admiral Willson announced that Navy would not challenge the composition of Cornell's roster. On Saturday, October 18, the Middies defeated their northern visitors 14–0 before forty-five thousand fans, including Adm. Chester Nimitz and other high-ranking naval brass. Snavely played Pierce for about five minutes in the second half, with no appreciable reaction from opposing players or the crowd. Yet Pierce did not completely escape racial discrimination while in Baltimore, as he was forced to stay at the black Young Men's Christian Association (YMCA) center while his teammates were housed at the exclusive Gilman School. A few weeks before the Cornell game the Naval Academy's shift in policy had been foreshadowed at a scrimmage between Navy's freshman football team and the Penn State first-year squad. The visiting team included Dave Alston, the most promising freshman athlete at Penn State in decades, and his brother Harry, who were the first African Americans to play football for the Nittany Lions. Because of the impending policy change and because the game was technically only a scrimmage, Navy permitted the two athletes to participate. Except for a group of black kitchen personnel from the academy who suddenly appeared to cheer for the Alstons, virtually no spectators were present, and the scrimmage was soon forgotten.[45]

Six days after the Navy–Cornell confrontation, a second football game, this time between Boston University and Western Maryland College, confirmed the further erosion of the athletic color line in Maryland. The 1941 contest was the third in a series between the two schools. The 1939 game had been staged in Baltimore, and Western Maryland had banned BU sophomore halfback Charlie Thomas from the match. Later that fall Boston University also left Thomas at home for a road trip to Florida to play the University of Tampa. The following year, when Western Maryland traveled to Boston, school officials yielded to BU's traditions and agreed that Thomas and sophomore Howard Mitchell could participate. But in 1941, as the series returned to Baltimore, Western Maryland instructed the visitors that Thomas and Mitchell could not play in the contest. On the Monday before the game BU athletic director John H. Harmon informed the two athletes that they would not make the Baltimore trip and excused them from practice for the rest of the week. But after the student newspaper reported that Thomas and Mitchell would be benched "because of southern sentiment," several student organizations and the Boston chapter of the NAACP sprang into action. When President Daniel L. Marsh returned to the city on Wednesday from a trip to the Midwest, several hundred irate students were waiting for him at the train station.[46]

President Marsh promptly set to work on defusing the controversy. After several discussions he finally convinced President Fred G. Holloway of Western Maryland to drop the school's traditional commitment to Jim Crow. The two presidents subsequently issued a joint statement declaring that a nondiscriminatory policy for the game would be a "wise course of action" and would promote "the best interests of sportsmanship." As a result, Mitchell and Thomas hastily rejoined the team at its Thursday practice and then departed with the squad by train. In Baltimore the two players actually stayed at the same hotel with their teammates. The next day, in a remarkable gesture, students at historically black Morgan State College invited Mitchell and Thomas to the campus for lunch, where they staged a small pep rally for the two in appreciation of their historic role. The Friday-night match between the two colleges unfolded without major incident, and Mitchell played one of his best games ever. Because Mitchell was light-skinned, however, many local fans and Western Maryland players apparently did not recognize him on the field. Since the Western Maryland defense seemed to concentrate excessively on stopping Charlie Thomas, Coach Pat Hanley played the senior halfback only sparingly. Mitchell later recalled that as both squads trudged off the field after Boston University's 14–0 victory, one Western Maryland player commented to another, "Well, we stopped that one nigger [Thomas], and if they had played the other one we would have stopped him too!"[47] The following year Johns Hopkins College allowed black halfback Leeland Jones of the University of Buffalo football team to play in a home game at Homewood Field in Baltimore, further confirming the new trend toward athletic democracy. Despite these important breakthroughs, the most prestigious football school in the state, the University of Maryland, did not immediately modify its Jim Crow policies for home games. As the northernmost member of the Southern Conference, the university continued to adhere to "southern rules" for its home games for another decade.[48]

World War II Further Undermines Jim Crow at the Margins

The arrival of World War II and the enormous war mobilization that followed dramatically reduced the size and scope of college sports. Thousands of athletes rushed to enlist, leaving their former teams shorthanded. Curtailed schedules, gasoline rationing, and travel restrictions eventually eliminated most intersectional contests. Many colleges reduced the number of athletic teams that they fielded, and some even dropped football for the duration of the war. Because of this different wartime environment, it is impossible to know if more southern schools would have followed the precedents established by such colleges as North Carolina, Duke, and SMU in abandoning the gentleman's agreement for games outside the South. The response of Major League Baseball and the National Football League during the war, however, serves as a warning about the continuing strength of racial exclusion in American sports. Despite a shortage of skilled white professionals, which even led to the signing of a one-armed white player, Major League Baseball declined to utilize the wartime situation to sign black professionals and integrate the major or minor leagues. Since no major league franchises were located in an ex-Confederate state (the Washington Senators were the unofficial "southern team"), this reluctance to break with tradition spoke volumes about continued racial conservatism in the North. The NFL likewise retained its whites-only policy, bringing former players out of retirement and adopting a free-substitution rule. Nonetheless, the war did loosen some racial barriers, and sporting activities at military bases within the United States occasionally departed from Jim Crow traditions.[49]

Athletic programs run by the military gave former college players the opportunity to remain active in sports and occasionally accepted integrated teams and competition. Most military installations encouraged team sports, and the larger posts and bases usually formed competitive football squads. These teams normally followed Jim Crow traditions in the South; after all, the U.S. armed forces were themselves tightly segregated. For example, the black Twenty-fourth Infantry Division at Fort Benning, Georgia, fielded a team but competed only against southern black colleges. Nonetheless, the unusual wartime situation sometimes permitted limited interracial competition. A white service team might occasionally borrow several players from a black squad for a special match. In some locations military teams seeking games from a limited number of potential opponents might dare to cross the color line and play a team from the other race. Most of the resulting integrated teams and interracial games did not receive press coverage, and their shadowy existence did not set any precedents. Yet they may have planted the seeds of later racial cooperation in sports. One military football team that received coverage in the black press was the Fort Knox Armoraiders, which played both college and professional teams. In the fall of 1942 the Fort Knox squad contained five black players, including former Morris Brown star fullback John "Big Train" Moody. The following year Camp Lee in Virginia also fielded an integrated team. Navy commanders initially segregated the football team at the Great Lakes Naval Training Center, but by 1945 Marion Motley, a former college star at Nevada, had joined the squad. In a few cases interracial contact may have been purely accidental. For example, in January 1943 a white high school basketball team in Virginia voted to defy local norms and play a black military team that had accidentally appeared at the school because of a scheduling snafu.[50]

The most unusual wartime event in southern college sports took place in Durham, North Carolina, where a white intramural basketball team from Duke University actually defied Jim Crow and played against a local black college team. Because of prevailing racial attitudes and the fear that they might have violated a law, the participants in this historic match kept its existence a secret for fifty years. In March 1944 the Eagles of North Carolina Central University, then known as North Carolina College for Negroes, wrapped up a highly successful basketball season with a 24-1 record. Their coach was the remarkable John B. McLendon, who had studied physical education at Kansas University with Dr. James Naismith and who would later become the first African American head coach of an integrated professional basketball team. At nearby Duke the Medical School fielded the champion intramural team, which was composed of former college players from around the country who were participating in military training programs. Apparently, a few local fans boasted that the talented Medical School team could beat the Duke varsity or any other college team in the state. Upon hearing these claims, someone from N.C. Central issued a challenge to the intramural squad. After brief negotiations the Medical School players agreed to a regulation match, complete with referee and clock, at the Central gymnasium. Fearful of police interference if news of the contest leaked out, McLendon and the Duke captain scheduled the game for eleven o'clock on Sunday morning, an hour when most people would be in church.

At the appointed time the two groups cautiously assembled at the North Carolina College gymnasium. As a precaution McLendon locked all the doors and windows to the building so as to exclude any spectators. Of course, a few curious students soon realized that something unusual was afoot, and several dozen eventually peeked through cracks in the windows to follow the action. After a nervous start, during which both teams repeatedly made unforced errors, the host Eagles finally unleashed their fast-break offense and pulled away for an easy 88–44 win. Not yet exhausted, the two sides swapped several players to create two more evenly balanced squads and then proceeded to hold a second contest with fully integrated teams. Afterward, the tired athletes held an informal "bull session" for a while before the Duke students finally drove back to campus. A reporter from the local black newspaper discovered the game but agreed not to print a word about it, a promise that he faithfully honored.[51]

Because of the total secrecy, this remarkable game had no influence on the general public, although it made a deep impression on the participants. Even though some of the Duke players were not southerners, the group's willingness to commit a major violation of the color line confirms that white players and students were not as deeply committed to Jim Crow in athletics as were politicians, educators, and fans. Although white athletes in the South were not eager to compete against African Americans, they were willing in many cases to temporarily accept them as members of an athletic brotherhood if the circumstances were right. Many white players also did not seem concerned about threats to their whiteness or their masculinity from competition with African Americans; rather, they worried more about retaliation from segregationists for their temporary acceptance of racial equality. In a larger sense, this unique game also suggests that the wartime rhetoric about democratic rights may have encouraged some whites to become more flexible in their behavior. The growing acceptance of interracial competition within the military, in military-civilian games, in special situations such as all-star games, and in college games held in the North seemed to suggest that older racial patterns were breaking down at the margins. Thus, at the war's end, proponents of athletic democracy were guardedly optimistic about the future. Their hopes would soon be rewarded. In the decade that followed the Japanese surrender in 1945, monumental changes swept over college and professional sports, destroying the gentleman's agreement and seriously wounding the practice of racial exclusion.

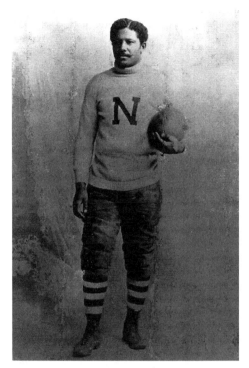

George A. Flippin of the University of Nebraska was one of the earliest black football players in the Midwest. The University of Missouri canceled its 1892 home game against Nebraska rather than compete against him. (Courtesy Media Relations, University of Nebraska)

The multitalented Paul Robeson lettered in four sports at Rutgers University, graduated at the top of his class, and was selected for Walter Camp's All-America team in 1917 and 1918. Yet during Robeson's first season the college president ordered him withheld from a home game against Washington and Lee College of Virginia. (Courtesy Rutgers University)

Defensive lineman Jack Trice, the first African American to play football at Iowa State University, is shown here with three of his teammates. Trice suffered internal injuries during a 1923 game at the University of Minnesota and died shortly thereafter, inspiring rumors that he had been deliberately injured because of his race. (Courtesy Special Collections, Iowa State University Library)

In 1937 the University of Maryland forced Syracuse University to bench its African American quarterback Wilmeth Sidat-Singh for their game in Baltimore. The following year, however, Maryland dropped its athletic color line and played against Sidat-Singh at Syracuse. (Courtesy Department of Athletics, Syracuse University)

Lou Montgomery was an elusive running back for Boston College in 1939 and 1940, but the university benched him six times during those two seasons for games against southern teams. (Courtesy University Archives, John J. Burns Library, Boston College)

The **CRISIS** December, 1941 • Fifteen Cents

CORNELL'S SAM PIERCE
He played against Navy

HITLERISM *without* **HITLER**
A Review by GEORGE S. SCHUYLER

DEMOCRACY *and the* **NEGRO**
PEARL S. BUCK

The Crisis, the monthly magazine of the NAACP, regularly featured on its covers photographs of black athletes who had broken color barriers in sports. The October 1941 issue honored Cornell's Samuel Pierce, who was the first African American to play against the U.S. Naval Academy at home in Maryland. (The author wishes to thank the Crisis Publishing Co., Inc., the publisher of the magazine of the National Association for the Advancement of Colored People, for the use of the magazine cover from the December 1941 issue of *The Crisis*)

Tackle Chester Pierce (#70) became the first African American to compete against a major white college team in the South when his Harvard squad played the University of Virginia in 1947 in Charlottesville. (Copyright 1947, Globe Newspaper Company, republished with permission)

Drake University halfback Johnny Bright shows reporters the wires holding his broken jaw together in this October 1951 photo. The previous week, in one of college football's most disgraceful incidents, an Oklahoma State lineman intentionally slugged Bright three times in the face, outside the view of officials, during their game in Stillwater, Oklahoma. Bright had been leading the nation in rushing, but the injury effectively ended his season. (Courtesy Special Collections at Coles Library, Drake University)

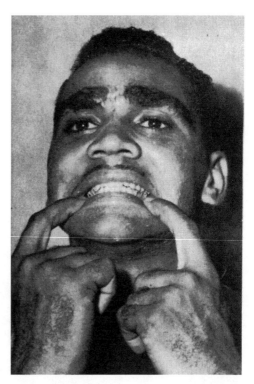

Charles Brown *(front left)*, Cecil Brown *(rear)*, and their Texas Western teammates cerebrate winning the Border Conference championship in the spring of 1957. The two Browns were the first African Americans to play basketball for a historically white major college in an ex-Confederate state. (Courtesy *El Paso Herald Post* and Special Collections Department, University of Texas at El Paso Library)

In the fall of 1957 University of North Texas halfback Abner Haynes, shown here, and teammate Leon King became the first African Americans to play for a major college football team in the ex-Confederate South. (Courtesy Media Relations, University of North Texas)

Sponsors of the enormously popular Dixie Classic Basketball Tournament in Raleigh, North Carolina, opened a new era in athletic competition in the region when they invited integrated teams from the North to participate in the 1958 event. This program from the 1960 tournament captures the paradox of progress and tradition that shaped North Carolina's athletic identity. (Courtesy Media Relations, North Carolina State University)

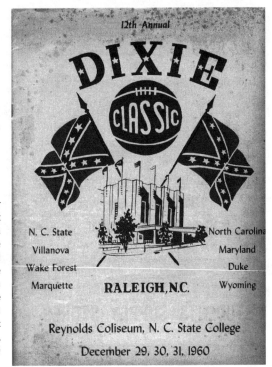

12th Annual

DIXIE CLASSIC

N. C. State   North Carolina
Villanova   Maryland
Wake Forest   Duke
Marquette   RALEIGH,N.C.   Wyoming

Reynolds Coliseum, N. C. State College
December 29, 30, 31, 1960

Excited University of Houston students carry halfback Warren McVea, the school's first African American football player, off the field in 1965 after McVea helped Houston upset the Ole Miss Rebels in the Astrodome. (Courtesy *Houstonian, 1966*, University of Houston)

Orsten Artis of Texas Western College carries the NCAA basketball championship trophy off the court after the Miners defeated Adolph Rupp's Kentucky Wildcats in the 1966 title game. Texas Western started five African Americans in the game, shattering stereotypes that black players would falter in high-pressure situations. (Courtesy Rich Clarkson, Rich Clarkson and Associates)

The cover of the 1973 *Football Media Guide* at North Carolina State University showed the growing importance of African American players at the school and reflected the changing face of southern college sports. (Courtesy Media Relations, North Carolina State University)

Henry Harris, the second black basketball player in the SEC, felt that his athletic skills were underutilized during his career at Auburn. (Courtesy Media Relations, Auburn University)

James Cash of Texas Christian University broke the color line in Southwest Conference varsity basketball during the 1966–67 school year. He later became a Harvard professor and a member of the TCU Board of Trustees. (Courtesy Department of Athletics, Texas Christian University)

Jerry LeVias of Beaumont, Texas, was the first African American athlete to accept a football scholarship to a Southwestern Conference school. LeVias poses with Coach Hayden Fry of Southern Methodist University shortly after signing his official agreement in May 1965. (Courtesy Media Relations, Southern Methodist University)

Captains Joe Dan Gold of Mississippi State and Jerry Harkness of Loyola of Chicago shake hands before their NCAA regional tournament game in 1963. The Mississippi State team had been forced to sneak out of the state in order to compete in the tournament because of a legal challenge to the trip filed by white segregationists. (Courtesy Rich Clarkson, Rich Clarkson and Associates)

Perry Wallace of Vanderbilt University was the first black varsity basketball player in the Southeastern Conference and one of the top rebounders in the league. (Courtesy Vanderbilt University)

In 1987 Wade Houston became the first African American head coach in the Southeastern Conference when the University of Tennessee hired him to direct its basketball program. (Courtesy Sports Information, University of Tennessee)

Confederate flags were a commonplace sight at most southern football games in the 1950s and the 1960s, although no school surpassed the University of Mississippi in their use. (Courtesy Special Collections, University of Mississippi Libraries)

Coach Paul "Bear" Bryant of the University of Alabama, shown here on campus in the mid-1960s, was slow to integrate his football teams but later established a special rapport with black players, who helped him win three national championships in the 1970s. (Courtesy Paul W. Bryant Museum, the University of Alabama)

Ben Williams, the first black varsity football player at the University of Mississippi, proved to be so popular with his fellow students that they elected him "Colonel Rebel" in 1975. Williams is shown here with "Miss Ole Miss," Barbara Biggs, in this photo that was risqué for its time. (Courtesy Special Collections, University of Mississippi Libraries)

As a freshman in 1980 Herschel Walker helped lead the Georgia Bulldogs to the national championship, and in 1982 he received the Heisman Trophy as the top college football player in the United States. (Courtesy Sports Communications, University of Georgia)

3

"Massive Resistance" and the
Fall of the Color Line, 1945–65

We at Penn State realize that there is only one way
to play football—the democratic way. Either all of our
players should participate—or none. . . . The ideals of
Democracy are more important than any football game.

—A Pennsylvania State University student,
November 1946

The South stands at Armageddon. . . . We cannot
make the slightest concession to the enemy in this
dark and lamentable hour of struggle. There is no
more difference in compromising the integrity of race
on the playing field than in doing so in the classroom.

—Georgia governor Marvin Griffin,
December 1955

Early in the evening of Monday, December 23, 1946, nearly twenty-six hundred sports fans in McKeesport, Pennsylvania, had assembled in the local high school gymnasium for an intersectional basketball game between Duquesne University and the University of Tennessee. As game time approached, the spectators became puzzled when the visiting team failed to take the court for warm-up drills. Unbeknownst to them, in another part of the building Tennessee coach John W. Mauer and Duquesne officials had been arguing for nearly two hours over the presence of African American center Charles "Chuck" Cooper in the Dukes' lineup. Mauer insisted that southern racial etiquette would not permit his Volunteer squad to compete against a black player and refused to send his team onto the court unless Cooper was withheld. When the two sides failed to reach a compromise, Duquesne officials reluctantly canceled the game. Later that night the Volunteers flew back to Knoxville, minus their financial guarantee for the match.

Embarrassed by national publicity over the game's cancellation, both universities publicly defended their behavior as consistent with the racial values of their home regions. Portraying the Volunteers as innocent victims of unfair treatment, Coach Mauer complained that it was unreasonable for Duquesne officials to expect a white college team from Dixie to play against an integrated team. Furthermore, the Tennessee coach added that his players, "all southern boys," had voted unanimously not to play against an African American and that he might lose his job if he permitted such a violation of southern customs to take place. Unmoved by Mauer's pleas, officials at Duquesne, a Roman Catholic institution, resolutely defended Cooper's right to play for his school. A World War II veteran, the talented Cooper was already a freshman sensation and in 1950 would become the first African American drafted by the National Basketball Association (NBA). Duquesne officials challenged Mauer's explanation of southern racial policy by pointing out that just three nights earlier Cooper had played without any controversy against Morehead State Teachers College in Louisville, Kentucky, in what was reportedly that state's first integrated basketball game. As a last-minute concession, Duquesne coach Chick Davies had offered to keep Cooper "out of the game as long as possible." When the Duquesne squad had learned about the dispute, Cooper faithfully played the role of the loyal team member and volunteered to sit out the game, but his teammates refused to take the court without him. Following the game's cancellation, Judge Sam Weiss, chairman of the Duquesne athletic council, explained to reporters that the college would not sacrifice its principles and permit discrimination based on "race, color, or creed." Weiss emphatically stated that "*the principle of the entire matter means more to us than a mere basketball game.*"[1]

The 1946 Tennessee–Duquesne incident exposed the intensifying postwar struggle between northern and southern universities over control of racial policy for big-time college sports. This new sectional conflict would last for another two decades before one uniform national policy of inclusion would finally be established. In the immediate postwar years most southern white universities assumed that their northern opponents would continue to follow "southern rules" and honor the gentleman's agreement for all intersectional games. Southern officials were initially unaware that racial attitudes on northern campuses had undergone a dramatic shift during World War II. A new discourse of democratic rights on the playing fields was spreading across the North, catching the University of Tennessee and other southern schools off guard.

The Second World War represented the turning point in this revolution in northern athletic policy. The democratic values that the United States repeatedly stressed in its wartime appeals, the contributions made by minorities to the war effort, and the shocking disclosure of the depths of the Holocaust exerted a powerful impact on racial attitudes in the North, especially on college campuses. Even though the American military had remained segregated during the war, many white veterans who flooded colleges under the G.I. Bill of Rights took the lead in defending the right of African Americans to compete on their schools' athletic teams. As a result of this tougher northern stand, the gentleman's agreement soon collapsed for games played in the North, and its future status in the South appeared uncertain. In fact, students at many northern universities eventually demanded that their schools cancel trips to the South rather than leave their black players at home. Faced with this new resistance, more southern colleges accepted integrated games in the North, and a few even did so at home. A desire to maintain access to the profits and prestige that popular intersectional games provided appeared to be slowly undermining southern schools' loyalty to the athletic color line.

This modestly liberal trend in Dixie was soon reversed following the United States Supreme Court's 1954 ruling in the *Brown v. Board of Education* case, which declared segregated public schools to be unconstitutional. In the wake of the *Brown* decision, southern segregationists launched a campaign of "massive resistance" to fight school integration. As part of a comprehensive effort to shore up the crumbling Jim Crow system, city governments, university governing boards, and one state legislature banned all integrated athletic contests. This white backlash temporarily resegregated sporting events, especially in the Deep South. After several years, however, moderate leaders reasserted their influence. The eventual resumption of integrated competition in the late 1950s and early 1960s showed that southern universities and most southern white fans preferred to participate fully in national sporting culture rather that isolate themselves within a shrinking segregated world. By 1965 virtually every major southern university had abandoned the color line for intersectional competition and was willing to play integrated teams on the road and at home. Next public attention would shift to internal color lines and the question of when these colleges might recruit black athletes for their own teams.

Postwar Challenges to Jim Crow in the North

The segregated nature of most American sports began to collapse after 1945. The three major professional team sports—football, basketball, and baseball—gradually dropped their exclusion policies and accepted African Americans into their ranks. Despite the historical emphasis on Jackie Robinson's entry into Major League Baseball in 1947, it was actually professional football that first abandoned the color line. In 1946 the newly created All-America Football Conference (AAFC) inaugurated a nondiscriminatory employment policy for the sport, thereby placing pressure on the more established National Football League to eliminate its twelve-year ban on black players. Unexpectedly, the Los Angeles Rams of the NFL became the first professional team to break the color line when they added former UCLA stars Kenny Washington and Woody Strode to their 1946 roster. The Rams took this action in order to head off an effort by civil rights supporters to block their use of the publicly owned Los Angeles Coliseum on grounds of racial discrimination. Later in 1946 the Cleveland Browns became the first AAFC team to sign African American players. Paul Brown, the team's head coach, had coached several black stars on military teams during World War II and jumped at the chance to add Marion Motley and Bill Willis to his squad. Despite the league's flexibility on race, the two Cleveland players were forced to sit out one conference game against the AAFC's franchise in Miami because of local laws. In 1947 five other AAFC teams signed black players. Among NFL clubs, however, another year passed before the New York Giants and the Detroit Lions added African Americans to their rosters, and most NFL squads waited until the 1950s to abandon their Jim Crow policies. National Basketball Association teams were also slow to open their doors to African Americans. Charles Cooper, Nat "Sweetwater" Clifton, and Earl Lloyd ended this exclusion during the 1950–51 season when they joined NBA teams.[2]

Despite the important breakthrough in professional football, baseball easily remained the number-one American sport in the late 1940s, and its traditional policy of racial exclusion offered an influential model for other athletic activities. No player identified as African American had participated in the major leagues since 1884. Furthermore, the affiliated minor leagues also continued to exclude black players. Branch Rickey shattered this long-standing policy in October 1945, when his Brooklyn Dodger organization signed Jackie Robinson, the former UCLA football star, to a contract. Robinson spent the 1946 season in the minor leagues before launching his illustrious career with the Dodgers in April 1947. Three months later the Cleveland Indians added outfielder Larry Doby to their roster, integrating the American League and making him the second black player in the big leagues. Most other clubs gradually took similar actions, although the Boston Red Sox did not field an integrated team until 1959. Major league clubs also assigned young black players to their minor-league affiliates, including those located in Dixie. According to historian Jules Tygiel, "By the end of the 1953 season, only the Southern Association of the higher minor leagues continued to bar blacks." Baseball integration thus served as a "powerful agent of racial reform" in the South and offered an alternative model to the racial exclusion still practiced in the college ranks.[3]

In the late 1940s resistance to southern efforts to exclude African American players from intersectional games increased, although there were still colleges that continued to respect the gentleman's agreement. During the 1946 season the University of Cincinnati provided a particularly egregious example of northern compliance. Cincinnati withheld senior end Willard Stargel, an army veteran, from a home game against Kentucky and a road match at the University of Tulsa during the fall. After the Bearcats finished with an 8–2 record, the Sun Bowl in

El Paso, Texas, invited the Ohioans to the January 1, 1947, event, and once again Cincinnati left Stargel behind. In another 1946 incident, Fresno State College benched several black players for a game at Oklahoma City University, but only after the Oklahoma school agreed to play against Fresno's full squad the following year in California. Other nonsouthern colleges, however, canceled contests against southern teams rather than accept racial exclusion. In November 1946 the University of Nevada refused to leave at home its two black starters, both military veterans, and instead called off its match against Mississippi State in Starkville. Nevada students, led by white veterans, had opposed any concessions to Mississippi State. Other intersectional games canceled in 1947 over the issue of racial exclusion included a basketball game between Duquesne and Miami and a football game between Ohio Wesleyan and Rollins College of Florida.[4]

The most widely publicized incident over racial policy between northern and southern colleges erupted in November 1946 and involved Pennsylvania State University and the University of Miami. The two teams had been scheduled to play their final regular-season game in the Orange Bowl Stadium in Miami. Penn State's unexpectedly firm stand reflected the growing insistence on democratic ideals in sports by northern students. During the fall Miami administrators informed Penn State that its team's two African American starters, fullback Wallace Triplett and end Dennis Hoggard, could not participate in the contest in the city-owned stadium, because an integrated game would violate local police department's rules and might cause "unfortunate incidents." Penn State students strongly opposed Miami's demand. One senior summed up this position in a letter to the student newspaper when he insisted, "We at Penn State realize that there is only one way to play football—the democratic way. Either all of our players should participate—or none." The writer then added, "*The ideals of Democracy are more important than any football game.*" Many members of the football squad agreed. At a team meeting called to discuss the game, the team captains, all of whom were veterans, declared that "this stuff has got to stop." The team then voted overwhelmingly against the Miami trip. "It was one of the high points of my life," Triplett later declared. Subsequently, the two colleges called off the game. Somewhat surprisingly, a few students and faculty at the University of Miami spoke out against their own school's racial policies. For example, a sports columnist in the student newspaper criticized the city of Miami for imposing an undemocratic racial policy on the university and depicted the cancellation as "a violation of the basic principles for which this last war was fought." In a similar vein, two political science professors, both World War II veterans, condemned the action as "contrary to the American tradition of democracy in education, and a perversion of the spirit of sport."[5]

Another related development in the Northeast was the increasing appearance of several African American players on teams in the elite Ivy League. Despite the conference's declining strength, the Ivy schools still carried considerable prestige and status. Princeton, the most conservative of the Ivy universities, accepted its first black students in 1944, including Arthur Wilson, who played on the basketball team for the next three years. During the 1945 and 1946 seasons Jay Swift appeared on the court for the Yale basketball team. The selection by Yale players of Levi Jackson, the first African American to play football at the college, as the captain of the 1949 grid squad carried far greater significance. The national press widely reported Jackson's selection and interpreted it as another sign of racial progress. The *New York Herald Tribune* noted that while the action did not carry quite "the measurable effects of a Supreme Court decision," it still represented in a sports-mad society "another precedent of real significance." *Life* also praised Jackson's selection, especially because it resulted from "a combination of things that transcended 'race'—technical competence, inspirational talent, personality, and character." Reflecting the influence of the cold war on racial issues, the magazine declared, "Stalin has probably never heard of the Ivy League, but the action taken by a few Yale students in 10 minutes' time has hit Joe a blow that will someday make him screech."[6]

In the late 1940s semiprofessional football teams in the Upper South began scheduling integrated games. In October 1947 the Staten Island Stapletons, a minor-league professional football team, visited North Carolina to challenge the Charlotte Clippers. The Stapletons brought along starting quarterback Bill Williams, one of three African Americans on their roster, who subsequently became the first African American to play in an integrated major athletic contest in the state. Two months later the Staten Island squad again crossed the Mason-Dixon line, in order to play in Virginia against the Norfolk Pioneers. This time all three of the black Stapletons made the trip and participated in the game. Also in the fall several black organizations in Durham, North Carolina, hosted an exhibition game between semiprofessional football teams from Philadelphia and Washington, D.C. Since the former squad was all-white and the latter all-black, the contest was unprecedented within the state. The sponsors stated that they arranged the match to promote racial goodwill and "to show subversive elements in foreign countries . . . that the members of the different races in American can play together as well as fight a common enemy together." Because of semiprofessional football's low status, however, these events did not directly influence the college game.[7]

Integrated College Games Begin in the South

The changing racial climate in American professional sports and on northern campuses made it less difficult for white universities in the Upper South to occasionally waive the gentleman's agreement for home games. In October 1947 the

University of Virginia became the first major white college to host an integrated football game in the ex-Confederate South. The Cavaliers' opponent was Harvard University, making its first trip ever below the Mason-Dixon line. The visit of an Ivy League team to the state itself constituted an unprecedented event. Since 1894 Virginia had played thirty-four games against the likes of Harvard, Yale, and Penn, but all of those contests had taken place in the North. The 1947 game attracted additional public interest because the Crimson squad included one African American, Chester Pierce, a senior tackle from New York City. In the preceding summer several Harvard players had informed the Virginia captain that Pierce would be accompanying the Crimson squad to Charlottesville. The captain replied that there would be no problem with his participation, since the Virginia team, which included several veterans, had voted unanimously to play against him. On the other hand, Virginia administrators were uneasy about Pierce's visit. Apparently under some local pressure, they unsuccessfully requested that Harvard leave Pierce behind. Nonetheless, President Colgate W. Darden urged UVa students to be gracious hosts in a speech at a campus pep rally.[8]

The Harvard squad encountered several unexpected situations after arriving in Charlottesville. At first the Monticello Hotel refused to permit Pierce to stay with the rest of the team, but eventually it agreed to let him and part of the squad share a plush guest lodge behind the main building. The hotel also conceded that Pierce could enter the central building through the same door as his teammates and eat his meals with them in the dining room. On game day an unanticipated greeting party welcomed the Crimson squad at the stadium. As one player later recalled, "It was eerie. There was a large crowd of black folks clustered along a cyclone fence by the players' entrance. They must have numbered about 200, and they cheered Chet as we passed through. It gave you goose bumps." Approximately five hundred black spectators eventually watched the game from a segregated seating section behind the north end zone in the stadium. The actual game proved to be a one-sided affair, as the superior Virginia team easily shut out the visitors 47–0. The Cavalier players treated Pierce quite fairly; in fact, at times they deliberately seemed to avoid his side of the line. When the Harvard tackle left the field in the third quarter, the crowd of twenty-four thousand gave him "a tremendous ovation." But not all Virginia fans were gracious hosts. Several of Pierce's teammates remembered hearing spectators shout racial slurs from the stands. Furthermore, several players and northern journalists complained about the widespread waving of Confederate flags at the game. Defending the South's customs, one white Virginia fan responded that "it is virtually standard operating procedure to unfold the flag of the gallant old Confederacy when this university plays a 'Yankee' eleven." Despite these minor conflicts, both black and white newspapers agreed that the game represented a major racial milestone in the Upper South.[9]

Most southern universities did not initially follow the example set by Virginia, except for a few colleges in Texas. Because of several lawsuits by black plaintiffs seeking admission to graduate and professional programs across the South, college officials remained cautious about taking any steps, even on the athletic fields, that might weaken their legal stand against school desegregation. Nonetheless, in September 1950 Duke University became the second major white university in the ex-Confederate South to host an integrated regular-season football game. When Duke president Dr. Hollis Edens and Coach Wallace Wade originally scheduled the contest against the University of Pittsburgh, they understood that the visiting squad might include black players. In a public statement the two officials explained that they had signed the game contract because they wished "to play on fair and even terms" against Pitt and because Duke had no right to exclude a visiting player "because of creed or color." Senior tackle Flint Green accompanied the Pitt squad to Durham but stayed in separate accommodations from his teammates. Green played almost half of the game in Pitt's uneventful 28–14 loss to Duke.[10]

Postseason Bowl Games Break Ranks with Jim Crow

Postseason college bowl games in the South also reconsidered their traditional policy of racial exclusion in the late 1940s. Since these New Year's Day events enjoyed considerable prestige and were controlled by civic elites, their endorsement of integrated competition carried considerable weight. The Rose Bowl classic in Pasadena, California, was the most prestigious college bowl game of that era. The Rose Bowl began in 1916 and was staged by the Tournament of Roses Committee in order to promote tourism to Southern California. The event soon became a smashing success, attracting huge crowds and providing generous payments to participating teams. During the mid-1930s ambitious promoters introduced four new postseason classics in southern cities: the Cotton Bowl in Dallas, the Orange Bowl in Miami, the Sugar Bowl in New Orleans, and the Sun Bowl in El Paso. These New Year's Day events were organized by businessmen and civic boosters who, seeking the holy grail of national press coverage, hoped to duplicate the Rose Bowl's success and expand tourism to their home cities. In Miami civic leaders formed the Orange Bowl Committee, which held its first contest on January 1, 1935. In New Orleans the Mid-Winter Sports Association organized its first Sugar Bowl game, also on January 1, 1935. One year later the Sun Bowl in El Paso hosted its first match between college teams. Texas oilman J. Curtis Sanford, inspired by Southern Methodist University's participation in the 1936 Rose Bowl, organized the first Cotton Bowl game in Dallas on New Year's Day in 1937.[11]

Although race relations in Southern California were far from ideal, the Rose Bowl accepted African American players from the start. In 1916 halfback Fritz Pollard of Brown played in the classic against Washington State, while in 1922 quarterback Charles West represented Washington and Jefferson against the University of California. The four new bowl games of the 1930s, however, were located in Lower South cities and therefore automatically excluded African American players. Until the late 1940s most northern universities seeking bowl invitations acquiesced to this policy. Thus, white southerners skillfully used the leverage that bowl games provided to force "southern rules" on ambitious northern schools. This pre-1945 capitulation by northern coaches and administrators also reflected their tolerance for racial discrimination, the small number of black players on their squads, the marginal status of black students on campus, and the growing lure of generous payouts and national prestige that bowl games provided.[12]

The first important defection by a bowl game from the traditional southern racial policy came with the 1948 Cotton Bowl clash in Dallas between Southern Methodist University and Pennsylvania State University. The city had previously displayed some flexibility concerning sports. In 1936 the city had hosted the Texas Centennial Olympic Games and in 1937 the Pan American Games, each time permitting integrated track and field competition. Nonetheless, the SMU–Penn State clash constituted the first integrated major college football game ever held in Texas. The game's substantial financial success and absence of political controversy demonstrated the advantages of cautious integration on the gridiron. The Penn State Nittany Lions had gone undefeated in the 1947 season and finished fourth in the Associated Press (AP) final poll. Unfortunately, the presence on the team's roster of fullback Wallace Triplett and end Dennis Hoggard, and the school's well-known stance against racial exclusion seemingly doomed the team's chances of receiving a bowl invitation. Local favorite Southern Methodist University delighted bowl officials by winning the Southwest Conference title and an automatic bid to the game. Led by All-American halfback Doak Walker, the 8-0-1 Mustangs finished the season with a number-three national ranking. Cotton Bowl representatives quickly grasped that by inviting Penn State without racial restrictions they could match the third- and fourth-ranked teams in the nation, creating "the top attraction in the nation on New Year's Day." Penn State officials accepted the subsequent invitation but raised questions about segregated hotels in Dallas. In response Cotton Bowl planners cleverly arranged for the visiting team to be housed together in the bachelor officer quarters of the Dallas Naval Air Station near suburban Grand Prairie, fourteen miles from downtown. For the postgame awards banquet, officials forced a downtown hotel to break local racial etiquette by allowing Triplett and Hoggard to attend with their teammates.[13]

The major Dallas newspapers initially reported the racial complications surrounding the possible selection of Penn State but later refrained from making any references to Triplett and Hoggard, apparently in order to avoid stirring up extreme segregationists. Finally, on the day of the game, the *Dallas Morning News* rediscovered Wallace Triplett, belatedly identifying him as Penn State's "star Negro fullback . . . who is both a fast and elusive runner, and a superb defensive player." The pairing of the eastern champion against local favorite SMU, as well as the enormous box-office appeal of the Mustangs' All-American halfback, Doak Walker, fulfilled bowl officials' dreams and produced more than one hundred thousand ticket applications during just the first four days of mail sales. On January 1, 1948, an overflow crowd of nearly forty-seven thousand packed the stadium for what one sportswriter described as "a hell of a game." SMU took an early lead, but Penn State rallied to tie the score at 13–13 on a third-quarter touchdown by Wallace Triplett. The game ended in a deadlock when a deflected last-second pass dramatically slipped off Dennis Hoggard's fingertips in the SMU end zone. Afterward, the *Christian Science Monitor* called the match "one of those milestones of history" and argued that the integrated game in Dallas "carries more significance than does a Supreme Court decision against Jim Crowism or would a Federal Fair Employment Practices Act." On a more practical level, the widespread enthusiasm generated by the contest allowed the bowl association to float a bond issue that financed expansion of the stadium's seating capacity to just over sixty-seven thousand seats.[14]

The Cotton Bowl attempted to replicate the game's success the following year. The SMU Mustangs, ranked ninth in the nation, again claimed the home-team invitation by winning the Southwest Conference. The selection of SMU's Doak Walker for the Heisman Trophy, awarded annually to the top college player, inspired even greater interest in the game. For the visiting slot the Cotton Bowl selected the University of Oregon Ducks, the first team from the Pacific Coast Conference to play in the Cotton Bowl. Led by flashy quarterback Norm Van Brocklin, Oregon had finished the season with a 9-1 record and the number-ten national ranking. More important, though, the Oregon squad contained three African American players. Oregon officials selected a downtown hotel as team headquarters, with the three black players staying separately at the private homes of prominent black Dallas residents. However, they joined their teammates at the main hotel for most of their meals. The bowl's main reception committee included several African Americans, a bold step for that era. The game itself was free of racial incidents, and an overflow crowd of seventy thousand applauded the Mustangs' exciting 21–13 victory. Clearly, the Cotton Bowl and SMU had followed a policy of racial moderation at a time and in a state where such flexibility was uncommon. This pragmatic gamble paid off handsomely, as the Cotton Bowl profited enormously from the two consecutive successes.[15]

In El Paso the Sun Bowl also confronted the problem of segregation in the late 1940s, but with less success than the Cotton Bowl. The contest was considered a notch below the major bowl games, and its payout barely covered team expenses. Despite its far West Texas location, the Sun Bowl had historically followed the southern custom of racial exclusion, in part because the annual event was held on the campus of the Texas College of Mines, a branch campus in the University of Texas system. The game's Jim Crow policy had not created any problems until the selection process began for the January 1, 1949, contest. After Border Conference champion Texas Tech declined an invitation, conference runner-up the Texas College of Mines agreed to replace Tech. As the visiting team the selection committee picked Lafayette College, which had just completed a 7-2 season. Because the Pennsylvania school had not played in a bowl game since 1923, its all-male student body responded enthusiastically to the news.[16]

An unanticipated racial problem concerning Lafayette's African American halfback, Dave Showell, soon disrupted the Sun Bowl's plans. Once El Paso officials learned about Showell, they informed Lafayette president Ralph C. Hutchison that UT regents' policies would not permit him to participate in the game. When informed about the rule, the popular Showell, a World War II veteran, urged his teammates to carry on without him. Subsequently, the Lafayette football squad and athletic council voted to accept the Sun Bowl invitation, but the college faculty unexpectedly voted overwhelmingly to reject the bid. Upset by this turn of events, nearly fifteen hundred angry students marched to the home of President Hutchison to protest the faculty decision. Hutchison, who had never been enthusiastic about the proposed trip, defended the faculty action by shifting blame to the Sun Bowl's racial policy. The beleaguered president declared, "It is fundamentally wrong for any team to go and play a game and leave any player behind because of his race, color or religion." Eventually, the frustrated students decided to march to downtown Easton, where they held a spontaneous rally against racial intolerance. West Virginia University eventually agreed to replace Lafayette in the bowl game.[17]

The national publicity over Lafayette's withdrawal created a public relations fiasco for the Sun Bowl and prompted local residents to rethink the wisdom of the exclusion policy. At the College of Mines the campus newspaper reported that most of the school's football players and students actually opposed the racial ban. Elsewhere in the city, many influential El Pasoans questioned why the Cotton Bowl could host integrated games inside the state of Texas but not the Sun Bowl. This question resurfaced two years later, when Loyola College of Los Angeles suddenly canceled its scheduled September 1950 regular-season contest against Texas Western College (the new name for the College of Mines) because of the exclusion policy. In the aftermath of the cancellation, university administrators, local civic leaders, and Sun Bowl officials begged the UT Board of Regents to grant the college an exemption from the racial ban. On October 27, 1950, the regents voted to grant Texas Western a special exemption so that integrated athletic events could be held on campus. This change now freed bowl officials to select teams from a much larger national pool. One year later the Sun Bowl hosted its first integrated contest, between California's College of the Pacific and Texas Tech.[18]

The Orange Bowl classic in Miami experienced similar problems during the late 1940s and early 1950s. Since Orange Bowl Stadium was owned by the City of Miami, the Orange Bowl Committee and the University of Miami lacked the authority to establish racial policies for their own athletic events held in the facility. Sports competition in Florida had traditionally been segregated by custom, and in the late 1940s the State Board of Control adopted a formal policy specifically prohibiting all public colleges from hosting integrated games. Despite a thriving tourist industry, both the City of Miami and its sister city Miami Beach were very much southern cities with extensive segregation. Furthermore, the Miami Police Department vigorously enforced the city government's policy against interracial athletics. In 1950, however, University of Miami administrators apparently convinced city fathers that the racial ban was hurting the college's athletic program. Consequently, the Miami *city* government reversed its position and permitted the *private* university to host integrated teams at Orange Bowl Stadium. On November 24 of that year the Hurricanes hosted a University of Iowa squad that included five African American players. The interracial game apparently did not upset students at the University of Miami, since the school's newspaper applauded the game as "a big, big step in the right direction."[19]

Despite the change in stadium policy, the Orange Bowl Committee avoided the racial issue for several more years by selecting all-white teams. Eventually, though, ambitious bowl officials adopted a color-blind policy when a major opportunity to enhance the event's national stature appeared. In 1953 organizers pulled off a major coup when they signed an agreement with the Big Seven Conference (later the Big Eight and now the Big Twelve) and the Atlantic Coast Conference to match their champions annually in Miami, starting in January 1954. This new arrangement earned the festival its first national television contract, greatly strengthening its financial position. Since most of the Big Seven schools except for Oklahoma and Missouri had recently begun to accept African Americans on their football teams, the new agreement also meant that most future Orange Bowl games would be integrated. The Orange Bowl Committee and the city government thus jettisoned Jim Crow in order to elevate the bowl's national visibility and increase its financial strength. The Orange Bowl's first integrated game took place on January 1, 1955, when the Nebraska Cornhuskers used two black players in their 34–7 loss to Duke. The local press did not take any special note of this racial milestone. Integrated games subsequently became the norm for the Orange Bowl in its city-owned stadium, but the University of Florida, Florida State University (FSU), other public colleges, and Florida high schools continued to prohibit mixed competition at their state-regulated facilities well into the 1960s.[20]

The occasional appearance of integrated football games in the South reflected a growing toleration of interracial contact by some southern white universities, most of which were located in areas lacking a large African American population. Colleges from the Deep South remained strongly opposed to any integrated games, however, regardless of where they were held. A few southern schools followed a third option—consistently playing integrated teams in the North without requiring a return match in the South. This approach allowed these universities to maintain their national profile through intersectional competition, but it placed them at a competitive disadvantage, since they always played this "big game" away from home. The University of Georgia and Georgia Tech provided the best examples of this strategy. Both colleges operated such successful athletic programs that they had easily rebuffed efforts by state educators in the early 1950s to deemphasize sports at the two institutions. Georgia was the first of the two schools to modify its Jim Crow policies. In September 1950 the Bulldogs traveled to San Francisco to challenge St. Mary's College. Led by black halfback John Henry Johnson, who ran back the second-half kickoff ninety yards for a touchdown, the Gaels battled the favored Georgians to a 7–7 tie. At Georgia Tech, Coach Bobby Dodd guided his teams to six consecutive bowl games and a share of the 1952 national championship. In October 1953 the Yellow Jackets challenged Notre Dame, the number-one ranked team in the nation, in South Bend, Indiana. That year Notre Dame fielded its first integrated team, but Georgia Tech never hesitated in scheduling the game. However, both Georgia and Georgia Tech prudently refrained from widely publicizing their new willingness to compete against black athletes outside Dixie.[21]

Major College Basketball and Race

After World War II growing interest in basketball turned the indoor game into the second most popular college sport after football. This lofty status was a far cry from the sport's humble origins nearly six decades earlier. James A. Naismith, a Canadian instructor at the Young Men's Christian Association school in Springfield, Massachusetts (now Springfield College), invented the game in the late nineteenth century in order to keep bored students busy during the winter months. The first actual contest played by one of his gym classes took place on December 21, 1891, with nine players on each side. The new activity excited students and YMCA members alike. Since most local YMCA directors received at least some of their training at the Springfield school, they became missionaries for the new game when they returned to their home communities around the country. The sport soon spread from YMCAs to settlement houses, athletic clubs, public schools, and universities. What may have been the first official college game took place in February 1895 between the Minnesota School of Agriculture and Hamline College. However, some writers have identified the March 1897 contest between Yale and the University of Pennsylvania as the first modern college game using five players per side. Because matches were not only played in gymnasiums but also in auditoriums, dance halls, and even warehouses, the court area was sometimes separated from the spectators by netting, chicken wire, and even a steel cage. Thus, "cagers" became one early nickname for participants in the sport.[22]

By about 1910 most eastern and midwestern colleges officially sponsored men's teams in basketball, but the sport generally lagged behind baseball and even track and field in spectator interest. Southerners, both white and black, were somewhat slow to embrace basketball. Influenced by the Nashville YMCA, Vanderbilt became one of the first southern universities to sponsor a team, playing mostly against YMCA teams during its inaugural 1900–1901 season. By the 1905–6 season a growing number of southern universities, including Virginia, Washington and Lee, William and Mary, Trinity College, Wake Forest, and Tulane, were competing in the sport. Out in the Southwest the University of Texas initiated a basketball program in 1906, while TCU and Baylor began an annual series in 1909. Following its formation in 1914, the Southwest Conference sponsored an annual championship in basketball as well as football. The sprawling Southern Conference, which numbered twenty members shortly after its formation in 1921, helped boost the popularity of the sport by staging an annual postseason tournament to determine the league champion. In the absence of national playoffs, the postseason conference tournament remained the primary focus of southern basketball fans into the 1930s.

Since basketball competition in Dixie developed several decades after football, the new sport followed the racial pattern already established by the older game. Although southern black colleges also developed basketball programs during the same period, any competition between white and black squads was unthinkable. Intersectional contests between northern and southern teams were less frequent than in football, but when teams from the two regions met, white southerners firmly insisted that the gentleman's agreement should be honored in the gymnasium, just as it was on the gridiron. Conflict over the issue was rare, since only a tiny number of African Americans appeared on northern teams before the 1930s. Nonetheless, a few distinguished themselves in the sport. Probably the first black basketball player at a white university was Samuel L. Ransom, who played from 1905 through 1908 at Beloit College in Wisconsin. At the University of Nebraska, Wilbur S. Wood enjoyed three excellent seasons beginning in 1908. Edward "Sol"

Butler at Dubuque College and Paul Robeson at Rutgers were multisport stars who displayed their prowess for their college teams during the World War I years. The first black All-American was George Gregory, who starred at Columbia University from 1929 to 1931 and was named to the Helms Foundation All-America team following his senior year. In February 1929 the Columbia captain led the Lions to a 32–31 home victory over the U.S. Naval Academy, marking the first time in its athletic history that the academy had ever competed against a black athlete. Still, for reasons that are not clear, the number of black basketball stars at white colleges remained proportionally smaller than the number of African Americans who distinguished themselves in football.[23]

These first African American basketball players at northern universities experienced the same discrimination and prejudice that their counterparts in football did. A few colleges would not allow blacks to participate on school teams at first, and other institutions sometimes refused to compete against them. By the 1920s such bias had mostly disappeared in New England, but many midwestern colleges continued to exclude black players. For example, the Big Ten Conference surprisingly maintained a rigid color line for basketball even though its members permitted African Americans to participate in many other sports. Conference basketball coaches cynically denied that any such agreement existed while at the same time upholding it. Why the conference ignored the example of football and started a policy of exclusion, let alone continued it during the 1930s and 1940s, is not clear. Although less violent than football, basketball was normally played indoors, in smaller and more intimate settings. Furthermore, players wore only brief uniforms that exposed much of the male body. Thus, it seems likely that uneasiness about physical contact between sweating, partially clad, clearly visible young men at times led to exclusion in basketball. Of course, it should be noted that many white coaches and school officials outside the Big Ten apparently did not share these same fears.[24]

An incident involving the University of Notre Dame sheds some light on these attitudes toward interracial competition on the basketball court. Allegedly because of its small-town location and the presence of students from the South, the Indiana college refused to admit black students until 1944. Although the Fighting Irish were willing to play against integrated football teams, the school drew the color line for basketball. In February 1934 the University of Detroit, also a Catholic institution, hosted the Irish cagers. Upon arrival in Detroit, Coach George Keogan discovered that the home team included Laurence Bleach, "the sensational negro sophomore." Keogan protested vehemently about this violation of racial etiquette but still allowed his team to play the game, which the Irish won 36–17. The Detroit athletic director, Gus Dorais, a former Notre Dame quarterback, immediately wrote to Father John O'Hara, acting president of Notre Dame, to apologize for the incident. Dorais pleaded that he was unaware "of this 'gentlemen's agreement' among coaches not to use colored boys" and was "mighty sorry" that the problem had arisen. However, he confessed that he could not see the logic of such a policy, since whites regularly competed against African Americans in football and track. Notre Dame officials themselves initially seemed puzzled as well. But after an investigation Father O'Hara replied to Dorais: "At first, I could see no objection to your using a negro on your team, but George [Keogan] pointed out to me that there is a difference in a game where there is such close physical contact between players scantily clad and perspiring at every pore."[25]

During the 1930s basketball achieved greater national popularity. Historian Benjamin Rader has suggested that this growth resulted in part from the efforts of big-city sports promoters, who had built large arenas in the 1920s to hold boxing crowds. Seeking to offset declining revenue from boxing during the Depression, these promoters began staging basketball doubleheaders at their facilities. College games at Madison Square Garden in New York City, which had a seating capacity of sixteen thousand, increasingly "served as a catalyst for the transformation of college basketball into a full-fledged spectator sport." In recognition of this increased popularity, three postseason championship tournaments were founded in the late 1930s. The first of these was the National Association of Intercollegiate Basketball (later Athletics) Tournament, which began in 1937 in Kansas City, Missouri. The NAIB (later NAIA) event appealed to smaller colleges and was sponsored by city leaders as a replacement for the national Amateur Athletic Union Tournament, which had recently moved from Kansas City to Denver. In 1938 the Metropolitan Basketball Writers' Association started the National Invitational Tournament (NIT) in New York City, which invited the top teams from around the country. Finally, in 1939 the NCAA launched its own national championship tournament, which remained in the shadow of the NIT for more than a decade.[26]

From its inception the NAIB Tournament in Kansas City practiced racial exclusion. Black colleges were not allowed to join the organization, and individual African Americans on white university teams were barred from the competition. The NAIB apparently imposed this prohibition in order to attract small colleges from the South and those areas of the Midwest where interracial competition on the court was not yet fully accepted. The pervasive segregation found in public accommodations in Kansas City also encouraged exclusion. The response to this policy in 1941 by two California institutions, San Jose State College and Santa Barbara State College, reveals the divided mind of white institutions when forced to choose between accepting racial exclusion in order to participate in a postseason tournament or standing up for equal treatment and staying at home. San Jose State took the more principled road and turned down its invitation to the tournament when its two black starters were barred by NAIB officials. Santa Barbara State took a more expedient route. Even though center Lowell Stewart, the team's leading scorer, was excluded from the NAIB event, the Gauchos remained a powerful squad without him and advanced to the tournament semifinals. The excitement of competing for a national championship apparently overwhelmed any guilt that players, coaches, and administrators felt over tolerating racial discrimination. Santa Barbara's actions in accepting Stewart's exclusion were even more curious since the college had canceled a 1938 football game against the Texas College of Mines because the team's two black players could not compete in El Paso.[27]

After World War II several smaller colleges in the North began to protest the NAIB's color line. In 1947 Indiana State University declined an invitation to the tournament. The school's head coach, John Wooden, who later coached UCLA to a record ten NCAA national championships, refused to take his team to Kansas City because the one African American squad member, Clarence Walker, would be barred from participating. Urban Catholic schools also played an important role in successfully challenging the tournament's racial policy. In the spring of 1948 Siena College and Manhattan College both withdrew from the event, with Manhattan officials explaining that the exclusion policy was inconsistent with Catholic teachings. Finally, one member of the United States Olympic Basketball Committee publicly suggested that NAIB players be excluded from the selection tournament that would be used to choose the 1948 Olympic team. Unnerved by this growing opposition, the executive committee of the NAIB conducted a special telegraph poll of members and announced that the ban on African Americans had been officially repealed.[28]

The next racial issue to confront the NAIB involved possible membership for historically black colleges and universities. The exclusion of such institutions from the NCAA and the NAIB demonstrated the extent of their marginalization within the overwhelmingly white college basketball world. In the late 1940s representatives from the four black intercollegiate conferences, led by Coach John McLendon of North Carolina Central, pressed the NCAA to admit black colleges to membership. Rebuffed by the association, these schools then turned to the NAIB, whose executive director, Al Duer, was quite sympathetic. In July 1951 the NAIB accepted historically black Central State College of Ohio as a provisional member. Then, in March 1952, the NAIB announced that membership was now completely open to black universities. Central State, North Carolina Central, and more than thirty other black schools soon established full membership, dramatically changing the public face of the NAIB.[29]

Basketball teams from black colleges first participated in the renamed NAIA Tournament in 1953. In order to gain a berth in the Kansas City event, participants had to win a qualifying tournament within their own geographical region. This policy would normally have matched the champions of the four African

American conferences against all-white teams from southern and border states. Such a policy was unacceptable to most southern white colleges in 1953. Therefore, the NAIB created a special region, Division 29, which was an all-black district not based on geography. This region's representative to the national tournament was selected by a special tournament exclusively for black colleges. In 1953 Tennessee A&I (later Tennessee State University) won the tournament in Nashville. The Tigers then surprised many white experts by advancing to the NAIA quarterfinals in their first visit to Kansas City.

Acknowledging the solid performances each year by the Division 29 winners, the NAIA created a second all-black district in 1956 and agreed to accept their champions automatically into the national tournament. That year Texas Southern University advanced to the national finals before losing to all-white McNeese State College, which had ignored threats from Louisiana segregationists in order to participate in the playoffs. The following year the powerful squad from Tennessee A&I, now coached by John McLendon and led by future NBA star Dick "Skull" Barnett, captured the championship and became "the first African American college team to win a national title against white competition in any sport." Tennessee A&I repeated as tournament champions in 1958 and 1959, and Grambling College claimed the 1961 championship. The NAIA's acceptance of individual black players in the late 1940s and its inclusion of all-black teams in the 1950s greatly expanded interracial competition on the small-college level. Southern white schools who would never schedule a black opponent now had to play one in Kansas City or surrender their dreams of athletic glory. Moreover, African American teams competed quite successfully with white squads, surprising many white coaches and undermining assumptions of white superiority. On the small-college level, Jim Crow had been placed on the defensive.[30]

The Midwestern Conferences Finally Integrate

In the late 1940s and early 1950s the three major midwestern conferences that had previously excluded African Americans from athletic competition finally dropped their racial restrictions. Most sports fans are unaware that Jim Crow ever dominated these conferences, and the universities themselves prefer to forget this embarrassing era in their institutional development. The Big Eight and Missouri Valley Conferences had traditionally maintained segregation in all sports, while the Big Ten rejected black athletes specifically in basketball. As long as these leagues enforced a color line, racial exclusion in college sports remained not just a southern custom but rather a broader American practice. The gradual rejection of these policies by midwestern colleges after World War II, however, left southern white universities increasingly isolated within the world of big-time college sports. Athletic integration in the Midwest also created further scheduling problems for southern teams, who found it more and more difficult to locate all-white teams as opponents.

The Big Ten Conference technically dropped its unofficial ban on black basketball players at the end of World War II, but it was not until the late 1950s that all members regularly fielded integrated teams. In the fall of 1944 the University of Iowa became the first conference school to eliminate its color line when Richard T. Culberson, a transfer from Virginia Union College, joined the Hawkeye squad. When he approached Hawkeye coach Lawrence "Pops" Harrison about joining the basketball team, Harrison encouraged him to do so. "I had no agenda," Culberson later recalled. "I just was someone who wanted to play basketball." Harrison realized that his newly integrated squad would face problems when traveling, so he always planned in advance to ensure that Culberson could eat and room with his teammates. Consequently, the Iowa team did not experience any major problems on the road, except when visiting Indiana University in Bloomington, where he stayed with a private family. The 6'3" center received his most substantial playing time as a junior on Iowa's 1945 team, which won the Big Ten championship, but he played less frequently as a senior. Overall, Culberson recalled his Iowa years as "a good experience." Because Culberson began his career at Iowa during the unusual conditions of World War II, and because he saw only limited playing time over his two years, his violation of the Big Ten color line did not completely undermine this policy, as other conference schools continued to ignore black basketball prospects.[31]

Indiana University became the second Big Ten member to break the league's informal ban on recruiting black players. In the summer of 1947 Coach Branch McCracken signed center Bill Garrett, who had recently led Shelbyville High School to the Indiana state championship, to a scholarship. Despite Garrett's obvious talent, though, not a single Big Ten college initially offered him a scholarship, and McCracken needed encouragement from President Herman B Wells before doing so. Because of Garrett's presence on the squad, the Hoosiers experienced some difficulty with hotels and restaurants when traveling. The university was well rewarded for its racial pragmatism, though, as Garrett led the team in scoring and rebounding during all three of his varsity seasons. As a senior in 1951 he earned all-conference first-team honors and was named to the All-America second team. Also that season Michigan State University became the third Big Ten school to field an integrated basketball team when 5'5" guard Ricky Ayala of New York joined the varsity. Other Big Ten schools gradually followed the lead of these schools, eventually eliminating the color line by the late 1950s. Notre Dame, a leading independent in the region, suited up its first two black basketball players, Joe Bertrand and Entee Shine, in 1952.[32]

The Missouri Valley Conference also reconsidered its racial policies after World War II. Conference members in 1946 included Drake University, Creighton University, Wichita State, St. Louis University, University of Tulsa, and Oklahoma State (then known as Oklahoma A&M). Bradley University and the University of Cincinnati joined the league in the early 1950s. Reflecting the strict segregation found in Oklahoma, Tulsa and Oklahoma State traditionally refused to admit black students and to compete against integrated teams at home. At a December 1947 league meeting, members nonetheless voted to end all racial discrimination in sports by September 1950. The subsequent recruitment of African American players did not end all complaints about racism, though. Many of the racial pioneers in the league encountered occasional discrimination and social isolation on their own campuses. More significantly, when competing on the road against the "southern" members of the conference, black players and sometimes their white coaches and teammates encountered verbal abuse from fans and discrimination in public accommodations. Most hotels and restaurants in St. Louis, Tulsa, and Stillwater refused to serve integrated groups throughout the 1950s. When the University of Houston (UH) and North Texas State College (NTSC) in Denton joined the league in the late 1950s, their inclusion added two more southern locations and produced additional complaints about hotel discrimination. Chet "the Jet" Walker of Bradley, a future NBA star, experienced many such problems from 1960 to 1962. He later recalled that these incidents, especially taunting from fans, only motivated him to play even harder. Oscar Robertson of Cincinnati, the top college basketball player in the country his junior and senior years, grew so frustrated that he once threatened to boycott a road trip to Texas unless he was guaranteed equal treatment in housing. Chet Walker also noted that despite these racial incidents, African American players "never discussed race with our white teammates," since everyone involved "would have been uncomfortable."[33]

A serious incident during a Missouri Valley football game between Drake and Oklahoma State demonstrated the dark side of athletic integration. In 1949 outstanding halfback Johnny Bright of Drake had been the most visible member of the first group of African Americans to break the league's color line, and that same year he was reportedly the first black player to compete at Oklahoma State. A fast, slashing runner, Bright set several conference records and led the nation in rushing for much of 1951. In October Bright suffered a fractured jaw in the first quarter of a road game against the Aggies (later known as the Cowboys) in Stillwater. Drake players, coaches, and officials were outraged by the incident and insisted that an Oklahoma State lineman had deliberately injured Bright by hitting him in the face on three separate occasions after Bright had handed off the ball and was standing far away from the action. Some of Bright's teammates claimed that they had overheard Oklahoma State students taking bets that the star halfback would not last the entire game. Two reporters for the Des Moines newspaper accidentally captured the incident on film. When their photographs were developed, they clearly showed that Bright had been intentionally assaulted by the OSU player away from the play while game officials were watching the actual ball carrier. The lead reporter later received the Pulitzer Prize for his photographs. Despite the clear evidence of deliberate foul play, which might have been encouraged by the Aggie coaching staff, Oklahoma State refused to punish the offending player or apologize for the incident. Drake then severed athletic relations with OSU and withdrew from the league. To black fans and sympathetic whites, the deliberate injury of Bright and the failure of the conference to take any action revealed continuing racism in major college football. The *Chicago Defender* contended that Bright "was the victim of the worst instance of foul play" in recent football history and that the incident made a mockery "of the ideals of sportsmanship and fair play." Despite the outcry, no punishment was ever imposed against Oklahoma State or its player. After several years Drake rejoined the Missouri Valley Conference and resumed its series with the Aggies.[34]

The last of the midwestern conferences to abandon Jim Crow was the Big Eight Conference, better known to modern fans as the Big Twelve. The league had been established on May 19, 1928, by six colleges—the University of Nebraska, the University of Kansas (KU), Kansas State University (KSU), Iowa State University, the University of Missouri, and the University of Oklahoma. The league's name changed from the Big Six to the Big Seven in 1947 with the admission of the University of Colorado, and it became the Big Eight when Oklahoma State joined in 1957. Nebraska, Kansas, and Iowa State had included African Americans on their athletic teams in earlier decades, but at the league's founding all six participating schools unofficially agreed to bar them from competition. The decision was apparently made at the insistence of Missouri and Oklahoma, who were adamantly opposed to integrated play. In 1946, following inquiries about this unwritten agreement, the conference unanimously adopted a formal policy that was slightly less restrictive. The new regulation stated that "the personnel of visiting squads shall be so selected as to conform with any restrictions imposed upon a host institution" by its regents or the state government. This meant that any Big Eight school hosting a conference game had the right to bar any black players on the visiting team, if there were an official regulation against such competition. Small wonder then that one critic dismissed the modification as meaningless and charged that the new wording simply represented "the gentleman's agreement in writing."[35]

The decision to adopt a formal exclusion policy upset many students at Nebraska, Kansas, Kansas State, and Iowa State. Even prior to the Big Eight action, the student governments at Kansas and Nebraska had adopted resolutions endorsing the participation of black athletes in the league. In November 1947 the student council at Nebraska adopted a resolution urging university officials to convince the Big Eight to repeal its racial ban and to consider withdrawing from the league "if the action is not taken." At a meeting of student representatives from five league schools in late November on the Nebraska campus, participants formally demanded that the Big Eight replace its exclusion clause with a new one that guaranteed that "any eligible student of a member institution shall be allowed to participate in all competitive athletic events at any member institution." Even the student government at the University of Missouri endorsed the resolution. The following month the athletic board of the University of Nebraska formally called upon the conference to delete the controversial clause. But when the council of Big Eight faculty representatives met a few days later at their annual gathering, it tabled the request.[36]

Kansas State University became the first Big Eight member to directly challenge the exclusion rule. With the approval of the athletic department, a campus organization at KSU tentatively offered a scholarship in the summer of 1948 to local football star Harold Robinson of Manhattan High School but then unexpectedly retracted the offer. Robinson nonetheless enrolled and played on the freshman team, paying for his expenses by washing dishes and mopping floors at local businesses. Following a coaching change at the end of the 1948 season, new head coach Ralph Graham decided to grant Robinson a scholarship. Graham then sent a letter to the next Big Eight meeting, declaring his intention to use Robinson during the fall season of 1949. "Since there is no ruling against the use of Negro players," he explained, "we plan to use Harold except at universities where there is a definite rule that decrees otherwise." When the league did not take action, Graham continued with his plan, and Robinson became a starter as a sophomore and junior. During his first year he experienced rough play and racial taunts in several games, and on trips to Oklahoma and Missouri he stayed separately from the rest of the team. For a road game at Memphis State, the coaching staff decided to leave him at home because of their uneasiness about challenging exclusion in a southern city. Just before the start of his senior season in 1951 Robinson was drafted into military service and left school. That fall sophomore Veryl Switzer, an outstanding player from Nicodemus, an all-black Kansas town, became the second African American to compete for the Wildcats. Since both young men had been high school stars inside the state and understood local racial etiquette, local whites were apparently more willing to accept their presence on the gridiron than if they had been outsiders.[37]

At the University of Kansas many campus groups and individual students supported the recruitment of black athletes, but university coaches were slower to act than their counterparts at Kansas State. When Oklahoma State applied to join the Big Eight in March 1947, sixteen student organizations sponsored a petition drive opposing membership because OSU refused to enroll African Americans. But in a campus referendum on the issue, students voted overwhelmingly in favor of admitting the Aggies. Eventually, the conference declined to act on Oklahoma State's request. Perhaps influenced by the campus debate, Kansas chancellor Deane W. Malott terminated the school's Jim Crow policy in May 1947. Malott announced that "any regularly enrolled student at KU may try out for intercollegiate athletics," provided he met conference eligibility requirements. The elimination of racial restrictions in sports did not mean that Jayhawk coaches immediately changed their behavior. Phog Allen, the highly successful basketball coach, publicly stated that his policies would remain the same and recommended instead that African Americans participate in track and field, because that sport "doesn't require as much body contact as basketball." Seven years actually passed before Allen finally recruited his first black player, guard Maurice King. In 1956, one year after King's arrival, Allen signed the school's most famous recruit ever, 7'0" center Wilt Chamberlain of Philadelphia, the top high school player in the country. University retirement rules forced Allen to step down after Chamberlain's freshman year, but in the 1957 season the giant center led the Jayhawks to a second-place finish in the NCAA Tournament. Color-blind recruiting in football likewise stalled until the arrival of a new coach in 1954. Chuck Mather, who had previously coached integrated prep teams in Massillon, Ohio, sought out black players from the start and fielded his first integrated varsity squad in 1955. New chancellor Frank Murphy strongly endorsed the recruitment of African Americans, hoping thereby "to promote racial tolerance through their athletic contributions to the university."[38]

The University of Oklahoma, where both football fever and a commitment to segregation were the strongest in the Big Eight, demonstrated the promptness with which an athletic program could change. In May 1955 the university announced that it would now accept any qualified African American for undergraduate classes and its athletic teams. Coached by Bud Wilkinson, the Oklahoma Sooners dominated Big Eight football and had won seven consecutive conference championships. Wilkinson did not fear athletic integration; in fact, in 1950 he stated that he would open the tryouts for his team to African Americans if the university should drop its racial restrictions. The Oklahoma coach waited only one year before awarding his first scholarship to an African American, halfback Prentice Gautt of nearby Oklahoma City. Gautt joined the Sooner varsity in 1957 and earned three letters while winning all-conference honors his senior season. The integration of the Oklahoma athletic program in 1957 and the University of Missouri program in 1958 delivered the final blows to the Big Eight's color line. With the Missouri Valley Conference, the Big Ten, and the Big Eight now accepting African Americans, public attention shifted to the three major conferences in the ex-Confederate South, where the color line still encircled the protected white space of the football field.[39]

"Massive Resistance" in the Deep South

The growing acceptance of integrated games by many southern universities and the integration of the midwestern conferences suggested that a new era in intercollegiate sports was at hand. This optimism was soon dashed by a militant segregationist backlash beginning in 1954. On May 17 of that year the United States Supreme Court issued its famous ruling in the case of *Brown v. Board of Education*, which reversed the 1896 *Plessy v. Ferguson* decision and declared that segregated public schools were unconstitutional. This death blow to "separate but equal" education applied not only to elementary and secondary schools but also to undergraduate studies in college. In May 1955 the high court confirmed the previous year's ruling and ordered school integration to proceed with "all deliberate speed." After a temporary lull, outraged segregationist politicians across the South launched a widespread counteroffensive, usually referred to as "massive resistance." Segregationists realized that the basic foundations of white supremacy were now endangered, and they viewed any deviation from 100 percent segregation, no matter how small, as a serious threat to the South's racial structure. According to one historian, "Legislatures in the former Confederate states enacted some 450 segregationist laws and resolutions" in the decade following the *Brown* ruling. In such a heated atmosphere, big-time college sports lost their privileged status and were now expected to conform completely to traditional racial norms.[40]

Demands for strict segregation in athletics were especially strong in the Deep South states of South Carolina, Georgia, Florida, Alabama, Mississippi, and Louisiana. Several cities and towns and one state adopted legal provisions banning integrated sporting events. Birmingham, Alabama, provided the most extreme case. In September 1950 promoters staged a National Football League exhibition between the Washington Redskins and the Detroit Lions in the city. Local officials insisted that the Lions leave their only African American player, Wallace Triplett, at home, but club officials protested. Eventually, city leaders and Lions management reached an understanding whereby Triplett could warm up with his teammates but would not be inserted into the contest. Shortly after the exhibition the city council adopted a municipal ordinance that prohibited whites and blacks from competing "with each other in any game of cards, dice, dominoes, checkers, baseball, softball, football, basketball, or similar game." This law prevented the New York Giants from using two black players in the following year's exhibition, after which the series was canceled. The loss of such athletic contests disappointed civic and business leaders. In January and March 1954 Mayor James Morgan convinced the city commission to amend the ordinance so as to exempt baseball and football matches from its provisions. Promoters then quickly scheduled two Major League Baseball exhibitions for the city in April.[41]

The council's revisions incensed Birmingham segregationists. Former state judge Hugh Locke organized a successful petition drive that forced a special referendum on the modifications to the ordinance. While the controversy raged across the city, more than twenty-one thousand fans, a majority of them African Americans, turned out in early April to see a series of major-league exhibitions featuring the Brooklyn Dodgers. Just over a month later in May, the Supreme Court's *Brown* decision added a sense of urgency to the segregationist campaign. One white supporter of revising the ordinance told a local newspaper that he favored complete segregation in sports, because "we must draw the line when it looks to us like this game might be the opening wedge to break down segregation." Hugh Locke went even further in providing the most explicit white supremacist warning against the ultimate dangers of integrated athletic events. The former judge passionately declared, "Allowing a few Negroes to play baseball here will wind up with Negroes and whites marrying." On June 1 Birmingham voters, almost all of whom were white, overwhelmingly repudiated the city commission's earlier action by a margin of 19,640 to 6,685. The vote technically restored baseball and football to the original ban and added to the list of prohibited activities golf, track, and "any mingling at the races, swimming pools, beaches, lakes, and ponds." White residents of Montgomery, the state's capital, declined to imitate Birmingham for several years while tolerating a few integrated minor-league baseball games. In 1957, however, the city commission finally adopted a sweeping ordinance banning competition between blacks and whites "in any game of cards, dice, dominoes, checkers, pool, billiards, softball, basketball, baseball, football, golf, track, and at swimming pools . . . or in any athletic contest."[42]

In Louisiana custom rather than law had prevented most interracial athletic competition, with the exception of prizefighting. During 1954 Loyola University and the Sugar Bowl both exploited this oversight to experiment with staging integrated sporting events in the city. In November Loyola announced that it had withdrawn all racial restrictions on opposing teams and eliminated segregated seating at its new sixty-five hundred–seat field house. The ambitious Jesuit institution officially dedicated its new facility on December 6 when it hosted the defending NCAA champion squad from LaSalle University of Philadelphia, which included one black player. The game apparently represented the first integrated major sporting event in the city in the twentieth century. The following year, in December, Loyola hosted two more integrated games. In a highly publicized matchup, the University of San Francisco Dons, the defending NCAA champion, easily defeated their hosts. Leading USF to victory was All-American center Bill Russell, a Louisiana native, whose family had moved to California during World War II to escape racism and seek better economic opportunities. After the game Russell told a reporter, "Playing against Loyola is better than twenty-five Supreme Court decisions." Loyola's contest against an integrated

Bradley University squad a few days later did not go so smoothly. During the visitors' stay in New Orleans, Bradley's Shellie McMillon was denied service at a local restaurant. When McMillon fouled out of the December 20 game, he angrily stuck out his tongue at the crowd and refused to shake hands with an opponent. McMillon's frustration may have been increased by the Loyola pep band, which struck up "Dixie" as he left the court. Embarrassed Loyola officials later announced that the band would refrain from playing "Dixie" during future contests against integrated teams.[43]

The Sugar Bowl Crisis

Loyola's repudiation of the color line may have encouraged the Mid-Winter Sports Association to modify its racial policies for the Sugar Bowl football game and its less well-known holiday basketball tournament. In the fall of 1954 the association sought to attract the U.S. Naval Academy to the January 1, 1955, Sugar Bowl football contest against the University of Mississippi. As a concession to Navy, bowl officials permitted unrestricted seating in the student, visitors, and armed forces sections. Taking advantage of the new policy, many black football fans in New Orleans purchased tickets for the visitors section. Encouraged by the Middies' 21–0 victory over the Rebels and the integrated seating available in part of the stadium, former college star Fritz Pollard declared that "Navy triumphed in more ways than one." The following year the Sugar Bowl moved even further away from Jim Crow by inviting integrated northern teams to its basketball tournament and its famous postseason football classic. The participation of Al Avant, an African American, on the Marquette University basketball team in the December 1955 tournament did not provoke any public protests, even though the Milwaukee college met Alabama in the third-place game. The selection of football teams for the January 1956 football classic proved to be far more complicated, however. Bowl officials selected the powerful Georgia Tech Yellow Jackets as the home team and the University of Pittsburgh Panthers as the visiting team. The latter choice greatly alarmed segregationists, because the Pittsburgh starting lineup included fullback Bobby Grier, potentially the first African American to compete in the New Year's Day classic. The ensuing controversy focused national attention on the Sugar Bowl and southern race relations while contributing to a heated political debate in the state legislatures of Louisiana and Georgia over the alleged dangers of integrated athletic competition.[44]

Before Georgia Tech administrators accepted the invitation, they prudently verified that key team boosters and Governor Marvin Griffin, a leader in the massive resistance movement, had no objections. Reportedly, Griffin reassured Tech coach Bobby Dodd by saying, "Bobby, I can't come out publicly and support this. But you go ahead and do it." A few days later, though, Governor Griffin unexpectedly reversed his position and urged the Board of Regents for the state university system to block Tech's participation. In apocalyptic terms the governor warned, "The South stands at Armageddon. The battle is joined. We cannot make the slightest concession to the enemy in this dark and lamentable hour of struggle. There is no more difference in compromising the integrity of race on the playing field than in doing so in the classroom. One break in the dike and the relentless seas will rush in and destroy us." Griffin's sudden reversal upset Georgia Tech football fans around the state. Angry Tech students staged two anti-Griffin rallies, and some of them marched on the governor's mansion. Even one prosegregation newspaper criticized the governor for tarnishing "the reputation of our two great state universities whose football teams have brought fame, glory, and prestige to Georgia." A few days later the state Board of Regents met and approved the trip. At the same time, the regents also adopted new guidelines requiring state colleges to retain segregation for in-state sporting events.[45]

The political controversy over Georgia Tech's participation in the Sugar Bowl helped focus widespread media attention on the January 1 contest and the changing racial patterns of the Deep South. An unusually large contingent of sportswriters descended on New Orleans, provoking one Atlanta journalist to accuse them of turning a "commonplace incident" into a front-page melodrama. Sugar Bowl officials again permitted integrated seating in the visitors section and even removed the "Caucasian race" label from tickets to the game. The actual contest turned out to be a low-scoring affair. Ironically, the game's outcome turned on a questionable pass-interference penalty called against Grier, which Pittsburgh fans strongly disputed as unwarranted. On the next play Georgia Tech scored the winning touchdown for a 7–0 victory. Grier did turn in a nice twenty-eight-yard run on one play and received a loud ovation from the crowd when he left the game in the fourth quarter. "I had no problems down there," Grier commented. "The only problem was that call on the field." After the game the Pitt fullback broke another color barrier by attending the awards banquet at the downtown St. Charles Hotel. Grier sat with several Georgia Tech players during the presentations but did not stay for the formal dance.[46]

The success of the 1956 Sugar Bowl failed to slow down the segregationist juggernaut that was sweeping across the South. If anything, the game's widespread publicity pointedly reminded ultrasegregationists that the color line had been violated in a Deep South state. Segregationists in Mississippi were particularly aggressive in fighting sports integration. To these activists, college athletics represented one battlefield in the much larger war to preserve white supremacy. Even one isolated integrated game could now set a dangerous precedent. "Being a little bit integrated is like being a little bit pregnant," warned the ultrasegregationist *Jackson Daily News,* pointing out that "a few short years ago only one Negro was in the National Baseball League!" Mindful of threats of financial retaliation from powerful legislators, the statewide board of trustees for higher education enforced what was called "the unwritten law" against integrated athletic competition. In late December 1956 officials at Ole Miss and Mississippi State obeyed this policy and ordered their basketball teams to withdraw from two separate out-of-state holiday tournaments and return home rather than play against integrated opponents. In 1959, 1961, and 1962 the Mississippi State basketball squad captured the Southeastern Conference championship but declined to participate in the NCAA Tournament, because it would have been required to play integrated teams. Black colleges in the Magnolia State were not exempt from the higher-education board's policy. In March 1957 the board ordered Jackson State College to drop out of the second round of the NCAA small-college basketball tournament, because the school was scheduled to compete against predominantly white teams. On March 5 President Jacob L. Reddix of Jackson State duly announced the withdrawal, noting that students as his school were "quite upset at the news."[47]

The Georgia Legislature Defends Jim Crow

Segregationists in Georgia and Louisiana attempted even more extreme measures than Mississippi to preserve white supremacy in sporting events, pressuring their state legislatures to adopt formal laws specifically banning integrated athletic contests. In 1955 and early 1956 state representatives introduced bills in the Georgia Assembly to prohibit all athletic events involving competition between blacks and whites, but no action was taken on them. During the next legislative session in early 1957, however, public anger at the federal government ran strong, and the assembly passed numerous bills designed to reinforce segregation. In their more extreme moments legislators even approved resolutions calling for the nullification of the Fourteenth and Fifteenth Amendments to the United States Constitution and the impeachment of Chief Justice Earl Warren. As part of the segregationist agenda, Senator Leon Butts of Lumkin introduced another bill to ban integrated athletics and related social activities. This sweeping proposal sought to prohibit all athletic matches, physical games, social functions, and entertainment events in which blacks and whites participated together. Emphasizing the symbolic importance of sports, Butts argued that interracial athletic competition would set a dangerous example for society, because "when Negroes and whites meet on the athletic fields on a basis of complete equality, it is only natural that this sense of equality carries into the daily living of these people." Governor Marvin Griffin strongly endorsed the proposal, explaining that he was against "Negroes and white folks playing any type of sport together." In mid-February 1957 the senate unanimously approved the measure and sent it to the house.[48]

The possibility that the bill might actually pass the house and become law alarmed the owners of minor-league baseball clubs, university officials, and sports fans. Baseball spokesmen warned that the bill would destroy the four Georgia teams in the Class A South Atlantic League, since major-league teams no longer tolerated such racial restrictions on their minor-league clubs. Determined to protect sports from political intervention, a small band of legislators quietly plotted to defeat the bill by preventing it from ever coming up for a final vote. Nonetheless, on February 22, the hectic last day of the legislative session, the proposal arrived for debate before the full house. At that point critics cleverly exploited parliamentary maneuvers to delay consideration of the bill until the exhausted legislators voted to close the session at the end of the day. A disappointed Senator Butts told reporters, "I think it's a shame the major league ball clubs and the NAACP have gotten control of the Georgia House."

The 1957 legislative session represented the high tide of segregationist efforts to regulate athletic activities by state law. Thereafter they concentrated their efforts on defending segregation in the state's educational institutions and in public accommodations. The legislature's failure to adopt a sports segregation law also meant that the Board of Regents of the state university system retained control over athletic policy. Furthermore, the bill's defeat helped Georgia and Georgia Tech avoid retaliation by northern states and universities, who were now threatening to boycott southern white teams. During the assembly debate, for example, three members of the Michigan legislature from Detroit publicly called upon the University of Michigan to cancel its scheduled 1957 home football game with the University of Georgia, because the college excluded African American students. Rejecting their complaint, Michigan officials announced that they would still host the Bulldogs in the fall. Nonetheless, Georgia administrators quietly modified their future schedules so that the university played against only one northern team over the next seven years. Other universities from the Deep South acted in a similar fashion, scheduling more southern opponents in order to avoid political controversy.[49]

Louisiana Bans Interracial Athletic Competition

Militant segregationists in the Louisiana legislature also moved to outlaw integrated athletic contests in the wake of the 1956 Sugar Bowl contest, but with far greater success. Conservative legislators there viewed "mixed" competition as a dangerous precedent for additional desegregation and vowed to do everything possible to protect the state's Jim Crow system. In 1952 a state senator had introduced a bill to prohibit whites and blacks from competing together in athletic events where an admission fee would be charged, but his colleagues ignored his proposal. After the *Brown* decision and the rise of massive resistance, however, Louisiana legislators became far more receptive. In July 1956, as part of a wave of regressive legislation designed to forestall any desegregation in Louisiana, the legislature adopted a dozen segregation bills. Among them were new laws that specifically required segregation in hotels and restaurants. One extreme segregationist even introduced an unsuccessful proposal to prohibit all television programs that showed blacks and whites together. Two of the new laws directly impacted amateur and professional sports. The first required segregated seating at all public performances, including athletic contests, while the second outlawed "dancing, social functions, entertainments, athletic training, games, sports or contests and other such activities . . . in which the participants or contestants are members of the white and Negro races." The senate rejected an amendment to exempt athletics from coverage by a vote of 30–2. Senator William Rainach, the powerful leader of segregationist forces in the legislature, frankly declared that the bill's purpose "is to wipe out integration in athletics. We consider it an opening wedge which would lead to integration in other things." The only concession that segregationists would make was to postpone the date on which the new laws would become effective until October 15, apparently in order to allow the Texas League to finish its baseball playoffs and Tulane University to host the Naval Academy's football team. After both houses quickly passed the measure, it went to the desk of Governor Earl Long, a moderate segregationist.[50]

The passage of the sports segregation bill caught the Mid-Winter Sports Association, the sponsor of the Sugar Bowl, off guard. Previously silent about the measure, the association quickly launched a public campaign against the legislation, taking out full-page advertisements in the New Orleans newspapers to argue its case. The executive committee of the association adopted a resolution urging the governor to reject the bill, warning that the measure would "seriously damage our sports program" by making the Sugar Bowl a mostly regional event. Apparently, many New Orleans business and civic leaders feared that a lower national profile for the postseason classic would reduce the game's financial benefits to the local economy. Baseball owners from the Texas League, which had a franchise in Shreveport, also criticized the proposal. Despite these lobbying efforts, Governor Earl Long reluctantly signed the bills into law, commenting that communications to his office had run four to one in favor of the measures. A few weeks later, though, a Long supporter secretly offered financial assistance to the New Orleans NAACP chapter if it would initiate a legal challenge to the sports ban, but the civil rights group responded that the governor and his friends should file their own lawsuit. Later in the year Sugar Bowl supporters made one last-ditch effort to escape the new law by endorsing a proposal to exempt cities with a population of more than three hundred thousand from its coverage, but the house tabled the bill by a vote of 67–15.[51]

The Louisiana sports segregation laws interfered with Sugar Bowl activities, college football and basketball games, minor-league baseball, and professional boxing inside the state. By requiring the Sugar Bowl to impose racial exclusion on the football field and segregated seating in the stands, the two main provisions made it virtually impossible to attract nonsouthern teams to the game. By default the Sugar Bowl, or what one black sportswriter termed the "Segregation Bowl," became an all-southern affair with a lower national profile. The frequent presence of the Southeastern Conference champion helped somewhat with attendance, especially when undefeated Louisiana State University (LSU) claimed the national championship in 1958. Nonetheless, bowl officials concluded that they were falling behind their main rivals, the Cotton Bowl and the Orange Bowl, which were not bound by such a restrictive policy.[52]

The sports segregation law also affected basketball scheduling. The Sugar Bowl basketball tournament and most Louisiana colleges found it difficult to attract northern teams to the state. The new law forced Loyola University to abandon its ambitious plans to bring one of the top college teams in the country to the city each year. In 1957 both Loyola and Centenary College in Shreveport had to revise their schedules after several northern teams refused to travel to Louisiana. Harvard University also announced that it would no longer play basketball games in the South, even if there were no African Americans on its team, so as to avoid conforming "to local prejudices." Several other northern universities announced that they would boycott athletic events in Louisiana. When Colorado State University officials revealed that they would leave the team's one black member behind for a three-game swing through the state in December 1957, student protests forced them to reverse course and cancel the trip.[53]

Athletic administrators at Louisiana universities, especially LSU and Tulane, also found their football scheduling disrupted by the new state laws. Even before the legislature acted in 1956, several schools began to back away from integrated athletic contests in order to avoid provoking segregationists. In March 1956 Louisiana Tech terminated discussions with the Air Force Academy over a football series because the academy had insisted that all game contracts guarantee that "no player be barred because of race or creed." After the sports segregation bill took effect, the Air Force Academy canceled plans to visit Tulane in 1958 and 1959. Tulane solved problems with scheduled home games against the U.S. Military Academy and Marquette in 1957 by moving both games to the North. Louisiana State University also encountered scheduling difficulties. In April 1956 the LSU boxing team hosted a Wisconsin team that included one black fighter, Orville Pitts. Nervous about staging an integrated bout in the state capital shortly before the upcoming legislative session, LSU forfeited the match against Pitts. The boxing exhibition had been part of the university's efforts to elevate its national profile by scheduling athletic contests with Big Ten schools, a strategy that was no longer possible. Many frustrated LSU and Tulane alumni feared that the sports segregation law would damage the national stature of both universities and might even turn them into virtual pariahs in college football circles.[54]

The Collapse of Massive Resistance in Sports

The summer of 1957 represented the high tide of massive resistance in college sports across the South. No significant new legislation or regulations were adopted after those months, and soon thereafter, a few southern teams cautiously resumed competition against integrated northern squads. The University of Virginia avoided a confrontation with the U.S. Military Academy that fall when it agreed to unrestricted seating in the visitors section of its own stadium, thereby guaranteeing that the Army football team would travel to Charlottesville. The University of North Carolina made similar concessions in order to secure a contest against the Naval Academy in Chapel Hill. Since both southern universities had recently admitted African American undergraduates, the seating issue had lost most of its emotional impact. Despite complaints from segregationists, Georgia ventured north to Ann Arbor in 1957 to challenge Michigan. Later that fall Georgia also played Navy in Norfolk, Virginia, after the game's promoters agreed not to segregate black spectators. As a concession to its conservative fans, however, Georgia officials agreed to sell its allotment of tickets for a special UGA section only to whites. In short, northern resistance to continued racial exclusion in intersectional games had forced concessions from some southern universities, but at the same time segregationist pressure also prevented others from pursuing their dreams of national glory through greater inaction with northern and western schools.[55]

In Louisiana Joseph Dorsey Jr., an obscure African American boxer, filed the main legal challenge to the sports segregation law. Dorsey's attorney argued that state boxing commission regulations and the 1956 statute unfairly restricted his economic opportunities and denied him equal protection under the law by preventing him from earning money by fighting white boxers. A three-judge federal panel, presided over by Judge John Minor Wisdom of the Fifth Circuit Court, heard arguments in January 1958. In November the judges ruled unanimously in Dorsey's favor and invalidated the sports segregation law because it violated the Fourteenth Amendment. Attorneys for the state immediately appealed to the United States Supreme Court, which in May 1959 affirmed the lower-court decision. "The ban on interracial sports of any type is eliminated," confessed a disappointed Louisiana attorney general, Jack Gremillion.[56]

Sugar Bowl officials applauded the Supreme Court ruling and optimistically predicted that it would greatly assist the New Year's Day classic. However, the section of the law requiring segregated seating at public events had not been challenged by Dorsey and became the source of continuing problems. Rather than accept segregation in the stands, northern universities maintained their boycott of the state. Furthermore, a few colleges now challenged the discrimination in hotels and restaurants that visiting teams encountered in Louisiana and the South. In January 1959 the Wisconsin Board of Regents adopted a policy that instructed the university's athletic teams not to play in cities and states where team members would be subject to discrimination of any kind in public accommodations. Finally, in 1960 sponsors of several local sporting events in New Orleans decided to defy the seating law. In February Loyola of New Orleans hosted an integrated basketball team from Loyola University of Chicago, while in April baseball promoters successfully staged two major-league exhibition games at City Park Stadium. Both events allowed unrestricted seating. A boycott campaign against the baseball games, led by the Southern Louisiana White Citizens Council, failed to have any financial impact. Local law enforcement made no attempt at any of these contests to enforce the segregated seating law.[57]

Shortly after the Loyola basketball game, the Associated Press surveyed the status of integrated competition in minor-league baseball and college sports across Dixie. The wire service reported that integrated professional baseball games had become commonplace but that many universities still were reluctant to host integrated contests. Seating in the stands for all sports often remained segregated. Except in the states of Alabama and Louisiana, formal laws and ordinances against integrated games had disappeared. Yet custom seemed almost as powerful as law; in fact, many whites still thought that segregation laws remained intact. The report explained the difficulty of changing this practice: "The segregation custom creates scheduling problems for many colleges in the Deep South. The subject is a touchy one, and coaches don't talk about it publicly. It is no secret, however, that fear of local opposition, particularly from politicians who control the purse strings for state-supported institutions, often prevents home-and-home series with integrated schools."

In the late 1950s and early 1960s federal courts continued to strike down laws and ordinances mandating segregation at athletic events. In September 1959 Judge Frank Johnson overturned the Montgomery municipal ordinance. Two years later in Birmingham, Judge H. H. Grooms ruled in favor of several African American plaintiffs and declared the city's ordinance prohibiting interracial athletic contests to be unconstitutional. These rulings came too late to save the AA

Southern Association baseball league, however. League franchises in Alabama and Mississippi had been caught between city ordinances banning integrated games and boycotts by black fans protesting these laws, crippling team finances. After several Southern Association teams in neighboring states switched to other minor leagues that did not bar black players, officials disbanded the league. As Bruce Adelson observed, "The Southern Association essentially committed suicide, with its segregation policy as the instrument of its destruction."[58]

As public school desegregation slowly advanced across the South in the early 1960s, southern universities became bolder in challenging the regulations and customs that blocked integrated athletic competition. In January 1961 the Gator Bowl postseason football game in Jacksonville broke with Florida custom and finally hosted its first integrated northern team. Florida State University abandoned its racial traditions in the fall of 1964 when the Seminoles played an integrated New Mexico State squad in Tallahassee. Even in Mississippi there were signs of change. In the spring of 1963 Mississippi State University officials defied the state's powerful segregationist leaders and allowed the school's basketball team, the SEC champion, to participate in the NCAA Tournament against integrated teams. That same spring the state Board of Regents in Georgia formally authorized Georgia Tech to host integrated teams at Grant Field in Atlanta. When organizers of the Blue-Gray all-star game in Montgomery continued to exclude African American players from its late-December football contest, they discovered that such segregation came with a stiff price, as NBC canceled its telecast of the 1963 game. After NBC officials refused to reconsider their action, Alabama governor George C. Wallace denounced the decision as "tragic and irresponsible."[59]

Finally, in July 1963 a three-judge federal panel in New Orleans struck down the Louisiana seating law and a related New Orleans ordinance requiring segregated recreational facilities. Speaking for the panel, Judge John Minor Wisdom wrote that southern cities must "face up to the facts of life." His opinion continued: "New Orleans, here and now, must adjust to the reality of having to operate desegregated public facilities. Time has run out. There is no defense left. There is no excuse left." Louisiana officials appealed to the U.S. Supreme Court, which in January 1964 affirmed the lower court's decision. The demise of the segregated seating law also terminated northern boycotts of Louisiana sporting events and enabled the Sugar Bowl to aggressively recruit highly ranked integrated teams for its annual game. For the January 1, 1965, contest, bowl officials targeted Syracuse University, undeterred by the presence of eight African Americans on the Orangeman squad. Ironically, administrators at the New York college had been under attack from campus activists because they would not rule out playing future games against all-white southern teams. Nonetheless, the Board of Athletics at Syracuse jumped at the opportunity to play LSU. Inside Louisiana the Syracuse invitation produced no public outcry, except for one complaint by the Southern Louisiana White Citizens Council. In a message to LSU officials the council expressed its "sincere concern" over the university's athletic future and admonished school administrators that "LSU owes its greatness, academically and athletically, to its Anglo-Saxon heritage." The ensuing January 1, 1965, contest attracted wider national attention to the Sugar Bowl, but it took several years before the stigma previously attached to the game finally dissipated.[60]

* * *

Over the twenty-year period from 1945 through 1965, historically white southern universities gradually abandoned their racial color line for intersectional athletic contests against northern and western colleges. After World War II the gentleman's agreement gradually broke down, as northern students rallied in defense of African American players on their school teams. In order to fully participate in national sporting culture and high-profile intersectional games, southern colleges were forced to accept integrated competition first in the North and then later at home. The white backlash against the Supreme Court's *Brown* decision temporarily reduced intersectional competition, but by the early 1960s most southern teams had resumed scheduling northern opponents. By 1965 undergraduate studies at all major southern universities were desegregated, but many vestiges of white privilege remained. An internal color line guaranteed that their football and basketball teams remained all-white. Full integration, rather than token desegregation, therefore necessitated the elimination of these remaining internal racial boundaries, especially the continued exclusion of African Americans from the protected white space of southern athletic teams. The following chapters will describe the process by which administrators, coaches, and students at southern universities, as well as black recruits, resolved what has been termed "the American Dilemma on the playing fields."

4

Cracks in the Solid South

Texas Western College
Abandons Jim Crow

The Negro race has many good athletes.
. . . [M]aybe we could get some of them.
—A Texas Western College student,
April 1955

Oh, how I can remember those last seven seconds! When
that clock started ticking off, it seemed like the whole
world just stood still. . . . Hey, we were Number One! I was
part of a team that was the best in the United States!
—Nevil Shed, February 1986

The championship game of the 1966 National Collegiate Athletic Association basketball tournament still stands today as a watershed in the social history of college basketball. This historic title contest matched the number-one ranked and heavily favored University of Kentucky Wildcats against the upstart Texas Western College Miners. The most successful college basketball program in the country, Kentucky had won four previous NCAA championships and numerous conference titles. Conversely, Texas Western was a relatively obscure school located on the U.S.-Mexican border and had not even participated in the NCAA playoffs before 1963. At the helm of the Kentucky basketball program stood the most renowned coach in college basketball—sixty-four-year-old Adolph Rupp. Known widely as "the Baron of the Bluegrass," Rupp had guided the Wildcats to sixteen NCAA tournament appearances and all four of their national titles. In contrast, the Miner squad was directed by thirty-six-year-old Don Haskins, a former school-bus driver and coach at several small West Texas high schools.

What made this 1966 matchup the most socially significant NCAA championship game ever played was not just these details, however, but rather the racial symbolism involved. For the fourteen thousand spectators crammed inside the University of Maryland's Cole Field House on March 19, as well as numerous fans watching the event on television sets at home, the game was truly a contest played in black and white. All twelve players on the Kentucky roster were white, while the five starters for the Miners were all African Americans. The racial composition of the Wildcats accurately reflected the social reality for most southern white college teams and the Southeastern Conference, seven of whose ten members were located in the Deep South. African American under-graduates had only recently gained admission to many of these universities, and every SEC member still maintained racial exclusion in its athletic programs. In contrast, Texas Western was an independent college lacking a conference affili-ation for the moment. More important, the TWC athletic program followed a radically different recruitment policy. The 1966 Miner squad contained seven African Americans, one Mexican American, and four Anglo Americans. In the championship game all five starters and the two substitutes who saw ac-tion for TWC were African Americans. Thus, the Miners' lineup contrasted dramatically with the Wildcats' and aptly captured the difference between an older, segregated South and the new world of fully integrated college sports that loomed on the horizon.

Most national sportswriters predicted that Kentucky would easily defeat the underdog Miners. But the actual game did not unfold as anticipated. After a nervous start the Miners broke a 9–9 tie midway through the first half. Then, on Kentucky's next two possessions, TWC guard Bobby Joe Hill skillfully stole the ball from the Wildcat guards and scored on uncontested layups, enabling the Miners to take control of the game. Displaying considerable poise and a tenacious defense, Texas Western continued to outplay Kentucky and finished with a convincing 72–65 win. After the game, shocked reporters acclaimed the Miner victory as the biggest upset in the history of the NCAA championship game. The world of college basketball would never be the same.[1]

The Texas Western triumph constituted a memorable athletic accomplish-ment, but the contest's broader significance lay in its social implications. As cultural critic Nelson George observed, "For liberals who sought social symbol-ism in sports, the 1966 NCAA title contest was perfection." The TWC victory inspired African American fans everywhere and sent a shock wave through the ranks of southern college basketball. No longer could white teams assume that they played a superior style of basketball or that basketball was a "white sport." Likewise, white sports fans could no longer claim that black players lacked the intelligence, discipline, or toughness under pressure to win major championships. By shattering these myths, the Miner victory constituted "the emancipation proclamation" of college basketball for African American players, especially in the South. The Texas Western win also sent a clear message to elite southern teams that continued segregation on the basketball court endangered their ability to compete successfully for national championships. Previous victories by integrated teams led by black stars had been dismissed as exceptions, but the triumph of an all-black starting lineup over such a highly regarded white program as Kentucky shattered these rationalizations. Moreover, Texas Western had challenged the old racial order from within, since the college was located in an ex-Confederate state. Members of the top conferences in Dixie now had reason to worry that their less prestigious southern rivals would tap a new source of talent and challenge the dominance of the elite teams. These fears were fully justified. Southern colleges lacking an elite conference membership, usually identified as "independents," and members of "blended" conferences that straddled the borders of the athletic South, did take the lead in recruiting African Americans and attempted thereby to gain a competitive advantage over better-known rivals. Athletic programs at nonelite colleges thus served as an opening wedge for sports integration across the South.[2]

Non-Elite Universities Take the Lead in Sports Integration

Opportunism, self-interest, pragmatism, ambition, and occasionally even a touch of idealism motivated a variety of non-elite southern universities to recruit African American players aggressively for their football and basketball teams by the mid-1960s. Athletic programs at the elite institutions of the Atlantic Coast Conference, the Southwest Conference, and especially the Southeastern Conference generally were much slower to seek out African Americans. This tardiness sprang from an assumption that the football field and the basketball court were primarily white spaces and that adding black athletes to their teams would demean their high social status. Taking the lead in recruiting African Americans were the University of Louisville, North Texas State College (NTSC), the University of Houston, and Texas Western College. These schools clearly hoped to gain a competitive edge over their elite rivals by tapping a new source of talent. Most of these colleges did in fact see their teams gain new success, at least temporarily. In addition to athletic glory, some of these colleges also hoped to elevate their institutional standing and public recognition. The University of Houston and especially Texas Western benefited the most from this strategy.

Athletic integration in the South actually started first with junior colleges and small regional colleges before spreading to larger state universities. Generally, these pioneering schools were located in predominantly white areas where local residents did not feel overly threatened by modest departures from traditional racial etiquette. In 1953 San Angelo Junior College in West-central Texas accepted its first three black students, one of whom, Benjamin Kelly, an army veteran, joined the football team. In 1954 Cecil Brown became the first black member of the basketball team at Amarillo Junior College in the Texas Panhandle, and the following year his uncle, Charles Brown, joined him there. St. Mary's College in San Antonio, a small Catholic institution, recruited its first African American basketball player in the fall of 1957 and with his help promptly upset Texas A&M of the Southwest Conference in an early-season game. Down on the lower section of the Texas-Mexican border, Pan American College in Edinburg quietly allowed several African American students to join the cross-country, baseball, and track teams during the 1954–55 school year, immediately after the *Brown* decision. New coach Sam Williams recruited the Broncs' first two black basketball players in 1959 and added several others in the following years, in addition to several white players from New York City. Pan American benefited enormously from this aggressive recruiting policy. Led by 6'9" center Lucious Jackson, the Texas team won the NAIA small-college championship in 1963 and finished second the following year. While coaches at the most prestigious southern universities tried to ignore such developments, their counterparts at nonelite colleges were not so blind.[3]

The University of Louisville was the first of these larger "independent" colleges to break the color line in sports. The university's location on the northern edge of a border state technically meant that the school was not literally a southern college. Although strict segregation lasted in Louisville through the mid-1950s, the city was economically linked to the Midwest, not the Deep South. Starting in the mid-1950s the university developed a "border" or "midwestern" identity in athletics and interplayed extensively with midwestern schools. Nonetheless, Louisville's athletic experiences are worth discussing because they contrast with the behavior of the state's leading institution, the University of Kentucky. Situated in Lexington in the so-called bluegrass area of the state, UK had histori-cally adopted a "southern" identity and looked southward as a member of the Southeastern Conference. In other words, in border states a university's self-constructed sectional identity determined whether it was culturally part of the South or another region and therefore what kind of racial policies concerning athletics it would follow.

The University of Louisville, a private institution at the time, maintained a segregated downtown branch for African American students until 1951, when the college opened up its main campus to all students. One black student briefly joined the 1952 football team but dropped out before playing in a game. In 1954 Coach Frank Camp launched the era of integration by recruiting local high school star Lenny Lyles and three other African Americans for his team. In that first year the team encountered frequent problems with restaurants and hotels when it traveled. Nonetheless, Camp continued to sign black prospects, in sharp contrast to his counterparts at the University of Kentucky. Lyles eventually de-veloped into an outstanding halfback and led the nation in rushing his senior year before going on to play professionally in the NFL. Louisville's basketball teams did not immediately follow suit, however. Coach Peck Hickman did not break the color line until the early 1960s, when the university president encouraged him to do so. In the fall of 1962 Hickman added three black players—Wade Houston, Eddie Whitehead, and Sam Smith—to the freshman squad. The trio made their varsity debuts the following year. Since Louisville abandoned its independent status in 1963 and joined the Missouri Valley Conference, which was well known for its outstanding, and integrated, basketball teams, Hickman may have felt pressured to recruit African Americans in order to compete effectively in the new conference. This shift in recruiting practices and the long-standing presence of black football players at UL made it easier for Hickman and his staff to subsequently recruit two of the most famous high school stars in Kentucky basketball history, Wes Unseld in 1964 and Butch Beard in 1965. As a result of a flexible racial policy and successful recruiting, Louisville became a nationally recognized basketball power, regularly received an invitation to the NCAA Tournament and established a heated rivalry with the University of Kentucky that still continues.[4]

The first major university in an ex-Confederate state to integrate its varsity football team was North Texas State College in Denton. Located just a few miles north of Fort Worth, the town had a small black population and was as much western as southern in character. North Texas accepted its first black graduate student in the summer of 1954 but did not admit African Americans as undergraduates until February 1956, when ordered to do so by a federal court. In September 1956 two new black students, Abner Haynes and Leon King, decided on their own to try out for the freshman football team. The son of a well-known minister, Haynes had grown up in Denton and had been a football and track star at a Dallas high school, where King also had been an accomplished player. Head coach Odus Mitchell gave the players a fair opportunity to display their ability and warned their white teammates that he would not tolerate any mistreatment of the two. Haynes quickly became the starting halfback and displayed exceptional running skills.

The presence of the two African Americans created problems during the freshman team's four relatively short road trips, mainly concerning meals. When one restaurant owner in Corsicana, a small town at the edge of East Texas, insisted that Haynes and King eat separately in the kitchen, the entire team stood up and walked out. Later that evening, when the NTSC squad arrived at the local junior college for their scheduled game, they received a hostile greeting from the home crowd. Enraged fans shouted racial abuse throughout the contest, frequently chanting "Get those niggers off the field!" and yelling "Nigger lovers!" at the white players. Several hurled rocks and bottles at the visitors. Haynes became even more unpopular after he scored four touchdowns. Following the final whistle, the victorious NTSC squad sprinted directly for the team bus and quickly left town. The experience brought black and white team members closer together, and an undefeated 5-0 season further strengthened morale. Nonetheless, despite eventually receiving scholarships, Haynes and King were not allowed to live on campus or eat in the main cafeteria for two more years, and white players did not socialize with them away from the practice field.

The success of the freshman team encouraged Mitchell to seek out additional black recruits in subsequent years. Since North Texas had just joined the Missouri Valley Conference, where most of their rivals were midwestern colleges fielding integrated teams, such a step did not create any scheduling problems with conference members. Moreover, Mitchell recognized the potentially large talent pool that he could draw from within Texas, where many white universities had not yet admitted any black students. President J. C. Matthews approved this recruiting strategy but initially limited the coaches to two new African Americans per year. Leon King played for two years on the varsity before temporarily dropping out of school, while Abner Haynes became the Eagles' star running back, earning All-America honors his senior year in 1959. That season NTSC finished with a 9-1 record and received an invitation to the Sun Bowl. The decision to accept a limited number of skillful African American players strengthened the North Texas football teams and helped them compete more successfully in the Missouri Valley Conference. However, their presence also forced NTSC to drop its traditional, and financially rewarding, opening game of the season at the University of Mississippi, when Ole Miss officials refused to permit the black players to participate. The contributions of several African American stars on the team may have caused many white students to view desegregation more favorably, but administrators did not grant black students equal access to campus housing until the 1960s.[5]

With the possible exception of Texas Western College, the University of Houston gained more from the racial integration of its athletic program than any other large university lacking membership in an elite conference. Founded as a junior college in 1927, the school expanded to become a locally funded four-year college in 1934, catering mostly to commuter students. The school's governing board approved the creation of athletic teams beginning in 1946, with the caution that they should remain "strictly subordinate to the academic purposes of the university." In the early 1960s President Philip G. Hoffman, supported by influential local businessmen who felt that the state's largest city deserved a major university, launched a campaign to elevate the modest institutional status of the college, which some local residents derisively referred to as "Cougar High." In 1961, after a spirited debate, the state legislature approved transferring the college to the Texas higher-education system, with state funding to commence in 1963. Hoffman and athletic director Harry Fouke viewed sports as one obvious vehicle through which to elevate the school's public standing. A little more than two months after admitting its first African American undergraduates for the fall semester of 1963, the university announced that any student who met the requisite academic standards would be eligible to compete for the Cougar athletic teams. This was not an empty public relations gesture, for Hoffman and Fouke had granted football coach William A. "Bill" Yeoman and basketball coach Guy V. Lewis permission to consider African American prospects for their teams. UH officials also made the first of many formal requests for admission to the prestigious Southwest Conference.[6]

Both Yeoman and Lewis expanded their recruiting efforts to include black high school prospects, and both eventually developed nationally ranked teams featuring African American stars. A talented football strategist, Yeoman was often credited with inventing the famous "wishbone" or triple-option formation. The Cougar football program also benefited enormously from the construction of the Houston Astrodome, which opened in 1964 as the largest domed stadium in the United States. The Cougars used the Astrodome as their home field and fully exploited it as a recruiting device. Yeoman's major coup came in the summer of 1964, when he signed high school sensation "Wondrous" Warren McVea of San Antonio to a scholarship. McVea was one of the most heralded running backs in Texas high school history and the target of football coaches from around the country. But because Southwest Conference members maintained segregation in sports, and because McVea's grades were mediocre, Houston was one of only a few Texas colleges to aggressively pursue him. During his career at UH, injuries prevented McVea from achieving his full potential, but he did receive second-team All-America honors as a senior. Furthermore, McVea helped the Cougars gain considerable recognition from Texas football fans, especially African Americans, and briefly attain a number-two national ranking in 1967. The number of black players on the UH roster expanded steadily throughout the 1960s, contrasting sharply with most Southwest Conference teams. At first local African Americans were suspicious of Houston's recruitment of black athletes, but the athletic staff eventually turned many of them into enthusiastic Cougar fans. Alexander Durley, the former head football coach at Texas Southern and a columnist for the *Houston Informer*, enthusiastically praised UH as a symbol of hope and change in college sports. Durley even contended that the school "is ideally located to become the educational and cultural center of the state and the South." The NCAA was less impressed with Houston, however, imposing major sanctions in 1966 on the football program and prohibiting the Cougars from appearing in bowl games or on television for three years.[7]

Guy Lewis took the Cougar basketball team to even greater heights than the football team during the 1960s. Acting on a tip from coaches at nearby Texas Southern University, a historically black college, Lewis tracked down and signed in May 1964 two outstanding black high school stars from Louisiana, 6'9" center

Elvin Hayes and 6'4" guard Don Chaney. Supported by other talented recruits, Hayes and Chaney led Houston to three consecutive appearances in the NCAA Tournament, reaching the Final Four in 1967 and 1968 before losing to eventual champion UCLA. In January 1968 the Cougars had upset UCLA star center Kareem Abdul-Jabbar (then Lew Alcindor) by a score of 71–69 in the Astrodome before 52,693 fans. This contest was sometimes called "the game of the century," and its attendance record stood for twenty-one years. Finally, in 1971 SWC schools voted to admit the University of Houston to full membership, effective in 1976. By dropping its racial barriers in sports in 1964, Houston had been able to tap a pool of previously ignored talent. African American athletes subsequently played a vital role in the newfound success of Cougar teams, thereby earning the university a highly prized membership in the Southwest Conference and the public recognition and institutional prestige that accompanied this step.[8]

Texas Western College Challenges the Color Line

Texas Western College provides the most successful story of an ambitious nonelite school that sought to gain regional and national prominence through athletic success. Progressive racial policies, naked self-interest, and pragmatic flexibility all combined to influence events at the college. Of course, TWC was not the first ambitious university to exploit athletics in order to achieve institutional advancement and recognition, nor were such efforts unique to the 1950s and 1960s. Earlier in the century the University of Chicago, Notre Dame, and Michigan State, among others, had used football success as a mechanism to make the names of their institutions familiar to a national audience. This approach proved particularly successful in the South, where the general public highly valued athletic success.[9]

In the mid-1960s the football and basketball programs at Texas Western enjoyed unprecedented success, while the track and field team won national recognition a few years later. African Americans played crucial roles in all of TWC's athletic accomplishments, rewarding the university for eliminating discrimination in recruiting. Ironically, though, Texas Western had firmly supported the color line earlier in the century. Founded as a mining school in El Paso in 1914, the college was located in the extreme western point of Texas. Known initially as the Texas College of Mines and Metallurgy, the school became Texas Western College in 1949 and the University of Texas at El Paso in 1967. Since TWC was administratively a branch of the University of Texas at Austin, the UT Board of Regents exercised final authority over academic and athletic policies. Because of its location the El Paso school belonged to the Border Conference, whose membership over the years included the University of Arizona, Arizona State in Tempe, Arizona State in Flagstaff, the University of New Mexico, New Mexico

State, Texas Tech, West Texas State, and Hardin-Simmons. In the late 1930s TWC became one of a handful of white southern universities that agreed to compete against African Americans *outside* the South, but the college retained the color line for all home games. El Paso residents, especially Anglo-Americans, fully supported this decision.

After World War II Texas Western encountered unexpected resistance to its traditional policy of racial exclusion, as national attitudes concerning integrated athletic competition became more liberal. As was noted previously, the Sun Bowl football classic in El Paso likewise experienced problems over its refusal to allow African American players to participate in the New Year's Day game. Because the annual event took place at Kidd Field on the TWC campus, the Sun Bowl found its racial policies controlled by the UT Board of Regents. During the late 1940s and early 1950s the regents aggressively defended segregation on the main campus in Austin against several legal attacks. The most prominent of these proceedings began in 1946, when the NAACP filed suit against the university on behalf of Heman M. Sweatt, who had been denied admission to the School of Law. During the next four years, while the *Sweatt* case made its way through the courts, the regents consistently opposed any retreat from Jim Crow elsewhere in the UT system.

This rigid approach did not transfer well to El Paso, where a bicultural population and a border location created a more fluid system of race and ethnic relations. In 1950 Anglo-Americans and Mexican Americans each constituted nearly one-half of the El Paso County population, while African Americans made up slightly less than 3 percent of local residents. After World War II support for segregation by Anglo-Americans weakened somewhat. Moreover, Mexican Americans, who themselves often experienced de facto segregation and employment discrimination, displayed little enthusiasm for the Jim Crow system. Nonetheless, Texas segregation laws still governed local policy. Since there was no specific state law requiring segregated athletic competition, the regents maintained an "unwritten rule" that prohibited integrated sporting events on university property.

The first major postwar challenge to Texas Western's color line arrived during the fall of 1947. The specific incident involved the football team from Arizona State College in Tempe, which was scheduled to meet the Miners on November 8 in El Paso. The Sun Devil squad included two African Americans, halfbacks Morrison "Dit" Warren, the team's star runner, and George "Dusty" Diggs. Texas Western administrators automatically barred the duo from the contest. To TWC's surprise ASC officials, coaches, players, professors, and students promptly denounced TWC for practicing racial discrimination. Several members of the athletic staff even briefly discussed flying Warren and Diggs into town on the day of the game, suiting them up, and daring Texas Western administrators to physically prevent them from playing. The ASC student newspaper went further and suggested that conference schools initiate a "sports boycott" against those Texas colleges that maintained Jim Crow policies. Missing the two players, the Sun Devils fell to the Miners by a score of 21–0. After the contest ASC team manager Tom Lillico again complained to the press about the racial ban. Pointing out the irony that the pre–Armistice Day ceremonies at halftime had honored American soldiers who had died in combat, Lillico emphasized, "We have two Negro players who were in the service. They were good enough to fight for Texas, but not good enough to play here." Many TWC faculty and staff members openly sympathized with the Arizona State complaints. Miner head coach Jack Curtice pointed out that no one had "objected when we played against [Warren and Diggs] in Tempe last year." Several members of the TWC team, including Joe Valencia and Santos "Kayo" Perez, publicly stated that they were willing to compete against an integrated squad in El Paso. A campus poll revealed that most students, especially World War II veterans, "overwhelmingly" opposed the racial ban. But President D. M. Wiggins, fearful that the campus dissent might offend state officials in Austin, announced that there would be no change in the long-standing policy.[10]

A second racial incident two weeks later involving the two Arizona State players further outraged school officials in Tempe and raised questions about the future of the Border Conference. On November 22 Warren and Diggs were again barred from a contest at West Texas State in Canyon. Following the incident the ASC athletic committee formally revised its position on game contracts. Under the new policy the university would not schedule a game unless all eligible members of the Arizona State team would be allowed to participate. TWC rejected these terms, and the Sun Devils dropped the Miners from their schedule for the next three years. But Hardin-Simmons College, a private church-related school in Abilene whose athletic policies were not governed by state authorities, accepted the new policy and remained on the Sun Devil schedule. Arizona State representatives also announced that they would raise the matter of racial exclusion at the Border Conference's next meeting, creating the possibility that the league might split in half, but they later decided not to force the issue. Since league members were required to play only a minimum of four conference games per season, Arizona State instead revised its future schedules so as to compete against only the four other non-Texas conference members plus Hardin-Simmons. This arrangement appeared to have solved the league's racial problem.[11]

Three years later, though, another incident over the color line at Kidd Field pushed the issue of racial exclusion back into the headlines. This time the controversy centered over senior halfback Bill English of Loyola University of Los

Angeles. The Lion team had been scheduled to play the Miners in El Paso on September 30, 1950. Earlier that year Loyola officials had corresponded with local hotels concerning accommodations, indicating that they might include several African Americans on their traveling squad. By the fall, however, English was the only African American still listed on the travel roster. Since the city's major hotels refused to accept African Americans, Loyola officials arranged for English and a black trainer to stay at a black-owned hotel but take their meals with the rest of the team in private dining rooms at two white hotels. When TWC officials eventually learned that English would be traveling with the team, they immediately informed Loyola that he could not participate in the contest. Although the game contract did not specifically exclude African Americans, Coach Jordan Olivar and school administrators apparently agreed to leave English behind in Los Angeles.[12]

Reports that Loyola would bench English for the game upset the African American community in Los Angeles. Edward Atkinson Jr., the only black member of the alumni association's board of directors, quickly organized a protest campaign with the help of several prominent black Catholic laymen and the *Los Angeles Tribune*, a weekly black newspaper. Embarrassed by the unexpected publicity, officials at the Catholic college quickly backtracked. After a series of telephone calls between the two universities failed to resolve their differences, the president of Loyola, the Reverend Father Charles S. Casassa, announced on September 27 that he had canceled the game. Father Casassa explained that "we cannot afford not to play the man in question." The game's last-minute cancellation touched off numerous complaints in El Paso. The college's administration defended its position as consistent with state policy and bitterly accused Loyola of reneging on a "gentleman's agreement" to leave English behind. TWC officials also complained that Loyola's late decision did not allow them sufficient time to find a replacement team and could cost the university up to seven thousand dollars. Many students vented their frustration on the regents' policy. In a campus poll conducted by the *Prospector*, 450 students opposed the racial ban, 50 favored it, and 60 abstained. One veteran explained his stand by stating, "A Negro hauled me out of the water at Normandy. Guess they can play football." In a biting editorial the *Prospector* pointed out that African American soldiers were at that moment fighting and dying in the Korean War and concluded emphatically that "a man is a man regardless of the color of his skin." This cold war appeal combining patriotism and racial equality was used occasionally by supporters of athletic integration in the late 1940s and 1950s. Both local daily newspapers also criticized the regents' policy and maintained that something must be done about its unfair restrictions. Several local organizations, including the Chamber of Commerce, the Sun Carnival Association, and the League of

United Latin American Citizens, as well as the city council, adopted resolutions urging the Board of Regents to repeal the racial ban.[13]

In October a New Mexico sportswriter launched a campaign against Texas Western's continued membership in the Border Conference. The sports editor of the *Santa Fe New Mexican,* Bill Bailey, publicly called for the Border Conference to expel TWC. "There is no place in American college football . . . for a school that draws the color line," he wrote. Bailey also urged the University of New Mexico to discontinue its annual contest with the Miners and suggested that other southwestern teams take similar action. Meanwhile, the issue of the color line at Kidd Field resurfaced when the University of Arizona traveled to El Paso for an October 14 match. The Arizona squad arrived minus halfback Fred Batiste, the Wildcats' first black player. Since the game contract included a racially restrictive clause, Arizona officials reluctantly concluded that they had no choice but to withhold Batiste. In so doing they rejected a plea from one Tucson newspaper to forfeit the game because of his exclusion. Despite this success in maintaining the color line, Texas Western officials worried that the incident had seriously damaged relations between the two schools and that the Border Conference might break up over the issue.[14]

The Board of Regents for the University of Texas system initially refused to consider adopting a special policy for Texas Western. In June 1950 the Supreme Court ruled against the university in the case of *Sweatt v. Painter,* ordering the School of Law to admit Heman Sweatt as its first black student. Despite the decision, the board subsequently desegregated only some of the professional and graduate programs at UT, and it remained determined to prevent any integration of undergraduate studies. The regents viewed its unofficial policy against integrated athletic contests as an import part of this larger defense of segregation. When TWC president W. H. Elkins delivered a personal request for a special dispensation from the athletic prohibition at the September 1950 board meeting, the regents rejected his request. Yet the numerous resolutions from El Paso organizations and influential civic leaders eventually forced the board to reconsider. At an October 27 meeting the regents reversed their position and by a 6–3 vote authorized Texas Western to host integrated competition at its facilities, because of the "peculiar conditions" in El Paso. However, the board clearly stated that this revised policy applied only to TWC and not to other campuses. Dudley Woodward, chairman of the board, acknowledged that failure to grant the waiver might "completely destroy intercollegiate athletics at Texas Western College." Woodward cited broad community support for change, including a petition signed by forty of the forty-three Miner football players. Immediately after the announcement, school officials contacted their counterparts at Arizona and Arizona State, and both universities agreed to resume competition with the

Miners. When Arizona State visited El Paso on November 17, 1951, Sun Devil players Jim Bilton and Cleveland Oden became the first African Americans to compete at Kidd Field.[15]

Texas Western eventually became the first major state-funded four-year college in Texas, and one of the very first in the ex-Confederate South, to openly admit African Americans to undergraduate study. Following the Supreme Court's *Brown v. Board of Education* ruling in 1954, the college received its first application from a black student, Thelma White, the valedictorian of the recent graduating class at El Paso's Frederick Douglass High School. Ignoring the *Brown* ruling, TWC rejected White's application. In March 1955 NAACP lawyers acting on her behalf filed suit in U.S. District Court in El Paso, seeking a court order requiring her admission to Texas Western because she had been denied equal rights under the law. Local reaction on campus was mildly supportive of White. One prointegration male student even recognized the potential contributions that African Americans might make to the Miner athletic program. He told the student newspaper, "Besides the humanitarian principles involved in considering such a question, we might also look at it from a selfish point of view. The Negro race has many good athletes. . . . [M]aybe we could get some of them." TWC administrators also responded favorably to the possibility of integration. The school's new president, Dr. Dysart E. Holcomb, reported in mid-June to Dr. Logan Wilson, president of UT-Austin, that local integration was probably inevitable. He recommended that it was preferable "to go ahead and adopt a desegregation policy rather than carry the present suit to the courts and have the College lose."[16] After federal district judge R. E. Thomason announced that he would hear arguments in the *White* case, the regents voted unanimously on July 8 to permit Texas Western to admit "qualified students, regardless of racial origin," to all educational programs. The board also voted to open all graduate and professional programs at the Austin campus to African Americans but to retain for one more year the racial restrictions on undergraduate enrollment there. At a special one-day hearing in July on White's suit, Judge Thomason issued a declaratory judgment for her and permanently enjoined the regents from denying African Americans the right to attend Texas Western College.[17]

Judge Thomason's ruling and the regents' new policy paved the way for the enrollment of African American students at Texas Western. As the fall semester of 1955 approached, college officials released as little information about the impending change as possible. President Holcomb spoke to several community groups, reassuring them that only a handful of African Americans would actually enroll. He also told reporters, "We are very proud to be the first senior college in Texas to admit Negro students." Eventually, a total of twelve African Americans quietly entered Texas Western, but surprisingly Thelma White was not among them. Uneasy over possible resentment toward her at TWC, White instead decided to return for her sophomore year at New Mexico State. During the fall term, integration in most campus activities proceeded smoothly, except for housing, which remained segregated for two more years. In September 1956 an additional dozen black students enrolled for the first time, attracting no special attention. The integration of Texas Western and the local public schools did not mean that all forms of local discrimination had disappeared. Responding to complaints from black students at the university in the spring of 1962, a local citizens committee, including several prominent Jewish civic leaders, encouraged the city commission to adopt a local public accommodations ordinance. In June the commission unanimously approved a municipal ordinance banning discrimination based on race, color, or religion at the city's hotels, restaurants, and motels. The ordinance was the first of its kind to be passed by a city in an ex-Confederate state and reflected a broader effort by local civic and business elites to create a progressive western identity for El Paso.[18]

Football's Glory Days at Texas Western

During the late 1950s and early 1960s ambitious administrators at Texas Western set out to achieve national recognition in football and elevate the university's shaky public standing. Initially, it seemed that the goal of gridiron prominence would not be too difficult. During the 1930s and 1940s the college had actually been a major power in the Southwest and regularly enjoyed winning seasons, earning five invitations to the Sun Bowl classic. But from 1957 through 1961 the Miners won only eighteen of forty-eight games. The decline of the football team helped convince college administrators and local civic leaders that the school badly needed a significant upgrade of its academic and athletic programs. Such improvements, these groups hoped, would elevate TWC's institutional profile, attract national publicity for the city, and boost the local tourist economy. During the late 1950s El Pasoans had become convinced that the state legislature and the UT Regents were neglecting Texas Western. In the fall of 1957 the Southern Association of Colleges and Secondary Schools startled community leaders when it issued a preliminary warning about TWC's continuing accreditation, citing inadequate funding by the state legislature. A study of average faculty salaries at public colleges in Texas, published in October 1959, revealed that TWC ranked sixteenth out of the eighteen schools examined. Only the state's two historically black colleges paid their professors even less than did Texas Western. Enrollment at TWC had increased steadily in the early and mid-1950s, but from 1958 to 1963 it suddenly soared from 4,592 to 6,745, straining college resources. Frequent turnover in the president's office created a leadership void that frustrated civic leaders. The inauguration of Dr. Joseph M. Ray, previously head of Amarillo Junior College, as the school's new president in August 1960 marked the end of this administrative turmoil. Although Ray mainly focused his attention on academic development, he shared with community leaders the belief that a successful athletic program was an integral part of a Texas university's broader mission and a reflection of its educational stature.[19]

The campaign to revamp the Texas Western athletic program involved constructing new facilities for football and basketball, expanding recruiting efforts, and hiring more innovative coaches. In the early 1960s the concern over TWC football coincided with a growing uneasiness by Sun Bowl officials about the future of their postseason game. University administrators, as well as local civic and political leaders, agreed that one immediate need was a modern football stadium. Such a facility would allow the Sun Bowl to attract higher-ranked teams and possibly gain a national television contract. Representatives of the various groups eventually agreed on a complicated plan to construct a new stadium in a rocky ravine at the edge of the university campus. The University of Texas system provided the title to the land, while the county commission secured the necessary funds through a local bond issue. Next the county supervised the actual construction of the project and then leased the structure back to Texas Western for ninety-nine years at a dollar per year. When the new Sun Bowl Stadium opened in September 1963, it contained thirty thousand seats, twice Kidd Field's capacity, and provided a dramatic setting for football games. A more aggressive recruitment policy targeting new sources of talent also figured prominently in Texas Western's plans. This strategy included identifying prospects from outside the Southwest, locating promising junior college players or transfers from senior colleges, accepting married athletes, and expanding the recruitment of African Americans. Such tactics reflected the reality of athletic recruiting in Texas, where Southwest Conference members enjoyed their pick of the best white players from the high school ranks but ignored black prospects. Thus, by following a color-blind recruitment policy, TWC could gain a competitive advantage over its more prestigious rivals and produce winning teams.[20]

The professional skills and recruiting abilities of several coaches contributed to the football program's success. In the fall of 1959 Coach Ben Collins broke with southern tradition and awarded the university's first football scholarship to an African American, end Leeford Fant of Corpus Christi, Texas. Texas Western became the second major white college in an ex-Confederate state to take such a leap in football. Fant saw action in several games that year but did not return for his sophomore season. The following year Collins recruited Robert Lincoln, another end, who received limited playing time and also did not come back for his second year. During their brief stays at TWC both players lived in the athletic dormitory and ate their meals with the rest of the team. For the fall of 1961 Collins expanded his recruiting and awarded scholarships to four black high school athletes: Louis James, Raymond Jackson, Don Mason, and Jim Nash.

Perhaps because there was strength in numbers, all of these recruits would play four years for the Miners. Unfortunately for Collins, the Miners finished with a disappointing 3-7 record, forcing his resignation. Texas Western then hired O. A. "Bum" Phillips, the colorful head coach at Amarillo High School. The tobacco-chewing Phillips rekindled football enthusiasm in El Paso. He immediately expanded the recruitment of junior college transfers and African Americans, and his first varsity squad in 1962 included a dozen black Miners. Since North Texas State and Texas Western were the only two major white southern colleges fielding integrated teams that year, the composition of the Miner roster was truly remarkable.[21]

Phillips got off to a modestly successful start in the fall of 1962, as Texas Western posted a 4-5 record. The new coach's folksy charm and enthusiasm rekindled hope that the team's recent slide would be reversed. At the end of the spring semester Phillips stunned El Pasoans when he unexpectedly resigned in order to become head football coach at a large public high school near Houston, an unusual career move for a college coach. President Joseph Ray unsuccessfully tried to retain Phillips by assuring him, "You don't have to resign. There's nobody after you. We want you." But Phillips, who later achieved notoriety as head coach of the Houston Oilers in the National Football League, told Ray that he was leaving because he believed that no individual, regardless of ability, could ever win consistently at Texas Western, given the limited financial resources available. The next head coach, Warren Harper, won only three games during his brief tenure at the college. His successor, Bobby Dobbs, finally ended fans' frustrations and led the Miners to two of their greatest seasons ever. Dobbs brought a different professional background to Texas Western, since he had most recently coached the Calgary Stampeders of the Canadian Football League, where teams employed a wide-open style of play. Dobbs emphasized the recruitment of junior college players and African Americans. He also accepted married players, a concession that many Southwest Conference schools refused to make. Star quarterback Billy Stevens later estimated that more than half of the starters on the outstanding 1967 squad were married. The wide-open, pro-style passing attack employed by Dobbs proved quite attractive to prospective recruits and brought local fans back into the Sun Bowl, as the "flying Miners" racked up a 7-3 record in 1965. In recognition of TWC's excellent season and local fan enthusiasm, the Sun Bowl invited the Miners to the annual classic, where they defeated Texas Christian University 13–12. Texas Western fans especially savored the victory over a team from the more prestigious Southwest Conference. The Miners' win became somewhat tarnished when in January 1967 the NCAA reprimanded the university for using in that game several junior college players that it deemed ineligible for postseason play, but the NCAA declined to place TWC on probation.[22]

In 1966 the Miners fell off slightly to a 6-4 record, but the following year the school fielded perhaps its most talented squad ever. The 1967 season was also important because, for the first time, the school operated under its new name, the University of Texas at El Paso. Led by quarterback Billy Stevens on offense and linebacker Fred Carr and halfback Charles West on defense, the Miners racked up an impressive 7-2-1 regular-season record. Their major disappointment came on November 18 in El Paso, when the University of Wyoming Cowboys escaped with a narrow 21–19 victory after a last-second Miner field-goal attempt sailed wide by only a few inches. Wyoming finished the season as the Western Athletic Conference champion and received a bid to the Sugar Bowl in New Orleans, while the Miners settled for another invitation to the Sun Bowl. As TWC's opponent bowl sponsors selected the University of Mississippi from the Southeastern Conference. In the December 30 matchup UTEP displayed a surprisingly strong defense to throttle the Rebels 14–7. El Paso fans again enjoyed seeing their local team defeat a representative from a more prestigious conference. Further recognition for the squad came in January 1968, when NFL teams drafted a total of eight Miner players, five of them in the first three rounds. First-round picks included Carr (the fifth choice overall) and guard George Daney. West and Bob Wallace went in the second round, while Stevens was chosen in the third round. Clearly, the implementation of an aggressive recruitment policy including acceptance of black athletes temporarily made Texas Western a regional football power and excited local fans. However, it was the Miner basketball team that eventually reached the pinnacle of success and gave the university the athletic prominence that it so desperately craved.[23]

Charles Brown and Cecil Brown Integrate Basketball at Texas Western

The successful integration of undergraduate studies at Texas Western College benefited basketball even more than football by helping create an athletic culture in which the 1966 national championship team could flourish. The somewhat flexible nature of local black-white relations, complicated by the presence of Mexican Americans, and the history of competition against integrated teams in the Border Conference made it easier for TWC to break the color barrier than for colleges located in the more conservative central and eastern parts of Texas. Constructing a winning basketball team was not an easy task in El Paso, though, since the lackluster Miner basketball program had enjoyed only seven winning seasons during the previous thirty-two years of official competition. Coach George McCarty, who was hired in 1953, revived interest in the basketball team. In early 1956 McCarty learned about an outstanding first-year player at Amarillo Junior College by the name of Charles Brown. The fact that Brown was African American did not deter McCarty, who talked many times by telephone with the 6'1" forward and also his nephew Cecil Brown, a 5'7" sophomore guard. Although he never personally saw them play, McCarty eventually offered scholarships to the two Browns. The TWC coach did not consciously intend to make a sweeping social statement by recruiting the two players. As he later commented, "All I could see was that [Charles Brown] was an outstanding player who could help us." When Charles and Cecil suited up for Texas Western in the fall of 1956, they became the first two African American basketball players at a historically white major college in an ex-Confederate state. In a sense, they were the Jackie Robinsons of southern college sports.[24]

The two Browns, especially Charles, were somewhat prepared for the adjustment facing them. Since Charles had grown up in a small town in East Texas, he fully understood the racial etiquette of Jim Crow and had learned the self-control necessary to avoid confrontations. In the early 1950s he served in an integrated U.S. Air Force unit during the Korean War and playing on military basketball teams. Charles subsequently joined his nephew Cecil at Amarillo Junior College in the predominantly white Texas Panhandle. Charles quickly emerged as the team's star and caught the attention of coaches across the Southwest. The fact that Charles was older and more mature than the typical freshman and that both Browns had already functioned successfully in a predominantly white environment made them promising candidates for breaking the color line at TWC. Charles and Cecil would also be able to provide companionship for each other in El Paso. Charles recalled that his nephew's presence "was a positive experience and made the transition easier." Cecil played a reserve role for the Miners, while his uncle became the Miners' star player and received almost all of the media attention. Since campus dormitories remained segregated during their first year, the two rented an off-campus apartment but ate their meals at the training table with the rest of the team. McCarty also made sure that a dormitory room originally intended for them remained unoccupied and then quietly arranged for the Browns to use the room on game days, so that they could be with their teammates.[25]

Most TWC students responded favorably to the Browns' arrival on campus. Charles made friends with many Mexican American and Anglo American students and became a popular figure at the school. Black students were especially supportive, and the two players were regularly invited to social functions in the small local black community. Senior Alvis Glidewell served as Charles's mentor when he arrived for summer school in 1956. During Brown's first week on campus Glidewell naively invited Charles to join him for a movie at the downtown Plaza Theater, forgetting that the theater had segregated seating. When theater employees tried to assign Brown to the separate balcony section, the two teammates walked away and subsequently restricted their movie trips to a local drive-in theater. In his classes Charles Brown experienced "a couple of minor disagreements" with two or three professors but encountered no harassment. Since Charles had more prior experience in such mixed settings than did local whites, he later pointedly observed, "I always said Texas Western was going through integration; I wasn't." Brown won numerous individual honors at TWC and led the Miners to three consecutive winning seasons. In the 1956–57 season, the "Amarillo Whiz" averaged twenty-one points per game, captured the Border Conference's "Most Valuable Player" (MVP) award, and paced the Miners to the league title. The student newspaper described Brown as "a fine gentleman and athlete." Charles won all-conference honors again during his junior and senior seasons. Over his three years Brown set a new career scoring record and established himself as the most outstanding player in the college's relatively short basketball history.[26]

Charles Brown's accomplishments were even more impressive when one considers the challenges that he faced on the road. For away games careful planning was needed in order to secure accommodations for the integrated Miner squad, and the Browns were sometimes forced to eat or sleep separately from their teammates. The two players also found themselves excluded from two games during their first year at TWC. In December 1956 the Browns missed the final two games of a five-game road trip through the Midwest and Upper South. While the Miners headed for Tennessee to play Memphis State and Tennessee Tech, Charles and Cecil returned to El Paso, "because of segregation practices in Tennessee." McCarty subsequently explained to reporters, "I just prefer not to put [them] in a position where [they] can be embarrassed." McCarty then rearranged the Miners' future schedules to avoid such conflicts. Another problem on the road was verbal abuse from belligerent fans. When Charles finally visited Tennessee Tech as a senior, fans were initially hostile but eventually applauded him because of his excellent performance. Charles and Cecil often talked privately about such racist behavior from fans, but neither they nor their white teammates felt comfortable openly discussing the issue with each other.[27]

Racial taunting from the bleachers and an occasional elbow from a rival player were not the only challenges that Charles had to overcome. During his senior year Brown's remarkably strong self-control almost broke down, and he briefly considered dropping out of college. In order to earn a combined elementary-secondary teaching certificate, Charles needed to perform part of his practice teaching at a local high school. But when he attempted to fulfill this requirement, the El Paso Independent School District rebuffed him. Although the EPISD had started integration of its classrooms in 1955, all of its black teachers were still restricted to teaching at Douglass Elementary School. Since the district had not yet placed an African American in charge of a class of white students, it would only agree to send Brown to Douglass Elementary. "My first reaction was to drop out of school," he recalled. Several education professors at Texas Western eventually worked out a compromise whereby Brown could do his secondary-level student teaching with the freshman physical education classes at the university, thereby meeting the certification requirement. After completing his degree, Brown enrolled in graduate school, in part because he could not obtain a full-time job. Eventually, he coached and taught for two years at Jefferson High School, a predominantly Mexican American school. He soon concluded that a black coach's prospects for advancement within the local school district were quite limited and moved to California, where he began a successful career with the San Francisco Unified School District.[28]

The arrival of Charles and Cecil Brown at Texas Western and the Miners' ensuing conference championship in the spring of 1957 had almost no immediate effect on recruiting practices at white Texas colleges, especially those in the elite Southwest Conference. Meanwhile, the racial experiment continued at Texas Western. In the fall of 1957 George McCarty added one additional black player, freshman center Harold Holmes of Lubbock, to his squad. Holmes displayed considerable promise on the court but found it difficult to adjust to the social environment of a predominantly white campus, and he dropped out of school in January. Reflecting the growing community interest in basketball, TWC moved its home basketball games from tiny Holliday Hall on campus to the El Paso County Coliseum, which seated nearly seven thousand fans. After Charles Brown graduated McCarty unexpectedly resigned as basketball coach and accepted an appointment as the dean of students. McCarty's replacement, Harold Davis, lasted for only two losing seasons before resigning. Just before his departure, however, he achieved one notable recruiting triumph when he convinced Nolan Richardson, TWC's fourth black basketball player, to enroll for the 1960–61 season. A multiple sports star at local Bowie High School, a predominantly Mexican American school, Richardson transferred back home from Eastern Arizona Junior College. During his first year at TWC Richardson was left behind when the Miners played in a holiday basketball tournament in Shreveport, Louisiana, where the city government still prohibited interracial games. Richardson supposedly had agreed to the arrangement without complaint when he enrolled at TWC. Shortly thereafter, the athletic department officially announced that in the future its teams would not participate in any such segregated events.[29]

Don Haskins Takes Texas Western Down Its "Glory Road"

In 1961 Texas Western hired another new coach and began construction of a new field house. The new indoor arena, Memorial Gymnasium, opened on campus the following year with seating for nearly five thousand fans, providing an attractive venue for Miner games. More important, in the summer of 1961, Texas Western hired Don Haskins as the Miners' new coach. Although he possessed no previous coaching experience on the college level, the thirty-one-year-old Haskins would eventually lead the Miners to the top of the college basketball world. Haskins had played basketball for the legendary Coach Henry Iba (known as "Mr. Iba") at Oklahoma State. After leaving college Haskins taught and coached at high schools in the tiny West Texas towns of Benjamin and Hedley, as well as the larger town of Dumas. To supplement his income at Benjamin, Haskins had also coached the girls' team and driven a school bus. At each of these schools his teams qualified for the state playoffs. George McCarty, now the dean of students but still President Joseph Ray's adviser on basketball matters, had followed Haskins's high school coaching career. Upon McCarty's strong recommendation, President Ray took a chance on the unknown coach and hired him, with the stipulation that he would also manage the school's athletic dormitory and keep the athletes under control.[30]

Under the leadership of Don Haskins the Miners immediately became a powerhouse in the Southwest, as their smooth-talking young coach convinced a variety of skilled players from around the country to come to El Paso. Through a Miner recruit Haskins met Hilton White, a supervisor of recreational programs in New York City who had been stationed in El Paso while in the army. White took a personal interest in the young men with whom he worked and encouraged them to escape their tough neighborhoods by accepting athletic scholarships at out-of-town colleges. With White's help Haskins recruited several key players from New York. He also developed contacts in several other big cities and on the junior college circuit. In Haskins's first season of 1961–62, the Miners went 18-6 and narrowly missed winning the Border Conference championship. Joining returning starter Nolan Richardson in the starting lineup were two additional black players, Willie Brown from New York City and JC transfer Bobby Joe Hill (the first of two players with the same name). At the end of the year the conference disbanded, with several members switching to the Western Athletic Conference. However, the new league snubbed Texas Western, forcing it to compete as an independent for the next five years.[31]

The Miner basketball team enjoyed even greater success during the 1963 and 1964 seasons. The star player on both of those teams was 6'8" center Jim "Bad News" Barnes, a transfer from Cameron (Oklahoma) Junior College. A dominating figure on the court, Barnes had been widely recruited while at Cameron by virtually every midwestern university but, because of his race, not a single Southwest Conference member. In Barnes's first season the Miners went 19-7 and were invited to the NCAA Tournament for the first time, a major milestone in the school's athletic history. However, the University of Texas eliminated the Miners in the first round. The following year Barnes averaging a school record twenty-nine points per game and also set a record for total rebounds. During the regular season the powerful Miner squad lost only two games and earned a number-nine ranking in the final United Press International (UPI) poll. Again selected for the NCAA Tournament, Texas Western defeated Texas A&M, the Southwest Conference champion, in a preliminary round. In the first game of the regional tournament against Kansas State, officials called three fouls on Barnes in the first five minutes of play, and the star center saw only eight minutes of action in a bitter 64–60 loss. A few months later the New York Knicks selected him as the number-one pick in the NBA draft. According to some knowledgeable fans, the 1964 team was just as talented as the famous 1966 squad but not as lucky.[32]

The ensuing two years brought further success to the Texas Western basketball program. In 1965 the Miners finished with a 16-9 record and received their first invitation to the National Invitational Tournament in New York City. The 1966 season proved to be the most exciting campaign in school history. The top two players for the Miners that year were 5'10" guard Bobby Joe Hill of Detroit (the second TWC player with that name) and 6'7", 240-pound center David Lattin of Houston. The other three starters came from a pool of five players, including Willie Cager, Nevil Shed, and Willie Worsley from New York City, and Orsten Artis and Harry Flournoy from Gary, Indiana. These seven athletes constituted the African American contingent on the squad and were also its most skillful players. Two other Miners saw regular action—Jerry Armstrong, a white farm boy from Hatfield, Missouri, and David Palacio, a Mexican American from El Paso. Rounding out the squad were three additional white reserves who received only limited playing time. From the first game of the season on, Haskins consistently started five black players, a pattern that surprised some sportswriters and fans. Yet because of the prevailing ideology of color blindness in sports, journalists almost never wrote about this development. Since only three other major colleges in the entire South were fielding integrated basketball teams that season, Haskins's policy was unprecedented. In fact, no other team from a major white university in any part of the country had ever started so many African Americans. The presence of so many black players did not mean that Haskins had changed his style of play, however. Unlike the wide-open, up-tempo style that many of the Miners had learned on urban playgrounds, Haskins insisted on the patterned, highly structured offense made famous by his mentor at Oklahoma State, Henry Iba, coupled with tenacious defense.[33]

The growing number of black players on the Texas Western team did not seem to bother students at the college but did upset some conservative whites in the area. During the 1963 season Andy Stoglin, an occasional starter for the Miners, had cautiously asked Haskins why he never seemed to start at home. According to Stoglin, Haskins opened a drawer in his desk, pulled out a stack of letters, and asked the player to read them while he stepped outside. In crude racist language the letters repeatedly criticized the Miner coach for recruiting too many African Americans. When Haskins returned Stoglin commented that he now understood the pressure that his coach was under. Clearly frustrated by the situation, Haskins told Stoglin, "We have to win enough games and then maybe someday we can change things." Three straight postseason appearances by the Miners seemed to have silenced this criticism. But in the fall of 1965 a few El Paso fans, uncomfortable with an even larger black presence, complained to President Joseph Ray. Concerned about their reaction, Ray instructed the school's athletic director to warn Haskins that it was not prudent to start so many African Americans. According to Ray, Haskins subsequently met with the president and defended his actions, explaining that he was merely starting his top players, who incidentally happened to be black. "They all know who the best players are, just as I do," he remarked. Ray agreed to think about the matter overnight, and the next day he told Haskins, "Don, you coach the basketball [team], and I'll try to do the rest of [the] job myself."[34]

The Texas Western squad opened the 1965–66 season in an impressive manner by winning eight consecutive games. The first real test for the team came on December 30 in El Paso, when TWC met the University of Iowa, ranked number six in the nation. Iowa's high ranking proved useless, however, as the Miners registered an easy 86–68 victory. Afterward, Texas Western jumped to the ninth spot in the Associated Press poll. During January and early February TWC continued its winning streak. On February 12 the Miners trailed the University of New Mexico by twenty points in the second half but rallied to win the game in overtime, 67–64. This amazing come-from-behind victory impressed sportswriters, who elevated the undefeated Miners to the number-three position in the national polls, the highest ranking ever for the school. Texas Western survived several more close games and extended its perfect record into early March. In the last regular-season contest the team made a long road trip to the Pacific Northwest, where a strong Seattle University squad upset the Miners by 74–72. Ironically, the number-one ranked Kentucky Wildcats also lost that same day, as both teams saw their twenty-three-game undefeated streaks end. With a record of 23-1 the Miners easily qualified for the NCAA Tournament. Since they did not represent a major conference, though, they were required to play a preliminary game in order to qualify for the midwestern regional tournament. Returning to form, TWC soundly defeated Oklahoma City University 89–74 to advance to the next round of play. At the regional tournament in Lubbock the Miners encountered their two toughest games of the playoffs. On opening night Texas Western faced the number-seven-ranked University of Cincinnati, NCAA champions in 1961 and 1962. In a nerve-racking contest the Miners finally edged the Bearcats 78–76 in overtime. The following night the Miners took on the fourth-ranked Kansas Jayhawks. The two teams were evenly matched, and after forty minutes of intense action the score was knotted at 69–69. In the first overtime Kansas star Jo Jo White appeared to have won the game at the buzzer with a desperation thirty-foot shot, but the referees ruled that he had stepped out of bounds before releasing the ball. In the second overtime the Miners grabbed an early lead and hung on for an exhausting 81–80 win. For the first time in the school's history TWC had qualified for the national championship tournament, to be held at the University of Maryland.[35]

Most sportswriters and coaches gave the Miners little chance of capturing the NCAA title and focused their attention on number-one Kentucky and number-two Duke. The Miners, who had finished third in the final polls, and the twelfth-ranked Utah Utes were treated like ugly ducklings when compared with the prestigious, elite programs from Kentucky and Duke. Most "experts," all of whom were white, predicted that the opening-night match between the Wildcats and the Blue Devils would actually determine the national championship, with the following night's contest against the winner of the Texas Western–Utah game just a formality. Such perceptions were based in part on the winning traditions maintained by Kentucky and Duke, as well as both teams' outstanding performances during the 1966 season. But there was another factor that also influenced the judgment of sportswriters, coaches, and fans—race. The reality that every player on the Kentucky and Duke rosters was white while the Miners' top seven players were black subtly affected most observers' judgments. With their all-white teams Kentucky and Duke accurately represented their respective conferences. In the spring of 1966 not one African American played varsity basketball in the entire Southeastern Conference. The situation was not much different in the Atlantic Coast Conference, where sophomore Billy Jones of Maryland was the lone black varsity player.

The Texas Western squad reflected a different racial model and embodied what eventually became the new athletic order in Dixie. By starting five African Americans, Haskins had dared to go further than any other coach at a predominantly white college. The racial subtext of the confrontation between two different philosophies of recruitment was like the proverbial five hundred–pound gorilla in the living room—everyone saw it, but no one dared to call attention to it. According to prevailing racial assumptions about sports held privately by many whites, black athletes lacked the intelligence, discipline, poise, and teamwork skills that white athletes possessed. African Americans obviously displayed individual talent, but this natural ability could not be harnessed into a consistent performance under pressure. Rather than state these beliefs in clear racial terms, writers occasionally referred to them through euphemisms or coded phrases. For example, in evaluating the four finalists one journalist depicted the TWC players as "uncoachable, if not incorrigible." Another sportswriter quoted an

NBA player who joked that the Miners "can do everything with the basketball but autograph it." A columnist for the *Baltimore Sun,* who obviously knew nothing about Haskins's great emphasis on tenacious defense and a patterned offense, actually wrote that the Miners "don't worry much about defense. . . . The running, gunning Texas quintet can do more things with a basketball than a monkey on a 50-foot jungle wire." This racial coding remained mostly in the shadows during the finals but was present nonetheless.[36]

For Don Haskins, worrying about how his squad could beat Kentucky or Duke was not his main concern. Instead, Haskins focused his energy on the opening-round game against a dangerous Utah team, led by its black star, Jerry Chambers. The Miner players were confident and even cocky at times, a trait that irritated their young coach, a perpetual pessimist. In the first half of the game Chambers, the eventual MVP of the tournament, scored almost at will against the Miners. Midway through the second half Haskins sent Jerry Armstrong into the game to try to stop Chambers. Although Armstrong did not completely shut down the Utah star, he did prevent him from dominating the rest of the game, and the Miners claimed an 85–78 win. The Texas Western victory set the stage for a showdown with Kentucky, which had defeated Duke 83–79. The championship game on Saturday, March 19, 1966, was a memorable one, for social as well as athletic reasons. As one writer later observed, "Never had there been such a clear confrontation in a national final between the haves and the have-nots, the establishment and the emerging newcomers." Kentucky's opening win over Duke had confirmed its role as the overwhelming favorite. Virtually every sportswriter present for the title match emphatically predicted that the Wildcats would claim the championship. Out of ten prominent coaches (all white) polled before the first night's games, just one had picked the Miners to win the tournament. Kentucky fans were equally confident. How could an unknown team from the desert Southwest, especially one featuring mostly black players, possibly upset their well-coached Wildcats? Their only uneasiness concerned the Miners' height advantage, since "Rupp's Runts" did not have a starter over 6'5". Ironically, Haskins in turn worried about the shorter Wildcats' overall quickness, so as a countermeasure he decided to go with a shorter lineup and unexpectedly started 5'7" Willie Worsley in place of 6'8" Nevil Shed.

The TWC strategy worked brilliantly, as the Miners' speed and tenacious defense consistently disrupted Kentucky's patterned offense. Miner guard Bobby Joe Hill especially frustrated the Kentucky guards. After he stole the ball from each of the guards on two consecutive possessions midway through the first half and converted the thefts into easy layups, the Miners' confidence soared. Hill eventually finished the night with twenty points to lead all scorers. On the backboards the Miners more than held their own. Center David Lattin scored on a thundering dunk early in the match and maintained an intimidating presence near the basket throughout the contest. While the game never lacked for excitement or intensity, the level of play was sometimes erratic. Repeated turnovers and missed field-goal attempts plagued both teams throughout the contest. Kentucky rallied twice in the second half to cut the Miners' lead to one point, but Texas Western kept its poise and opened up an eleven-point lead with just over three minutes left. Forward Nevil Shed recalled the final seconds of the Miners' 72–65 victory: "When that clock started ticking off, it seemed like the whole world just stood still, and the only thing that I could see was that five, four, three, two, one. Hey, we were Number One! I was part of a team that was the best in the United States!"[37]

The Texas Western win surprised coaches, sportswriters, and basketball fans around the country. At the time many believed that the TWC triumph constituted the biggest upset in the history of the national finals. Over the following three decades sportswriters continued to agree that the Miner victory was a historic event. On the surface, of course, it seems odd that writers would depict as anything more than mildly surprising a game in which the number-three team in the nation, which had lost only one contest all year, upset the number-one team. Several contrasts between the two teams help explain why so many people did not anticipate a Kentucky loss—Rupp's vast experience and Haskins's inexperience, the Wildcats' long winning tradition and Texas Western's lackluster history, Kentucky's national presence versus TWC's geographical isolation, and especially the sharp racial difference between the starting lineups. Disappointed UK fans were reluctant to admit that these factors had caused them to underestimate the Miners. Instead, some of them excused their team's unexpected loss by arguing that the Wildcats had exhausted themselves against Duke the previous night. Coach Adolph Rupp took the loss especially hard, lamenting to reporters that "the pressure got to us" and that illness had weakened his players' stamina. The week following the game one Kentucky sportswriter, still struggling with the painful loss and its racial overtones, crudely commented, "There is no disgrace in losing to a team such as was assembled by Texas Western after a nationwide search that somehow escaped the recruiting of the Globetrotters." In later years Rupp became even more bitter over the loss and voiced exaggerated accusations against TWC, in essence denouncing the Miners for denying him what rightfully should have been his fifth national championship.[38]

The Miner victory also delivered a powerful message about the dangers of continued athletic segregation to coaches at white southern universities. As one black journalist noted, Kentucky "missed out on the opportunity of proving that there are schools who can still win the big title without Negro players." It now seemed clear that if southern basketball teams wished to remain nationally competitive, they would have to finally accept African Americans or place their teams at a disadvantage. The Kentucky–Texas Western game did not cause the racial structure of southern college basketball to change overnight, of course, but it did make a dramatic statement about the perils of Jim Crow. One month after the final in College Park, Vanderbilt University signed center Perry Wallace of Nashville's Pearl High School to a basketball scholarship, the first ever awarded to an African American by a member of the Southeastern Conference. Although athletic integration was inevitable at some future date, the Texas Western victory helped accelerate the process and offered the Miners as a model for other schools to imitate. Since Texas Western was technically a southern college, its success served as a warning to elite schools elsewhere in the South that lesser-known regional rivals could gain a competitive advantage over them by abandoning segregation.[39]

The Kentucky–Texas Western matchup carried great significance for African Americans. As far as many black fans were concerned, Adolph Rupp was "the basketball version of Birmingham police chief Bull Connor and the embodiment of segregation's lingering hold on the South." (Connor became infamous in the early 1960s for his opposition to civil rights protests in Birmingham.) The unexpected presence of five African Americans in the title match was itself exhilarating. A columnist in the *Pittsburgh Courier* recalled that one local fan watching the game on television leaped from his seat when the fifth Miner starter was announced and excitedly screamed, "Man, this is out of sight!" For African American sports fans, the ability of the Miners to withstand two second-half rallies by the Wildcats and not break under pressure proved that black players possessed the mental toughness and poise needed for athletic success. Butch Beard, the 1965 high school player of the year in the state of Kentucky, watched the championship game from his dormitory at the University of Louisville. Beard, who turned down the opportunity to become the first black basketball player at Kentucky, was deeply impressed by the Miners. "I felt like they had proved, once and for all, that black players could win big games at that level," he recalled. For African American players, then, the game represented "the emancipation proclamation" of southern college sports.[40]

Back in El Paso jubilant students danced through the streets and built several bonfires on campus to celebrate the victory. Nervous Texas Western officials finally summoned local police in order to keep the celebration from getting completely out of hand. An estimated ten thousand exuberant El Pasoans welcomed the team home the next day at the airport. Letters of congratulations poured in from around the country. However, the college's obscure status and lack of previous national recognition confused a few writers. One northern industrialist sent a congratulatory letter to President Ray in which he expressed his satisfaction at seeing the national championship won by "a small Negro college." But not all fans were so complimentary. Almost immediately Haskins began to receive a flood of hate mail. Eventually, he received hundreds of letters and postcards denouncing him in crude racist language for selling out the white race by using black players to win a championship. The nonpolitical coach was so shaken by this display of bigotry that he sometimes wished that the Miners had lost the title contest. Nonetheless, the Texas Western victory could not be undone, and the game had a greater impact on southern college sports than any other event since the Supreme Court's *Brown v. Board of Education* ruling.[41]

In the early 1960s under the leadership of President Joseph Ray, Texas Western had set out to upgrade its academic and athletic programs. Local civic elites strongly supported such goals, believing that the city deserved something more than an underfunded, lowly regional college. By 1967 their efforts had accomplished a great deal. New physical facilities had sprouted across campus, including Sun Bowl Stadium and a modern air-conditioned classroom building. The football team's recent successes had caught the eye of traditional Texas sports fans. Most important, the Miners' championship basketball team of 1966 had given TWC the national prominence that school administrators and civic leaders coveted. While not the only factor in the Miners' rise to prominence, the essential contributions of African American players, especially in basketball, had played a vital role in these athletic developments. The school's new status was confirmed by two developments in 1967. First, the Western Athletic Conference offered the college a highly desired membership invitation. TWC thereby rejoined several of its traditional southwestern rivals, including New Mexico, Arizona, and Arizona State, in a nationally prominent conference. Second, the regents of the UT system voted to change the name of the college to the University of Texas at El Paso, thereby adding prestige to the school and eliminating its regional designation. The athletic and academic future of the university appeared bright indeed.

The Downside of Success at Texas Western

Athletic success brought considerable national recognition to UTEP, but in 1968 much of this publicity turned negative. Since most of the ensuing criticism focused on racial issues, university officials were outraged and embarrassed. During 1967 a few black Miners became mildly assertive and complained to the athletic department about several minor grievances. As racial tensions intensified across the United States during 1968, African American students and athletes on numerous college campuses increasingly voiced their dissatisfaction over the status quo, especially after the assassination of Dr. Martin Luther King Jr. in April. At UTEP most of the controversy during the spring of 1968 focused on the track and field team, directed by young head coach Wayne Vandenburg. Hoping to duplicate the success of its football and basketball teams, the university had given Vandenburg a generous budget in order to recruit the top athletes available. Many of these Miner tracksters were African Americans. The UTEP track squad first attracted national criticism in February 1968 over an indoor meet sponsored by the New York Athletic Club. Vandenburg refused to honor a widespread boycott of the event organized by civil rights activists to protest the club's discriminatory membership policies and forced his athletes to participate. In April most of the team's black members announced that they would boycott a scheduled track meet at Brigham Young University over Easter weekend. The runners insisted that this was a matter of high principle to them, because of the allegedly antiblack teachings and practices of the Church of Jesus Christ of Latter-day Saints, which operated BYU. In response to this challenge Vandenburg promptly kicked eight athletes, including NCAA long-jump champion Bob Beamon, off the team and revoked their scholarships, provoking an outcry from black activists around the country and some TWC students and faculty. Despite the protests Vandenburg refused to change his decision, believing that his fundamental authority as coach had been challenged.[42]

The UTEP athletic program came under even more fire during the summer when *Sports Illustrated* devoted one segment of its famous multipart series "The Black Athlete" to the university. Part 3 of the controversial set of articles, authored by radical sportswriter Jack Olsen, focused on the racial atmosphere at UTEP and in El Paso in order to demonstrate that "there are harsh and perhaps inescapable consequences when status-conscious universities seek fame by importing Negro athletes." The article surveyed the entire athletic program and rendered a harsh verdict. To prove his thesis that UTEP and other major predominantly white universities callously exploited African Americans, Olsen quoted several athletes who expressed frustration and anger over conditions at the university and in the city. Their complaints included the use of racial slurs by coaches and administrators, a lack of emphasis on academic progress for athletes, limited social opportunities available in the city, alleged prohibitions against interracial dating, exclusion from fraternities, an absence of good jobs for athletes' wives, and discrimination in housing. University officials challenged many of Olsen's charges, arguing that some of them were factually wrong and others exaggerated. A few of the athletes quoted later retracted their comments or explained that they had been taken out of context. Despite their disclaimers UTEP administrators and coaches did make some concessions in hopes of reducing discontent among African Americans, especially in the area of monitoring academic progress. The number of complaints from black athletes declined the following year, and no national boycott of the university took place. Yet the negative publicity definitely hampered recruiting for several years, especially in basketball. Nonetheless, Don Haskins continued to produce strong teams, and Vandenburg's revamped track squads eventually won several NCAA team championships. The football team's results were not so favorable, however. From

1970 on the Miners went into a sharp decline for the next several decades, never again enjoying the level of success that they had achieved in the mid-1960s. Bum Phillips's comment upon his resignation in 1963—that no coach would ever be able to win consistently in El Paso—proved prophetic, at least through the start of the twenty-first century.[43]

Officials and coaches at UTEP were ill-prepared for the criticism they received in 1968 and felt betrayed by the turn of events. The transformation of the university's image from enlightened pioneer to callous exploiter in just two years proved difficult for most whites to understand. UTEP representatives were especially irritated that the school's earlier efforts at racial inclusion were so readily dismissed at a time when most historically white southern universities still maintained segregated athletic programs. Clearly, the university had benefited enormously from the early and courageous integration of its sports programs. But by incorporating so many African Americans onto its teams, UTEP also guaranteed that it would unwillingly participate in "the revolt of the black athlete" during the late 1960s. Eventually, racial tensions subsided on most campuses. At the same time, sportswriters, civil rights activists, and even the federal government began to look more closely at those southern universities that continued to maintain all-white sports programs. The next two chapters will investigate how members of the Atlantic Coast Conference, the first of the three major southern white conferences to abandon the color line, responded to the racial challenges of the 1960s and early 1970s.

5

Hold That (Mason-Dixon) Line

The Atlantic Coast Conference and Football

Voluntary acceptance of Negroes because they can fulfill a valuable service for a school will break down the barriers of prejudice much more quickly than the compulsory enrollment of a James Meredith.

—University of Michigan *Michigan Daily*, February 1963

State College, if it is to continue to participate in athletics on a big-time basis, is being hypocritical, short-sighted, and slightly foolish in not approaching and offering scholarships to Negro athletes.

—North Carolina State University *Technician*, February 1963

On the afternoon of November 16, 1963, a long-standing racial barrier in college sports fell when Clemson University hosted the University of Maryland in a historic Atlantic Coast Conference football game. Although both teams had been already eliminated from the conference championship race, most spectators present that Saturday still realized that they were witnessing an important athletic milestone. What made this particular game significant was the presence in the Maryland starting lineup of wide receiver Darryl Hill, the first African American to play varsity football in the ACC. Hill's appearance at Clemson took place against a backdrop of widespread white resistance to public school desegregation across the state of South Carolina. Earlier that year Clemson had reluctantly admitted its first black student under a federal court order, after several years of legal delays. Adding to the drama, no black player had previously been allowed to set foot on the playing field inside Memorial Stadium, unofficially known by the ominous nickname of "Death Valley." Moreover, seating in the stands remained totally segregated. Consequently, many

Tiger fans resented both Hill's presence on this sacred ground and the new racial order that he represented, and some of them let him know it by shouting racial epithets at him throughout the game.

This hostile atmosphere did not intimidate Hill, but a racial incident involving his mother almost caused him to boycott the contest. At the last minute Mrs. Palestine Hill had decided to drive to Clemson in order to see her son play, but university policies restricted African American spectators to a segregated seating area on a grassy hill behind the east end zone. At the gate Mrs. Hill presented a complimentary ticket from her son for the visitors' section, where other Terrapin parents were seated, but stadium personnel refused to accept her ticket. After Darryl Hill was informed about the situation, he rushed to the stadium entrance and unsuccessfuly attempted to negotiate his mother's admission. Furious over her treatment, he started toward the locker room to remove his equipment. Fortunately, the president of Clemson appeared at that moment and resolved the situation by personally escorting Mrs. Hill into the stadium. Darryl Hill then rejoined his teammates, determined to channel his anger into a strong performance. During the game Hill set a new school record by catching ten passes despite being double-teamed. However, the Clemson defense accomplished its goal of preventing him from scoring a touchdown, and the Tigers posted a 21–6 win.[1]

The 1963 Maryland–Clemson football game represented a crucial turning point in the history of the Atlantic Coast Conference. The presence of Darryl Hill at Memorial Stadium on that November afternoon signaled the end of the era of complete segregation in big-time ACC sports and the start of the age of racial integration. Since the late nineteenth century, when the eight conference members had established their first football teams, every single player on those squads had been white, until Hill's arrival in 1963. Over the following eight years the remaining seven ACC members would gradually integrate their athletic teams as well. The real loser that November afternoon at Clemson was not the Terrapin football team but rather Jim Crow.

Origins of the Atlantic Coast Conference

The Atlantic Coast Conference was the first of the three major southern conferences to begin the process of integrating its football and basketball teams in the 1960s. Black athletes first appeared in the so-called minor or nonrevenue sports, such as tennis, soccer, wrestling, and swimming, in the late 1950s and early 1960s. These sports did not normally provide scholarships, and there was only modest public concern about interracial competition in them. Football and basketball were a different matter entirely. The general public viewed these two sports as representing the core of university activities, and many school alumni, white state residents, and political leaders all agreed on the necessity of preserving the color line. But when Maryland in 1962 and Wake Forest in 1963 announced that they would no longer exclude African Americans from their athletic programs, proponents of integration grew hopeful. The student newspaper at the University of Michigan captured this optimism in 1963 when it argued that there existed a "world of difference" between the involuntary, court-ordered admission of a black student like James Meredith at Ole Miss and the voluntary recruitment of a black athlete. "Voluntary acceptance of Negroes because they can fulfill a valuable service for a school will break down the barriers of prejudice much more quickly than the compulsory enrollment of a James Meredith," it asserted. The newspaper warned that "those teams which now can afford the luxury of not having Negro players will not be so fortunate in the future."[2] In the ACC this scenario unfolded more slowly than predicted, since conservative league members did not immediately rush to follow in Maryland's footsteps. Indeed, it was not until the fall of 1971 that the last two conference members, Clemson and Virginia, finally sent integrated varsity teams onto the gridiron. Thus, the hallowed "white space" of big-time sports remained closed to African Americans long after other racial barriers on campus had fallen.

The Atlantic Coast Conference sprang to life out of a schism among members of the Southern Conference in the late 1940s and early 1950s. Seventeen colleges scattered between Maryland to the north and South Carolina to the south belonged to the Southern Conference. This internal dispute was part of a much larger debate within higher education over the financing of college athletics, especially the issue of scholarships for athletes. Some colleges wanted to retain a semblance of pure amateurism under the so-called sanity code, but others preferred the new, more commercialized model of open subsidies for athletes. Within the Southern Conference the larger state universities with more successful athletic programs embraced the new model and eventually decided to form a separate elite league in order to pursue big-time sports more aggressively. In May 1953 five public universities and two private colleges formally withdrew from the Southern Conference. The following month representatives from these institutions met in Raleigh, North Carolina, and officially established the Atlantic Coast Conference. Charter members of the new league were the University of Maryland, the University of North Carolina, North Carolina State, Wake Forest, Duke, the University of South Carolina (USC), and Clemson. These seven "founding fathers" also wished to create a more geographically compact conference of eight teams. The University of Virginia appeared to be the most attractive possibility for the final slot, but in Charlottesville there was strong sentiment for retaining the school's independent status. After lengthy discussions President Colgate W. Darden and the Board of Visitors concluded that the university's athletic future would best be served by joining the new league. On December 4, 1953, the ACC officially admitted Virginia to membership.[3]

As part of the ACC's drive to gain national recognition, the conference sought to combine academic excellence, athletic success, and financial profitability. This evolving universe of college sports in the early 1950s was, of course, almost exclusively a man's world. The original conference bylaws made this perfectly clear by explicitly stating that "athletic participation is limited to male student-athletes." This requirement was not repealed until February 1973. Even then it took another four and a half years before conferencewide competition for women in tennis and basketball commenced in the fall of 1977. In 1961, hoping to give additional emphasis to academics and to help clean up the conference's image following several recruiting scandals, the ACC adopted a requirement that all prospective athletes must have scored at least 750 on the Scholastic Aptitude Test (SAT) in order to qualify for an athletic scholarship. Four years later league members voted to raise the required score to 800. This decision irked many coaches and administrators, especially at Clemson and South Carolina, because their state's high school graduates tended to perform poorly on standardized tests. The requirement was finally dropped in August 1972.[4]

In November 1953 the new conference achieved an important milestone when it signed an agreement with the Orange Bowl to send its football champion to the postseason classic. There the ACC winner would meet the champion of the Big Eight Conference, creating an exciting contest that would attract national interest. Pleased with the television ratings for the matchup, CBS signed a new multiyear contract with the Orange Bowl and the two conferences in December 1954 that substantially increased the payout to the participating teams. The popular bowl game and its national television audience provided the ACC with greater national exposure for the rest of the 1950s and boosted the conference's prestige. In the disappointing 1960s, however, teams from other conferences increasingly defeated ACC football squads, and the league lost its automatic spot in the Orange Bowl when the old contract expired. Many football coaches blamed this decline in football on the new academic requirements, which imposed higher standards on ACC athletes than was the case of most other southern colleges, especially those who belonged to the Southeastern Conference.[5]

The original ACC regulations did not impose any formal racial restrictions on athletic participation, since all eight member schools were already segregated by law. After classroom integration arrived in the 1960s, though, the possible recruitment of black athletes by ACC universities became a new concern. On such matters conference members eventually divided into two blocs. Maryland was the leader of the moderate faction, which also included the four "Tobacco Road" schools of North Carolina, North Carolina State, Duke, and Wake Forest.

Virginia, Clemson, and South Carolina constituted the conservative faction and displayed the greatest resistance to racial change in sports. Led by Maryland, all five universities in the moderate group had integrated both their varsity football and their varsity basketball programs before any of their three conservative brethren accepted African Americans on their teams in either sport.

The University of Maryland Takes the Lead

Since the University of Maryland was the only Atlantic Coast Conference member located in a border state, the school appeared the most likely candidate to liberalize its athletic policies. Historically, Maryland had been a slave state, but in 1861 it rejected secession and remained part of the Union. Despite this loyalty most white residents strongly endorsed white supremacy. In the early twentieth century the state government constructed an extensive system of legal segregation in public accommodations and education, just like its counterparts across the South. However, this Jim Crow system eventually began to unravel sooner than in the Confederate South. Because of several lawsuits the University of Maryland accepted one black law school student in 1935, another black professional student in 1950, and its first black undergraduate, in electrical engineering, in 1951. Regents finally removed all racial restrictions on admissions in 1954. Although these developments hardly made Maryland a racial paradise, they did indicate that the state possessed a somewhat more flexible racial system than was found in the Deep South. Moreover, its geographical location meant that the state's athletic teams often competed against northern colleges that sometimes included black players on their squads.[6]

Football began in 1892 at College Park, when the school was known as the Maryland Agricultural College. Once derided by critics as "a football field with a few academic buildings attached," the college fielded rather average teams over the decades. Despite its border location Maryland joined the old Southern Conference and followed "southern rules." The advent of integrated games against northern teams did not present a major problem for the Terrapin players, a majority of whom came from Pennsylvania and other northern states. During the 1950s, under the leadership of Coach Jim Tatum, Maryland enjoyed its best era ever. The undefeated 1951 team finished number three in the regular-season polls, while in 1953 the Terrapins again went undefeated during the regular season and finished first in the AP poll. After Tatum left in 1956 for the University of North Carolina, however, the Terrapins' fortunes fell on hard times. Concerned about possible criticism from civil rights activists, university officials informed Coach Tom Nugent in 1962 that there were no longer any racial restrictions on his recruiting. When freshman coach Lee Corso learned that Darryl Hill, a wide receiver on the Naval Academy freshman team, was planning to transfer to another college, he quickly contacted him. Hill had been a star player at a private high school in the District of Columbia and clearly possessed the academic and social skills that most universities sought in their pioneering black athletes. After sitting out the 1962 season because of transfer rules, Hill officially became the first African American to play ACC football in September 1963.[7]

Hill's enrollment at Maryland did not create any controversy on campus. Once they saw his obvious ability, his teammates readily accepted him. Coach Tom Nugent and his staff let Hill and the other players work out their relationships without any close supervision. An assistant coach did speak to Hill once about shaving off a mustache. On another occasion the coaching staff warned against interracial dating. Travel to ACC schools created potential racial problems, so Nugent paid careful attention to local arrangements. When two hotels at which the team had previously stayed refused to accept Hill, Nugent moved the entire team to new facilities. On road trips Hill roomed with linebacker Jerry Fishman, whom southern fans sometimes insulted because he was Jewish. Since Hill was the first black athlete to set foot on the football fields at both the University of South Carolina and Clemson, and one of the first African Americans to do so at several other schools, local fans were often hostile. In fact, one rival team captain even apologized to him for the crude behavior of his school's fans.[8]

In the second week of the 1963 season Hill became the first black player to compete in Carolina Stadium against the University of South Carolina, less than three weeks after the school had admitted its first black students under a federal court order. Hill scored one touchdown in a 21–13 loss, and the Gamecock players treated him like any other opposing player. However, many South Carolina fans, still unhappy about the university's recent integration, were openly hostile. As the Maryland players left the field, a large group of fans blocked their path and engaged them in a shoving match. One angry spectator tossed a drink on Hill. The following week's stay in Durham also proved stressful. When Hill and several other players lined up to order ice cream at a Woolworth's lunch counter downtown, an employee announced that Hill would not be served. Led by Fishman, the players walked out of the restaurant in protest. Also in Durham a different group of players noticed two antique pistols prominently displayed in a restaurant window. Asked about the gun's significance, the owner replied, "I'm going to use them to shoot that nigger after the game tomorrow!" Despite these incidents the actual game proved uneventful and resulted in another Terrapin loss. Two weeks later at home Maryland finally won a game, narrowly defeating the Air Force Academy. On the last play of the game Hill caught a thirty-six-yard touchdown pass from quarterback Dick Shiner to pull out a dramatic victory, solidifying his popularity with Maryland fans.[9]

Hill's pass-catching skills were repeatedly demonstrated over the ensuing weeks, as he and quarterback Shiner settled into their roles in Coach Tom Nugent's wide-open offense. On October 26 the Terrapins won their second straight game, with Hill catching two touchdown passes from Shiner in a 32–0 shutout of hapless Wake Forest. After two consecutive losses Maryland then made its toughest trip of the year on November 16 to Clemson. The temporary exclusion of Hill's mother from the stands disrupted his concentration before the game. Then during pregame drills Clemson coach Frank Howard walked to midfield and glared directly at Hill for several minutes, apparently seeking to intimidate him. Despite these distractions Hill turned in a successful performance on the field, catching a school record ten passes in the Terrapin loss. In late November Maryland closed its disappointing season with a 21–6 road win over Virginia. Hill ended the season with forty-three pass receptions, which placed him fifth in NCAA statistics. His seven touchdown receptions for the year tied him for first place in the ACC in that category, and he lead the conference in kickoff-return average. The following year Hill encountered less hostility on ACC fields, but injuries sidelined him for most of the 1964 season. Nonetheless, Maryland's experiment in breaking the color line was off to a successful start.[10]

At the end of the 1963 season, Maryland signed two local stars from Baltimore Polytechnic High School to scholarships. In the fall of 1965 Ernie Torain, a fullback, and Alvin Lee, a halfback, both joined the varsity, becoming the second and third African Americans to play for the Terrapins and demonstrating that Maryland was fully committed to an integrated football program. As a sophomore Torain ended up as the team's leading rusher for the year. Maryland continued to recruit African Americans in subsequent years. By the fall of 1969 eight African Americans suited up for the Terrapin varsity. During that same season three ACC schools—Virginia, Clemson, and South Carolina—still did not have a single African American on their football teams. The integration of Maryland's football teams did not catapult the Terrapins to the top of the conference; instead, the school remained somewhere in the middle of the league standings in most years. Nonetheless, Maryland had demonstrated to ACC rivals that an integrated team could work together and win games.[11]

Pragmatic Integration at Wake Forest University

In 1965 Wake Forest became the second ACC member to integrate its varsity football team. This pragmatic decision resulted mostly from a desire to end several seasons of ignominious failure on the football field. A Baptist-affiliated college, Wake Forest moved into its spacious new campus in Winston-Salem in 1956. This small industrial city in the west-central section of the state provided a flexible and modestly progressive racial climate. Following the *Brown* decision in 1954, the university continued to reject admission requests from African Americans, even though the state Baptist convention had urged church schools to open their doors to all qualified students regardless of race. President Harold W. Tribble, a racial moderate, moved slowly on the issue because he feared offending conservative trustees and major donors. During 1961 the Board of Trustees removed racial restrictions on graduate programs, summer school, and evening classes. Finally, in April 1962, the board voted 17–9 to open undergraduate studies to all students. The school's first black undergraduate, Edward Reynolds of Ghana, promptly enrolled in June.[12]

Athletics occupied an important place at Wake Forest, especially with the school's alumni, but the college's football teams were consistently mediocre. From 1956 through 1969 the Demon Deacons enjoyed only one winning season, and in 1970 they captured their first and only ACC football title. Thus, by the 1960s, "Wake Forest had become a revolving door" for football coaches. The football program hit rock bottom in 1962 and 1963. After the Demon Deacons went 0-10 and 1-9 during those seasons, the school fired Coach Bill Hildebrand in December 1963. Worse yet, the athletic department recorded its biggest financial deficit ever for the 1962–63 school year. This financial crisis forced Wake Forest officials to conduct a painful reappraisal of athletics, discussing numerous options before eventually reaffirming the university's commitment to big-time sports.[13] The recruitment of African American athletes eventually became part of the university's strategy to reinvigorate its football program. In early 1963 President Tribble announced that Wake Forest would no longer maintain a color line for its athletic teams. However, the administration did not authorize the football staff to offer any scholarships to black high school prospects. Moreover, Coach Bill Hildebrand told the student newspaper that few local African American athletes could qualify academically for Wake Forest anyway. At the end of the year university officials notified Hildebrand shortly before he was fired that the college's policy had changed and that promising black recruits could now be offered athletic scholarships.[14]

New head coach Bill Tate, a thirty-six-year-old assistant coach at Illinois, aggressively sought to resuscitate Wake Forest football. Tate had grown up in the North and had no emotional loyalties to the segregated athletic order in Dixie. Furthermore, he desperately needed to do something to attract more talented athletes to the undistinguished Wake Forest program. Recruitment of junior college athletes and African Americans was one avenue that he actively pursued. Shortly after being hired in February 1964, Tate announced that he would seek out African American prospects, "provided that they meet the academic, moral, and athletic qualifications of the college." Despite some negative reaction to his announcement, the new head coach quickly demonstrated that he was serious about seeking out the best high school athletes regardless of race. In early April Tate announced that Kenneth "Butch" Henry of Greensboro, a 6'3", 185-pound quarterback, had accepted a scholarship to the college. The son of two public school teachers, Henry told reporters that he selected Wake Forest because he wanted to acquire a good education. Henry acknowledged that he might encounter a few problems as the first black athlete at the school, but he quickly added that "times are changing, and everything should be all right at a school like Wake Forest." The following day William "Butch" Smith of Greenville, South Carolina, announced that he had signed with the Demon Deacons, rejecting offers from several Big Ten schools. The following month end Robert Grant of Jacksonville, North Carolina, became the third African American to sign with Wake Forest. Tate's experiment was off to a strong start.[15]

During the fall of 1964 Henry, Smith, and Grant all played on the freshman team without encountering any major problems. On the varsity level Bill Tate coached the Deacons to a surprising 4-3 conference record and a 5-5 overall mark, earning him the league's "Coach of the Year" award. Although Smith transferred after his freshman year, Henry and Grant both played on the varsity squad during the 1965 season, joining Maryland's Eddie Torain and Alvin Lee as the only four African American football players in the ACC. Henry moved from quarterback to wide receiver and finished the season as the team leader in pass receptions. During the 1966 season three black sophomores joined Henry and Grant on the Deacon varsity, giving Wake Forest the largest black contingent in the conference. Somewhat surprisingly, no other ACC team immediately copied the example of Wake Forest and Maryland, and again in 1967 those two universities were the only league members fielding integrated teams. In 1967 Tate crossed another racial boundary when he started Freddie Summers, a transfer from McCook (Nebraska) Junior College, at quarterback. By starting Summers Tate directly challenged the prevailing white stereotype that African Americans lacked the intelligence and leadership ability required at this key position. After losing their first six games of the 1967 season, the surprising Deacons then swept their four final conference games. Summers finished the year as the conference leader in total offense and was named to the All-ACC first team at the quarterback spot. The following year he bettered his 1967 statistics, but his inconsistency in key situations, and that of his teammates, resulted in another losing season. Overall, the addition of African Americans to the Maryland and Wake Forest teams provided only a modest boost to their season records. Nonetheless, Maryland and Wake Forest had demonstrated that it was possible for southern universities to field integrated squads without destroying team unity or splitting up their conference.[16]

Black Tar Heels in Chapel Hill

Because of the relatively liberal atmosphere found in Chapel Hill, the University of North Carolina appeared to be the next logical choice to pursue football integration. Yet the Tar Heel football team did not send its first African American varsity player onto the field until 1968, five years after Darryl Hill had joined the Maryland squad. Despite its tardiness UNC still acted sooner than five other conference schools. North Carolina had achieved considerable success on the gridiron over the decades, winning Southern Conference championships in 1922, 1934, and 1937. Beginning in the 1930s the Tar Heels sought greater national recognition by scheduling high-profile intersectional games, even against northern teams that included African Americans. North Carolina's first integrated home game came in November 1953 against a Notre Dame team that had just added its first two black players. UNC enjoyed its "golden era" of football success in the late 1940s under Coach Carl Snavely. Paced by fabulous halfback Charlie "Choo Choo" Justice, twice the runner-up for the Heisman Trophy, the Tar Heels won the Southern Conference championship in 1946 and 1949 and played in three bowl games. But during the 1950s and 1960s Carolina's football fortunes declined sharply.[17]

Like other white colleges across the South, the University of North Carolina continued to reject black applicants for admission after World War II. In 1951, however, a federal appeals court ordered the School of Law to admit qualified black applicants, despite the existence of a separate law school for African Americans at North Carolina Central College. The ensuing integration of the law school indirectly led to an embarrassing incident concerning segregated seating in Keane Stadium. In September 1951, when five African American law students decided to attend a football game there, they were issued tickets to the segregated all-black section in the stadium end zone, rather than the student section. The five boycotted the September 22 home game against North Carolina State in protest and threatened to sue the college. Fourteen campus groups, the *Daily Tar Heel,* and the NAACP all endorsed their stand. Chancellor Robert B. House initially defended the seating policy, explaining that the school would treat the five in a fair manner "but on an extremely conservative basis." He added that there was a "difference between educational services to Negro students and social equalization." Three weeks later, however, he relented and issued student-ticket booklets to the group. After skipping the next home game, the law students quietly sat together without incident in the student section for the Tar Heels' November 3 game against Tennessee.[18]

The Supreme Court's *Brown* ruling in 1954 placed further legal pressure on the University of North Carolina and the state university system. In May 1955 three black high school graduates from nearby Durham—Leroy B. Frasier, Ralph Frasier, and John Lewis Brannon—filed suit in federal court seeking admission to undergraduate studies at Chapel Hill. In September a three-judge federal panel ordered the university to accept them immediately. On Monday, September 19, the three attended their first classes without incident. North Carolina thus became the second university in the ACC and the first major white institution in the Southeast to admit African Americans to undergraduate work. The admission of the three students did not have any effect on the recruiting policies for the football and basketball teams. Eventually, in 1963, Edwin Okoroma, a chemistry major from Nigeria, lettered in soccer, a non-scholarship sport, but the major sports remained segregated until the late 1960s.[19]

A coaching change helped speed up the integration of the Tar Heel football team. In December 1966 North Carolina hired Bill Dooley as its new head coach. A native Alabamian and a graduate of Mississippi State University, the thirty-three-year-old coach nonetheless approached the racial issue in a pragmatic manner. Aware that several talented African Americans from the state had gone north to play in the Big Ten, Dooley told his staff to "keep the good players at home." The UNC coaches especially looked for strength of character and good citizenship in black prospects, since these players would be subjected to intense public scrutiny. Dooley soon signed the team's first black scholarship player, Ricky Lanier, an outstanding quarterback from Williamston, North Carolina, who enrolled in September 1967. Although Dooley received a few crank letters from die-hard segregationists, most Tar Heel fans supported his new recruitment policy. During his first semester Lanier started several games for the freshman team at quarterback. As a sophomore and junior he occasionally started at the position but failed to establish himself as the number-one quarterback. For his senior year in 1970 the coaching staff shifted Lanier to wide receiver, where he saw regular action during the season. Suspicious African American students at Chapel Hill and black sports fans questioned this move and feared that influential white donors would never accept black quarterbacks. Of course, white quarterbacks sometimes resisted being switched away from the most glamorous position on the field too, but they were not concerned over subtle racial bias. The quarterback issue resurfaced at UNC in 1973 when another African American quarterback, Charles Baggett, transferred after his sophomore year, in part because coaches wanted to move him to wide receiver.[20]

During the 1969 season two additional African Americans, sophomores James Webster and Judge Mattocks, joined Lanier on the varsity squad. Webster's route to Chapel Hill illustrated how racial change in the public schools affected college sports. Just before the start of Webster's senior year, Winston-Salem school officials transferred him from a segregated black high school to predominantly white Parkland High School as part of a local desegregation plan. Had he remained at his previous school, he probably would have been ignored by most ACC recruiters, but by distinguishing himself at Parkland, Webster received several scholarship offers. His decision to attend UNC was partially influenced by the presence of Ricky Lanier, but he also wanted to stay close to home and to show skeptics that he could succeed athletically and academically in the prestigious ACC. Webster saw only limited playing time as a defensive back during the 1969 and 1970 seasons because of injuries. During his senior year in 1971 his misfortunes continued when he suffered a broken neck immediately prior to the season. Miraculously, Webster was able to return for the final three regular-season games and the Tar Heels' postseason trip to the Gator Bowl, where sportswriters selected him as the most valuable defensive player in the contest. The ACC also honored him with the Brian Piccolo Award in recognition of his courageous battle against adversity. After graduation Webster returned to UNC in 1973 as the team's first black assistant coach. Judge Mattocks's career at North Carolina followed a different trajectory. A 6'4", 190-pound end, the talented Mattocks earned All-ACC first-team honors as a sophomore, but his performance declined somewhat during his junior year. Increasingly, he found himself drawn into discussions of social and racial issues, as student protests swept the campus. Mattocks also became more religious, and he eventually concluded that these wider concerns were of far greater importance than college athletics. As a result he quit the football team in 1971 in order to focus on personal and social issues.[21]

As the 1970s unfolded, the number of black football players at Chapel Hill grew slowly but steadily, as the revitalized Tar Heels claimed three ACC championships. Ronnie Robinson, a 250-pound defensive tackle, and Charles Waddell, an imposing tight end at 6'6", 230 pounds, were outstanding performers at North Carolina from 1972 to 1974. As a senior Waddell became the first black Tar Heel to receive All-America honors. The university was able to recruit these and other African American players despite entrance requirements that were slightly higher than the ACC standard and considerably higher than the NCAA minimum. When the ACC dropped its requirement of an 800 SAT score in 1972 and the NCAA changed its eligibility requirements in 1973, North Carolina maintained its previous standards. These institutional requirements sometimes created a barrier to incorporating more African Americans into the athletic program. Balancing the desire to maintain academic standards with a commitment to pursuing athletic success and to opening doors for black students proved complicated. In 1967 the university administration quietly began permitting a limited number of noncompetitive admissions for prospective athletes who met all ACC and NCAA requirements but fell just short of UNC's higher standards. At first only white athletes entered the university through this back door, but in the 1970s black athletes also utilized the policy as well.[22]

North Carolina State Takes the Lead in Minor Sports

North Carolina State University (commonly referred to as N.C. State or "State" by area residents) was the first ACC school to accept African American students onto its athletic teams in minor sports. Despite this initial flexibility N.C. State did not field an integrated varsity football team until the fall of 1969, the same year that Duke University took similar action. These developments that year meant that all of the "Big Four" ACC schools from the state of North Carolina had fully integrated both their football and basketball squads before the two conference members in neighboring South Carolina had desegregated either sport. NCSU had been founded in 1889 as a land-grant institution and was officially named the North Carolina State College of Agricultural and Mechanical Arts. For many years the college accepted only male applicants and provided compulsory ROTC training for all students. Women did not receive complete equality in admissions and housing until the 1960s. In such a robust male environment sports proved extremely popular with students. From the early 1920s through the late 1950s, however, N.C. State rarely produced winning football teams. In hopes of remedying this problem, several coaches recruited athletes from Pennsylvania and other northern states. This limited use of "Yankee" players from various ethnic backgrounds irritated some white North Carolinians, who felt that the purity of southern sports had been stained by these "League of Nations" teams. One nativist white fan warned against the purported dangers of recruiting Italian American athletes: "It is all right to have one or two on the squad, but when there are as many as three Italian players they are liable to gang up on the coach. The most experienced coaches are afraid of Italian football players and try to avoid having more than two of them on the squad at the same time." Regardless of its football players' geographical origins, though, N.C. State teams continued to lose.[23]

Legal rulings concerning discriminatory admissions at the University of North Carolina in the 1950s applied equally to North Carolina State, since both were part of the state university system. The demise of the "separate but equal" principle for graduate education led in 1953 to the enrollment of two African American engineering students. In June 1956 freshmen engineering majors Manuel H. Crockett Jr. and Edward Carson enrolled in summer school, thereby becoming NCSU's first black undergraduates. Four additional African Americans joined them in the fall. At first these students continued to live at home, but in the spring of 1957 Irwin R. Holmes Jr. and Walter V. Holmes (no relation) desegregated campus housing when they moved into a dormitory. Walter Holmes broke another barrier when he joined the marching band. The integration of undergraduate studies in turn led to the integration of minor sports. The university administration took the position that since black students were legally enrolled, they could therefore try out for (almost) any school team. As a result, Irwin Holmes and Manuel Crockett became the first African Americans to participate in any ACC sporting event, albeit on the freshman level, when they joined the indoor track team. In February 1957 the two competed in a meet against UNC, with Crockett finishing third in the 600-yard run. While Crockett entered several additional meets, Holmes switched to the freshman tennis team. After the local press inquired about the two young men's participation in sports, athletic director Roy Clogston announced that Holmes and Crockett were being "treated just the same as any other student." Holmes's season with the freshman tennis team proved uneventful, except when one high school team showed up in Raleigh unaware that the NCSU squad was now integrated. Upon discovering that Holmes was listed as the top seed for the Wolfpack, the visitors forfeited the number-one singles and doubles matches rather than compete against an African American.[24]

During each of the following three years Holmes lettered on the varsity tennis squad. At the start of his senior year team members elected him a cocaptain, making him the first African American to captain an ACC team in any sport. Students and administrators at NCSU apparently accepted this racial change without complaint, but officials at the University of South Carolina and Clemson were upset over Holmes's participation. The Wolfpack team encountered a major problem on two occasions when it was scheduled to play dual matches against these two universities. Both the USC and Clemson coaches informed N.C. State that Holmes could not play at their tennis facilities, because of a state policy against integrated competition. But tennis coach John F. Kenfield, a man of principle, refused to travel to South Carolina without Holmes. In a compromise, both Clemson and USC finally agreed to move their home matches against NCSU to Raleigh, thereby avoiding a forfeit while still maintaining Jim Crow at home.[25]

Although NCSU was the first conference member to integrate minor sports, school officials displayed no interest in opening up football and basketball to African Americans. As Irwin Holmes later recalled, "One thing that I was not encouraged to do was to go out for basketball." Despite the integration of undergraduate studies the admissions office did not make any efforts to recruit African American students. Consequently, in 1960 there were only 15 black undergraduates among the 6,510 students enrolled at the university. During the ensuing decade the NCSU student newspaper periodically criticized the slow growth in black enrollment. In February 1963 the *Technician* specifically attacked the university administration for failing to recruit black athletes for major sports, charging that N.C. State was "being hypocritical, short-sighted, and slightly foolish in not approaching and offering scholarships to Negro athletes." The newspaper also warned that by "neglecting a source of athletic talent which could improve its teams," N.C. State was also hurting itself. The issue of black enrollment eventually caught the eye of the Department of Health, Education, and Welfare. In February 1970 HEW issued a report that charged that N.C. State and the University of North Carolina had not fully complied with the Civil

Rights Act of 1964. The report found the small presence of African American students, about 200, and the lack of black faculty at NCSU to be disturbing. Also noting the tiny number of African American athletes, the report suggested that the university hire a black coach who could assist with recruiting. The *Technician* agreed and noted that the absence of black athletes also made it easier for white students at campus sporting events to maintain southern customs that offended African American students. One black freshman told the newspaper that he had enthusiastically attended the fall semester's first pep rally, but his school spirit quickly evaporated when he encountered an oversized Confederate flag. Another black student stated that she was "completely insulted" when the school band played "Dixie" at football games.[26]

In the late 1950s and 1960s Coach Earle Edwards successfully rebuilt the NCSU football program. Edwards came to Raleigh from Michigan State in 1954. After a slow start Edwards directed the Wolfpack to ACC championships in 1957, 1963, 1964, 1965, and 1968, but he did not aggressively seek out black recruits. The college's first African American football players, Marcus Martin and Clyde Chesney, actually enrolled at N.C. State for academic reasons and did not participate in sports during their freshman year. But eventually their love of football and the challenge of making the varsity squad as walk-ons motivated them to return to the football field. Martin was the first African American at N.C. State to play on the Wolfpack varsity. The valedictorian of his small segregated high school in West Virginia, Martin came to Raleigh in the fall of 1966 to pursue a double major in chemical engineering and pulp and paper technology. During the spring of his freshman year he participated in football drills and then earned a spot on the practice squad during the fall. In 1968 Martin made the varsity team, seeing action in five games on the kickoff team and as a defensive halfback. At the end of the season an upbeat profile of him published in the *Technician* suggested that "perhaps the most significant breakthrough of this year's team is the fact that finally the color barrier has been broken." The newspaper did take note of Martin's complaint that "every other school in the ACC is ahead of us" in awarding scholarships to African Americans. In the fall of 1969 Martin expected to receive expanded playing time, but the coaching staff unexpectedly moved a white scholarship player ahead of him. Disappointed over the lack of encouragement from coaches and determined to earn high grades in order to retain his academic scholarship, Martin quietly quit the team.[27]

Clyde Chesney eventually became the first African American to receive a football scholarship at N.C. State. Chesney had ranked second in his high school graduating class in Fayetteville, North Carolina. An outstanding linebacker, he turned down an athletic scholarship to the Hampton Institute in order to major in landscape architecture at NCSU. After earning good grades in the fall of 1967, Chesney realized that he missed football and decided to go out for spring training. Chesney wanted to prove that he could be both a good student and a successful football player. He also welcomed the challenge of seeking to become the first African American to earn a football scholarship at NCSU. He later recalled that the experience of "being a black at a predominantly white university offered me a challenge that quickly dispelled my idea of not playing." Chesney impressed coaches during spring drills. After redshirting for the 1968 season, he earned a scholarship the following year and played in most games as a defensive end. He gained more playing time his junior year and was projected to be an all-conference performer as a senior in 1971. Unfortunately, a series of knee problems left him unable to finish the season, although he still made the academic All-ACC team. The coaching staff strongly supported Chesney's academic pursuits, but he reluctantly switched his major to conservation in the School of Forestry in order to have time for afternoon practices. For part of his career he was the only African American player on the varsity, which left him somewhat isolated despite support from his fellow black students. Two black staff employees, the assistant trainer and the equipment manager, provided frequent encouragement. Chesney found that most of his northern teammates completely accepted him once he demonstrated his ability, although a few southern players remained distant.[28]

In the fall of 1971 two additional black scholarship players joined the Wolfpack varsity. Willie Burden and Charles Young were both outstanding running backs from Raleigh who offered a combination of speed and power, qualities that the N.C. State squad often lacked. Furthermore, as local residents the two young men already had in place a support system of family and friends, an important asset given the limited social opportunities for African Americans on the overwhelmingly white NCSU campus. The recruitment of Burden and Young also muted growing criticism that the football program was uninterested in recruiting black athletes. Both players enjoyed considerable success during their careers, in part because the team's fortunes improved immediately after new head coach Lou Holtz arrived in 1972. In Holtz's first season N.C. State finished second in the conference, and the following year the Wolfpack captured the ACC title. Willie Burden contributed significantly to those teams' success, earning all-conference first team honors both years and the ACC "Player of the Year" award in 1973.[29]

The football team's accomplishments and the key contributions made by black players eventually prompted campus discussion about the changing roles of minority athletes. In the fall of 1973 an article in a campus magazine directly addressed this issue. Utilizing a series of interviews with African American players, the article contrasted the frustrations that Marcus Martin had experienced only five years earlier with the generally positive and upbeat attitudes expressed by fullback Charles Young, basketball star David Thompson, and several other black athletes. Although the players agreed that campus race relations could still be improved, they praised the considerable progress of the past few years. Thompson even suggested that the high visibility of successful black athletes at N.C. State had helped black high school graduates around the state identify with the university and increased the possibility that they might choose to attend NCSU. The football team's success, and the NCAA championship won by the 1974 basketball squad, made white students and fans increasingly appreciative of integrated teams. In the fall of 1973 the photograph on the cover of the school's football brochure dramatically captured, perhaps unintentionally, the symbolism of the new racial order in NCSU sports. There, in full color, were four Wolfpack running backs, three of them black and one of them white, stacked vertically like pancakes, with Stan Fritts's shoulders and white face peering forth from the stack below Roland Hicks and above Charles Young and Willie Burden. Clearly, the "face" of NCSU football had entered a new and more inclusive era.[30]

Black Blue Devils at Duke

Duke University faced many of the same problems as did the other North Carolina colleges in integrating its athletic program, as well as the additional burdens of high academic standards and an elitist atmosphere. The college was founded in the nineteenth century as Trinity College and historically was affiliated with the Methodist Church, South. After receiving a huge endowment from the tobacco fortune of James B. Duke, the trustees reorganized the college and renamed it Duke University in 1924. In 1931 Duke lured Coach Wallace Wade away from the University of Alabama by offering him a large increase in salary. Under the successful leadership of Wade and his temporary wartime replacement, Eddie Cameron, the Blue Devils won the Southern Conference championship ten times during the next two decades and were twice invited to the Rose Bowl. During the first ten years of ACC competition Duke won or tied for six conference titles before beginning a gradual descent into mediocrity.[31]

Over the decades Duke had displayed considerable flexibility concerning competition against African American players. Despite these pioneering actions, this progressive attitude did not carry over to the actual integration of the university itself. In fact, Duke was rather slow to accept African Americans for undergraduate study, primarily because of its conservative Board of Trustees. In the late 1940s a majority of students and faculty at the divinity school endorsed the admission of African Americans as day students in their program, but the trustees ignored their request. Led by U.S. Senator Willis Smith, an outspoken segregationist, the board resisted any change in enrollment policy until March 1961, when it voted to desegregate all graduate and professional studies. Two black graduate students enrolled the following year. In June 1962 the trustees dropped all racial restrictions on undergraduate admissions. Still, it was not until September 1963 that the color line totally disappeared when five African American freshmen actually enrolled. Douglas M. Knight, selected as the school's new president in 1963, was a "young, liberal northerner" who promptly eliminated any remaining vestiges of segregation on campus, such as separate bathrooms, and initiated efforts to attract black students. But the college's expensive tuition, high entrance requirements, and overwhelmingly white atmosphere made recruitment difficult, and African American enrollment remained quite low.[32]

The admission of black undergraduates brought no immediate changes in the racial composition of Blue Devil athletic teams. While most administrators and students remained complacent, a small but growing number of students, often from the North, began publicly to voice complaints about the absence of black players. In November 1964 a sportswriter for the Duke *Chronicle* accused the administration of continuing to follow "its backward policy of by-gone years" in athletic recruiting. The author pointed out that African Americans competed for football teams in the Ivy League, Big Ten, and other major conferences and that "some of these students are athletically and academically qualified for admission to Duke." By failing to take a leadership role in sports integration, he warned, the university was "losing out on the talented Negro student-athlete all over the South and the nation." The following year sports editor Jon Wallas likewise chastised the athletic department for ignoring African American athletes. Wallas asserted that the current football team sorely lacked speed and that the recruitment of black players could help resolve that deficiency. Furthermore, Wallas insisted that athletic integration was morally the right thing to do, arguing that "Duke has a moral responsibility to try to recruit regardless of color. How can Duke be a leading university in the nation if they refuse to actively seek the Negro on the athletic field as well as in the class room?"[33]

The arrival in 1966 of new head coach Tom Harp, a northerner, eventually led to a shift in recruiting patterns at Duke. After several possible recruits changed their minds at the last minute, the school finally awarded its first athletic scholarships to African Americans in the spring of 1968. The two recipients, Ernest Jackson, a defensive back from Hopkins, South Carolina, and Clarence Newsome, an offensive end from Ahoskie, North Carolina, played on the freshman team that fall and moved up to the varsity in 1969. The following year Nat Bethel, a fullback, and Willie Clayton, an offensive tackle, joined them on the varsity squad. The number of black players at Duke continued to grow during the 1970s, although not as rapidly as at other ACC schools because of the school's stiff entrance requirements. Ernest Jackson became the most successful of these black Blue Devils, enjoying a spectacular senior season in 1971 and earning the nickname of the "Can Do Kid." Against the University of South Carolina in the second game of the season, the veteran defensive halfback returned a punt for one touchdown and ran an intercepted pass back for a second score in a 28–12 Duke victory. The win was especially sweet to Jackson, a former high school football star in South Carolina, because USC had declined to offer him a scholarship. When mounting injuries decimated the Duke offensive, the versatile senior was pressed into service as a running back. In his first start at halfback he scored Duke's first two touchdowns in a 41–13 thrashing of North Carolina State. The following week in a 15–14 loss to Navy, Jackson played both offense and defense for most of the game and turned in a remarkable display of skill and endurance. At the end of the season sportswriters selected Jackson as the ACC "Player of the Year," the first defender to be so honored, and later as a consensus All-American defensive back.[34]

Jackson's remarkable performances and the contributions of his black teammates won respect from white students and fans. Still, individual athletic accomplishments did not always lead to close relationships between these pioneering black athletes and white students. Black teammate Clarence Newsome attributed some of this social distance to whites' lack of previous contact with African Americans and their blindness to blacks' inner feelings. He later recalled, "I think many of the fellows I played with, and many of the coaches, had never really dealt first hand with blacks on an extended basis. . . . Many was the time that I'd walk on that field alone, and walk off that field alone, while all the other players kind of clustered around the coaches. And the same was experienced [by] the other black football player. We were not a part of the 'in group.'" Dr. Samuel DuBois Cook, a political science professor who in 1966 became the first African American faculty member at Duke, remembered individual black players standing by themselves on the sidelines during football games and sensed a distance between them and most of their white teammates. The small contingent of black undergraduates at Duke often experienced similar feelings of social isolation. In February 1969 a group of African American students temporarily seized the administration building in order to press for acceptance of an eleven-point plan to end racial tokenism at the university. Although none of these demands specifically addressed the athletic program, the protest did eventually make the Duke administration think about the need to hire an African American coach. In 1972 the football staff selected Bishop Harris, a former star player at North Carolina Central College, as a graduate assistant. The following year he accepted a full-time position, making him one of the first black assistant coaches in the ACC.[35]

South Carolina and the Conservative Bloc Take Their Time

The University of South Carolina was the first member of the racially conservative bloc of ACC schools to integrate its football teams, beating out Clemson

University and the University of Virginia by one year. The state of South Carolina provided an especially conservative climate for educational institutions, given the state's long history as a leading defender of the southern racial order. Chartered in 1801 the University of South Carolina had exclusively served white students except for a brief period during Radical Reconstruction. In its athletic contests the university traditionally drew the color line, reflecting the view of white South Carolinians that interracial competition should never be allowed in any sport under any circumstances. An October 1947 amateur football game held off-campus in Columbia fully illustrated these extreme beliefs. The contest matched a city all-star team of former high school and college players against a visiting squad from the Greenville Army Air Base. When the military team unexpectedly included five African Americans, the home team protested. After some delicate negotiations, the Columbia players agreed to play the match, provided that their fans did not object. When the game's sponsors asked members of the crowd for their opinions, the vast majority of the eight hundred spectators "overwhelmingly opposed" any integrated contest. These fans apparently believed that protecting the special white space of the gridiron was far more important than obtaining three hours of sports entertainment. After checking with their superior officers, the army squad refused to compromise its team unity, forcing cancellation of the contest.[36]

Since the university was located in Columbia, the state capital, the state's political leaders paid close attention to university affairs, especially racial policies. When African American students started to seek admission to the university in the late 1950s, USC administrators vigorously resisted their efforts. In 1963 the university finally exhausted its legal options, and a federal court ordered it to admit qualified African Americans. Consequently, three black students, Henri Monteith, Robert G. Anderson Jr., and James L. Solomon Jr., registered for classes in September 1963. Anxious to avoid the violence that had accompanied integration at the University of Georgia and Ole Miss, USC officials restricted press coverage of their enrollment and took special precautions to minimize possible disruptions by segregationists. The three new students encountered no harassment on their first day, and several white students even welcomed them to the campus.[37]

During the 1950s and 1960s South Carolina usually fielded competitive football teams, but the school did not win its first ACC title until 1969. Paul F. Dietzel served as head football coach and athletic director from 1966 through 1974. Earlier in his career at Louisiana State University, he had coached the Tigers to the national championship in 1958. His arrival in Columbia temporarily revived hope for the football program. As other ACC schools fielded integrated teams, however, Dietzel came under fire for the continued all-white makeup of his squad. Many African Americans believed that influential USC alumni did not want to see the football team integrated and doubted Dietzel's interest in black recruits. According to journalist Jack Bass, Dietzel defended his recruiting policies in 1967 before an integrated ministerial group by announcing that he had scouted five black prospects in the state. The Gamecock coach quickly cautioned that four of the young men could not meet ACC academic standards and that the fifth lacked athletic promise. The black ministers present remained skeptical, however, especially since they believed that Ernest Jackson, the fifth athlete, was an excellent prospect. Apparently, they were better judges of talent than Dietzel, since Jackson eventually attended Duke and won the ACC Player of the Year award as a senior.[38]

There was ample evidence for the ministers' belief that the state's black high schools produced many talented and academically qualified athletes. Northern universities had been recruiting in the state for many years and had strengthened their teams with southern black players. The best example of this "brawn drain" from the Palmetto State was J. C. Caroline. An outstanding performer at the University of Illinois in the early 1950s, the powerful halfback played his high school football in Columbia only a few miles from the USC campus and was reportedly the first native of that city to earn All-America honors. In 1953 he led the NCAA in total rushing yardage and was subsequently honored by the city fathers with a hometown parade witnessed by an estimated fifteen thousand South Carolinians. Of course, Caroline had not been eligible at the time to attend the University of South Carolina because of his race. Most black sports fans believed that there were other black high school stars in the state who could likewise compete successfully on the major college level.[39]

In the spring of 1968 USC coaches came under criticism on campus for their failure to recruit African Americans. George Terry, assistant athletic director, denied these charges, asserting that the major problem for coaches was finding white or black athletes "who qualify on the field and in the classroom." The following spring complaints over recruiting resurfaced amid growing student protest at the university. In April 1969 the student senate debated and later tabled a thirteen-point proposal calling for the elimination of racial injustice at the university. One of these points specifically called for the inclusion of African Americans on all school athletic teams. That same month Paul Dietzel assured the student newspaper that school trustees had never pressured him to avoid recruiting blacks and that he had "been highly encouraged to recruit Negro athletes by the administration, the faculty, and the student body." The athletic director also disputed reports of racial friction between white athletes and black students on campus and accusations that USC fans had verbally harassed black basketball players on visiting teams. The awarding of two athletic scholarships, one in football and one in basketball, to black recruits later that spring undercut some of these attacks. At the end of the fall sports editor Bruce

Honick defended the athletic department in the *Gamecock*. Apparently basking in the glory of South Carolina's recent ACC football championship, won by an all-white team, Honick crudely asked, "What difference does it make whether there are black athletes or not as long as the football and basketball teams are doing well?" The sports editor further insisted that school coaches were color-blind and that African American players were themselves partially responsible for the minuscule number of black athletes on campus, because some of them were reluctant to attend a Deep South university. Honick reiterated that student critics were overemphasizing the race issue and that the Gamecocks should not "sign someone just because he is of a certain color."[40]

Dietzel and university officials eventually exploited the issue of recruiting minority athletes as part of their continuing dispute with the ACC over the conference's high scholarship requirements. They may also have felt pressured by recent inquiries from the U.S. Department of Health, Education, and Welfare concerning integration at the school, including the athletic program. Many ACC football coaches and administrators at USC and Clemson had complained bitterly about this issue since 1965, when the conference raised the minimum SAT score for scholarship athletes from 750 to 800. Football coaches believed that this requirement, the highest among the major national conferences, unfairly diverted talent to rival leagues, especially the Southeastern Conference. The extremely poor showing by ACC teams in nonconference games compounded their unhappiness. Initially, of course, all of the athletes denied admission were white. But as critics began to question the lack of black athletes on campus, USC officials increasingly blamed the 800 rule as the principal barrier to their inclusion. In the fall of 1970 the student government president, Mike Spears, proposed lowering the university's entrance requirements for African Americans, arguing that the second-class education provided by the state left many of them initially behind their white classmates. Spears stressed that the university "needs to recruit black students, particularly athletes." The sports editor of the *Gamecock,* Bill Currie, attacked the 800 rule and identified misguided academics as the real culprits. "The very professors who weep for the black man in the classroom are the same ones who are keeping so many first class black athletes out of the ACC schools," he argued.[41]

The athletic department's campaign for relief from the 800 rule took a dramatic turn in 1970. On October 23 the Board of Trustees authorized university officials to ignore the ACC policy and instructed coaches that they could begin recruiting under the lower NCAA requirements in September 1971. Trustees at Clemson University subsequently approved a similar policy for their institution, declaring that "the ACC cut-off rule is educationally unsound and athletically unsound." This decision came after five years of repeated conflict between the university and the ACC. For example, in 1966 the conference had ordered the

Gamecocks to forfeit all of their 1965 football victories after it was discovered that two players on the team had not earned the minimum SAT score. The new action taken by the trustees guaranteed a confrontation with the ACC. Trying to avert secession by the two colleges from South Carolina, conference members approved a limited concession. The new ACC provision stated that prospective athletes scoring between 700 and 799 on the SAT could still be eligible if their projected college grade point average (determined by an NCAA formula) was slightly higher than the NCAA minimum. USC administrators and trustees rejected this modification and announced that the university would officially withdraw from the ACC on August 15, 1971.[42]

While the University of South Carolina was engaged in its fight with the ACC, public school desegregation finally became a reality across the state. In September 1969 only twelve of the state's ninety-three public school districts contained an integrated school, as state and local politicians fought to the bitter end against desegregation. But by the fall of 1970 a majority of these districts had completely exhausted their legal options and began to desegregate their schools. With whites and blacks now starting to play together on high school teams, the racial composition of the state's college teams no longer seemed quite so controversial. Ironically, it was not the state's premier public university but rather many of the state's high schools who were the racial pioneers in athletic integration. These changes on the secondary level in turn made it easier for USC to modify its traditional recruiting policies for athletics.[43]

In 1969 and 1970 Paul Dietzel finally issued South Carolina's first athletic scholarships to African Americans. Carlton Haywood, a halfback from Macon, Georgia, became his first black recruit. Haywood played on the 1969 freshman team but then sat out the following year. Consequently, the first African American to earn a varsity letter in football was Jackie Brown. A wide receiver from Jonesville, North Carolina, Brown originally came to USC in 1969 on a baseball scholarship but switched to football in the fall of 1970. The following year Brown, Haywood, and sophomore Thad Rowe all saw considerable playing time on the Gamecock varsity squad. In 1972 Brown, Rowe, and four more black players suited up for USC and earned varsity letters. One year later, with freshmen now eligible after an NCAA rule change, ten black Gamecocks reported for fall drills, a remarkable change from the 1969 season, when every player on the school's ACC championship team had been white. The presence of African Americans forced a few changes by the athletic department. In the spring of 1972 Dietzel slightly relaxed team rules concerning personal appearance and permitted football players to have neat mustaches, after black players complained that facial hair was part of their cultural heritage. Another change came in 1973, when South Carolina hired its first African American assistant coach, Oree Banks.[44]

USC administrators and Dietzel had anticipated that by withdrawing from the ACC and thereby escaping its 800 SAT rule, the Gamecock athletic teams would be able to improve their performance. Despite the eventual addition of black athletes as well, their hopes were not fulfilled. In August 1972 the ACC hastily dropped the 800 SAT requirement, after a federal judge unexpectedly ruled in favor of two white plaintiffs who had challenged the requirement's legality. The conference then replaced the 800 rule with the lower NCAA standard. South Carolina's departure from the league now seemed rash, and the school lost its temporary recruiting advantage over its former conference rivals. On the grid-iron the Gamecock football team achieved no more success as an independent than it had as an ACC member. Moreover, the elimination from the schedule of all games against traditional ACC rivals except for Clemson hurt spectator interest in football and especially basketball. In 1980 the Gamecocks did record one impressive milestone, however, when black running back George Rogers led the NCAA in rushing and won the Heisman Trophy. Rogers was the first player from one of the eight original ACC schools to receive the prestigious award, an honor that had eluded all of the conference's white players during the era of segregation. Despite this achievement, South Carolina's decision to abandon the ACC proved disastrous for the school's athletic program.[45]

Clemson Delays Athletic Integration

Clemson University and the University of Virginia were the last two ACC members to field integrated varsity football teams, finally abandoning the color line in the fall of 1971. Clemson had been founded in 1888 as Clemson Agricultural College of South Carolina and named for Thomas Green Clemson, the son-in-law of Senator John C. Calhoun, the state's most famous political leader. In 1964 school officials simplified the official name of the institution to Clemson University. Like other land-grant institutions, Clemson required its all-male student body to enroll in military training, retaining the requirement until 1955. Clemson's small-town location, its emphasis on agricultural and manual training, and its military orientation combined to create an especially conservative social and cultural atmosphere on campus. As a result, the college "was one of the last land grant schools to admit women and abandon the military emphasis." In such a traditional and heavily masculine environment, intercollegiate athletics traditionally received strong support from students and alumni.[46]

Clemson administrators strongly resisted any efforts to desegregate the university after World War II. In 1948 they rejected two black applicants, a policy that they continued to follow throughout the following decade. During the 1960s and 1970s President Robert C. Edwards presided over the transformation of the school "from a small, segregated agricultural and military college for men into a coeducational, racially integrated university with a diversified curriculum." Although the state's leading politicians vehemently opposed desegregation of higher education, they also did not want racial violence to harm the state's image or frighten away outside investors. After losing a protracted legal battle in federal court, Edwards and his staff developed a carefully managed plan for peaceful integration. On January 28, 1963, Harvey Gantt, a native of Charleston, quietly enrolled as the first African American student at Clemson. So successful was the university's strategy that the *Saturday Evening Post* titled its report on the event "Integration with Dignity." An architecture major, Gantt became the first black student to attend a white public college within the state since Reconstruction. The personable young man eventually won "*almost* complete acceptance" from Clemson students and four years later became the school's first black graduate. The number of applications from black students remained modest, though, and by the fall of 1969 there were only an estimated seventy-five African Americans enrolled. The athletic department showed no interest in recruiting black athletes until the late 1960s, a position apparently supported by many of its key financial supporters.[47]

Prior to the 1950s Clemson athletic teams had consistently refused to compete against African Americans. The school's dual commitment to winning football games and maintaining the color line hit a snag in late 1956, however, when Clemson captured its first ACC title and received an automatic invitation to the Orange Bowl. University officials became concerned when they discovered that their opponent, the University of Colorado, had two African Americans on its team. Their fears were justified, as anti-integration sentiments dominated political discourse within the state after the *Brown* decision. Earlier in 1956 ultraconservatives had completely controlled the so-called segregation session of the state legislature, which adopted a wide array of laws buttressing the state's Jim Crow system. Yet white South Carolinians also passionately loved their football and the glory that gridiron victories brought to their state. Moreover, the Tigers' unexpected success each week during the fall had steadily increased public support for the team. Consequently, Governor George B. Timmerman Jr., a strong segregationist, allowed the Tigers to go to Miami. Clemson's participation in the Orange Bowl demonstrated that, even at the high point of political resistance to integration, the state's political leaders, unlike those in Mississippi, were still willing to allow big-time football a partial dispensation from Jim Crow, provided that the integrated contest took place outside the state. This special exemption for football testified to the strong grip that the sport retained on the hearts and minds of white South Carolinians.[48]

Despite the Orange Bowl trip, Clemson officials made it perfectly clear that they had no intention of modifying their commitment to racial exclusion at home. An incident in October 1957 involving the marching band from North

Carolina State demonstrated their resolve. While at Clemson to perform during a football game, the entire N.C. State band, including its first black member, Walter Holmes, ate a special meal in a reserved section of the student cafeteria. Apparently, this was the first time that an African American had ever been served in a Clemson dining hall. After learning about the meal, outraged segregationists condemned the incident as "a foot in the door" for integration and collected several thousand signatures on petitions to the governor criticizing Clemson's behavior. Embarrassed university officials responded that the lunch had been a separate, private meal and that the band had not physically mixed with Clemson students. Nevertheless, they still apologized publicly for this breach of racial etiquette. Clemson president Robert F. Poole even felt it necessary to meet with the state attorney general, after which he reaffirmed that the college would continue to refuse to play "racially mixed" teams at home.[49]

Clemson officials maintained the athletic color line on campus into the early 1960s, but they were eventually forced to accept integrated competition. In the spring of 1958 and 1960 university administrators had refused to allow the integrated N.C. State tennis team to play on the USC courts. After Harvey Gantt enrolled in January 1963, formal resistance to competing against black athletes declined. In September 1963 the Tiger football team made a road trip to the University of Oklahoma and played what was apparently Clemson's first integrated regular-season contest. Later that season Clemson hosted the Maryland Terrapins and wide receiver Darryl Hill, the ACC's first black football player. Many Tiger fans were outraged over what they viewed as the desecration of their sacred playing field, and they, along with Coach Frank Howard, gave Hill a hostile reception. Howard, a large and somewhat intimidating man, headed the Tiger football program from 1940 to 1969. In the late 1960s the once popular coach came under fire because of the absence of African Americans from his football team, his old-fashioned personal style, and his antagonism toward social change on campus. After the 1969 season Howard stepped down as coach and was appointed athletic director.[50]

Complaints about the absence of African Americans from Clemson athletic teams mounted in 1969 and 1970, as black students increasingly criticized conditions at the university. President Robert C. Edwards denied that the football program rejected black high school prospects. Instead, he blamed the ACC requirement of a minimum score of 800 on the SAT, calling the rule "a major obstacle in the recruiting of black athletes." Hootie Ingram, Howard's successor as head coach, supervised the actual integration of the football team. The first African American to receive an athletic scholarship at Clemson was Marion Francis Reeves, a defensive back from Irmo, South Carolina. As a sophomore in 1971 Reeves eventually earned a starting position on the varsity. In 1972 four additional black players joined Reeves on the varsity squad. One year later, with the 800 rule gone and freshman now eligible for varsity competition, the Tiger roster included a dozen African Americans, and the number of African American players grew steadily thereafter.[51]

Clemson's football fortunes slowly improved in the late 1970s. Under Coach Danny Ford, the Tigers went undefeated during the 1981 regular season and beat Nebraska in the Orange Bowl to claim the national championship. Black athletes made up nearly half of that team, exactly ten years after Marion Francis Reeves had become the first African American to join the Tiger varsity. This dramatic change in the racial composition of the Clemson football team surprised many fans who remembered the university's earlier resistance to integrated competition. Darryl Hill, the former Maryland star, watched the Orange Bowl game on television. He was stunned to see the large number of black players on the Clemson team, since he remembered quite clearly the hostile atmosphere that existed at the university back in 1963. Unfortunately, other athletic problems dating from the era of all-white teams continued. In the 1970s the NCAA put the Tiger basketball team on probation for improper financial aid to players. After another investigation in the early 1980s the NCAA also placed the football program on probation and banned the Tigers from bowl games for two years. Illegal payoffs, an obsession with winning at any cost, and lack of institutional control continued to plague college athletics in the post–civil rights era. Integration changed the racial composition of Clemson teams, but it did not resolve these perennial problems in big-time college football.[52]

Virginia Finally Integrates Its Football Team

Along with Clemson, the University of Virginia was the last ACC member to finally abandon racial exclusion for its football team. Founded by Thomas Jefferson in 1819, the university enjoyed a strong reputation for academic excellence. Virginia fielded its first official football team in 1888, but the golden years of Cavalier football came after World War II under the leadership of Coach Art Guepe. From 1946 through 1952 Guepe compiled a record of forty-seven wins and seventeen losses, making him the most successful coach in the university's history. But academic critics worried that football had assumed too dominant a role on campus, and in 1951 a special university committee recommended that the sport be discontinued. Although school officials rejected this drastic proposal, they did issue a ban on postseason bowl games. Guepe promptly departed for Vanderbilt in disgust, and UVa's football fortunes declined sharply. From 1953 through 1982 the Cavaliers achieved only two winning seasons and suffered the further indignity of a twenty-eight-game losing streak from 1958 to 1960. Virginia's high academic standards, serious intellectual atmosphere, and upper-class image did not always prove attractive to white football players, many of whom came from working-class backgrounds. Decades of losing seasons made successful recruiting even more difficult. Unlike Wake Forest, UVa coaches did not consider the early recruitment of African American athletes as an acceptable strategy to improve their teams' performances.[53]

After World War II black Virginians increasingly challenged segregation at the university as part of a larger attack on the inequities of graduate education in the state. In 1950 the university admitted its first African American students to the School of Law and the Graduate School. In September 1955, following the *Brown* decision, Virginia allowed its first black undergraduates to enroll specifically in the School of Engineering. However, no African Americans were admitted into the School of Arts and Sciences until 1961. The slowness of these changes did little to improve the negative image that black Virginians held toward the university. In 1967 there were only 19 black undergraduates among the entire student body, and by 1970 the number had grown only to 121 undergraduates. Because of the tiny size of the black cohort on campus and the university's traditional image as a bastion of white privilege, talented black athletes were understandably hesitant to enroll. The first brief effort to integrate the Cavalier football squad occurred in early 1956. On February 27 George Harris, a freshman engineering major and one of three black undergraduates at the university, reported for spring training along with 60 other students. Harris's second day of drills was cut short when coaches learned that he was on academic probation and hence ineligible to practice. Harris's limited appearance still lasted long enough to provoke one letter of protest to President Colgate W. Darden. J. W. Hudson, a Cavalier fan and ardent segregationist, indignantly wrote, "Just why should this 'Nigger' be issued a shirt in the first place?" Although the exchange was private, President Darden did not hesitate to defend Harris's brief appearance, responding that the athletic department had treated Harris just like any other student. "This is as it should be," he asserted.[54]

In the early 1960s two minor sports were integrated at Virginia. During the 1963–64 school year freshman George King III, a former high school football player, took up wrestling and then lacrosse, primarily to keep in shape. Despite his lack of experience, he earned letters in both of these non-scholarship sports. King's coaches and teammates strongly supported his participation in athletics, but he dropped out of the university after three semesters because of academic difficulties. King's brief career did not alter recruitment practices for football and basketball. By the mid-1960s the continuing absence of African Americans from Cavalier teams provoked several attacks on the university. In March 1966 both the state office of the NAACP and the Virginia Council on Human Relations publicly accused the school of racial discrimination in athletics. As one black spokesman complained, "While Duke, UNC, Wake Forest, V.P.I. [Virginia Tech], and other surrounding institutions are actively seeking Negro recruits on the same basis as whites, UVA has not even advanced as far as its usual position of tokenism." Liberal white students on campus formed a protest organization, Students for Social Action, which pressed for an end to racial "tokenism" at the university. The group reported that several coaches had privately admitted that they had not actively recruited blacks, because "we have not been given the green light." The reason for this hesitancy, the group charged, was "the fear of a drop in contributions from alumni to the Student Aid Foundation," which funded athletic scholarships.[55]

President Edgar F. Shannon (1959–74) denied the charges of intentional discrimination and reaffirmed a commitment to equality of opportunity for athletics. Shannon subsequently instructed the athletic department to make sure that its coaches did not overlook any potential athlete and to document all contacts with potential black recruits. Football coaches made several scholarship offers to black athletes over the next three years, but none of them accepted. In the spring of 1969 Nat Lucas, a non-scholarship athlete, competed in the high jump for the track team, and thereafter a few other black students tried out for the freshman football and basketball teams. Head football coach George Blackburn finally broke the color line in 1970 by awarding scholarships to four African American athletes, all of them from Virginia. In the fall of 1971 the group made their debut on the Cavalier varsity, along with walk-on Gary Ham. Several of them had an immediate impact. Harrison Davis III earned a starting berth as quarterback for much of the season, while halfback Kent Merritt led the squad in rushing yardage and was later voted the team's MVP. Stanley "Bubba" Land, an end, started every game on defense for the Cavs. Virginia recruited additional African American players over the following years. The gradual growth in black enrollment aided this expanded recruiting by creating a more comfortable social setting for prospective athletes. Still, it took another decade before black high school athletes in the state thought more positively about Mr. Jefferson's university.[56]

* * *

During the period from 1963 to 1980 sweeping change took place on the gridiron within the Atlantic Coast Conference. When junior wide receiver Darryl Hill took the field for the University of Maryland in 1963, he became the first African American to play football in the ACC. Maryland's decision to drop its internal color line did not immediately inspire or scare fellow conference members into taking similar action. With the exception of Wake Forest in 1965, it would take five more years before any additional ACC college fielded an integrated varsity team and eight years before the last two conference holdouts, Clemson and Virginia, finally completed the conference's integration. The black athletes who became racial pioneers welcomed the challenge of succeeding in an overwhelmingly white atmosphere in order to prove their masculinity in a physically demanding sport and to demonstrate their intelligence in a competitive academic setting. This process was not unique to football, of course. ACC basketball also faced similar challenges during this period. Sometimes basketball culture proved more flexible in its race relations than did the more traditional sporting culture associated with football, but hostile fans crammed into a compact gymnasium could also harass black players more effectively than in a large football stadium. The next chapter will explore the racial dynamics of athletic integration in basketball, where once again ACC members acted somewhat sooner than their counterparts in the other two major southern conferences.

6

"Two at Home and Three on the Road"

The Atlantic Coast Conference and Basketball

I think that the more Charlie Scotts we have, the easier it
will be for the South to change its mind about Negroes.

—A University of North Carolina professor,
March 1969

"Dixie" is not the song for athletics.
We should let it die.

—University of South Carolina *Gamecock*,
February 1970

In March 1957 the University of North Carolina Tar Heels captured
their first National Collegiate Athletic Association basketball title with a thrilling
54–53 triple overtime victory over the Kansas Jayhawks and seven-foot center
Wilt Chamberlain. Coached by the flamboyant Frank McGuire, a New York City
native, the undefeated Tar Heels represented the Atlantic Coast Conference in
the NCAA tournament, and their national championship inspired widespread
pride among North Carolinians and many other southerners as well. Yet several observers noted that there was an ironic aspect to the squad's role in promoting regional pride, since all five Tar Heel starters, including All-American
Lenny Rosenbluth, hailed from the New York metropolitan area. In jest fans
sometimes humorously referred to McGuire's players as the "Noo Yawk Tar
Heels" or the squad of "four Catholics and a Jew." Except for the geographical
background of these "Rebel Yankees," however, the 1957 North Carolina team
closely resembled its counterparts at every other major southern university in
one important respect—its whiteness.[1]

In the spring of 1957 big-time college basketball in the eleven ex-Confederate
states was remarkably white. Not only was every ACC basketball team all-white,

but only three conference members—Maryland, North Carolina State, and the University of North Carolina—had fully desegregated their undergraduate student bodies. Within the rival Southeastern Conference, which included many schools in the Deep South, only the University of Kentucky permitted African American students to attend undergraduate classes. Therefore, when compared to other southern conferences and the major southern independents, the ACC's racial profile appeared quite normal. In fact, during that spring semester of 1957 every major historically white university located in the eleven ex-Confederate states, with the lone exception of Texas Western College in El Paso, maintained all-white basketball teams. The pervasiveness of Jim Crow policies in college sports demonstrated just how thoroughly racial segregation permeated virtually every aspect of southern life in the 1950s.

Seventeen years later another ACC champion captured the NCAA basketball title, but the racial composition of this North Carolina State team differed considerably from that of the 1957 UNC squad. In March 1974 N. C. State upset the defending champion UCLA Bruins in the semifinals and then defeated the Marquette Warriors 76–64 in the finals to claim the national championship. Leading the integrated Wolfpack squad to victory was national collegiate Player of the Year David Thompson, an African American and native North Carolinian. Three other African Americans joined him on the NCSU roster. Because of their race, however, none of the four could have played for their school back in 1957, the year of the North Carolina championship. The differences between the UNC and NCSU championship teams illustrated the historic changes that swept over ACC basketball during the late 1960s and early 1970s. Despite foot-dragging by several universities, all conference members had incorporated African Americans into their basketball teams by 1972. N.C. State's championship team of 1974 therefore accurately reflected the new, more inclusive world of southern universities, just as the 1957 UNC team had symbolically represented the older era of racial exclusion.[2]

This dramatic shift from rigidly segregated competition in the 1950s to the fully integrated structure of the 1970s is one of the least-remembered consequences of the civil rights era, and one of its most permanent accomplishments. The subsequent emergence in the ACC of such black basketball stars as Ralph Sampson, Michael Jordan, Grant Hill, and Tim Duncan in the 1980s and 1990s could not have occurred without this earlier racial transformation. From its beginnings in the first decade of the twentieth century through the 1960s, big-time southern college basketball had been exclusively the preserve of white athletes. Only after World War II did those schools that eventually formed the ACC begin to play against integrated northern teams. Even when the first black players joined conference schools, there still was some resistance to their full participation. Rumors of a quota system whereby African Americans would not be allowed to outnumber white players on the court, at least in front of the home fans, circulated widely. This glass ceiling for blacks was captured by the phrase "two at home and three on the road." The eventual appearance of black players wearing their school colors not only undermined old stereotypes about African Americans' ability to play in the highly competitive ACC but also focused attention on the continued use at athletic events of such traditional southern symbols as the Confederate battle flag and the song "Dixie." These remnants of an earlier and whiter age slowly retreated into the background, as black students increasingly challenged their legitimacy for a biracial student body. Eventually, racially inclusive teams themselves became a new symbol behind which both whites and blacks could unite, thus helping speed the process of reconciliation after two decades of racial conflict.

For the first half of the twentieth century basketball did not enjoy the widespread popularity that it later achieved across the ACC region. Most southern white universities formed their first organized teams in the first two decades of the twentieth century, but interest in the new sport lagged far behind football and even baseball for many years. After World War II basketball's popularity increased substantially, solidifying its position as the number-two sport on American college campuses. Enthusiasm ran much stronger at universities in the South Atlantic region and the states of Kentucky and Tennessee than in the Deep South and Southwest. Early successes by several future ACC teams, especially the N.C. State squads of the legendary Everett Case, stimulated greater interest in the sport. In 1946 the University of North Carolina advanced to the finals of the NCAA Tournament, losing the championship to Oklahoma A&M. When North Carolina won the NCAA championship in 1957, the first ever by an ACC club, the conference received increased national recognition and respect. From 1960 through 1969 ACC representatives in the NCAA playoffs advanced to what is now called the Final Four in seven out of ten seasons, though none of them was able to bring home a championship trophy. Basketball developed a vast army of passionate fans, especially in the state of North Carolina. Unlike the situation in other southern conferences, basketball in the ACC enjoyed near-equal status with football.[3]

The NCAA's tournament playoff system made it more difficult for southern white basketball teams to avoid facing integrated northern rivals than was the case with college football and its postseason bowl games, most of which were located in the South and historically had excluded African Americans. For the NCAA Tournament the ACC schools were automatically assigned to the eastern region because of their geographical location. This meant that they frequently had to compete against teams from the New York and Philadelphia metropolitan areas. These two cities produced some of the best high school and college basketball players in the country, and teams from there reflected the ethnic and racial diversity of the area. By the early 1950s many of these northern teams included one or two African American players. In order to pursue basketball glory ACC schools pragmatically accepted integrated competition. Moreover, scheduling regular-season games against nationally ranked northern teams, especially in such prestigious venues as Madison Square Garden in New York and the Palestra in Philadelphia, gave conference members additional media exposure. With the exception of Clemson and South Carolina, most ACC teams soon came to view integrated games as a minor cost of maintaining big-time basketball programs. This flexible policy contrasted with the strong resistance to integrated play often found in the Deep South. In North Carolina a holiday basketball tournament involving four ACC teams provided an important transition from segregated to integrated competition in the heart of ACC country.[4]

The Dixie Classic Breaks the Color Line

In the late 1940s and early 1950s the academic and corporate supporters of big-time basketball in the state of North Carolina made several decisions that greatly affected the sport's future. First, they gained funding for the construction of a new state-of-the-art basketball facility in Raleigh. Reynolds Coliseum opened in December 1949 with a seating capacity of 12,400 and was reportedly the largest field house in the Southeast. Next, basketball boosters established a major holiday tournament, the Dixie Classic, held annually in Raleigh between Christmas and New Year's Day. The remarkably popular event lasted from 1949 through 1960 and consistently drew overflow crowds to the coliseum. Finally, this coalition launched an aggressive campaign to host the annual NCAA regional tournament. The NCAA awarded the tournament to Raleigh beginning in 1951, a substantial victory for North Carolina tourism but one that also meant accepting integrated basketball teams assigned to the venue by the national organization.[5]

The Dixie Classic aggressively recruited the top teams from around the country. The event's format called for an eight-team tournament, with each of the four local colleges—Duke, Wake Forest, North Carolina, and North Carolina State—taking on one of the four visiting teams in the opening round. The tournament became an instant hit. "It was the Sugar Bowl and the Rose Bowl rolled into one," one administrator observed. Shortly after Christmas each year, carloads of die-hard basketball fans from across the region descended on Reynolds Coliseum for three nights of outstanding basketball and heavy partying. In addition to generating considerable revenue for the participants and positive publicity for the state, the tournament also played an important role as a pathbreaker in interracial competition. The tournament's founders agreed from the first that black players could not be excluded if they wanted a highly successful tournament. Nonetheless, for the first few years officials discouraged visiting squads from bringing along African Americans, because of the inconveniences they would face in a segregated city. For example, Pennsylvania State University agreed to participate in the inaugural classic in 1949, but tournament organizers convinced the school to leave its one African American player at home. In 1950 the University of Oregon faced the same dilemma, but after much discussion the college decided to skip the tournament rather than exclude a team member because of his race.[6]

By 1952 basketball sponsors in Raleigh worried less about the difficulty of accommodating black athletes. In February the Boston Celtic team, which included Charles Cooper, the first African American drafted by the National Basketball Association, broke the color line in Reynolds Coliseum during a special NBA game. One month later in the NCAA regional tournament, Penn State's Jesse Arnelle became the first black collegian to play in the arena. In order to minimize problems with segregated local businesses, the Penn State squad stayed on the N.C. State campus and took their meals in a private dining room in the campus cafeteria. This policy was personally approved by NCSU chancellor Carey H. Bostian, who commented to the school's athletic director, "I hope that this policy will enable you to entertain visiting teams having Negro players without any embarrassment to them." Sponsors of the Dixie Classic aggressively used this arrangement to convince integrated northern teams to participate in their tournament.

In 1958 organizers scheduled the most exciting tournament field ever, with black stars Oscar Robertson of Cincinnati and Johnny Green of Michigan State leading their number-one and number-two nationally ranked teams into Reynolds Coliseum. Both schools had been assured that their squads would receive first-class treatment in Raleigh. Robertson turned in a series of spectacular performances, awing the crowd with his deft moves and accurate shooting. The Cincinnati star so impressed Coach Everett Case of NCSU that Case began to think back to 1947, when Jackie Robinson had broken the color line in Major League Baseball. Comparing Oscar Robertson to Robinson, Case joked to reporters, "I know a lot of southern coaches who would like to pull a Branch Rickey with that boy." Because of the presence of Cincinnati and Michigan State, the tournament turned into a financial gold mine for its sponsors, who sold a record seventy-three thousand tickets for the three-day event. To the delight of local fans, N.C. State defeated Cincinnati in the semifinals and Michigan State in the finals to capture the tournament title. As far as sponsors were concerned, the 1958 edition of the classic had been a tremendous success.[7]

For Oscar Robertson and the Cincinnati Bearcats, however, the experience had been considerably less satisfying. The loss of two consecutive games upset Coach George Smith, who blamed hometown officiating in part for his team's defeats. Back in Ohio, Smith and Robertson both complained publicly about eating and housing conditions in Raleigh, as well as crowd behavior. Robertson was personally indignant that the Cincinnati squad could not stay at a downtown hotel like the other teams and instead were housed at an N.C. State dormitory, along with the four black players from Michigan State. Smith and Robertson were also upset about an incident in the opening game against Wake Forest, when Robertson and the Deacons' Dave Budd became involved in what was variously described as a "tussle," a "shoving match," and a "fight" as they struggled for a rebound. Officials and coaches quickly intervened to prevent the skirmish from escalating into a full-scale brawl, and both players were permitted to remain in the game. Despite Cincinnati's complaints the Dixie Classic's sponsors invited the Bearcats back the following year, but Cincinnati officials instead chose to compete in a holiday tournament in New York City, where there was no segregation in public accommodations.[8]

The Dixie Classic eventually became a victim of its own success. By the late 1950s administrators at several conference schools worried that the event had gotten out of control. The freewheeling atmosphere at the event raised fears about contact between players and professional gamblers, a serious concern given recent point-shaving scandals. The increasingly commercialized aspect of the tournament and its extensive utilization by coaches as a recruiting device further troubled university administrators. In fact, the NCAA subsequently placed the University of North Carolina on probation for violations that included excessive entertainment of prospective recruits at the classic. Several ACC members also complained that N.C. State gained a competitive recruiting advantage from hosting the tournament on its campus. Anxious to reassert their control of athletics, administrators in the North Carolina higher-education system unexpectedly canceled the tournament in 1961. They further decided to limit temporarily the number of out-of-state athletes that N.C. State and UNC could recruit. These actions were part of a larger reform movement within the ACC, which resulted in a new requirement mandating that prospective athletes score at least a 750 (later raised to 800) on the SAT. Despite its untimely death the Dixie Classic had achieved its goal of greatly increasing basketball enthusiasm in the region by bringing together many of the top college teams in the nation, regardless of their racial composition. The tournament, along with the continuing successes of North Carolina's four ACC schools, also helped transform college basketball into "one of the state's most beloved institutions" and "a cherished component of Tar Heel identity."[9]

During its twelve-year lifetime the Dixie Classic served as a useful transition in race relations for the four North Carolina participants, undermining basketball's commitment to segregation. This acceptance of integrated games was increasingly important, because by the late 1950s black players had achieved a major role in the college game nationally. In 1955 and 1956 Bill Russell led the

University of San Francisco Dons to back-to-back NCAA championships. In 1958 the Associated Press named four African Americans—Oscar Robertson of Cincinnati, Elgin Baylor of Seattle, Wilt Chamberlain of Kansas, and Guy Rodgers of Temple—to its All-America first team, the most ever. The National Basketball Coaches Association also selected those four, plus Bob Boozer of Kansas State, for its All-America squad, creating the first all-black national All-America team. If the ACC wished to remain one of the premier conferences in the country, its members would need to play integrated teams on a regular basis. By the early 1960s several ACC coaches quietly began contemplating the possibility of recruiting talented African American players for their own teams.[10]

Maryland Breaks the Color Line in Basketball

Just as it had done in football, the University of Maryland played a pioneering role in the integration of ACC basketball. Since public school desegregation had started much earlier in the state than elsewhere in the ACC, the idea of integrated college teams did not seem unusual by 1960. The Terrapins traditionally had produced average basketball teams in the tough ACC competition, so the recruitment of African Americans offered the school the opportunity to strengthen its program. The head coach at Maryland was H. A. "Bud" Millikan, a Missouri native and former All-America college player at the University of Oklahoma. Millikan directed the Terrapin program from 1950 to 1967 and won the ACC Tournament championship in 1958, the school's only title until 1975.

Maryland dropped all racial barriers to its athletic teams in the early 1960s, but it took several years before the university successfully recruited its first black basketball players. In the spring of 1962 Millikan announced that the basketball squad was now open to any student and that he was actively scouting black high school prospects. Over the next two years a few African American students practiced with the team as walk-ons, but none displayed enough skill to earn a scholarship. One promising recruit turned down Millikan in order to sign a minor-league baseball contract. Finally, in April 1964, the university announced that Billy Jones, a 6'1" guard from predominantly white Towson (Maryland) High School, had accepted a scholarship offer. An all-state selection, Jones had scored forty-one points and thirty-two points in the two games of the state Class AA high school tournament, leading his team to second place. Millikan praised Jones as a "high class young man" and a conscientious student who had made a good score on his SAT. Just over a month later, Maryland signed a second African American player, 6'0" guard Julius "Pete" Johnson of Fairmont Heights, Maryland. Johnson had averaged more than twenty-three points per game as a senior for the Class A state champions. The Maryland high school basketball tournament had been held for several years in Cole Field House on the Maryland campus, so Jones and Johnson were already familiar with the school's athletic facilities. Jones had also attended a Boys State conference at the university. Since Maryland had signed two black high school football stars earlier in the year, Jones and Johnson knew that they would not be completely alone on the UM campus.[11]

Millikan took no special measures to ease Jones and Johnson into the athletic program, nor did he hold any lengthy discussions with them about their unique role as racial pioneers. For their part, neither player specifically set out to break the ACC's color line. Being a racial trailblazer "never entered my thoughts," Jones later recalled. "I was kind of naive, and I guess in some ways I'm glad I was." Perhaps because he had attended integrated schools since the seventh grade, Jones was not intimidated by a predominantly white university. He selected the University of Maryland, a popular destination for many of his high school classmates, because "I saw no reason why I shouldn't go there." The veteran white Terrapin players greeted their two new black teammates in a friendly manner once school began and quickly incorporated them into pickup games. Their freshman season went smoothly, with Jones and Johnson each averaging nearly twenty points per game. Except for publishing several articles about the students' decision to attend Maryland, the local press did not devote any special attention to them.[12]

While Pete Johnson sat out his second year at Maryland in order to improve his academic record, Billy Jones became the first African American to see varsity action in the ACC during the 1966 season as a sophomore. Before the Terrapins made their annual trip south to play Clemson and the University of South Carolina, Millikan did have a rare talk with Jones about the fact that he would be the first black collegian to play on those schools' basketball courts, which Jones had not realized. On these road trips southward his white teammates were very protective of him. Prior to one such departure an older teammate put his arm around Jones and told him, "Don't worry about a thing." Such firm support made a deep impression on Jones and gave him additional confidence on the court. Still, he played sparingly in away games his sophomore year, and he later concluded that Millikan had probably limited his exposure before hostile crowds in order to shield him from any undue pressure or racial incidents. On most of his ACC road trips Jones avoided potential problems over lingering segregation in local entertainment spots by spending much of his free time socializing with students at nearby black colleges.

Both Jones and Pete Johnson made valuable contributions to the Terrapins over the next two years. In Jones's senior season he served as cocaptain, while Johnson led the Terrapins in scoring. During their careers at College Park, the two racial pioneers did not encounter any major racial incidents at rival schools, although fans did occasionally yell racial slurs at them. Jones speculated that because ACC fans "really loved their basketball," they tended to overlook race. "As long as you had a road uniform on, they weren't particularly fond of you," he later recalled. "But they didn't care what color your skin was." In College Park, Jones and Johnson socialized informally with their white teammates in the dormitories and elsewhere on campus. Unlike most of their teammates, however, they were never invited to pledge a fraternity or attend fraternity parties, making them feel at times like they were only "partial citizens" on campus. Despite their closeness, team members never discussed race relations with each other, perhaps because they had no precedents or models to guide them. In later years both players revealed that they had been less content at the university than they had indicated at the time, hiding their true feelings from all but their closest friends.[13]

Despite the addition of Jones and Johnson, Maryland's basketball fortunes continued to languish through several mediocre seasons. Millikan retired in 1967 and was briefly replaced by assistant coach Frank Fellows. The university next hired Charles "Lefty" Driesell, a highly successful coach from Davidson College, for the 1970 season. A consummate showman, Driesell "reinvigorated" Maryland basketball through his dramatic personality, elaborate theatrics, and aggressive recruiting. In one of his first decisions Driesell hired George Raveling for the position of senior assistant coach, the highest post filled by a black coach in the ACC to that date. Raveling would later serve as head coach at Iowa and the University of Southern California. Driesell's first team finished at 13-13, but he then proceeded to post sixteen consecutive winning seasons. The flamboyant coach actively sought out the best available talent, black or white, and by the 1973 season Maryland listed eight African Americans on its varsity roster, reflecting black players' significant presence in the college game, even in the South.[14]

Duke Is Number Two

After Maryland broke the ACC's color line in basketball, the four conference members from North Carolina began to look more closely at potential black recruits. Anxious to remain competitive in the tough ACC, these schools did not let the conference's 800 SAT requirement, political opposition to school desegregation, or the diffidence of some athletic boosters deter them. Duke University soon became the second league member to abandon the color line in basketball. The Blue Devils were a regional power of long standing, having suffered only one losing season between 1928 and 1972. Under the leadership of Vic Bubas in the 1960s they enhanced their national stature by winning four straight regular-season ACC titles. In three of those years Duke also won the conference tournament and advanced all the way to the NCAA Final Four, but the Blue Devils fell short of the national championship each time. Although

Duke eliminated all racial restrictions on admissions in 1962, only about two dozen black undergraduates were enrolled as of September 1966. An affluent white atmosphere, as well as Duke's high entrance requirements and previous history of segregation, did not create an attractive environment for African American students or athletes. Beginning in 1964 a few students began to question whether Coach Vic Bubas was really willing to recruit African Americans. The whiteness of the Duke basketball program also received unwelcome national attention in December 1965 when *Sports Illustrated* reported that three black UCLA players had been the targets of "crude racial taunts" when Duke hosted the Bruins in Durham. President Douglas M. Knight and athletic director Eddie Cameron promptly denied that the school ignored prospective black athletes and placed the blame for the fan abuse on members of a visiting junior college basketball team.[15]

Complaints about the absence of black athletes eased somewhat after Claudius B. Claiborne enrolled at Duke in the fall of 1965. Claiborne's arrival on campus did not attract media attention, since the Danville, Virginia, native entered Duke on an academic scholarship in order to study engineering. However, the basketball staff also had encouraged him to enroll, and he became a steady performer on the freshman team. He was unable to attend the 1966 basketball honors banquet, though, because it was held at the segregated Hope Valley Country Club. As a sophomore during the 1967 season, the 6'2" guard became the first African American to appear in a varsity game for the Blue Devils, eventually earning an athletic scholarship. The following year Claiborne played frequently as a substitute, and as a senior he started several contests but played less in the second half of the season after attracting Bubas's disfavor for growing a large Afro. During Claiborne's first two years at Duke he felt that (in contrast to Billy Jones at Maryland) he played more minutes in road games than he did at home in front of the Blue Devils' white fans. Fans in the Deep South seemed more hostile than elsewhere. Once in a game at Tuscaloosa, Alabama fans stood behind the backboard waving Confederate flags and voicing "rebel yells" when he attempted to shoot free throws. On the Duke campus Claiborne socialized some with his white teammates and his fellow engineering students, and as a sophomore he became one of the first African Americans to pledge a fraternity at Duke. For additional social opportunities he frequently visited nearby North Carolina Central College, a historically black university. Claiborne eventually earned a degree in engineering, having proved that he could compete both on the basketball court and in the classroom at a prestigious ACC university.[16]

During his three-year career with the Blue Devils, Claiborne remained highly visible because he was the only black scholarship athlete on either the varsity football or the varsity basketball team. By the 1968–69 school year African American students, despite their tiny numbers, and sympathetic whites publicly questioned many racial practices on campus. These activists focused less on sports than did their counterparts at most other southern schools, but they did challenge some of the cultural traditions closely associated with Blue Devil athletics. In particular they criticized the display of the Confederate battle flag and the playing of "Dixie" at athletic events and other school functions, even though Duke did not utilize these two cultural icons as extensively as did many other southern colleges. In October 1968 a campus race relations committee publicized a long list of student complaints concerning racial conditions. In the area of athletics the committee reported that African Americans were disturbed by the use of the flag and the song, which they believed "was a symbolic display of support of Old Southern race codes." The committee report touched off a testy campus debate over this issue. Many faculty and some white students, especially those from the North, saw no need to continue using the flag and the song, while other white students, especially native southerners, many band members, and several cheerleaders, strongly opposed dropping the traditional symbols. They argued that both were part of their southern heritage and that they had been misinterpreted by critics. As one white undergraduate explained, "When someone plays 'Dixie' or waves a Rebel flag, he is not boasting of Confederate suppression of Negroes. . . . He does it now to tell the world that he is from the South and proud of it." As the dispute continued the only black member of the marching band threatened to resign if the band continued to play "Dixie," while several white members in turn threatened to drop out if the band stopped performing the song. After much equivocation President Douglas M. Knight finally asked band officials and the cheerleaders to abandon the two disputed symbols. Heated arguments about racial discrimination continued throughout the year, however, and eventually culminated in the temporary seizure of the administration building by black students and their removal by local police.[17]

Meanwhile, Duke's efforts to recruit African American players proceeded very slowly. During Claudius Claiborne's senior season in 1968–69 Duke awarded an athletic scholarship to Don Blackman, a high school All-American from Brooklyn. Blackman displayed great potential during his two years with the Blue Devils, but he chose not to return for the 1971 season, making Duke and Virginia the only two ACC varsity teams without black members that year. Sam May of Tacoma, Washington, started on the Duke freshman team that season, but he in turn chose not to return for the 1972 season. Partially in response to these recruiting and retention problems, second-year head coach Bucky Waters hired Jim Lewis in 1971 as the college's first black assistant coach. Lewis had played for Waters at West Virginia University and was the first full-time black assistant at any of the Big Four North Carolina colleges. In 1972 the Blue Devils recruited 6'9" center Willie Hodge from San Antonio, Texas. An NCAA rule that year made freshmen eligible for varsity play, allowing Hodge eventually to become one of the first four-year lettermen at Duke. Over the following years Duke experienced more success in attracting black players, but the school's unique circumstances continued to make athletic recruiting quite challenging.[18]

Athletic Success and Social Isolation at Wake Forest

During the 1967–68 season two more ACC teams fielded integrated basketball teams. Unlike Duke, both Wake Forest and the University of North Carolina immediately attracted black stars who contributed substantially to their teams' success. Despite its weak football program Wake Forest consistently produced successful and widely popular basketball teams. In the late 1940s Wake Forest began to play northern basketball teams in such venues as Madison Square Garden and the Palestra in Philadelphia, as part of a drive for national prominence. The university accepted the occasional presence of an African American on these northern teams without protest. Horace "Bones" McKinney, a colorful and popular figure, coached Wake Forest to even greater success from 1957 to 1965. McKinney's strong 1962 squad advanced to the NCAA finals, where they finished third. Wake Forest officials subsequently informed McKinney that he could now recruit black athletes. Although many of the university's older graduates expressed concern over the decision, other basketball fans pragmatically supported the recruiting change since it might strengthen the Deacon team.[19]

The possibility of becoming the first basketball coach in the ACC to break the color line appealed to Bones McKinney. He and his staff soon discovered Herb Gilliam, a talented player at a local high school. Assistant Coach Billy Packer, a former basketball star for the Deacons and future television sports commentator, initially convinced Gilliam to attend Wake Forest. Since the first SAT test score by the Winston-Salem native did not meet the ACC minimum, Packer encouraged him to take an SAT review course. On his second try Gilliam narrowly missed the mandatory score, much to Packer's dismay, and subsequently accepted a scholarship from Purdue University of the Big Ten, where he became an all-conference performer. Packer spent considerable time over the next two years in New York City, a fertile source of basketball talent. Eventually, he convinced Norwood Todmann, a 6'3" star at Power Memorial who had broken several school scoring records set by Lew Alcindor (Kareem Abdul-Jabbar), to enroll at Wake Forest. Todmann's recruitment opened the doors for a series of African American players at Wake Forest. The following year, two more highly recruited black players, Charles Davis from New York City, a childhood friend of Todmann, and Gil McGregor from Raeford, North Carolina, joined the Demon Deacon squad. Without Todmann's presence Davis might have gone elsewhere, since he had not seriously thought about playing for a southern university while growing up. As a racial pioneer on the court, Davis understood that the opportunity to play for a big-time ACC school was "a major break" and that his success there would open up additional opportunities for African Americans.[20]

Todmann, McGregor, and especially Davis, a 6'1" guard, had a major impact on the Deacon basketball program. In an outstanding sophomore season in 1968–69, Davis averaged twenty-three points per game, set a new Wake Forest single-game scoring mark of fifty-one points, finished fifth in the nation in free-throw accuracy, and earned first team All-ACC honors. Gil McGregor, a 6'7" inside player, also started on the varsity at times as a sophomore and provided defensive strength, while Todmann added eleven points per game. The Demon Deacons posted an 18-9 record, their best since 1962, en route to a third-place finish in the conference. Davis continued to dazzle opponents during his junior and senior seasons, earning All-ACC first-team honors both years. In 1971 sportswriters selected him as the league's most valuable player, the first African American to receive that honor. Davis led the league in free-throw shooting all three seasons and finished with a career average of twenty-five points per game, a Wake Forest record. Although injuries limited Todmann's playing time his senior season, McGregor continued his solid rebounding during his junior and senior years, nicely complementing Davis's outside game.[21]

As three of the first nine African American players in the ACC, Todmann, Davis, and McGregor occasionally encountered vestiges of earlier racism. Davis later recalled seeing a few "Whites Only" signs on campus when he arrived, but they soon disappeared. Although white students were not hostile, black players had only superficial interaction with them at first. During Davis's and McGregor's sophomore year of 1968–69, the campus experienced a variety of student protests. Black students and athletes joined liberal white students in specifically criticizing the use of Confederate symbols at the school. In November 1968 an integrated group dramatized the issue by burning a Confederate flag on the school plaza after chapel services. The ensuing discussion of race relations at the school revealed a wide gap between the expectations of black and white students. In criticizing conditions at the school, Davis, McGregor, and other black athletes specifically exempted the athletic program. As one football player remarked, "The Athletic Department here is good, but the campus isn't." In a series of interviews with reporters from the school newspaper, a group of black athletes candidly expressed disappointment over their marginal status on campus. Although white students seemed friendly, the players lamented, they tended to view African Americans almost exclusively as one-dimensional figures. "I can never talk to a student without him bringing up the subject of basketball," McGregor told one reporter. Davis voiced similar concerns. "It is difficult to know who is accepting me as Charlie Davis, the person, and who is accepting me as Charlie Davis the basketball player," he said. "Many people give me the impression that they're speaking or smiling at me because I'm a black athlete." Another complaint focused on the tiny number of black female students on campus. As McGregor explained, "The biggest social problem the black athlete . . . faces is the ratio of girls on the campus." Consequently, many of these athletes went off-campus for social outlets. In the black community of Winston-Salem they found a significant source of encouragement. Aware of the pioneering role that these athletes were performing, local African Americans welcomed them with open arms, providing social opportunities and emotional support lacking on campus.[22]

The three athletes also worried about the influence that wealthy, influential donors had on Wake Forest athletics. They assumed that some of these older white fans were opposed to the pace of racial change in basketball. During the 1968–69 season, the first year that Todmann, Davis, and McGregor were all on the varsity together, they noticed that the three of them were rarely on the court at the same time. The following year the same arrangement continued, with Todmann, a senior, the odd man out. This substitution pattern, captured by the famous phrase "two at home and three on the road," raised fears that a quota system might be at work. According to this concept no more than two black players could be on the court at the same time at home, in order to avoid the appearance that African Americans had "taken over" the program. On the road, however, it was acceptable to start three blacks in order to try to win the game. Head coach Jack McCloskey did not discuss the issue with his players, but they worried that he might be under pressure to restrict their playing time. When the three did in fact play together for much of one game, several fans reportedly complained to McCloskey. Nonetheless, the continued success of African American players wearing the school's black and gold colors eventually won wide acceptance for athletic integration at Wake Forest.[23]

Dean Smith and Charles Scott Transform North Carolina Basketball

At the University of North Carolina at Chapel Hill, basketball fans supported their Tar Heel team with a near-religious fervor. The university had been known for its winning basketball teams since the 1920s, and its legendary 1924 squad won all twenty-three of its games for a perfect season. In order to compete with the strong teams produced by Everett Case at N.C. State after World War II, North Carolina lured Frank McGuire, the successful coach of St. John's University in New York City, to Chapel Hill in 1952. A gifted recruiter with a flamboyant, brash personality, McGuire regularly imported high school stars from the playgrounds of New York City. One of the thirteen children of a New York City policeman, McGuire possessed a special rapport with young men from urban, working-class, Catholic families. In the 1956–57 season McGuire coached his famous collection of "Noo Yawk Tar Heels" to the NCAA championship, defeating Wilt Chamberlain and the Kansas Jayhawks in triple overtime to cap a perfect 32-0 season. Despite his success on the court, McGuire's brash personality and his generous spending on entertainment irritated many people. Recruiting violations that resulted in a one-year sanction from the NCAA also upset several key UNC officials. After the 1960–61 season, McGuire abruptly left North Carolina to coach the Philadelphia franchise in the NBA. He later returned to the ACC in 1964 as head coach at archrival South Carolina, embittering many Tar Heel fans.[24]

Dean Smith, a young assistant to McGuire, became the new head coach for the 1962 season and eventually presided over the integration of the UNC basketball program. An individual with strong religious convictions, Smith was one of the few southern coaches who viewed athletic integration as an ethical and moral responsibility. Although he was not an immediate success at UNC, Smith eventually surpassed McGuire by leading the Tar Heels to a pair of NCAA championships in 1982 and in 1993. During Smith's first year as head coach, he came close to recruiting black prep star Lou Hudson of Greensboro, who eventually attended the University of Minnesota. In May 1966 he achieved one of the college's most important recruiting victories ever when he signed forward Charles Scott to a scholarship agreement. Scott was the perfect choice to break the color line at a southern university, since according to popular belief a racial "pioneer had to be better than average." The talented 6'6" forward was definitely above average. As one local sportswriter later commented, "Scott is everything the university could want: not only splendid on the court, personable, a 'regular' guy, but a good student too." A New York City native, Scott had spent his senior year in North Carolina at the Laurinburg Institute, where he was the valedictorian of his graduating class. Scott had initially considered attending Davidson College, but his enthusiasm cooled considerably after a nearby restaurant refused to serve him and his Laurinburg coach in the white seating area during an unannounced visit to the college. UNC recruiters made a more positive impression on the young man by bringing him to campus for a festival weekend, during which several nationally prominent black musical groups performed. Smith also took Scott to Sunday services at his church. Influenced by the greater social opportunities in Chapel Hill, Scott chose UNC. As he explained to the press, "I don't want to be just a basketball player. I want to be a part of student life." At North Carolina he became the first African American to receive an athletic scholarship in any sport.[25]

Tar Heel fans expected great things from Scott, and he did not disappoint them. In his first season of varsity play in 1968, the sophomore forward averaged almost eighteen points per game and earned all-conference first-team honors. Led by senior star Larry Miller, the ACC player of the year, the Tar Heels eventually advanced to the finals of the NCAA Tournament, where they lost to UCLA. During the year Scott received a few hostile letters, and rival fans sometimes verbally harassed him on the road. The following year UNC captured the ACC Tournament title again and advanced to the semifinals of the NCAA Tournament. Unfortunately, an unpleasant incident at the University of South Carolina marred his season. In Columbia unruly white fans yelled numerous racial insults at him and even threw coins onto the floor. Although Scott again earned all-conference first-team honors, league sportswriters unexpectedly selected South Carolina's star guard John Roche as player of the year and Gamecock coach Frank McGuire as coach of the year. In a postseason interview Scott candidly stated his opinion that Dean Smith deserved the coaching award. When pressed by reporters he added that he deserved the player-of-the-year honor as well. Several journalists chastised Scott for his blunt comments, causing some Tar Heel fans to wonder if a white player would have been treated similarly. When Dean Smith learned about Roche's selection and that several sportswriters had curiously left Scott's name off their ballots for the all-conference first team, he responded, "Either the writers are ignorant, or it's bigotry." In his senior year the Tar Heels stumbled to a second-place finish, despite another impressive performance from Scott. The senior forward led the conference in scoring with an average of twenty-seven points per game and was named to both the All-ACC first team and the ACC all-academic team. Furthermore, sportswriters selected him for first-team All-America honors and also for the academic All-America squad, a rare double accomplishment. But in another controversial decision ACC journalists again narrowly chose South Carolina's John Roche, who likewise had earned All-America first-team honors, as the conference player of the year.[26]

During Scott's senior year Bill Chamberlain, a sophomore from New York City, joined him on the varsity. Chamberlain averaged just over eleven points per game as a sophomore and improved to fourteen points per game as a junior, when he also made the dean's list. At the end of his second varsity season, the Tar Heels won the National Invitational Tournament, and sportswriters selected Chamberlain as the tournament's most valuable player. For the 1972 season transfer Robert "Bob" McAdoo of Greensboro joined the Tar Heels. The first junior college player recruited by Smith at Carolina, the 6'9" center made the most of his one-year stay at the school. McAdoo averaged nearly twenty points per game for the season, leading UNC to both the regular-season and ACC Tournament championships. Once again the Tar Heels advanced all the way to the NCAA Tournament finals, finishing in third place. For his efforts McAdoo earned all-conference first-team honors. He then skipped his senior year and joined a professional team.[27]

The process of racial change in basketball was a relatively uneventful one at Chapel Hill. Charles Scott's friendly personality and solid academic performance made him a popular figure on campus and encouraged wider acceptance of integration. The UNC band apparently dropped its use of the song "Dixie" during Scott's sophomore year, and the athletic program never became a major target for racial protests on campus. During the NCAA Tournament in March 1969 the *New York Times* carried a lengthy feature about Scott and his beneficial effect on North Carolina race relations. The article reported that because of his outstanding performance on the basketball court the Tar Heel star enjoyed "a public esteem not often accorded to Negroes" in the South. This new respect seemed to reflect a partial shift in white opinions about African Americans. As one young UNC professor commented, "I think that the more Charlie Scotts we have, the easier it will be for the South to change its mind about Negroes." An accompanying photograph of several young white boys seeking Scott's autograph reinforced this message. But the newspaper also cautioned that a few white sports fans had only superficially changed their attitudes. When the junior forward played poorly in North Carolina's national semifinal loss to Purdue, one erstwhile Scott fan crudely responded, "It just proves 'niggers' choke in the clutch." The integration of Tar Heel basketball under Dean Smith helped an already strong program retain its prominence and, if possible, increase the fanatical loyalty of its supporters. But there were also limits on the extent to which integrated college athletics could change the racial attitudes of white North Carolinians.[28]

North Carolina State's Road to a National Championship

North Carolina State University followed close behind Wake Forest and North Carolina in abandoning the color line in basketball. After World War II NCSU teams became the dominant power in the South Atlantic area until the 1960s. The architect of this success was Everett Case, an Indiana native who served as head coach from 1946 through 1964. Case played a key role in the creation of the Dixie Classic basketball tournament and also helped work out the agreement by which visiting teams with African American players could stay together on the N.C. State campus when playing in the classic. In the early 1950s the Wolfpack made three straight NCAA Tournament appearances, representing the Southern Conference. After joining the ACC in 1953 NCSU captured three regular-season conference titles and four ACC postseason tournament championships during the remainder of the decade. But because of NCAA penalties over recruiting violations, N.C. State had to sit out the national playoffs in 1955 and 1959. Case recruited most of his top players from the Midwest, but he was aware of the growing number of black basketball players making an impact on the game nationally. In 1955 he reportedly was willing to risk outraging southern segregationists by offering a scholarship to Wilt Chamberlain. In the 1960s

Case's teams became somewhat less successful, and he suddenly retired in late 1964 because of health reasons. Assistant Coach Press Maravich replaced him for the next two years.[29]

In 1966 Norman Sloan became the new head coach and led North Carolina State to even greater triumphs on the basketball court. Sloan also presided over the shift from an all-white program to one that was racially inclusive. An Indiana native and former NCSU player, he eventually spent fourteen years at the helm of the Wolfpack. In the spring of 1967 Sloan awarded the first basketball scholarship in the school's history to an African American—guard William Cooper of Raleigh. During the 1968 season guard Alfred Heartley of Smithfield, North Carolina, joined Cooper on the freshman team as a walk-on. Midway through the season, freshman coach Sam Esposito moved Heartley into the starting lineup alongside Cooper, ahead of several white players. After the school year ended Cooper transferred to another college, and Sloan awarded Heartley a full scholarship, thus making him the first African American member of the varsity squad. The presence of the two black players on the freshman team did not escape the notice of those white fans who opposed athletic integration. One irate NCSU booster wrote Sloan a bitter letter, complaining that in only one year the new coach had "introduced dagos and niggers to the program" and declaring that he would make no further contributions to the athletic fund.[30]

Much like Claudius Claiborne at Duke, Al Heartley selected N.C. State primarily because of its academic programs. An applied-mathematics major, Heartley had been student government president and valedictorian of his high school class. His parents and high school teachers had emphasized the importance of earning a college degree, yet as a competitive player he also wanted to test his skills against other athletes at NCSU. During his sophomore and junior years Heartley was a part-time starter on the varsity before becoming a regular in his final season. During his senior year he served as team captain and received the Alumni Award as the outstanding student-athlete. Heartley did not encounter any serious racial incidents except for one freshman game at a junior college, where a group of students repeatedly yelled racial slurs at him and teammate William Cooper. Off the court Heartley mostly socialized with black students at NCSU and the area's several black colleges. Since he had grown up in the state he understood local racial etiquette and avoided potentially confrontational settings. The year following Heartley's arrival in Raleigh, Sloan awarded another basketball scholarship to an African American player, Edward Leftwich, a talented forward from New Jersey. As a sophomore and junior Leftwich proved to be an explosive offensive player, but just before the 1971 ACC Tournament he unexpectedly quit the team for personal and academic reasons. The following year Sloan scored a recruiting triumph when he signed Tommy Burleson, a towering 7'4" white center, to a scholarship.[31]

During the 1971 season the NCSU staff participated in an intense recruiting battle for a black high school star who was arguably the most talented prep basketball player in the state's history. Earlier in the year a report by the U.S. Department of Health, Education, and Welfare had criticized N.C. State and other North Carolina colleges for their failures to enroll more minority students and had recommended the recruitment of additional black athletes and the hiring of black coaches. Sloan and his staff hardly needed such encouragement, as they organized an extensive recruiting campaign aimed at David Thompson from Shelby, North Carolina. A 6'4" forward, Thompson possessed an awesome forty-two-inch vertical leap, exceptional quickness, and a deft shooting touch near the basket. Recruiters from all over the nation descended on his parents' small, weathered farmhouse outside of town. The competition for Thompson was so intense that the NCAA eventually banned both Duke and North Carolina State from postseason play for one year over recruiting violations. A quiet, shy young man, Thompson had anticipated playing for one of North Carolina's black colleges but signed with the Wolfpack because of the ACC's greater national exposure. Moreover, the presence of Burleson, the 7'4" center, meant that the foundation of a powerful team was already in place.[32]

For the next four years David Thompson delighted N.C. State fans with his spectacular performances. In his 1972 freshman season he averaged almost thirty-six points per game, and the freshman team sometimes played before a larger crowd in Reynolds Coliseum than did the varsity. As a sophomore Thompson teamed with Tommy Burleson to lead the Wolfpack to a perfect 27-0 regular-season mark, the conference regular-season championship, and the ACC Tournament title. Sportswriters chose Thompson as the conference player of the year and as an All-America first-team selection as well. Because of the NCAA probation, however, the Wolfpack was ineligible for the national playoffs. Prior to the start of that season Sloan had added Wilbert Johnson to his staff, making him the first black assistant coach at NCSU. Johnson proved especially helpful in resolving communication problems between his white fellow coaches and several black players. During the 1974 campaign North Carolina State fielded another powerful team. Thompson continued his brilliant play, while Burleson dominated opposing teams under the basket. Monte Towe, a 5'7" white guard, and black junior college transfers Phil Spence and Morris Rivers added strength to the squad. After an early-season loss to defending NCAA champion UCLA, the Wolfpack never tasted defeat again, completing their second consecutive undefeated ACC schedule, the only team ever to accomplish this two-year feat. Thompson was once more voted the ACC player of the year and again earned All-America first-team honors. Towe earned first team All-ACC honors, and Burleson made the second team.[33]

N.C. State swept through the ACC Tournament and the NCAA regionals. At the NCAA finals in nearby Greensboro, with thousands of fans cheering them on, the Wolfpack squad gained a rematch in the semifinals with the UCLA Bruins. Led by seniors Bill Walton and Keith (later Jamaal) Wilkes, the Bruins were favored to claim a record eighth consecutive championship for Coach John Wooden. Led by Thompson and Burleson, NCSU upset the defending champions 80–77 in double overtime. The following night N.C. State defeated Marquette 76–64 to claim the school's first NCAA basketball championship and the second by an ACC team. Following the tournament the Associated Press selected Sloan as national coach of the year and Thompson as the national player of the year. The following season, despite a 22-6 record, the defending champions failed to earn an invitation to the NCAA Tournament after finishing second in both the regular-season standings and the ACC Tournament. Despite this disappointment Thompson was named the conference player of the year for the third time, a remarkable achievement. National sportswriters again honored him as the player of the year for the second time and as an All-American for the third straight year.[34]

The great success of David Thompson and the N.C. State basketball team united many black and white North Carolinians behind the Wolfpack. More so than Charles Davis of Wake Forest and Charles Scott at UNC, Thompson became the great black superstar in the ACC and a hero to countless sports fans in the region. The example of black and white players working together to achieve a common goal offered a practical model of interracial cooperation rarely found in North Carolina or the South at that time. As one history of N.C. State observes, "The presence of black players like Thompson helped to change racial stereotypes held by numerous North Carolina whites." Moreover, as Thompson himself once noted, the presence of black athletes at NCSU encouraged African Americans across the state to identify with an institution to which they had no previous ties. The fact that Thompson was a native son also resonated with many North Carolinians. Previous ACC stars such as Lenny Rosenbluth, Charles Davis, John Roche, and Charles Scott had all hailed from the North. Thompson's numerous accomplishments suggested that black residents of the state could make major contributions to college athletics and presumably other areas of public life as well. Still, a few white boosters grumbled privately about these racial changes. While they did not demand that Sloan return to the days of all-white teams, several informed him that N.C. State should "be known as a predominantly white basketball program." Such complaints represented the last gasps of the old racial order, one that David Thompson had helped destroy.[35]

Racial Conflicts and Embarrassing Scandals at Clemson

Clemson University, the University of South Carolina, and the University of Virginia constituted the conservative bloc of the ACC and lagged behind the rest of the conference in desegregating their varsity basketball teams, just as they had done in football. At Clemson football inspired great passion from fans, while basketball, as one historian dryly noted, represented only "a winter interlude" between the end of the fall football season and the start of spring drills. Over the years the Tiger basketball team rarely achieved success, regardless of the strategies employed by a string of perennially optimistic but ultimately unsuccessful coaches. Over the first twenty years of ACC competition, for example, the Clemson squad suffered through seventeen losing seasons and finished in last place more frequently than any team. In fact, the Tigers did not win their first regular-season ACC title until 1990. The arrival of racial integration in conference basketball offered Clemson one possible avenue to upgrade its basketball teams, but many alumni remained hostile to the recruitment of African Americans. Moreover, the university's dogged resistance to desegregation had left bitter memories with most black South Carolinians, making it difficult at first for athletic recruiters to "sell" Clemson to the families of black high school prospects.

Although Clemson had the most conservative social atmosphere of any ACC university, the university still experienced campus turmoil during the 1968–69 and 1969–70 school years. Many of these sometimes heated debates focused on the Vietnam War or the controversial youth culture of the 1960s. Another major topic of conflict concerned race relations on campus, especially complaints over the absence of African American athletes and the use of Confederate symbols at sporting events. In February 1968 the student senate overwhelmingly passed a resolution urging that all racial restrictions for university athletic squads be dropped. Although the student government may have been more concerned about improving the records of the football and basketball teams than promoting racial egalitarianism, the vote demonstrated student dissatisfaction with the athletic department's recruiting patterns. In February 1969 the debate over race and athletics intensified when unknown parties stole a large Confederate flag used at football games. Several black students expressed delight at the theft, explaining that its prominence at football games and the absence of African Americans from Clemson teams made them ashamed of their school. One student asked, "How can I enjoy the game when a giant flag, half the size of the field . . . reminds me of Negro slaves?" Other black students expressed their distaste for the continued all-white nature of Tiger squads by refusing to stand for the national anthem at basketball games. Students also denounced the widespread use of racial epithets by spectators to harass players on rival teams. One white student reported that at a basketball game between Clemson and Florida State she heard Tiger fans shout such vicious racial slurs as "Pickaninny, Nigger, Jungle Bunny, Boy, Willie, LeRoy, and Coon" at the visiting team.[36]

In October 1969 many of Clemson's estimated seventy-five black students temporarily withdrew from campus during an outbreak of racial tensions. The Student League for Black Identity articulated several black complaints, including a demand that the Confederate flag be retired at the school. The Clemson student newspaper agreed, stating, "The Confederate flag is symbolic of a whole system of inhumanity to black men. It represents racism, bigotry, oppression, and brutality. Are black students wrong to ask that a symbol of indecent treatment of their race not be flaunted at football games? We think not." In response, more than three thousand white students signed a petition endorsing the use of the flag and "Dixie." Eventually, though, the controversy died down, and university administrators quietly phased out the semiofficial use of the contested symbols. Then, in the fall of 1970, school officials unveiled a new symbol for Clemson athletics—a Tiger paw. New head coaches also took over the leadership of the football and basketball programs that autumn. These changes were part of a campaign to revive enthusiasm for Tiger athletics but also carried with them the subtext that a new, modern era in university sports had arrived.[37]

In the midst of these controversies the basketball program finally attracted its first African American scholarship athletes. In July 1969 Coach Bobby Roberts signed the school's first black basketball player, Craig Mobley, a guard from Chester, South Carolina, who turned down an appointment to the U.S. Military Academy in order to break the color line at Clemson. Mobley had averaged twenty points per game as a high school senior, but, more important, he had been president of the National Honor Society and wished to major in chemical engineering. During Mobley's freshman year Johnny Moon also joined the track and field team as its first black scholarship member. The appearance of these two athletes somewhat eased student fears that the athletic program would not accept African Americans. In the fall of 1970 Tates Locke, a thirty-three-year-old Indiana native, replaced Roberts. Since the state produced few highly talented basketball players who could score at least 800 on their SAT, Locke searched widely for possible recruits, especially in northern cities. The young head coach quickly realized that the college's small-town southern location did not appeal to urban basketball players, especially African Americans. Locke also discovered that "probably [his] largest handicap was the general lack of support at Clemson for recruiting black athletes," especially from influential alumni. After he had once assembled a group of possible recruits, most of whom were black, for a campus visit, he was asked by one unhappy member of IPTAY (I Pay Ten Dollars a Year), the school booster organization, "How many of dem niggers you plan on signing?" After Clemson finished last in the ACC in 1971, Locke intensified his recruiting efforts. For his second season he added guard Anthony "Jive" Brown from Anderson (South Carolina) Junior College to the squad. When Craig Mobley quit the team later that year in order to concentrate on his studies, Brown became the only black player on the Tiger varsity. At the end of the season the team again rested at the bottom of the conference standings. Locke's recruiting base expanded considerably after 1972, when the NCAA made freshmen eligible for varsity competition and the ACC subsequently dropped its 800 SAT rule. During the 1974 season Wayne "Tree" Rollins, a 7'1" freshman center from

Cordele, South Carolina, and junior college transfer Jo Jo Bethea injected new life into Tiger basketball. Nearly two hundred colleges had contacted Rollins as a high school senior, and his enrollment "put Clemson basketball on the national map." The towering center eventually became the university's best inside player ever and twice led the ACC in rebounding during his four years as a Tiger.[38]

Locke's growing success in attracting talented players, especially African Americans, to Clemson was based in part on illegal payments to athletes' families and eventually brought disgrace to the university. At first Locke attempted to make the social environment at Clemson look more desirable to visiting black prospects from the North by quietly funding several weekend parties hosted by the black student organization for local high school students. After the ACC abandoned its SAT requirement, the pool of southern black players eligible for admission to Clemson expanded considerably. This reduced the need for recruiting northern players; in fact, the school's location now became a plus in attracting black high school stars from the Southeast. More important, the attitudes of most white boosters had changed to an acceptance of integration. In fact, a few of them privately agreed to assist the basketball program by secretly providing illicit financial aid to the top black players and a few white ones too. These boosters made such payments directly to the players or their families, so that Locke would not have any direct personal knowledge of specific illegal actions. Tree Rollins later estimated that he and his family received nearly sixty thousand dollars in cash and benefits (such as car payments) while he was at Clemson. Locke's unethical recruiting produced improved results for the Clemson basketball team. In the 1975 season the Tigers tied for second place in the ACC and received an invitation to the NIT. After reports surfaced concerning the illegal payments to players' families, however, the university forced Locke to resign. The NCAA eventually placed Clemson on probation and barred the basketball team from postseason play for three years because of the "significant benefits and inducements" illegally provided to players. Once excluded because of their race, African American players now found themselves at the center of Tiger basketball, both on the court and in newspaper headlines. Earlier scandals in the ACC had involved only white players, but now black players could share in the glory of big-time basketball, and in its infamy as well. Although the Clemson case was an extreme example, it confirmed that the collapse of the color line in ACC sports had not eliminated all ethical problems from college athletics.[39]

Frank McGuire Revitalizes South Carolina Basketball

At the University of South Carolina in Columbia football had traditionally overshadowed basketball and other school sports. Over the years South Carolina basketball teams rarely posted winning seasons, and in the first decade of

ACC competition they regularly joined Clemson and Virginia at the bottom of the league standings. The Gamecocks' basketball fortunes experienced a major turning point in 1964 when the school stunned its conference rivals by hiring Frank McGuire, the former North Carolina coach. The flamboyant McGuire had grown tired of the NBA and wanted to return to college coaching. At South Carolina McGuire's first two teams suffered through losing seasons, but from 1967 on the Gamecocks regularly challenged for the ACC title. His outstanding 1970 squad, led by John Roche and Tom Owens, compiled a 25-3 record, went undefeated in conference play, and finished sixth in the national polls. Just as he had done at North Carolina, McGuire concentrated on recruiting hard-nosed white ballplayers from the asphalt courts of New York City. In 1970, for example, nine of the thirteen members on his championship team hailed from the New York–New Jersey area. Because McGuire was not a native southerner, some thought that he might be willing break the color line. Since McGuire's pipeline to northern playgrounds regularly brought outstanding white players to Columbia, however, he apparently saw no immediate need to challenge the conservative racial structure of South Carolina sports. He also displayed little interest in recruiting local prospects regardless of race, irritating some native South Carolinians.[40]

McGuire's focus on northern big-city players sometimes ran afoul of the ACC's tighter eligibility requirements during the 1960s. The conference's decision to raise the minimum SAT score required for athletic eligibility to 800 in 1965 led to a bitter confrontation with the ACC. In late 1965 McGuire had convinced Mike Grosso, a 6'8" New Jersey high school star, to enroll at USC. Unfortunately, Grosso scored only 789 on his SAT, but the ACC commissioner's office initially permitted him to enroll at USC because of a technicality. The existing league rule specifically banned athletic *scholarships* to prospective athletes scoring below 800 but only implied that such athletes would automatically be ineligible due to their low scores. Since Grosso's parents stated that they would pay his expenses at South Carolina, and USC certified that he met all normal entrance requirements, the ACC was forced to permit Grosso to enroll because of this ambiguity in the rules. The conference quickly revised the wording of its SAT requirement, making it clear that athletic eligibility, not just receipt of an athletic scholarship, required an 800 score. Therefore, in October 1966, the conference's executive committee ruled the New Jersey star ineligible. USC officials appealed to the NCAA, which in early 1967 not only decided against Grosso but also imposed a two-year ban from postseason play on the South Carolina football and basketball teams. In addition to several other violations, the NCAA sanctioned USC over Grosso's private financial aid, which, it had now been revealed, came not from his parents but instead from a restaurant and bar operated by a relative.[41]

During the late 1960s the University of South Carolina experienced considerable student protest over social issues, especially the Vietnam War. As was the case at Clemson, the continued absence of African Americans from university athletic teams and the persistent use of Confederate symbols increasingly angered black students and some white students as well. The two issues were often intertwined on the Columbia campus, which experienced a wider range of student opinion than did Clemson. By the spring of 1968 a growing number of students openly criticized the coaching staff for the absence of African Americans. In particular, they also expressed surprise that such a distinguished coach as Frank McGuire would be unable to recruit outstanding African American players unless "his hands were tied." The debate over the lack of black Gamecocks was subsumed during the 1968–69 school year within the larger campus controversy over the Confederate battle flag and "Dixie," the unofficial fight song of the university. The perceived lack of loyalty to USC athletic teams by some black undergraduates also became an issue that was linked to the use of these traditional southern white symbols. In February 1969 the Association of Afro-American Students requested that the student affairs office ban the flag and the song from all university functions. As campus debate over the issue quickly spread, a radical interracial group demonstrated its opposition to the symbols by dramatically burning a Confederate flag in front of the president's house. An editorial in the student newspaper conceded that the battle flag was "sacred" to many white South Carolinians and that to them it represented "God, Mother, apple pie, and hominy grits." But the *Gamecock* went on to argue that the flag and the song "have as much place in the athletic arena of the present as have Rhett Butler and Scarlett O'Hara."[42]

Many white students rushed to defend the two symbols. One student pointed out to the *Gamecock* that "Dixie" always inspired an enthusiastic response from fans at USC basketball games, demonstrating that the traditional song was "loved and cherished by the majority of the student body." He also warned that the wishes of most South Carolina students should not "be ruled by the selfish whims of the minority." Another white correspondent invoked the memories of Confederate soldiers to defend the public use of the two symbols. He explained that "to those of us whose great-grandfathers, uncles, and cousins so bravely and gallantly gave their lives under Confederate colors, the Flag and 'Dixie' provide nostalgic reverie through which we may pay respect to their memories, and we Europo-Americans shall not disavow our blood kin by striking their colors and silencing their anthem." White students also complained that African Americans "are doing nothing to try to understand us" and questioned their loyalty to USC because some of them cheered for black players on rival teams. Furthermore, several white alumni threatened to withhold their financial support from the university if the two symbols were abandoned. The largest expression of proflag sentiment came when a group of students staged a rally before the Confederate monument at the state capitol, where they sang "Dixie" and the school's alma mater.[43]

The February 26, 1969, visit by the North Carolina Tar Heels and star Charles Scott to the Carolina Coliseum resulted in an embarrassing incident and triggered further reflections about the state of campus race relations. The Tar Heels inflicted a rare home-court loss on a McGuire team, due to what the *Gamecock* described as a "fantastic performance" by Scott. During the game university officials had to escort off the coliseum floor a group of students trying to parade a Confederate flag around the court. Throughout the contest spectators yelled insults at Scott. Near the end a group of angry fans actually threw coins into an area of the court where Scott and a referee were standing. Several embarrassed USC students wrote the student newspaper to express their disgust at this unruly behavior by their fellow Gamecock fans. One white student attributed much of the racial abuse aimed at Scott to students, suggesting that their behavior proved that "racism is alive and well at the university." He stated that he had personally heard students shout such slurs as "black ape," "black bastard," "nigger," and "Leroy" at Scott. Another student pondered what would happen if South Carolina eventually attracted its own black players. "Will they be bombarded with pennies and epithets when they come onto the court," he asked, "or will they be accepted as Fighting Gamecocks?" Athletic director and head football coach Paul Dietzel denied most of these accusations. He insisted that the students who threw coins onto the court were protesting a questionable call by the referee and that it was an accident that Scott happened to be nearby. Subsequently, Dietzel worked with other school officials to produce a new fight song for the Gamecock teams, one that white and black students could both support. Trying to put the endless debate over "Dixie" to rest, the *Gamecock* suggested in February 1970 that "the old ballad has outlived its time." Noting that "Dixie" had regrettably become "a trademark for racism," the newspaper concluded that it was time to retire the song. "'Dixie' is not the song for athletics," it declared. "We should let it die." Campus debates over racism and protests against the Vietnam War, however, did not mean that all forms of traditional male behavior at USC had been replaced by heightened social consciousness. During the fall semester of 1969, for example, hundreds of male students staged at least nine "panty raids" on women's dormitories.[44]

In September 1969 the first African American to receive a basketball scholarship to USC enrolled at the university. Casey Manning, a high-scoring guard from Dillon, South Carolina, seemed a logical choice to break the color line, since as a senior he had been voted the state's player of the year. Manning had also graduated in the top 10 percent of his class. In his first season at South Carolina, he averaged a solid sixteen points per game on the freshman team.

The following year Manning received only modest playing time on the Game-cocks' 1971 ACC Tournament championship team. Just before the start of his junior season he suffered an injury and missed practice for several weeks, but eventually he saw steady action as a reserve and became a crowd favorite. Under McGuire's system, however, the starters normally played almost the entire game unless they fouled out, so Manning and other top substitutes received only limited playing time. A few black students grumbled that McGuire had turned Manning from a high-scoring shooter in high school to a low-scoring reserve in college. In Manning's senior season of 1973 he served as McGuire's number-one reserve but still could not crack the starting lineup for the Gamecocks, which finished the year ranked sixteenth in the country. In his final college match against Southwestern Louisiana in the NCAA regionals, he played extensively and scored thirteen points. After college Manning attended law school and became a family court judge.[45]

During Manning's senior year another African American player joined the Gamecocks. Freshman Alex English of Columbia promptly quelled concerns that McGuire was reluctant to start an African American. Taking advantage of the new NCAA ruling making freshmen eligible, English immediately moved into the starting lineup. The 6'8" forward went on to start all 111 games of his four-year career and set a USC career scoring record. Surprisingly, the gradual addition of southern black players did not sustain the Gamecocks' high level of success. After leaving the ACC following the 1971 season South Carolina enjoyed three more outstanding seasons, but then the Gamecocks' fortunes slowly declined. Although all of these later teams managed winning records, they failed to match the outstanding performances of the early 1970s and never again qualified for the NCAA Tournament under McGuire. The decision to withdraw from the ACC now appeared to be a mistake, as it eliminated estab-lished rivalries from the schedule and made it more difficult to attract high school stars. McGuire finally retired after the 1980 season, having won 283 games in sixteen seasons at USC.[46]

Black Cavaliers at Last

The University of Virginia achieved the dubious distinction of becoming the last member of the ACC to integrate its basketball team. Prior to World War II the college usually fielded strong basketball teams, but this success disappeared after the war. During the period from 1950 through 1970 Virginia fans found little to cheer about, as the Cavaliers consistently ended up in the bottom half of the ACC standings and finished dead last on six occasions. This dismal re-cord should have made Virginia's basketball program receptive to new sources of talent, but such was not the case. Beginning in 1966 liberal students at UVa and black civil rights leaders openly criticized the whiteness of the Cavalier football and basketball teams. But even when the coaching staff became more attentive to black high school athletes, the Old South atmosphere in Charlottesville and the tiny number of black students on campus created social barriers to the recruitment of African Americans.[47]

William J. "Hooter" Gibson, the Virginia head coach from 1963 to 1974, initially failed to improve the team's performance and was slow to seek out prospective black players. In the spring of 1969 Gibson survived a player revolt and convinced the university administration to make a stronger financial commitment to the basketball program. One year later he finally signed the team's first black player, Al Drummond, a 6'3" guard from Waverly, New York. As a sophomore during the 1972 season Drummond watched mostly from the bench. As a junior and senior he earned a starting position in the backcourt and became known as a defensive specialist. Since every other ACC member had integrated their basketball teams prior to Virginia, Drummond's presence on the Cavaliers had no social impact outside of the state. The ACC's decision in 1972 to drop its 800 SAT rule did little at first to help Virginia's recruiting, since the university retained its high entrance requirements for all athletes. Even when the basketball team did add several more African Americans, none of them matched the success of black players at rival schools. Junior college transfer Lamont Carr played for the 1975 and 1976 Cavalier squads, mostly as a reserve. Tom Briscoe began his career in the 1975 season but remained a substitute during his four years. Guard Bobby Stokes started for three seasons from 1977 to 1979, served as team captain his final year, and made the all-conference academic team. Despite their routine careers these four athletes, through their presence on the Cavalier team, slowly helped modify the negative view that many black Virginians held toward the university and its athletic programs.[48]

The change in Virginia athletics to a new multiracial order was solidified in 1979 by the most important signing in the school's athletic history. In the spring Coach Terry Holland won an intense recruiting contest for Ralph Sampson, a Virginia native and the top high school prospect in the nation. Over the next four years the towering 7'4" center led the school into its most successful basketball era ever. In Sampson's freshman year the Cavaliers finished 24-10 and captured first place in the NIT. In 1981, as a sophomore, Sampson paced Virginia to the ACC championship and an eventual trip to the NCAA Final Four. In 1982 and 1983 the Cavaliers tied for first in the ACC and advanced to the regional round in the NCAA Tournament. Acknowledging Sampson's dominating performances, sportswriters selected him as the ACC player of the year and also the national player of the year for three straight seasons. The success of Sampson and the Cavaliers permanently altered the public's perception of Virginia basketball. Now the Cavaliers were seen as a basketball power, one that regularly challenged for the ACC title. The university also finally lost its reputation as the special preserve of white athletes, a struggle that took even longer than it did for Clemson and South Carolina. Both in racial composition and in success, the Cavalier squads of the 1980s were quite different from their counterparts some twenty years earlier.[49]

The changes in Virginia basketball during the 1970s reflected on a modest scale the broader shift taking place across the ACC. The number of African American players on league squads grew steadily in the latter part of the decade and increased in the 1980s. Their growing prominence became clear in 1977, when sportswriters for the first time selected an all-conference team that consisted entirely of African American players. Over the years talented stars like David Thompson of N.C. State, Ralph Sampson of Virginia, and Michael Jordan of North Carolina displayed remarkable skills to adoring fans. They and other black players helped the conference develop a faster-paced, more wide-open style of play. The number of African Americans holding ACC coaching positions also increased but much more slowly. By the late 1970s black assistant coaches had become standard at most schools. A major coaching milestone took place in 1986, when Maryland selected Bob Wade, a respected coach at Baltimore Dunbar High School, to head its basketball program. Wade thus became the conference's first African American head coach, some twenty-two years after Maryland had fielded the conference's first integrated team. His hiring served as a reminder that athletic integration was not a onetime event but rather an extended process that included not only the gradual appearance of African American players but the hiring of black assistant coaches and head coaches as well.

* * *

Between 1957, when the North Carolina Tar Heels won the ACC's first national championship, and 1974, when David Thompson led N.C. State to the league's second NCAA title, the racial structure of ACC basketball underwent a radical transformation. The inclusion of African American athletes on conference basketball and football teams represented an important step toward full acceptance of black students on campus. Within the world of ACC athletics basketball coaches seemed to be slightly more amenable to racial change than football coaches, and the eventual recruitment of black players helped the league maintain its premier status as one of the nation's top basketball conferences. Despite the small differences between basketball and football cultures, a more fundamental division occurred between the conference members who were more flexible on race (Maryland, Wake Forest, UNC, N.C. State, and Duke) and the three more conservative members (Virginia, South Carolina, and Clemson). Since the latter three teams were traditionally weak in basketball, they logically should have been willing to recruit African Americans aggressively, in order to gain parity with their more successful rivals. Nonetheless, these three schools were actually the last ones to incorporate black players into their teams. Their desire to maintain whiteness on the basketball court thus trumped opportunism and self-interest, as their athletic programs remained trapped in cultural captivity to the broader racial views of their states.

ACC schools were not alone in facing racial challenges in the 1960s and 1970s. Out on the western border of the South, universities in Texas and Arkansas that belonged to the Southwest Conference also confronted similar problems. Whether their location would produce less resistance to athletic integration than in the ACC will be explored in the next chapter.

7

The Eyes of Texas
Are (Not) upon You
The Southwest Conference and Football

[Integration] is not going to help you that much
in football. There aren't enough Negro football
players around with the athletic and academic
qualifications to make a great deal of difference.

—A Southwest Conference coach,
November 1963

An eighty-yard run by a fleet Negro halfback will
do wonders in dissolving racial antipathy.

—University of Texas *Daily Texan*,
November 1963

On a rainy Saturday afternoon in late November 1966, a capacity crowd of just over thirty thousand football fans assembled on the campus of Texas Christian University in Fort Worth to watch the home team take on the visiting Southern Methodist University Mustangs. At stake for SMU that day was the undisputed conference championship and an automatic invitation to the Cotton Bowl on New Year's Day. For the underdog Horned Frogs, who had won only two games so far that fall, the contest represented their last opportunity to salvage some pride in front of their fans. Leading the SMU squad into Amon Carter Stadium were veteran quarterback Mac White and wide receiver Jerry LeVias. Although the 1966 season represented LeVias's first year of varsity competition, the "sophomore whiz kid" had attracted widespread media attention because of his dramatic game-winning performances and, more important, his historic status as the first African American football player to break the color line in the Southwest Conference.

As fans gradually filled the stands, an unusually large number of uniformed policemen and plainclothesmen in trench coats, many of them carrying two-way radios, monitored their movements. Although the TCU–SMU game was a classic end-of-the-season rivalry contest, this extensive law enforcement presence stemmed from death threats made against LeVias, not fear of rowdy fans. Four days prior to the contest an anonymous caller had telephoned the SMU campus and crudely announced, "We're going to shoot that dirty nigger LeVias on Saturday." Obscene telephone calls and occasional threats of personal violence were nothing new to LeVias, who had been a marked man ever since he signed a scholarship agreement with SMU in May 1965. But since this particular caller had specified when and where his threat would be carried out, SMU administrators prudently contacted local police. Later in the week the Fort Worth Police Department also received a message about a possible shooting attempt at the game. Perhaps because the death threats arrived immediately following the third anniversary of President John F. Kennedy's assassination in downtown Dallas, law enforcement officials decided to take extra security measures for the game but not to inform the press.

Administrators at TCU and SMU also remained quiet about the threats until game day. As a precaution SMU coach Hayden Fry made LeVias do his pregame warm-ups in the locker room rather than on the field, an unusual move that his star player assumed was some type of motivational strategy. Shortly before kickoff time, though, Fry finally told LeVias about the death threat and offered him the option of sitting out the game, with the complete support of the university. Although slightly unnerved by the news, LeVias, a fierce competitor, insisted on taking the field with his teammates. During the contest he followed instructions to stand in the middle of the SMU huddle, and at the line of scrimmage the Mustangs executed their offensive plays quickly so as to avoid making their star end stand still for very long. On the SMU sideline plainclothesmen constantly hovered near LeVias whenever he was resting. To the relief of both colleges, police never detected any unusual behavior in the crowd, and the game proceeded normally. After a sluggish start the Mustangs methodically ground out a 21–0 victory, clinching the school's first SWC title since 1948 and a Cotton Bowl invitation. The pressure on LeVias did not hurt his performance. In fact, he scored on the game's most exciting play, a sixty-eight-yard touchdown pass from Mac White. Back in Dallas that night, while many of his teammates celebrated into the early morning hours, LeVias reluctantly spent the night on campus because of security concerns.[1]

In the state of Texas sports fans took their football very seriously, but death threats against players were not normally part of the annual pageantry. Although the specific threat to Jerry LeVias was unusual, in another sense it represented an extension of the relentless abuse that he had endured since enrolling at SMU in September 1965. Because the Mustangs' wide receiver had been the first African American to receive a football scholarship in the Southwest Conference and had proved to be a "big-play" competitor during his initial year of varsity action, he served as a lightning rod for racist outrage over social change. Even more than other racial pioneers in the Atlantic Coast Conference and the Southeastern Conference, LeVias experienced repeated harassment on the gridiron. Why he seemed to attract such abuse is not clear. Perhaps SWC coaches may have misjudged the degree of antagonism that their players would direct at LeVias and therefore failed to take preemptive action at the start of the season. In any case, the difficulties that LeVias faced on and off the field, as well as the continuing reluctance of SWC coaches to recruit black athletes, demonstrated that in the mid-1960s the states of Texas and Arkansas were strongly southern in terms of their athletic culture and that football fans there viewed the gridiron as a special space reserved exclusively for white males.

Football Expands into the Southwest

At the start of the twentieth century higher education in the Southwest (defined herein as the states of Texas and Arkansas) was relatively underdeveloped and received only limited public support. As educators struggled to justify an expansion of higher education, they discovered that athletic teams provided one important mechanism through which to create and mobilize a larger off-campus constituency. University students in the Southwest were anxious to validate themselves by replicating traditions and practices from eastern schools. As part of the steady cultural diffusion of football across the United States, the sport entered the region in the 1890s and quickly won many converts. By the time of the First World War, football had become permanently rooted on college campuses in Texas, Arkansas, and Oklahoma. The first major college in the Lone Star State to organize an official football team was the University of Texas in 1893. Not to be outdone, archrival Texas A&M University fielded a squad the following year, as did the University of Arkansas (UA). Texas Christian University launched its football program in 1896, followed by Baylor University in 1899. When additional colleges and universities sprang up during the next three decades, administrators at these new schools usually formed a football team as soon as possible, in order to inspire school spirit and to demonstrate to the public that they were a modern, progressive institution of higher learning. The first official intercollegiate football game held in the state took place in the fall of 1894 in Austin, when a more experienced Texas squad easily defeated Texas A&M by a score of 38–0. The two schools soon developed a spirited rivalry. In fact, the competition between the two became so intense that after a wild 1911 contest in Houston, university officials canceled the series for the next three years.[2]

Regulating the new athletic competition proved to be a challenge. Several Texas colleges formed the state's first football conference in 1904, but eventually a group of the larger, more competitive southwestern universities became concerned about the growing disregard of eligibility rules. On December 8, 1914, representatives from eight colleges met in Houston and officially created a new elite league known as the Southwest Intercollegiate Athletic Conference, later known simply as the Southwest Conference. Original members included Texas, Texas A&M, Baylor, Arkansas, Southwestern University, Oklahoma, Oklahoma A&M, and Rice University (then Rice Institute). SMU joined the conference in 1918, while TCU signed on in 1923. By the mid-1920s Southwestern, Oklahoma, and Oklahoma A&M had all withdrawn, leaving behind a stable seven-team conference. No new members were accepted until 1958, when the league added Texas Technological University in Lubbock. During the period from 1923 to 1958 five of the six SWC members from Texas were located in the east and central areas of the state, where southern white culture dominated towns and cities alike. Only Fort Worth, the home of TCU and "the city where the West begins," offered some slight regional diversity. The University of Arkansas likewise found its social policies controlled by the state's dominant southern heritage.[3]

The quality of football displayed in the Southwest Conference did not impress eastern and midwestern sportswriters and coaches until the 1930s. In the early years of play southwestern schools mostly scheduled opponents from within the region. Notre Dame became the first major national opponent to visit Texas. In November 1915 the Irish trounced Rice 55–2 and the University of Texas 36–7 during a two-game swing through the state. In the 1930s Southwest Conference teams finally won national recognition and became renowned for their wide-open passing attacks and rugged physical play. By the end of the decade most SWC squads had played major intersectional contests in New York, Philadelphia, Chicago, or Los Angeles, thereby attracting greater attention from the national press. In 1931 the University of Texas recorded an important athletic milestone when Harvard hosted the Longhorn team in Cambridge. The willingness of the venerable New England college to establish athletic relations with a southwestern university bestowed enhanced cultural recognition and educational status on the Austin school. The league's growing stature was also reflected in the increasingly high rankings that southwestern teams earned in the national polls during the 1930s. In a remarkable demonstration of strength by the conference, three different SWC schools claimed the mythical national championship during the decade: SMU in 1935, TCU in 1938, and Texas A&M in 1939. The 1935 SMU team also earned a lucrative invitation to the Rose Bowl in Pasadena, California, further enlarging the conference's national profile. Outstanding All-Americans like TCU quarterbacks Davey O'Brien, the 1938 Heisman Trophy winner, and "Slinging Sammy" Baugh, as well as Texas A&M's rugged halfback "Jarrin' John" Kimbrough, became national sports celebrities and brought further acclaim to the conference.[4]

Until the mid-1930s SWC schools consistently refused to compete against black players, but most of them were willing to play against other nonwhite groups, especially Native Americans. For example, the University of Texas played the Haskell Institute squad eleven times before World War I. At Texas A&M the 1909 squad included two American Indian students who had transferred from the Carlisle Institute, while the 1924 and 1925 teams included Taro Kishi, a Japanese American. In the mid-1930s, though, three SWC schools opportunistically dumped racial exclusion in order to pursue profits and prestige. SMU, TCU, and Texas A&M all jettisoned racial exclusion in order to play UCLA and its black stars in Los Angeles, hoping to impress Rose Bowl sponsors. Despite this moderation outside the state, all of these colleges rejected any alterations to their Jim Crow policies at home. The integrated track and field competition that the city of Dallas permitted when hosting the 1936 Centennial Games and the inaugural Pan American Olympic Games in 1937 did not have any immediate effect on racial policy for football games held in the Southwest.[5]

After World War II the growing refusal by northern colleges to leave their black players behind when visiting the South forced Southwest Conference members to reassess their priorities. Private colleges such as SMU possessed more flexibility on this issue than public universities, who had to answer to the state legislature. The major postseason bowl game in Texas, the Cotton Bowl, played a key role in overcoming the political and social barriers to interracial competition inside the state. By matching integrated teams from Penn State in 1948 and the University of Oregon in 1949 against SMU, the Cotton Bowl shattered the color line inside Texas and served as an opening wedge for expanded integrated competition. As part of an effort to maintain a national profile, SMU officials scored quite a coup for 1949 when they convinced Notre Dame to begin a home-and-home series with the Mustangs. The integration of the Irish football team in 1953 did not disrupt this relationship, and in 1954 SMU hosted an integrated squad for the first time in Dallas. SMU administrators had once again indicated that they valued the prestige and profits of big-time college football more dearly than the preservation of Jim Crow on the gridiron.[6]

Professional football also brought a brief dose of racial change to Dallas and the state. In 1952 a group of Texas investors purchased a financially struggling National Football League franchise, the New York Yankees. They subsequently relocated the Yankee team to Dallas, cleverly renamed it the Texans, and scheduled home games in the Cotton Bowl stadium. The new owners inherited three black players with the club, two of whom they retained. White fans disliked the team's integrated status. Black fans were also dissatisfied when they found themselves restricted to a Jim Crow end-zone section, creating the irony of a segregated audience viewing an integrated athletic event. Consequently, the team struggled financially, as neither white nor black fans showed up in large numbers. At the end of the season the owners sold the franchise to new investors, who moved it to Baltimore and renamed the team the Colts. Nonetheless, for one year the city's residents had witnessed an integrated professional team. The Texans had set a precedent for future athletic events, even if southwestern colleges chose not to utilize it.[7]

In Austin the University of Texas avoided hosting integrated football games until the mid-1950s. In addition to their general commitment to white supremacy, the Board of Regents barred integrated competition at Memorial Stadium so as to avoid undermining its legal defense of educational segregation on the UT campus. In August 1954 the athletic department discovered that the Washington State squad, which was scheduled to visit Austin in the fall, included one African American. Rather than risk a confrontation with Washington State, the regents set aside their unofficial rule. In October fullback Duke Washington of the Cougars thus became the first African American to compete against the Longhorns in Austin. After Washington scored a touchdown on a spectacular seventy-three-yard run, the crowd gave him what the *Daily Texan* termed "a thundering ovation." In 1955 the regents permanently abandoned their exclusion policy so that the university could have the honor of hosting the Olympic trials for the U.S. track and field team the following year.[8]

By the mid-1950s most Southwest Conference members had accepted competition against African American players for home and away games. Compared to the continuing refusal by several members of the Atlantic Coast Conference and the Southeastern Conference to host integrated contests, the SWC appeared fairly progressive. Moreover, Texas political leaders lent only modest support to the massive resistance movement that followed the *Brown v. Board of Education* ruling in 1954. For a while it seemed that the conference might move toward recruiting African American athletes much sooner than the other elite southern conferences, but the "moderate resistance" campaign in Texas masked prolonged opposition to racial integration by segregationists, especially in education. Many public colleges, especially those in East Texas, did not accept their first black undergraduates until 1963 and 1964, much like universities in Alabama and Mississippi. Texas A&M, for example, enrolled its first African American students only in 1963. Since this moderate resistance never became violent, the tardiness of many Texas colleges in desegregating their campuses mostly escaped national censure. Even after the integration of undergraduate studies, athletic programs at SWC schools continued to avoid recruiting black athletes, lagging far behind those at independent Texas universities and most small colleges as well. In the state of Arkansas, the more extreme form of massive resistance initiated by Governor Orval Faubus kept University of Arkansas officials on the defensive throughout the 1960s. In short, SWC colleges failed to demonstrate progressive leadership in desegregating their classrooms and their athletic programs. At most conference athletic programs until the late 1960s, a color line continued to encircle the football field.[9]

In the early 1960s continued segregation in Southwest Conference athletics attracted special attention from liberal students, African Americans, and journalists. Each fall a few sportswriters would speculate over when the SWC might finally drop its color line, usually noting various black high school players who had left the state to become stars elsewhere. In the spring of 1961 rumors circulated that outstanding halfback Junior Coffey from the small Panhandle town of Dimmit might attend an SWC school and break the color line. But conference recruiters mostly ignored Coffey, who eventually enrolled at the University of Washington. Meanwhile, as the civil rights movement gradually toppled racial barriers across the South and public school integration became more commonplace, the whiteness of Southwest Conference teams increasingly stood out. Student activists who challenged lingering discrimination on their campuses often included the issue of athletic integration among their grievances. In September 1961 approximately six thousand University of Texas students signed petitions urging the Board of Regents to sanction athletic integration at the university. Three months later, the student government presidents of the seven Texas members of the SWC met in Dallas just before the Cotton Bowl. The group discussed the league's racial practices and adopted a resolution urging that "capable athletes of all races" be permitted to compete on conference athletic teams. But SWC officials ignored their appeal.[10]

Toward the end of 1963 members of the Southwest Conference finally dumped their unwritten policy, but not yet their practice, of excluding African Americans from their football teams. Several SWC schools had enrolled their first black undergraduates that fall, and Rice and TCU would complete the full integration of their classrooms the following year. A decision by the UT Board of Regents proved to be the catalyst for action. The ultraconservative board had doggedly resisted integration on the Austin campus for decades. In early November 1963, though, the regents unexpectedly adopted a resolution stipulating that the UT athletic department and individual coaches would now set their own policies on student participation. Other SWC members soon followed in Texas's footsteps. Two weeks later the athletic council at Baylor voted unanimously to allow African Americans to participate in the school's athletic programs. Administrators at SMU, TCU, Texas Tech, and Rice eventually made similar announcements. In the state of Arkansas, however, continuing political resistance to court-ordered school desegregation blocked any change in policy, as Governor Orval Faubus announced that he opposed any use of black athletes at the state university.[11]

Despite these encouraging signs from Texas colleges, most observers doubted that any significant racial change would be immediately forthcoming. Sportswriter Roy Edwards of the *Dallas Morning News* surveyed SWC coaches and athletic department officials about the issue. His contacts generally agreed that in the short run there would not be any "sweeping changes" in recruiting patterns. In fact, one administrator confessed that his program had not even discussed when their coaches might approach potential African American recruits. In words that today sound remarkably shortsighted, this unnamed official confidently asserted that integration "is not going to help you that much in football. There aren't enough Negro football players around with the athletic and academic qualifications to make a great deal of difference." One slightly more optimistic coach predicted that when integration finally arrived, "We will look for a boy whose athletic ability, academic achievement, and character are beyond question. And he will be from our immediate area." Most of the individuals interviewed agreed that the major barrier to recruitment of black high school players was their limited academic preparation, a claim that black sports fans strongly disputed. Edwards concluded that only African Americans who were "the bluest of the blue chips" would be recruited and that the first black athlete to play SWC football would be investigated as carefully by his coach as Jackie Robinson had been by Branch Rickey of the Brooklyn Dodgers. African American sports fans were outraged by such negative comments from whites, since they were familiar with many black high school stars who had left the state and achieved success at northern or western colleges. For example, the industrial city of Beaumont produced two especially gifted athletes in the early 1960s, Charles "Bubba" Smith at Michigan State and Mel Farr at UCLA. Both graduated from high school in 1963, earned All-American honors in college, enjoyed successful professional careers, and had been ignored by SWC schools.[12]

Athletic Integration Begins with Small College and High School Teams

While Southwest Conference schools delayed in recruiting African Americans, sports integration preceded steadily at the state's major independent colleges, small colleges, and various high schools. Since the late 1950s major independents North Texas State and Texas Western had featured black players on their football squads. Houston, an ambitious upstart, fielded its first integrated football and basketball teams in the fall of 1965. Several junior colleges in the southern and western parts of Texas had also recruited African Americans for their football teams by the early 1960s. The most important small-college league in the state was the Lone Star Conference (LSC), which was affiliated with the National Association of Intercollegiate Athletics (NAIA). Members included Texas A&I, Southwest Texas State, Sul Ross, and three public colleges in the eastern part of the state: East Texas State, Sam Houston, and Stephen F. Austin. The first conference member to drop its color line was Texas A&I College, now known as Texas A&M–Kingsville. Texas A&I won the NAIA national championship in 1959 and was a perennial national power throughout the 1960s. The college's first African American player, halfback Sid Blanks of Del Rio, enrolled in the fall of 1960, eventually earned NAIA All-America honors, and played professionally for several years. A small but steady stream of black football players followed Blanks to Texas A&I, including lineman Eugene Upshaw, a future all-pro guard for the Oakland Raiders. Other LSC teams gradually incorporated African Americans into their football programs. By the fall of 1967 even conference members in eastern Texas had added black players despite the conservative racial attitudes of their surrounding communities. African Americans frequently praised these colleges while condemning SWC members. *Houston Informer* columnist Alexander Durley, a former coach, regularly singled out Texas and Texas A&M for criticism, warning that the state's two premier universities "are not the symbols that future generations will look to." On the other hand, Durley and many black fans were delighted when Texas A&I, Arlington State, and West Texas State all started black quarterbacks in the late 1960s.[13]

The spread of integration in the Texas public school system and the resulting changes in high school athletic competition during the late sixties undermined the old athletic status quo. High schools in southern and western Texas, where the African American population was small, mostly integrated in the middle and late 1950s. Integrated athletic competition was common in these areas by 1963, but the Dallas and Houston school districts, as well as those located in East Texas, continued to fight desegregation. Therefore, most of the state's black athletes still competed for all-black schools that were part of the Prairie View Interscholastic League. Since Southwest Conference coaches did not deign to scout PVIL games, they overlooked many promising young athletes. In May 1965 the University Interscholastic League began preparing to incorporate some of these black high schools into its ranks by deleting the word *white* from its constitution. During the 1967–68 school year many black high schools switched to the UIL, creating a surge in interracial competition, especially in state play-offs. SWC coaches therefore could no longer ignore the skills of black athletes. Athletic integration had its greatest immediate impact on basketball. In March 1968 the all-black Houston Wheatley Wildcats unexpectedly (to whites) captured the state championship of the UIL big-school division by defeating the all-white Dallas Jefferson Rebels 85–80 in overtime. Jefferson fans waved Confederate flags throughout the game, while Wildcat supporters responded with miniature

American flags. Houston Wheatley repeated as the state champion in 1969 and 1970, a remarkable feat. The growing public acceptance of integrated high school competition, plus the excellent performances of black stars, made it easier for SWC members to start or expand the integration of their athletic programs.[14]

The first black athletes to compete in Southwest Conference sports appeared in track and field, followed eventually by football and basketball. In the spring of 1964 junior Oliver Patterson represented the University of Texas in the first varsity track meet of the season, while James Means competed in the freshman division. Neither runner had a scholarship that year, but UT awarded Means one the following year, making him the first African American to receive an athletic scholarship in the SWC. The first black athletes to receive scholarships in football and basketball appeared on the freshman level during the 1965–66 school term and, more important, in varsity play the following season The three church-related members of the conference, SMU, TCU, and Baylor, were the first to integrate their major sports programs. In football, though, it was not until the fall of 1970 that the conference's three elite members, Texas, Texas A&M, and Arkansas, at last fielded integrated football teams. Overall, the SWC concluded the process of athletic integration marginally sooner than did the Southeastern Conference and the ACC, where members from such Deep South states as Mississippi, Alabama, and South Carolina were especially slow to eliminate Jim Crow. Arkansas's extreme political climate explains the inaction of the state university there. But why the Texas members of the SWC did not eliminate racial exclusion more rapidly is a complicated question and the subject of the next section.

The Integration of SWC Basketball

Basketball occupied a decidedly secondary position within the states of Texas and Arkansas, as well as in the Southwest Conference. Football's domination on both the high school and the college levels in the region was aptly captured by the famous cliché about Texas athletics: "There are only two sports in Texas—football and spring football." Public interest in the development of basketball integration also remained modest. Sportswriters, including those in the black press, paid only limited attention to this topic while devoting enormous space to football news. Within the SWC, church-related schools took the lead in breaking the color line on the basketball court. In early 1965 TCU chancellor M. E. Sadler informed basketball coach Buster Brannon that it was now acceptable to recruit black athletes. Although one member of the school's Board of Trustees resigned over this policy change, the board backed Sadler's decision. Brannan eventually convinced 6'6" center James Cash, who led Fort Worth Terrell High School to the state championship of the PVIL that spring, to enroll at TCU. Since Cash lived only a few miles from the university, he was familiar with racial etiquette in the city and already had a social network in place. Furthermore, he ranked near the top of his senior class. Cash experienced predictable problems with meals and lodging during his first year when the freshman team traveled to central and east Texas. At a game against Kilgore Junior College, fans were so hostile that several policemen escorted him to and from the court. As a sophomore Cash had his nose broken in an unusually rough nonconference game in Mobile, Alabama, forcing Brannon to remove him from the contest for his own safety. However, in three years of SWC varsity competition, Cash experienced relatively few problems with rival players and did not attract the repeated harassment that Jerry LeVias, the conference's first black scholarship football player, had to endure. During his sophomore season, junior college transfer John Ed White, the second African American to play varsity SWC basketball, joined him on the Frog squad for one year. As a junior Cash helped the Frogs win the conference championship, and in his final year he led the team in scoring and rebounding, earning all-conference second-team honors.[15]

TCU's abandonment of the color line in basketball opened the door for other Southwest Conference teams to take similar action. In the spring of 1966 Baylor signed Tommy Bowman from Athens, Texas, who went on to win all-conference honors as a sophomore and junior. Somewhat surprisingly, given the political climate in that state, the University of Arkansas also awarded its first ever scholarship to a black athlete, Thomas Johnson, that same spring. Both Bowman and Johnson began varsity play during the 1967–68 season. Over the next two years, however, only SMU and then Texas Tech added African Americans to their rosters, as the pace of racial change in basketball seemed to slow. Then in the 1970 season Rice and Texas joined the mainstream of the SWC with integrated squads. This left Texas A&M as the last holdout. Finally, Mario Brown, a 6'2" junior college transfer, joined the Aggies for the 1972 season. The racial integration of SWC teams eventually improved the overall quality of play in the conference, especially when the University of Houston became a full-fledged member in 1976. Two years later Arkansas took third place in the national tournament, and in 1982, 1983, and 1984 Houston advanced to the Final Four, twice losing in the championship game. Nonetheless, football continued to reign as the king of SWC sports, and in that sport the issue of athletic integration provoked considerable controversy.

Hayden Fry and Jerry LeVias Break the Color Barrier at SMU

Southern Methodist University was the pioneering institution that courageously broke the color line in the Southwest Conference in football. Although the college was located in an affluent area of Dallas and enrolled numerous students from wealthy and upper-middle-class backgrounds (hence one nickname of Southern Money University), its administrators and athletic officials were willing to depart from southern customs in order to maintain a nationally recognized football program. In the 1930s and 1940s SMU displayed more flexibility than any other southern university in accepting games against integrated teams, including two Cotton Bowl appearances against Penn State and Oregon. The school's conservative alumni and wealthy donors accepted this pragmatic policy, although presumably some of them must have disliked it. Following the 1948 season, though, the football team went into decline and did not win another conference title for eighteen years. The hapless 1960 squad even set a new low in futility by failing to win a single game. To reverse this slide, the university turned to a young coach named Hayden Fry as its savior. A native of West Texas, Fry had previously served as an assistant coach at Baylor and Arkansas, earning a reputation as "a dedicated salesman and recruiter." He arrived at Southern Methodist in 1962 just as the undergraduate college prepared to accept its first black applicants. The initial step away from an all-white student body had taken place in 1952, when the Perkins School of Theology, a semiautonomous Methodist divinity school physically attached to SMU, had accepted its first full-time African American students. This action did not immediately modify racial policies for other components of the university, however. In 1962 SMU admitted Paula Jones as its first full-time black undergraduate. No additional black undergraduates arrived until 1965, when two men, one of whom was Jerry LeVias, and two women enrolled.[16]

Despite their conservative political views, many SMU students supported an end to segregated athletics in the Southwest Conference. Student government president Gary Cadenhead addressed the issue in December 1961, commenting, "It is a great loss for Southwest Conference athletics that Negro athletes are prevented from participating." Two months later, 75 percent of 1,837 students participating in a special campus election voted in favor of ending racial restrictions in sports. Because of this student support and the elimination of admission barriers at the university, Fry felt emboldened to challenge the SWC's color line. Fry had grown up in modest economic circumstances in Odessa and had interacted with African American playmates during his youth, thereby acquiring a greater racial sensitivity than most white coaches of his generation. Moreover, since the SMU program was in shambles, personal self-interest and professional survival gave him a powerful incentive to seek out new sources of talent. At the time of his hiring Fry outlined his plans to President Willis M. Tate and athletic director Matty Bell, both of whom indicated their support. Many influential donors to the athletic program were unhappy with Fry's decision, and a few even threatened to withhold their support from the athletic department.[17]

The SMU coaching staff soon began to scout the top African American players in the state, including those competing in the Prairie View Interscholastic

League. In 1963 they discovered a promising junior halfback by the name of Jerry LeVias at all-black Hebert High School in Beaumont. During his final two years in high school, LeVias scored a remarkable forty-three touchdowns and twice led Hebert to the PVIL title game. Equally important, LeVias maintained high grades, and school officials described him as a role model for his classmates. SMU coaches soon concluded that he was the perfect choice to break the color line. LeVias received more than ninety scholarship offers, however, and took his time before finally selecting the Mustangs. What attracted him to SMU was not the opportunity to become a racial pioneer but rather the solid academic programs available there. "I didn't go to the Southwest Conference to break any racial barriers," LeVias later recalled. "My intent was to get an education." He was also impressed by the successful corporate executives he met while visiting Dallas and the future business connections that SMU graduates could develop through such alumni. LeVias signed a scholarship agreement with SMU in May 1965. In a formal press release Fry stated, "I hope this signing will open the door for future Negro student-athletes in the Southwest Conference." The SMU coach later joked to reporters that he would not be too upset if his SWC rivals delayed their recruitment of black players a little longer, though, "until we get all the good ones."[18]

In his four years at Southern Methodist, Jerry LeVias consistently produced outstanding athletic performances while enduring frequent racial harassment and abuse, especially during his sophomore season in 1966. Although Hayden Fry had tried to provide LeVias with an honest appraisal of the difficulties he would face as a racial pioneer, neither the coach nor the young recruit fully anticipated the deep hostility that awaited him. Both also underestimated the extent of his social isolation on campus, where he was just one of five black un-dergraduates during his first semester. As he moved into his formerly all-white dormitory at the start of his freshman year, a few white families mistook him for a custodian. Several other parents informed SMU officials that they did not want their sons living next to an African American, and his initial roommate moved out after one day. Lineman Terry May became his roommate for the next two years. LeVias eventually began to receive obscene telephone calls and hostile letters. As the volume of vicious communications increased, athletic department employees started screening LeVias's mail, separating out the hate letters, which were turned over to him at his graduation.

LeVias played only sparingly on the freshman team during his first year at SMU, but as a sophomore in 1966 he stunned opposing fans with several daz-zling performances. Unexpectedly joining him in SWC varsity competition that fall was John Westbrook, a former walk-on at Baylor whose hard work in spring training had earned him a football scholarship. Westbrook's relatively unknown presence as a second-string halfback for Baylor did not defuse the animosity that the high-profile LeVias attracted as a star player and the first black scholarship recipient in the conference. In SMU's home opener against the University of Illinois, LeVias quickly impressed fans by catching two touchdown passes from quarterback Mac White in leading the Mustangs to a 26–7 upset. Three weeks later the sensational sophomore led his team to a come-from-behind victory over the Rice Owls by catching a touchdown pass in the game's final seconds. Despite increased attention from opponents' defenses, LeVias still scored a touchdown in each of the Mustangs' next two victories over Texas Tech and Texas. By November SMU fans were dreaming of the school's first Southwest Conference title since 1948. Against Texas A&M LeVias returned an Aggie punt eighty-three yards for the winning touchdown, and against Baylor he scored on a scintillating one hundred–yard kickoff return, confirming his growing reputation as "a game-breaker." SMU then clinched the Cotton Bowl invitation with a 21–0 shutout of TCU in Fort Worth, completing the school's best record since 1948. LeVias ended the season as the SWC leader in total scoring, made the all-conference team as a wide receiver, and was named "most valuable line-man" on the honorary team.[19]

Jerry LeVias's outstanding performances were even more remarkable in light of the verbal abuse and physical punishment that he endured on and off the field during the season. On the SMU campus the volume of hostile telephone calls increased until LeVias finally obtained an unlisted number. Despite efforts by the athletic department to screen his mail, a few hate letters still slipped through. On the gridiron rival players often targeted him because of his skill and his race. Players from every SWC team hurled racial slurs at him during pileups, as well as an occasional knee or fist if they could escape detection. In the third game of the season LeVias was even embarrassed by one of his teammates on the sidelines, who yelled, "Stop that nigger!" when a Purdue halfback broke past the line of scrimmage on a long run. Against Baylor LeVias was further disheartened to hear his white opponents mutter racial insults at him, despite the presence of John Westbrook on their team. In Austin a few Texas Long-horn fans waved ropes tied in hangman's nooses at LeVias. When SMU played Texas A&M cadets dumped several black cats on the field in order to razz him. In the fourth quarter an Aggie defender surreptitiously voiced several racial insults at LeVias. The Mustang star responded a few minutes later by fielding an A&M punt and returning it eighty-three yards for the winning touchdown. Although some of the older SMU players were cool toward LeVias, harassment by opponents brought the team closer together. Nonetheless, the continuous racial abuse took a toll on LeVias, who considered quitting the team on several occasions. Hayden Fry often talked with him late into the evening, reassuring him that he could handle the pressure. Overall, Fry provided more emotional support for LeVias than did any other southern coach during the process of athletic integration. At the end of November a frustrated Fry went public with details about the weekly mistreatment of LeVias. Rival coaches quickly denied that any of their players had acted improperly, of course. At a SWC coaches meeting in early December, though, the group took the unusual step of issuing a call for better sportsmanship from member schools, but without mentioning LeVias or the race issue.[20]

During the winter LeVias considered transferring but eventually decided to remain at SMU. Perhaps because of publicity over his harassment, the number of racial incidents on the playing field declined substantially over his last two years. Yet the 1967 season proved disappointing for other reasons. Most of the defensive standouts on SMU's championship team the previous year had graduated, and injuries further weakened the squad. The Mustangs eventually finished the season with a disappointing 3-7 record. Despite regularly facing double coverage as a pass receiver, LeVias still led the conference in total receptions. At the end of the season, sportswriters selected him for the All–Southwest Conference first team. In his final year LeVias again performed brilliantly, and the Mustangs rebounded to post an 8-3 record. The senior wide receiver broke the SWC record for total receptions in a season by catching eighty passes that year, finishing second in the nation in that category. In the fourth game of the season, against TCU, LeVias experienced one more disgraceful incident when a tackler spat on him and uttered a racial slur as the two got up from the turf. LeVias took himself out of the game and threw his helmet on the ground in disgust. After TCU failed to advance the ball, however, he reentered the game with the punt-return unit after promising Fry that he would get revenge by scoring on the play. Leaving would-be tacklers sprawled all over the field, LeVias dramatically returned the punt eighty-nine yards for the winning touchdown. Fry later described the run as "the most inspirational football play I've ever seen." The Mustangs finished third in the SWC behind nationally ranked Texas (third) and Arkansas (sixth). Sportswriters heaped numerous honors on LeVias, including All-SWC first team, All-America first team, and academic All-America. He also received the conference sportsmanship award and was named the most valuable player in two postseason all-star games. In May LeVias graduated with a degree in business and went on to play in the NFL for six years.[21]

Coach Hayden Fry continued to seek out black high school prospects for the Mustangs in the years following LeVias's arrival. His willingness to break the SWC color line in 1965 had earned him much respect among black Texans and made recruiting somewhat easier. In 1966 SMU signed three African Americans to scholarship agreements—Rufus Cormier and Lee McElroy from Beaumont and Walter Haynes from Baton Rouge. During LeVias's last two years at SMU he roomed with Cormier, an outstanding student. The presence of Cormier and other black players on the Mustang team, as well as a slow increase in the number of black undergraduates on campus, reduced some of the social isolation that LeVias had experienced during his first two years in Dallas. In the spring of LeVias's senior year, many of these new students formed the Black League of Afro-American and African College Students (BLAACS) and pressured the SMU administration with demands for racial change on campus. When LeVias did not join the movement several BLAACS members labeled him an "Uncle Tom." Cormier assumed a leadership role in the group, and SMU president Willis M. Tate later credited him with keeping the often heated negotiations between student activists and administrators from escalating out of control. After his senior season Cormier won a prestigious Rhodes Scholarship to study at Oxford University, and he later graduated from Yale Law School.[22]

The willingness of Southern Methodist to aggressively recruit African American football players earlier than rival SWC teams clearly brought benefits to the Mustang program. To the extent that one athlete can make a difference, Jerry LeVias personally revitalized Mustang football. The African Americans who followed him to SMU also contributed to the Mustang cause, but they did not have the same impact as LeVias. Despite SMU's pioneering actions and its initial success on the field, the university did not secure a permanent advantage over conference rivals, once they also recruited African Americans. Thus, football integration did not permanently alter the balance of power in the SWC, and SMU football struggled during the 1970s. In the 1980s SMU returned to prominence and captured three conference championships. Unfortunately, the team's coaches and wealthy boosters committed numerous major violations of NCAA regulations, including direct payments to players. Consequently, the NCAA imposed the so-called death penalty on the university, banning the Mustangs from competition for the 1987 season. This scandal created a negative image for the SMU football program, obscuring the earlier progressive image that the university had acquired during the 1960s under Coach Hayden Fry.

John Westbrook Struggles to Integrate Baylor Football

The second member of the Southwest Conference to integrate its football program was Baylor University. Located in the central Texas town of Waco, the university was affiliated with the (Southern) Baptist General Convention of Texas. Traditional southern white culture dominated race relations in Waco, which in 1916 had been the site of the infamous mutilation and lynching of Jesse Washington at the downtown square. Baylor established its first school football team in 1899, and the rough new sport proved quite popular with students. Over the decades the college team, known as the Baptists and later the Bears, achieved only moderate success in the Southwest Conference. Baylor's conservative trustees displayed no interest in the late 1950s in integrating the study body, but by 1962 faculty members, several administrators, and the student government were urging them to do so. In April of that year a straw poll of students found substantial support for desegregation on campus, except in the area of housing. In November 1963 the Board of Trustees ended its resistance and approved a new policy stating that "neither race nor color [will] be a factor to be considered in the admission of qualified students." At the end of the month the athletic council announced that the college's sports teams would be open to all qualified students.[23]

Despite this change in athletic policy, Baylor's first African American football player would not arrive on campus for two more years, and then somewhat by accident. Since the new policy did not require Bear coaches to actively seek out African American high school prospects, the football staff continued to ignore them for the next two recruiting seasons. Then in September 1965 the first African American to play football at Baylor quietly enrolled without an athletic scholarship. John Westbrook, a 190-pound halfback, had been an excellent player at Booker T. Washington High School in the small Texas town of Elgin, ninety miles south of Waco. The son of a teacher who also served as a part-time minister, Westbrook was an unusually serious young man. At the age of fifteen he had been ordained as a Baptist preacher, and he ranked second in his high school graduating class. Westbrook received scholarship offers from several historically black universities, but he was interested in competing for Baylor. Although he had contacted the athletic department before his senior year, the football staff neglected to scout any of his games. During the summer of 1965 he again spoke with the athletic department and confirmed that he would at least be allowed to try out for the team.[24]

Unlike Jerry LeVias's brilliant record at SMU, Westbrook experienced a disappointing athletic career at Baylor. His first semester proved especially daunting. Westbrook selected the Baptist school because of its religious atmosphere and its solid academic programs. Although he was not primarily motivated by a desire to become a racial pioneer, he did consciously wish to prepare himself to function in an increasingly diverse society. As he later told an interviewer, "I figured at that time, 1965, if I was going to compete in the world that was becoming more and more integrated, I should go to an integrated college." Lacking an athletic scholarship, Westbrook patched together a small church-related scholarship, a student loan, some modest financial assistance from his parents, and a part-time job in order to pay for his first year. He reported to freshman football practice at the start of classes, two weeks after the scholarship freshmen had commenced workouts. Because of this late start it took time for his performance to catch the attention of the coaches. As one of the fastest members of the team, however, his ability could not be totally ignored. Nonetheless, freshman coach Catfish Smith resisted giving Westbrook much playing time in games, probably because he wanted to see what his scholarship players could do and because was unhappy with having an African American on his squad. Westbrook appeared briefly in only a few games, accumulating a grand total of three minutes of playing time during the 1965 freshman season. An auspicious beginning it was not. Away from the football field, he found his social opportunities limited. The absence of black females on campus frustrated Westbrook, who clearly understood the racial etiquette of the time, even before a coach cautioned him to "watch yourself with girls." Fortunately, he discovered that he could hold his own with white students in the classroom. His freshman English teacher, Sherry Castello, provided academic encouragement and even invited him to dine with her family, a bold action in Waco. When spring training arrived, his spirits improved. Head coach John Bridgers, who was widely respected for his integrity, insisted that Westbrook be given a fair chance, and the freshman delivered several impressive performances. Although several assistant coaches downplayed his efforts, Westbrook later recalled, Bridgers "overrode all the coaches and gave me a full scholarship." Finally, it seemed, Westbrook had turned a corner in his young career.[25]

During the 1966 varsity season Westbrook showed flashes of considerable promise when given a chance, but he also suffered an injury that handicapped him for the rest of his career. In the nationally televised season opener against Syracuse, one week before Jerry LeVias's debut for SMU, Westbrook entered the game in the fourth quarter, as the stadium announcer blurted out, "Colored football for color TV." In the next four games Westbrook continued to see limited action, although he did score a touchdown against Washington State. Finally, in the sixth contest of the season against TCU, Westbrook received more playing time because of an injury to one of the starters. Unfortunately, on his best run of the day, a fourteen-yard gain, a tackler crashed into his right knee, seriously injuring it and in effect ending his season. In the spring of 1967 doctors performed surgery on the knee, but by the start of the fall season it had not fully healed. Westbrook sat out the first two games before playing extensively in a 10–7 victory over Washington State. He saw less action in the Bears' next two games, as his knee clearly hindered his movement. Worse yet, Westbrook then suffered a concussion during practice, forcing him to sit out Baylor's final five games. Worried that prejudiced assistant coaches were trying to run him off the team and fearful that his knee might never heal properly, he became further depressed. Late one fall evening he hit an emotional low and swallowed a handful of aspirin in a halfhearted suicide attempt. Fortunately, Westbrook survived this incident, but his future as a football player appeared bleak.[26]

Despite his injury problems, lack of support from assistant coaches, and the death of his mother at the start of classes, Westbrook returned for his senior season. The previous spring he had discussed quitting the team with Bridgers, but the compassionate head coach had encouraged him to remain on the squad.

The player's strong religious faith and his determination to prove that he could compete physically and intellectually at Baylor helped him persevere. Nonetheless, as the season progressed, Westbrook found his role limited mostly to duty with the kickoff and punting units. He continued to worry that running backs coach Pete McCulley was prejudiced against him and had given up on him when he first injured his knee. In the final game of the season against Rice, Bridgers sent Westbrook onto the field in the fourth quarter. As the Bears marched down the field, the senior halfback carried the ball five times and scored Baylor's second touchdown to clinch a 16–7 victory. Although he said nothing publicly at the time, Westbrook privately believed that he should have played more during the 1967 and 1968 seasons. On the other hand, some unsympathetic white Baylor fans grumbled that Bridgers's desire to make a symbolic racial statement had caused him to be too generous with a halfback whose knee injury had effectively ended his career. Away from the gridiron Westbrook found more support from his teachers and some of his fellow students, and he continued to earn good grades. In May 1966 he graduated with a degree in English, fulfilling at least one of his original goals in selecting Baylor.[27]

Several other African Americans followed Westbrook to Baylor, making the Baptist school one of the two pioneering institutions in the conference, along with SMU. Tommy Reaux, a defensive lineman, entered Baylor one year after Westbrook and played for three years on the varsity. Reaux had been scheduled to attend Tennessee State University on a scholarship but instead enrolled at Baylor at the last minute. After his excellent performance on the freshman squad, Bridgers awarded him a scholarship. Reaux experienced few of the racial problems during his varsity career that Westbrook had encountered, as coaches and players had begun to adjust to integration. Reaux's obvious football prowess, which twice earned him second-team All-SWC honors, also furthered his acceptance on the team. Roland Hunter, a tight end, enrolled in 1967 and also played three seasons for the Bears. Thus, in the fall of 1968, the varsity football team at Baylor included three African Americans on scholarships, at a time when five Southwest Conference schools did not have even one black scholarship athlete on their varsity squads. Baylor's religious ties apparently made it somewhat easier to overcome opposition to recruiting African American athletes. Furthermore, the football team's average performance may have motivated coaches to accept a new source of talent. Nonetheless, Baylor failed in the long run to take full advantage of its pioneer role in SWC integration.[28]

TCU Fails to Capitalize on Its Early Athletic Integration

In 1968 TCU became the third member of the Southwest Conference to integrate its varsity football team. Founded in 1873, the university moved to its permanent location in southwestern Fort Worth in 1911 and was affiliated with the Disciples of Christ denomination (known informally as the Christian Church). Despite the misgivings of many faculty and administrators, TCU formed its first football team in 1896. The Horned Frogs, as the school's athletic teams were known, gained admission to the Southwest Conference in 1923 and had captured the conference football title four times by the end of World War II. In 1938 American sportswriters selected the undefeated TCU squad, led by Heisman Trophy winner Davey O'Brien, as the national champion. Under the direction of Coach Abe Martin, the Horned Frogs dominated the SWC in the 1950s, winning or sharing the league title four times. After 1959, however, the football team struggled, achieving only four winning seasons over the next thirty years and no SWC championships.[29]

TCU occasionally violated southern racial customs in the 1940s and 1950s by enrolling a few African Americans in special classes. During World War II the university participated in a joint program with the armed forces and offered selected courses for servicemen on campus, which black soldiers were permitted to attend. For a decade after the war TCU continued to provide off-campus courses to active-duty military personnel. However, an occasional science class had to be held on the main campus at night, and black servicemen were again allowed to participate. In the early and mid-1950s TCU also offered education courses exclusively to black teachers at a local public school. Since all of these programs involved special situations, they did not establish a precedent for other academic programs at the university. A more important milestone occurred in September 1952, when the trustees of Brite College of the Bible, a Disciples of Christ seminary that functioned as a semiautonomous unit on campus, voted to accept African Americans. Despite this action TCU trustees and administrators consistently refused to remove the racial restrictions on enrollment in the regular undergraduate programs. Yet many students, even in the early 1950s, expressed support for additional integration. In October 1952 the student newspaper interviewed 100 students and found that three-fourths of them supported the admission of black undergraduates. Several voiced the opinion that a person could not profess a belief in basic Christian principles and support racial exclusion in the classroom. One pragmatic male student even argued that the athletic accomplishments of African Americans merited their access to equal education. Ten years later TCU students again debated the issue. In March 1962 seminary students at Brite College resolved that "all areas of university life be made available to all qualified persons regardless of race or color." The following month, in a student opinion poll, a majority of students endorsed full integration by a margin of 1,088 to 722.[30]

Because of continued resistance from several conservative members of the Board of Trustees, TCU eventually followed a slow two-stage process for undergraduate integration. In the fall semester of 1962 the university specifically opened the nursing college to all applicants and enrolled three African American women. In June 1963 Dr. J. M. Moudy, vice chancellor for academic affairs, circulated a long memorandum supporting full undergraduate integration. Moudy argued that racial exclusion in education was unscriptural and that there were no valid scientific or educational reasons to continue such restrictions. At a special board meeting in January 1964 Chancellor M. E. Sadler endorsed complete integration of all university programs. Despite some continued opposition from conservatives, the trustees overwhelmingly approved the elimination of all racial restrictions on enrollment. During the following week twelve black students registered for undergraduate classes in the evening program.[31]

Although Texas Christian lagged behind most other Texas universities in fully integrating its undergraduate programs, the university soon became one of the first Southwest Conference schools to aggressively recruit minority athletes. Chancellor Sadler personally encouraged Horned Frog coaches to seek out black prospects who had the grades, talent, and character necessary to be the "first" at TCU. In football new head coach Fred Taylor (1967–70) did not have much immediate success. Since the Horned Frogs won only fifteen of the forty-one games played during Taylor's four years on the job, few top prospects, black or white, wished to play at TCU. Nonetheless, in 1968 TCU became the third SWC school to field an integrated varsity football team with the arrival of the team's first black recruit, Linzy Cole, a JC All-American. The speedy wide receiver enjoyed two productive years at TCU. As a senior Cole led the Horned Frogs in scoring and received the team's MVP award. Coach Fred Taylor later recalled that "the other players accepted him right from the start" and socialized some with him off-campus. Taylor continued to recruit African American players from the area. His 1970 varsity team included five talented black sophomores and a junior college transfer. All six of these players played important roles during the season. Unfortunately, the team won only four games, and Taylor was forced to resign.[32]

Several more losing seasons, two coaching changes, and growing complaints from African American students about campus life created additional challenges for the TCU football program. To replace Taylor, the college hired Jim Pittman from Tulane University for the 1971 season. While at the New Orleans school Pittman and his staff had failed to recruit any African Americans. A stern disciplinarian, the new head coach soon clashed with several players. In late October 1971 Pittman tragically suffered a fatal heart attack during a game. Assistant coach Billy Tohill assumed the head coach position, but conflict between players and coaches continued. To complicate matters further, African American students at TCU became more outspoken in 1970 and 1971, demanding that the administration devote greater attention to racial issues and establish a black cultural center. Because of dissatisfaction with the new coaching staff, academic problems, and a new racial sensibility on campus, five of the six black players on the previous year's squad chose not to return for the 1971 season. TCU thus became the only SWC school where internal dissension resulted in significant defections by black players. In 1974 Jim Shofner replaced Tohill as head coach. Because of the turmoil in the program, the Horned Frog team that year included only nine African Americans, fewer than any other SWC squad. Except for the University of Texas team, which included ten African Americans, the rosters of the remaining SWC members all listed between twenty and twenty-nine black players. Thus, the positive legacy of TCU's progressive enrollment history and its early recruitment of black players did not continue past 1971. Worse yet, TCU finished last or next to last in the SWC for the next twelve years. The integration of the football program thus failed to produce any long-term changes in the team's mediocre performances, and internal racial tensions between black players and white coaches initially made winning seasons even harder to achieve.[33]

Texas Tech and Rice Enjoy a Quiet Integration

In contrast to TCU, athletic integration at both Texas Tech and Rice was a relatively quiet process, lacking in drama. Although neither school dared to take the lead in accepting African American players, both still managed to field integrated varsity squads before Texas, Texas A&M, and Arkansas, the three elite members of the Southwest Conference, did so. Texas Technological University officially opened its doors in September 1925, two weeks after the school's football team had started practice. The key figure in the development of Texas Tech football was Coach "Pete" W. Cawthon, who headed the program from 1930 through 1940. The colorful coach set out to win national recognition for the Red Raiders by scheduling intersectional games all over the country. In fact, the team traveled so widely that "Join the Raiders and see the U.S.A." became the team's informal recruiting slogan. After Cawthon used two ineligible players who had transferred from the Haskell (Indian) Institute during the 1938 season, though, the Border Conference expelled Tech for "repeated violations of the conference eligibility rules." School trustees became further dissatisfied with Cawthon when the team's 1940 schedule failed to include even one contest against a Texas opponent and forced him to resign. Texas Tech eventually rejoined the Border Conference, which included integrated teams from Arizona. Although the Red Raiders had been willing to play against black players on the road since 1934, university officials stubbornly refused to allow African Americans to compete at home, even after fellow conference members Texas Western and Hardin-Simmons agreed to do so. Facing the growing threat of another expulsion from the conference,

Tech's Board of Directors finally voted on December 6, 1952, to cancel the rule. Four years later school officials saw their greatest athletic dream fulfilled when the Southwest Conference voted to admit the university to membership, fully effective in 1960. Apparently intimidated by influential board member J. Evetts Haley, an independent historian and influential right-wing political figure, Tech officials continued to deny admission to African Americans until 1961, after Haley retired. Then, fearing a lawsuit, they dropped all racial restrictions on enrollment. The school's athletic teams remained closed to black students for another two years, though, until the Board of Directors voted unanimously in December 1963 to allow their participation.[34]

It took another three years before Coach J. T. King (1961–69) found an outstanding high school prospect who was willing to break the color line at Texas Tech. In the spring of 1967 King signed Danny Hardaway of Lawton, Oklahoma, to a football scholarship. The elusive halfback was also a great pass receiver and had been one of the top players in the state. During his freshman year Hardaway performed successfully on both the football and the basketball squads. After sitting out the 1968 football season, he returned in 1969, starting at halfback and leading the team in rushing. His playing time declined somewhat during his junior year, but he became the team's main punt- and kickoff-return specialist. Since Hardaway had grown up in a military family and had previously interacted with whites, he adjusted fairly well to the overwhelmingly white environment in Lubbock. His athletic skills and weekly soul music show on the university radio station made him a well-known figure on campus. Unfortunately, low grades forced him to transfer to Cameron State College in Oklahoma for his final season. In 1969 Jim Carlen replaced King as head coach and expanded the recruitment of African Americans. The 1970 varsity squad included Hardaway and three other black athletes. The integration of Red Raider football did not appear to have altered the team's fortunes, as Tech fielded solid but unspectacular teams until 1976, when the school earned a share of the SWC title for the first time in school history.[35]

The advent of integrated athletic teams at Rice University proved to be relatively uneventful as well. The college owed its existence to the generosity of William Marsh Rice, a wealthy nineteenth-century cotton merchant. In order to finance a private, nonsectarian university "of the first order," Rice created a trust that upon his death converted his huge estate into an endowment of nearly ten million dollars, the seventh largest in the United States at the time. What was initially known as the Rice Institute opened its doors in Houston in 1912, subject to two key restrictions in its charter: (1) no tuition would be charged, and (2) enrollment would be limited to white male students from Harris County. University officials eventually admitted women, and over the years they also allowed a few Asian and other nonblack minority students to enroll. In the early

1960s Rice administrators and trustees attempted to reinterpret the charter's restrictions as part of a long-term plan to raise revenue and elevate the university's national academic standing. Ever-increasing expenses had strained the school budget and necessitated new sources of funding, such as tuition, unless administrators wanted to shelve their ambitious plans. Research funds from the federal government and major private foundations represented a growing share of the school's revenue, but the university's racial restrictions endangered their continuation. Consequently, the Board of Trustees concluded that it was imperative to legally reinterpret the trust's language, in order to charge tuition and admit black students. In February 1963 the trustees filed suit in local court, seeking legal permission to modify these restrictions, but a small group of alumni and heirs of Rice contested the suit. In March 1964 a trial jury returned a verdict in favor of the university. Because the next entering class had been mostly selected and the jury finding was appealed, officials delayed implementation of the new policies until 1965. Unofficially, though, one black graduate student, Raymond L. Johnson, had quietly attended classes during the 1963–64 school year. Because Rice administrators feared that Johnson's enrollment might undermine their legal efforts to revise the charter, they created the fiction that the research assistant was only auditing selected classes and later retroactively awarded him credit for those courses.[36]

The Rice football team had traditionally finished in the lower half of the conference standings in the early years of the SWC. Under the leadership of Coach Jess Neely from 1940 through 1966, however, the Rice teams improved their performance and actually won the conference championship three times. After Neely departed for Vanderbilt, Rice went through four coaches over the next eleven years, achieving only one winning season. Although the school's high academic standards made recruiting difficult, the Owls desperately needed skilled football players, regardless of race. In the spring of 1968 Coach Harold "Bo" Hagan awarded scholarships to the first African American football players in the school's history. Rodrigo Barnes and Mike Tyler of Waco and Stahle Vincent of Greensboro, North Carolina, were all outstanding high school prospects who contributed significantly to the Owl team during their careers at Rice. As sophomores in 1969 all three earned starting positions. Barnes was the most prominent of the three, and after the season sportswriters selected him as the SWC sophomore defensive player of the year. After sitting out the 1970 season because of academic probation, Barnes returned the following year and anchored the Rice defense, earning all-conference first-team honors. Vincent, an honor roll student, became the first black quarterback in the Southwest Conference when he started for the Owls as a sophomore during the 1969 season. Since the talented athlete was a better runner than passer, Harold Hagan moved him to halfback for his final two years. Vincent thrived in his new position, leading the team in total rushing yardage both years. As a senior he was selected for the All-Southwest Conference first team and named the Owls' most valuable player. In the early 1970s Bill Peterson and Al Conover, Hagan's successors, recruited additional African American players who met the university's high entrance requirements. Rice officials broke another barrier in 1972 when they hired McCoy McLemore as the school's first black assistant coach in both basketball and football. Overall, the university's quiet recruitment of black athletes created no public controversies and had no long-range effect on Rice's regular position in the lower half of the conference football standings.[37]

"Orange and White Lack Black"

The last three Southwest Conference schools to add African Americans to their varsity rosters, all in 1970, were the league's three highest-status members—the University of Texas, Texas A&M, and the University of Arkansas. Of the three, Texas attracted far more media attention than the other two. In fact, no other conference member inspired such a sustained public controversy over the racial composition of its football teams. Because of UT's status as the state's preeminent public university and its location in Austin, the state capital, the school found itself at the center of public discourse over sports integration in the 1960s and early 1970s. During those years the Longhorn football team enjoyed phenomenal success on the gridiron, but many Texans repeatedly criticized the coaching staff and the athletic department for their alleged indifference toward minority athletes. Despite UT's elite status, and to some extent because of it, the university failed to take a leadership role on the issue. In 1893 the University of Texas became the first college in the state to establish an official football team, and in 1914 it became a charter member of the Southwest Conference. During the 1940s and 1950s the Longhorn football program achieved national prominence. Under famous coach Dana X. Bible, UT captured the SWC title three times in the forties, and his successors added four more championships in the 1950s. From 1957 through 1976 Darrell Royal developed the Longhorns into the dominant power in the SWC. Over this twenty-year period Texas won or shared the conference title eleven times, and wire-service polls twice picked the Longhorns as the consensus national championships. Despite this remarkable success, accusations that Royal preferred to recruit only white players eventually came to haunt UT athletics and tarnish his reputation.[38]

During the 1950s the federal courts dealt a series of fatal blows to UT's traditional exclusion of African Americans. As historian Joe B. Frantz later observed, "Integration at UT came slowly, painfully, with much unnecessary resistance and embarrassment." In 1950 the United States Supreme Court ordered the School of Law to admit Heman Sweatt, accepting the NAACP argument that the state did not provide a "separate but equal" legal education for black Texans. The regents responded with an evasive strategy that opened only some of the university's graduate and professional programs to black applicants. Following the *Brown v. Board of Education* ruling in May 1954, UT temporarily admitted five African Americans for undergraduate work. One of them, Marion Ford, a chemical engineering major, boldly announced that he planned to try out for the freshman football team. Ford never made it to the practice field, though, because university officials abruptly canceled the five students' admission three months later and told them to attend one of the state's black colleges. In 1955 the board removed all restrictions on graduate work in Austin and allowed Texas Western College to admit black undergraduates. However, the regents also declared that African American students could not enroll as undergraduates on the main campus for one more year. However, in a highly unusual action, President Logan Wilson secretly permitted three black undergraduates to register immediately for summer school on an individual basis. Only one of them, plus another who entered the university in the fall, lasted until June 1956, when the two were openly allowed to enroll and the official ban on black undergraduates was dropped.[39]

The admission of African Americans to academic programs at the university did not mean that all campus activities and facilities were automatically desegregated. As historian Amilcar Shabazz has observed, "Desegregation did not mean inclusivity." Although UT enjoyed the most liberal campus atmosphere of any white Texas college, some school organizations, musical and drama productions, campus housing, and intercollegiate athletics retained their racial restrictions. In a sense, the university was technically desegregated but not fully integrated. Many students nonetheless strongly supported athletic integration. In May 1958 the *Daily Texan* called for an end to continuing segregation on campus, specifically urging the athletic department to remove its racial barriers. In the spring of 1961 the student assembly voted 23-0 to recommend that the Board of Regents permit qualified athletes of any race to participate in intercollegiate athletics. In May and again in September 1961 UT students submitted several petitions to the board that urged the "immediate integration of the athletic program." One unorthodox regent, Sterling Holloway, actually sided with the students and urged his fellow board members to at least permit the integration of the track and field team. Holloway cleverly noted that in track "no bodily contact is involved and . . . only the effort or performance of the individual is the measure of excellence." Unmoved by these requests, the regents responded that no significant changes in policy were needed, since the board had "probably gone further than a majority of the citizens of Texas and the members of the Legislature would approve." Undeterred, the *Daily Texan* continued to hound the board over the issue, warning that if UT did not act promptly, "it will soon find itself hopelessly behind in both athletics and the granting of human rights."[40]

Over the next two years UT students continued to lobby for the elimination of racial restrictions in athletics. In April 1963 a committee of the student assembly reported that intercollegiate sports remained the only area of campus life from which African Americans were still totally excluded. In November the regents finally surrendered. Darrell Royal, the head football coach and athletic director, announced the new policy by stating that any qualified UT student could now try out for the Longhorn athletic teams. Royal seemed to suggest that his staff would soon start scouting black prospects, but other UT coaches quickly pointed out possible problems under the new policy. "The first boy who plays for Texas will really have to be something special to do anything," one coach candidly stated. "He must be a fine athlete as well as have the ability to take jibes and ridicule." Another coach noted that segregation in the athletic dormitory would cause problems, adding, "I can't recruit a boy and tell him he can't live with the rest of the team." The *Daily Texan* applauded the new openness in athletics and predicted that "an eighty-yard run by a fleet Negro halfback will do wonders in dissolving racial antipathy."[41]

At first some journalists speculated that the University of Texas might take the lead in recruiting African Americans. In December 1964 three non-scholarship black students worked out with the track and field squad. One of them, freshman James Means, eventually earned an athletic scholarship and received his initial varsity letter in 1966, becoming the first African American to letter in any SWC sport. By the fall of 1966, though, with Jerry LeVias starring at SMU and John Westbrook playing at Baylor, no additional black athletes had received scholarships at UT. In the spring of 1967 the Texas staff announced that Mike Williams, a linebacker from El Paso, had verbally committed to the Longhorns. Unfortunately, he allegedly missed the minimum SAT score required by UT and instead accepted a scholarship from SMU. This continuing absence of black athletes at the university disappointed many students, especially those African American students who belonged to the Negro Association for Progress (NAP). In May 1967 members of the group met with assistant basketball coach Leon Black, who assured them that the athletic staff seriously considered African American prospects when awarding scholarships. Regrettably, he explained, most did not qualify for admission for a variety of reasons, including low college entrance-exam scores. Despite his openness NAP members remained convinced that UT coaches had failed to make "a sincere effort" concerning black athletes. In October the group picketed outside Memorial Stadium before a home football game. NAP's message was succinctly stated on one student's sign, which read: "Orange and White Lack Black." Later that same month a *Daily Texan* special feature reported that there were only two African Americans currently receiving athletic scholarships, both in track. The newspaper asked, "Can it be that there is only a half-hearted effort in recruitment?"[42]

The Texas athletic program finally awarded its first football scholarship to an African American in 1968, but charges of tokenism and indifference, as well as bad luck, continued to plague the Longhorns well into the 1970s. One non-scholarship student, E. A. Curry of Midland, earned some playing time on the 1967 freshman team, even scoring one touchdown. He practiced with the varsity throughout the 1968 season but failed to make the traveling squad and eventually dropped out of school. Earlier that year linebacker Leon O'Neal of Killeen accepted a scholarship to UT, making him the school's first black recruit in football. O'Neal played extensively on the 1968 freshman team but left the university because of low grades. His departure meant that the great 1969 Longhorn varsity team, which went undefeated and won the national championship, would be an all-white squad. Thus, at the high point of a brilliant career, Coach Darrell Royal found himself the frequent target of criticism from black sports fans. Writers in the *Houston Informer,* an African American newspaper, regularly castigated Royal for his alleged indifference toward the state's black players. Remarks attributed to Royal in a 1967 *Sports Illustrated* article especially rankled African American coaches. When quizzed by writer Dan Jenkins about the large number of outstanding black running backs that year, the Texas coach replied that the top black athlete seemed to be blessed with great speed. He added, "Now he is getting good coaching in our part of the world because of integrated schools. The result is a lot of spectacular backs." When black coaches read this comment, they interpreted it as a major insult to their abilities. In response, Royal insisted that Jenkins had misunderstood his remarks and that he was merely pointing out that black athletes at tiny segregated schools where one coach handled all sports would benefit from attending larger integrated schools with a full staff of specialized coaches. Despite his explanation Royal's reputation suffered further damage among black Texans.[43]

Another controversy erupted in January 1970 when an Associated Press writer quoted Royal as telling colleagues at a football convention that the typical "black coach has not reached the point where his coaching is as scientific as it is in the major colleges." The Longhorn coach demanded a retraction, which he received after the journalist admitted that the quotation had come from a questionable source. In November 1972 the UT football program, which finally included several African Americans, again found itself under attack when the *Austin American* published a five-part series about the status of black members of the Longhorn squad. The six black players interviewed for the series openly voiced suspicions that several of the Longhorn coaches were racially prejudiced. None of them, however, cited a clear example of discriminatory treatment and mostly pointed out cultural misunderstandings. Furthermore, five of the six players also indicated that they would still choose to play for the Longhorns if given the chance again to select a university. Upset by the articles, Royal and his assistants strongly denied that there was any racial friction on the team. Nonetheless, the series, as well as additional rumors such as the claim that Royal had once privately bragged that UT did not need to recruit black athletes in order to win, circulated widely among African Americans and were taken seriously. Coaches from many SWC rivals naturally exploited such reports during the annual recruiting season, reportedly depicting the UT coach at times as virtually "George Wallace in the schoolhouse door." Influenced by these controversies, some black coaches deliberately steered their top prospects away from UT for many years.[44]

Despite these recurring controversies, the Texas football team gradually began to attract a few African American players. In 1969 Longhorn coaches convinced Julius Whittier from San Antonio to accept a scholarship to UT. Reports that the athletic department was unfriendly to black athletes did not intimidate the young recruit, who welcomed the challenge of proving himself at the university. An independent-minded philosophy major, Whittier refused to allow the initial coolness of many teammates to affect his performance. He displayed considerable promise on the freshman squad and as a sophomore earned a varsity letter. He eventually started most of his junior and senior seasons, helping the Longhorns claim their fourth and fifth consecutive SWC championships. Whittier's presence on the team also aided Texas in recruiting several more African Americans. In 1970 the Longhorns signed halfback Lonnie Bennett, and the following year three additional black players, Roosevelt Leaks, Donald Ealey, and Howard Shaw, joined the team. In 1972 Royal hired defensive back Alvin Matthews of the Green Bay Packers as a part-time coach to assist with spring training. Ironically, UT failed to sign a black recruit that year, another embarrassment for the university.[45]

The Longhorns acquired their first African American star when Roosevelt Leaks emerged as an outstanding running back during his sophomore season in 1972. The following year Leaks experienced a spectacular season, setting new SWC records for individual-game and single-season rushing yardage, earning All-America first-team honors, and finishing third in balloting for the Heisman Trophy. Although a serious injury limited his playing time as a senior, Leaks's high profile removed some of the suspicion that black Texans felt toward the UT program. Yet the school still lagged far behind most of its SWC rivals in the recruiting contest. A 1974 study of varsity football rosters in the conference found that only TCU with nine black players (the result of player-coach conflict) had fewer African Americans than UT, which had ten. Leading the SWC in total numbers were SMU with twenty-nine African Americans and Arkansas with twenty-eight.[46]

The arrival of halfback Earl Campbell in 1974 initiated a series of events that permanently altered the perceptions of many southwestern sports fans about

Table 1. Black football players in the Southwest Conference, 1974

University	Number	Percentage of all players
SMU	29	27.4
Arkansas	28	22.8
Rice	26	20.8
Texas A&M	22	22.2
Baylor	21	24.1
Texas Tech	20	22.5
Texas	10	8.8
TCU	9	7.7
Total/Average	165	19.5

Source: Charles M. Tolbert II, "The Black Athlete in the Southwest Conference: A Study of Institutional Racism" (master's thesis, Baylor University, 1975), 40.

the Longhorns. Campbell, a native of Tyler, soon eclipsed Leaks with his awesome performances. The powerful running back earned All-SWC honors three times and was twice named to the All-America first team. In 1977 he won the Heisman Trophy, becoming the first African American from a southern university to receive the prestigious award. Ironically, ten years earlier he would not have been recruited by the Longhorns and probably would have left the state to play for Oklahoma or a Big Ten school. Campbell's status as a superstar who was also a native son helped alleviate much of the suspicion that black Texans had felt toward UT. Royal's sudden retirement in 1976 also removed him from the continuing debate. Over time the Longhorns eventually came to resemble their counterparts in the SWC, as African Americans increasingly dominated football in the 1980s and 1990s. Yet rumors persisted into the mid-1990s that UT would never allow a black player a fair chance to win the quarterback position, which was reserved for whites. By the time that the 2005 Longhorn team, led by sensational quarterback Vince Young, an African American, won the national championship, the issue finally seemed to have been buried, although not totally forgotten by older black sports fans.[47]

In retrospect, Darrell Royal and the UT football program missed a golden opportunity to assume a historic leadership role in SWC integration. Royal's hesitancy grew not out of conscious racism but rather from his own remarkable success under the established sports system. Like other winning coaches in the Atlantic Coast Conference and the Southeastern Conference, he saw little reason to change his traditional and highly successful recruiting habits once African Americans became eligible for SWC competition. When the UT coach finally did seek out African American prospects, he displayed no sense of urgency. Neither did he seem aware of the suspicion with which many black

Texans viewed the University of Texas. Moreover, he also seemed to be search-ing for the perfect racial pioneer, and when he failed to sign such a player, he delayed even longer. Eventually, this procrastination itself became a recruiting barrier. There was also an element of luck involved; a change of mind by just one or two eighteen-year-old athletes could have altered Royal's reputation. Follow-ing his retirement and the arrival of new coaches, the Texas football program eventually constructed a new image for itself, one that combined receptiveness to black athletes with high aspirations for success on the gridiron.

Can African Americans Be Real Aggies?

The other two members of the Southwest Conference to fully integrate their football teams in 1970 were Texas A&M University and the University of Arkan-sas. Founded in 1876 under the Morrill Act as the Agricultural and Mechani-cal College of Texas, A&M served as the land-grant institution for the state. Admission was limited to young white men, and all students were required to join the Corps of Cadets. The university fielded its first football team in 1894. Within a few years the Farmers, as A&M teams were initially known, became an archrival of the University of Texas Longhorns. Most sports fans in the re-gion regarded the annual showdown between the two teams on Thanksgiving Day as the high point of the football season. Under Coach Homer Norton in 1939 Texas A&M enjoyed its greatest season ever. Led by All-American half-back "Jarrin' John" Kimbrough, the Aggies were voted the number-one team in the country and defeated Tulane in the Sugar Bowl to cap an undefeated season. The college prided itself on turning boys into men, and this emphasis on promoting masculinity contributed to a great interest in sports. Extensive hazing of first-year cadets coupled with strict discipline either drove students away or turned them into true believers in the school's mission. Since African Americans could study agriculture and some technical fields at Prairie View A&M, the state's separate and unequal land-grant school, the NAACP devoted its limited financial resources to legal efforts aimed at desegregating other public colleges, especially the University of Texas.

In the early 1960s major changes in fundamental policies dramatically altered Texas A&M and reshaped its future. By 1960 many administrators and members of the Board of Directors had concluded that A&M was lagging behind other public universities in the region and needed to modify its policies in order to attract more students. Their main concerns focused on the admission of women and the abandonment of mandatory participation in ROTC, two cornerstones of Aggie tradition. Previously, women could attend summer school but were not allowed to take day classes during the regular academic year. In addition, it was clear that the university could no longer avoid racial integration. But all three of these potential changes were unpopular with many of the school's conservative white alumni. Nonetheless, in the spring of 1963 the board announced that thenceforth both women and African Americans were eligible for admission to any of the university's academic programs. In June two black graduate students and one black undergraduate enrolled at A&M. In keeping with similar actions at other SWC schools, the directors voted in late November to remove all racial restrictions on participation in intercollegiate athletics. It took two more years, however, before the board dropped the requirement that all students must join the Corps of Cadets for at least two years.[48]

The new admission policies at Texas A&M did not immediately attract many African Americans to the university. The school's somewhat isolated location in East Texas, its emphasis on science and engineering programs, the limited potential for social life, and the aggressive white masculinity of the student body did not appeal to many African Americans. In athletics A&M coaches preferred to wait for their counterparts at other schools to assume the lead in integration. Coach Gene Stallings took over the football program in 1965 and vowed to restore the Aggies to prominence, but his plans for rebuilding the team's fortunes did not initially include African Americans. As Stallings once explained privately, A&M needed "a team that will work, pull, and fight together and really get a feeling of oneness. . . . I don't believe we could accomplish this with a Negro on the squad." Stallings apparently later changed his mind, but nonetheless the first African American football players at Texas A&M were non-scholarship athletes. In the fall of 1967 Sammy Williams made the practice squad as a wide receiver, and the following year he received an honorary letter like other Aggie seniors. A second walk-on, wide receiver Hugh McElroy, made the varsity football squad in 1969. Although he never started, McElroy played in most games as a junior and senior and eventually earned a scholarship. In the spring of 1971 Stallings finally recruited his first black scholarship player from the high school ranks, halfback Jerry Honore from Louisiana. Emory Bellard, who took over as head coach in December 1971, quickly changed the negative attitudes of black high school prospects toward Texas A&M. His outstanding freshman class of 1972 contained many high school stars, including several top black recruits. By 1974 the A&M squad had joined the conference mainstream in its racial composition. Under Bellard the Aggies also became regular contenders for the SWC championship, with African Americans playing key roles in the team's improvement. Bubba Bean, an All–Southwest Conference halfback in 1974 and 1975, emerged as the Aggies' first black star. Under Bellard's leadership, A&M successfully created a new biracial identity for its athletic program and reversed the older negative image that black sports fans held toward the college.[49]

From White Razorbacks to "Razorblacks"

Political pressure from powerful segregationists and a strong attachment to traditional southern culture guaranteed that the University of Arkansas would be one of the last Southwest Conference schools to eliminate its color line in athletics. Administrators at Arkansas had to deal with a far more volatile political environment than did their counterparts at SWC schools in Texas. In 1871 the university opened its doors in Fayetteville in a dual capacity as the land-grant institution for Arkansas and also as the state university. One year later the Board of Trustees, appointed during Radical Reconstruction when Republicans controlled state government, officially announced that the institution was "open to all without regard to race, sex, or sect." Apparently, two or three African American males enrolled in 1872. The president of the university personally taught them, in order "to save embarrassing the teachers." The students did not return for a second year, and the legislature subsequently authorized a branch campus at Pine Bluff for "the poorer classes," which became the segregated college for African Americans. The university continued to exclude black students until 1948, when three black applicants won admission to the law school and the medical school. However, the school rejected black applications for undergraduate study until 1955, when officials faithfully implemented the *Brown* ruling.[50]

In 1957 the bitter political crisis over court-ordered integration of Central High School in Little Rock put the state at the heart of the massive resistance movement in the South and attracted media attention from around the world. As Governor Orval Faubus exploited this situation for political gain, public school integration ground to a halt within the state. By the fall of 1963 only one-third of 1 percent of African American public school students attended classes with whites. In such a hostile political climate University of Arkansas officials exercised extreme caution when contemplating any changes in their educational policies. After several Texas universities dropped their racial restrictions on athletics in late 1963, Governor Faubus announced that he opposed any similar action in Arkansas. Supporting the governor, the Board of Trustees then reaffirmed its policies of excluding African Americans from athletics and dormitories. Black students went to court to challenge these exclusionist policies, and in May 1965 a federal district judge ruled that it was unlawful for the university to discriminate in any area of student life, including housing and sports.[51]

Despite the ruling coaches at the University of Arkansas did not immediately attempt to recruit African Americans for Razorback teams. One brave black student, Darrell Brown, did play on the freshman football squad in 1965, but he received so much harassment from players and coaches that he did not try out for the varsity. In early 1966 basketball coach Glen Rose told reporters that he would be willing to break the color line, if he could find the right player, but influential trustee Dallas P. "Pete" Raney privately reiterated to coaches the trustees' strong opposition to integration. Frank Broyles, the head football coach, had directed Razorback teams to seven SWC titles between 1958 and 1975, as the school became a national power. But for Broyles, athletic integration "was a matter that was out of my hands, and I didn't think about it much." Furthermore, a shift in recruiting policy would have challenged the prevailing southern orientation of the team's most devout supporters. Arkansas fans frequently expressed their support for the Razorbacks by waving Confederate flags and responding enthusiastically when the school band played "Dixie," customs that were uncommon at other SWC schools. Black sports fans despised such displays and often criticized Broyles for his failure to seek out African American recruits. In the late 1960s the trustees at last dropped their opposition to athletic integration, and in 1969 Broyles signed halfback Jon Richardson to a football scholarship. The Little Rock high school star had not previously considered attending the university and was shocked when Broyles contacted him. His enrollment at Arkansas angered some white fans but also brought accusations from a few blacks that he had "sold out." Richardson lived a somewhat lonely existence during his first two years on campus, but eventually he and many white players became close. Each year following Richardson's arrival in Fayetteville, Broyles unexpectedly accelerated his recruitment of African American players, especially from inside the state. By the mid-1970s he had become so successful in attracting black athletes to Arkansas that a few disgruntled white fans even referred to the 1975 SWC championship team as the "Razorblacks." Thus, the long delay by the UA athletic department in implementing football integration did not prevent Broyles and his successor, Lou Holtz, from eventually recruiting the best athletic talent inside the state, regardless of color.[52]

* * *

From 1966 through 1970 the Southwest Conference experienced a difficult process of racial adjustment on the gridiron and the basketball court. The SWC's three church-affiliated members—SMU, Baylor, and TCU—all added African Americans to their football teams before any of the secular universities did so, but the timing of athletic integration did not have any significant long-term effect on the balance of power within the conference. The league's three elite schools—Texas, Texas A&M, and Arkansas—were the slowest to incorporate black athletes but continued to dominate the annual standings. The absence of a massive resistance campaign against school desegregation in Texas should have made it easier for the seven SWC teams located there to abandon their racial restrictions. In reality, though, SWC coaches acted ahead of their counterparts in the Southeastern Conference by only one or two years, hardly a monumental difference. This slowness revealed a strong southern cultural identity, not a separate western identity, for Southwest Conference sports. In Arkansas the state's massive resistance movement led by Governor Orval Faubus was more typical of the Lower South and clearly delayed athletic integration in football. The following two chapters will investigate how the football field and the basketball court at universities in the Southeastern Conference collectively became the "final citadel of segregation" in the larger struggle for full racial equality in higher education.

8

From Exclusion to Prominence

The Southeastern Conference
and Basketball

It is no safer to mix with negroes on the
ball courts than in the classroom.
—A Mississippi legislator, 1963

It is one thing to take in a few colored students
under demands from the federal government and the
unconstitutional Civil Rights Law, and quite another
to give them a free ride as it were. The desire to win a
ball game at any price is a terrible thing.
—An Auburn University fan, 1968

It was the first week of March 1963, and the Mississippi State University basketball team had just clinched its third straight Southeastern Conference championship and an automatic bid to the NCAA Tournament. As Coach James H. "Babe" McCarthy plotted strategy for his team's next game, the biggest challenge confronting him was not the Maroons' probable first-round opponent, the Loyola University Ramblers from Chicago. Instead, the state of Mississippi's rigid color line in sports, which prohibited any "mixed" competition between white and black athletes, constituted a far more formidable barrier. This long-established racial boundary remained so sacrosanct that previous Mississippi State championship teams had been forced to decline invitations to the NCAA Tournament in 1959, 1961, and 1962 in order to avoid playing against integrated teams. In the spring of 1963, however, many MSU students, alumni, and fans publicly argued that the time had come to resume normal athletic competition against northern universities. Encouraged by this grassroots support for the team, President Dean W. Colvard announced on Saturday, March 2, that he would accept the NCAA invitation, unless "hindered by competent authority."[1]

Die-hard segregationists immediately set out to block Mississippi State's trip to the NCAA Tournament. Governor Ross Barnett and several influential legislators warned that accepting "race-mixing" in any area of public life, including college basketball, would greatly undermine the state's united front against federal desegregation efforts and endanger its "southern way of life." But when the Board of Trustees of the State Institutions of Higher Learning met on Saturday, March 9, the trustees unexpectedly rejected a resolution barring MSU from the tournament. Refusing to accept the board's decision as final, two ultraconservative legislators eventually convinced a segregationist state judge on Wednesday, March 13, to issue a temporary injunction that barred university officials from allowing the team to participate in the NCAA playoffs. In order to avoid being served with legal papers blocking the trip, Mississippi State administrators and coaches literally sneaked out of Starkville on Wednesday evening. The next morning, after making sure that sheriff's deputies were not lurking nearby, MSU players departed on a chartered flight to Nashville. There they joined McCarthy and his assistants, and the combined party then boarded a flight to East Lansing, Michigan. The next evening, March 15, Mississippi State squared off against the Loyola Ramblers, whose lineup included four black starters. MSU took an early lead in the contest, but the Ramblers eventually pulled away in the second half to win the game. Despite the loss the Maroons' struggle for the opportunity to compete in the NCAA Tournament won the respect of sports fans around the country. More significantly, their tournament adventure demonstrated that many white Mississippians had turned their backs on the state's extreme segregationists and were anxious to rejoin the rest of the athletic nation, even if it required some modification to their Jim Crow traditions.[2]

Southeastern Conference Basketball and the Color Line

The 1963 controversy over Mississippi State's participation in the NCAA tournament briefly focused national attention on basketball in the South, a region where "King Football" reigned supreme. Basketball apparently first arrived in Dixie in 1893 in Nashville, where Vanderbilt students learned the new sport at a downtown YMCA. Vanderbilt established its own official college team during the 1900–1901 school year, while the University of Kentucky fielded a team in early 1903. Basketball had spread to the Deep South by the 1905–6 school term, when Auburn, Georgia Tech, and Tulane began organized play. In 1921 a group of major southern universities who emphasized "big-time" sports formed the Southern Conference. Eventually, the league accepted so many additional colleges that it lost its cohesiveness. As a result, thirteen ambitious universities from the mid-South and Deep South withdrew in December 1932 and created the Southeastern Conference. The founding members of the SEC included the state universities of Alabama, Florida, Georgia, Kentucky, Mississippi, and Tennessee, as well as Auburn, Georgia Tech, Louisiana State, Mississippi State, Tulane, the University of the South (Sewanee), and Vanderbilt University. Sewanee soon withdrew from the league in 1940, followed much later by Georgia Tech in 1964 and Tulane in 1966.[3]

Unlike Southeastern Conference football teams, few SEC basketball squads traveled north for major intersectional games until after World War II. Hence, conference schools rarely encountered any direct challenges to their policy of racial exclusion on the court until well into the 1950s. Instead, the SEC placed great emphasis on its original postseason conference tournament, which lasted from 1933 through 1952. Because of transportation difficulties during winter months and the size of the conference, member schools did not play a complete round-robin schedule. Thus, an end-of-the-year tournament determined the actual league champion and heightened public interest. Of the nineteen tournaments held from 1933 through 1952, Kentucky captured thirteen championships, Tennessee three titles, and Georgia Tech, Alabama, and Vanderbilt one each. The creation of the NCAA postseason basketball tournament in 1939 created one possible challenge to the traditional southern policy of racial exclusion. In the NCAA's national playoff format, participating southern teams could not negotiate where or against whom they might play. Furthermore, most tournament sites were located outside the South and did not automatically honor southern racial etiquette. For the first twenty years of the NCAA tournament, however, this problem failed to materialize, for two reasons. First, many northern basketball teams lacked African American players until the 1950s. Second, Kentucky so consistently dominated the Southeastern Conference that the school in effect shielded all of its fellow SEC members except Mississippi State from possible interracial competition.[4]

Following the Supreme Court's *Brown v. Board of Education* ruling, the issue of competition against integrated athletic teams now became part of the larger struggle to defend Dixie's traditional racial structure. White resistance to integration ran especially strong in the Deep South states, where nine of the twelve SEC schools were located. For many white politicians, intersectional athletic competition had become too sensitive an issue to be left in the hands of mere educators. University administrators had no choice but to modify their scheduling practices in order to avoid political retribution. By 1960, however, these passions had cooled somewhat, although opposition to integrated home games remained strong. As the *New Orleans Times-Picayune* reported, "The segregation custom creates scheduling problems for many colleges in the Deep South. The subject is a touchy one, and coaches don't talk about it publicly. It is no secret, however, that fear of local opposition, particularly from politicians who control the purse strings for state-supported institutions, often prevents home-and-home series with integrated schools." By middecade, though, SEC members came to regard competition against teams that included African Americans as an acceptable cost of maintaining a nationally recognized athletic program. Yet this decision did not mean that SEC coaches were anxious to take the next step and recruit African Americans for their own squads. On southern campuses the basketball court and the football field remained special areas of "white space" protected from the larger racial changes that were sweeping across Dixie. Small wonder then that some critics viewed SEC sports as one of the last strongholds of segregation in the region.[5]

During the latter half of the 1960s sportswriters around the country, representatives of the U.S. Office of Education, and the growing number of black students on southern campuses increasingly pressured Southeastern Conference universities to recruit black athletes. Beginning in 1965 presidents of universities receiving federal funds were required to certify that their institutions adhered to the nondiscrimination provisions of the Civil Rights Act of 1964. Charles Morgan Jr. of the American Civil Liberties Union officially requested in 1966 that the U.S. Office of Education investigate SEC members to determine if they "practice racial discrimination in their athletic programs," explaining that the importance of football and basketball at southern colleges "cannot be overemphasized." Although federal officials did not initiate any special investigations of college sports, they did begin collecting information on athletic scholarships as part of their regular duties.[6]

African American students also voiced growing concern over the absence of black athletes on their school teams. At Kentucky black students picketed Memorial Coliseum in December 1967 to protest the failure of Adolph Rupp to recruit any African Americans for the Wildcats. Elsewhere in the SEC, newly formed black student associations aggressively criticized racial practices on campus, always listing the lack of minority athletes as one of their major complaints. To most African American students, especially males, the continued absence of blacks from athletic teams stigmatized all minority students as second-class citizens. On the other hand, equal participation in this core university activity would create a new level of acceptance and generate public respect for their presence on campus. Through sports black men could prove their manliness, character, and usefulness, thus demonstrating their equality with whites and generating pride among all African Americans. This "muscular assimilation," to borrow historian Patrick Miller's term, would validate African Americans in a region where athletic success ranked as one of the highest possible achievements for males. Many white students also endorsed athletic integration by the late 1960s, but usually on more pragmatic or opportunistic grounds.[7]

Most SEC basketball coaches preferred to avoid political controversies and waited for someone else to take the lead in integrating the conference. Because of his preeminent status as the most successful college basketball coach in the country, Kentucky's Adolph Rupp attracted considerable speculation about whether he would sign a black recruit, and also much criticism when he failed to do so. Virtually all head coaches faced pressure from wealthy donors, influential alumni, and segregationist politicians against integrating their teams. When quizzed by reporters, many coaches claimed that they did not know of any African American prospects who possessed both the athletic and the academic ability necessary to succeed in the conference. These comments about academic performance were somewhat ironic, since the SEC itself had been often criticized over the years for maintaining low academic standards. Frank Howard, the head football coach at Clemson, once referred sarcastically to the SEC as "the knucklehead league." In 1963 the conference tightened its policies by requiring scholarship recipients either to post a B average in high school or to achieve a minimum SAT score of 750. Race was not a factor at the time, since all SEC athletes were white. By 1970, though, the SAT requirement had become a barrier for those coaches who genuinely wished to recruit African Americans.[8]

Within the Southeastern Conference university presidents and the commissioner's office mostly failed to exert any progressive leadership concerning the league's color line during the early and middle 1960s. Presidents Frank G. Dickey and John W. Oswald of Kentucky were the only college leaders bold enough to openly endorse athletic integration prior to 1965, although Chancellor Alexander Head at Vanderbilt worked quietly behind the scenes to promote the recruitment of African Americans at his university. While occupying the Office of the Commissioner, Bernie H. Moore (1948–66) and A. M. Coleman (1966–72) ducked the potentially divisive issue and never took a public position supporting the incorporation of black athletes into the conference. In their defense it should be noted that the commissioner's office did not possess much independent power, since the presidents' council was the body that officially established league policy. The conference's regularly scheduled meetings of college presidents and athletic directors likewise avoided any formal discussions about integration, although many attendees privately shared their concerns during social functions. So strong was this unofficial taboo about mentioning race in public that at a January 1968 SEC meeting in Tampa, neither the commissioner's annual report nor the formal agenda acknowledged that black players had made their first appearances that fall in varsity competition.[9]

It is not surprising that such institutional foot-dragging, nurtured by the fierce political resistance to desegregation in the Lower South, made the SEC the last major southern conference to abandon its racial barriers. Nonetheless, by the spring of 1973 all SEC members finally had admitted African Americans into the previously protected spaces of the football field and the basketball court. The actual desegregation process lasted roughly from 1966 through 1973. Tulane University technically recruited the first African American to break the color line in any major SEC varsity sport. Sophomore outfielder Steve Martin of Marrero, Louisiana, who held an academic scholarship, started for the Green Wave baseball team during the spring 1966 season. Because Tulane officially withdrew from the conference immediately after Martin's first varsity season ended, southern sports fans and journalists soon forgot his participation. Not surprisingly, SEC members in the Upper South generally acted sooner to integrate their squads than did their counterparts in the Lower South. In football the University of Kentucky became the first school to break the color line in the fall of 1967, with Tennessee taking similar action one year later. Vanderbilt took the lead in SEC basketball integration when Perry Wallace became the first African American to compete in SEC varsity basketball during the 1967–68 season. No conference member followed Vanderbilt's lead the following year, and during the 1969–70 season only Auburn's Henry Harris joined Wallace in varsity competition. The pace of basketball integration accelerated during the 1970–71 season. That year Alabama, Georgia, and Kentucky fielded their first integrated teams, meaning that half of all SEC squads now included African Americans. The following year LSU, Tennessee, Florida, and Ole Miss added black players to their varsity teams. Mississippi State, the last conference member with an all-white roster, added two black recruits to the Maroon squad during the 1972–73 season, completing the initial phase of basketball integration in the SEC.[10]

Once this color line dissolved the number of African Americans participating in SEC basketball and football increased steadily. A change in NCAA eligibility standards accelerated this process. In 1973 the association adopted a new lower eligibility rule requiring incoming freshmen to a have earned only a C average in high school in order to qualify for an athletic scholarship. NCAA members had approved this policy in part because it would facilitate the greater incorporation of African Americans into southern athletic programs. The new eligibility rule definitely assisted SEC coaches in recruiting increasing numbers of African American athletes and eliminating fears of "tokenism" in athletic participation. By 1980 it was clear that the basketball court and the gridiron no longer served as special areas reserved exclusively for white males. The expanding presence of minority athletes literally changed the "face" that SEC universities presented to the general public, an important symbolic action. Player recruitment in turn led to the hiring of black assistant coaches, as the concept of "integration" now took on a broader meaning. During the 1980s the number of black assistants slowly increased, but no SEC university seemed eager to hire an African American head coach. Eventually, in April 1989, the coaching fraternity expanded its elite membership when the University of Tennessee selected Wade Houston to direct its basketball program. Houston's hiring opened up a new era in SEC basketball history, one that was far removed from the days when Jim Crow controlled the sport. An examination of the individual experiences of each SEC school helps explain how national changes in civil rights policy, competitive athletic pressures, shifting student values, and black activism combined to reshape institutional practices and eliminate the color line in basketball. African American players occupied a central role in this drama, struggling to achieve their individual goals and to "advance the race" through their athletic accomplishments in a strange and often hostile college environment.[11]

Perry Wallace Leads a Lonely Life at Vanderbilt

The first member of the Southeastern Conference to desegregate its basketball program was Vanderbilt University in Nashville. The university's urban location in the Upper South, its private legal status, and its resulting freedom from dependency on state funding should have facilitated the acceptance of African American students. This was not the case, however. Named after benefactor Cornelius Vanderbilt, the college opened its doors in 1873 and maintained an affiliation with the Methodist Episcopal Church, South, until 1914. During the 1950s and early 1960s Vanderbilt underwent a protracted and painful debate over its racial restrictions on admissions. Under the prodding of Chancellor Harvie Branscomb, the conservative Board of Trustees reluctantly voted in 1953 to permit a local African American minister to enroll in the School of Religion. Three years later the board allowed the School of Law to admit its first two black students. These two young men were not allowed to compete in intramural sports, but they were permitted to sit with their fellow students at football and basketball games. Nonetheless, African Americans remained excluded from undergraduate studies until May 1962, when the trustees announced that thenceforth university admissions would be conducted "without regard to race or creed." Still, it was not until September 1964 that the college's first black students, nine in all, finally registered for undergraduate classes.[12]

Vanderbilt had been one of the pioneers in college basketball in the South, fielding its first team during the 1900–1901 school year. During the 1920s the Commodores began scheduling athletic contests against northern or western squads, and in the late 1940s Chancellor Branscomb quietly dropped the color line for these games, if held outside the South. The 1960s were especially good years for Vanderbilt basketball. Under Coach Roy Skinner the 1965 squad went 24-4 and captured the SEC championship, while the 1966 and 1967 teams each finished second in conference play. During these same years the athletic department began its trek toward desegregating the school's sports teams. Dr. Alexander Heard, a well-known southern political scientist, replaced Branscomb as chancellor in 1963. A visionary educator who headed the university for the next twenty years, Heard sought to transform Vanderbilt into a nationally competitive school by upgrading its academic programs and diluting some of its southern traditions. As part of this vision the new chancellor supported racial liberalization in every area of campus life, including sports.[13]

Basketball coach Roy Skinner did not have to look very far to locate an outstanding athlete who met the prerequisites for becoming a racial pioneer. At Nashville's all-black Pearl High School, a nationally renowned basketball powerhouse, center Perry Wallace literally stood head and shoulders above his classmates. In the spring of 1966 Wallace helped lead his team to a 31-0 record and the state championship in the first year of fully integrated competition. Even more impressively, he ranked first academically in his senior class. More than eighty universities, including several historically white southern schools, attempted to recruit him. In May 1966, less than two months after Texas Western College and its all-black starting lineup defeated SEC champion Kentucky for the national title, Wallace signed with Vanderbilt. Wallace selected the university because his parents wanted him to stay close to home, because he admired the Commodores' recent success on the court, and especially because he valued the school's high academic standing. Skinner was not finished recruiting, though, as he soon signed another black prep star, guard Godfrey Dillard of Detroit. The two athletes were the first African Americans to receive basketball scholarships at an SEC school, and their arrival temporarily placed Vanderbilt, along with the Kentucky football program, in the vanguard of racial change in the league.[14]

Wallace and Dillard experienced a difficult first year at Vanderbilt, both on and off the court. There were only ten additional African Americans in their entering freshman class, and many white students remained aloof. Consequently, both athletes experienced bouts of loneliness. Wallace's family ties offered some relief, but he and Dillard found their social life mostly nonexistent. The athletic program made no special provisions for them, treating them exactly like other players. This proved to be a well-intentioned but naive decision. On the basketball court Wallace and Dillard were accepted by their teammates and Vanderbilt fans, but road games in the South proved to be an emotional ordeal. Because of careful planning by coaches, there were only minimal problems with restaurants and hotels, but opponents' home courts were another matter. Hostile fans at Auburn, Tennessee, and especially Mississippi State created an intimidating and threatening atmosphere for the two freshmen. When the Vanderbilt freshman squad ventured into Starkville in early 1967, Mississippi State fans unleashed a torrent of racial insults and threats at Wallace and Dillard. The two players were so shaken that they held hands in the dressing room during halftime in order to find the courage to return to the court for the second half. Sometimes fearful about his personal safety, Wallace nonetheless had an excellent season, scoring seventeen points per game and hauling down twenty rebounds per contest. Vanderbilt students turned out in large numbers to view what the student newspaper termed Wallace's "dazzling play" and "his personalized dunk shot." Dillard also enjoyed a productive season, finishing the year as the number-three scorer on the freshman squad. Despite their individual success, though, both considered transferring to another school because of the abuse they had received on the road and their loneliness on campus.[15]

During the 1967–68 season Perry Wallace earned a starting position on the varsity squad, but Godfrey Dillard sat out the year because of a serious knee injury. Wallace thus became the first African American to break the Southeastern Conference color line in varsity competition. The 1968 Commodores enjoyed yet another successful season, finishing third in the SEC. While home fans strongly applauded Wallace's performances, he again encountered several exceptionally hostile crowds on the road, especially at Ole Miss and Mississippi State. White fans at Oxford even chanted "We're gonna lynch you!" Keenly aware of his role as a racial pioneer, Wallace kept his emotions under tight control during games and afterward refused to complain publicly. Wallace remained a strong defender and rebounder for the Commodores, but his offensive contribution declined because of a new NCAA rule prohibiting the dunk shot, his favorite offensive weapon. To make matters worse, his mother's serious medical problems also proved a distraction at times. In the late fall of 1968 Wallace lost an important source of support when Godfrey Dillard quit the team after being relegated to the varsity B-team in preseason drills. Dillard viewed his demotion as punishment for his political activism as president of the newly formed Afro-American Association (AAA) on campus, a charge Skinner vehemently denied. During the ensuing season Wallace continued to be a defensive stalwart, but his performances were solid, not spectacular. Although Commodore fans remained supportive, he sensed their disappointment that he was not fulfilling their earlier expectations.[16]

In his senior year Wallace encountered a noticeably less hostile reaction from rival SEC fans, and his teammates elected him captain. He finally seemed relaxed on the court, in part because he now felt safe when Vanderbilt traveled to Alabama or Mississippi. Perhaps the belated appearance of the conference's second black player, sophomore guard Henry Harris of Auburn, relieved some of the pressure. Nonetheless, as one of only two African Americans among approximately 120 varsity basketball players in the SEC, Wallace would hardly go unnoticed by rival fans. The Commodores fared poorly during the 1970 season, finishing with a disappointing 12-14 record. Wallace improved his free-throw shooting and offensive production while maintaining his defensive presence, averaging an outstanding eighteen points and fourteen rebounds per contest. In his final game as a Commodore, he collected a season-high twenty-seven rebounds and scored a career-high twenty-nine points in a 78–72 win over Mississippi State. Some fifteen thousand fans gave him a lengthy standing ovation at the end of the game. Both the Associated Press and the United Press selected him for the all-conference second team. Off the court his fellow students displayed their respect for him when they elected him the "Bachelor of Ugliness," the highest student-based award handed out to a male student each year. Wallace also earned his degree in May, completing a difficult double major in electrical engineering and engineering mathematics.[17]

Shortly after the end of the season Wallace shocked the Vanderbilt community by granting two interviews in which he expressed his dissatisfaction with several aspects of his career. Previously he had tactfully avoided any controversial public statements. Now Wallace shared with reporters for the *Nashville Tennessean* and the Vanderbilt student newspaper his numerous frustrations and disappointments. He revealed new details about just how vicious the harassment by rival SEC fans at road games had been and how hurt he felt when university officials, coaches, and teammates never publicly denounced such despicable behavior. Wallace emphasized his loneliness and social isolation on campus, suggesting that most of his fellow students viewed him only as a symbol, not a real person. An encounter with racism at the University Church of Christ, located near the campus, also had left psychological scars. Church elders there had politely asked him to stop attending Sunday services, because older whites in the congregation were threatening to withhold their contributions if he continued to worship there. While Wallace stressed that he greatly valued the education that he had received at Vanderbilt and did not wish to appear ungrateful, he confessed that if he had the opportunity to revisit his original decision he would probably select a college in the North or West.[18]

Wallace's revelations may have reinforced several changes that were already under way at Vanderbilt. In January 1970 the university hired its first African American for a coaching position. Harold Hunter, the former head coach at Tennessee State University in Nashville, joined the athletic department as a part-time basketball coach and recruiter. At the start of the summer, though, he turned down a full-time job offer and left for another position. University officials also expanded their efforts at recruiting minority students and mentoring them once they arrived on campus. Later in the spring Roy Skinner finally recruited another black high school prospect, Bill Ligon of Gallatin, Tennessee. Ligon had been president of his senior class, a National Merit Scholarship finalist, and salutatorian of his graduating class. The following year two high school stars from New York City, Ben Skipper and Billy Smith, joined Ligon at Vanderbilt. Over the following decades the Commodores regularly attracted a few African American players. However, once other SEC members initiated more aggressive recruitment efforts, they soon surpassed Vanderbilt in the total number of minority athletes on their rosters, especially after the NCAA lowered its academic requirements. With its high entrance standards and modest minority enrollment, Vanderbilt struggled to attract the top black prospects, and white ones too, despite its pioneering role in breaking the SEC's color line.[19]

Henry Harris Struggles at Auburn

Two years after Vanderbilt broke the league's color line, Auburn University surprised many southern sports fans, including some of its own alumni, when it became the second Southeastern Conference school to add an African American player to its varsity basketball team. The university's location in a small, predominantly white town in the Deep South did not appeal to many potential black recruits. Moreover, Auburn maintained a long tradition of racial exclusion in sports. The institution had first opened its doors in 1859 as East Alabama Male College. After the Civil War the state acquired the private school and turned it into Alabama's land-grant college, with the new name of the Agricultural and Mechanical College of Alabama. Officials later changed the school's name to Alabama Polytechnic Institute in 1899 and to Auburn University in 1960. Women were first admitted on a limited basis in 1892, but the campus atmosphere remained heavily masculine and sports oriented.[20]

During the 1950s and early 1960s Auburn escaped much of the controversy over segregation in the state's higher-education system, since the key legal battles took place at the University of Alabama. As historian Wayne Flint once pointed out, Governor George Wallace "didn't try to block any doorways at Auburn." The successful desegregation of the state university in June 1963 also destroyed the legal basis for continued segregation at Auburn. For many years the school had dealt with prospective African American students by simply discarding their applications. After Wallace's defeat in Tuscaloosa, though, Auburn president Ralph B. Draughon recommended that the university admit a black student who would be "less bad than the others." Draughon was concerned about protecting the several million dollars that Auburn received annually from the federal government to administer the state agricultural extension service and other farm programs. But the conservative Board of Regents stubbornly refused to desegregate unless explicitly ordered to do so by a federal judge. In the fall of 1963 an African American applicant, Harold Franklin, filed suit in federal court seeking admission for graduate work in history, and Judge Frank Johnson ruled in his favor. Amid tight security measures, Franklin quietly enrolled in January 1964. In September the first two black undergraduates, Anthony Lee and Willie Wyatt Jr., joined him at the university.[21]

Intercollegiate sports, especially football, traditionally enjoyed great popularity with Auburn's overwhelmingly male student body. Over the years the school's athletic teams were known at as Plainsmen, War Eagles, and Tigers. Until the arrival of Coach Joel Eaves in 1949, Auburn's basketball teams were usually rather mediocre, but Eaves slowly turned the Tigers' fortunes around. In 1960 his squad compiled an outstanding 19-3 season record and captured the first SEC championship in school history. However, the team had to sit out the NCAA Tournament because the university was on NCAA probation for violations committed by the football program. In the mid-1960s, once undergraduate studies had been successfully integrated, public attention eventually turned to the university's continuing color line in athletics. Several die-hard members of the Board of Regents still opposed any voluntary desegregation in sports, and new president Harry M. Philpott (1965–80) did not initially press the issue. Even if he had, Tiger coaches faced several recruiting disadvantages when approaching black prospects. Minority enrollment at the university remained small throughout the 1960s, and this tiny African American presence provided limited social opportunities on campus. In fact, African American students were often forced to travel to Tuskegee Institute, located some twenty miles away, for social activities.[22]

Despite these obstacles Tiger coaches initially identified a few promising black high school players during the 1967–68 school year. This new attention may have been encouraged by a visit to campus earlier that year by several representatives of the Department of Health, Education, and Welfare, who had inquired about the participation of African Americans in sports. Basketball coach Bill Lynn took the lead in actively pursuing black prospects. He was especially impressed by Henry Harris, a high-scoring guard with a good academic record at Green County Training School in the western Alabama town of Boligee. After receiving President Philpott's approval to offer him a scholarship, Lynn aggressively courted the young player. In March 1968 he announced that Harris, by then an all-state and All-America high school selection, had accepted a basketball scholarship to Auburn. This news upset many Auburn alumni, fans, and even university trustees. Philpott had previously informed the governing board about the impending development. One unhappy trustee immediately responded, "We can't do that. The state is not ready for that yet." To his surprise several other trustees disagreed with him, explaining that athletic integration was inevitable. One board member even confessed that he had recently assisted the Tigers' recruitment efforts by taking a black prospect to dinner. Yet not all Auburn fans were as tolerant of this historic shift in recruitment policy as were the trustees. Several voiced their displeasure directly to Philpott. One correspondent from Florida informed the Auburn president that he and his friends had reacted "with a sense of real shock and dismay" at the news of Harris's scholarship. The disgruntled fan continued, "It is one thing to take in a few colored students under demands from the federal government and the unconstitutional Civil Rights Law, and quite another to give them a free ride as it were. The desire to win a ball game at any price is a terrible thing."[23]

When Henry Harris arrived on campus in September 1968, he discovered that he was the only African American living in the athletic dormitory. Since he had been selected as the most valuable player in the Alabama high school all-star game and had participated in a national all-star contest as well, Tiger basketball fans held high expectations for his performance. They were not disappointed. Harris led the freshman squad in scoring and quickly became a favorite with the student section at home games. When Harris advanced to the varsity the following season, however, he became frustrated with his more modest role. Lynn moved him to a forward position, where his jumping ability did not fully compensate for his lack of height. Instead of Harris, the featured performer for the Tigers in the 1969–70 season was guard John Mengelt, a deadly shooter who averaged twenty-seven points per game and set the all-time single-game scoring record for an Auburn player with sixty points against Alabama. Harris contributed a solid supporting performance to the team that year and again as a junior, when Mengelt averaged more than twenty-eight points per game for the Tigers. The limitations of this supporting role, as well as continued social isolation on campus, caused him to become increasingly bitter. As a senior Harris underwent knee surgery during the summer but recovered to become a valuable though not spectacular all-round performer and team captain. The Tigers struggled throughout the season, finishing in a tie for seventh place in the SEC. Nonetheless, the Associated Press named Harris to the all-conference third team. Happy to leave Auburn behind, Harris next pursued a professional career in the NBA. Unfortunately, he failed to make the Houston Rockets and then played minor-league basketball while clinging to his NBA dreams, becoming increasingly despondent over his lack of success. Tragically, in 1974 he committed suicide. After Harris's departure the number of black basketball players at Auburn jumped dramatically, and in 1975 four of the five starters were African Americans. Unfortunately, Harris did not live long enough to see the long-term results of his pioneering role at Auburn.[24]

Adding Black to the Crimson Tide

During the 1970–71 basketball season three more Southeastern Conference members, the University of Alabama, the University of Georgia, and the University of Kentucky, fielded their first integrated varsity teams. Alabama and Georgia faced several disadvantages in the recruitment of black athletes for their basketball teams, including Deep South locations and long-standing institutional support for segregation, while Kentucky's location in a border state and its national prominence in basketball provided the university with several potential advantages. The University of Alabama first opened its doors in 1831, with enrollment restricted to young men until 1893. The school experienced its most unpleasant example of intersectional conflict in 1865, when an invading Union army unit burned down most of the buildings on campus. Both the university and the state strongly emphasized their southern heritage and once again became important battlefields during the civil rights era. In February 1956, following a legal victory in federal court, the school's first black student, Autherine J. Lucy, enrolled for undergraduate study. An angry mob soon forced her to flee the campus, however, and university officials later expelled her. When additional African Americans sought admission in the following years, UA administrators employed a variety of evasive tactics to ignore, discourage, or reject them and preserve the university's segregated status. The election of George C. Wallace as governor in 1962 further complicated federal efforts to desegregate the university and eventually damaged the school's reputation. In his strident inaugural speech, Wallace had vowed "Segregation now! Segregation tomorrow! Segregation forever!" The fiery governor soon came to personify white defiance of federal desegregation efforts. In June 1963 he physically blocked the main door of Foster Auditorium to prevent, for a few hours, the registration of Vivian Malone and Jimmy Hood as Alabama's first permanently enrolled black students. Although a modest number of African Americans joined Malone and Hood in the years immediately following Wallace's unsuccessful "stand in the schoolhouse door," most black Alabamians continued to regard the campus as a bastion of white privilege.[25]

The Alabama basketball program enjoyed success in the 1950s but fell on hard times during the 1960s. Under Coach Johnny Dee, the Tide went undefeated in league play in 1956 and finished with a 21-3 record. Unfortunately, the team became trapped in a technical dispute between the SEC and the NCAA over freshman teams and varsity eligibility. As a result, all five Alabama senior starters were ruled ineligible for the NCAA Tournament. Shortly thereafter, Dee left the university, and the basketball team did not achieve the same level of success again until the 1970s. After the Tide won only three conference games in 1968, the university hired C. M. Newton as the new head coach. A former player for the Kentucky Wildcats under Adolph Rupp, the thirty-eight-year-old Newton had coached for twelve years at Transylvania College in Kentucky, where he had signed the school's first African American player. Upon arriving in Tuscaloosa, Newton informed President Frank Rose and athletic director Paul "Bear" Bryant that his recruiting approach would be to seek out the best available prospects inside the state of Alabama, regardless of race. Newton immediately contacted several of the state's top black high school players, including Henry Harris, but he failed to sign any of them. During the ensuing 1968–69 school year the young coach's job became somewhat easier when the state's two separate high school athletic associations merged into one combined group. White and black athletes now competed against each other on a regular basis, and the change was most obvious in basketball. In the finals of the state tournament in March 1969, predominantly black Parker High School of Birmingham defeated predominantly black Carver High School, also of Birmingham, to claim the state title. Integrated high school competition thus highlighted for white coaches the previously overlooked skills of black players and helped prepare white Alabamians for the desegregation of college sports.[26]

In the spring of 1969 Newton signed his first African American recruit. The young Alabama coach was not a social reformer; rather, he viewed athletic integration as a pragmatic experiment that would yield positive results. Newton was impressed by a member of Parker High School's 1969 championship team, 6'6" center-forward Wendell Hudson, who had been overlooked by other coaches. In late April the *Tuscaloosa News* announced that Hudson had signed with Alabama, noting that the athletic program had "quietly broken the color barrier . . . in a moment that proved as undramatic as it was historic." Hudson's mother was unhappy with her son's decision because she feared for his safety in Tuscaloosa, and some black fans criticized him as a sellout for selecting a white college. During the fall of 1969 Hudson stood out as the only black resident of the athletic dormitory. After football coach Bear Bryant deliberately sat down next to him in the dormitory cafeteria for an evening snack, white athletes understood that he was not to be picked on. When the basketball team traveled Newton made sure that there would be no conflicts over hotels or restaurants. On the court Hudson fulfilled Newton's confidence in his potential, emerging as the freshman team's number-two scorer and number-one rebounder.[27]

Newton continued to sign African American players, mostly from within the state, over the following years. A few white fans voiced their objections, but as the team won more games, such criticism declined. During the 1971 season two more African Americans joined the Alabama basketball program—guards Raymund Odums and Ernest Odom from Birmingham. Meanwhile, Hudson started on the Tide varsity as a sophomore and displayed improved offensive skills before being injured. Early in the season the student newspaper referred to him as "perhaps the most exciting sophomore in 'Bama cage history." Meanwhile, Odums established a new season scoring record for the freshmen, averaging twenty-four points per game and creating further excitement among fans. The 1972 Tide roster featured Hudson, Odums, and Odom, while Charles Cleveland, another Alabama native, starred on the school's last freshman team. Hudson emerged as the varsity's key player and subsequently earned a spot on the All-SEC first team. The following year these four athletes, plus center Leon Douglass, played together on the varsity squad, with four of them starting together at times. Sportswriters selected Hudson as the conference player of the year, a remarkable achievement for someone who four years earlier had received only one scholarship offer. After a slow start during his first three years, Newton then coached his teams to the top echelon of the conference, eventually winning the SEC championship in 1976. These achievements validated Newton's pragmatic recruiting strategy. The fact that the team's black stars were Alabama natives helped gain the support of a growing number of white fans. Despite what initially seemed to be a difficult environment at Tuscaloosa, Newton had made basketball integration work.[28]

Georgia Accepts Athletic Integration

Much like the University of Alabama, the University of Georgia did not appear to offer a favorable setting for athletic integration. Founded in 1801, the college did not admit women on an equal basis until the early twentieth century and historically excluded African Americans, even during Radical Reconstruction. After the *Brown* decision in 1954, black applicants continued to encounter a veritable stone wall of administrative and legal resistance. By 1960, however, the federal courts had lost patience with the endless delays. On January 6, 1961, U.S. District Judge William A. Bootle ordered the university to admit two African Americans, Hamilton Holmes and Charlayne Hunter, to undergraduate studies. The two officially enrolled on Tuesday, January 10, and Hunter moved into a dormitory amid considerable tension on campus. The next evening, following an emotional home basketball game against archrival Georgia Tech, several hundred students and town residents rioted on campus for two hours and attacked Hunter's dormitory. For their safety, both Hunter and Holmes were temporarily removed from Athens but returned the following Monday and successfully resumed their studies. With the legal battle for integration now won, a few more black students enrolled at the university in the following semesters, but African Americans continued to view the campus as an inhospitable locale for several years.[29]

Georgia's first basketball team took to the court in 1907, but the Bulldogs' mediocre performances over the decades did little to endear the sport to students. After helping establish the SEC in 1932, Georgia consistently finished near the bottom of the standings for several decades and did not win its first regular-season title until 1990. In the late 1960s Georgia's basketball and track programs signed their first black recruits. In 1969 Forrest "Spec" Towns, the track and field head coach, issued the school's first scholarship to an African American athlete. The recipient, Maxie Foster, had been one of the first black students to graduate from predominantly white Athens High School and initially lived at home while attending the university. When Foster was rejected by the freshman basketball team coach, Spec Towns welcomed him onto the track squad and soon placed the young runner on scholarship. Towns also kept a watchful eye on Foster, stopping several football players from harassing him on one occasion. Changes soon began in the basketball program as well. In the spring of 1969 head basketball coach Ken Rosemond hired a new assistant, John Guthrie, who had been coaching at George Washington University. Guthrie possessed a thorough knowledge of prep basketball in the Washington metropolitan area, where many of the top prospects were African Americans. Guthrie's recruitment strategy successfully targeted guard Ronnie Hogue, the team captain at McKinley Technical High School, the city champions. On a campus visit Hogue revised some of his previous stereotypes about the Deep South, impressed by the wide variety of UGA educational programs and the school's modern athletic facilities. The self-confident young man also welcomed the challenge of breaking the basketball color line for the Bulldogs.[30]

During his career at the university Hogue earned many honors, and his success made it easier for the basketball program to recruit additional African Americans. An outgoing student, Hogue got along fairly well with the other athletes, but his social life was somewhat limited. In his three years of varsity competition Hogue displayed outstanding offensive skills and twice led the team in scoring. As a sophomore he established a new UGA individual record by scoring forty-six points in one game. In his junior year Hogue was joined by the team's second African American member, center Tim Bassett, a junior college All-American. For the season Hogue averaged just over twenty points per contest and won All-SEC second-team honors. The following year as a senior, Hogue turned in another strong performance, but his teammate Bassett did even better and was selected for the All-SEC second team. In September 1973 Guthrie was promoted to head coach, and two years later he hired the team's first black assistant coach, Calvin "C. C." Jones, a well-known high school coach in Atlanta. By the following year African Americans constituted a majority of the Georgia squad. While Guthrie's teams never won the SEC championship during his five years as head coach, the successful integration of the Bulldog team partially undermined the negative image that black Georgians held toward the university.[31]

Adolph Rupp and the Black Athlete at Kentucky

Compared to other members of the Southeastern Conference, the University of Kentucky faced relatively few obstacles when pursuing athletic integration in the 1960s. Charlie Bradshaw, the head football coach, exploited the school's natural advantages to become the first SEC coach to recruit African American players, while basketball coach Adolph Rupp was repeatedly faulted for his slowness in adding black athletes to his outstanding teams. The University of Kentucky's location in a border state was one obvious factor that helped facilitate the school's abandonment of its color line. Moreover, Kentucky's relatively small African American population, 7 percent of the state's total population in 1950, did not pose a significant threat to white political domination. Finally, in the early 1960s students and administrators at UK tended to be less conserva-tive on racial matters than their counterparts at most SEC campuses. On the other hand, Kentucky had been a slave state until 1865, and many men from its divided population fought with the Confederate army. After the war the state legislature eventually imposed segregation on all public activities, including education. In a sense, as some historians have quipped, Kentucky waited until Reconstruction to secede from the Union. Despite the presence of several miti-gating factors, most of the state's white residents continued to strongly embrace southern racial values through the end of World War II.[32]

Founded in Lexington in 1865 as an agricultural and mechanical college for white males, the school accepted its first female students in 1880 and became officially known as the University of Kentucky in 1916. Beginning in the 1930s African Americans periodically challenged educational segregation at the uni-versity. In 1949 a federal judge ruled in favor of plaintiff Lyman T. Johnson and ordered UK to admit qualified African Americans into the graduate school and the Colleges of Law, Pharmacy, and Engineering. Despite the ruling the university continued to reject black applicants for undergraduate studies until September 1954, when some twenty black undergraduates were permitted to reg-ister for classes.[33] Kentucky's public school system also began to desegregate in the mid-1950s, although there was "passive resistance" from some local districts for a while. In the spring of 1957 teams from predominantly black high schools competed for the first time in the previously white state basketball tournament. These developments created a far more supportive environment for racial change in athletic policy than could be found in the Deep South states.[34]

University of Kentucky basketball attracted phenomenal support from state residents for most of the twentieth century. In 1930 the university took some-thing of a gamble by hiring a relatively unknown twenty-eight-year-old high school coach named Adolph Rupp, a native of Kansas. Over the next forty-two years he produced forty-one winning seasons and collected 876 victories, a career record that lasted until North Carolina's Dean Smith surpassed it in 1997. Rupp's teams dominated the SEC for more than three decades, capturing NCAA championships in 1948, 1949, 1951, and 1958. One symbol of Kentucky's repeated success and its extensive fan support came in 1950 when the univer-sity constructed a new facility, Memorial Coliseum, known informally as the "House That Rupp Built," which contained the then enormous seating capacity of 11,500. Just over six months after capturing the 1951 NCAA championship, Kentucky suffered a near-fatal blow to its basketball program. During the fall three former players and one current team member confessed to taking bribes from gamblers in order to "shave" points (win by a smaller margin than the betting line predicted) in Wildcat games. As a result of a federal investigation that faulted Rupp and Kentucky for ignoring the influence of gamblers and the university's ensuing refusal to fire Rupp, the SEC banned the Wildcats from all conference play for the 1953 season. The Wildcats rebounded in 1954 by winning the SEC championship and going undefeated with a 25-0 record. But the NCAA then ruled three UK starters ineligible for postseason play on technical grounds, causing Kentucky to decline the tournament invitation. In 1958 the Wildcats recovered and captured their fourth NCAA title. As the decade ended Rupp stood atop the coaching profession as undeniably the top collegiate coach in the nation.[35]

Kentucky's athletic teams had traditionally followed southern racial etiquette by refusing to compete against African Americans, but after World War II the university opportunistically abandoned the policy. Since Rupp aspired to make Kentucky the top basketball program in the nation, he had little choice but to play an occasional northern team that included a black player. Also, Rupp's selection as one of the coaches of the U.S. Olympic team in 1948 led to an important change in Lexington. A special exhibition contest held there in July matched two separate squads that collectively made up the U.S. team. One unit was built around Rupp's Wildcats, the 1948 college champions. The other consisted of amateur players from industrial league teams, including Don Barksdale, the first African American to make the Olympic team. Rupp apparently suggested that the former UCLA star sit out the contest, in deference to local custom, but Amateur Athletic Union (AAU) officials refused. On July 9 some 14,000 fans watched Barksdale lead the amateurs to a 56–50 victory in the precedent-shattering outdoor game at Stoll Stadium.[36]

At the start of the 1951–52 season Rupp scheduled eastern power St. John's University of New York for a December matchup in Lexington. When the national polls were released a few days before the contest, the St. John's squad occupied the number-one spot, while the Wildcats were rated number two. A new member of the St. John's squad, African American guard Sol Walker, almost caused the contest to be canceled. According to St. John's coach Frank McGuire, when Rupp learned that Walker would be traveling with the team to Kentucky, he telephoned McGuire and declared, "You can't bring that boy down here." The fiery McGuire supposedly responded, "Then cancel the game." Rupp backed down, and the Wildcats soundly defeated the Redmen 81–40 without any incidents. In fact, one newspaper reported that "Walker received a round of applause from the crowd each time he left the game." St. John's gained its revenge later in the season, though, when the New York team upset the Wildcats in the NCAA regional finals. Rupp's strategy of playing the toughest teams available, regardless of their racial composition, seemed to work throughout the 1950s. During the 1960s, however, several developments in college basketball, especially the rise of the black athlete, created new challenges that threatened Rupp's elevated status within the basketball world.[37]

In the early 1960s University of Kentucky administrators boldly took the lead in challenging the color line in the Southeastern Conference. President Frank G. Dickey publicly raised the possibility of accepting African American players in December 1961. Complaints from SEC members in Alabama and Mississippi forced him to postpone his plans, but in the spring of 1963 Dickey renewed his call for the conference to address the issue. Dickey also pressured the directors of the University of Kentucky Athletic Association to take a public stand. Subsequently, the directors voted in May to drop all racial restrictions on UK athletic programs. The new university policy did not immediately produce any changes in the racial composition of the Wildcat athletic teams. Eventually, in the fall of 1966, the school's first two black football recruits enrolled at Kentucky, and the following year the university became the first SEC member to field an integrated varsity football team. Also in the fall of 1967, track coach Press Whelan welcomed his first black recruit, Kentucky high school sprint champion James Green. Since freshmen were eligible for varsity competition in track and field, UK and Green broke a racial barrier in yet another SEC sport in the spring. These developments focused further attention on the continued failure of Adolph Rupp to add any black players to the Wildcat basketball squad.[38]

A new university president, various sportswriters, liberal white students, and black students repeatedly urged Rupp to recruit African Americans. Dr. John W. Oswald, a former Phi Beta Kappa scholar and football team captain at De-Pauw College, arrived on campus in the summer of 1963 as President Dickey's replacement. Oswald, who soon joined the board of directors of the local Urban League chapter, sought to develop the university into a nationally renowned institution. To him such a campaign included purging UK of any vestiges of prior discrimination, including racial exclusion in sports. Furthermore, the new president did not hesitate to press Rupp about his recruiting policies, which the veteran coach did not appreciate. After one meeting at which they discussed black athletes, Rupp complained to his assistants, "That son of a bitch is going to drive me crazy. He's unreasonable." The Wildcat coach also complained about athletic and academic deficiencies on the part of African American prospects, alleging privately that "them who can play can't qualify and them who can qualify can't play." Rupp, who turned sixty-five in 1966, also faced more general problems in his approach to recruiting, since he disliked flattering eighteen-year-old athletes regardless of color. His obvious awkwardness around African Americans further handicapped his sporadic efforts to recruit black athletes. Yet despite these limitations Rupp did seriously approach a few black high school stars. Apparently, the first African American prospect that Rupp pursued was center Wesley Unseld, the star of the 1964 state championship team, but the future NBA player politely declined UK's scholarship offer. Unseld may have been negatively influenced by an incident at the state tournament in Lexington earlier that year, when fans had booed him from the stands. The next year Rupp sought out Butch Beard, who has been selected as "Mr. Kentucky Basketball." After some soul-searching, Beard ultimately selected Louisville, concluding that Rupp's overtures were mostly designed to appease Oswald. "We decided that Rupp was under pressure to recruit a black player, but he didn't really want one," he later recalled.[39]

Rupp's repeated failures concerning African American players were viewed in a harsher light after his number-one-ranked 1966 squad lost in the NCAA finals. The Wildcat team, dubbed "Rupp's Runts" because of its lack of size, advanced to the championship game, where they were upset 72–65 by a relatively unknown Texas Western College squad from El Paso. All seven players who saw action in the game for the Miners were African Americans, highlighting the continued whiteness of the Kentucky team. The unexpected loss was an extremely painful one for Rupp and many Kentucky fans. At a banquet honoring the team a few weeks later, one local journalist attempted to console the audience by declaring, "At least we're still the best white team in the country." His comment horrified university officials, and Oswald personally complained to his newspaper's editor. Rupp's critics seized upon the Texas Western victory as proof that his inability to recruit black athletes would endanger the Wildcats' future success. In the summer of 1967 the Kentucky coach appeared on the verge of a major breakthrough when he quietly signed Felix Thurston, an all-state forward from Owensboro, to an SEC scholarship agreement. But Thurston eventually changed his mind and accepted a scholarship to Trinity College, a small school in San Antonio. Since the university chose not to issue a news release about his initial signing, most sports fans never learned about Thurston. Had he enrolled at Kentucky, Rupp's historical reputation and subsequent recruiting strategy might have been different. Instead, by the fall of 1967 student complaints mounted. Members of the newly formed African American student group Orgena ("a Negro" spelled backward) charged that Rupp had failed to make a sincere effort to attract black recruits. In December several dozen members of the group picketed outside Memorial Coliseum during two home games in order to draw attention to the continued whiteness of the Wildcat squad.[40]

It took another year and a half before Adolph Rupp finally landed his first African American recruit. In the summer of 1969 Rupp signed Tom Payne, a seven-foot center from the Louisville area, to a scholarship. Payne's father, a former sergeant in the U.S. Army, deliberately steered his son to Kentucky so that he could break UK's racial barrier in basketball. Since Payne's grades and test scores did not meet SEC minimum requirements, his family paid for his first year at the university, during which he played on a local AAU squad. In the fall of 1970 Payne joined the Wildcat varsity, giving Rupp the towering center that he had long hoped for. With Payne making a significant contribution, the

1971 team claimed yet another SEC title. In the NCAA Tournament, though, Western Kentucky and its seven-foot black center, Jim McDaniels, a Kentucky native, handed the Wildcats an embarrassing defeat. At the end of the spring semester Payne unexpectedly dropped out of school and signed a contract as a "hardship case" with the Atlanta Hawks of the NBA. As a result the 1972 Wildcat team again lacked any African American scholarship players, although two black football players briefly joined the team to provide depth. Still, Kentucky tied for the SEC championship and claimed the automatic NCAA berth. The Wildcats were eventually eliminated in the regional finals by Florida State, which, like Texas Western in 1966, started five African Americans. The contest turned out to be Rupp's final game at Kentucky, since the Board of Trustees refused to waive the university's mandatory retirement rule for the seventy-year-old coach.[41]

Rupp's replacement, former assistant coach Joe B. Hall, faced the difficult challenge of replacing a legendary coach but nonetheless managed to produce winning teams while eliminating the controversy over racial bias in recruiting. Hall's prior experience in coaching integrated high school and college teams, as well as his relative youth, made him an appealing counterweight to the elderly Rupp. Hall's first recruiting class in 1972 included Reggie Warford of Drakesboro, the second African American to receive a basketball scholarship from Kentucky. Warford had earned all-state second-team honors as a senior and had also been a member of the National Honor Society. In signing him Hall ignored conventional wisdom that a college's first black recruits must be superstars in order for integration to work. The next year Hall added two more African Americans to the UK roster, guard Larry Johnson and forward Merion Haskins, both Kentucky natives. The presence of these three athletes in UK's blue and white jerseys helped demonstrate, especially to African Americans, that the basketball program had truly become racially inclusive.[42]

In 1974 Hall assembled an outstanding incoming group of freshman, including 6'10" centers Mike Phillips and Rick Robey, who were white, and African Americans Jack "Goose" Givens and James Lee, both of Lexington. He also hired Leonard Hamilton as an assistant, making him the first African American member of the coaching staff. Givens's enrollment at Kentucky helped modify black perceptions of the basketball program. While growing up just a few miles from the university, Givens had never identified with the Wildcats because of the school's lack of black players, and many of his neighbors actively discouraged him from signing with the university. At UK Givens became the leading scorer for three straight years. During Givens's senior season of 1978, Kentucky started three black players for the first time in school history, and the team accumulated twenty-nine wins in advancing to the NCAA title game against Duke. In the best game of his career Givens scored forty-one points to lead the Wildcats to the school's fifth NCAA title. The Kentucky victory clinched Hall's stature as a worthy successor to Rupp, and the contributions of UK's black players, especially Givens, displaced any lingering doubts that UK basketball was hostile to black athletes. Another racial milestone occurred in 1997, when the university hired Tubby Smith as the school's first black head coach. Smith soon won much support from Wildcat fans with his unpretentious, down-to-earth demeanor. Perhaps more importantly, his first team advanced all the way to the 1998 NCAA finals, where they defeated Utah to claim Kentucky's seventh national title. Smith's success on the court and his acceptance by Wildcat fans established his special position in Kentucky basketball history and helped lay to rest any remaining ghosts still haunting Kentucky basketball from the days of Adolph Rupp.[43]

Tennessee Hires the First Black Basketball Coach in the SEC

During the 1971–72 school year four more Southeastern Conference colleges joined the five previously integrated SEC members by incorporating African Americans onto their basketball squads. Such actions by the University of Tennessee, the University of Florida, Louisiana State, and Ole Miss left Mississippi State all alone as the only conference school with an all-white team. The University of Tennessee's urban location in Knoxville and the state's Upper South mentality provided a somewhat less hostile environment for racial change than existed in the Lower South. Nonetheless, conservative university administrators moved cautiously when contemplating any changes in academic or athletic policies. Founded in 1794, the University of Tennessee did not enroll any African Americans during its first century and a half of operations. In 1869 a Republican state government did adopt a law that guaranteed that no state citizen could be denied admission to the college because of race or color, but no African Americans apparently enrolled under this policy. Once conservative whites regained political control, they institutionalized racial segregation at all levels of public education. This dual system remained firmly entrenched until 1951, when a federal district judge ordered the university to admit African Americans to all graduate and professional programs. The Board of Trustees nonetheless delayed accepting the desegregation of undergraduate studies until November 1960, when it announced that "there shall be no racial discrimination in the admission of qualified students." Two months later, in January 1961, Theotis Robinson Jr., Charles E. Flare, and Willie Mae Gillespie quietly registered for classes on the Knoxville campus. This historic change in UT admissions policy did not mean, however, that the athletic department had also abandoned its color line.[44]

During the first half of the twentieth century University of Tennessee athletic teams had consistently refused to compete against African Americans in any sport, even in the North. The university organized its first official basketball squad in 1909, and over the decades the Volunteers were usually one of the best teams in the South. During the 1940s Tennessee regularly traveled to New York, Pennsylvania, and Ohio for games against strong opponents. This ambitious scheduling reflected the school's commitment to maintaining a nationally recognized basketball program, a rarity in the football-oriented SEC. On one such trip to New York just after World War II, university officials apparently convinced Coach Clair Bee of Long Island University to withhold his two black players from the contest with the Volunteers. The next year in Pennsylvania, when Duquesne University refused to take similar action and bench Charles Cooper, the Tennessee team refused to take the court, forcing the game's cancellation. In the early 1950s, as resistance to racial exclusion became more widespread, UT officials quietly dropped their stand against integrated competition in the North.[45]

Tennessee's continuing refusal to permit integrated athletic contests in Knoxville caused the university to stumble into an embarrassing incident in April 1961, when the Eastern Kentucky College track squad arrived for a dual meet. Upon discovering that there were two black runners among the visiting athletes, Tennessee officials demanded that the Eastern Kentucky coach withdraw the two from competition. When he refused to do so, UT administrators canceled the dual meet just minutes before it was slated to begin. Bowden Wyatt, the assistant athletic director and head football coach, explained to the press that Tennessee had no choice but to call off the meet, since it was "our policy not to compete against Negro athletes at Shield-Watkins Stadium." The cancellation embarrassed the university and drew unwanted attention to Tennessee's continued policy of racial exclusion at home. Despite this negative publicity school officials and the Board of Regents nonetheless retained their exclusion policy for two more years. The trustees belatedly dropped the restriction in 1963 in order to schedule future football games against integrated teams. As a result, the Volunteers hosted major intersectional games in the fall of 1965 against integrated teams from UCLA and the University of Houston. The appearance of black athletes competing against the Volunteers inspired the *Daily Beacon,* the student newspaper, to criticize the continuing exclusion of African Americans from SEC teams. The newspaper urged Tennessee to drop its ban on recruiting black athletes, since "the school that takes the first step will have its choice of the top Negro talent in the South."[46]

The growing desegregation of the public schools in the Knoxville metropolitan area and the incorporation of predominantly black high schools into statewide athletic competition during the 1965–66 school year helped reduce white opposition to interracial competition in sports. No longer fearful of a negative reaction from alumni, the athletic department announced in early 1966 that it would offer scholarships to any qualified athletes regardless of race. In the fall of 1967 the first three African Americans to accept athletic scholarships to

Tennessee arrived on campus. The first black football player, Lester McClain, had attracted some attention from the press, but the two runners on the track squad, Audry Hardy of Memphis and James Craig of Birmingham, were virtual unknowns. The two Tennessee runners, along with James Green of Kentucky, became the first African Americans to compete in track for an SEC university later in the year. For Hardy, the outstanding facilities at UT made his decision to attend the university an easy choice. As he later explained, "I grew up in a poor section in Memphis. Now, all of a sudden instead of running in tennis shoes on pavement, I was running in leather shoes with a tartan track beneath my feet. I'll never forget that feeling." Although Hardy and Craig experienced a few minor problems at Tennessee, they generally found their teammates to be supportive. On one occasion, when a restaurant owner in Georgia refused to serve the black members of the track squad, the entire team walked out of the restaurant together, an action that deeply touched Hardy.[47]

Efforts to integrate the Tennessee basketball team began in 1966, but because of several factors, including bad luck, the Volunteers did not field an integrated squad until the 1972 season. Coach Ray Mears, who had previously led Wittenberg University of Ohio to the NCAA College Division title in 1961, presided over this transition. Mears represented a trend among some southern universities to hire younger head basketball coaches, often from a northern or border state, who had prior experience coaching integrated teams. Beginning in 1966 Mears actively sought to recruit several outstanding African American players, including Perry Wallace. The following year Mears pursued an even bigger high school star, 6'8" center Spencer Haywood from Detroit. Haywood, who had been born in Mississippi and relished the idea of becoming a racial pioneer, agreed to attend Tennessee. Unfortunately, he had not yet met NCAA and SEC eligibility requirements. As part of the effort to attract Haywood to the South, Mears apparently encouraged his high school counselor to apply for a position with the Knoxville Public Schools. If Haywood qualified for admission, the school proposed to hire the counselor on a part-time basis to assist Haywood with his first year of college work. In the meantime, the basketball staff discussed hiring a different tutor for Haywood to help him prepare for the American College Test in August, but they were forced to drop these plans after receiving a negative ruling from the SEC commissioner. In June 1967 Haywood moved to Knoxville and took what he later called a token job at a local car dealership. However, he eventually failed to gain admission to UT. Rejecting the idea of attending a local junior college for a year and then transferring to Tennessee, he left town and enrolled in a Colorado junior college. In the summer of 1968 Haywood earned a starting position on the U.S. Olympic team and helped lead the Americans to the gold medal in the Mexico City Games. In the fall he enrolled for his sophomore year at the University of Detroit, where he led the nation in rebounding while scoring thirty-two points per game. Haywood then left school and became a star in professional basketball. How large an impact he might have made on the SEC if he had ever become eligible at Tennessee is impossible to know, but his presence could have altered the dynamics of athletic integration.[48]

Mears continued to pursue several black prospects over the next two years but without any success. In the fall of 1969 the Tennessee coach announced that Rupert Breedlove, a 6'11" sophomore center, had transferred from Cincinnati and would be eligible after sitting out the 1970 season. Despite high hopes, Breedlove left the team before the 1971 season began and never played for the Volunteers. Finally, in 1971, Mears convinced junior college All-American forward Larry Robinson to enroll at Tennessee. Robinson immediately became a starter for the 1972 Volunteer squad. Wilbert Cherry, a 5'11" guard and non-scholarship player from Knoxville, also made the varsity that same season as a walk-on and saw brief action in four games during that season. Then in the fall of 1974 freshman Bernard King, a highly regarded prep All-American selection from Brooklyn, arrived on campus. King immediately became UT's first African American superstar. In an unprecedented performance as a freshman, the 6'6" forward averaged more than twenty-six points per game and earned the SEC player of the year award from one wire service.[49]

Black athletes continued to grow in numbers at Tennessee and other SEC schools in the late 1970s, and by the early 1980s a majority of conference basketball players were African American. Black assistant coaches gradually appeared, but the head-coaching ranks remained all-white. Finally, at the end of the decade, Tennessee became the first conference school to hire an African American head coach. In the spring of 1989 athletic director Doug Dickey announced the hiring of Wade Houston, a longtime assistant at the University of Louisville and a native of Alcoa, Tennessee, located just outside of Knoxville. News of Houston's hiring was well received locally. The *Knoxville News-Sentinel* summed up the positive feelings of many Volunteer fans when it declared, "Welcome Home, Coach." Houston's hiring also appeared to show that race had become almost irrelevant in southern college sports. Within a week, though, charges of racial discrimination appeared when it was learned that the exclusive Cherokee Country Club had not extended a membership to the new head coach. The university had traditionally paid individual membership fees to the club for several athletic department officials. Although Houston discreetly commented that he was too busy hiring his staff and organizing his schedule to play much golf, President Lamar Alexander announced that the university could not be a party to unequal treatment of its coaches. Consequently, the head football coach, Johnny Majors, and the athletic director, Doug Dickey, both resigned from the club. In the midst of the furor Pat Summitt, head of the UT women's basketball coach since the program began in 1974, added gender considerations to the controversy, revealing that she too had never been invited to join the Cherokee Country Club, because it did not offer individual memberships to women. Houston's hiring and the ensuing country club incident demonstrated both the declining importance of race and the continuing existence of subtle racism, despite the growing dependency of most SEC football and basketball programs on African American athletes.[50]

Black Gators Were Long Delayed

Traditional southern white racial values dominated the political landscape in Florida for the first seven decades of the twentieth century, despite later efforts to construct a more progressive and less southern identity for the state. Following the *Brown v. Board of Education* ruling in 1954, Florida's political leadership pursued a familiar Deep South pattern in stubbornly resisting all federal efforts to eliminate racial discrimination, including segregation in public education. The University of Florida's location in the town of Gainesville in the northern and more traditional part of the state further encouraged conservative views on social and racial issues. Although the state would lose much of its southernness by the end of the twentieth century, the earlier athletic history of the state university was intertwined with cultural and political developments in the Deep South.

The state legislature created the modern University of Florida in 1905 as part of a sweeping consolidation of higher education. Over the following decades, school administrators and state officials tirelessly defended Jim Crow in the college classroom, fully matching similar legal resistance at the University of Alabama and Ole Miss, but with much less national press coverage. The school received its first inquiry from an African American applicant in 1920, and in the late 1940s several more African Americans applied to the university, only to be swiftly rejected. Even after a 1950 decision by the U.S. Supreme Court opened up most graduate and professional programs across the South to African Americans, Florida administrators simply ignored the ruling. Only in September 1958, after a federal judge specifically ordered all university graduate programs opened to minorities, did school officials comply with the 1950 ruling. Yet recalcitrant school officials and trustees continued to reject black applicants for undergraduate study. It was not until September 1962, the same month that James Meredith finally gained admission to Ole Miss, that the first seven black undergraduates registered for classes at Florida. Over the ensuing years the enrollment of minority students expanded very slowly on campus. In early 1968 an HEW study identified only 87 full-time black students at UF, out of a total enrollment of 15,221. Not surprisingly, black Floridians displayed little support for the university.[51]

In 1916 Florida became the last Southeastern Conference member to establish a basketball team, and student interest in the sport remained quite modest
until the 1960s. At the height of integration fears in the 1950s the state Board
of Regents officially banning any interracial competition at public educational
institutions. Consequently, it was not until 1966 that the university finally hosted
its first integrated athletic event on campus—a football game against Northwestern University. Coaches Norm Sloan (1961–66) and Tommy Bartlett (1967–73)
improved the performance of the Gator basketball teams, but neither could win
an SEC championship. Sloan also assisted with the football team, indicating the
lack of importance that the university placed on basketball. He experienced
considerable frustration as a recruiter when he apparently became the first
Florida coach to approach potential black recruits. Despite representing the
state's flagship university, Sloan encountered unexpected resistance from the
parents of several black prospects when he approached their sons, because they
remained bitter over the university's long history of racial exclusion. Neither
Sloan nor Bartlett succeeded in signing black players, and in 1968 the entire
UF athletic program came under attack for allegedly refusing to recruit African
American athletes. Over the next two years local African Americans directed
most of their anger at Ray Graves, the head football coach, allowing Bartlett to
remain in the background.[52]

The Florida track and field squad took the first steps to desegregate the
university's athletic program. In May 1968 Coach Jimmy Carnes awarded the
school's first scholarship to an African American, high school star Ron Coleman, who specialized in the triple jump. The student newspaper enthusiastically welcomed Coleman's signing, commenting, "It's about time." In the fall
of 1968 John Brown, a non-scholarship athlete, joined the cross-country squad
and technically became the first black athlete to actually compete for the Gators. The enrollment of two additional African American track athletes further
highlighted the absence of black athletes on the basketball and football teams.
The athletic program finally quieted some of its critics when it produced an
integrated varsity basketball squad for the 1971–72 season. Tommy Bartlett
awarded athletic scholarships to forward Steve Williams and guard Malcolm
Meeks in the spring of 1970, hoping that the two would support each other in
an unfamiliar environment. Williams eventually started on the Gator varsity
for three years, but Meeks quit the team as a sophomore. During the 1972–73
season forward Gene Shy, the Gators' third African American player, joined
him in the starting lineup. The following season Florida started three African
Americans when Norm Caldwell earned a starting guard position alongside
Williams and Shy. Despite the change in the racial composition of the Gators,
the team continued to struggle in SEC competition. Florida's delay in recruiting African Americans may also have made it more difficult for coaches to

recruit the best black prospects during the remainder of the 1970s because of the university's historical unpopularity with black Floridians.[53]

The dilatory process by which the University of Florida incorporated African Americans into its basketball team contrasted sharply with the approach of two other schools in the state, Florida State University and Jacksonville University. In contrast to UF, Florida State fielded its first integrated basketball team in the fall of 1966. Sadly, Lenny Hall, a junior college transfer, suffered a career-ending leg injury literally in his first FSU game and never returned to the team. Other African Americans followed Hall to Tallahassee, and by the 1969–70 season the Seminoles started four black players. The 1972 team, which knocked Adolph Rupp's final Kentucky team out of the NCAA Tournament, actually started five African Americans. Unfortunately, the school's aggressive recruiting policy included a negative side, as the NCAA banned FSU from postseason play in 1969 for several rule violations. Jacksonville University, another ambitious school, enjoyed spectacular success beginning in 1969. That year's team included two African American players more than seven feet tall, Artis Gilmore and Pembrook Burrows III. Led by these towering inside players, the 1970 squad lost only one regular-season game and advanced to the NCAA finals before losing to defending champion UCLA. Compared to the record of these other two colleges, the University of Florida's slowness in recruiting African Americans confirmed that elite institutions retained their traditional policies of racial exclusion much longer than did their less prestigious and more aggressive counterparts.[54]

Collis Temple Jr. Brings LSU into the Mainstream of College Basketball

Louisiana State University joined Tennessee and Florida in fielding an integrated varsity basketball team during the 1971–72 season. In the mid-1950s LSU administrators had displayed some flexibility by allowing the Tiger basketball team to risk playing integrated teams in the NCAA Tournament. But the intensity of Louisiana's massive resistance movement blocked any desegregation of undergraduate studies for a decade, and athletic integration was delayed even longer. Founded just before the Civil War as an institution for white males, LSU eventually served as both the state university and the state land-grant college. Since LSU stood at the apex of higher education in the state, civil rights activists made it an important target after World War II. Despite the creation in 1948 of a new law school at all-black Southern University in Baton Rouge, a federal court in 1950 still ordered LSU to admit African Americans to its School of Law, as well as its other graduate and professional schools. In 1953 one black undergraduate temporarily gained entrance to undergraduate classes until a federal circuit court overruled his admission. By the spring semester of 1956, an unusually large number of 117 black graduate and professional students were enrolled at the university. Elsewhere in the state, three white public colleges in predominately Catholic southern Louisiana accepted black students by the fall of 1955, and the New Orleans branch of LSU admitted African Americans when it opened its doors in 1958. However, LSU continued to stonewall the admission of black undergraduates until 1964, almost two years after James Meredith's admission to Ole Miss.[55]

LSU established its first official basketball team in 1909, and over the next three decades the Tigers established themselves as one of the top programs in the South. In 1935, under Coach Harry Rabenhorst, LSU finished undefeated in SEC competition and went on to defeat the University of Pittsburgh in an unofficial national title game held in Atlantic City. Rabenhorst got another chance to compete for a national title in 1953, when the Tigers went 13-0 in the SEC and advanced to the NCAA semifinals before losing to Indiana. The following year, led by future Basketball Hall of Fame selection Bob Pettit, the Tigers returned to the playoffs. In the NCAA regional tournament LSU fell to a powerful Penn State team 78–70. What made this 1954 contest especially significant was the fact that the Nittany Lion squad included four black players, an unusually high number for that era, and was led by African American star Jesse Arnelle. Neither LSU administrators nor Louisiana's political leaders attempted to block the tournament trip, indicating that "big-time" sports enjoyed a partial dispensation from strict Jim Crow etiquette. Significantly, the NCAA Tournament took place two months before the Supreme Court's momentous *Brown* decision in May 1954.[56]

Louisiana's protracted massive resistance campaign *after* the *Brown* ruling disrupted LSU's athletic plans for nearly a decade. In 1956, as part of a flood of legislative actions designed to shore up the state's Jim Crow system, the assembly passed the so-called sports segregation bill, which prohibited the staging of racially mixed athletic contests or social events. Although the federal courts struck down the actual legislation after several years, LSU officials remained afraid to challenge the underlying policy until well into the 1960s. The ban on integrated competition made it almost impossible for the Tigers to schedule northern schools. In addition, the team experienced a string of disappointing seasons. To revive the school's basketball fortunes, LSU in 1967 hired as its new head coach Press Maravich, a native of Aliquippa, Pennsylvania, who had just completed two seasons at North Carolina State. Since Maravich's son Pete, a precocious basketball talent with unprecedented dribbling and passing skills, had failed to meet ACC entrance standards but did qualify for SEC play, the veteran coach had sought a position where he could coach his son. The two Maraviches rescued LSU basketball from the doldrums and turned home games into popular spectacles. Sportswriters three times selected Pete as the SEC player of the year, and in 1969 and 1970 he earned All-America first-team honors. After setting a national scoring record of 44.5 points per game as a senior, he was named the national player of the year. Despite's Pete's exceptional individual performances, Press Maravich made little progress in recruiting black players. In fact, it was the LSU track and field team, not the football or basketball programs, that broke the school's athletic color line when Charles Steward and Lloyd Wells joined the squad during the 1969–70 season.[57]

In 1970 Maravich finally signed his first black recruit, reducing suspicions that he was indifferent toward African American players. As a senior in Kentwood, Louisiana, 6'8" center Collis Temple Jr. was hard to overlook. Governor John McKeithen even personally visited the Temple home to encourage the young athlete to enroll at LSU. Ironically, Collis Sr. had been rejected by LSU when he applied to the graduate school in the early 1950s, because of his race. Influenced by his parents, both of whom were educators and valued the academic programs available at the state university, Temple elected to join the Tigers. Some enthusiastic white fans referred to the new recruit as LSU's "great black hope," but not all whites were happy to see him on campus. Temple experienced several brief confrontations with white teammates and occasionally received hate mail. On the road he suffered a few racial insults and one death threat, and there were several physical altercations in the heat of close games. For social activities he prudently visited nearby Southern University and maintained a low profile away from the basketball court. After Dale Brown replaced Maravich as head coach for the 1973 season, the number of African Americans at LSU slowly increased, but it took several more years before black Louisianans came to fully identify with the team. Despite some negative experiences during his career, Temple remained supportive of the university. In fact, three decades later he proudly watched two of his sons join the Tiger basketball team.[58]

Rebels of a Different Color at Ole Miss

Much like the case at LSU, athletic policy at the University of Mississippi was controlled during the 1950s and 1960s by the state's overwhelming commitment to white supremacy. The state's political leaders so fervently demanded that strict segregation be maintained in all areas of public education, including sports, that university officials occasionally referred to this doctrine as the "unwritten law," an unofficial but binding policy that prohibited all interracial competition in athletics. Racial exclusion historically had flourished at Ole Miss. African Americans started applying to the university in the 1950s, but state and university administrators waged a determined and protracted campaign to deny them admission. Finally, in September 1962, federal marshals enforcing a court order escorted James Meredith to campus, touching off the infamous Ole Miss riot. Two people died in the violence, which President John F. Kennedy quelled by sending in National Guardsmen and federal troops. The small number of black students who enrolled at the university over the next few years faced continuing hostility from many whites. Thus, the likelihood that UM coaches would now start recruiting black athletes for the "Rebel" athletic teams seemed quite remote.

Throughout the twentieth century basketball had remained a second-class sport at Ole Miss, barely edging out baseball in popularity among students. The basketball program dated from 1908, and over the decades the Rebels consistently finished near or at the bottom of the conference standings. The basketball team and the university briefly attracted unwelcome national attention at the end of December 1956, when a racial controversy erupted around the All-American City Tournament in Owensboro, Kentucky. The Rebels lost their opening game in the holiday event and were scheduled to meet the Iona College Gaels of New York in the consolation match, but the Iona squad included one black player, guard Stanley Hill. Ole Miss coach Bonnie Graham informed tournament officials that his team would not play Iona if Hill was in the lineup. Ole Miss president Dr. J. M. Williams and athletic director C. M. "Tad" Smith backed up Graham's decision. Equally steadfast in his convictions, Iona coach James McDermott refused to compete without Hill. Tournament officials therefore had no choice but to forfeit the game to the Gaels. Hill was shocked and humiliated by the cancellation, although he was also touched when the Rebel players came by Iona's hotel and personally apologized for their university's action. Back in Mississippi, several prominent state legislators praised school officials for their "honorable" decision, which one state senator claimed had shown America that "Mississippi is not going to tolerate integration in any phase of education." Over the following decades the incident was gradually forgotten, however, and the Ole Miss basketball press guide did not even list the contest as part of the 1957 team's record.[59]

In the wake of the 1956 Iona incident, political leaders and higher-education officials reaffirmed their commitment to maintaining the athletic color line. A little more than a year later the exclusion policy forced the basketball team at Jackson State College, an all-black school, to withdraw from the NCAA small-college tournament. Jackson State had defeated another black college in the opening round and would have been matched against predominantly white teams in the Upper Midwest in the next round of play. However, the state coordinating board for higher education concluded that "under current conditions" it was best for Jackson State to remain at home. In the spring of 1959 the Ole Miss baseball team ran afoul of the same rule. The Rebels won the SEC championship but had to skip the NCAA playoffs because they might have encountered an integrated team. Ole Miss had previously participated in the 1956 playoffs, finishing third in the College World Series that year. In 1960 the Rebels captured their second consecutive SEC baseball title, and again they were forced to stay home. Finally, in 1964, university officials allowed the team to participate in the playoffs after it won yet another conference championship.[60]

During the late 1960s Ole Miss gradually modified its racial policies concerning athletics. In January 1967, though, Ole Miss canceled a home basketball game against the Vanderbilt freshman team, which included the first two black basketball players in the SEC, because of a "scheduling conflict." The spreading integration of athletic teams at other conference schools eventually drew attention to the continued whiteness of the Rebel teams. With encouragement from administrators, basketball coach Robert "Cob" Jarvis quietly started to scout possible black recruits for his team in the late sixties. In August 1970 Jarvis announced that Coolidge Ball, a forward from Indianola, had accepted a basketball scholarship, making him the university's first black athlete. Ball proved to be a valuable addition to the Rebels, as he led the varsity team in scoring during his three years of play. Over the course of Ball's career sportswriters twice selected him for the All-SEC second team. A quiet and easygoing student, Ball got along well with his teammates and went out of his way to avoid potential conflicts. He later insisted that he never experienced any racial problems during his four years at the university, perhaps because as a Mississippi native he understood the state's racial etiquette. As a junior Ball was joined on the varsity by the team's second black player, guard Dean Hudson of Greenville. Additional black recruits followed, and by 1976 African Americans constituted a majority of the team. In 1992 the university hired Rob Evans to direct the basketball program, making him the first black head coach at Ole Miss. After the 1998 season Evans left to coach at Arizona State, and Rod Barnes assumed the job, giving Ole Miss its second black head coach. Barnes's outstanding 2001 team qualified for the NCAA Tournament and ironically was assigned a first-round game in the regional tournament against none other than Iona College.[61]

The 2001 Mississippi–Iona matchup briefly revived interest in the 1956 incident in Owensboro. In searching for information about previous meetings between the two schools, sportswriters stumbled across the old 1956 controversy. Once he learned about the earlier incident, Ole Miss chancellor Robert Khayat invited Stanley Hill to the regional tournament as a special guest of the university. This time, though, the circumstances surrounding the game were quite different. A majority of the Ole Miss players were black, as was their head coach. The team met privately with Hill, by then a retired labor union officer in New York, and presented him with a basketball autographed by the entire squad. This time nothing interfered with the actual game, which Ole Miss narrowly won. The social and athletic dimensions of the 2001 contest highlighted the distance that Ole Miss basketball had traveled since the Rebel basketball team had walked away from the 1956 Owensboro tournament and a young Stanley Hill.[62]

Mississippi State Violates the "Unwritten Law"

Mississippi State University was the last Southeastern Conference member to incorporate black athletes into its basketball team. The college had also been the last conference school to admit black students to undergraduate classes. The state legislature originally chartered the Agricultural and Mechanical College of Mississippi in Starkville in 1878 as the land-grant institution exclusively for whites. In early 1909 the university established its first official basketball team. During the following two decades Mississippi State regularly enjoyed winning seasons, but after joining the SEC the Maroons' fortunes fell on hard times. For nonconference games the team normally played nearby white colleges, thereby avoided the thorny issue of interracial competition. During the late 1950s and early 1960s a new basketball coach brought unprecedented success on the court to the Maroons, but the state's insistence on maintaining an athletic color line repeatedly frustrated the team and its fans. In July 1955 MSU officials made what was arguably their most successful hiring ever when they selected James H. "Babe" McCarthy as the school's new basketball coach. A former high school and U.S. Air Force coach currently working in sales for an oil company, McCarthy proved to be a silver-tongued recruiter who successfully lured a stream of talented southern boys to Starkville. With this recruiting pipeline flowing smoothly, McCarthy's teams quickly emerged as an SEC power and challenged Kentucky for basketball supremacy. Six of McCarthy's first seven teams enjoyed winning seasons, with two of them posting remarkable 24-1 records. During this stretch the Maroons claimed four SEC championships. In the final regular-season national poll conducted by the Associated Press, MSU finished third in 1959, fourth in 1962, and sixth in 1963.[63]

The Maroons' remarkable success created growing frustration over their inability to compete in the NCAA postseason basketball tournament. The almost total commitment by white Mississippians to the massive resistance movement after the *Brown* decision and key legislators' imposition of the "unwritten law" on Ole Miss and Mississippi State placed a strain on MSU's basketball program. In order to prepare his team for SEC competition, McCarthy began scheduling one out-of-state tournament each December. In late 1956 the Maroons traveled to Indiana for the Evansville Invitational Tournament. On Friday, December 28, MSU slipped past a surprisingly tough University of Denver squad in the opening round by a score of 69–65. The contest would normally have received scant newspaper coverage had it not been for the presence on the Denver team of two

African Americans, Bill Peay and Rocephus Sligh. Although caught off guard by their appearance, McCarthy agreed to play the game, and he naively hoped that news about the two Denver players would not filter back to Mississippi. His hopes were quashed the next day when the *Jackson Daily News* reported on the game under the headline "State's Team Plays Negroes." To further complicate matters, MSU's victory qualified the Maroons for the championship game against host Evansville, whose roster included one black player. Since several other Mississippi newspapers also reported this information, MSU president Ben Hilbun and athletic director C. R. Noble telephoned McCarthy and ordered him to leave the tournament immediately. Noble explained his decision by commenting, "It's always been our policy that our teams would not compete against Negroes."[64]

Hilbun and Noble's decision to reject interracial competition foreshadowed similar actions by the university in 1959, 1961, and 1962, after the Maroons had won the SEC championship. In 1959 future NBA star Bailey Howell led MSU to a sensational 24-1 record, and the Maroons beat out the number-two-ranked team in the nation, the Kentucky Wildcats, for the league title. But after the season finale against Ole Miss, Hilbun confirmed that MSU would decline its automatic invitation to the NCAA Tournament. Placing the pursuit of athletic glory in the context of the state's battle against racial integration, the president explained that "there are great issues involved which transcend mere athletic competition." Babe McCarthy and team members accepted this decision without protest, but a few disgruntled students responded by hanging Hilbun in effigy. In 1961 the basketball team produced a 19-6 record and claimed its second SEC title in three years. In early March new president Dean W. Colvard announced that MSU would again reject the NCAA invitation. Although students were upset by his decision, there was little public complaint, perhaps because of deepening fears among white Mississippians over the possibility of federally enforced public school integration in the state.[65]

The following year Mississippi State once again finished at the top of the SEC standings. The 1962 team posted another near-perfect 24-1 record and finished with a number-four ranking in the final wire-service polls. This time MSU students and fans expressed guarded optimism that the traditional ban might be lifted. Writers in the student newspapers at both Mississippi State and archrival Ole Miss endorsed acceptance of the NCAA bid. The editor at Ole Miss pointed out that even the state's famous beauty pageant contestants, including Ole Miss coeds, participated in the Miss America contest in Atlantic City with black women. After the final regular-season game Babe McCarthy broke his public silence and argued that his team should be allowed to participate in the NCAA Tournament and "play against integrated teams away from home." McCarthy's public support for integrated games, if held outside Mississippi, had no effect on the state's political leadership, however, which was now desperately trying to prevent James Meredith from gaining admission to Ole Miss. Thus, President Colvard reluctantly concluded that MSU must continue to honor the unwritten law. As the *Jackson Daily News* subsequently noted, only an unlikely "change of heart by Mississippi's politicians" offered any hope for MSU's gaining permission for postseason play.[66]

In 1963 the Maroons captured their third consecutive Southeastern Conference championship, inspiring renewed appeals that the unwritten law be dumped. Led by seniors Joe Dan Gold, Leland Mitchell, and Red Stroud, the Maroons finished first in the SEC with a 12-2 conference record. During the final week of the regular season MSU students held several rallies supporting the team, the student senate adopted a resolution endorsing the tournament trip, and more than three thousand students signed petitions urging acceptance of the NCAA invitation. Coach Babe McCarthy openly campaigned on behalf of a change in policy, commenting that it made him "sick" to think that his players might again be denied a chance to compete for the national title. At the end of the week President Colvard announced his decision to break with tradition. His formal statement declared that "unless hindered by competent authority I shall send our basketball team to the NCAA competition." MSU basketball fans enthusiastically celebrated the announcement, while hardcore segregationists around the state sounded the alarm, especially when they learned that MSU's probable first-round opponent would be Loyola University of Chicago, a team that featured four black starters. Several politicians immediately threatened to slash appropriations for the university if the Maroons played Loyola. At first Governor Ross Barnett remained uncharacteristically subdued, but he eventually spoke out against the trip, stating that such participation was "not in the best interests of Mississippi State University, the State of Mississippi, or either of the races."[67]

Colvard eventually received about 350 letters, postcards, and telegrams commenting on his decision. Approximately 100 of these were highly critical messages from outraged white Mississippians. These communications, as well as editorials in various newspapers around the state, stressed three major themes: (1) the school was overemphasizing the selfish pursuit of sports success, (2) Colvard was selling out "our cherished southern way of life," and (3) interracial competition would give dangerous groups like the NAACP an opening wedge for further desegregation. One writer charged that MSU administrators were placing "personal pleasures before moral principles," while another distressed correspondent asked, "Can we sacrifice the principles we profess for a few moments of glory on a basketball court?" The *Meridian Star* endorsed these sentiments, warning that "dear as the athletic prestige of our schools may be, our southern way of life is infinitely more precious." The *Jackson Clarion-Ledger,* a tireless defender of segregation, warning that such dangerous interracial competition would have a domino effect in behalf of racial integration within the state: "If Mississippi State U. plays against a Negro outside the state, what would be greatly different in bringing the integrated teams into the state? And then why not recruit a Negro of special basketball ability to play on the Mississippi State team? This is the road we seem to be traveling." Encouraged by such public support, several highly conservative trustees forced an emergency meeting of the Board of Trustees of the Institutions of Higher Learning of the State of Mississippi on Saturday, March 9, in hopes of preserving the "unwritten law."[68]

Despite strong support from university alumni and several newspapers, President Colvard remained unsure if his decision would be sustained by the trustees. When the full board eventually met, influential board member M. M. Roberts introduced a resolution barring MSU from competing in the NCAA Tournament. To his surprise, the board rejected the motion by an 8–3 vote. When Roberts then moved that the trustees ask President Colvard to resign, his motion failed for lack of a second. Instead, the board approved a resolution expressing continued support for the MSU president by a 9–2 vote and then adjourned. The "unwritten law" had finally died. Or had it? The next day, a few die-hard segregationists refused to accept its demise and launched a last-ditch effort to block the Mississippi State trip. On Wednesday, March 13, just one day before the team was slated to depart for East Lansing, Michigan, state senator F. W. "Billy" Mitts filed legal papers in a state court in Jackson seeking to prevent the Maroons from leaving the state. Judge L. D. Porter, a strong segregationist, quickly granted a temporary injunction barring university officials from allowing the team to compete in the NCAA Tournament or authorizing the expenditure of any state funds on such a trip. News of the legal action quickly reached the MSU campus, where school officials promptly left town in order to avoid being served with any legal papers. Late that evening, when Deputy Sheriff Dot Johnson led deputies from Jackson to McCarthy's and Colvard's homes, the two men were no longer in town.[69]

The Maroon players remained unsure if any further efforts would be made to prevent them from leaving for the tournament. The next morning, March 14, an assistant coach first sent the reserve players and a few freshmen to the airport to make sure that no law enforcement officials were waiting there. When the team's chartered plane finally appeared after a weather delay, the full squad rushed over from the campus and hastily climbed into the aircraft. As the flight left the ground, one Maroon player quipped, "Now I know how those East Berliners feel when they make it past the wall." McCarthy met the squad in Nashville, and the full party boarded a flight to East Lansing, where relieved tournament officials and local fans gave them a warm welcome. Back in Mississippi, while the team had been in the air, Justice Robert G. Gillespie of the state supreme court had dissolved the temporary injunction against MSU, making the trip legitimate once again.[70]

On Friday night the Maroons finally took on the high-scoring Ramblers from Loyola in the first round of the mideastern regional tournament. Loyola entered the contest ranked third in the AP final season poll, while Mississippi State held down the number-six spot. When captains Joe Dan Gold of MSU and Jerry Harkness of Loyola shook hands at center court before the game, so many photographers' flashbulbs went off that a few spectators briefly thought a bomb had exploded. Both head coaches had lectured their players about the need to maintain their composure during the contest, and all the players displayed excellent sportsmanship throughout the evening. Mississippi State raced off to an early 7–0 lead, but the Ramblers went ahead 26–19 by halftime. State briefly closed the deficit to three points midway through the second half, but after Leland Mitchell fouled out late in the game, Loyola controlled the final minutes and clinched a 71–61 victory. The following evening MSU defeated Bowling Green in the third-place game. Loyola then easily defeated the University of Illinois to win the regional championship, and the following week the Ramblers defeated Duke and the University of Cincinnati to capture the national championship.[71]

Mississippi State's unique struggle to get to East Lansing earned the university new respect at home and around the nation, but hard-core segregationists remained bitter about their defeat. The *Rebel Underground,* a mimeographed newspaper published anonymously by Ole Miss and MSU students opposed to all integration, characterized the loss to Loyola as "one of the worst defeats ever" for a Mississippi team. The newspaper declared, "Any citizen of Mississippi who knowingly supports an act to integrate our school [such] as playing basketball against niggers cannot but live in shame. A severe blow has been made at our great way of life in Mississippi." Other segregationists were less hostile, and a few confessed that they had even rooted for the Maroons. Despite the loss MSU fans continued to strongly support the team; in fact, more than five hundred supporters swamped the airport to welcome the players back to Starkville. When asked if he would be willing to play another integrated team in a future NCAA Tournament, Coach McCarthy responded, "There'll either have to be a law forbidding us to come, or we'll be back." Several sportswriters expressed hope that the MSU trip had finally restored sanity to the state's intercollegiate athletic programs. As one sports information director later commented, State's NCAA participation represented "a momentous step out of the dark ages." To be sure, most white Mississippians had not abandoned their commitment to segregation inside the state. Yet the NCAA Tournament controversy had demonstrated that moderate whites were now willing to modify their personal convictions in order to rejoin the larger sporting nation and resume the pursuit of athletic success.[72]

Participation in the NCAA Tournament did not alter the fact that Mississippi State remained a segregated institution. President Colvard continued to worry that a qualified African American would apply to the university and that the state government would intervene, endangering the school's accreditation and perhaps even inciting an outbreak of violence. Consequently, the MSU president did not publicly advertise the fact that he was now willing to admit any qualified black applicant. In early 1965 Colvard submitted to several federal agencies a formal pledge of nondiscrimination in the use of grant funds, despite some grumbling from trustees. The president then approved the school's first evening classes at nearby Columbus Air Force Base, for which several black airmen quietly registered. Finally in June Colvard informed the trustees that a black applicant had met all admission requirements and would soon enroll on the main campus. To his relief, no political leader challenged this decision, although the *Rebel Underground* did unsuccessfully call for student resistance to the change. On July 19 Richard Holmes, a Starkville native, quietly registered for undergraduate classes in the second summer session, becoming the university's first African American student. Holmes returned for the fall semester, when he was joined by two additional black undergraduates. Black enrollment slowly crept upward over the following years, with MSU eventually surpassing Ole Miss in minority enrollment.[73]

After the Mississippi State team fared poorly over the next two seasons, Coach Babe McCarthy resigned in 1965 and was replaced by Joe Dan Gold, his former player. Gold's first two squads compiled winning records, but his teams slumped badly over the next three years. After the 1970 Maroons won only three SEC games, he resigned his position. During his five years as head coach Gold failed to recruit any African American players. Although this was not unusual at the start of his tenure, by the summer of 1970 every conference member except MSU had issued at least one basketball scholarship to a black athlete. Gold's replacement, Kermit Davis, initially failed to sign any African American recruits, but in the spring of 1972 he convinced two outstanding high school prospects, Larry Fry of Lexington, Tennessee, and Jerry Jenkins of Gulfport, Mississippi, to enroll at Mississippi State. Both players enjoyed highly successful careers for the Maroons. When the two players suited up for the 1972–73 varsity season, MSU finally joined the rest of the Southeastern Conference in fielding an integrated basketball team. Davis expanded the number of black recruits over the following years, and the 1975 Maroons included six African Americans on the varsity squad. Mississippi State's tardiness in recruiting black players did not seem to hamper later recruitment, although the team rarely finished in the top half of conference standings. In one exception to this trend, the unusually successful 1979 Maroon team was invited to participate in the National Invitational Tournament and hosted a first-round game against Alcorn State College, the land-grant university that had been the black counterpart to MSU during the era of segregation. In an additional irony, all ten starters in the contest were African American. The dramatic change since 1963 in athletic policy for MSU athletics, and the state of Mississippi, could not have been more clearly demonstrated.[74]

* * *

The racial integration of Southeastern Conference basketball unfolded from 1966 through 1973. Despite the leadership displayed by Vanderbilt and to some extent Auburn, other SEC schools, especially those located in the Deep South, were slow to incorporate African Americans into their basketball teams, despite their obvious ability. Hence, it was clear that athletic programs at southern universities could not stray very far from the mainstream of their state's social and racial norms. Even after African Americans won admission to undergraduate classrooms at southern universities, a retreating color line still encircled the basketball court and preserved the whiteness of its special space. Thus, the physical presence of African Americans on campus did not automatically lead to their full inclusion in all campus activities. Football, that most powerful representation of southern manliness, also remained initially closed to black participation. The challenges that confronted southern football programs during the racial crosscurrents of the 1960s, and the struggles of black athletes to demonstrate their ability and character on the gridiron, will be explored in the next chapter.

9

The "Final Citadel of Segregation"

The Southeastern Conference and Football

The faster they run, the more touchdowns
they make, the whiter they get!
—A member of the Board of Regents
of Auburn University, 1969

Thank God for Earl Warren.
—A Georgia sportswriter, 1981

On Saturday, September 12, 1970, a crowd of more than seventy-two thousand excited football fans, the second largest in stadium history, crammed into Legion Field in Birmingham to cheer for the University of Alabama Crimson Tide against the visiting University of Southern California Trojans in the season opener for both schools. The highly publicized appearance by the Southern California team, ranked number three in the Associated Press preseason poll, inaugurated a new era in Alabama football. Since 1951 no major northern or West Coast football squad had ventured into the state to play the Crimson Tide, and the UA athletic staff believed that the absence of such high-profile intersectional contests had harmed the Tide's national rankings. The Trojans' visit also constituted an important racial milestone for college athletics in Alabama, because nearly twenty players on the Southern Cal travel squad were African Americans. Never before had an integrated team with so many African American players been allowed to challenge the all-white Crimson Tide squad within the state. Determined to avoid any racial incidents, university administrators granted final approval for the contest only after Birmingham civic leaders assured them that the Trojans would not encounter any discrimination in lodging or other public accommodations during their visit. As a further gesture of goodwill, the UA band even volunteered not to play "Dixie" until the second half.

The game's unexpected results dealt a bitter blow to Alabama pride, as Southern California "overwhelmed, mauled, and battered" the Tide en route to an easy 42–21 victory. USC's black stars played key roles in demolishing the Alabama squad, stunning many white football fans across the Deep South. Sophomore fullback Sam Cunningham gained 135 yards, scored two touchdowns, and sometimes literally ran over the smaller Alabama defenders. Halfback Clarence Davis, ironically a native of Birmingham who once dreamed of playing for the Tide, rushed for 76 yards and one touchdown, while quarterback Jimmy Jones deftly directed the Trojan offense and passed for a touchdown. According to popular accounts, Alabama coach Paul "Bear" Bryant visited the Southern California dressing room following the game. After graciously congratulating the victors, the legendary coach specifically sought out Clarence Davis and confirmed that the USC halfback had spent his early years in Birmingham. Then, as he left the room, Bryant turned and remarked, "Ain't no more of y'all ever going to get out of here again." Later that night, according to yet another story, Bryant supposedly confided to one of his assistants, "We're going to have to make some changes. To compete, we're going to have to have black players." The 1970 USC game thus supposedly marked the historic turning point in the long struggle to integrate the playing fields of the Deep South. As one white assistant coach later proclaimed, "Sam Cunningham did more for integration in Alabama than Martin Luther King did in twenty years."[1]

The 1970 Alabama–Southern California game was indeed a historic event in southern and American sports history, but many of the legendary stories and anecdotes about the contest have somewhat exaggerated its impact. Bear Bryant did not suddenly decide to recruit African American athletes because of his defeat, since there was already one black player on the Alabama freshman team that fall. Furthermore, other SEC coaches had not waited for Bryant to act before deciding to integrate their own squads. As of September 1970 six of the ten SEC varsity squads already included African American players. Contrary to legend, then, Bear Bryant was more of a follower than a leader in athletic integration within the conference. Nonetheless, the USC game did constitute an important episode in sports history and southern history. First, the fact that Bryant and Alabama administrators had scheduled the contest revealed that the university was now anxious to rejoin the larger integrated world of college sports. Second, the Tide's humiliating defeat, as well as two consecutive mediocre seasons in 1969 and 1970, encouraged many die-hard 'Bama fans to accept the recruitment of African Americans as a practical necessity. The considerable success of Bryant's subsequent teams, which contained growing numbers of black players, further helped legitimize athletic integration inside the state. During the 1970s Bryant's teams captured three national championships, further enhancing his status as an American sports icon.

At the time of Bryant's retirement in 1982, the racial composition of Alabama football teams and other Southeastern Conference squads had changed dramatically from that found at the start of the century. During the period from the 1890s through 1966, not even one African American had ever competed on the varsity level for any SEC school. Yet by 1980 black football players constituted approximately one-third of all conference lettermen and many of the league's top stars. This new racial structure clearly marked a significant departure from the sport's earliest days in the Dixie, when white supremacy and racial exclusion had dominated all areas of southern life, including the football field.[2]

Southeastern Conference Football and the Color Line

From the founding of the Southeastern Conference in 1932, SEC schools had religiously "held the line" against any competition with African Americans on the football field. From 1950 through the mid-1960s, though, conference members gradually accepted integrated competition outside their states and eventually on their own campuses. Meanwhile, legal action by the federal government finally desegregated southern college classrooms. With black students now a reality on campus, the issue of whether conference schools might recruit black players for their own squads moved to the forefront. SEC football coaches viewed athletic integration with considerable uneasiness and were reluctant to take action ahead of their peers. Such nationally prominent coaches as Bear Bryant, John Vaught of Ole Miss, and Ralph "Shug" Jordan of Auburn chose not to use their stature to challenge the long-standing southern tradition of all-white teams. Members of an older southern generation that had known only segregation, these coaches were conservative in their values and believed that their only social responsibilities were to win football games and develop toughness in young men. In addition, many wealthy donors, influential alumni, and segregationist politicians urged them not to surrender to integration. Many of these coaches quietly reassured their supporters that they would never recruit a black player. Privately, they also worried that they did not know how to relate to black athletes on a personal basis and that mixing blacks and whites together would disrupt fragile team harmony.

The University of Kentucky and the University of Tennessee eventually became the first two SEC schools to accept black football players. The fact that both colleges were located outside the Lower South made it easier for them to abandon the color line. In December 1965 Kentucky announced that it had awarded football scholarships for the 1966–67 school year to two African American recruits, Greg Page and Nathaniel "Nat" Northington. In the fall of 1967 Northington became the first African American to play in an SEC varsity contest. Earlier that year, the University of Tennessee joined Kentucky in abandoning Jim Crow when it issued a grant-in-aid to Lester McClain, who made his varsity debut in the fall of 1968. It took two more years before four additional SEC members—Auburn, Vanderbilt, Mississippi State, and Florida—added black players to their varsity football squads. Alabama joined their ranks in 1971, leaving Louisiana State, Ole Miss, and the University of Georgia as the remaining holdouts. Finally, in the fall of 1972 these three universities fielded integrated varsity teams, ending the age of segregation in the SEC. The "final citadel of segregation" had surrendered.[3] Why some SEC members moved faster than others to eliminate Jim Crow and incorporate African Americans into their football programs is a complicated story that the rest of this chapter will attempt to answer.

A Personal Tragedy Almost Derails Athletic Integration at Kentucky

The northernmost member of the Southeastern Conference, the University of Kentucky, took the lead in the integration of SEC athletics. The university's geographical location in a border state and the progressive racial attitudes of Presidents Frank G. Dickey and John W. Oswald combined to provide a supportive environment in which to eliminate Jim Crow from UK athletics. In May 1963, under pressure from President Dickey, the UK athletic association announced that it had lifted all racial restrictions on athletic participation at the university. Unfortunately, the Wildcats' traditional lack of success in the SEC made it difficult to recruit the state's top high school prospects. Therefore, the recruitment of African American players offered Kentucky a unique opportunity to gain a competitive advantage over its rivals. The desegregation of the state's main high school sports association in the late 1950s made interracial competition familiar if not necessarily popular with whites across the state. Complicating the university's efforts was the reality that many of the state's top black players came from Louisville, the largest city and least "southern" part of the state, while UK was located in Lexington in the bluegrass section, which emphasized its southern heritage. Nonetheless, Kentucky administrators were determined to upgrade the university's national image and viewed sport as one mechanism to achieve that goal. The arrival of a new president, Dr. John W. Oswald, in 1963 reinforced the move toward athletic integration, since Oswald supported Dickey's liberal policies on race. In 1964 Coach Charlie Bradshaw predicted that the first black Wildcat would come from within the state, "because we owe it to the taxpayers who support this institution." The coaching staff pursued several potential black recruits over the next two years but without any success.[4]

The Kentucky football program finally succeeded in beginning the actual integration of its varsity football team and the Southeastern Conference in December 1965. During the fall Wildcat coaches focused their recruiting efforts on several prospects, including halfback Nat Northington, an all-state football player and "A" student at Jefferson High School in Louisville. Governor Edward T. Breathitt Jr., who sat on UK's Board of Trustees, assisted the recruiting campaign. Along with President Oswald, the governor personally escorted the young athlete around the Lexington campus on his official visit. On December 19, 1965, Northington signed a scholarship agreement with Kentucky, becoming the first African American to receive a football scholarship to an SEC school. Oswald, Breathitt, and Bradshaw all attended the ceremony, with Oswald telling reporters that the event represented "a great and historic day for Kentucky, for its athletic program, and for the Southeastern Conference." Northington's family soon had second thoughts about his decision, and his mother wrote Governor Breathitt that she was "apprehensive as to Nat's safety as the first Negro to play in the Southeastern Conference." Breathitt and university officials reassured her that her son would be fully protected on all Deep South trips, and the new recruit remained in the Kentucky fold. That same week Bradshaw announced the signing of a second black player, all-state end Greg Page of Middlesboro. Page and Northington would room together at Kentucky, thereby providing the emotional support that they would need as racial pioneers.[5]

During the fall of 1966 both Northington and Page enjoyed successful seasons on the freshman team. Since first-year squads played only a limited schedule and were open to non-scholarship students, most sports fans did not consider SEC football to have been truly integrated. The following spring Charlie Bradshaw signed three more African Americans, Wilbur Hackett and Albert Johnson of Louisville and Houston Hogg of Owensboro, offering further proof that the Wildcat football program had eliminated racial restrictions on recruiting. When classes began in the fall of 1967 there were five African Americans enrolled on football scholarships at Kentucky, plus state sprint champion James Green in track.[6] As the new season arrived, considerable attention focused on the anticipated appearance of either Page or Northington as the SEC's first African American varsity player. But during preseason drills an unexpected tragedy cast a shadow over the Wildcat football program and endangered the integration experiment. At an August 22 session Bradshaw instructed the varsity to execute a special pursuit drill in which the entire defensive team gang tackled and piled on top of an offensive ball carrier. In one round of this brutal drill Page hit the runner first, and then both of them were buried under an avalanche of their teammates. While the other players staggered back to their feet, Page lay motionless on the ground. Emergency personnel rushed him to the university medical center, where doctors determined that he had suffered a broken neck and was paralyzed from the shoulders down. Page's terrible injury emotionally devastated Northington. He and the three black freshman players were further shaken when they heard rumors that Page had been deliberately injured for daring to integrate the football team, even though they did not really believe these reports.[7]

Nat Northington somehow found the emotional strength to continue practicing. In the season opener against Indiana University on September 23, he unfortunately dislocated his shoulder, which did not heal immediately. Northington's spirits sank even lower the following week when Greg Page died on September 29. The Wildcats were scheduled to host the Ole Miss Rebels the next day in Lexington, and after consulting with Page's parents the university went ahead with the game, which Ole Miss won 26–13. Despite considerable physical and emotional pain, Northington started the game at defensive halfback. He played for only a little more than three minutes against the Rebels before he once again dislocated his shoulder, which sidelined him indefinitely. Nonetheless, in that brief appearance Northington had become the first African American to play in a SEC football game. On the following Monday, Page's funeral was held in his hometown of Middlesboro, with a crowd so large that the service had to be moved to the white First Baptist Church. Local government officials, UK administrators, and Governor Edward Breathitt were among those who attended the service.[8]

In the wake of Page's death Kentucky's great integration breakthrough teetered on the brink of disaster. Physically battered and emotionally drained, Northington decided to quit the team and drop out of school. When tracked down by a reporter for the student newspaper, he explained that he was not leaving due to racial problems but because of all the personal difficulties he had faced on and off the gridiron. As the discouraged young man removed his possessions from his dormitory, he stopped by the room of Wilbur Hackett and Houston Hogg. Northington told them that he could not stay any longer but urged them "not to leave" in order to keep the integration experiment going. Away from home for the first time and in a new environment, the two freshmen discussed their future with teammate Albert Johnson and sprinter James Green. Eventually, the four athletes agreed that they could not quit just because times were tough. With their decision Kentucky's effort at athletic integration had narrowly survived. Meanwhile, the Wildcat football team continued its downward slide, finishing the year with only two wins.[9]

The 1968 season at Kentucky opened on a more optimistic note. Although Albert Johnson eventually left the team because of injuries, Hackett and Hogg returned with renewed dedication, and Hackett soon became a starter on defense. The two athletes became the first black Wildcats to venture into the Deep South when Kentucky traveled to Jackson for a September 28 meeting with Ole Miss. Because of concerns about their safety, several Mississippi highway patrolmen were specifically assigned to protect them at the stadium. When Hackett and Hogg arrived in Jackson they were relieved to discover that local people treated them just like their white teammates. The Rebel players likewise treated them fairly the next day during their game. But the behavior of the state highway patrolmen assigned to protect the Wildcats was another matter. As they stood on the sidelines, these hefty law enforcement agents regularly shouted out lines from a racist football joke that was circulating within the state. According to the joke, two black football teams were playing, and late in the game the losing team gained an opportunity to score near their opponent's goal line. The coach yelled to his quarterback, "Give 'at ball to LeRoy!" On the ensuing play the quarterback instead handed off to a different runner, who was slammed hard to the ground at the line of scrimmage. "Give 'at ball to LeRoy!" the coach shouted in a louder voice. Again the quarterback handed off to another player, and this time the ball carrier was knocked down behind the line of scrimmage and had to be helped off the field. Screaming at the top of his lungs, the frustrated coach yelled one last time, "Give 'at ball to LeRoy!" This time the quarterback turned toward the sidelines and shouted back, "LeRoy say he don't want 'at ball!" Hackett and Hogg were not familiar with the joke, but they grasped its anti-black message. As the patrolmen continued to yell out references to "LeRoy," the two furious players barely avoided attacking their alleged protectors.[10]

Hackett and Hogg experienced several other minor racial incidents during their careers at Kentucky, but none of them upset the duo as much as did the situation with the highway patrolmen in Jackson. In a generally upbeat interview with the student newspaper after his senior season, Hackett recalled hearing opponents occasionally utter racial slurs during games, more so at Hogg because the fullback attracted considerable attention as a ball carrier. Hackett also recounted an unpleasant incident when he and several teammates were denied service at a hamburger joint in Baton Rouge after a game. Despite some occasional misunderstandings with his white teammates, they elected him a co-captain both his junior and senior years, reflecting the respect that they held for him. Unfortunately, the Wildcats struggled on the field. After Kentucky finished with a 3-7 record in 1968, Charlie Bradshaw resigned as head coach. His replacement, John Ray, continued to recruit African Americans, but his teams never won more than three games in a season. Despite the university's bold action in breaking the SEC color line, Kentucky failed to gain any long-term advantage from recruiting African Americans, once rival schools changed their policies. Nonetheless, the University of Kentucky had taken a courageous stand in favor of fair play on the gridiron at a time when no other SEC school dared to act.[11]

Tennessee Embraces the New Racial Order in Football

The University of Tennessee became the second member of the Southeastern Conference to accept African American players on its varsity football team. Football traditionally dominated the campus scene at UT, and the Volunteer teams enjoyed enormous popularity across the state. Under the leadership of legendary coach Robert R. Neyland, famous for his single-wing offense, Tennessee became a national power. In 1938, 1940, and 1951 at least one poll selected his teams as national champions. At the time of his retirement Neyland had accumulated a career record at UT of 173 wins, 31 losses, and 12 ties. Despite the Volunteers' national prominence, Neyland refused to accept intersectional games against integrated teams after World War II. In the early 1950s, though, school officials quietly dropped their stand against interracial competition *outside* the state for other school teams. The university's continuing ban on interracial competition in Knoxville remained in place until the summer of 1962, when athletic officials tentatively scheduled two intersectional football games for 1965. They approved these contests with the knowledge that the visiting teams would probably include African Americans. When the 1965 season arrived Tennessee hosted UCLA and the University of Houston, both of which featured African American running backs. Although there were complaints that UCLA's Mel Farr and Houston's Warren McVea had been subjected to racial taunts during their games, Tennessee had entered a new era in its athletic history. Finally, in February 1966, the athletic department announced that it would now offer scholarships to any qualified athletes regardless of race.[12]

Tennessee's announcement focused media attention on the Knoxville school and its likely role as the next SEC school to embrace African American athletes. The desegregation of public high schools in the Knoxville area in 1963 and 1964 helped create a more tolerant atmosphere for similar changes at the university. The Volunteers' young head coach, Doug Dickey, who was hired in 1964, had coached an integrated football team while serving in the U.S. Army and seemed more flexible than older coaches. Nonetheless, criticism of the athletic department appeared after Dickey failed to sign any black prospects during 1965 or 1966. In January 1967 the campus newspaper suggested that UT coaches had focused too narrowly on only a few black high school superstars and instead needed to scout a wider pool of prospects. Several months later Dickey signed the top high school player in the state, halfback Albert Davis of nearby Alcoa, Tennessee, to a scholarship. When Davis attended a Volunteer basketball game on campus, fans had chanted "We Want Albert." The following month, Dickey convinced another black recruit, halfback Lester McClain of Nashville Antioch High School, to sign with Tennessee. A minister's son and honor student, McClain had transferred as a senior to Antioch, where he was the only African American on the team. Unfortunately, Davis failed to earn the minimum standardized test score required by the SEC, leaving McClain as the first African American to receive a football scholarship at UT.[13]

An outgoing, cheerful person, McClain got along fairly well with his white teammates, but the presence of two other black freshman athletes, Audry Hardy and James Craig from the track team, helped provide special companionship during his sometimes lonely first year on campus. Coaches soon moved him from halfback to wide receiver, and he led the freshman team in total pass receptions. McClain joined the varsity in 1968, becoming the second African American to play football in SEC competition. A three-year letterman, he proved to be a reliable pass receiver, and his seventy career catches left him ranked fifth on the all-time list at Tennessee. In 1969 three additional African Americans joined McClain on the Tennessee varsity, and by his senior year there were a total of seven black athletes on the varsity roster. In 1972 UT broke another barrier when sophomore Conredge Holloway started at quarterback for the Volunteers, making him and Mississippi State's Melvin Barkum the first two African Americans to start at quarterback in the SEC.[14]

As the university's first African American football player, McClain experienced considerable pressure to prove that black athletes could compete in the rugged Southeastern Conference. He sometimes felt discouraged and thought about leaving school, but he realized that his role as a racial pioneer required him to remain on campus and succeed. As he later recalled, "I just couldn't [drop out]. I knew the next day the headline would say: 'Lester McClain, first black athlete, quits UT.'" McClain also understood the informal integration script that called for a racial pioneer to be a "good Negro," that is, quiet, hardworking, and noncomplaining. Although the young athlete overheard a few teammates use racial epithets and had to endure occasional racial slurs from opposing teams, he diplomatically refrained from making any public comments about this treatment. At the end of his senior year, however, McClain touched off a small controversy when he candidly told a reporter for the school newspaper about the extra pressures he had endured as an African American player and also mentioned several problems with UT athletics. According to the reporter, he also claimed that newly promoted head coach Bill Battle had discriminated against him. After the article appeared McClain publicly complained that his comments had been taken out of context and adamantly denied that Battle had ever acted improperly. He further explained that he had identified several minor problems in the athletic program not out of personal bitterness but so that they could be corrected. Battle and McClain later reached a rapprochement after a private meeting, but the brief incident revealed that white coaches and administrators did not fully comprehend the myriad challenges faced by the first black athletes on their teams.[15]

James Owens Lives a Lonely Life at Auburn

Despite the examples of Kentucky and Tennessee, the remaining members of the Southeastern Conference continued to postpone the integration of their varsity football teams. Two years passed before a group of four additional schools—Auburn, Vanderbilt, Mississippi State, and Florida—finally sent African Americans wearing their school colors onto the football field. Their actions meant that for the first time a majority of SEC schools had integrated teams and that the conference was at last joining the mainstream of American college sports. Auburn University had long maintained a tradition of racial exclusion in sports, and the shift to athletic integration proved painful. Football competition at the college began in 1892, and over the years the school teams achieved considerable success. During the 1920s President Spright Dowell undertook a major effort to upgrade academic standards and de-emphasize football, which he labeled "a continuous problem" that diverted attention from "the more serious work of the institution." But when the school team went winless in 1927, the Board of Regents fired the embattled president. Dowell was neither the first nor the last southern educator to learn that providing a winning football team constituted an essential duty for public universities. After World War II, Coach Ralph "Shug" Jordan established the Tigers as a conference power. Under his leadership from 1951 to 1975 Auburn regularly finished at or near the top of the SEC standings and made twelve bowl appearances.[16]

Auburn enrolled its first African American students in 1964, inaugurating a series of racial changes on campus during the rest of the decade. In October 1966 the Tigers defeated Wake Forest in the first integrated game held in the Auburn stadium. Despite the shifting racial climate Shug Jordan did not make any immediate plans to alter his recruiting patterns. A native of Selma, Jordan represented a generation of white southern coaches who were quite comfortable with the status quo and viewed athletic integration with trepidation. When basketball coach Bill Lynn unexpectedly announced in 1968 that he had awarded a scholarship to Henry Harris, Jordan privately complained to President Harry M. Philpott that Lynn's action had placed unwelcome pressure on him to integrate his team. At the next meeting of the university's Board of Trustees, one member bitterly criticized Harris's signing, but several other members disagreed, arguing that athletic integration was inevitable. One trustee, a dedicated football fan, jokingly dismissed such resistance to black football players by asserting, "The faster they run, the more touchdowns they make, the whiter they get!"[17]

During the fall of 1968 Auburn coaches carefully evaluated several possible African American recruits and eventually concentrated their attention on James Owens. A 195-pound halfback, Owens had transferred as a sophomore to predominantly white Fairfield High School, where he was the only African American on the team. Influenced by his parents, he signed with the Tigers in December 1968. In his first year at the university Owens turned in a solid performance as a running back on the 1969 freshman squad. During the 1970 season the versatile sophomore played mostly on defense, but he did return a punt eighty-nine yards for a touchdown against Florida. During his first two years Owens lived a somewhat lonely existence as one of only two black athletes in the athletic dorm. As a junior and senior Owens became a starter at the fullback position. However, he spent much of that time blocking for Terry Henley, the team's star white halfback.[18]

Over the next three years only two more black recruits joined the Tigers. In 1970 Thomas Gossom enrolled at Auburn in hopes of becoming the second African American to make the varsity football team. A successful sprinter and football player at Birmingham's predominantly white John Carroll (Catholic) High School, the speedy Gossom soon impressed coaches and was rewarded with a scholarship. In the fall of 1972 halfback Mitzi Jackson of DeFuniak Springs, Florida, enrolled as the third black scholarship player at Auburn. The arrival of these athletes provided Owens with badly needed support and companionship. By his junior year Owens discovered that many white players had become much friendlier. In fact, he even found himself invited to a few white fraternity parties. Most of the time, though, Owens, Harris, and Gossom sought social life in the small black community in the town of Auburn, where they were treated as heroes, and also at nearby Tuskegee Institute. At times Owens and Gossom heard coaches and teammates use racial epithets, but both saw relations between blacks and whites improve steadily from year to year. Because of their status as racial pioneers, the two experienced extra pressure on the field and in the classroom, but they refused to quit because they felt a special obligation to open doors at the university for future black athletes.[19]

The presence of African Americans in Auburn sports increased steadily throughout the remainder of the 1970s. By the early 1980s black players made up more than 40 percent of the Auburn roster. In 1983 the Tigers, coached by Pat Dye, captured the SEC championship, their first league title since 1957. Among the star players on that team was popular halfback Vincent "Bo" Jackson, who later won the Heisman Trophy in 1985. The dramatic shift in the racial composition of Auburn football teams could also be seen by the mid-1980s in the photographs of former stars proudly displayed at the Grille, a traditional student hangout located on historic Toomer's Corner directly across from the campus. There one could view along the walls a long row of player photographs, which featured only whites at its beginning. In the latter half of the display, however, photographs of black faces appeared, underscoring the racial shift that had taken place on the Tiger squad. Missing from this wall of honor, though, was a photograph of James Owens, whose perseverance helped open the doors for many of these later stars.[20]

Vanderbilt Students Push for Athletic Integration

As the only private college in the Southeastern Conference, Vanderbilt University enjoyed relative freedom from the demands of segregationist politicians during the era of massive resistance. Yet Vanderbilt's different legal status did not prevent the university from fully embracing southern white values concerning segregation. The university held its first official football match in 1890 and soon developed into "the southern powerhouse in football." The undefeated 1904 team won all nine of its games and outscored its opponents by a remarkable total of 474–4. After the retirement of veteran coach Dan McGugin in 1934, however, Vanderbilt's fortunes suffered a gradual decline. During the dismal 1960s the inept Commodores endured three seasons in which they won only one game. Frustrated by such wretched performances, a few students and faculty members even urged the university to drop football. Before World War II Vanderbilt enforced the color line for all intersectional games, but after the war Chancellor Harvie Branscomb secretly modified this policy. In 1947 the Commodores opened the season against an integrated Northwestern team in Evanston, Illinois, but school administrators and sympathetic Nashville sportswriters helped cover up this breach of the color line. The following year, though, Vanderbilt ventured north to challenge Yale, which was led by star halfback Levi Jackson, an African American. Branscomb approved the game for both academic and athletic reasons. After several influential alumni complained about southern boys having to play against Jackson, a conciliatory Branscomb privately replied, "I don't think any of us enjoyed the experience of playing against Levi Jackson." But in the campus newspaper, the chancellor took a different stand, openly praising Jackson as a "fast and courageous" opponent who had "earned the respect of the Vanderbilt players and everyone in the stands."[21]

An energetic new chancellor, Dr. Alexander Heard, succeeded Branscomb in 1963 and helped liberalize the university over the next twenty years. The football program proved to be one of his most difficult challenges. Following the end of the 1966 season the university fired coach Jack Green and hired thirty-four-year-old Bill Pace as his replacement. At the same time, the school hired as its new athletic director sixty-five-year-old Jess Neely, a 1922 Vanderbilt graduate who had just retired as head coach at Rice University. To improve the team's fortunes, many students suggested that Pace should expand traditional recruiting patterns and seek out African American prospects. Their hopes were partially influenced by the pioneering actions of basketball coach Roy Skinner, who had broken the SEC's color line in that sport in 1966. Bill Pace briefly restored some success to the football program but attracted student criticism over the failure to integrate his squad. His 1968 team achieved a 5-4-1 record, the school's first winning season in nine years, but the Commodores quickly reverted to their previous level of mediocre performances. In late 1967 the tiny contingent of black students at the school formed the Afro-American Association. The group subsequently voiced complaints over subtle discrimination on campus, the lack of social opportunities, and the absence of black athletes outside the basketball team. When Pace failed to sign any minority athletes in the spring of 1968, white students became more vocal in their criticism. An incident involving a white football player served as a catalyst for a campus debate on racial attitudes within the athletic department. In early April junior Terry Thomas publicly claimed that Pace had warned him not to take a black woman as his date to the spring football banquet at a local country club. Interpreting the incident as proof of the athletic department's racial insensitivity, more than four hundred students signed an open letter to Chancellor Heard, dismissing the basketball team's integration as "a token experiment" and criticizing football coaches for not recruiting African Americans.[22]

Athletic director Jess Neely and Bill Pace repeatedly defended the athletic department against such accusations. Neely met with a delegation of students and informed them that his coaches had evaluated more than two dozen black prospects for the coming year, but most of them failed to met Vanderbilt's demanding entrance requirements. The school eventually had offered scholarships to two of them, he revealed, but both declined. His actions temporarily quieted the protests, but the following spring similar complaints resurfaced. The editor of the student newspaper, Henry Hecht, launched a personal campaign to convince Vanderbilt to rethink its staffing priorities. Hecht argued that "good intentions" were not enough and that the university should deliberately hire a black coach, because "the system will never open up to qualified black men without a conscious effort." His stand was publicly endorsed by undergraduate Walter Murray, a cofounder of the Afro-American Association and an informal adviser to Chancellor Heard on race relations. Murray contended that such a hiring was important because it could help recruit minority athletes and "would certainly be a new and valuable experience for the football players, almost all white, to have to take orders from a black man." Chancellor Heard viewed the integration of the athletic program as an important public symbol of the university's racial progress, but he privately worried that Neely, the product of an older South, did not appreciate the symbolic value of athletic integration. In a related matter, Heard also became frustrated with Neely when the athletic director failed to hire any minorities for clerical work or ticket sales within the athletic department. As a result, two groundskeepers remained the department's only black employees during 1969.[23]

During the spring of 1969 Bill Pace finally awarded the school's first football scholarship to an African American, Taylor Stokes of Clarksville, Tennessee. Stokes told the press that he welcomed the chance to break racial barriers at the university, since "Vanderbilt is suited to a black athlete looking for academics as well as athletics." Criticism of the athletic program eased somewhat after Neely hired Harold Hunter as a part-time assistant coach with the basketball team in January 1970. In the fall of 1970 Taylor Stokes advanced to the Vanderbilt varsity but suffered an injury and was forced to sit out the season. Joining him on the varsity that fall was another African American, junior James Hurley, a non-scholarship player. Hurley had attended the prestigious Phillips Academy in Andover, Massachusetts, and played freshman football at the University of Georgia before transferring to Vanderbilt. Also in the fall of 1970 defensive back Doug Nettles of Panama City, Florida, and wide receiver Walter Overton of Nashville became the second and third African Americans to enroll at Vanderbilt on football scholarships. Overton, who grew up just a few blocks from the university, told the student newspaper that playing for the Commodores was "a childhood dream which I thought was impossible" until recently. The following year Nettles, Overton, and Stokes all played on the varsity squad. After several more African Americans joined the Commodores over the next two years and the university hired its first black assistant football coach, Fred Malone, the debate over the football squad's racial composition subsided. The Commodores' inept performance in the Southeastern Conference, however, remained the same. Neither a shift in recruiting practices nor a revised undergraduate curriculum designed to make it easier for football players to pursue a degree managed to have any major effect on Vanderbilt's football fortunes over the next thirty years.[24]

Mississippi State Recruits a True Scholar-Athlete

At first glance, Mississippi State University did not seem a likely candidate to become one of the earlier Southeastern Conference members to integrate its athletic program. The school's location in the small town of Starkville, its historic role as an agricultural college, and white Mississippians' extreme opposition to school desegregation were all factors that appeared to rule out any flexibility in race relations by the university. Yet somewhat surprisingly, Mississippi State joined Vanderbilt, Auburn, and Florida in the second wave of SEC schools to field integrated varsity football teams in 1970. Created in 1878 as the state's land-grant institution for white males, the college formed its first intercollegiate football team in 1895. The Maroons never became one of the stronger squads in the Deep South, although the 1917 team lost only one game. In the season finale that year MSU edged the Haskell Institute by a score of 7–6. The fact that this game was held in race-conscious Mississippi showed that a Native American team could be viewed as an honorable opponent even though its players were not of European origins. Competition against even one African American, however, was completely unacceptable and dishonorable.[25]

From 1926 through 1949 Mississippi State regularly scheduled intersectional contests against northern and western squads. Following World War II the possible presence of black players on these non-southern teams created a dilemma for the school. In November 1946 MSU officials became upset when Nevada canceled its scheduled game in Starkville after they had denied the visitors the right to use their two black players in the game. In 1946 and 1947 Mississippi State was more successful in two games against Michigan State, forcing their hosts to bench their one African American player on both occasions. The two schools did not renew the series after 1947, perhaps because Michigan State would no longer honor the gentleman's agreement. Mississippi State significantly modified its football schedule policy after 1949 by replacing all northern and western teams with southwestern and southern colleges in order to avoid encountering any black players. Thus, the intense turmoil within Mississippi from 1955 to 1965 over massive resistance to school desegregation had no additional impact on football. In the fall of 1963 the MSU squad finished the season with a 6-2-2 record and received an invitation to meet North Carolina State in the Liberty Bowl in Philadelphia. The invitation of an all-white team from a segregated southern university upset some city residents, and the Philadelphia branch of NAACP unsuccessfully filed an official protest of the invitation with the bowl sponsors.[26]

Mississippi State continued to avoid scheduling integrated teams until the school had actually enrolled its first African American students. An ongoing football series with the University of Houston led to the actual break with tradition. MSU opened the 1965 season against Houston and that school's first black player, halfback Warren McVea, in the new Astrodome Stadium and unexpectedly blanked the Cougars 36–0. The following year the two teams again met in the Astrodome, and in the fall of 1967 the Maroons hosted the annual game in Starkville. Houston's black players were somewhat apprehensive about visiting such a small town in the Deep South, since this would be the first integrated home game for MSU. University officials went out of their way to ensure that the visitors received a friendly welcome. The football squad also proved to be a generous host, losing to the Cougars 43–6. Immediately after the game, a mob of spectators unexpectedly rushed toward the Houston bench and McVea, who had sat out the contest because of injuries, briefly alarming security guards. In a sign that white Mississippi attitudes had changed, however, it turned out that these individuals were merely fans seeking McVea's autograph.[27]

With African Americans attending classes and home games against integrated teams now a reality, attention shifted to the composition of the Mississippi State football squad. Except for the successful 1963 season, the Maroons continued to struggle throughout the sixties. From 1966 through 1969 the team failed to win a single SEC contest. Even the school's rowdy fans, infamous for loudly ringing cowbells in the stands, could not awaken the Maroons from their slumber. MSU administrators and trustees regularly lamented the demoralizing "football situation." In 1966 Charley Shira took over as head coach and lasted through the 1972 season, despite posting only one winning record. Because of State's repeated losses, Shira may have become more open-minded about recruiting than more successful coaches. During the 1968 high school season his staff identified two outstanding black prospects in the state. The first, Frank Dowsing, was in his second year at Tupelo High School, where he and a few other black students had enrolled the previous year under the state's "freedom of choice" plan. The other athlete, Robert Bell, attended an integrated high school in Meridian. Both were in the first small group of African Americans allowed to play football in the white high school athletic association. Their good grades and exposure to a predominantly white environment suggested that they could adjust to the campus atmosphere in Starkville. Dowsing and Bell both wished to stay close to home for college, and in December they signed with Mississippi State, becoming the school's first black athletes in any sport. Bell, a defensive lineman, had a reasonably successful career as a part-time starter and became something of a crowd favorite. He credited the Fellowship of Christian Athletes and the black student association with providing him emotional support during his four years, a near necessity given the limited social life available on campus for black students at that time.[28]

Frank Dowsing enjoyed a remarkable career at MSU, one that gave real meaning to the term *scholar-athlete*. As a sophomore in 1970 Dowsing quickly earned a starting role as a defensive back. As a junior the Associated Press named him to its All-SEC team, while UPI selected him for its all-conference team the following year. Also in 1972 the *Football News* picked Dowsing for its All-America team. To add to his honors, the SEC named the premed major to its all-academic squad for each of his three varsity seasons, and he received All-America academic honors as a senior. Finally, the National Football Foundation selected Dowsing as a Hall of Fame scholar-athlete in 1972, the only SEC player to be so honored that year, and awarded him a graduate scholarship. In one unique additional honor, students at MSU voted Dowsing "Mr. Mississippi State" in October 1972, the highest accolade that students could bestow on a male student. Dowsing's selection for this special award indicated that race relations at Mississippi colleges, though far from perfect, had evolved considerably since James Meredith's arrival at Ole Miss some ten years earlier.[29]

Two more African Americans joined Bell and Dowsing on the Maroon squad over the next two years. Fullback James Smith moved up to the varsity in 1971, and Melvin Barkum, a talented player at several positions, began varsity play in 1972. Barkum alternated with Rocky Felker, who was white, at the quarterback position on the freshman team and also during their sophomore year, creating a minor "quarterback controversy." Along with Conredge Holloway of Tennessee, Barkum became one of the first two African Americans to start at quarterback in the SEC. Midway through the 1973 season, Coach Bob Tyler, Shira's replacement, moved Barkum to wide receiver because of his versatility and installed

Felker as the permanent quarterback. The various shifts in who started at this position provoked a few complaints from both white and black fans, revealing a special sensitivity over the quarterback slot because of its prominence. Eventually, the controversy abated, especially after Felker enjoyed an outstanding senior year in 1974, earning All-SEC first-team honors while leading the Maroons to a 7-3 regular season record and a Sun Bowl invitation. The 1974 squad's excellent record demonstrated that integration had aided the Maroons in improving the competitive performance of their teams. But after losing a protracted legal battle with the SEC over a player-eligibility dispute, MSU later had to forfeit eighteen wins from the 1975, 1976, and 1977 seasons. Thereafter, the team consistently finished in the bottom half of the conference standings. Some three decades later, however, Mississippi State did establish an important racial milestone for the conference when in December 2003 it hired the league's first black head football coach, Sylvester Croom.[30]

Athletic Integration Moves Slowly at Florida

The fourth and final member of the Southeastern Conference to field an integrated varsity football team in the fall of 1970 was the University of Florida. Although the Sunshine State lost much of its Deep South identity over the final two decades of the twentieth century, its earlier political culture remained strongly southern well into the 1970s. Florida began sponsoring intercollegiate football in 1906 and was a charter member of the SEC. Until the 1960s the Gators compiled a rather average record, having failed to win even one SEC title. After the Supreme Court's *Brown* ruling, the state Board of Regents reinforced its segregation policy for sports, formally prohibiting all interracial competition at public university facilities. Yet in 1958 the athletic department leaped at the chance to play a high-profile game in Los Angeles against UCLA, even though the Bruin squad included several African Americans. This contest carried special meaning because it was the first time that the Gators had ever competed against an integrated team. As resistance to desegregation eased in the 1960s, Florida officials subsequently agreed to a home-and-home series with Northwestern University. In the opening game of the 1966 season the Gators hosted the Wildcats in their first integrated game at home in Gainesville.[31]

During the 1960s Coach Ray Graves led Florida to unprecedented success on the football field but encountered criticism over the racial composition of his team. During his ten years as head coach from 1960 through 1969, Graves suffered through only one losing season and took the Gators to five postseason bowl games. In 1965 Graves, who also served as athletic director, announced that any eligible student could try out for the Gator athletic teams. By early 1968, however, when no African Americans had appeared on any university team, critics began to attack the athletic department for racial discrimination. The local chapter of the NAACP, led by the Reverend T. A. Wright, took the lead. The group blamed the absence of African Americans primarily on the Gator head coach. Reverend Wright also emphasized that many black high school athletes in the state had received football scholarships to comparable universities around the country but were never invited to play at Florida, thus demonstrating racial bias at the university. Graves denied the accusations and in turn warned that Wright's negative remarks made it harder to attract black recruits to Gainesville. Graves further blamed most of his difficulty in locating eligible black athletes on their inadequate scores on the state's Senior Placement Examination, a standardized entrance test required of all UF applicants. Graves told one reporter that he had "found fifteen Negroes who I thought had good enough grades and ability to play for me," but none remained eligible after taking the test.[32]

The small contingent of black students at Florida soon joined the criticism of the athletic department. In the spring of 1968 the Afro-American Student Association and individual students decried a variety of problems on campus, including discrimination by professors, the absence of social activities and special support services for African Americans, and the deliberate exclusion of black athletes from the university's sports teams. The AASA also condemned the state entrance examination as racially biased. During the 1968–69 school year the first black athletes appeared on campus in cross-country and track and field, but the football program failed to add any black recruits, further inciting Graves's critics. Some of them unfavorably compared the university with in-state rival Florida State, where the recruitment of minority athletes had advanced more rapidly.[33]

In December 1968 Graves finally convinced two young black athletes to sign scholarship agreements with Florida. Leonard George of Tampa and Willie B. Jackson of Sarasota became the first African Americans to break the color line in Gator football. George, a halfback, and Jackson, an end, arrived on campus in September 1969 and played on the Gator varsity for three years beginning in 1970. Jackson especially enjoyed a successful career, displaying considerable skill as a pass receiver. Both players felt considerable pressure to succeed at Florida. George later explained that as a racial pioneer, "You've got a big responsibility, because there are a lot of people out there in the black community who . . . are depending on you. They're pushing you. They've got their hopes and dreams in you." A series of campus protests by African American students in April 1971 brought additional stress to UF's black athletes. After 66 protesters were arrested when they refused to halt a sit-in demonstration in the president's office, more than 120 African Americans, nearly half the school's black enrollment, withdrew from the college in protest. The departing students begged the 10 athletes to join them. After much reflection, the players decided not to leave, fearing that they would be unable to compete in their sports at another school and that their ability to finance a college education would be endangered. Willie Jackson, the group's representative, announced they had decided to "give this thing a chance here. There's got to be somebody left here to keep the pressure on so changes can be made."[34]

Despite the 1971 upheaval the hiring of new head coach Doug Dickey eventually led to changes in football recruiting and improved race relations. Dickey expanded Graves's efforts and steadily recruited a growing number of black prospects. His prior success at integrating the Tennessee football squad and the fact that he was a fresh face may have allayed the suspicions of some black Floridians. The appearance in 1973 of Don Gaffney as the Gators' first black quarterback may also have helped. Over his nine years as head coach, Dickey took three teams to bowl games and compiled a 58-43-2 record. Athletic integration did not appear to have affected Florida's fortunes very much during the 1970s, other than to assist the Gators in maintaining their moderate success on the gridiron.[35]

Bear Bryant Was a Follower, Not a Leader

Although several members of the Southeastern Conference eventually achieved national prominence in football, none of them equaled the remarkable success enjoyed by the University of Alabama Crimson Tide. Male students at the university established the school's first official football team, known initially as the "thin red line," in 1892, one year before women were first admitted to classes on campus. During the 1920s Alabama emerged as the first Deep South team to gain national recognition. The famous 1925 Crimson Tide squad went undefeated and received the first invitation ever extended to a southern team to compete in the Rose Bowl. Alabama eventually received five more invitations to the New Year's Day classic, before Rose Bowl officials signed an exclusive contract with the Big Ten Conference to provide its visiting team. After World War II Alabama exercised considerable care in scheduling its few intersectional matches, so as to avoid integrated teams. In 1952 the Crimson Tide finished with a 9-2 record and accepted an invitation to the Orange Bowl in Miami. When school officials learned that their opponent would be Syracuse, whose teams had featured several black players in recent years, they became alarmed. Reluctant to sacrifice the prestige and revenue expected from the contest, President John M. Gallalee nonetheless instructed Coach H. D. "Red" Drew to threaten to pull his team off the field if Syracuse inserted an African American into the game. These racial fears proved unwarranted, as the Orangeman roster did not include any black players that year, and Alabama easily won the match, 61-6.[36]

In 1957, after four straight losing seasons, Alabama hired former player Bear Bryant away from Texas A&M in order to rebuild the football team and direct the athletic program. In Bryant's second year back in Tuscaloosa, the Crimson Tide finished the season with a 7-1-2 record and received an invitation to play Penn State in the Liberty Bowl at Philadelphia, its first postseason opportunity in six years. This offer was complicated by the presence of one African American starter in the Penn State lineup. Bryant wanted to accept the bid because it would renew excitement about his program and reward his players for their hard work. Sensitive to the state's political climate, Bryant and university administrators first cleared the trip with Governor John Patterson and then the Board of Trustees, who gave their consent. One trustee even suggested that the school band play such southern favorites as "Dixie" and "My Old Kentucky Home." On the other hand, a few die-hard segregationists opposed the Philadelphia trip. Two chapters of the White Citizens Council admonished school officials that competition against an African American would undermine the larger fight to maintain complete segregation inside the state. As one council chapter stated, "It is very difficult to explain why we indulge in integrated football and draw the line in other places." In the North not everyone approved of the Tide's participation either. The Philadelphia branch of the NAACP unsuccessfully protested the Liberty Bowl's invitation to Alabama, charging that the university was "perhaps the most racially bigoted and illiberal educational institution in this country."[37]

During the 1960s the racial violence that accompanied the civil rights struggle in Alabama and the controversial political stands of Governor George C. Wallace turned the state into something of a national pariah. In such an atmosphere the Crimson Tide football program could not escape at least some political fallout. Outside critics especially derided the Tide's unwillingness to invite any integrated squads to play in Tuscaloosa. The growing political problems that Alabama's football program faced were highlighted at the end of the 1961 season. The Tide compiled a perfect 10-0 record, captured the SEC championship, and finished the season ranked number one in the country. Meanwhile, a unique opportunity presented itself in Southern California. The formal contract by which the Big Ten provided the visiting team for the Rose Bowl game each January 1 had expired, and negotiations for a new contract were stalled. As a result, several bowl officials explored the idea of inviting the highest-ranked available team to challenge the host West Coast champion, in order to create something resembling a national championship game. The idea of luring Alabama to the classic quickly caught on. The most likely opponent for the Crimson Tide appeared to be the UCLA Bruins. However, in Los Angeles, African American groups, liberal UCLA students, several black Bruin players, and sports columnist Jim Murray of the *Los Angeles Times* launched a counterattack that derailed the Alabama campaign. Murray repeatedly used his acerbic writing skills to skewer the Deep South, the state of Alabama, southern football, and southern racism.

Since one faction of the bowl association preferred to continue to invite a Big Ten team in hopes of negotiating a renewed contract the following year, the attack on Alabama's racial policies strengthened their position. When it became obvious that the embarrassing public controversy would only grow worse, disappointed UA officials abandoned their California dreams and accepted a bid to the Sugar Bowl, where the Tide defeated an all-white team from the University of Arkansas, solidifying its claim to the national championship.[38]

Bryant's teams continued to excel, claiming two more national championships in 1964 and 1965. According to one historian, this impressive feat delighted white Alabama fans, who viewed "the Crimson Tide as a natural rallying point for the embattled white South" and "a potent symbol of pride and cultural vitality." Yet critics like sports columnist Jim Murray continued to belittle the Tide's accomplishments. "'National' Champion of what?" Murray once thundered in a column: "The Confederacy? This team hasn't poked its head above the Mason-Dixon Line since Appomattox." At the end of the 1966 season, politics again caught up with the Tide. That year Bryant produced yet another undefeated team and again beat Nebraska in the Sugar Bowl in January 1967. But voters in the final wire-service polls refused to select the Tide as the national champion, instead picking Notre Dame, even though the Irish had tied Michigan State. This rejection hurt Bryant and convinced white Alabamians that an anti-southern bias by sportswriters had cost the school its well-deserved national championship.[39]

Once the University of Kentucky broke the color line in Southeastern Conference football, Bear Bryant publicly acknowledged that integration would someday extend to the entire league. Yet despite his widespread popularity within the state, which at times rivaled that of Governor Wallace, Bryant proceeded cautiously on the race issue. In 1965 he told an official from the University of Florida that Alabama would be willing to host any integrated SEC team at Tuscaloosa without complaint, but he continued to schedule only southern white teams for *non-conference* home games. In the spring of 1967 five African American students joined the Tide for spring workouts, and two of them participated in the formal spring game. None were offered athletic scholarships, however. Also during that spring Bryant informed the school's basketball and track coaches that they could begin recruiting African Americans if they wished. It was not until January 1968, though, that Bryant's assistant coaches started to scout black prospects as well as white ones. At the end of the 1968 season Alabama offered scholarships to black high school stars Frank Dowsing and James Owens, but both athletes instead signed with other SEC teams.[40]

African American students eventually challenged the continuing whiteness of the UA football team. Despite Bryant's claim that he did not consider race in his recruiting, his failure to sign any black prospects by the spring of 1969 upset black students on campus. During the summer the school's Afro-American

Association, aided by the NAACP, filed suit in federal court, charging the university with racial discrimination in athletics. Both sides in the case agreed to numerous postponements, with the result that no action was taken for nearly a year. Meanwhile, the integration of the basketball team at Alabama failed to pacify the AAA, which described the action as "tokenism" and argued that only the integration of the football team would indicate a substantive transformation in policy. In October 1969 some fifty black students staged a sit-down demonstration in the university cafeteria to draw attention to a list of seven major proposals articulated by the AAA. These demands included the creation of a black studies program, the hiring of minority professors, and the establishment of an African American center. The group also called for the recruitment of black football players and specifically criticized the school's "white racist football team." Changing racial conditions in the state's high schools helped set the stage for the integration of the Bryant's team. The court-ordered merger of the black high school sports association into its white counterpart created integrated competition across the state during the 1968–69 school term. Newly desegregated white high schools also added a few African American players to their teams that year. These changes allowed black athletes to demonstrate their skills in a traditional environment, making them no longer outsiders to white college coaches.[41]

Bear Bryant's second year of recruiting black prospects proved more successful than the first. In the fall of 1969 assistant coach Pat Dye identified wide receiver Wilbur Jackson of Carroll High School in Ozark, Alabama, as a scholarship candidate. Jackson had recently transferred to Carroll after his former school was closed under a federal desegregation order. When Jackson visited the Tuscaloosa campus, Bryant assured him that the coaching staff would treat him fairly, and Jackson eventually signed with the Tide. His decision was primarily a pragmatic one, since Alabama was initially the only major college to offer him a full scholarship. Although Jackson certainly understood the significance of becoming the first African American football player at Alabama, he later explained, "I just wanted to go to college, get an education, and play football. I didn't want to be Jackie Robinson." Perhaps to protect the young recruit from excessive media attention, Alabama officials kept publicity about his signing and enrollment to a minimum. However, during the summer they did cite his recruitment to gain another postponement in the sports discrimination lawsuit brought by the Afro-American Association. In May 1971, after Alabama handed out football scholarships to four more black players, the suit was finally dismissed.[42]

Despite Jackson's enrollment the legendary contest between the Tide and the University of Southern California Trojans in September 1970 in Birmingham came to symbolize racial change in college athletics in Alabama and the Deep South. Bear Bryant and school officials specifically scheduled the game as part of their desire to create an improved national image for the athletic program and the university, one free from the stigma of racial segregation and the politics of George Wallace. To a large extent Alabama accomplished that goal, despite absorbing a humiliating defeat on the field. None other than the Tide's number-one critic, columnist Jim Murray of the *Los Angeles Times,* praised the university's shift in policy, albeit in a backhanded manner. "The bedsheet-and-burning cross conference is coming out in the daylight of the twentieth century," Murray wrote in his usual flamboyant style. Reflecting on the contest, he declared that "bigotry wasn't suited up" and that "hatred got shut out." The final score itself, he emphasized, "was less a defeat for Alabama than a victory for America. Birmingham will never be the same. And, brother, that's a good thing."[43]

The Southern California game also produced several legends and misconceptions about Bryant and Alabama football. Since Bryant had already started to recruit African American players, the game did not force this policy upon him. The USC contest was actually the second integrated home game for Alabama, after the Tennessee game the previous year. The principal differences between the two contests were that Tennessee started only one black player and was a conference opponent that Alabama was required to play, while the Trojan lineup contained some twenty African Americans, including most of the game's offensive stars, and was a contest that 'Bama had elected to schedule. It is true that the USC loss clearly shocked many white fans and made many of them more willing to accept Bryant's new policy of recruiting African Americans. White Alabamians' desire to win football games would subsequently triumph over their historical preference for maintaining the whiteness of the Tide football team. Finally, the Southern California game also revealed that Alabama was ready to rejoin the larger sporting nation and embrace American rather than southern principles concerning integrated competition.

At the end of the 1970 season Bryant's staff intensified their recruiting efforts. By January of the new year they had issued scholarships to three more black high school prospects—Sylvester Croom of Tuscaloosa and Ralph Stokes and Mike Washington of Montgomery. These three athletes had all attended black schools until their senior year, when they were reassigned to previously white high schools as part of a surge in public school integration. Their recruitment demonstrated that Bryant was not interested in mere tokenism. Even more significant in the short run was the signing of defensive end John Mitchell from Eastern Arizona Junior College. Mitchell had been a Tide fan as a youngster and jumped at the opportunity to play for Bryant. When Alabama opened the 1971 season in Los Angeles in a rematch with Southern California, Mitchell appeared in the starting lineup and played a valuable role in the Tide's 17–10 upset victory. Alabama went on to compile an 11-0 record that season, before losing to Nebraska in the Orange Bowl.[44]

The highly successful 1971 season demonstrated that Bryant's teams could return to the top ranks of college football. However, this accomplishment had initially been achieved with an overwhelmingly white squad, since twenty-one of the twenty-two starters that year were white. Obviously, integration had not yet significantly affected the Tide's fortunes. Alabama's return to glory had also been aided by a new offensive formation—the wishbone—which Bryant had secretly installed in preschool workouts. The following season Alabama went 10-1, with Mitchell earning all-conference and All-America honors. The 1973 season proved even more successful, as one wire service selected the Tide as the regular-season national champion. There were nine African Americans on this squad (not counting freshmen), and three of them including Wilbur Jackson earned all-conference honors. Bryant's black players trusted and respected their head coach, and his Alabama squads avoided most of the racial tensions found on some teams during the 1970s. Furthermore, these integrated teams became one of the few public symbols around which both white and black Alabamians could rally, helping narrow the wide racial gap that had historically divided them. And the Tide continued to win year after year. In 1978 and 1979 Bryant again coached Alabama to national titles, with rosters featuring even more African Americans. When he retired after the 1982 season, Bryant had won 323 games, the most by any major college coach to that date. His six national championship teams constituted another remarkable career record.[45]

Bear Bryant's decision to recruit African Americans for his Crimson Tide teams, while not a pioneering action, obviously brought results in the long run. His own hardscrabble background may have enabled him to establish a special rapport with minority athletes. Yet other SEC coaches were adding African Americans to their teams during the same period. According to one study, the number of black scholarship athletes and lettermen increased by about 50 percent per year in the first half of the 1970s and then at a slower pace for the remainder of the decade. Hence, the recruitment of African Americans alone does not explain Bryant's success. Bryant clearly possessed a superior combination of necessary coaching skills, plus a deep-seated drive to succeed in his life's work. His knowledge of the game, ability to inspire exceptional performances, skill at recruiting, and talent at making integrated squads work together propelled his teams to the top of college football. In almost every category he achieved remarkable success. Except for one: in the area of racial integration, Bryant was a follower, not a leader.[46]

A Governor Helps Open the Doors at LSU

Three Southeastern Conference members, LSU, Ole Miss, and Georgia, lagged behind the rest of the conference in embracing athletic integration. LSU faced special difficulties, because the state of Louisiana erected more formal legal barriers against integrated football games than did any other state. While Mississippi had its "unwritten law" against whites and blacks competing against each other, the Louisiana legislature adopted an actual state statute prohibiting *any* integrated public athletic, social, or recreational event. Since the university and the state capital were both located in Baton Rouge, LSU administrators could not avoid constant scrutiny from the state's ultraconservative political leaders. Therefore, the Fighting Tigers had to overcome two opponents in their quest for national prominence, their rivals on the gridiron and segregationist politicians in the state government. The university's most impressive season came in 1958, when both national polls selected the undefeated Bengal team as the national champion. By the early 1970s LSU had won an impressive total of five SEC championships. Beginning back in 1930 the Tigers had normally scheduled one major intersectional game each year, reflecting the desire of school officials to produce a nationally prominent football program. While many southern white schools were eliminating such matchups in the 1950s, LSU administrators tried to continue playing northern teams until politics intruded onto the gridiron.[47]

The controversy in late 1955 surrounding the integrated Sugar Bowl contest between Pittsburgh and Georgia Tech significantly impacted LSU athletics. Despite segregationists' demands for a halt to such games inside the state, the LSU Board of Supervisors voted in February 1956 to continue scheduling northern teams, even if they should include black players. The board justified its decision by stating that a successful college sports program required playing highly rated opponents, including those from other regions of the country. This action temporarily confirmed an existing contract for a home-and-home series with the University of Wisconsin to begin the following year, which would have resulted in LSU's first integrated football games ever. Over the next six months, however, the supervisors slowly retreated from this position. At a board meeting in April 1956 one conservative member introduced a resolution to prohibit any athletic competition between blacks and whites. The proposal would also have required the athletic department to include a special clause in all contracts for home games, stating that "members of the Negro race shall not be allowed to participate with members of the white race." Perhaps hoping that the issue would go away, the board tabled the proposal. At their next meeting the supervisors struggled to find some way of preserving both intersectional games and Jim Crow. This time a different board member introduced another resolution to ban athletic contests against teams that regularly included African Americans, regardless of the game's location. When the resolution came to a vote, the result was a 7–7 tie vote, which caused the measure to fail.[48]

During the summer of 1956 extreme segregationists took control of the Louisiana legislature and passed a series of sweeping measures designed to strengthen the state's extensive system of legal segregation. Included in this legislation was a sports segregation law that banned individuals, groups, schools, or corporations from sponsoring any public athletic contests, social functions, or entertainments that included white and black participants. The law also required segregated seating and drinking fountains at public events. As a result of the law, LSU officials had to abandon their tentative plans to schedule more home-and-home series with midwestern universities.[49]

The new segregation law also severely restricted LSU's postseason options. The outstanding 1958 and 1959 Tiger teams could play only in the Sugar Bowl, where participation was limited to white teams. In December 1961, however, as the political strength of extreme segregationists weakened somewhat, the Board of Supervisors became bolder and approved a trip to the January 1962 Orange Bowl in Miami. There LSU defeated the University of Colorado in the university's first integrated football contest ever. After the Supreme Court struck down the last remaining provisions of the Louisiana sports segregation law in 1964, scheduling became much easier for LSU. In January 1965 the Tigers participated in the first integrated Sugar Bowl contest in nine years, and officials began to make plans to host integrated teams in Baton Rouge. Although most LSU fans accepted the change, one chapter of the Citizens Council protested the decision, arguing that "LSU owes its greatness, academically and athletically, to its Anglo-Saxon heritage."[50]

By the fall of 1970 as a majority of SEC members fielded football teams including African Americans, the LSU athletic program increasingly stood out because of its inaction. In March 1968 Norbert Godchaux, an African American student from New Orleans, reported for spring drills with the Tigers. At the end of the spring he participated in the traditional Purple and Gold intrasquad match. According to the student newspaper, his entrance onto the field "set off a rancorous cacophony of high-pitched 'Leroy' [calls], contemptuous laughter, and just plain booing" from some white fans. His treatment at the Purple and Gold game upset a group of African American students who had just formed Harambee, a black student organization, and who were protesting the absence of black scholarship athletes at the university. Over the next three years black students staged periodic rallies and demonstrations to draw attention to their proposals for campus improvements, including the creation of a black cultural center, the hiring of minority faculty and clerical workers, and the recruitment of black football players. Even the resumption of the long-delayed football series with the University of Wisconsin in the fall of 1971 inadvertently highlighted the continued absence of African Americans from the LSU varsity. Because the Tiger squad was all-white, the Wisconsin student newspaper accused the LSU athletic department of being "racist," while a columnist for the *Madison Capital Times* worried that UW might have "prostituted itself and tainted one of its dearest ideals" by playing a segregated team.[51]

LSU coaches eventually stepped up their recruitment efforts aimed at black prospects. By September 1970 both the track team and the freshman basketball squad included African Americans, even though there were far fewer scholarships available in these sports than for football. In February 1971 an editorial in the student newspaper argued that "it should not have taken the university this long" to get serious about recruiting black athletes. As a result, the editorial stated, "LSU finds itself in the position of having to catch up with other schools . . . because it failed to take any initiative in this area earlier." In response, athletic director Carl Maddox insisted that Coach Charlie McClendon and his staff were pursuing prospective black recruits "more vigorously" than before. Their efforts to stem the flow of black talent away from the state were joined by none other than the governor of Louisiana, John McKeithen. The governor publicly expressed his hope that the top black prospects from Louisiana would stay within the state, preferably at LSU. McKeithen even addressed an assembly at predominantly black St. Augustine High School in New Orleans on the issue, encouraging three highly recruited football players at the school to consider LSU. McKeithen also personally telephoned possible recruits to ask them to come to Baton Rouge.[52]

Later in 1971 LSU finally signed its first two African Americans to football scholarships. The first to commit to the Tigers was Lora Hinton, a halfback from Virginia. Hinton had attended integrated schools since the seventh grade and was vice president of the student body at his high school. He had seen LSU play on television and became interested in the school after a white teammate received a scholarship offer from the Tigers. In the summer McClendon signed a second black prospect, all-state defensive back Mike Williams from Covington, Louisiana. Because Hinton missed most of his freshman season due to a knee injury and then redshirted the following year, Williams became the first African American to actually play on the Tiger varsity in the fall of 1972. Both found their fellow players to be unexpectedly supportive; in fact, the two roomed with white teammates rather than each other. There were several more African American recruits over the next two years, including talented halfback Terry Robiskie, who went on to become the first great black running back at LSU. Despite the Tigers' late start in recruiting African Americans, the team did not suffer any long-term competitive disadvantage and eventually successfully tapped into the rich vein of local football talent that it had historically ignored. In fact, much of LSU's subsequent football success derived from its new African American heritage.[53]

Black Rebels at Ole Miss?

The University of Mississippi was the last Southeastern Conference team to issue a football scholarship to an African American player, and one of the last three, along with LSU and Georgia, to field an integrated varsity squad. No other SEC member, not even the University of Alabama, more fully embodied the cultural heritage of the Old South than did Ole Miss. Through the extensive use of such evocative symbols as the song "Dixie," the Confederate battle flag, the mascot "Colonel Rebel," and the team nickname of Rebels, the university created a remarkable fusion of school traditions and Deep South imagery. Even the school's informal name of Ole Miss, a term that referred to the mistress of a plantation, recalled the antebellum era. Furthermore, several widely publicized developments during the 1960s, including the state's extreme resistance to public school desegregation, the deadly riot over the arrival of the school's first black student, James Meredith, in 1962, and repeated violence against civil rights workers, combined to make Mississippi the epicenter of southern white resistance to racial change. Moreover, despite Meredith's enrollment and eventual graduation, race relations on the Oxford campus remained strained for the rest of the 1960s.

The University of Mississippi opened its doors in 1848 but temporarily suspended operations in 1861 when most of its all-male student body rushed to enlist in the Confederate army. After the Battle of Shiloh in April 1862, Confederate authorities used the campus buildings as a hospital for wounded soldiers, literally tying the university's history to the Lost Cause. The university formed its first football squad in 1893, but the team name of Rebels was not actually adopted until 1936. The Dixiecrat Revolt of 1948 against President Harry S. Truman and the national Democratic Party inspired further use of Confederate symbols at Ole Miss. The States Rights Democratic Party adopted the Confederate battle flag as it unofficial symbol, leading to a revival of its display across the South. That fall the UM marching band unveiled a gigantic Confederate flag, measuring sixty feet by ninety feet, for use during halftime pageantry. In 1959 cheerleaders began giving out free miniature Confederate flags at home games, further expanding the flag's display. During the civil rights crisis of the 1960s these symbols took on even greater meaning. In the summer of 1962 the federal courts ordered Ole Miss to admit James Meredith, a native Mississippian and air force veteran, for fall classes. On Saturday, September 29, just before Meredith's impending registration, Governor Barnett delivered an emotional address at halftime of the Ole Miss–Kentucky football game in Jackson. Surrounded by a sea of Confederate flags, Barnett raised a clenched fist and proclaimed, "I love Mississippi! I love her people! I love her customs! I love and respect our heritage!" On Sunday evening, after federal marshals escorted Meredith to campus, a full-fledged riot broke out. When the violence finally ended, a French reporter and a local resident lay dead. Despite the rioting Meredith quietly registered for classes the next day.[54]

Struggling to keep the university operating, school administrators hoped that football games would provide a social and emotional outlet for its distracted students. Uneasy about permitting a crowd of more than twenty-five thousand whites to assemble in Oxford, federal officials forced the university to move its upcoming October 6 homecoming contest to Jackson, but they allowed the rest of the season to continue. Football did seem to help calm down Ole Miss students. In fact, head coach Johnny Vaught later argued that the football team saved the university from shutting its doors and "helped to ease tension throughout the state." Support for the Rebels grew dramatically week by week, and the squad finished the season undefeated, captured the SEC championship, and earned a trip to the Sugar Bowl. The football team's outstanding success in 1962 and again in 1963 provided a source of deep satisfaction to white Mississippians during a time of crisis. Although the federal government had forced the university to accept integration in the classroom, the football field remained a protected space where white Mississippians could demonstrate their athletic prowess and celebrate their cultural pride. Football thus became an important symbol of an unchanging white Mississippi and its southern white heritage.[55]

The ongoing love affair between white Mississippians and Ole Miss football had originated early in the twentieth century, but its greatest years came after the arrival of Coach Johnny Vaught in 1947. Under Vaught's leadership the Rebels would capture six SEC titles and one national championship in 1960. But in the mid-1950s, as more northern schools acquired African American players, Ole Miss withdrew from intersectional competition in order to protect the exclusive whiteness of its football program and did not challenge another non-southern foe until 1971. Rejecting Ole Miss's example, Jones County Junior College in Laurel ignored tradition and accepted an invitation in November 1955 to play in the Junior Rose Bowl contest in California against an integrated Compton Junior College squad. This violation of segregationist principles infuriated several influential state legislators, who threatened in early 1956 to adopt a law punishing college officials for any violation of Jim Crow. In order to head off legislative action, administrators at Ole Miss and other state colleges subsequently pledged to obey an "unwritten law" against all interracial athletic competition.[56]

The "unwritten law" survived until 1963. Then in March the Board of Trustees of the State Institutions of Higher Learning declined to overrule Mississippi State president Dean W. Colvard's decision to allow the MSU basketball team to participate in the NCAA Tournament. At several subsequent meetings the trustees failed to reach an agreement on a new policy that would specify when integrated contests could be permitted. In 1964 Ole Miss administrators exploited this inaction to regain control over athletic scheduling, but fear of interracial contact continued. In September the university opened the new season at home against Memphis State. Although MSU brought an all-white team to Oxford, rumors circulated before the game that the travel party would include a group of black students who were planning "an invasion" of the Ole Miss cafeteria and other campus facilities. The Board of Trustees responded by authorizing white cafeteria workers to arrest any African Americans who attempted to use the facility, unless they were Ole Miss students or employees. Several ultraconservative trustees even unsuccessfully proposed that all future contracts for football games specifically bar black students, employees, and faculty at opposing schools from accompanying their teams to Oxford. The rumored Memphis invasion never materialized, however.[57]

At the end of the 1964 season the Ole Miss administration finally placed opportunism ahead of ideological purity and made the momentous decision to retire the school's tradition of racial exclusion on the gridiron. After the final game UM officials accepted an invitation to play in the Bluebonnet Bowl contest in Houston. They took this action even though the opposing team from the University of Tulsa included several African Americans, including star defensive lineman Willie Townes, ironically a Mississippi native. The results of the historic contest proved disappointing to Ole Miss fans, as Tulsa upset the Rebels 14–7. Sportswriters selected Townes, who on several occasions tackled Mississippi running backs behind the line of scrimmage, as the most valuable lineman in the game. Townes's outstanding performance inspired a widely circulated joke spoofing Ole Miss's switch to integrated competition. The joke came in the form of a question, which asked, "Who was the first Negro to integrate the Ole Miss backfield?" The answer: "Willie Townes!" The Ole Miss schedule for the next three years confirmed that the Tulsa game represented a permanent shift in policy for games played outside the state. In 1965 Ole Miss elected to continue its rivalry with the University of Houston, even though the Cougars would be fielding their first integrated team. This decision revealed that the university was ready to rejoin the mainstream of college football in order to assert its stature as one of the nation's top football programs. At the game in the Astrodome, though, the Cougars' new black star, halfback Warren McVea, scored two touchdowns in Houston's 17–3 upset win, and excited white students literally carried him off the field on their shoulders. In 1966 Houston met Ole Miss in Memphis, with the Rebels gaining revenge by 27–6. Afterward, McVea complimented the Ole Miss players on their sportsmanship, but he complained that Rebel fans had hurled many racial insults, and occasionally a few empty beer cans and rocks as well, at the Cougar bench.[58]

In the fall of 1967 Ole Miss dropped all of its racial restrictions concerning opposing teams. On September 30 the Rebels opened their conference schedule against Kentucky in Lexington. Wildcat defensive halfback Nat Northington played part of the first half against the Rebels, as the two squads staged the first integrated SEC football contest. The following month the Houston Cougars and McVea visited Oxford, the first time that an African American had been permitted to compete in Hemingway Stadium. Aided by several costly Cougar mistakes, the Rebels eked out a 14–13 victory. By the end of the 1967 season, then, the Ole

Miss athletic program, if not all Rebel fans, had reluctantly accepted the reality of integrated competition both outside and inside the state. This new flexibility on race did not initially extend to the recruitment of African Americans for the university's teams, however. But as other SEC schools pursued black athletes, Coach Johnny Vaught and his staff reevaluated their recruiting practices. In May 1969 Vaught surprised many fans when he announced that J. T. Parnell, a half-back from Jackson, had committed to joining the Rebels. Parnell later accepted a scholarship to Southern Illinois University, though, and eventually enrolled there instead. Thus, the effort to recruit Parnell not only failed but instead focused more attention on the continued whiteness of the Ole Miss team.[59]

Beginning in the spring of 1969 African American students, a few liberal white classmates, and several faculty members grew more outspoken about racial issues linked to the athletic program. They focused in particular on the continuing absence of black football players, the use of Confederate imagery, and the shouting of racial insults at Rebel football games. The approximately 120 black students at Ole Miss, who had remained fairly quiet theretofore, now voiced numerous complaints about conditions on campus. In March they received a charter for a Black Student Union (BSU), which took the lead in articulating black concerns, including demands for the creation of a black studies program, the hiring of black faculty and staff, and the recruitment of black athletes. At the beginning of the fall semester of 1969 both Mississippi State and the University of Southern Mississippi (USM) enrolled their first African American football players, further highlighting their absence from the Rebel team. During the winter and spring of 1970 the BSU took a more confrontational approach, staging several demonstrations and even disrupting a musical performance on campus. Sports remained an important concern, and one BSU member publicly charged that "the Ole Miss athletic department is the main breeding ground in Mississippi for racism." Black students also voiced their disapproval of the Confederate battle flag as a symbol for the university's athletic teams, dramatically burning several of them on campus. Letters to the student newspaper likewise condemned racially inflammatory language at football games, citing as an example one group of rowdy UM students who allegedly chanted "Kill that nigger!" during a fall game.[60]

These negative factors caused African American students to feel considerable alienation from the Ole Miss athletic program. Many skipped the Saturday football games, and others turned the stands into a forum for protest, periodically holding up signs reading "Racist Athletic Department" and "Ole Miss = Racism." Occasionally, a few of them cheered outstanding efforts by African Americans playing against the Rebels. For black students, then, the football team, more than any other sector of the university, had come to symbolize the continued emphasis on whiteness at Ole Miss and their outsider status. The growing problem of Confederate imagery and its possible effect on recruiting was also noted in 1970 by a white sportswriter for the *Jackson Clarion-Ledger*, who warned that "there will be no Negro flashes in the Ole Miss backfield, or lightning-fast black flankers in the flats or tough Negro troopers in offensive or defensive lines so long as the Stars and Bars of the Confederacy remains the true standard of the school." The issue of African American players also appeared during the seemingly jinxed 1970 season. In October Ole Miss hosted Southern Mississippi, a 69–7 victim of the Rebels the previous year, but this time Southern Mississippi stunned the previously undefeated Rebels by 30–14. Even more shocking, halfback Willie Heidelburg, one of the first two black players at USM, scored two touchdowns on the Rebels. Critics of the athletic department seized upon Heidelburg's performance as proof that the failure to integrate the Rebel squad was slowly undermining its competitive ability.[61]

The loss to Southern Mississippi added to the athletic department's mounting woes. On Thursday before the Southern Mississippi game, athletic director Tad Smith suffered a heart attack. Three days after the upset Coach Johnny Vaught also suffered a heart attack. Both men eventually retired from the university during the winter. Another disaster arrived in November, when star quarterback Archie Manning broke his arm against the Houston Cougars, dashing hopes of another SEC championship. After the end of the season university trustees selected Billy Kinard as the Rebels' new coach. Despite the coaching change the 1971 Rebel varsity and freshman football teams remained as white as ever. Worse yet, Ole Miss appeared to be isolated even within the SEC, since every other conference football team had now given out at least two football scholarships to African Americans. During the fall Kinard aggressively targeted six top black prospects within the state and eventually convinced two of them to play for the Rebels. The continuing desegregation of the Mississippi public school system and its athletic programs greatly aided this change. Integrated high school competition also lessened the social and cultural shock that a change in recruitment policies at Ole Miss would have on fans and alumni. On December 11, 1971, tackle Robert J. "Ben" Williams of Yazoo City and halfback James Reed of Meridian signed with Ole Miss, eventually becoming the first African Americans to compete for the Rebels. The era of racial exclusion in Ole Miss football had finally ended.[62]

Williams and Reed were reasonably well prepared for the challenges that they would encounter at the university. Both were serious students who had attended integrated high schools, and Williams had even served as captain of his team. The two became roommates in the athletic dormitory, although Williams had a white roommate on road trips their first year. Because a new NCAA rule in 1972 permitted freshmen to compete on varsity teams and because the Rebels were shorthanded in the defensive line, UM coaches advanced Williams to the varsity.

Meanwhile, Reed spent the fall on the newly created junior varsity, which had replaced the old freshman team. In the third game of the season on September 30, exactly ten years to the day after the infamous Ole Miss riot, Williams took the field in Hemingway Stadium against Southern Mississippi, to the cheers of most Rebel fans. By the end of the year the young athlete had moved into the starting lineup, and he became a standout performer for the next three years, earning All-America honors as a senior. Although James Reed never attracted as much attention as did Williams, he still experienced a successful career for the Rebels as a part-time starter at running back.[63]

It was difficult to overlook Ben Williams on the football field or on campus. The easygoing, relaxed young man soon became quite popular with white as well as black students. In the fall of his senior year students elected him to the special position of "Colonel Rebel," the highest honor bestowed upon a male student. To many white students his selection demonstrated the tremendous racial progress that had taken place at Ole Miss. But many African Americans experienced a more bittersweet reaction, since they feared that the honor would be used to exaggerate the level of racial acceptance on campus. They also resented the fact that the football program, which had been one of the last bastions of white exclusiveness, would now receive undeserved praise for improving university race relations. The yearbook photograph of Williams with "Miss Ole Miss," Barbara Biggs, symbolically (but unintentionally) captured the ambiguous status of African Americans at the university in 1976. The photograph shows the couple posing in a rural setting, with Williams standing behind and slightly to the right of Biggs. Both are leaning on a wooden fence, which subtly but clearly separates the two from physical contact. Like blacks and whites on the Oxford campus, Williams and Biggs were so close yet so far away.[64]

The integration of the Ole Miss football program grew rapidly during the remainder of the 1970s. By the fall of 1976 sixteen African American players appeared in the football media guide, and UM now employed its first black assistant coach, Tommy Thompson. Despite these changes, however, the Rebels failed to find much success on the gridiron after 1971. The school's small-town location and distance from rapidly growing metropolitan areas of the South undoubtedly hindered recruiting. By the early 1980s an additional explanation gained prominence. University administrators and football coaches concluded that the school's continued embrace of Old South traditions had created a competitive disadvantage in recruiting, since most of the outstanding black players across the South, and especially their parents, did not identify with those Confederate symbols.[65]

Campus controversies erupted periodically over the role of these traditional images. In the fall of 1982 Ole Miss's first black cheerleader refused to carry the Confederate flag onto the football field, touching off a debate that eventually forced Chancellor Porter Fortune to officially dissociate the university from use of the flag. A clever effort to create a modified flag for the university by rearranging the traditional cross and stars to form the letters "UM" failed to win much support. Finally, in 1997 the school banned from university events all dangerous items, including sticks and flagpoles, in part to make it difficult to display the Confederate flag. When "Dixie" also came under attack in the 1980s Ole Miss officials deflected some of the criticism by borrowing a performance technique from Elvis Presley and merging the song with "The Battle Hymn of the Republic" into a continuous musical montage. In the early 1980s school officials removed Colonel Rebel's iconic image from the football team's helmets, but the durable colonel survived as the university mascot until the fall of 2003, when the school officially retired him from active duty. All of these changes provoked protests from a few conservative white alumni and students, who complained that the university was repudiating its southern heritage.[66]

The effect that these symbols and the controversies over them had on football recruitment was difficult to calculate. Certainly, most UM coaches worried that it prevented them from attracting some of the most talented African American players in the area. With the passage of time and the maturing of a new generation of black Mississippians who had no direct personal memory of the civil rights struggles and white resistance, the negative impact declined but did not totally disappear. Nonetheless, it is a fact that after the arrival of racial integration in the SEC, the Rebels never again won a conference championship for the remainder of the twentieth century. Of all the SEC schools, Ole Miss appeared to have lost the most by its stubborn resistance to integration, both in the classroom and on the gridiron.

Herschel Walker Leads Georgia to a National Championship

The University of Georgia was one of the last three Southeastern Conference schools to integrate its football program. Unlike the Ole Miss Rebels, though, the Georgia athletic program eventually recruited a number of talented black athletes who helped improve the Bulldogs' competitive performances and significantly contributed to winning a national championship. Georgia's football history began in 1892, when male students formed the school's first official team. Under Coach Wally Butts, the Bulldogs gained national prominence during the 1940s. The powerful 1942 team, led by Heisman Trophy winner Frank Sinkwich, lost only one game and earned the college's only invitation to the Rose Bowl. Anxious to maintain the team's national standing, university officials in the late 1940s modified their traditional opposition to competition against African Americans outside the South. In 1950 the Bulldogs played St. Mary's College in California in their first integrated contest. But because of political turmoil in the state over the desegregation of public schools and the university itself, school officials scheduled only an occasional northern or western opponent over the next fifteen years. In the mid-1960s the Board of Regents dropped all racial restrictions on scheduling, and in September 1968 Georgia hosted the University of Houston in the first integrated game held on campus.[67]

Questions about when the university might recruit African Americans for the Bulldog team surfaced in the mid-1960s. During the spring of 1966 Savannah State transfer Kenneth Dious worked out with the team during off-season drills, but he did not return in the fall. In September 1967 James Hurley made the freshman team as a non-scholarship player, but he transferred the next year to Vanderbilt. As the Bulldogs continued to be all-white, black undergraduates and a few liberal white students became impatient. Some of them blamed wealthy supporters of the athletic program for pressuring coaches not to seek out black recruits. Retiring president O. C. Aderhold apparently shared their concerns and in 1967 publicly criticized the athletic department's main support organization for opposing the recruitment of African Americans. In the midsixties occasional letters complaining about the absence of black players on the Bulldog team appeared in the student newspaper, the *Red and Black*. In January 1966, for example, senior economics major Harold Black expressed dismay that some of the state's finest athletes, because of their race, were limited to playing for historically black colleges or at northern schools, because UGA had refused to take a leadership role on the issue. Reflecting the egalitarian rhetoric of 1960s liberals, he urged that "athletes be recruited on the basis of merit and not color."[68]

In the fall of 1968 black students at Georgia became more vocal. During a regionally telecast football game, a group unfurled a banner that condemned the athletic department for its failure to recruit minority athletes. In March 1969 the Black Students Union presented the administration with a list of twenty-two demands. The first demand called for the creation of a Department of Afro-American and African Studies. The second item on the list urged the active recruitment of both black scholars and black athletes, indicating the priority that African American students attached to athletic integration. Along with the Young Democrats and the campus chapter of Students for a Democratic Society, the BSU also repeatedly called for discontinuing the use of the Confederate battle flag and the song "Dixie" at football games and other university functions. Joel Eaves, director of athletics, responded that the athletic department had already expanded its recruitment efforts aimed at predominantly black high schools nearly two years earlier. To clear up any uncertainties about the university's position, though, he issued a formal memo reminding all UGA coaches that the university now recruited athletes without regard to race, creed, or color.[69]

During 1969 the university's basketball and track and field teams issued their first scholarships to African Americans, drawing more attention to the football team's continued whiteness. In February 1970 the university announced that a black prospect, fullback John King, had signed an SEC scholarship agreement to play for the Bulldogs, but King later changed his mind and instead enrolled at Minnesota. At the end of the year Coach Vince Dooley finally announced that five black high school stars had agreed to play at Georgia. Three of these athletes came from Clark Central High School in Athens, a new school created by the merger of the town's black and white high schools. Since they were local residents, Horace King, Richard Appleby, and Clarence Pope had family and friends close at hand and therefore faced relatively few social adjustments as freshmen. Chuck Kinnebrew of Rome and Larry West of Albany also signed scholarship agreements with UGA. Each of the five except Pope eventually started for the Bulldogs, whose first integrated varsity team took the field in the fall of 1972. During the next several years the number of African American players steadily increased. In 1975 Calvin Jones, a former high school coach from Atlanta, joined the staff as an assistant coach and counselor in both football and basketball. Apparently reflecting the changing racial composition of the football team and the student body, the UGA band discontinued playing "Dixie" in the fall of 1974, despite a few complaints from white students.[70]

Concerns over whether white Georgia fans would support an integrated football team eventually disappeared, as Vince Dooley regularly coached the Bulldogs to winning seasons and bowl game invitations. In April 1980 Dooley won one of the biggest recruiting battles over a high school athlete in the history of the state when Herschel Walker, an exceptionally talented running back from Wrightsville, accepted a UGA scholarship. During his high school career Walker scored eighty-six touchdowns (a national prep record), won the hundred-yard dash in the state track meet, and earned the valedictorian spot in his graduating class. In his first year at Georgia the sensational running back set an NCAA freshman rushing record, led the Bulldogs to an 11-0 regular season record and the Southeastern Conference championship, and finished third in the Heisman Trophy balloting. Walker concluded his remarkable season by scoring two touchdowns and earning the game's most valuable player award in Georgia's 17-10 Sugar Bowl victory over Notre Dame, which earned the Bulldogs the national championship. In 1981 and 1982 Walker again paced the Bulldogs to the SEC championship. During Walker's three-year career Georgia compiled a 33-3 record. Walker finished second in the Heisman Trophy race in 1981 and finally received the prestigious award in 1982.[71]

Herschel Walker's phenomenal career made him the most popular athlete in Georgia and a hero to sports fans across the nation. Walker thus personally exemplified the triumph of "muscular assimilation" in southern college football. Polite and well mannered, he overcame the suspicions of even most conservative whites. When his hometown of Wrightsville experienced racial troubles in the early 1980s, however, Walker remained discreetly silent. His athletic accomplishments, obvious intelligence, and exemplary public behavior made him the perfect role model to unite blacks and whites inside the state and a powerful symbol of racial change at the university. Furthermore, the image of black and white teammates working together on a shared mission offered a new model of interracial cooperation to Georgians. Had integration not yet reached southern college sports when Walker graduated from high school, he probably would have left the state and spent his college career at Southern California or Michigan. But as one journalist pointed out, if Walker had entered the local public schools before the Warren Court's *Brown v. Board of Education* ruling was finally implemented in Georgia, he might not even have played football. Doc Kemp High School, the all-black school in Wrightsville, was so small and poorly funded that it did not field a football team. Integration thus made available to Walker the modern athletic and academic facilities of Johnson County High School, where he perfected his skills. Small wonder then that Atlanta journalist Jim Minter ironically wrote after Georgia's 1980 national championship, "Thank God for Earl Warren."[72]

Walker did not always play the perfect role of the "'good' black hero." His decision to skip his senior season and sign a multimillion-dollar contract with the New Jersey Generals of the new United States Football League irritated some Bulldog fans and produced a few racist comments. Walker also attended his hometown's Herschel Walker Appreciation Day in December 1982 accompanied by white girlfriend Cindy DeAngelis, whom he later married. Still, as a native son who brought national glory to his university and state, Walker provided a common bond for black and white Georgians whose athletic pasts, to say nothing of their social and political traditions, had been separate and unconnected. Nothing could better illustrate the unifying force of big-time college sports. But, as the outbreak of racial conflict in his hometown of Wrightsville during his glory days at Georgia illustrated, the Walker story also revealed the limitations of sports integration in solving the broader racial problems in southern society.[73]

Conclusion
The Accomplishments and Limitations of Athletic Integration

What tremendous champions might come out of the
Southeast, with such recruits to build upon, and what
quiet miracles might be worked in better race relations?

—*New York Times,* April 21, 1963

Sports may have opened doors,
but it didn't open minds.

—James Webster, 1994

From 1890 through 1980 remarkable racial change swept over southern
and American college sports, leaving them permanently transformed. During
this ninety-year period two competing ideologies struggled for control of collegiate athletic policy. The first of these, the American credo of equal opportunity
in sports, or "democracy on the playing fields," drew on athletic traditions from
Great Britain as adapted by all-male preparatory schools and private colleges in
New England. This ideology maintained that athletic competition should offer
a level playing field to all participants and that fair play based on character and
merit, not raw talent or outside social status, should determine the ultimate
winner. One black sportswriter for the *Atlanta Daily World* summed up this
idealistic view: "On the playing field, it doesn't matter whether your parents
came over here on the Mayflower or a slave ship. If you've got guts, a competitive
heart, lightning speed, and the will to compete, then brother you're in the game."[1]
Northern and western colleges embraced this creed in theory, but in practice
many of them repeatedly compromised its tenets concerning the treatment of
African American athletes. White southerners articulated a radically different
philosophy, demanding that a rigid color line excluding African Americans be
imposed on all games involving southern teams. These southerners defined
athletic competition as a form of social relations and asserted that any breach of
the color line, even for a few hours on the football field or the basketball court,

would constitute social equality, thereby dishonoring the white participants and endangering the social structure and "natural" racial hierarchy of the South. With the complicity of northern universities, they succeeded in imposing a color line on much of college athletics in the early twentieth century.

Over the ensuing decades opponents of this policy of racial exclusion waged a protracted struggle on several fronts. As sociologist Herbert Blumer astutely observed several decades ago, "As a metaphor, the color line is not appropriately represented by a single, sharply drawn line but appears as a series of ramparts, like the 'Maginot Line,' extending from outer breastworks to inner bastions." Blumer added, "Outer portions of it may . . . be given up only to hold steadfast to inner citadels."[2] This depiction of a retreating color line protecting a central core of white supremacy provides a perceptive overview of the ninety-year period during which African American athletes advanced from marginality to full inclusion in college sports. From 1890 to 1980 college campuses represented, both symbolically and literally, contested terrain where many battles, small and large, prominent and obscure, successful and unsuccessful, were waged to challenge, modify, and ultimately destroy Jim Crow's tenacious grip on the athletic arena. At the start of the period in the late nineteenth century, historically white southern universities excluded African Americans from enrollment and refused to compete against them in athletic competition. However, southern schools also desperately wanted to participate in national sporting culture and earn institutional recognition from their more prestigious counterparts located in the North. Intersectional games offered southern schools the opportunity to pursue these goals, but the occasional presence of an African American on a northern team posed a potential roadblock to this quest for status and profits.

In order to avoid any potential conflict over integrated games, southern officials eventually convinced their northern counterparts to honor the so-called gentleman's agreement. According to this informal but widely accepted policy, northern schools would act as gracious hosts or thoughtful visitors by automatically withholding any black player on their squads when competing against a southern college, eliminating the need for an explicit request from the southerners. The complicity of many northern schools in this arrangement is not surprising, since the few black students enrolled there were treated as second-class citizens and excluded from some campus activities. Worse yet, prior to World War II, at least two dozen northern colleges drew their own internal color line for athletic competition. For example, both the Big Six Conference and the Missouri Valley Conference excluded African Americans from their teams during the 1930s and for most of the 1940s. Thus, racial exclusion should not be narrowly viewed as exclusively a "southern" custom but instead seen more broadly as an "American" practice.

During the 1930s and 1940s northern students increasingly defended the rights of African Americans on their school teams and demanded that they be permitted to participate in all home games against southern teams. A few southern universities responded by taking a more legalistic approach. In signing game contracts with northern universities some southern administrators now added so-called "No Negroes" exclusion clauses, making official and legal what had previously been informal and unstated. Despite their efforts, this new resolve by northern colleges gradually forced many ambitious southern schools to modify the gentleman's agreement and accept an occasional integrated contest in the North as the cost of seeking national recognition in big-time college sports. University trustees and political leaders in the South in effect granted southern colleges a special dispensation for these violations of Jim Crow etiquette, revealing the social importance and privileged status that successful athletic teams enjoyed in Dixie. However, southern schools stood firm in their refusal to accepted mixed athletic competition at home. Furthermore, the establishment of several postseason football bowl games in the South during the 1930s gave white southerners new leverage over ambitious northern universities. Several such schools, most notably Boston College, callously placed the benefits and prestige of securing a bowl invitation ahead of the rights of their African American athletes. When an integrated northern team agreed to play a regular-season or especially a postseason game in the South, the black member of the team was expected to play the role of the "good Negro" and follow an informal script whereby he would graciously sacrifice his individual desire to participate for the greater good of his team. Black athletes suffered deep emotional wounds from such exclusion, and, to make matters worse, unsympathetic black critics sometimes questioned their masculinity for not quitting their teams in protest.

After World War II more and more northern students embraced the democratic values and egalitarian principles that wartime culture had inspired, endangering the color line in athletics. Often led by war veterans, northern students demanded that democracy on the playing fields be practiced on both sides of the Mason-Dixon line. One consequence of this heightened sensitivity came in the Lower Midwest, where racial exclusion remained widespread in 1945. Starting in the late 1940s basketball coaches in the Big Ten slowly began to recruit African American players for the first time. The Big Six and Missouri Valley Conferences, which included teams from Iowa, Kansas, Nebraska, Missouri, and Oklahoma, dropped their bans on black athletes in the late 1940s. It still took another ten years, however, before the last holdouts in each conference incorporated African Americans into their teams. In addition, pressure from northern students, sportswriters, and black organizations soon halted racial exclusion for intersectional games held in the North. Furthermore, these groups now demanded that northern schools include all team members on road trips to the South or cancel the contests.

Faced with this resistance, many southern universities grudgingly accepted the new terms and hosted integrated games on their own campuses rather than lose the opportunity to obtain "gate receipts and glory" through intersectional competition. Beginning in 1955, though, the widespread massive resistance movement unleashed by southern politicians against the United States Supreme Court's *Brown v. Board of Education* ruling the previous year interrupted this modest liberalizing trend for several years. Alarmed segregationists now worried that even one seemingly minor action by a southern college might undermine their larger struggle to defend white supremacy and racial segregation from federal attack. As the editor of one Mississippi newspaper explained, "Dear as the athletic prestige may be, our southern way of life is infinitely more precious."[3] In one extreme action in 1956 the Louisiana legislature went so far as to adopt legislation making it illegal to sponsor an integrated athletic event. Some Deep South teams temporarily suspended intersectional contests because of this pressure, but by the early 1960s this white resistance had lost its strength. In 1963 the Mississippi State basketball team defied the state's political leadership and sneaked out of the state in order to play an integrated opponent in the first round of the NCAA Tournament. Once the federal government succeeded in requiring white universities across the Deep South to admit African American undergraduates, school policies prohibiting integrated games on campus no longer seemed relevant.

The final phase in dismantling the color line's inner citadel—the actual integration of southern college athletic teams—began in the mid-1960s. Universities that lacked a major conference affiliation for their athletic teams, the so-called independents, or those who belonged to a conference that included nonsouthern schools led the way. Texas Western College in El Paso sent an integrated basketball squad onto the court in the fall of 1956, while North Texas State College, located just north of Fort Worth, fielded an integrated varsity football team in the fall of 1957. The more elite conferences and teams took longer to summon the courage to act. Led by the University of Maryland in 1963, the Atlantic Coast Conference became the first of the three major southern athletic conferences to accept African American participants. The Southwest Conference followed slightly behind the ACC, while the Southeastern Conference, where seven of its ten members in 1966 were located in the Lower South, was the last of the three leagues to fully shed its old racial restrictions.

Geography, opportunism, institutional religious affiliation, and on a few rare occasions idealism were important factors in university decisions to accept integrated competition and eventually to recruit African Americans for their own athletic teams. Geography clearly played a significant role. Except for the University of Virginia, colleges located near the borders of the South, where African Americans usually constituted a modest percentage of the total population, generally accepted competition against African Americans much earlier than their Lower South counterparts. These schools also took the lead in seeking out black recruits for their teams. The University of Maryland and the University of Kentucky, both technically located in border states but with conference ties that linked them to the states of the Old Confederacy, enjoyed a flexibility not available to their counterparts in Alabama, Georgia, or Mississippi. The location of Texas Western College at the far western edge of its state and the South, as well as its position on the U.S.-Mexican border, created a unique situation that was favorable to athletic integration.

Opportunism and complacency likewise shaped institutional decision making, sometimes in unpredictable ways. Coaches at successful, high-status athletic programs were occasionally willing to schedule integrated games in order to preserve their national prominence. In 1938 Duke University willingly agreed to play a road game against Syracuse and its African American quarterback, Wilmeth Sidat-Singh, in order to improve its chances of receiving a Rose Bowl invitation. Accepting competition against an integrated opponent from time to time was one thing, but tolerating the integration of one's own team was something quite different. Elite institutional status and prior success in winning championships made some athletic programs and individual coaches complacent about rethinking their recruiting strategy. Successful coaches like Texas's Darrell Royal in football and Kentucky's Adolph Rupp in basketball preferred to stick with their traditional recruiting practices, since they had previously fared so well with those policies. On the other hand, pragmatic coaches who were hired to rebuild unsuccessful athletic programs, like Hayden Fry at SMU, Bill Tate at Wake Forest, or Don Haskins at Texas Western, took a more aggressive approach to recruiting and searched for previously untapped sources of talent in hopes of gaining a competitive edge over their more successful rivals. A generational gap in the coaching ranks often reinforced these tendencies. Older coaches, especially if raised in the Deep South, sometimes found it difficult to seek out African Americans, while younger coaches tended to be more color-blind when it came to recruiting.

There were some noticeable differences at times between public and private universities as well. Private colleges were generally slower to fully desegregate undergraduate education than were public institutions, because their different legal status partially protected them under existing law from federal court action. Moreover, presidents and deans at these schools also discovered that the wealthy, conservative individuals who sat on their boards of trustees were often dignified segregationists no more interested in racial change that were demagogic politicians. Once those private universities that were church related opened their undergraduate programs to all students, they generally moved more rapidly to accept black athletes than did their secular rivals. In the Southwest Conference, Southern *Methodist* University first broke the color line in football, along with Baylor University, a *Baptist* institution. In basketball Texas *Christian* University took the lead in that sport. Away from church-affiliated schools, idealism lagged far behind self-interest in athletic integration, but it did exist. Frank Porter Graham, the liberal president of the University of North Carolina, strongly supported North Carolina's historic 1936 trip to New York City to play a NYU football squad that included halfback Ed Williams. This pathbreaking contest was the first instance in which a major southern university voluntarily accepted integrated football competition in the North. In the 1960s University of Kentucky presidents Frank G. Dickey and John W. Oswald, as well as Vanderbilt chancellor Alexander Heard, strongly supported athletic integration as part of their ambitious plans to modernize their respective universities. Football and basketball coaches traditionally avoided social issues and did not see themselves as agents of social change. Yet Hayden Fry at SMU, John Bridgers at Baylor, and Dean Smith at North Carolina were examples of socially conscious coaches who fully understood the broader symbolic importance of integrating southern teams. There was also, of course, an element of contingency or random chance involved in all of these developments. Especially in the sixties, the failure of an individual athlete to achieve a minimum test score on the SAT or a last-minute change of heart concerning his college preference could significantly affect the public image of a coach and a university.

The long campaign to eliminate the color line from intercollegiate athletics had both a "top-down" and a "bottom-up" dimension to its social dynamics. Complaints from the small number of black students on northern campuses and pressure from their more numerous white classmates belatedly convinced college administrators there to take a firm moral stand against racial exclusion, eventually forcing southern teams either to accept integrated competition or to abandon their pursuit of prestige and profits from intersectional games. On the other hand, the internal decision by southern athletic programs to recruit African Americans resulted mostly from a "top-down" approach. To be sure, white and black liberal students exercised some agency by frequently urging their administrations to require their coaches to recruit black prospects. White students usually emphasized the pragmatic benefits that would result from athletic integration. As one prescient student at Texas Western College bluntly commented in 1955 after endorsing integration of the school in a student newspaper poll, "Besides the humanitarian principles involved in considering such a question, we might also look at it from a selfish point of view. The Negro race has many good athletes. . . . [M]aybe we could get some of them."[4] A few white students also asserted that it was morally wrong to limit access to intercollegiate athletics solely because of race. Black students consistently stressed the principle of equal access, contending that the inclusion of African American males in the university's most important public activity would permit black men to prove their masculinity while bestowing higher status on all minority students. A black student organization at the University of Alabama even filed a lawsuit in federal court charging the athletic department with racial discrimination for refusing to recruit African American football players.

Most southern administrators and coaches remained relatively unmoved by idealistic complaints over fairness and access. Instead, what caught the attention of many administrators were visits from federal officials representing the U.S. Office of Education, which by the latter part of the 1960s required college presidents to certify that their universities did not discriminate on the basis of race in order to receive federal funds. Southern coaches, for their part, were far more concerned about the opinions of wealthy donors and influential politicians than students. Yet a few of them also worried by the mid-sixties that their teams' national reputations and standings in the polls could be harmed by continued segregation in their programs. Some coaches also feared that integrated teams in other parts of the country, as well as more flexible rivals in their own conferences, could gain a competitive advantage over them via the addition of black stars. The court-mandated desegregation of local public school systems, which automatically affected high school sports, reduced the fears of university administrators and coaches that their schools might suffer political reprisals if they integrated too early. Integrated prep competition also created a sense of inevitability about the addition of African American players. Unlike civil rights campaigns to integrate lunch counters, hotels, school classrooms, and other public spaces in the South, though, the campaign for athletic integration did not feature black athletes beating on stadium gates, demanding to be allowed inside. Instead, once Jim Crow had been sent to the sidelines, white coaches still had to entice African American prospects to enroll at their universities, since they retained the option of playing at regional black colleges or major universities in the North and West. Ultimately, a combination of these factors convinced the last coaching holdouts to abandon their old recruiting habits and embrace equality of opportunity on a level playing field.

African American athletes stood symbolically at the center of the racial discourse over intersectional competition but were literally relegated to the margins of the southern college sports world until the early 1970s. For those black athletes who fell victim to the gentleman's agreement before World War II, the denial of the opportunity to demonstrate their honor, athletic prowess, and manhood through competition against southern whites must have wounded them to the core, yet they were expected to endure their humiliation in silence. Much more is known about the experiences of those racial pioneers who broke the color line at southern colleges in the 1960s and 1970s. Such individuals were usually selected because of a combination of athletic ability, academic skills, and strong character, since they would face an unprecedented situation upon their arrival on an overwhelmingly white campus. Unfortunately, most players and their coaches greatly underestimated the difficult challenges that awaited them. Many of these athletes initially experienced social isolation and suffered insensitive comments from coaches and teammates. On the road they sometimes encountered problems at hotels and restaurants, and opposing fans often welcomed them with crude racial taunts. The continued use of Confederate symbols at athletic contests constantly reminded black athletes, as well as their fellow black students, of their outsider status. All of this harassment and smaller social snubs left hidden scars that were rarely revealed to their teammates, let alone their coaches. Yet through their courage and perseverance, these racial pioneers opened the door for the next generation of black athletes who were fortunate enough to escape such flagrant indignities.

It would be difficult to overlook the remarkable contributions that African Americans made to southern college athletics, once afforded an opportunity to compete on a level playing field. In April 1963 the *New York Times* predicted that "tremendous champions" would appear in the South after integration, if only athletic programs there would accept African Americans. The subsequent accomplishments of such stars as Jerry LeVias, Earl Campbell, George Rogers, Herschel Walker, and Bo Jackson in football and Charles Scott, David Thompson, Ralph Sampson, and Michael Jordan in basketball confirmed this prediction. Their brilliant individual performances, and the victories won by integrated teams in the 1970s and the early 1980s, helped validate athletic integration and win the loyalty of most white fans. For example, when freshman running back Herschel Walker led the University of Georgia to the school's first national championship in football in 1980, Bulldog fans were ecstatic. Had Walker been born ten years earlier, he would probably not have been able to play for Georgia, as the Bulldog team had not been integrated in 1970. No wonder one exuberant journalist proudly proclaimed, after reflecting on the long-term impact of the Warren Court's *Brown v. Board of Education* ruling on southern sports, "Thank God for Earl Warren." In basketball the national championship won by Texas Western College and its five black starters in 1966, when this unheralded school defeated the all-white University of Kentucky Wildcats, awakened white coaches to the very real threat to their success that the arrival of black players could mean. Integrated teams could also bring together a historically divided population, at least temporarily. As journalist Nadine Cohodus observed about residents of Mississippi, but in words that applied equally well across the South, "Black and white Mississippians had a shared history, but they had a deeply divided heritage."[5] The national championship won in 1974 by the North Carolina State basketball team provided the region with a new general model for success—blacks and whites working together to achieve a common goal. Successful integrated teams also served as racially inclusive symbols around which white and black southerners could unite in a common cause, thereby fostering racial reconciliation and inventing a new shared tradition.

Not all white sports fans responded positively to these racial changes, of course. A few whites simply stopped attending games because African Americans were participating. The athletic world of complete whiteness that they had known for so long was rapidly slipping away from them, shattering the emotional ties that had previously linked them to their favorite college team.[6] The specter of sexual contact, real and imagined, between black male athletes and white coeds also alarmed some whites. Earlier in the century, before African Americans actually appeared on southern teams, white racists had warned about the domino effect that any interracial contact in athletics would have, ultimately leading to sexual relationships and racial intermarriage. Southern whites continued to issue such warnings into the 1950s. For example, in 1954 an Alabama judge led a movement to ban integrated athletic contests in Birmingham because "allowing a few Negroes to play baseball here will wind up with Negroes and whites marrying." Because of this racial taboo, pioneering black athletes at southern colleges were often warned by their coaches to avoid any contact with white females. Even after whites reluctantly accepted the principle of athletic integration, some fans argued that African Americans should be restricted to limited participation through the use of informal quotas. In basketball circles the phrase "two at home and three on the road" reflected the fears of many black players that their coaches would not risk angering influential donors and alumni by playing three of them at the same time in a home game. One concerned fan articulated this perspective when he bluntly informed North Carolina State coach Norm Sloan that the Wolfpack should "be known as a predominantly white basketball program." Eventually, most whites made their peace with the new racial order and enthusiastically cheered on their teams publicly, but some privately continued to make negative and occasionally racist comments about black athletes. James Webster, a racial pioneer at the University of North Carolina and subsequently a Division I assistant football coach, later reflected on the transition period of the 1970s. "Sports may have opened doors," he suggested, "but it didn't open minds."[7]

African Americans themselves experienced mixed feelings about the changing nature of southern college sports. In principle they strongly supported the elimination of all racial barriers in sport, but some of them also voiced misgivings about the human costs involved in the process. A few hoped to see black high school stars continue to join their favorite black college teams, while others feared that these young men would be mistreated at white colleges. The mother of Wendell Hudson, Alabama's first black basketball recruit, literally cried when she learned that her son wanted to enroll at the Tuscaloosa school. The sister of basketball player Collis Temple Jr. repeatedly begged her brother not to attend LSU, because of her concern that he would be mistreated at the university.[8] Other African Americans worried more about neglect than mistreatment, fearing that white coaches could not provide the emotional support that such pioneering athletes would need in their unprecedented roles. For coaches at historically black colleges, athletic integration represented a bittersweet process that eventually stripped them of most of their best players. During the late 1950s and 1960s National Football League scouts had belatedly discovered black colleges and the talented athletes there. By the end of the 1960s, for example, Coach Eddie Robinson of Grambling College had seen more than 150 of his players drafted by the NFL or the Canadian Football League. Ten years later, though, the quality of competition and the number of professional prospects in the black southern conferences had declined noticeably. Black coaches also lamented that athletic integration was a one-way street, since white stars would not enroll at historically black colleges. A few major universities in the Midwest and on the West Coast also were losers in athletic integration. In the 1950s and 1960s teams like Illinois, UCLA, and especially Michigan State under Coach Duffy Daugherty had been able to augment their recruiting classes by adding a small but highly talented group of African American players from the South. After southern white colleges finally opened their doors to black prospects, however, this recruiting pipeline to the North and West mostly shut down. Grambling's Eddie Robinson once famously quipped that "integration in the South would hurt Grambling and Michigan State more than any other schools."[9]

Not everything went smoothly as athletic integration began to transform southern college sports. Many African American students resented the slow pace associated with the recruitment of black athletes. African Americans also worried that black players were being "stacked" at certain positions in football and being forced to play out of position in basketball. The purpose of such decisions, they feared, was to limit the number of black starters to a number acceptable to influential whites. The quarterback position especially generated controversy. Despite the successes of Freddie Summers at Wake Forest during the 1967 and 1968 seasons and Conredge Holloway at Tennessee from 1972 to 1974, few African Americans appeared at that position for major southern colleges before the 1980s. Since the quarterback position allegedly required both intelligence and leadership skills, black critics felt that by excluding African Americans white coaches were reinforcing racial stereotypes about African Americans' alleged deficiencies. In basketball black fans complained that African Americans were often given the toughest defensive assignment so that a white player could be the team's offensive star. These critics also suspected that many coaches preferred a white player at the point-guard position, basketball's closest position to the quarterback slot.

By the early 1980s African American students and fans, as well as a few white supporters, regularly questioned the limited number of black assistant coaches and staff members in athletic departments, as well as the absence of African Americans in head-coaching positions. This new concern over staffing indicated that the process of athletic integration had been redefined to include issues beyond just the number of black players in the starting lineup. Changes in hiring patterns appeared earlier in basketball than in football. The Southwest Conference witnessed its first black head coach in 1985 when Arkansas hired Nolan Richardson to take charge of its basketball team. At Maryland in the ACC Bob Wade became the head basketball coach in 1987. The Southeastern Conference, the most conservative of the three major southern conferences, did not have an African American head basketball coach until 1989, when Tennessee hired Wade Houston. Football culture remained more traditional than basketball, though, and the absence of black head coaches in that sport was particularly noticeable. The Southwest Conference disbanded in 1996 without ever having an African American head football coach at one of its member institutions. Mississippi State did not hire the Southeast Conference's first black head coach, Sylvester Croom, a former star player at Alabama under Bear Bryant, until 2003. Two years earlier, in a further sign that the inner citadels of institutional power were finally opening up, Virginia hired Craig Littlepage as its athletic director, making him the first African American to hold such a position at a major southern university. Critics also attacked southern colleges for exploiting black athletes by not encouraging them to finish their degrees. During the mid-1980s the University of Georgia became mired in an embarrassing public scandal concerning low academic expectations and support for its black football players. From time to time influential white donors were caught making disparaging remarks about African Americans. Other types of problems periodically embarrassed southern athletic programs, including illegal payments to players, use of recreational drugs, academic corruption, and arrests of athletes on various criminal charges.

Earlier in the century, black and white racial liberals had optimistically assumed that the elimination of racial restrictions in sports would inspire the similar dissolution of social and economic barriers to black advancement in other areas of southern and American society. In April 1963 the *New York Times* had not only predicted an advent of champions after integration but also pondered "what quiet miracles might be worked in better race relations?" Once whites experienced more contact with African Americans through sports, liberals argued, they would see through the fallacy of old racial stereotypes and realize that African Americans could make positive contributions to their communities in other areas as well. Athletic competition mattered a great deal, then, to both black leaders and white segregationists, because of its important symbolic value and its potential role as an opening wedge for further social change. As *The Crisis* remarked in 1939, "Fair play in sports leads the way to fair play in life." In a similar vein, the student newspaper at the University of Texas suggested in a November 1963 editorial that "an eighty-yard run by a fleet Negro halfback will do wonders in dissolving racial antipathy."[10]

The extent to which sports integration produced "quiet miracles" in southern race relations beyond campus boundaries is another matter. As early as 1974 journalist John Egerton advanced this argument in his popular book *The Americanization of Dixie,* when he wrote, "Athletics may be doing as much to influence racial attitudes in the United States as the emergence of economic and political black power." Egerton argued that the desire to win a conference title or earn a high national ranking had overwhelmed segregation's lingering appeal and that "even the most racist fans now appear to accept, however cheerfully, the lofty status of black heroes as well as white ones." During the 1980s many southern educators and politicians regularly cited college athletics as a prime example of racial progress in the South. As Dr. Wilford S. Bailey, an Auburn professor and a former president of the NCAA, remarked at the end of the decade, "I am of the opinion that sports integration has been the single greatest contributor to racial progress and development in the South."[11]

This narrative of unimpeded racial progress through college athletics has gained even wider acceptance over the ensuing decades as part of the construction of historical memory at southern universities. Yet many scholars and African Americans remained more pessimistic about how much had really changed in the region and the nation, especially since inherited economic patterns and institutional structures continued to limit black advancement. Reflecting this skepticism, historian Patrick Miller concluded that "the principal sites of racial change lay beyond the playing fields."[12] Moreover, the nostalgia sometimes expressed for an older and simpler era of college sports partially reflected uneasiness over the prominent role played by black athletes in recent years. Ironically, the breadth of this black athletic success also served to reinforce older negative assumptions about African Americans' "natural" physical abilities and intellectual skills, a development not anticipated by traditional racial liberals. On campus, some white students came to view black athletes as hired mercenaries rather than genuine classmates. Nonetheless, the establishment of equal access to college sports reaffirmed their democratic nature and allowed African Americans to establish a revised model of southern masculinity. Furthermore, despite its many flaws, college sport remains one of the most integrated activities today in the American South, and its model of whites and blacks working together to achieve common goals provides a positive example for all Americans.

Notes

Introduction

Research for this project was funded in part by a grant from the National Endowment for the Humanities.

1. *Nashville Banner,* April 5, 1989; *Knoxville Journal,* April 6, 26, 1989; *Knoxville News-Sentinel,* April 5, 1989; *El Paso Times,* April 10, 11, 1989; Wade Houston, interview by author, Knoxville, Tenn., August 10, 1989; Wade Houston, telephone interview by author, December 8, 2009. Houston had been warned in advance that there might be a problem with the Cherokee Country Club over his membership. President Lamar Alexander's firm response reassured him that he had the full support of the university.

2. Thomas G. Dyer, *The University of Georgia: A Bicentennial History, 1785–1985* (Athens: University of Georgia Press, 1985), 185; Andrei S. Markovits, "Reflections on the World Cup '98," *French Politics and Society* 16 (Summer 1998): 2, 20–23. General accounts of these developments include Ronald A. Smith, *Sports and Freedom: The Rise of Big-Time College Athletics* (New York: Oxford University Press, 1988); and Mark F. Bernstein, *Football: The Ivy League Origins of an American Obsession* (Philadelphia: University of Pennsylvania Press, 2001).

3. Andrew Doyle, "'Causes Won, Not Lost': College Football and the Modernization of the American South," *International Journal of the History of Sport* 11 (1994): 231–51.

4. *Richmond Times,* January 12, 1900; Dale Somers, *The Rise of Sports in New Orleans, 1850–1900* (Baton Rouge: Louisiana State University Press, 1972), 286–90; Grace Elizabeth Hale, *Making Whiteness: The Culture of Segregation in the South, 1890–1940* (New York: Pantheon, 1998), xi–xii. Hale curiously omits any reference to the role of sporting events in the construction and performance of whiteness. On racial segregation in northern public school systems, see Davidson M. Douglas, *Jim Crow Moves North: The Battle over Northern School Segregation, 1865–1954* (New York: Cambridge University Press, 2005); and Thomas J. Sugrue, *Sweet Land of Liberty: The Forgotten Struggle for Civil Rights in the North* (New York: Random House, 2008).

5. *Richmond Times-Dispatch,* October 9, 1923.

6. James Insley Osborne and Theodore Gregory Gronert, *Wabash College: The First Hundred Years* (Crawfordsville, Ind.: R. R. Banta, 1932), 272; Charles H. Martin, "The Color Line in Midwestern College Sports, 1980–1960," *Indiana Magazine of History* 98 (June 2002): 85–112; *New York Times,* May 31, 1959, 8.

7. Robert M. Hutchins, "Gate Receipts and Glory," *Saturday Evening Post,* December 3, 1938, 23.

8. Peter Wallenstein, introduction to *Higher Education and the Civil Rights Movement: White Supremacy, Black Southerners, and College Campuses,* edited by Peter Wallenstein (Gainesville: University Press of Florida, 2008), 6–8; Paul Conkin, *Gone with the Ivy: A Biography of Vanderbilt University* (Knoxville: University of Tennessee Press, 1985), 215. For examples of how the popular press used games involving Carlisle and Haskell to reinforce negative and essentialized views of Indian character, see Michael Oriard, *Reading Football: How the Popular Press Created an American Spectacle* (Chapel Hill: University of North Carolina Press, 1993), 229–47; and Oriard, *King Football: Sport and Spectacle in the Golden Age of Radio and Newsreels, Movies and Magazines, the Weekly and the Daily Press* (Chapel Hill: University of North Carolina Press, 2001), 283–91. On Mexican Americans, see Neil Foley, "Partly Colored or Other White: Mexican Americans and Their Problem with the Color Line," in *Beyond Black and White: Race, Ethnicity, and Gender in the U.S. South and Southwest,* edited by Stephanie Cole and Alison Parker (College Station: Texas A&M Press, 2004), 123–44; and Jorge Iber and Samuel O. Regalado, eds., *Mexican Americans and Sports: A Reader on Athletics and Barrio Life* (College Station: Texas A&M Press, 2007).

9. *Crisis* 46 (November 1939), 337; Patrick B. Miller, "Muscular Assimilationism: Sport and the Paradoxes of Racial Reform," in *Race and Sport: The Struggle for Equality On and Off the Field,* edited by Charles K. Ross (Jackson: University Press of Mississippi, 2004), 146–49, 156–58.

10. A brief overview of desegregation at public universities in the South is Peter Wallenstein's essay "Black Southerners and Nonblack Universities: The Process of Desegregating Southern Higher Education, 1935–1965," in *Higher Education and the Civil Rights Movement,* edited by Wallenstein, 17–59; Melissa Kean, *Desegregating Private Higher Education in the South: Duke, Emory, Rice, Tulane, and Vanderbilt* (Baton Rouge: Louisiana State University Press, 2008); and Amilcar Shabazz, *Advancing Democracy: African Americans and the Struggle for Access and Equity in Higher Education in Texas* (Chapel Hill: University of North Carolina Press, 2004).

11. Pioneering studies on the integration of college sports in the South include Richard Pennington, *Breaking the Ice: The Racial Integration of Southwest Conference Football* (Jefferson, N.C.: McFarland, 1987); and Ronald E. Marcello, "The Integration of Intercollegiate Athletics in Texas: North Texas State College As a Test Case, 1956," *Journal of Sport History* 14 (Winter 1987): 286–316. Books that emphasize the impact of key games on encouraging athletic integration include Frank Fitzpatrick, *And the Walls Came Tumbling Down: Kentucky, Texas Western, and the Game That Changed American Sports* (New York: Simon and Schuster, 1999); and Don Yaeger, with Sam Cunningham

and John Papadakis, *Turning of the Tide: How One Game Changed the South* (New York: Center Street, 2006).

12. One rare microhistory of athletic integration at a junior college is Bill Elder, *All Guts and No Glory: An Alabama Coach's Memoir of Desegregating College Athletics* (Montgomery, Ala.: NewSouth Books, 2007).

13. On the early development of competitive sports for males at historically black colleges, see Patrick B. Miller, "To 'Bring the Race along Rapidly': Sport, Student Culture, and Educational Mission at Historically Black Colleges during the Interwar Years," *History of Education Quarterly* 35 (Summer 1995): 111–33; and Ocania Chalk, *Black College Sport* (New York: Dodd, Mead, 1976). Other general studies about black college sports include Edwin Bancroft Henderson, *The Negro in Sports,* rev. ed. (Washington, D.C.: Associated Publishers, 1949); and Arthur R. Ashe Jr., *A Hard Road to Glory: A History of the African-American Athlete,* 3 vols. (New York: Warner Books, 1988).

14. The now forgotten Association for Intercollegiate Athletics for Women, mostly controlled by female physical educators and designed to avoid the NCAA's commercialized approach, sponsored many championships for college women in the 1970s. The NCAA seized control of women's sports from the AIAW in the early 1980s. On physical activities for southern college women, see Pamela Grundy, *Learning to Win: Sports, Education, and Social Change in Twentieth-Century North Carolina* (Chapel Hill: University of North Carolina Press, 2001); and Pamela Dean, "'Dear Sisters' and 'Hated Rivals': Athletics and Gender at Two New South Women's Colleges, 1893–1920," *Journal of Sport History* 24 (Fall 1997): 341–57. On Title IX and its impact on youth and college sports, see Debby Schriver, *In the Footsteps of Champions: The University of Tennessee Lady Volunteers, the First Three Decades* (Knoxville: University of Tennessee Press, 2008); and Sarah K. Fields, *Female Gladiators: Gender, Law, and Contact Sport in America* (Urbana: University of Illinois Press, 2004). On modern women's sports, see Susan K. Cahn, *Coming on Strong: Gender and Sexuality in Twentieth-Century Women's Sport* (New York: Free Press, 1994).

15. Wilford S. Bailey, interview by author, Auburn, Ala., July 28, 1990; Miller, "Muscular Assimilationism," 174.

Chapter 1. White Supremacy and American College Sports

1. Ronald A. Smith, *Sports and Freedom: The Rise of Big-Time College Athletics* (New York: Oxford University Press, 1986), 3–119.

2. Elliott J. Gorn and Warren Goldstein, *A Brief History of American Sports* (New York: Hill and Wang, 1993), 88–97, 103, 111–13, 129–31, 141–64; Smith, *Sports and Freedom,* 8–28, 83–84, 95–98; Benjamin G. Rader, *American Sports: From the Age of Folk Games to the Age of Televised Sports,* 6th ed. (Upper Saddle River, N.J.: Pearson, 2009), 93–97; Richard O. Davies, *Sports in American Life: A History* (Oxford: Blackwell, 2007), 63–71, 77–82; John S. Watterson, "The Death of Archer Christian: College Presidents and the Reform of College Football," *Journal of Sport History* 22 (1995): 158; Edward L. Ayers, *The Promise of the New South* (New York: Oxford University Press, 1992), 314; Dale A. Somers, *The Rise of Sports in New Orleans, 1850–1900* (Baton Rouge: Louisiana State

University Press, 1972), 261; Jim L. Sumner, "John Franklin Croswell, Methodism, and the Football Controversy at Trinity College, 1887–1894," *Journal of Sport History* 17 (1990): 8. On "muscular Christianity" during this era, see Clifford Putney, *Muscular Christianity: Manhood and Sports in Protestant America* (Cambridge: Harvard University Press, 2001).

3. A Canadian team from McGill University first introduced Harvard players to rugby in May 1874. Smith, *Sports and Freedom,* 67–98; Rader, *American Sports,* 89–100, 177–92; Patrick Miller, "The Playing Fields of American Culture," unpublished book manuscript; Mark F. Bernstein, *Football: The Ivy League Origins of an American Obsession* (Philadelphia: University of Pennsylvania Press, 2001), 17.

4. Charles R. Wilson and William Ferris, eds., *The Encyclopedia of Southern Culture* (Chapel Hill: University of North Carolina Press, 1989), s.v. "football"; Ayers, *Promise of the New South,* 313; *ACC Football Media Guide* (1992), 20, 26, 44, 50, 56, 62, 68; *Georgia Tech Football Media Guide* (1992), 252–53; Sumner, "John Franklin Crowell," 5; Germaine M. Reed, "Charles Holmes Herty and the Establishment of Organized Athletics at the University of Georgia," *Georgia Historical Quarterly* 77 (1993): 536.

5. L. Andrew Doyle, "Science and Chivalry: The Cultural Syncretism of Early Southern College Football," paper presented at the Southern Historical Association Convention, New Orleans, November 1995; William J. Baker, *Playing with God: Religion and Modern Sport* (Cambridge: Harvard University Press), 85–107.

6. Smith, *Sports and Freedom,* 118–46; Jesse Outlar, *Between the Hedges: A Story of Georgia Football* (Huntsville, Ala.: Strode Publishing, 1973), 14–18; Robert C. McMath Jr. et al., *Engineering the New South: Georgia Tech, 1885–1985* (Athens: University of Georgia Press, 1985), 124, 138, 272–74, 390; Al Thomy, *The Ramblin' Wreck* (Huntsville, Ala.: Strode Publishers, 1973), 22–23; Somers, *Rise of Sports in New Orleans,* 265–68.

7. Reed, "Charles Holmes Herty," 534–35; W. Baker, *Playing with God,* 102–3; Sumner, "John Franklin Croswell," 5–20; Walter B. Edgar, *South Carolina in the Modern Age* (Columbia: University of South Carolina Press, 1992), 38; Clyde Bolton, *Unforgettable Days in Southern Football* (Huntsville, Ala.: Strode Publishers, 1974), 128–29; *ACC Football Media Guide*; George Washington Paschal, *History of Wake Forest,* 4 vols. (Wake Forest, N.C.: Wake Forest College, 1943), 2:311–16.

8. Outlar, *Between the Hedges,* 25–26; Bolton, *Unforgettable Days,* 130–35; Jack A. Powers, "A History of the Furman University Football Program, 1889–1965" (master's thesis, Furman University, 1966), 5–8.

9. Smith, *Sports and Freedom,* 191–200; Rader, *American Sports,* 179–80; Eugene W. Baker, *To Light the Ways of Time: An Illustrated History of Baylor University, 1845–1986* (Waco: Baylor University, 1987), 105–6; Kent Keeth, *Looking Back at Baylor* (Waco: Baylor University, 1985), 67.

10. Smith, *Sports and Freedom,* 202–8; Watterson, "Death of Archer Christian," 150–52; Rader, *American Sports,* 181–82; Robin Lester, *Stagg's University: The Rise, Decline, and Fall of Big-Time Football at Chicago* (Urbana: University of Illinois Press, 1995), 73–77.

11. E. Baker, *To Light the Ways of Time,* 106–7; "Death, Burial, and Resurrection," 67; Paschal, *History of Wake Forest,* 3:110–11.

12. A total of eight college players reportedly died from injuries received during the 1909 season. Rader, *American Sports,* 181–82; Watterson, "Death of Archer Christian," 149–65.

13. Watterson, "Death of Archer Christian," 165–67; Ayers, *Promise of the New South,* 313; Edgar, *South Carolina in the Modern Age,* 38; Thomas G. Dyer, *The University of Georgia: A Bicentennial History, 1785–1985* (Athens: University of Georgia Press, 1985), 185, 246, 285.

14. Arthur R. Ashe Jr., *A Hard Road to Glory: A History of the African-American Athlete,* 3 vols. (New York: Warner Books, 1988), 1:94–98; Ocania Chalk, *Black College Sport* (New York: Dodd, Mead, 1976), 197–203, 218, 275–77; Patrick B. Miller, "To 'Bring the Race along Rapidly': Sport, Student Culture, and Educational Mission at Historically Black Colleges during the Interwar Years," *History of Education Quarterly* 35 (Summer 1995): 111–33.

15. Ashe, *Hard Road to Glory,* 1:96–98, 2:103; Chalk, *Black College Sport,* 275; "Run for Respect," reprint, *Atlanta Constitution,* September 7–14, 1986, 6.

16. Miller, "To 'Bring the Race along Rapidly,'" 111–25.

17. Ashe, *Hard Road to Glory,* 1:70–71, 77, 90–92; Chalk, *Black College Sport,* 145–46; Fred Burwell, e-mail to author, August 29, 2001.

18. Martin Bauml Duberman, *Paul Robeson* (New York: Ballantine Books, 1989), 20–24; John Behee, *Hail to the Victors!* (Ann Arbor: Ulrich's Books, 1974), 18–19.

19. Chalk, *Black College Sport,* 71; Ashe, *Hard Road to Glory,* 1:108–9; Lester, *Stagg's University,* 40; Bernstein, *Football,* 106–7.

20. Carol Medlicott, e-mail to author, July 26, 2002; James Insley Osborne and Theodore Gregory Gronert, *Wabash College: The First Hundred Years* (Crawfordsville, Ind.: R. R. Banta, 1932), 272; *Wabash,* December 1903, 215–16, December 1904, 183; Johanna Herring to author, July 22, 1997; *DePauw,* October 22, November 12, 19, 1904; Ashe, *Hard Road to Glory,* 1:92; *New York Times,* November 22, 1903, 13.

21. A small regional college in Massachusetts later hired Bullock as its coach, apparently making him the first African American head football coach at a predominantly white college. William Jewett Tucker to William Hayes Ward, November 7, 1903, Special Collections, Dartmouth College Library; Henry Beach Needham, "The College Athlete," *McClure's,* July 1905, 271; Michael Oriard, *Reading Football: How the Popular Press Created an American Spectacle* (Chapel Hill: University of North Carolina Press, 1993), 296; *New York Times,* October 25, 1903, 13; Bernstein, *Football,* 72.

22. Ashe, *Hard Road to Glory,* 1:102; John M. Carroll, *Fritz Pollard: Pioneer in Racial Advancement* (Urbana: University of Illinois Press, 1992), 19; *New York Times,* October 25, 1908, sec. 4, p. 1; November 8, 1908, sec. 4, p. 1; November 15, 1908, sec. 4, p. 1; *Dartmouth,* November 6, 10, 1908; Chalk, *Black College Sport,* 165.

23. After Pollard led Brown to an upset of Harvard, the Brown president exuberantly declared, "There is no bigger white man on the team than Fritz Pollard." Bernstein, *Football,* 108; Ashe, *Hard Road to Glory,* 1:102–3; Carroll, *Fritz Pollard,* 70–73, 100; Jay Barry, "A Rose Bowl Star—56 Years Ago," *Ebony,* January 1972, 106.

24. Steven A. Riess, *City Games* (Urbana: University of Illinois Press, 1989), 115–18; David W. Zang, *Fleet Walker's Divided Heart: The Life of Baseball's First Black Major*

Leaguer (Lincoln: University of Nebraska Press, 1995), 44–47, 60–64; Rader, *American Sports,* 69–71.

25. Somers, *Rise of Sports in New Orleans,* 96, 120, 180–83, 222–24, 286–90; Riess, *City Games,* 113–14.

26. Somers, *Rise of Sports in New Orleans,* 183.

27. University of North Carolina *Daily Tar Heel,* October 14, 1938; Andrew Doyle, "'Causes Won, Not Lost': College Football and the Modernization of the American South," *International Journal of the History of Sport* 11 (1994): 231–51; Michael Oriard, *King Football: Sport and Spectacle in the Golden Age of Radio and Newsreels, Movies and Magazines, the Weekly and the Daily Press* (Chapel Hill: University of North Carolina Press, 2001), 88–92.

28. Lester, *Stagg's University,* 115–20.

29. Against the advice of their coach, Nebraska players elected Flippin the team captain. Robert N. Manley, *Centennial History of the University of Nebraska* (Lincoln: University of Nebraska Press, 1969), 1:293–94; Mary K. Dains, "University of Missouri Football: The First Decade," *Missouri Historical Review* 70 (1975): 28–34; *Hesperian,* November 1, 1892; "Big Meet Off," *Missouri Alumnus,* April 1939, 10; Richard Lapchick et al., *Pioneers: African-Americans Who Broke Color Barriers in Sport* (Morgantown, W.Va.: Fitness Information Technology, 2008), 328.

30. Dains, "University of Missouri Football," 34–35; Dick Lamb and Bert McGrane, *75 Years with the Fighting Hawkeyes* (Dubuque: W. C. Brown, 1964), 11, 45; *Cedar Rapids Gazette,* June 30, 1996; *Iowa City Daily Republican,* November 12, 1896, clipping in Board of Curators Records, and William G. Manly, "History of Athletics in the University of Missouri, 1890–1898," unpublished manuscript, both in Western Historical Manuscript Collection, Ellis Library, University of Missouri–Columbia; *University of Missouri Football Media Guide* (1995), 188–89; Earl M. Rogers to author, August 5, 1997. For more details on racial exclusion in the Midwest, see Charles H. Martin, "The Color Line in Midwestern College Sports, 1890–1960," *Indiana Magazine of History* 98 (June 2002): 85–112.

31. During the 1890s the Howard University baseball team played games against white colleges including Trinity College of Connecticut and the Yale Law School. After 1900, however, these schools drew the color line and refused to schedule Howard. Ashe, *A Hard Road to Glory,* 1:78–79; Miller, "Playing Fields of Academe"; Chalk, *Black College Sport,* 11–17, 22–23.

32. Ashe, *Hard Road to Glory,* 1:100–101; Duberman, *Paul Robeson,* 20–23; Dorothy Butler Gilliam, *Paul Robeson, All-American* (Washington, D.C.: New Republic Books, 1976), 18–19; Jerry Izenberg, "Hall of Fame Doors Finally Swing Open for Robeson," copy in author's possession; *New York Times,* November 12, 1916, sec. 7, p. 3. Ashe incorrectly states that Robeson was again benched against Washington and Lee in his senior year, but no such game took place.

33. Rader, *American Sports,* 184, 186–92.

34. Lester, *Stagg's University,* 126–33; Doyle, "'Causes Won, Not Lost,'" 243–44; *University of Georgia Football Media Guide* (1993), 130–31; Temple Pouncey, *Mustang Mania: SMU Football* (Huntsville, Ala.: Strode Publishers, 1981), 53.

35. Rader, *American Sports*, 184, 192; Thomy, *The Ramblin' Wreck*, 104.

36. Until the mid-twentieth century, sportswriters selected the "national champion" based on regular season records, excluding bowl game results. Thomy, *The Ramblin' Wreck*, 18, 59; Wilson and Ferris, *Encyclopedia of Southern Culture*, s.v. "football"; Harvard vs. Pennsylvania program, November 16, 1991, 44.

37. Doyle, "'Causes Won, Not Lost,'" 231–46; Bolton, *Unforgettable Days*, 39, 92–93; *Atlanta Constitution*, January 2, 1929; Anthony C. DiMarco, *The Big Bowl Football Guide*, rev. ed. (New York: G. P. Putnams, 1976), 2–3.

38. Ashe, *Hard Road to Glory*, 2:94, 100–101; Chalk, *Black College Sport*, 234–35, 239, 241–43; Raymond Wolters, *The New Negro on Campus* (Princeton: Princeton University Press, 1975), 313.

39. Wolters, *New Negro on Campus*, 315–17; *Pittsburgh Courier*, September 27, 1930; Emma Lou Thornbrough, *Indiana Blacks in the Twentieth Century* (Bloomington: Indiana University Press, 2000), 8–12, 161.

40. *Pittsburgh Courier*, October 13, November 17, 1923; *Iowa State Student*, October 10, 1923; *Minnesota Daily*, October 9, 1923; *Iowa State Daily*, October 5, 1973, July 22, 1997; Chalk, *Black College Sport*, 236. On Trice's legacy, see Jaime Schultz, "The Legend of Jack Trice and the Campaign for Jack Trice Stadium, 1973–1984," *Journal of Social History* 41 (Summer 2008): 997–1029. The Iowa State stadium was renamed for him in 1997.

41. Chalk, *Black College Sport*, 179–86; *Pasadena Star News*, September 19, 1974, *Los Angeles Times*, September 19, 1974, *Seattle Post-Intelligencer*, August 1974, all in Brice Taylor File, Office of Sports Information, University of Southern California.

42. In the mid-1920s, the University of Pittsburgh added the school's first black athletes to its track team but withheld them from meets at the U.S. Naval Academy. Column by Ed Sullivan, n.d., C. M. Snelling Papers, Hargrett Rare Book and Manuscript Library, University of Georgia; *Pittsburgh Courier*, January 2, October 30, November 26, 1926, December 4, 1937, October 15, 1938; Chalk, *Black College Sport*, 186–87; Ashe, *Hard Road to Glory*, 2:94; *Butler College Yearbook*, 1926, 1929. Chalk also reported that NYU left Joe Washington at home for a baseball trip to the South in 1923 and that Colgate left J. L. Hart behind for another football game at Vanderbilt in 1929.

43. *Richmond Times-Dispatch*, October 7, 1923; *Pittsburgh Courier*, October 13, 1923; *New York Age*, October 23, 1923; *New York Tribune*, October 7, 1923.

44. *Richmond Times-Dispatch*, October 9, 1923.

45. *Richmond Times-Dispatch*, October 7, 9, 1923; *Pittsburgh Courier*, October 13, 1923; *New York Age*, October 23, 1923; Ashe, *Hard Road to Glory*, 2:93.

46. *New York Times*, December 26, 1924, 12; February 10, 1929, sec. 9, p. 3; *1925 El Rodeo* (yearbook), 426–27; Wolters, *New Negro on Campus*, 316; *El Paso Times*, December 25–26, 1924; Chalk, *Black College Sport*, 104–6.

47. In 1931 the Carnegie Foundation report on excessive professionalism in college sports singled out NYU as one of the chief violators. Ken Rappoport, *The Syracuse Football Story* (Huntsville, Ala.: Strode Publishers, 1975), 76–77; Outlar, *Between the Hedges*, 11–12, 40–41; *New York Times*, October 13, 1929, sec. 3, p. 2, sec. 11, p. 1.

48. Sullivan column, n.d.; Emanuel Celler to Elmer E. Brown, November 4, 1929,

Snelling Papers; *Pittsburgh Courier,* November 2, 9, 23, 1929; *New York Times,* October 6, 1929, sec. 11, p. 3; *New York Herald Tribune,* November 5–7, 1929.

49. University of Georgia *Red and Black,* November 1, 1929; Brown Buford to C. M. Snelling, October 25, 1929; Snelling to Buford, October 28, 1929; W. T. Nettles to Snelling, October 28, 1929; Snelling to Nettles, October 30, 1929; Snelling to C. R. Spence Jr., October 25, 1929; James Thayer Pate to Snelling, November 5, 1929; William H. Nichols to Emmanuel Celler, November 6, 1929, all in Snelling Papers; Dyer, *University of Georgia,* 233; *Atlanta Constitution,* November 9, 10, 1929; *Pittsburgh Courier,* November 16, 1929; *New York Herald Tribune,* November 8–10, 1929.

50. *Atlanta Constitution,* November 10, 1929; *Pittsburgh Courier,* November 9, 16, 30, 1929; *Crisis* 37 (January 1930): 30.

Chapter 2. "Fair Play" versus White Supremacy

1. *Pittsburgh Courier,* January 27, 1934, December 23, 1939; Arthur R. Ashe Jr., *A Hard Road to Glory: A History of the African-American Athlete* (New York: Warner Books, 1988), 2:56, 94–99, 3:129, 398; Thomas G. Smith, "Outside the Pale: The Exclusion of Blacks from the National Football League, 1934–1946," *Journal of Sport History* 15 (1988): 255–81; Charles K. Ross, *Outside the Lines: African Americans and the Integration of the National Football League* (New York: New York University Press, 1999), 46–51.

2. *University of Minnesota Football Media Guide* (1995), 176; *Pittsburgh Courier,* November 21, 1936; Penelope Krosch, e-mail to author, October 5, 1998.

3. *New York Times,* February 10, 1929, sec. 11, p. 3; Walter White to George Rightmire, November 3, 1930; Rightmire to White, November 5, 1930; Rightmire to L. W. St. John, November 5, 1930; Perry Jackson to Rightmire, November 9, 1930; Rightmire to Jackson, November 12, 1930; unsigned to L. E. Judd, November 17, 1930; Ellsworth G. Harris to Samuel Willaman, November 17, 1930, all in George W. Rightmire Papers, RG 3/f/6/2, University Archives, Ohio State University Library.

4. In 1934 officials at the United States Coast Guard Academy in Connecticut barred a black member of a New Hampshire boxing team from a series of bouts at the academy, explaining that a majority of their trainees were white southerners. *Pittsburgh Courier,* October 17, November 7, 14, 21, 1931, February 3, 1934; Henderson, *Negro in Sport,* 113; John Behee, *Hail to the Victors!* (Ann Arbor: Ulrich's Books, 1974), 22, 27; *Chicago Defender,* October 17, November 14, 1931.

5. During the 1930s Michigan State actually took two versions of its official team photo, one including all its players and another with only its white players. *Atlanta Constitution,* October 18, 1934; *New York Age,* October 26, 1934; *Pittsburgh Courier,* November 5, 1932; Baylor University *Daily Lariat,* November 18, 23, 1937; *Houston Informer,* July 29, 1967; John Matthew Smith, e-mail to author, August 27, 2006; Paulette Martis, e-mail to author, April 20, 1999; anonymous manuscript, 1953, on early black players at Michigan State, copy in possession of the author; Kevin A. Grace, e-mail to author, October 15, 1998.

6. Behee, *Hail to the Victors!* 18–19, 23, 33; W. A. Alexander to Fielding H. Yost, January 3, 1934; Alexander and A. H. Armstrong to Yost, March 17, 1934; Dan E. McGugin

to Yost, May 2, 1934; Roy Wilkins to Harry Kipke, September 20, 1934, all in Board in Control of Athletics Papers, Michigan Historical Collections, Bentley Historical Library, University of Michigan; Wilkins to Alexander G. Ruthven, October 11, 1934, Ruthven Papers, Michigan Historical Collections; *Atlanta Daily World,* September 26, 30, 1934; *Pittsburgh Courier,* October 6, 28, 1934; *Atlanta Constitution,* October 18, 1934, "Run for Respect" (reprint), *Atlanta Constitution,* September 7–14, 1986, 1; *New York Age,* October 13, 1934; Howard H. Peckham, *The Making of the University of Michigan, 1917–1967* (Ann Arbor: University of Michigan Press, 1967), 190.

7. Alexander to Yost, January 8, 1934, Board in Control Papers; *Atlanta Constitution,* October 20–21, 1934; *Georgia Tech Alumnus* 13 (November–December 1934): 26; *Atlanta Daily World,* October 21, 1934; Bobby Dodd, interview by August W. Giebelhaus and Larry Foster, July 5, 1983, Georgia Tech Archives, Atlanta.

8. Hoot Gibson was also hurt by his benching and remained "bitter until his death bed" over the incident. Bobby Dodd, interview by Scott Anderson, May 28, 1980, Georgia Tech Archives, Atlanta; Dodd, interview by Giebelhaus and Foster; *Crisis* 41 (November 1934): 333; *Atlanta Daily World,* October 3, 21, 1934; *Pittsburgh Courier,* October 27, 1934; Behee, *Hail to the Victors!* 29–30; Ashe, *Hard Road to Glory,* 2:94; *Atlanta Constitution,* October 18, 1934.

9. University of North Carolina *Daily Tar Heel,* October 16, 17, 1936; *Crisis* (November 1938): 361; *Durham Morning Herald,* October 16, 1936; Frank P. Graham to H. W. Chase, October 16, 1936, Presidents Office Records, Graham Files, Manuscripts Department, Wilson Library, University of North Carolina at Chapel Hill; Patrick Miller, "The Playing Fields of American Culture," unpublished manuscript, chap. 8.

10. *Durham Morning Herald,* October 18, 1936; Frank P. Graham to Walter White, November 4, 1936; White to Graham, November 30, 1936; White to Bernie Bierman, November 30, 1936, Graham Presidential Files; *New York Amsterdam News,* October 24, 1936; *Pittsburgh Courier,* October 24, 1936; Donald Spivey, "'End Jim Crow in Sports': The Leonard Bates Controversy and Protest at New York University, 1940–1941," *Journal of Sport History* 15 (Winter 1988): 292.

11. University of North Carolina *Daily Tar Heel,* October 14–16, 1938; *Pittsburgh Courier,* October 16, 1937, October 22, 29, 1938.

12. J. W. Cantrell to Graham, November 1, December 7, 1938, Graham Presidential Papers.

13. Sidat-Singh was also an outstanding basketball player, but in February 1939 the U.S. Naval Academy apparently barred him from a basketball game between the two schools in Annapolis. James R. Coates Jr., "Gentleman's Agreement: The 1937 Maryland–Syracuse Football Controversy" (master's thesis, University of Maryland, 1982), ii–iii, 31–46; Ken Rappoport, *The Syracuse Football Story* (Huntsville, Ala.: Strode Publishers, 1975), 124–35; Rod MacDonald, *Syracuse Basketball, 1900–1975* (Syracuse: Syracuse University Printing Services, 1975), 35–36, 135; Marty Glickman, with Stan Isaacs, *The Fastest Kid on the Block: The Marty Glickman Story* (Syracuse: Syracuse University Press, 1996), 50–52; *Pittsburgh Courier,* October 22, 1938.

14. Wallace Wade, interview by Patrick Miller and William E. King, September 21, 1981, Duke University Archives; *Crisis* (November 1938): 361; Miller, "Playing Fields

of American Culture," chap. 8; *Carolina Times* (Durham), October 29, 1938; *Pittsburgh Courier,* November 19, 1938.

15. *Crisis* 45 (November 1938): 361; *Carolina Times* (Durham), November 26, 1938; *Pittsburgh Courier,* November 19, 1938; Duke University *Chronicle,* November 18, 1938; Miller, "Playing Fields of American Culture," chap. 8.

16. Ralph L. Sellmeyer and James E. Davidson, *The Red Raiders: Texas Tech Football* (Huntsville, Ala.: Strode Publishers, 1978), 11–14; *Pittsburgh Courier,* March 3, November 3, 1934; Sellmeyer and Davidson, *Red Raiders,* 48–54, 82–95, 124–29.

17. Temple Pouncey, *Mustang Mania: SMU Football* (Huntsville, Ala.: Strode Publishers, 1981), 9, 53; Mary Martha Thomas, "Southern Methodist University, the First Twenty-five Years, 1915–1940" (Ph.D. diss., Emory University, 1971), 324–28.

18. Pouncey, *Mustang Mania: SMU Football,* 75–85; Thomas, "Southern Methodist University," 328–29; *Eugene (Ore.) Register Guard,* December 28, 1948.

19. *Pittsburgh Courier,* December 4, 1937, October 29, 1938; Southern Methodist University *Campus,* November 17, 20, 1937; *Eugene (Ore.) Register Guard,* December 7, 1948.

20. Many years later, one former UCLA student recalled that SMU players had inflicted tremendous physical abuse on Washington, but contemporary accounts make no such references. *Pittsburgh Courier,* December 4, 1937, October 29, 1938, October 5, 1940; Southern Methodist University *Campus,* November 24, 1937, September 28, 1940; Steve Springer and Michael Arkush, *60 Years of USC–UCLA Football* (Stanford, Conn.: Longmeadow Press, 1991), 52, 60–61.

21. *Pittsburgh Courier,* October 7, 1939; Texas Christian University *Skiff,* September 22, October 6, 1939.

22. *Pittsburgh Courier,* October 19, 1940; *New York Times,* October 12, 1941, sec. 5, p. 1; *Crisis* 48 (November 1941): 343.

23. The first black athlete at Arizona State, Harvey was not allowed to eat in the campus cafeteria or live in the school dormitories. Athletic officials also neglected to give him a letterman's blanket upon his graduation. *Arizona Republic* (Phoenix), August 4, 1980; Arizona State University *State Press,* April 14, 1977; *El Paso Herald-Post,* October 13, 1938; *Pittsburgh Courier,* December 9, 1939; Karen Underhill, e-mail to author, September 3, 1998; Ellen Brown, e-mail to author, October 22, 1998.

24. In November 1937 Loyola College of California left two black team members behind when the school played Baylor University in Beaumont, Texas. *El Paso Herald-Post,* October 13, 1938; *El Paso Times,* October 13, 1938; Texas College of Mines *Prospector,* October 15, 1938; miscellaneous clippings in University Archives, University of California, Santa Barbara; Neil Bethke to author, September 2, 1998.

25. *El Paso Times,* October 13–15, 30, 1938; *El Paso Herald-Post,* October 13–14, 1938; Texas College of Mines *Prospector,* October 22, November 5, 1938; *UTEP Football Media Guide* (1990); *San Diego Tribune,* October 15, 1938; miscellaneous newspaper clippings in University Archives, University of California, Santa Barbara.

26. In October 1940 the football team from St. Mary's College of San Antonio, a small Roman Catholic institution, played a game at Ebbets Field in Brooklyn against Long Island University, which was led by black star William "Dolly" King. The Communist

Party's *Daily Worker* quoted one of the Texas players as saying that "the color of a man's skin don't make no mind to us." *Chicago Defender,* October 14, 1939; *Pittsburgh Courier,* October 14, 1939; *Daily Worker,* October 25, 1940; *New York Age,* October 26, 1940; *Crisis* 46 (November 1939): 337.

27. *Pittsburgh Courier,* April 15, 1939; *New York Times,* April 5, 1939, 34; April 9, 1939, sec. 5, 2.

28. *Trenton Evening Times,* February 15–16, 1935; Trenton State Teachers College *State Signal,* February 8, 21, 1935. Alito's son, Samuel Alito Jr., was appointed to the United States Supreme Court in 2005 by President George W. Bush.

29. *Daily Worker,* January 22, 25, 1938; *Pittsburgh Courier,* November 30, 1940, September 6, October 11, December 6, 1941; *New York Age,* February 10, December 7, 1940, January 4, 1941; *New York Times,* October 12, 1941, sec. 5, p. 5; *Baltimore Afro-American,* October 11, 1941.

30. Glen Stout, "Jim Crow, Halfback," *Boston Magazine,* December 1987, 124; *Pittsburgh Courier,* January 11, 1941.

31. Stout, "Jim Crow, Halfback," 124–31; *Chicago Defender,* November 4, 11, 1939.

32. Stout, "Jim Crow, Halfback," 133; Jack Falla, *'Til the Echoes Ring Again: A Pictorial History of Boston College Sports* (Boston: Stephen Green Press, 1982), 20–21; Auburn University *Plainsman,* November 3, 1939.

33. In mid-January 1940 the Boston Veterans of Foreign Wars presented Montgomery with a special medal, in recognition of his "sportsmanship, citizenship, and athletic ability." Stout, "Jim Crow, Halfback," 131–33; Falla, *'Til the Echoes Ring Again,* 21; *Pittsburgh Courier,* December 23, 30, 1939; *Chicago Defender,* November 11, December 23, 1939, January 6, 1940; *New York Times,* December 17, 1939, sec. 5, p. 5; December 23, 1939, 40; December 24, 1939, sec. 5, p. 10.

34. Stout, "Jim Crow, Halfback," 133; Falla, *'Til the Echoes Ring Again,* 21–22; *Pittsburgh Courier,* August 31, October 5, 1940; *Chicago Defender,* October 5, 1940; *New York Age,* September 28, 1940; *Montgomery Advertiser,* November 25, 1940; Auburn University *Plainsman,* November 22, 26, 1940.

35. Stout, "Jim Crow, Halfback," 133–34; Falla, *'Til the Echoes Ring Again,* 22–23; *Pittsburgh Courier,* January 11, 1941.

36. Spivey, "'End Jim Crow in Sports,'" 285–90; *New York Times,* October 31, 1940, 34; *Daily Worker,* October 19, 23, 1940; *New York Age,* October 5, 26, 1940.

37. Spivey, "'End Jim Crow in Sports,'" 290–98; *New York Times,* October 19, 1940, 13; October 27, 1940, sec. 5, p. 1; November 1, 1940, 34; *New York Age,* November 9, 1940; *Pittsburgh Courier,* October 26, November 2, 9, 1940.

38. *Carolina Times* (Durham), January 18, 1941; University of North Carolina *Daily Tar Heel,* January 17, 19, 1941; A. Heningburg to Harry Chase, January 20, 1941, Graham Presidential Papers; *Pittsburgh Courier,* January 11, March 15, 1941; *New York Age,* January 11, 18, February 1, 1941.

39. Spivey, "'End Jim Crow in Sports,'" 299–302; *New York Times,* April 4, 1941, 23; April 14, 1940, 4; May 4, 2001, 1; *Pittsburgh Courier,* March 15, April 5, 1941.

40. *New York Times,* October 12, 1941, sec. 5, p. 1; October 19, 1941, sec. 5, p. 4; October 28, 1941, 31; November 4, 1941, 33; November 6, 1941, 31; November 18, 1941,

36; November 22, 1941, 25; November 25, 1941, 37; November 30, 1941, sec. 5, p. 1; Spivey, "End Jim Crow in Sports,'" 302–3.

41. *Long Beach Independent,* July 17, 1945; Ralph E. Shaffer, e-mail to author, January 20, 2008.

42. Harding accompanied the team to Washington in 1938 and sat on the bench during the game, irritating some white fans. *Pittsburgh Courier,* October 15, 1938, October 21, 1939; Howard Caldwell, *Tony Hinkle: Coach for All Seasons* (Bloomington: Indiana University Press, 1991), 49–51, 100; *Butler Collegian,* October 7, 12, 1938, October 13, 17, 18, 24, 1939; *New York Times,* October 15, 1939, sec. 5, p. 5.

43. *Baltimore Sun,* December 25, 1994; Patrick B. Miller, "Harvard and the Color Line: The Case of Lucien Alexis," in *Sports in Massachusetts: Historical Essays,* edited by Ronald Story (Westfield: Institute for Massachusetts Studies, 1991), 142–56; George H. Callcott, *A History of the University of Maryland* (Baltimore: Maryland Historical Society, 1966), 352–53.

44. Also in the spring of 1941, Navy apparently refused to allow NCAA sprint champion Barney Ewell of Penn State to compete at a dual track meet in Annapolis, so the schools moved the event to Pennsylvania. *New York Age,* October 5, 26, 1940, April 19, 26, 1941; *Baltimore Afro-American,* October 25, 1941; *Baltimore Sun,* December 25, 1994; Miller, "Harvard and the Color Line," 147–56; Ocania Chalk, *Black College Sport* (New York: Dodd, Mead, 1976), 11; *Pittsburgh Courier,* January 27, 1934, April 19, 1941; *New York Times,* April 19, 1941, 34; *Centre (Pa.) Daily Times,* November 6, 1946.

45. In recognition of the racial milestone, *The Crisis* published a photograph of Samuel Pierce on the cover of its December 1941 issue. A Phi Beta Kappa graduate of Cornell, Pierce later served as secretary of housing and urban development under President Ronald Reagan. *Baltimore Afro-American,* October 25, November 1, 1941; *Baltimore Sun,* December 25, 1994; Robert J. Kane, *Good Sports: A History of Cornell Athletics* (Ithaca: Cornell University Press, 1992), 51–52; *Star-News,* October 25, 1941, and "Alston Brothers Remembered," clippings supplied by the Penn State Office of Sports Information.

46. Howard E. Mitchell to author, July 11, 1996; miscellaneous clippings, n.d., supplied by Howard E. Mitchell; *Pittsburgh Courier,* October 28, 1939; *Boston University News,* October 21, 28, 1941.

47. Howard Mitchell to author, June 11, 1996; *Baltimore Afro-American,* November 1, 1941; *Pittsburgh Courier,* November 1, 1941; Donald Spivey, "The Black Athlete in Big-Time Intercollegiate Sports, 1941–1968," *Phylon* 44 (1983): 120.

48. *Baltimore Afro-American,* November 7, 1942.

49. Ross, *Outside the Lines,* 70–71.

50. *Baltimore Afro-American,* January 30, 1943; *Pittsburgh Courier,* October 24, November 21, 1942, September 18, October 9, 1943, October 7, 1944, January 20, September 22, 1945, January 12, 1946; A. S. "Doc" Young, *Negro Firsts in Sports* (Chicago: Johnson Publishing, 1963), 253.

51. Scott Ellsworth, "The Secret Game," *New York Times Magazine,* March 31, 1996, 19–22; Milton S. Katz, *Breaking Through: John B. McLendon, Basketball Legend and Civil Rights Pioneer* (Fayetteville: University of Arkansas Press, 2007), 40–46, 111–15; *Durham Herald-Sun,* March 31, 1996.

Chapter 3. "Massive Resistance" and the Decline of the Color Line

1. *Lexington Herald,* December 21, 24, 1946; *Knoxville Journal,* December 24, 1946, May 22, 1989; miscellaneous clippings, Duquesne University Archives (emphasis added).

2. Several African Americans did play in the National Basketball League, a different professional league, during the 1930s and 1940s. Thomas G. Smith, "Outside the Pale: The Exclusion of Blacks from the National Football League, 1934–1946," *Journal of Sport History* 15 (Winter 1988): 273–81; Charles K. Ross, *Outside the Lines: African Americans and the Integration of the National Football League* (New York: New York University Press, 1999), 75–117; Arthur Ashe Jr., *A Hard Road to Glory: A History of the African-American Athlete* (New York: Warner Books, 1988), 3:129–31, 398–99; *New York Times,* September 25, 1997, C26; Nelson George, *Elevating the Game: Black Men and Basketball* (New York: Harper Collins, 1992), 95–102; *Washington Post,* February 1, 1976.

3. Jules Tygiel, *Baseball's Great Experiment: Jackie Robinson and His Legacy* (New York: Oxford University Press, 1983), 71, 120–43, 173–226, 269–76; Bruce Adelson, *Brushing Back Jim Crow: The Integration of Minor-League Baseball in the American South* (Charlottesville: University Press of Virginia, 1999), 257–71.

4. *Lexington Herald,* December 24, 1946; *New York Times,* November 6, 1946, 33; January 10, 1947, 26; November 25, 1947, 41; October 18, 1951, 39; Kevin Grace, "The Stargel Story: One Measure of Progress," *UC Currents,* October 23, 1992, 2; *El Paso Herald-Post,* December 6–7, 1946; *Pittsburgh Post-Gazette,* January 10, 1947; *New York Herald Tribune,* October 31, 1946; University of Miami *Hurricane,* January 9, 1947; *Pittsburgh Courier,* February 12, 1949. Bradley University's 1951 game at Florida State was also canceled because of the exclusion issue.

5. *Centre (Pa.) Daily Times,* November 6, 1946; *New York Times,* November 6, 1946, 33; *Atlanta Constitution,* November 6, 1946; Pennsylvania State University *Daily Collegian,* November 1, 6, 1946 (emphasis added), July 29, September 26, November 25, December 10, 16, 19, 1947, January 9, 1948; University of Miami *Hurricane,* November 8, 15, 22, 1946.

6. Jackson, a married World War II veteran, was tapped for Skull and Bones but declined the honor. *New York Herald Tribune,* November 24, 1948, Amistad Collection, Tulane University; *Life,* December 6, 1948, 50; Ashe, *Hard Road to Glory,* 2:423; Neil D. Isaacs, *All the Moves: A History of College Basketball,* rev. ed. (New York: Harper and Row, 1984), 188.

7. In December 1950 fullback Fred Cooper, an African American, actually played with a southern white semiprofessional team, the Richmond Rebels, in an exhibition game against a team of former Southern Conference all-stars. *New York Times,* October 13, 1947, 34; November 24, 1947, 25; November 27, 1947, 51; *Pittsburgh Courier,* December 27, 1947.

8. Robert F. Kennedy, Harvard's left end, missed the Virginia trip because of an injury. George Sullivan, "Remembering a Barrier Broken," in Harvard versus Pennsylvania football program, November 16, 1991, 54–56; special series, "Breaking the Color Barrier,"

Roanoke Times, October 5, 1997; *University of Virginia Football Media Guide* (1992), 132–35; *Pittsburgh Courier,* October 18, 1947; *Baltimore Afro-American,* October 18, 1947.

9. Sullivan, "Remembering a Barrier Broken," 54–55; *Roanoke Times,* October 5, 1997; *Pittsburgh Courier,* October 18, 1947; *Baltimore Afro-American,* October 18, 1947; University of Virginia *College Topics,* October 14, 1947; *Time,* October 20, 1947, 25; November 10, 1947, 8; unidentified clipping from Portland, Maine, in Colgate W. Darden Jr. Presidential Papers, Manuscripts Department, University Archives, University of Virginia Library.

10. *New York Times,* October 24, 1948, sec. 5, p. 6; University of Pittsburgh *Pitt News,* October 3, 1950; *New York Times,* October 1, 1950, sec. 5, p. 3; *Pittsburgh Courier,* October 7, November 25, 1950, January 20, 1951.

11. Anthony C. DiMarco, *The Big Bowl Football Guide,* rev. ed. (New York: G. P. Putnams, 1976), 3–4; Carlton Stowers, *The Cotton Bowl Classic: The First Fifty Years* (Dallas: Host Communications, 1986), 7–16; Loran Smith, *Fifty Years on the Fifty: The Orange Bowl Story* (Charlotte: East Woods Press, 1983), 3–10. For a more detailed account of southern bowl games, see Charles H. Martin, "Integrating New Year's Day: The Racial Politics of College Bowl Games in the American South," *Journal of Sport History* 24 (Fall 1997): 358–77.

12. DiMarco, *Big Bowl Football Guide,* 1–3; Joe Hendrickson, *Tournament of Roses: The First 100 Years* (Los Angeles: Knapp Press, 1989), 1–42; John M. Carroll, *Fritz Pollard: Pioneer in Racial Advancement* (Urbana: University of Illinois Press, 1992), 79–90.

13. *New York Times,* November 6, 1946, 33; November 27, 1947, 51; Pennsylvania State University *Daily Collegian,* November 1, 6, 1946, July 29, September 26, November 25, December 10, 16, 19, 1947, January 6–9, 1948; *Pittsburgh Courier,* October 18, December 13, 1947; *Dallas Morning News,* November 24–27, December 21, 24, 1947, January 6, 1948; *Dallas Times Herald,* November 25, 27, December 9, 1947; Felix R. McKnight, telephone interview by author, April 23, 1996; Rich Donnell, *The Hig: Penn State's Gridiron Legacy* (Montgomery, Ala.: Owl Bay Press, 1994), 186–87, 201–2.

14. *Dallas Morning News,* December 1–31, 1947, January 1–2, 6, 1948; *Dallas Times Herald,* December 1–31, 1947; *Dallas Express,* January 10, 1948; *Pittsburgh Courier,* December 13, 1947, January 3, 10, 1948; McKnight interview; *Christian Science Monitor,* January 3, 1948, 22; Lee Cruse, *The Cotton Bowl* (Dallas: Debka Publishers, 1963), 36–39; Stowers, *Cotton Bowl Classic,* 77–78; McKnight interview; Ridge Riley, *Road to Number One: A Personal Chronicle of Penn State Football* (New York: Doubleday, 1977), 305.

15. *Pittsburgh Courier,* December 4, 11, 1948; *Dallas Express,* December 11, 25, 1948, January 8, 1949; Cruse, *The Cotton Bowl,* 39–41.

16. Sun Bowl program (1983), 44–47; Texas College of Mines *Prospector,* November 20, 1948; *El Paso Times,* November 16, 19, 1948.

17. The *Pittsburgh Courier* reported a rumor that state officials in Austin were worried that permitting an integrated football game in El Paso might undermine the University of Texas's defense against a lawsuit seeking to integrate the UT School of Law. *El Paso Times,* November 22–26, 1948; *El Paso Herald-Post,* November 22–24, 1948; Faculty

Minutes, November 23, 1948, and Statement by the President, November 24, 1948, College Archives, Skillman Library, Lafayette College; *Pittsburgh Courier,* January 1, 1949; *New York Times,* November 24, 1948, 27; Lafayette College *Lafayette,* December 3, 1948; Albert W. Gendebien, *The Biography of a College* (Easton, Pa.: Lafayette College, 1986), 234–35.

18. Texas Western College *Prospector,* December 4, 1948, September 30, October 7, 14, 28, 1950; *El Paso Herald-Post,* November 24, 1948, September 29, October 11, 12, 28, 1950, December 26, 1951, January 2, 1952; *Pittsburgh Courier,* January 1, 1949; *Oklahoma City Black Dispatch,* November 11, 1950; *El Paso Times,* September 30, October 11, 13, 23, 28, 1950; Larry L. King, *Confessions of a White Racist* (New York: Viking, 1971), 68.

19. The five black Iowa players were required to stay at a different hotel from their teammates. *Pittsburgh Courier,* November 25, 1950, January 20, October 20, 1951; University of Iowa *Daily Iowan,* November 25, 1950; University of Miami *Hurricane,* December 1, 8, 1950; Charlton W. Tebeau, *The University of Miami: A Golden Anniversary History, 1926–1976* (Coral Gables: University of Miami Press, 1976), 176–78, 236; Howard Kleinberg, telephone interviews by author, August 18, 23, 1997; Howard Kleinberg to author, August 29, 1997.

20. In November 1958 the University of Buffalo rejected an invitation to play in the Tangerine Bowl in Orlando, because the local school district, which owned the city's major stadium, refused to waive its ban against African American players. A. S. "Doc" Young, *Negro Firsts in Sports* (Chicago: Johnson Publishing, 1963), 254; Bruce A. Corrie, *The Atlantic Coast Conference* (Durham: Carolina Academic Press, 1978), 49–50; *El Paso Times,* January 2, 1955; *New York Times,* November 29, 1958, 22; Vaughn Mancha to author, January 31, 1995; Howard Kleinberg to author, August 27, 1997; L. Smith, *Fifty Years on the Fifty,* 83, 91, 178–79, 231.

21. Robert C. McMath Jr. et al., *Engineering the New South: Georgia Tech, 1885–1985* (Athens: University of Georgia Press, 1985), 284–85; Thomas G. Dyer, *The University of Georgia: A Bicentennial History, 1785–1985* (Athens: University of Georgia Press, 1985), 288–89; University of Georgia *Red and Black,* September 29, October 6, 1950; *Los Angeles Mirror,* October 2, 1950; *Atlanta Constitution,* December 1, 1955; Georgia Tech *Technique,* November 27, 1953; *Pittsburgh Courier,* October 31, December 5, 1953; *Atlanta Constitution,* December 1, 1955; John E. Heisler to author, June 24, 1994. Notre Dame's first black student enrolled in 1944 and competed on the track team.

22. Isaacs, *All the Moves,* 19–22; Benjamin G. Rader, *American Sports: From the Age of Folk Games to the Age of Televised Sports,* 6th ed. (Upper Saddle River, N.J.: Pearson, 2009), 106–8.

23. Ocania Chalk, *Black College Sport* (New York: Dodd, Mead, 1976), 70–117.

24. Ibid., 71; *Pittsburgh Courier,* January 27, 1934; *Chicago Defender,* December 15, 1951.

25. Charles E. Dorais to John O'Hara, February 3, 1934; J. Leonard Carrico to Dorais, February 6, 1934; O'Hara to Dorais, February 20, 1934, UVOH 2/9, Archives of the University of Notre Dame; Christine Yancy, e-mail to author, May 20, 1999.

26. Rader, *American Sports,* 285–88; Isaacs, *All the Moves,* 165–66.

27. *Pittsburgh Courier,* March 15, 1941; Santa Barbara State College *El Gaucho,* February 28, March 7, 1941; *Santa Barbara State College Yearbook,* 1941.

28. Isaacs, *All the Moves,* 277; *New York Times,* March 4, 1948, 37; March 6, 1948, 17; Milton S. Katz, *Breaking Through: John B. McLendon, Basketball Legend and Civil Rights Pioneer* (Fayetteville: University of Arkansas Press, 2007), 70–72.

29. A frustrated John McLendon complained privately that NCAA stood for "No Colored Athletes Allowed." In later years he praised Al Deur as "the Abraham Lincoln of college sports" for his key role in integrating the NAIA. *Los Angeles Tribune,* January 13, 1951; *Pittsburgh Courier,* December 30, 1950, February 9, March 22, May 24, September 20, 1952; *Baltimore Afro-American,* December 22, 1951, March 22, 1952; Katz, *Breaking Through,* 66–73, 109.

30. *Pittsburgh Courier,* February 2, 1952, January 17, 1953, January 2, 1954, January 14, March 24, 1956, March 23, 1957, *Atlanta Daily World,* February 12, March 19, 1957; *New York Times,* March 13, 1960, sec. 5, p. 3; March 19, 1961, sec. 5, p. 2; George, *Elevating the Game,* 86–91.

31. Richard T. Culberson, telephone interview by author, July 23, 2001; *University of Iowa Basketball Media Guide* (1944–45, 1945–46).

32. On Bill Garrett's experiences and racial discrimination in Indiana high school basketball, see Tom Graham and Rachel Graham Cody, *Getting Open: The Unknown Story of Bill Garrett and the Integration of College Basketball* (New York: Atria Books, 2006). Indiana University *Indiana Daily Student,* April 17, 1997; news release, Indiana University News Bureau, February 24, 1986; *Lansing State Journal,* February 16, 1988; *Pittsburgh Courier,* December 8, 1951.

33. *New York Times,* December 14, 1947, 4; Chet Walker, with Chris Messenger, *Long Time Coming: A Black Athlete's Coming-of-Age in America* (New York: Grove Press, 1995), 64–72, 77–81, 119–24; Oscar Robertson, *The Big O: My Life, My Times, My Game* (n.p.: Rodale, 2003), 88–90.

34. In 2006 Drake University named the playing surface of its stadium Johnny Bright Field. *Chicago Defender,* October 13, 27, November 10, December 8, 15, 1951; *Baltimore Afro-American,* October 27, November 17, December 8, 1951; miscellaneous clippings in possession of author; *Moment of Impact: Stories of the Pulitzer Prize Photographs,* TNT Channel documentary (1999).

35. Minutes of the Meeting of the Faculty Representatives of the MVIAA, May 17, 18, 1946, 2–3, courtesy of Prentice Gault; *New York Times,* May 19, 1946, sec. 5, p. 2; Clifford S. Griffin, *The University of Kansas: A History* (Lawrence: University Press of Kansas, 1974), 661, 767.

36. *New York Times,* April 18, 1946, 32; November 20, 1947, 42; November 23, 1947, sec. 5, p. 4; November 30, 1947, sec. 5, p. 2; December 11, 1947, 50; December 14, 1947, sec. 5, p. 3.

37. *Kansas Industrialist,* September 22, 1949; *Manhattan Mercury,* November 20, 1991; *Wildcat Weekly,* February 18, 1995; Tim Fitzgerald, *Kansas State Wildcat Handbook* (Wichita: Wichita Eagle and Beacon Publishing, 1996), 54–57; miscellaneous clippings in University Archives, Kansas State University. Although Robinson carefully avoided

violating local racial customs, he temporarily eloped with the daughter of a university art professor shortly after he received his draft notice.

38. One critic of Phog Allen sarcastically commented that the veteran coach "would rather lose every game on the schedule than allow a Negro to play on his team." *New York Times,* March 30, 1947, sec. 5, p. 2; Kristine M. McCusker, "'The Forgotten Years' of America's Civil Rights Movement: The University of Kansas, 1939–1961" (master's thesis, University of Kansas, 1987), 101–2, 107–10; Mike Fisher, *Deaner: Fifty Years of University of Kansas Athletics* (Kansas City, Mo.: Lowell Press, 1986), 204–6, 269–71.

39. Jimmie L. Franklin, *A History of Blacks in Oklahoma* (Norman: University of Oklahoma Press, 1971), 75–85; *Los Angeles Tribune,* June 24, 1950; *El Paso Times,* June 9, 1955; *Louisiana Weekly,* September 14, 1957.

40. Numan V. Bartley, *The New South, 1945–1980* (Baton Rouge: Louisiana State University Press, 1995), 187–260. Recent studies of massive resistance include Clive Webb, ed., *Massive Resistance: Southern Opposition to the Second Reconstruction* (New York: Oxford University Press, 2005); and George Lewis, *Massive Resistance: The White Response to the Civil Rights Movement* (New York: Oxford University Press, 2006).

41. Adelson, *Brushing Back Jim Crow,* 120–23; *New York Times,* March 24, 1954, 29.

42. Adelson, *Brushing Back Jim Crow,* 123–26, 204; *New York Times,* June 3, 1954, 25; March 20, 1957, 40; William Warren Rogers et al., *Alabama: The History of a Deep South State* (Tuscaloosa: University of Alabama Press, 1994), 539.

43. *Pittsburgh Courier,* November 27, December 11, 1954; *New York Times,* January 24, 1953, 20; November 26, 1954, 18; *New Orleans Louisiana Weekly,* December 11, 1954, December 24, 31, 1955, January 7, 1956; Walker, *Long Time Coming,* 119.

44. *New Orleans Louisiana Weekly,* January 8, 1955, January 14, 1956; *New York Age,* January 15, 1955. For a more detailed description of the Sugar Bowl controversy, see Charles H. Martin, "Racial Change and 'Big-Time' College Football in Georgia: The Age of Segregation, 1892–1957," *Georgia Historical Quarterly* 80 (Fall 1996): 550–59.

45. Bobby Dodd, interview by August W. Giebelhaus and Larry Foster, July 5, 1983, Georgia Tech Archives, Atlanta; *Atlanta Constitution,* December 3–6, 1955; *Atlanta Journal,* December 3, 5–6, 1955; "Tempest o'er the Sugar Bowl," *Tech Alumnus,* December 1955, 8; *Atlanta Daily World,* December 1, 7, 1955; McMath et al., *Engineering the New South,* 283.

46. Bobby Grier, telephone interview by author, June 23, 1994; *Atlanta Constitution,* January 5, 1956; *Atlanta Daily World,* January 3, 1956; *Pittsburgh Courier,* December 10, 1955, February 11, 1956; *Pittsburgh Press,* February 5, 1956; *New York Times,* January 1, 1956, 42; January 3, 1956, 33; Minutes, Board of Administrators Meeting, Tulane University, December 14, 1955, University Archives, Tulane University. For a survey of American newspaper reactions to the Sugar Bowl controversy, see Michael Oriard, *King Football: Sport and Spectacle in the Golden Age of Radio and Newsreels, Movies and Magazines, the Weekly and the Daily Press* (Chapel Hill: University of North Carolina Press, 2001), 308–12.

47. In March 1956 Delta State College yielded to segregationist threats and withdrew its all-white basketball team from the NAIA Tournament rather than risk competing

against integrated or all-black teams. *Atlanta Daily World,* March 6, 1957; *New York Times,* December 29, 1957, 1; December 30, 3; December 31, 1956, 13; March 6, 1957, 25; Oriard, *King Football,* 310.

48. *Atlanta Constitution,* February 15–21, 1957; *Atlanta Journal,* February 16–21, 1957; *New York Times,* February 15, 1957, 1; February 23, 1957, 1; *Memphis Commercial Appeal,* February 1, 1956, University Archives, Mitchell Memorial Library, Mississippi State University; Adelson, *Brushing Back Jim Crow,* 154–55, 204–6.

49. *Atlanta Constitution,* February 16, 21–23, 1957; *Atlanta Journal,* February 16, 21–23, 1957; *New York Times,* February 16, 1957, 10; February 23, 1957, 1; University of Georgia *Red and Black,* February 28, 1957; Adelson, *Brushing Back Jim Crow,* 205–6.

50. *Baton Rouge Morning Advocate,* July 6, 1956; *New Orleans Times-Picayune,* July 14, 1956; *New York Times,* June 4, 1952, July 15, 1956, sec. 1, p. 5; Adelson, *Brushing Back Jim Crow,* 187–90.

51. *New York Times,* July 17, 1956, 13; July 22, 1956, sec. 4, p. 8; September 1, 1956, 6; October 16, 1956, 14; *New Orleans Times-Picayune,* January 1, 1984; Adam Fairclough, *Race and Democracy: The Civil Rights Struggle in Louisiana, 1915–1972* (Athens: University of Georgia Press, 1995), 205–6, 232–33; "Football: Segregation Snafu," *Newsweek,* July 30, 1956, 79; Adelson, *Brushing Back Jim Crow,* 190–91; Paul E. DeBlanc to Rufus C. Harris, July 16, 1956, University Archives, Tulane University.

52. *Pittsburgh Sun-Telegram,* July 24, 1956; *Pittsburgh Post-Gazette,* n.d., Edward H. Litchfield Papers, University Archives, Hillman Library, University of Pittsburgh; *Pittsburgh Courier,* March 24, April 14, November 17, 1956; *New York Times,* July 29, 1956, sec. 5, p. 4; July 31, 1956, 11; October 6, 1956, 20; October 26, 1956, 21; December 13, 1957, 31; November 29, 1958, 22; *Baton Rouge State Times,* July 30, 1956; *New Orleans Louisiana Weekly,* October 13, 1956; University of Georgia *Red and Black,* November 15, 1956; Fairclough, *Race and Democracy,* 219, 335–36; *New Orleans Times-Picayune,* January 1, 1984; *Atlanta Daily World,* January 2, 1957.

53. *New York Times,* July 29, 1956, sec. 5, p. 4; July 31, 1956, 11; October 6, 1956, 20; October 26, 1956, 21; December 13, 1957, 31; *Baton Rouge State Times,* July 30, 1956; *New Orleans Louisiana Weekly,* October 13, 1956; University of Georgia *Red and Black,* November 15, 1956; Fairclough, *Race and Democracy,* 219, 335–36.

54. Louisiana State University *Daily Reveille,* September 13, 1956; *Pittsburgh Courier,* March 24, April 14, November 17, 1956; *New York Times,* September 17, 1957, 1, 22; Minutes, Athletic Advisory Committee, September 9, November 5, 1957, Rufus C. Harris Papers, University Archives, Tulane University.

55. University of Georgia *Red and Black,* October 4, 1957; *Atlanta Journal and Constitution,* October 20, 1957.

56. *Dorsey v. State Athletic Commission* 168 F. Supp. 149 (1958); Jeffrey T. Sammons, *Beyond the Ring: The Role of Boxing in American Society* (Urbana: University of Illinois Press, 1988), 190; *New Orleans Times-Picayune,* January 14, 1958, vertical file, Louisiana Collection, University Library, Louisiana State University; *New York Times,* November 29, 1958, 1, 22; May 26, 1959, 1.

57. *New York Times,* November 29, 1958, 22; January 18, 1959, 52; February 22, 1959, 2; *New Orleans Times-Picayune,* March 6, 1960; Adelson, *Brushing Back Jim Crow,* 238.

58. *New Orleans Times-Picayune,* March 6, 1960; Adelson, *Brushing Back Jim Crow,* 227–28, 238–42; *New York Times,* August 19, 1961, 18.

59. Georgia Tech *Technique,* April 26, 1963; *New York Times,* November 9, 1963, 53; November 14, 1963, 71; November 15, 1963, 34; December 4, 1963, 95.

60. *Bynum v. Schiro,* 219 F. Supp. 204 (1963); *New York Times,* July 3, 1963, 10; January 7, 1964, 20; February 18, 1964, 20; May 16, 1964, 52; *New Orleans Times-Picayune,* January 1, 1984; Fairclough, *Race and Democracy,* 335–36; Ken Rapport, *The Syracuse Football Story* (Huntsville, Ala.: Strode Publishers, 1975), 254–56; "Sugar Bowl History," in *Sugar Bowl Media Guide* (1985).

Chapter 4. Cracks in the Solid South

1. Ray Sanchez, *Basketball's Biggest Upset* (El Paso: Mesa Publishing, 1991), 115–38; Frank Fitzpatrick, *And the Walls Came Tumbling Down: Kentucky, Texas Western, and the Game That Changed American Sports* (New York: Simon and Schuster, 1999), 198–217; Don Haskins, with Dan Wetzel, *Glory Road: My Story of the 1966 NCAA Basketball Championship and How One Team Triumphed against the Odds and Changed America Forever* (New York: Hyperion, 2006), 177–88; Bryan Woolley, "The Game," *Nova* 26 (Summer 1991): 12–17.

2. Nelson George, *Elevating the Game: Black Men and Basketball* (New York: Harper Collins, 1992), 135–37; Fitzpatrick, *And the Walls Came Tumbling Down,* 228–35.

3. A. S. "Doc" Young, *Negro Firsts in Sports* (Chicago: Johnson Publishing, 1963), 253; *El Paso Times,* July 3, 2006; Charles Brown, interview by author, El Paso, Tex., July 14, 1989, Oral History Collection, University of Texas at El Paso; *San Antonio Express,* December 8, 1957; Maurice Harris, telephone interview by author, June 30, 1990; *Valley Evening Monitor* (McAllen), February 22, 1999; D. Joe Williams, interview by author, El Paso, Tex., August 7, 2000; Sam Williams, telephone interview by author, February 27, 1989.

4. Gary Tuell, *Above the Rim: The History of Basketball at the University of Louisville* (Louisville: University of Louisville Athletic Association, n.d.), 123–46; William J. Morison, e-mail to author, April 12, 1999; Lenny Lyles, telephone interview by author, May 4, 2000, Oral History Center, University of Louisville; Wade Houston, interview by author, Knoxville, Tenn., August 10, 1989.

5. Ronald E. Marcello, "The Integration of Intercollegiate Athletics in Texas: North Texas State College as a Test Case, 1956," *Journal of Sport History* 14 (Winter 1987): 286–316; Marcello, "Reluctance versus Reality: The Desegregation of North Texas State College, 1954–1956," *Southwestern Historical Quarterly* 99 (October 1996): 152–85; *Yucca Yearbook* (1958, 1959, 1960, 1961, 1962).

6. Patrick J. Nicholson, *In Time: An Anecdotal History of the First Fifty Years of the University of Houston* (Houston: Pacesetter Press, 1977), 12, 85, 296, 368–88; Amilcar Shabazz, *Advancing Democracy: African Americans and the Struggle for Access and Equity in Higher Education in Texas* (Chapel Hill: University of North Carolina Press, 2004), 206–7; Richard Pennington, *Breaking the Ice: The Racial Integration of Southwest Conference Football* (Jefferson, N.C.: McFarland, 1987), 26–27; University of Texas *Daily Texan,* November 20, 1963; University of Houston *Cougar,* April 8, 17, May 6, 8, 1964.

7. Pennington, *Breaking the Ice*, 27–49; *Pittsburgh Courier,* January 2, 1965; *Dallas Express,* March 11, 1967; Dan Jenkins, "You've Got to Have Some 'O,'" *Sports Illustrated,* October 16, 1967, 41–44; *New York Times,* January 11, 1966, 25. On McVea's recruitment and career, see Katherine Lopez, *Cougars of Any Color: The Integration of University of Houston Athletics, 1964–1968* (Jefferson, N.C.: McFarland, 2008).

8. Lewis assigned white roommates to Hayes and Chaney as part of his strategy to help them adjust to an overwhelmingly white campus. *Houston Informer,* May 30, 1964; *Houston Post,* February 3, 1966; *Dallas Express,* January 20, 27, 1968; Pennington, *Breaking the Ice,* 30; Lopez, *Cougars of Any Color,* 42–43, 63–64, 78–83.

9. For details, see Murray Sperber, *Shake Down the Thunder: The Creation of Notre Dame Football* (New York: Henry Holt, 1993); and Robin Lester, *Stagg's University: The Rise, Decline, and Fall of Big-Time Football at Chicago* (Urbana: University of Illinois Press, 1995).

10. Morrison Warren played football at Phoenix (Junior) College in 1941 and 1942 before entering military service. In Warren's first season the Phoenix team was forced to leave him behind when they played New Mexico Military Institute in Roswell. In 1946 Arizona State also left Warren at home when the Sun Devils visited Hardin-Simmons in Abilene, Texas. Arizona State University *State Press,* November 7, 14, 1947; Phoenix *Arizona Republic,* n.d., 1947, August 2, 1981; *El Paso Herald-Post,* November 4, 10, 11, December 22, 1947; Morrison Warren, telephone interview by author, April 1, 2000; *El Paso Times,* November 4, 1947, September 29, 30, October 2, 1950; Texas College of Mines *Prospector,* November 1, 8, 1947.

11. On a 1947 trip to Wichita State, Warren and Diggs were initially denied service at a small restaurant in Amarillo. After the rest of the team vehemently protested, the entire party was served together. Arizona State University *State Press,* November 21, December 5, 1947; *Dallas Morning News,* November 26, 1947; *El Paso Herald-Post,* November 26, December 20, 22, 1947; Warren interview.

12. Red Hopkins to Rt. Reverend Monsignor G. W. Caffery, n.d.; Frank Murray to Red Hopkins, May 26, 1950; *Loyola University Football Media Guide* (1950); miscellaneous team rosters, all in University Archives, Loyola-Marymount Universiy; *El Paso Times,* September 29–30, 1950.

13. *Los Angeles Loyolan,* October 3, December 5, 12, 1950, January 16, 1951; *Los Angeles Tribune,* October 7, 1950; *El Paso Times,* September 30, October 11, 13, 23, 27, 1950; *El Paso Herald-Post,* September 30, October 11, 12, 25, 1950; Texas Western College *Prospector,* September 30, October 7, 20, 1950; *People's World* (San Francisco), October 2, 1950.

14. *Santa Fe New Mexican,* September 29, October 1, 3, 1950; *El Paso Herald-Post,* September 30, October 11, 14, 25, 1950; *El Paso Times,* September 30, 1950; University of Arizona *Wildcat,* October 11, November 15, 22, 1950; Tucson *Arizona Daily Star,* October 4, 8, 9, 11, 12, 1950.

15. Technically, the first African Americans to compete in an athletic activity on the Texas Western campus were two members of a military basketball team that played the TWC freshman squad during the 1950–51 season. *El Paso Times,* October 28, 1950, November 18, 1951; *El Paso Herald-Post,* October 11, 28, 31, 1950, November 20, De-

cember 26, 1951, January 2, 1952; Texas Western College *Prospector,* October 7, 28, 1950, December 1, 1951; *Oklahoma City Black Dispatch,* November 11, 1950.

16. Several junior colleges in Texas integrated before the *Brown* ruling, and two four-year community colleges not directly under a state board did so in 1954. The first major public university in the South to admit black undergraduates on a continuing basis appears to have been Virginia Tech in 1953. Texas Western College *Prospector,* April 2, 16, 1955; *El Paso Times,* March 31, April 2, 1955; Shabazz, *Advancing Democracy,* 159–61, 197; Dysart E. Holcomb to Logan Wilson, July 1, 1955, President's Files, Barker Texas History Center, University of Texas at Austin.

17. *El Paso Times,* June 1, July 9, 16, 19, 20, 28, August 24, 1955; *El Paso Herald-Post,* July 8–9, 1955; *Austin Statesman,* July 8, 1955; Minutes, University of Texas Board of Regents, July 8, 1955, Barker Texas History Center, University of Texas; J. M. Whitaker, telephone interview by author, February 5, 1991.

18. Administrators at the University of Texas in Austin secretly admitted three black undergraduates in 1955 but refused to acknowledge their presence publicly or to officially register black students until 1956. *El Paso Times,* July 14, September 10, 1955; *El Paso Herald-Post,* September 9, 13, 1955; "Louise Resley Wiggins," in *Diamond Days: An Oral History of the University of Texas at El Paso,* edited by Charles H. Martin and Rebecca M. Craver (El Paso: Texas Western Press, 1991), 128; Joe Atkins, telephone interview by author, January 29, 1991; Whitaker interview; Dysart E. Holcomb to Judge Scott Gaines, April 20, 1956, Barker Texas History Center; Shabazz, *Advancing Democracy,* 158–59; Will Guzman, "On the Border of the South, on the Border of the West: The 1962 Anti-Discrimination Ordinance of El Paso," graduate seminar paper, copy in possession of author; El Paso City Ordinance 2698, copy in possession of author.

19. *University of Texas at El Paso Football Media Guide* (1999), 139–42; Francis Fugate, *Frontier College* (El Paso: Texas Western Press, 1964), 117–29, 149, 157; Texas Western College *Prospector,* October 31, 1959; "Joseph M. Ray," in *Diamond Days,* edited by Martin and Craver, 174–76.

20. "Joseph M. Ray," 176; Texas Western College *Prospector,* September 7, 21, 1963.

21. Texas Western College *Prospector,* September 14, 26, 1959; Bob Ingram and Ray Sanchez, *The Miners* (El Paso: Mesa Publishing, 1997), 38–40, 50–55, 79–80; Marcello, "Integration of Intercollegiate Athletics in Texas," 286–316; *The Flowsheet, 1962, 1963* (yearbook).

22. Several teams from major conferences, including the University of Southern California, also ignored the NCAA's strict rules on eligibility for junior college transfers. Ingram and Sanchez, *The Miners,* 80–84; Texas Western College *Prospecter,* February 16, 1963; *New York Times,* January 9, 1967, 41; "Joseph M. Ray," 175; "William S. Stevens," in *Diamond Days,* edited by Martin and Craver, 82–84.

23. Carr, Daney, West, and Wallace were African Americans. Ingram and Sanchez, *The Miners,* 84–90; "William S. Stevens," 184–85; University of Texas at El Paso *Prospector,* September 11, 1967, February 9, 1968; *El Paso Times,* April 21, 1991.

24. Texas Western College *Prospector,* November 28, 1956, February 13, 20, 1957; Ingram and Sanchez, *The Miners,* 57; "Charles T. Brown," in *Diamond Days,* edited by Martin and Craver, 145–46. For the full text of the Brown interview, see Charles T.

Brown, interview by author, July 14, 1989, Interview no. 776, Institute of Oral History, University of Texas at El Paso.

25. "Charles T. Brown," 145–46; Texas Western College *Prospector,* March 24, 1956, March 13, 1957. For profiles of Charles Brown, see Bill Knight, "Crossing the Line," *El Paso Times,* June 2, 1991; and Charles H. Martin, "Charlie Brown," *Nova* 25 (Spring 1990): 7–9.

26. Alvis Glidewell, telephone interview by author, July 20, 1989; "Charles T. Brown," 146–47; Texas Western College *Prospector,* February 27, March 2, 13, 1957, March 7, 1958, March 7, 14, 1959.

27. "Charles T. Brown," 146–47; *El Paso Times,* December 13, 14, 1956; *El Paso Herald-Post,* December 13, 17, 1956.

28. Brown interview; "Charles T. Brown," 147–48.

29. Texas Western College *Prospector,* October 18, December 6, 1957; *El Paso Herald-Post,* December 30, 1960; *El Paso Times,* December 27, 1960.

30. Don Haskins and Ray Sanchez, *Haskins: The Bear Facts* (El Paso: Mangan Books, 1987), 17–28, 38–49, 64; Haskins, *Glory Road,* 81–82.

31. Haskins and Sanchez, *Haskins: The Bear Facts,* 49–51, 60–61, 64; Haskins, *Glory Road,* 86–96, 131–36.

32. Haskins and Sanchez, *Haskins: The Bear Facts,* 56–58; Haskins, *Glory Road,* 109–11.

33. The first NCAA championship team to start three African Americans was the University of San Francisco in 1955. The 1963 NCAA champion, Loyola of Chicago, started four African Americans but did not set off complaints like Texas Western did. Fitzpatrick, *And the Walls Came Tumbling Down,* 24–26, 61.

34. "Joseph M. Ray," 178–79; Haskins and Sanchez, *Haskins: The Bear Facts,* 59–66; Alexander Wolff, "The Bear in Winter," *Sports Illustrated,* March 1, 1999, 64; Fitzpatrick, *And the Walls Came Tumbling Down,* 120; Haskins, *Glory Road,* 113–17.

35. Haskins and Sanchez, *Haskins: The Bear Facts,* 65–68; Sanchez, *Basketball's Biggest Upset,* 64–111; Robert Stern, *They Were Number One: A History of the NCAA Basketball Tournament* (New York: Leisure Press, 1983), 224–25; Haskins, *Glory Road,* 146–68.

36. The Disney film *Glory Road* (2006), a popular movie about the 1966 team that took many liberties with the actual facts, depicted journalists and broadcasters publicly talking at length about the racial dimensions of the title game. In 1966, though, the reality was just the opposite. George, *Elevating the Game,* 135–38; Sanchez, *Basketball's Biggest Upset,* 125–26; Fitzpatrick, *And the Walls Came Tumbling Down,* 5–6, 26, 38–43; Barry Jacobs, *Across the Line: Profiles in Basketball Courage—Tales of the First Black Players in the ACC and the SEC* (Guilford, Conn.: Lyons Press, 2008), 16–18.

37. Sanchez, *Basketball's Biggest Upset,* 116–17, 128–38; Haskins, *Glory Road,* 177–87; *New York Times,* March 20, 1966, sec. 5, p. 1; Stern, *They Were Number One,* 232–33; "Nevil Shed," in *Diamond Days,* edited by Martin and Craver, 169; "The Miners Major Upset," *Newsweek,* March 25, 1966, 63; videotape of game, in possession of author.

38. Fitzpatrick, *And the Walls Came Tumbling Down,* 218–21; Sanchez, *Basketball's Biggest Upset,* 3–4; Haskins, *Glory Road,* 194–96; *USA Today,* April 1, 1988, E2.

39. *Pittsburgh Courier,* April 2, 1966.

40. George, *Elevating the Game*, 137; *Pittsburgh Courier*, April 2, 1966; *New York Times*, December 21, 1994, B9; *El Paso Times*, March 16, 1990, January 4, 1996; *El Paso Herald-Post*, April 1, 1991; Billy Jones, telephone interview by author, October 5, 1994; Houston interview.

41. "Joseph M. Ray," 179; Wolff, "The Bear in Winter," 64–66; *El Paso Times*, April 2, 1988; Haskins, *Glory Road*, 193–94.

42. University of Texas at El Paso *Prospector*, February 23, March 22, April 18, 26, 1968; Harry Edwards, *The Revolt of the Black Athlete* (New York: Free Press, 1970), 84–88, 150–53. On other protests, see David K. Wiggins, "'The Year of Awakening': Black Athletes, Racial Unrest, and the Civil Rights Movement of 1968," in *Glory Bound: Black Athletes in a White America*, by David K. Wiggins (Syracuse: Syracuse University Press, 1997), 102–22. Bob Beamon recalled his experiences at UTEP in *The Man Who Could Fly: The Bob Beamon Story* (Columbus, Miss.: Genesis Press, 1999).

43. Jack Olsen, "In An Alien World," *Sports Illustrated*, July 15, 1968, 30–43; Ad Hoc Committee on Athletic Re-evaluation, *Final Report* (El Paso: University of Texas at El Paso, 1969).

Chapter 5. Hold That (Mason-Dixon) Line

1. Darryl Hill, telephone interview by author, July 26, 1993; *Washington Star*, November 17, 1963; Clemson University *Tiger*, November 22, 1963; Wright Bryan, *Clemson: An Informal History of the University, 1889–1979* (Columbia, S.C.: R. L. Bryan, 1979), 215; John Greenya, "Black Man on a White Field," *Washington Post Magazine*, February 1, 2004, 17–18.

2. University of Michigan *Michigan Daily*, February 13, 1963.

3. John S. Watterson, *College Football: History, Spectacle, Controversy* (Baltimore: Johns Hopkins University Press, 2000), 209–18, 236–40; Bruce A. Corrie, *The Atlantic Coast Conference, 1953–1978* (Durham: Carolina Academic Press, 1978), 28–29, 43–52; *New York Times*, May 9, 1953, 16.

4. Corrie, *Atlantic Coast Conference*, 72–73, 86, 115–18, 122, 141.

5. Ibid., 49–51, 57, 66–67, 97; Marvin Francis, telephone interview by author, September 20, 1994.

6. George H. Callcott, *Maryland and America, 1940–1980* (Baltimore: Johns Hopkins University Press, 1985), 145–52; Callcott, *A History of the University of Maryland* (Baltimore: Maryland Historical Society, 1966), 306–7, 351–53; Peter Wallenstein, "Black Southerners and Nonblack Universities: The Process of Desegregating Southern Higher Education, 1935–1965," in *Higher Education and the Civil Rights Movement: White Supremacy, Black Southerners, and College Campuses*, edited by Peter Wallenstein (Gainesville: University Press of Florida, 2008), 26–29; Anne Turkos, e-mail to author, August 24, 2006.

7. Callcott, *History of the University of Maryland*, 354–56, 385; *University of Maryland Football Media Guide* (1972), 119, 158–59; Hill interview; *Baltimore Sun*, May 31, 1964; Greenya, "Black Man on a White Field," 26.

8. Hill interview.

9. Before the South Carolina game, Coach Tom Nugent received several hate letters and one death threat. University of Maryland *Diamondback,* September 24, October 1, 1963; *Washington Star,* September 29, 1963; *Washington Post,* October 20, 1963; Hill interview; Greenya, "Black Man on a White Field," 27.

10. Hill interview; *Baltimore Sun,* November 29, 1963; *Washington Star,* November 13, 1963; University of Maryland *Diamondback,* October 15, 1964.

11. African Americans also began participation in nonrevenue sports at Maryland during the mid-1960s, with John Williams competing on the swimming team in 1964 and 1965. *Baltimore Sun,* February 23, 1964; *University of Maryland Football Media Guide* (1966, 1967, 1968, 1969); *ACC Football Media Guide* (1992); University of Maryland *Diamondback,* May 17, 1965, March 11, 1966; *The Terrapin, 1964, 1965* (yearbook).

12. Bynum Shaw, *The History of Wake Forest College* (Winston-Salem, N.C.: Wake Forest University, 1988), 4:71, 113, 130–34.

13. Ibid., 4:113, 325, 331; *Wake Forest Football Media Guide* (1992).

14. Wake Forest University *Old Black and Gold,* December 9, 18, 1963; "Report of the Special Committee on Intercollegiate Athletics," August 22, 1964, Harold Wayland Tribble Papers, Reynolds Library, Wake Forest University.

15. *Winston-Salem Journal,* April 2, May 7, 1964; Wake Forest University *Old Black and Gold,* February 10, 17, March 16, April 13, 1964; Francis interview.

16. *Wake Forest University Football Media Guide* (1967, 1968, 1969, 1992); *Atlantic Coast Conference Football Media Guide* (1992); Francis interview.

17. *University of North Carolina Football Media Guide* (1994), 170; Ken Rappoport, *Tar Heel: North Carolina Football* (Huntsville, Ala.: Strode Publishers, 1976), 138, 148–52, 243, 258–66; Player Time Sheets, 1953, 1954, Office of Sports Information, University of Notre Dame.

18. Neal Cheek, "An Historical Study of the Administrative Actions in the Racial Desegregation of the University of North Carolina at Chapel Hill, 1930–1955" (Ph.D. diss., University of North Carolina at Chapel Hill, 1973), 61, 118, 136–47, 159, 173–76; *Pittsburgh Courier,* October 6, 20, 1951; *New York Times,* October 13, 1951, 7; October 14, 1951, 39.

19. Cheek, "Historical Study of the Administrative Actions," 189–200; *New York Times,* September 16, 1955, 25; September 20, 1955, 35; William S. Powell, *The First State University,* 3rd ed. (Chapel Hill: University of North Carolina Press, 1963), 285; Richard A. Baddour, "A Study of Non-competitive Athletic Admissions at the University of North Carolina at Chapel Hill" (master's thesis, University of North Carolina, 1975), 22.

20. *University of North Carolina Football Media Guide* (1967, 1968, 1969, 1970); Rappoport, *Tar Heel,* 196, 203; Ronald W. Hyatt, interview by author, Chapel Hill, N.C., July 15, 1993; James Webster, telephone interview by author, November 29, 1994; Bill Dooley, telephone interview by author, December 9, 1994.

21. *University of North Carolina Football Media Guide* (1971); *ACC Football Media Guide* (1992); Hyatt interview; Webster interview.

22. Rappoport, *Tar Heel,* 254–55; *University of North Carolina Football Media Guide* (1969, 1970, 1971, 1972, 1973, 1974); *ACC Football Media Guide* (1992); *Wake Forest*

Football Media Guide (1991); Hyatt interview; Baddour, "Study of Non-competitive Athletic Admissions," 20–22.

23. Bill Beezley, *The Wolfpack: Intercollegiate Athletics at North Carolina State University* (Raleigh: North Carolina State University, 1976), 89, 102, 117–21, 327–37.

24. Alice E. Reagan, *North Carolina State University: A Narrative History* (Ann Arbor: Edwards Brothers, 1987), 163–65; *Raleigh News and Observer,* June 19, 1956, January 30, February 11, 1957; *Sioux Falls Argus-Leader,* October 28, 1956; *Greenville News,* October 17, 1957; Irwin R. Holmes Jr., telephone interview by author, October 12, 1994; Beezley, *Wolfpack,* 227.

25. Holmes interview; *Raleigh News and Observer,* April 2, 1960; Beezley, *Wolfpack,* 227.

26. James J. Steward Jr. to L. M. Wright Jr., October 18, 1960, vertical files, University Archives, North Carolina State University; Holmes interview; North Carolina State University *Technician,* February 7, 1963, November 14, 1969, February 6, April 17, 1970; Marcus Martin, telephone interview by author, October 23, 1994.

27. Beezley, *Wolfpack,* 89, 102, 117–21, 227, 327–37; Martin interview; North Carolina State University *Technician,* n.d. [1968], November 21, 1969.

28. *North Carolina State University Football Media Guide* (1969, 1970, 1971); Clyde E. Chesney, "Experiences at N.C. State as a Football Walk-on, 1968–1972," August 18, 1993, in possession of the author; *Clyde and Pride,* football program, North Carolina State University versus Kent State University, September 11, 1971, University Archives, North Carolina State University.

29. Beezley, *Wolfpack,* 227–35; *ACC Football Media Guide* (1992); *North Carolina State University Football Media Guide* (1971, 1972, 1973).

30. *North Carolina State University Football Media Guide* (1973); "Black Athletes Make Impact," unknown clipping, n.p., 1973, in possession of author.

31. Robert F. Durden, *The Launching of Duke University, 1924–1949* (Durham: Duke University Press, 1993), 1–3, 236–43; *New York Times,* October 1, 1950, sec. 5, p. 3; *Duke University Football Media Guide* (1993).

32. Don Yannella, "Race Relations at Duke University and the Allen Building Take-over" (senior honors thesis, Duke University, 1985), 1–5; Jorge Kotelanski, "Prolonged and Patient Efforts: The Desegregation of Duke University, 1948–1963" (senior honors thesis, Duke University, 1990), 14–19, 48, 122–25, 133–38; Duke University *Chronicle,* February 10, 1989; Melissa Kean, *Desegregating Private Higher Education in the South: Duke, Emory, Rice, Tulane, and Vanderbilt* (Baton Rouge: Louisiana State University Press, 2008), 38–42, 139–49, 192–95.

33. Duke University *Chronicle,* November 20, 1964, November 12, 1965.

34. *Duke University Football Media Guide* (1967, 1968, 1969, 1970, 1971); *New York Times,* January 11, 1966, 24; *ACC Football Media Guide* (1992); football program, Duke versus University of North Carolina, November 20, 1971; Glenn E. Mann, *A Story of Glory: Duke University Football* (Greenville, S.C.: Doorway Publishers, 1985), 231–32.

35. Yannella, "Race Relations at Duke University," 6; *Durham Morning Herald,* July 8, 1973; mimeographed flyer, n.d., Herbert C. Bradshaw Papers, University Archives, Duke University.

36. *New York Times,* October 29, 1947, 39.

37. University of South Carolina *Gamecock,* March 1, 15, 1968; *New York Times,* September 11, 1963, 3; Walter Edgar, *South Carolina: A History* (Columbia: University of South Carolina Press, 1998), 391–92, 424, 538–39.

38. Jack Bass, interview by author, Oxford, Miss., March 23, 1994.

39. *Pittsburgh Courier,* December 5, 12, 19, 26, 1953, January 2, 1954; Walter B. Edgar, *South Carolina in the Modern Age* (Columbia: University of South Carolina Press, 1992), 99.

40. University of South Carolina *Gamecock,* April 26, 1968, April 11, 15, 25, May 2, December 5, 1969, March 23, 1970.

41. University of South Carolina *Gamecock,* March 23, October 16, 28, November 2, December 9, 11, 1970.

42. Corrie, *Atlantic Coast Conference,* 85–88, 104–10; University of South Carolina *Gamecock,* October 26, 1970.

43. Edgar, *South Carolina in the Modern Era,* 98, 124–27.

44. University of South Carolina *Gamecock,* September 30, 1970, March 15, October 12, 1972; *University of South Carolina Football Media Guide* (1970, 1971, 1972, 1973, 1994); football program, University of South Carolina versus North Carolina State University, October 28, 1972; football program, Clemson University versus the University of South Carolina, November 24, 1973.

45. Corrie, *Atlantic Coast Conference,* 115–18, 139; *University of South Carolina Football Media Guide* (1994); Edgar, *South Carolina in the Modern Era,* 98, 124–27.

46. Bryan, *Clemson,* 3–11, 22–28, 192–94.

47. Donald M. McKale, ed., *Tradition: A History of the Presidency of Clemson University* (Macon: Mercer University Press, 1988), xiv, 187, 196–201; Bryan, *Clemson,* 154–62; Taites Locke and Bob Ibach, *Caught in the Net* (West Point, N.Y.: Leisure Press, 1982), 40–43.

48. *Atlanta Daily World,* January 1, 2, 5, 1957; Edgar, *South Carolina: A History,* 523–29.

49. *Greenville News,* October 17, 1957.

50. Holmes interview; *Clemson University Football Media Guide* (1994).

51. Clemson University *Tiger,* September 4, 1970; *Clemson University Football Media Guide* (1971, 1972, 1973, 1974, 1975).

52. *Clemson University Football Media Guide* (1983); Hill interview; McKale, *Tradition,* 230–31.

53. *University of Virginia Football Media Guide* (1992).

54. "An Audacious Faith: Report of the Task Force on Afro-American Affairs," University of Virginia, June 1987, 4, 174, Manuscripts Department, University Archives, University of Virginia; Kenny Lucas, "The Right to Compete: George King III, the First African American Athlete at the University of Virginia" (student paper, University of Virginia, December 6, 1994), 2–5, courtesy of Julian Bond; *New York Times,* February 29, 1956; J. W. Hudson to Colgate W. Darden, February 1956; Darden to Hudson, March 1, 1956; unidentified clipping, February 28, 1956, all in Colgate W. Darden Presidential Papers, Manuscripts Department.

55. Lucas, "Right to Compete," 6–10, 20–32; *New Orleans Louisiana Weekly,* March 19, 1966; Students for Social Action, mimeographed flyer, n.d., Edgar F. Shannon Presidential Papers, Manuscripts Department.

56. Paul Saunier Jr. to Steve Sabo, March 16, 1966; memo to Edgar F. Shannon, June 25, 1967, Shannon Papers; *University of Virginia Football Media Guide* (1970, 1971, 1972, 1973); Lucas, "Right to Compete," 12.

Chapter 6. "Two at Home and Three on the Road"

1. *New York Times,* March 24, 1974, sec. 5, p. 1; *Raleigh News and Observer,* March 13–25, 1957; "Tobacco Road Rebels," *Time,* January 7, 1957, 54; Neil D. Isaacs, *All the Moves: A History of College Basketball,* rev. ed. (New York: Harper and Row, 1984), 229–34; Robert Stern, *They Were Number One: A History of the NCAA Basketball Tournament,* rev. ed. (New York: Harper and Row, 1984), 119–23, 127–30; Nelson George, *Elevating the Game: Black Men and Basketball* (New York: Harper Collins, 1992), 114.

2. Stern, *They Were Number One,* 352–55; Bill Beezley, *The Wolfpack: Intercollegiate Athletics at North Carolina State University* (Raleigh: North Carolina State University, 1976), 318–22.

3. The ACC sent the winner of its postseason tournament, not the regular season champion, to the NCAA playoffs. Pamela Grundy, *Learning to Win: Sports, Education, and Social Change in Twentieth-Century North Carolina* (Chapel Hill: University of North Carolina Press, 2001), 190–96; *Atlantic Coast Conference Basketball Media Guide* (1988–89).

4. Marvin "Skeeter" Francis, telephone interview by author, September 20, 1994.

5. Beezley, *Wolfpack,* 167–68, 248–56; Grundy, *Learning to Win,* 197.

6. Bruce Corrie, *The Atlantic Coast Conference, 1953–1978* (Durham: Carolina Academic Press, 1978), 30; Ron Morris, *ACC Basketball: An Illustrated History* (Chapel Hill: Four Corners Press, 1988), 60; Beezley, *Wolfpack,* 328–29; Barry Jacobs, *Across the Line: Profiles in Basketball Courage—Tales of the First Black Players in the ACC and the SEC* (Guilford, Conn.: Lyons Press, 2008), 208; Francis interview.

7. In addition to concerns over segregated housing, tournament organizers also worried about how the young white women presiding over tournament social festivities and the presentation of individual and team awards would interact with black players. Grundy, *Learning to Win,* 289; Beezley, *Wolfpack,* 328–29; *Raleigh News and Observer,* December 29–31, 1958, January 1, 1959; Beezley, *Wolfpack,* 290.

8. Morris, *ACC Basketball,* 54, 58–62; *Raleigh News and Observer,* December 30, 1958; *Cincinnati Enquirer,* December 30, 1958; *Pittsburgh Courier,* January 17, 1959; Randy Roberts, telephone interview by author, November 2, 1998; Francis interview; Oscar Robertson, *The Big O: My Life, My Times, My Game* (n.p.: Rodale, 2003), 98–101.

9. Francis interview; Beezley, *Wolfpack,* 328–29; Corrie, *Atlantic Coast Conference,* 73–77; Grundy, *Learning to Win,* 205, 214–16.

10. *New York Times,* March 13, 1958, 36.

11. Billy Jones, telephone interview by author, October 5, 1994; *Washington Post,* January 28, 1964; *Baltimore Sun,* February 23, 1964; *Washington Star,* April 7, May 13,

1964; Morris, *ACC Basketball,* 99, 108; University of Maryland *Diamondback,* October 22, 1964; *University of Maryland Basketball Media Guide* (1993).

12. Jones interview; Morris, *ACC Basketball,* 98–99.

13. Jacobs, *Across the Line,* 1–21; Morris, *ACC Basketball,* 98–99; Jones interview; *University of Maryland Basketball Media Guide* (1967, 1968, 1969, 1970).

14. Morris, ACC Basketball, 98–99; Stern, *They Were Number One,* 325–26; *University of Maryland Basketball Media Guide* (1969, 1970, 1973, 1993).

15. *Duke University Basketball Media Guide* (1993–94); Frank Deford, "Lost Weekend in Carolina," *Sports Illustrated,* December 20, 1965, 32; Douglas M. Knight to Gerald C. Lutton, January 5, 1966; E. M. Cameron to Lutton, January 7, 1966; Knight to D. C. Tosteson, January 12, 1966; Herman Hill to Dick Friendlich, April 9, 1966, Douglas M. Knight Papers, University Archives, Perkins Library, Duke University.

16. Jacobs, *Across the Line,* 55–74; Duke University *Chronicle,* April 23, 1965; *Duke University Basketball Media Guide* (1967, 1968, 1969); Claudius B. Claiborne, telephone interview by author, September 14, 1999.

17. Claiborne participated in the student takeover of the administration building and thus missed a road game, but Vic Bubas permitted him to remain on the basketball team. Yannella, "Race Relations at Duke University," 8–18; Duke University *Chronicle,* October 16, 19, 22, 24, November 1, 1968, February 13, 1989; Claiborne interview; Jacobs, *Across the Line,* 65, 70–71; Larry Watson to Vann V. Secrest, October 21, 1968; Secrest to Douglas M. Knight, October 31, 1968; John Altrocchi to Jim Henry, November 4, 1968, in Knight Papers.

18. *Duke University Basketball Media Guide* (1970, 1971, 1972, 1973, 1974, 1975, 1994).

19. *Wake Forest University Basketball Media Guide* (1993, 1994); Don Payne to Harold W. Tribble, January 18, 1962, Tribble Papers; Francis interview.

20. Billy Packer, with Roland Lazenby, *Hoops! Confessions of a College Basketball Analyst* (Chicago: Contemporary Books, 1985), 52–55; *Wake Forest University Basketball Media Guide* (1968, 1969); Charles Davis, interview by author, Winston-Salem, N.C., July 21, 1993.

21. *Wake Forest University Basketball Media Guide* (1969, 1970, 1971); Morris, *ACC Basketball,* 157.

22. Davis interview; Wake Forest University *Old Black and Gold,* October 22, November 19, 26, 1968; Jacobs, *Across the Line,* 161–64.

23. Davis interview; Jacobs, *Across the Line,* 147, 157–59.

24. *New York Times,* October 12, 1994, A16, B10; Stern, *They Were Number One,* 119–23, 127–30; *ACC Basketball Media Guide* (1993); Morris, *ACC Basketball,* 122–23; *ACC Basketball Media Guide* (1993).

25. One nonscholarship black student, William Cooper, played on the 1965 UNC freshman team, but he quit basketball to concentrate on earning his degree. Morris, *ACC Basketball,* 108, 120–21; Packer, *Hoops!* 53; Dean Smith, with John Kilgo and Sally Jenkins, *A Coach's Life* (New York: Random House, 1999), 172–77; *Chapel Hill Weekly,* May 4, 1966; Ronald Hyatt, interview by author, Chapel Hill, N.C., July 15, 1993; *North*

Carolina Anvil, January 20, 1968, clipping file, North Carolina Collection, University of North Carolina.

26. Curry Kirkpatrick, "One More War to Go," *Sports Illustrated,* March 2, 1970, 12–15; *University of North Carolina Basketball Blue Book* (1968–69, 1969–70, 1970–71); *ACC Basketball Media Guide* (1992–93); Morris, *ACC Basketball,* 109; Jack Williams, "Charlie Scott," February 1970, copy in possession of author; University of South Carolina *Gamecock,* April 15, 25, 1969; Thad Mumau, *Dean Smith: A Biography* (Winston-Salem, N.C.: John F. Blair, 1990), 67; Smith, *A Coach's Life,* 201–4.

27. *University of North Carolina Basketball Media Guide* (1970–71, 1971–72); *ACC Basketball Media Guide* (1992–93).

28. For an evaluation of Scott's career at North Carolina, see Gregory J. Kaliss, "Uncivil Discourse: Charlie Scott, the Integration of College Basketball, and the 'Progressive Mystique,'" *Journal of Sport History* 35 (Spring 2008): 98–117; Duke University *Chronicle,* November 1, 1968; *New York Times,* March 22, 1969, 20; *North Carolina Anvil,* January 20, 1968, North Carolina Collection; Williams, "Charlie Scott"; Morris, *ACC Basketball,* 121.

29. Beezley, *Wolfpack,* 239–98; *ACC Basketball Media Guide* (1992–93), 42, 53; Corrie, *Atlantic Coast Conference,* 119; Stern, *They Were Number One,* 123; Holmes interview.

30. Norman Sloan, with Larry Guest, *Confessions of a Coach* (Nashville: Rutledge Hill, 1991), 122–24; Alfred Heartley, telephone interview by author, July 25, 1998; Beezley, *Wolfpack,* 301–2; University of Maryland *Diamondback,* April 24, 1967.

31. Heartley interview; *North Carolina State University Basketball Media Guide* (1968, 1969, 1970, 1971, 1993); North Carolina State University *Technician,* February 18, 1970; Jacobs, *Across the Line,* 205–16; Beezley, *Wolfpack,* 302–5; Sloan, *Confessions of a Coach,* 87, 123.

32. North Carolina State University *Technician,* February 6, April 17, 1970; Sloan, *Confessions of a Coach,* 23–25, 87–88; Corrie, *Atlantic Coast Conference,* 118–19; "Black Athletes Make Impact," unidentified clipping, 1973, in possession of author.

33. Sloan, *Confessions of a Coach,* 24–26, 124–25; *North Carolina State University Basketball Media Guide* (1973, 1974); Beezley, *Wolfpack,* 306–20; Stern, *They Were Number One,* 337–38.

34. Beezley, *Wolfpack,* 306–10; *ACC Basketball Media Guide* (1992–93); Stern, *They Were Number One,* 337–41, 366–67.

35. Sloan, *Confessions of a Coach,* 137; Heartley interview; Francis interview; Alice E. Reagan, *North Carolina State University: A Narrative History* (Ann Arbor: Edwards Brothers, 1987), 224.

36. On the contested use of the Confederate flag, see John M. Coski, *The Confederate Battle Flag: America's Most Embattled Emblem* (Cambridge: Harvard University Press, 2005); Donald M. McKale, ed., *Tradition: A History of the Presidency of Clemson University* (Macon: Mercer University Press, 1988), 207; and Clemson University *Tiger,* February 16, 1968, February 14, 1969, February 18, 1977.

37. *Greenville News,* October 28, 1969; Clemson University *Tiger,* October 24, November 7, 14, 1969, February 18, 1977.

38. In soccer Coach Ibrahim I. Ibrahim had started recruiting foreign players of various racial and ethnic backgrounds in 1967. Clemson University *Tiger,* July 25, 1969; *Greenville News,* December 31, 1969; *Clemson University Basketball Media Guide* (1969–70, 1970–71, 1971–72, 1972–73, 1973–74); Tates Locke and Bob Ibach, *Caught in the Net* (West Point, N.Y.: Leisure Press, 1982), 32–33, 40–68; Morris, *ACC Basketball,* 184–85.

39. Locke and Ibach, *Caught in the Net,* 41–47, 56–72, 102–3; McKale, *Tradition,* 208–9; Corrie, *Atlantic Coast Conference,* 132.

40. *New York Times,* October 12, 1994, A16, B10; Morris, *ACC Basketball,* 122–23; *ACC Basketball Media Guide* (1992–93).

41. Corrie, *Atlantic Coast Conference,* 85–88.

42. University of South Carolina *Gamecock,* May 3, November 22, 1968, February 11, 14, 18, 28, 1969.

43. Ibid., February 14, 18, 1969.

44. Ibid., March 7, 11, April 15, 25, October 1, 17, November 24, 1969, February 9, 11, 13, 16, 1970, February 7, 9, 11, 18, 1972.

45. *University of South Carolina Basketball Media Guide* (1969–70, 1970–71); *ACC Basketball Media Guide* (1993); University of South Carolina *Gamecock,* April 15, 1969.

46. *ACC Basketball Media Guide* (1993); *University of South Carolina Basketball Media Guide* (1995).

47. *University of Virginia Basketball Media Guide* (1992–93); Kenny Lucas, "The Right to Compete: George King III, the First African American Athlete at the University of Virginia" (unpublished student paper, University of Virginia, December 6, 1994, 6–12); *New Orleans Louisiana Weekly,* March 19, 1966.

48. *University of Virginia Basketball Media Guide* (1970–71, 1971–72, 1972–73, 1973–74, 1992–93); Morris, *ACC Basketball,* 94–95; Rich Murray to author, January 4, 1995.

49. *University of Virginia Basketball Media Guide* (1992–93); *ACC Basketball Media Guide* (1992–93).

Chapter 7. The Eyes of Texas Are (Not) upon You

1. *Fort Worth Star-Telegram,* November 25–27, 30, 1966; Richard Pennington, *Breaking the Ice: The Racial Integration of Southwest Conference Football* (Jefferson, N.C.: McFarland, 1987), 95–97; *El Paso Times,* November 27, 1966; Willis M. Tate, *Views and Interviews,* edited by Johnnie Marie Grimes (Dallas: Southern Methodist Press, 1978), 167; Jerry LeVias, interview by Daniel U. Sanchez, April 17, 2006, Southwest Collection, Texas Tech University; *Jerry LeVias: A Marked Man,* Fox Sports Net Documentary (2003).

2. *Southwest Conference Football Media Guide* (1994). On Texas high school football, see Ty Cashion, *Pigskin Pulpit: A Social History of Texas High School Football Coaches* (Austin: Texas State Historical Association, 1998); and H. G. Bissinger's classic best-seller, *Friday Night Lights: A Town, a Team, and a Dream* (New York: Addison Wesley, 1990).

3. *Aggies: A Century of Football Tradition* (New York: Professional Sports Publications, 1994), 10–16, 24–30; *Southwest Conference Football Media Guide* (1994), 5–6. The Southwest Conference was dissolved in 1996, after Texas, Texas A&M, Baylor, and Texas Tech defected to the Big 8 and formed the Big 12 Conference.

4. *Aggies,* 30–33, 46–47; *Southwest Conference Football Media Guide* (1994); Michael Oriard, *King Football: Sport and Spectacle in the Golden Age of Radio and Newsreels, Movies and Magazines, the Weekly and the Daily Press* (Chapel Hill: University of North Carolina Press, 2001), 93–100; Will Grimsley, *Football: The Greatest Moments in the Southwest Conference* (Boston: Little, Brown, 1968), 4–7.

5. *Aggies,* 14; *El Paso Herald-Post,* June 18, 1936; *Pittsburgh Courier,* July 31, 1937.

6. Playing Time Sheets, 1953, 1954, Sports Information Office, University of Notre Dame; *Notre Dame Football Media Guide* (1994), 223.

7. Charles K. Ross, *Outside the Lines: African Americans and the Integration of the National Football League* (New York: New York University Press, 1999), 128–30.

8. In 1956 Cornelius Roberts, a halfback for the University of Southern California, became the second black player to compete against UT in Memorial Stadium. When an Austin hotel refused to allow Roberts to stay with the rest of the USC team, Coach Jess Hill moved the entire squad to another facility. University of Texas *Daily Texan,* October 3, 1954; Pennington, *Breaking the Ice,* 115–16; Tim Tessalone to author, June 10, 1994.

9. On the integration of state-supported junior and senior colleges in Texas, see Amilcar Shabazz's outstanding study, *Advancing Democracy: African Americans and the Struggle for Access and Equity in Higher Education in Texas* (Chapel Hill: University of North Carolina Press, 2004).

10. *New York Times,* March 12, 1960, 10; October 27, 1961, 65; December 31, 1961, 51; University of Texas *Daily Texan,* July 28, August 1, October 26, 1961, February 1, October 17, November 20, 1963; Pennington, *Breaking the Ice,* 9.

11. Remarkably, the UT Regents nonetheless continued to permit some segregation in campus housing and dining halls until May 1964. University of Texas *Daily Texan,* November 3, 10, 19, 20, 24, 1963, May 17, 1964; *Dallas Morning News,* November 13, 1963; *New York Times,* November 10, 1963, 77; December 8, 1963, 14; Minutes, Board of Regents, University of Texas, November 9, 1963.

12. *Dallas Morning News,* November 13, 1963; *Houston Informer,* May 23, July 11, 1964; February 5, 26, July 2, 23, September 10, 1966; *Dallas Express,* July 22, 1967; Pennington, *Breaking the Ice,* 9–10.

13. A. S. "Doc" Young, *Negro Firsts in Sports* (Chicago: Johnson Publishing, 1963), 253; *Houston Informer,* October 15, November 12, 1966, April 1, September 30, 1967, August 17, 31, December 28, 1968, January 4, June 14, 1969; *Dallas Express,* September 30, December 30, 1967; Pennington, *Breaking the Ice,* 11–12.

14. The PVIL disbanded in 1970. *Houston Informer,* October 15, 1966, March 2, 16, April 15, May 18, 1968, March 15, 1969; *New York Times,* May 18, 1964, 24; University of Texas *Daily Texan,* April 21, May 11, 1965; *Dallas Express,* January 7, 28, August 19, December 30, 1967, January 6, 1968.

15. James Cash, telephone interview by author, November 7, 1988; Pennington, *Breaking the Ice,* 37–39, 84–85; *New York Times,* May 23, 1965, sec. 5, p. 5; *This Is T.C.U.* (Winter 1976): 24; *TCU Basketball Media Guide* (1966, 1969); *Fort Worth Star-Telegram,* n.d., Special Collections, Main Library, Texas Christian University.

16. Mary Martha Thomas, "Southern Methodist University: The First Twenty-five Years, 1915–1940" (Ph.D. diss., Emory University, 1971), 324–29; Temple Pouncey, *Mustang Mania: SMU Football* (Huntsville, Ala.: Strode Publishers, 1981), 9, 76–81, 91–97, 122–23, 189, 195; *Pittsburgh Courier,* December 4, 1937, October 29, 1938; Southern Methodist University *Daily Campus,* November 17, 1937, October 14, 1970, February 10, 1994.

17. Southern Methodist University *Daily Campus,* January 5, March 2, 1962; Pennington, *Breaking the Ice,* 78–79; Hayden Fry, with George Wine, *Hayden Fry: A High Porch Picnic* (Champaign: Sports Publishing, n.d.), 67–70.

18. Pennington, *Breaking the Ice,* 80–86; *Dallas Times Herald,* August 4, 1985; Temple Pouncey, "A Pioneer in the SWC," in SMU football program, September 29, 1990; unidentified clipping, May 29, 1965, Jerry LeVias File, Office of Sports Information, Southern Methodist University; LeVias interview, Southwest Collection, Texas Tech University; *Dallas Morning News,* February 5, 2007; Fry, *Hayden Fry,* 69–71.

19. *Dallas Times Herald,* August 4, 1985; Pennington, *Breaking the Ice,* 85–97; Pouncey, *Mustang Mania: SMU Football,* 203–11; *Southern Methodist University Football Media Guide* (1993); *Southwest Conference Football Media Guide* (1994).

20. An examination of the minutes of the regularly scheduled Southwest Conference administrative meetings during the mid-1960s did not turn up even one agenda discussion about possible problems or consequences of the SWC's racial integration. *Dallas Times Herald,* August 4, 1985; Pennington, *Breaking the Ice,* 88–97; Pouncey, "Pioneer in the SWC," 64; *Fort Worth Star-Telegram,* November 21, 25, 1966; *Dallas Morning News,* February 5, 1997; Southwest Conference Files, Southwest Collection, Texas Tech University.

21. More than thirty years later, Hayden Fry told a Sun Bowl luncheon crowd, "The thing I'm proudest of in my 47 years of coaching is recruiting Jerry LeVias to SMU." Pennington, *Breaking the Ice,* 101–11; Pouncey, "Pioneer in the SWC," 64; *El Paso Times,* December 31, 1999; *Houston Chronicle,* December 22, 2008; Fry, *Hayden Fry,* 80–81.

22. *Southern Methodist Football Media Guide* (1967, 1968, 1969); unidentified clipping, 1966, LeVias File; *Dallas Times Herald,* August 4, 1985; Dr. Willis Tate, interview by Gerald McGee, October 12, 1973, DeGolyer Library, Southern Methodist University; Southern Methodist University *Daily Campus,* April 29, May 2, 6, September 10–12, 1969.

23. Eugene W. Baker, *To Light the Ways of Time: An Illustrated History of Baylor University, 1845–1986* (Waco: Baylor University, 1987), 105–6; *Southwest Conference Football Media Guide* (1994); University of Texas *Daily Texan,* April 6, 1962, November 3, 24, 1963. On racial violence in Waco, see Patricia Bernstein, *The First Waco Horror: The Lynching of Jesse Washington and the Rise of the NAACP* (College Station: Texas A&M University Press, 2005).

24. Pennington, *Breaking the Ice,* 50–55; Oral Memoirs of John Westbrook, Institute of Oral History, Baylor University, Waco, Tex., 46–50.

25. Pennington, *Breaking the Ice,* 56–63; Oral Memoirs of Westbrook, 43, 55–59, 90, 102; *Houston Informer,* April 16, 1966.

26. At the Syracuse game a teammate blurted out to Westbrook that he had told several Syracuse players that "our nigger's gonna be better than their nigger [star halfback Floyd Little] today." Pennington, *Breaking the Ice,* 63–71; Oral Memoirs of Westbrook, 89–90.

27. Pennington, *Breaking the Ice,* 71–75; Oral Memoirs of Westbrook, 84–86, 101–5, 112–13.

28. Tommy Reaux, telephone interview by author, August 8, 2000; *Baylor Roundup, 1966, 1967, 1968, 1969, 1970* (yearbook); Pennington, *Breaking the Ice,* 74.

29. *Texas Christian University Football Media Guide* (1993).

30. Texas Christian University *Skiff,* November 2, 1951, September 19, 26, October 3, 1952, February 19, 1954, March 10, May 23, 1961, March 20, April 20, 1962; Jerome A. Moore, *Texas Christian University: A Hundred Years of History* (Fort Worth: Texas Christian University Press, 1973), 225.

31. Moore, *Texas Christian University,* 225; Texas Christian University *Skiff,* September 18, 25, 1962, December 6, 1963, February 4, 1964; Memorandum by J. M. Moudy, June 7, 1963, Moudy Papers, Special Collections, Main Library, Texas Christian University.

32. *Texas Christian University Football Media Guide* (1968, 1969, 1970, 1993); *Fort Worth Star-Telegram,* May 9, 1993.

33. *Texas Christian University Football Media Guide* (1970, 1971, 1972, 1973, 1993); Charles M. Tolbert II, "The Black Athlete in the Southwest Conference: A Study of Institutional Racism" (master's thesis, Baylor University, 1975), 38–40; Pennington, *Breaking the Ice,* 138; Texas Christian University *Skiff,* October 20, 1970, February 9, May 7, September 8, 1971.

34. Ralph L. Sellmeyer and James E. Davidson, *The Red Raiders: Texas Tech Football* (Huntsville, Ala.: Strode Publishers, 1978), 11–14, 46–54, 85, 124–29; Elmer Tarbox, interview by David Murrah, August 3, 1973; *Arizona Daily Star,* May 14, 1939; *Lubbock Daily Times,* May 21, 1939; miscellaneous clippings, all in Southwest Collection, Texas Tech University; *New York Times,* December 14, 1952, sec. 5, p. 2; December 8, 1963, 14; *Pittsburgh Courier,* February 16, December 20, 1952; Shabazz, *Advancing Democracy,* 205–6; Texas Tech *Daily Toreador,* December 9, 11, 1952, December 10, 1963.

35. Pennington, *Breaking the Ice,* 138–41; *La Ventana, 1968, 1969, 1970, 1971* (yearbook).

36. Kerri D. Gantz, "On the Basis of Merit Alone: Integration, Tuition, Rice University, and the Charter Change Trial, 1963–1966" (master's thesis, Rice University, 1991), 2–4, 6, 35–113; Fredericka Meiners, *A History of Rice University: The Institute Years, 1907–1963* (Houston: Rice University, 1982), 198–201; Melissa Kean, *Desegregating Private Higher Education in the South: Duke, Emory, Rice, Tulane, and Vanderbilt* (Baton Rouge: Louisiana State University Press, 2008), 169–75, 220–33.

37. *Rice University Football Media Guide* (1969, 1970, 1971, 1972); Pennington, *Breaking the Ice,* 143–45.

38. Denne H. Freeman, *Hook 'Em Horns: A Story of Texas Football* (Huntsville, Ala.: Strode Publishers, 1974), 13, 19, 40, 46–59, 156–59; *Southwest Conference Football Media Guide* (1994); Reaux interview.

39. Joe B. Frantz, *The Forty-Acre Follies* (Austin: Texas Monthly Press, 1983), 199, 206–8; Richard B. McCaslin, "Steadfast in His Intent: John W. Hargis and the Integration of the University of Texas at Austin," *Southwestern Historical Quarterly* 95 (July 1991): 20–35; Shabazz, *Advancing Democracy,* 115–17, 156–59; University of Texas *Daily Texan,* August 24, September 15, 1954, July 12, 1955; *Houston Post,* August 22, 1954; *Austin Statesman,* June 10, 1963; Minutes, University of Texas Board of Regents, July 8, 1955. See also Michael L. Gillette, "Blacks Challenge the White University," *Southwestern Historical Quarterly* 86 (1982): 321–44; and Dwonna Goldstone, *Integrating the 40 Acres: The 50-Year Struggle for Racial Equality at the University of Texas* (Athens: University of Georgia Press, 2006), esp. 36–89.

40. University of Texas *Daily Texan,* May 16, 1958, December 4, 7, 1960, April 11, May 12, July 28, August 1, October 1, 26, 27, 1961; *New York Times,* March 12, 1960, 10; October 27, 1961, 65; Minutes, University of Texas Board of Regents, July 22, September 29, 1961; Goldstone, *Integrating the 40 Acres,* 120–26. On the UT civil rights movement, see Martin Kuhlman, "Direct Action at the University of Texas during the Civil Rights Movement, 1960–1965," *Southwestern Historical Quarterly* 98 (April 1995): 550–66.

41. University of Texas *Daily Texan,* April 10, November 10, 19, 1963, January 29, March 20, May 17, September 15, 1964; Minutes, University of Texas Board of Regents, November 9, 1963.

42. *Dallas Morning News,* November 13, 1963; University of Texas *Daily Texan,* December 4, 1963, February 7, May 12, 14, October 8, 22, 1967; Pennington, *Breaking the Ice,* 120–21; Goldstone, *Integrating the 40 Acres,* 112–27.

43. University of Texas *Daily Texan,* February 15, 1968; Pennington, *Breaking the Ice,* 124–30; *Houston Informer,* October 1, 1966, April 1, 1967, March 2, 1968; Freeman, *Hook 'Em Horns,* 156–59; Jimmy Banks, *The Darrell Royal Story* (Austin: Shoal Creek Publishers, 1973), 89–90; Ken Rappoport, *The Syracuse Football Story* (Huntsville, Ala.: Strode Publishers, 1975), 212–18; Dan Jenkins, "You've Got to Have Some 'O,'" *Sports Illustrated,* October 16, 1967, 41; *Dallas Express,* November 4, 1967.

44. Banks, *The Darrell Royal Story,* 154–63; Pennington, *Breaking the Ice,* 119, 129–35; Goldstone, *Integrating the 40 Acres,* 129–33; *Austin American,* November 14–17, 19, 1972; Reaux interview; Freeman, *Hook 'Em Horns,* 156–59; Jan Reid, "Coach Royal Regrets," *Texas Monthly* 10 (December 1982): 250–52.

45. Pennington, *Breaking the Ice,* 127–30; Almetris Marsh Duren and Louise Iscoe, *Overcoming: A History of Black Integration at the University of Texas at Austin* (Austin: University of Texas, 1979), 28.

46. Pennington, *Breaking the Ice,* 130–33; Freeman, *Hook 'Em Horns,* 162–63; Tolbert, "Black Athlete in the Southwest Conference," 40.

47. Tim Layden, "High Stakes Gambler," *Sports Illustrated,* August 25, 1997, 85–88; Ivan Maisel, "Urban Cowboys," *Sports Illustrated,* February 18, 2002, 78–79.

48. *Aggies,* 7–16, 36–37, 52–53; University of Texas *Daily Texan,* June 4, 1963; *New York Times,* November 29, 1963, 52; Shabazz, *Advancing Democracy,* 208–9.

49. Alexander Wolff, "Ground Breakers," *Sports Illustrated,* November 7, 2005, 60; *Houston Informer,* April 1, 1967; Texas A&M University *Aggieland,* 1968, 1969, 1971, 1972, 1973, 1974 (yearbook); Pennington, *Breaking the Ice,* 137.

50. Guerdon D. Nichols, "Breaking the Color Barrier at the University of Arkansas," *Arkansas Historical Quarterly* 27 (1968): 3–21; *New York Daily Worker,* August 25, 1948.

51. *New York Times,* May 18, 1964, 1; *Dallas Morning News,* November 13, 1963; University of Texas *Daily Texan,* October 27, 1961, May 7, 1965; Steve Narisi, e-mail to author, August 19, 2001.

52. Frank Broyles, with Jim Bailey, *Wild Hog: The Autobiography of Frank Broyles* (Memphis: Memphis State University Press, 1979), 108–9, 179–80; Pennington, *Breaking the Ice,* 145–46; Richard Pennington, "The Racial Integration of College Football in Texas," in *Invisible Texans: Women and Minorities in Texas History,* edited by Donald Willett and Stephen Curley (Boston: McGraw-Hill, 2005), 220–25.

Chapter 8. From Exclusion to Prominence

1. Dean W. Colvard, *Mixed Emotions: As Racial Barriers Fell—a University President Remembers* (Danville, Ill.: Interstate Printers & Publishers, 1985), 64–66.

2. The most important articles on the 1963 controversy are Russell J. Henderson, "The 1963 Mississippi State University Basketball Controversy and the Repeal of the Unwritten Law: 'Something More than the Game Will Be Lost,'" *Journal of Southern History* 63 (November 1997): 827–54; Alexander Wolff, "Ghosts of Mississippi," *Sports Illustrated,* March 10, 2003, 61–71; Paul Attner, "The Defiant Ones," in *The Sporting News 1995–96 College Basketball Yearbook* (St. Louis: Sporting News, 1995), 30–35; Bill Finger, "Just Another Ball Game," *Southern Exposure* 7 (Fall 1979): 74–81. On Loyola's championship season, see Ron Fimrite, "It Was More than Just a Game," *Sports Illustrated,* November 18, 1987, 106–15.

3. *Southern Conference Basketball Media Guide* (1994–95); *Southeastern Conference Basketball Media Guide* (1990–91), 17–18; *Vanderbilt University Basketball Media Guide* (1993–94); Christopher J. Walsh, *Where Football Is King: A History of the SEC* (Lanham, Md.: Taylor Trade Publishing, 2006), 9–18.

4. *Southeastern Conference Basketball Media Guide* (1990–91), 179–80; Bert Nelli and Steve Nelli, *The Winning Tradition: A History of University of Kentucky Basketball,* 2nd ed. (Lexington: University Press of Kentucky, 1998), 59–76, 254–56.

5. *New Orleans Times-Picayune,* March 6, 1960.

6. *Dallas Express,* June 17, 1967; Charles Morgan Jr. to Harold Howe II, May 12, 1966, copy in possession of author; *New York Times,* May 15, 1966, 63; Charles F. Simmons to Willard F. Gray, August 15, 1969, Harry M. Philpott Papers, University Archives, Ralph B. Draughon Library, Auburn University; *Atlanta Constitution,* February 15, 1968; *Atlanta Journal,* February 15, 1968; Rix N. Yard to Herbert E. Longenecker, April 4, 1967, Herbert E. Longenecker Papers, Howard-Tilton Memorial Library, Tulane University.

7. University of Georgia *Red and Black,* November 12, 1968, March 27, 1969; *Birmingham Post-Herald,* July 23, 1969; University of Mississippi *Daily Mississippian,* March 27, 1969; Louisiana State University *Daily Reveille,* January 21, 1972; Patrick B. Miller, "Muscular Assimilationism: Sport and the Paradoxes of Racial Reform," in *Race and Sports: The Struggle for Equality On and Off the Field,* edited by Charles K. Ross (Jackson: University Press of Mississippi, 2004), 146–58.

8. Harry M. Philpott Oral History Transcripts, University Archives, Ralph B. Draughon Library, Auburn University, Auburn, Ala., 328; Bernie Moore to Earl M. Ramer, June 19, 1963, Andrew D. Holt Presidential Papers, University Archives, Hoskins Library, University of Tennessee, Knoxville; Barry Jacobs, *Across the Line: Profiles in Basketball Courage; Tales of the First Black Players in the ACC and the SEC* (Guilford, Conn.: Lyons Press, 2008), 256.

9. Bernie Moore to Earl M. Ramer, Holt Presidential Papers; Wilford S. Bailey, interview by author, Auburn, Ala., July 28, 1990; Alexander Heard, telephone interview by author, October 5, 1990; Minutes of [Tulane] Athletic Advisory Committee Meeting, June 4, 1963, Longenecker Papers; Minutes of Annual Meeting, January 26, 1968, Osward Papers; Philpott Oral History Transcripts, 327–28.

10. *New York Times,* March 9, 1966, 32.

11. Bailey interview; *Nashville Tennessean,* April 4, 1989.

12. Paul K. Conkin, *Gone with the Ivy: A Biography of Vanderbilt University* (Knoxville: University of Tennessee Press, 1985), 80–81, 136–41, 214–17, 307–11, 430–31, 540–80, 641; Melissa Kean, *Desegregating Private Higher Education in the South: Duke, Emory, Rice, Tulane, and Vanderbilt* (Baton Rouge: Louisiana State University Press, 2008), 70–76, 99–104, 160–65, 207–9; Vanderbilt University *Hustler,* November 2, 1962; Minutes, Board of Trust, November 13–14, 1964, University Archives, Jean and Alexander Heard Library, Vanderbilt University.

13. *Vanderbilt University Basketball Media Guide* (1993–94); *Southeastern Conference Basketball Media Guide* (1990–91).

14. *Lexington Herald,* December 20, 1965; *Chicago Defender,* May 7, 1966; *New Orleans Louisiana Weekly,* May 14, 1966; Conkin, *Gone with the Ivy,* 641; Roy Skinner, interview by author, Nashville, Tenn., August 17, 1989.

15. Vanderbilt University *Hustler,* December 2, 1966, April 21, 1967, September 24, 1968; Alexander Heard to Rob Roy Purdy, August 19, 1966, Chancellor's Records, Alexander Heard Papers, Heard Library; *Atlanta Constitution,* January 12, 1988; Roy M. Neel, *Dynamite! 75 Years of Vanderbilt Basketball* (Nashville: Burr-Oak Publishers, 1975), 169–70; Jacobs, *Across the Line,* 42–45.

16. Vanderbilt University *Hustler,* May 7, 17, September 20, November 26, 1968, March 21, 1969, March 18, 2005; *Atlanta Constitution,* January 12, 1988; Neel, *Dynamite!* 170; Jacobs, *Across the Line,* 23–24, 46; Skinner interview.

17. Vanderbilt University *Hustler,* March 9, 18, 1970; *Santa Monica Outlook,* February 12, 1970; *Vanderbilt University Basketball Media Guide* (1993–94).

18. *Nashville Tennessean,* March 9, 1970; Vanderbilt University *Hustler,* March 18, 1970; Jacobs, *Across the Line,* 24–26, 42, 47–48.

19. Vanderbilt University *Hustler,* January 9, November 6, December 11, 1970, February 2, 5, 9, 1971.

20. Malcolm McMillan and Allen Jones, *Through the Years: Auburn from 1856* (Auburn, Ala.: Auburn University, 1977), 1–3, 7–9, 29.

21. Franklin completed all of his course work for the M.A. degree but left the university after the initial draft of his master's thesis was rejected by his adviser. Auburn

University *Plainsman,* September 25, 1964, February 26, 1981; unidentified clipping, Harold Franklin File, University Archives, Auburn University; Minutes of Informal Board Meeting, July 17, 1963, Joseph B. Sarver Collection, University Archives, Ralph B. Draughon Library, Auburn University; Allen Barra, *The Last Coach: A Life of Paul "Bear" Bryant* (New York: W. W. Norton, 2005), 379.

22. *Auburn University Basketball Media Guide* (2004), 188–95; Harry M. Philpott Oral History Transcripts, University Archives, Draughon Library, Auburn University, 244, 326; Auburn University *Plainsman,* May 16, 1968; *Anniston Star,* December 24, 1991.

23. Philpott Oral History Transcripts, 28–29, 243–45, 325–26; George Kennedy to Harry M. Philpott, March 15, 1968; Bettie M. King to Philpott, March 20, 1968; Charles F. Simmons to Willard F. Gray, August 15, 1969, Philpott Papers; Auburn University *Plainsman,* March 28, 1968; Bailey interview.

24. Auburn University *Plainsman,* January 30, 1969; James Owens, telephone interview by author, August 3, 2005; *Auburn University Basketball Media Guide* (1972, 1973, 1974, 1975, 1976, 2004).

25. E. Culpepper Clark, *The Schoolhouse Door: Segregation's Last Stand at the University of Alabama* (New York: Oxford University Press, 1993), 40–113, 213–37.

26. Years later some sports fans would incorrectly claim that Alabama had boycotted the 1956 tournament in order to avoid playing integrated teams, but the issue of freshman eligibility, not race, kept the Tide cagers at home. University of Alabama *Crimson White,* February 21, 28, March 6, 13, 1956; Nelli and Nelli, *Winning Tradition,* 75; C. M. Newton, interview by author, Lexington, Ky., August 7, 1989; unidentified clipping, March 2, 1969, Basketball File, Media Relations Department, University of Alabama.

27. *Tuscaloosa News,* April 26, 1969; *Birmingham News,* April 26, 27, 1969; University of Alabama *Crimson White,* March 17, 1970; Sherry Tatom, "A Man of Many Firsts," *'Bama,* February 1982, 24–25; Newton interview; Jacobs, *Across the Line,* 126–30, 141.

28. University of Alabama *Crimson White,* December 14, 1970, February 1, 25, March 11, 1971; *Birmingham Post-Herald,* n.d., 1970; *Tuscaloosa News,* April 16, 1971; Newton interview.

29. Holmes once expressed an interest in trying out for the football team, but an administrator warned him not to try. However, when the Bulldogs experienced a losing season that fall, one white fan crudely joked about the sturdy Holmes, "The more I look at that nigger, the whiter he gets." Thomas G. Dyer, *The University of Georgia: A Bicentennial History, 1785–1985* (Athens: University of Georgia Press, 1985), 165, 173, 185, 246, 285, 303–34; http://www.uga.edu/uga/history.html; Francis M. Wilhoit, *The Politics of Massive Resistance* (New York: George Braziller, 1973), 149, 191–92; Charlayne Hunter-Gault, *In My Place* (New York: Farrar, Straus, Giroux, 1992), 177–91, 237–38. See also Robert Cohen, "'Two, Four, Six, Eight, We Don't Want to Integrate': White Student Attitudes toward the University of Georgia's Desegregation," *Georgia Historical Quarterly* 80 (Fall 1996): 616–45. A recent study is Robert A. Pratt, *We Shall Not Be Moved: The Desegregation of the University of Georgia* (Athens: University of Georgia Press, 2005).

30. John Guthrie, interview by author, Birmingham, Ala., April 25, 1994; *Athens Daily News,* October 3, 1991.

31. *Athens Daily News,* May 7, 1971; Guthrie interview; *University of Georgia Basketball Media Guide* (1973, 1976, 2005).

32. Charles Gano Talbert, *The University of Kentucky* (Lexington: University Press of Kentucky, 1965), 174; David C. Roller and Robert W. Twyman, eds., *The Encyclopedia of Southern History* (Baton Rouge: Louisiana State University Press, 1979), s.v. "Kentucky." On antiblack violence in Kentucky, see George C. Wright, *Racial Violence in Kentucky, 1865–1940* (Baton Rouge: Louisiana State University Press, 1990); and J. Michael Rhyne, "Rehearsal for Redemption: The Politics of Racial Violence in Civil War Era Kentucky," C. Ballard Breaux Public Conference, Filson Institute, Louisville, Ky., May 19, 2001, copy in possession of author.

33. In one highly unusual case, an undergraduate transfer student was able to gain entry to the engineering school under the 1949 court order. His enrollment did not otherwise affect UK's undergraduate admissions policy. Talbert, *The University of Kentucky,* 174–76; George C. Wright, *A History of Blacks in Kentucky: In Pursuit of Equality, 1890–1980* (n.p.: Kentucky Historical Society, 1992), 2:170–83; Peter Wallenstein, "Black Southerners and Non-black Universities: Desegregating Higher Education, 1935–1967," *History of Higher Education Annual* 19 (1999): 130; *Lexington Leader,* October 13, 1954; *Lexington Herald,* May 5, 1981; *Fifty Years of the University of Kentucky African-American Legacy, 1949–1999* (Lexington: University of Kentucky, 1999), 6, 47, 49.

34. *New York Times,* January 24, 1957, 30; Numan V. Bartley, *The New South, 1945–1980* (Baton Rouge: Louisiana State University Press, 1995), 163, 196; Steven A. Channing, *Kentucky: A Bicentennial History* (New York: W. W. Norton, 1977), 203–4; Wright, *History of Blacks in Kentucky,* 193–205.

35. Nelli and Nelli, *Winning Tradition,* 6–8, 14–30, 33–37, 65–73.

36. In another violation of racial etiquette during the 1948 game in Lexington, several white AAU players shared a water bottle with Barksdale during a time-out, shocking many of the white spectators. Ron Thomas, *They Cleared the Lane: The NBA's Black Pioneers* (Lincoln: University of Nebraska Press, 2002), 120–24; *New York Times,* May 20, 1994, B14; Nelli and Nelli, *Winning Tradition,* 50.

37. *New York Times,* December 18, 1951, 44; October 12, 1994, B10; Thomas, *They Cleared the Lane,* 116–24; University of Kentucky *Kentucky Kernel,* December 14, 1951; *Lexington Herald,* December 18, 1951; *New York Amsterdam News,* December 22, 1951; *New York Age,* August 18, 1951; Nelli and Nelli, *Winning Tradition,* 76.

38. University of Kentucky *Kentucky Kernel,* December 15, 1961, April 16, 18, 30, May 14, 17, July 5, 1963, April 7, 1964, September 5, October 3, 1967; *Lexington Herald,* May 30, 1963, December 20, 23, 1965; *New York Times,* April 13, 1963, 14; April 30, 1963, 40; May 30, 1963, 13; *Jacksonville Journal,* June 31, 1962; Minutes, Board of Directors Meeting, University of Kentucky Athletic Association, April 29, 1963, Frank G. Dickey Papers, King Library, University of Kentucky; Frank G. Dickey to author, September 4, 1990.

39. While at a high school in Illinois, Rupp did coach at least one African American player. *Louisville Courier Journal,* May 17, 1963; *Lexington Herald-Leader,* December 13, 1977, December 12, 2002; Nelli and Nelli, *Winning Tradition,* 76; *New York Times,* December 21, 1994, B9; Russell Rice, interview by author, Lexington, Ky., August 8,

1989; Robert L. Johnson to Bernie Shively, March 29, 1966, John W. Oswald Papers, King Library, University of Kentucky; Robert L. Johnson to author, December 16, 1998; Frank Fitzpatrick, *And the Walls Came Tumbling Down: Kentucky, Texas Western, and the Game That Changed American Sports* (New York: Simon and Schuster, 1999), 142–45; University of Kentucky *Kentucky Kernel*, April 29, 1966. For recent reviews of the debate over Rupp's racial views and recruiting policies, see University of Kentucky *Kentucky Kernel*, March 24, 2005; and "Adolph Rupp: Fact and Fiction," http://www.ukfans.net/jps/uk/rupp.html.

40. Nelli and Nelli, *Winning Tradition*, 85; Russell Rice, *The Wildcat Legacy: A Pictorial History of Kentucky Basketball* (Virginia Beach: JCP Corporation, 1982), 113; Adolph F. Rupp to B. A. Shively, July 14, 1967; Shively to John W. Oswald, July 14, 1967; Inter-Conference Letter of Intent, July 14, 1967, Oswald Papers; University of Kentucky *Kentucky Kernel*, September 7, October 24, December 5, 11, 1967.

41. Rice, *Wildcat Legacy*, 129–33; Rice interview; University of Kentucky *Kentucky Kernel*, June 19, 1969; Nelli and Nelli, *Winning Tradition*, 90; *Atlanta Constitution*, June 29, 1973; *El Paso Times*, November 14, 1986; Chuck Walse, e-mail to author, August 8, 2005; Jacobs, *Across the Line*, 178–79, 191–92. Following one season with the Atlanta Hawks, Payne spent almost all of the next three decades in prison, after being convicted of rape and sexual assault in Kentucky, Georgia, and California.

42. *Lexington Herald-Leader*, May 24, 1979, December 12, 2002; Nelli and Nelli, *Winning Tradition*, 111.

43. After Rupp's forced retirement, a new facility, Rupp Arena, was eventually constructed in 1976 with twenty-three thousand seats. *Lexington Herald-Leader*, December 12, 2002; Nelli and Nelli, *Winning Tradition*, 8, 111–21, 148, 152–53, 168–73, 202–6, 219–20, 240–46; *New York Times*, May 13, 1997, C23; November 18, 1997, C32. In 2007, Smith accepted the head coaching position at the University of Minnesota.

44. Tennessee's first African American graduate student, Gene Mitchell Gray, registered for classes in January 1952. James Riley Montgomery, Stanley J. Folmsbee, and Lee Seifert Green, *To Foster Knowledge: A History of the University of Tennessee, 1794–1970* (Knoxville: University of Tennessee Press, 1984), 75, 81, 88, 199, 228–30, 267–69; Minutes of Special Meeting, Board of Trustees, University of Tennessee, November 18, 1960, University Archives, University of Tennessee, Knoxville; University of Tennessee *Daily Beacon*, January 27, 1968.

45. *Lexington Herald*, December 24, 1946; *Knoxville Journal*, December 24, 1946; *Pittsburgh Courier*, January 4, 1947; *Knoxville News-Sentinel*, December 26, 1946; *Memphis Commercial Appeal*, February 1, 1956; University of Tennessee *Orange and White*, January 8, 1947.

46. *Knoxville News-Sentinel*, April 23, 1961; University of Tennessee *Orange and White*, April 28, 1961; University of Tennessee *Daily Beacon*, May 12, September 29, 30, October 8, 26, 27, November 4, 1965; Minutes, Board of Athletics Meeting, April 28, 1961, May 4, 1963, Samuel R. Tipton to Andrew D. Holt, April 25, 1961; Max H. Freeman to Holt, April 23, 1961; Freeman to Robert R. Neyland, April 23, 1961; Tom Elam to Holt, March 19, 1962; and other letters, A. D. Holt Presidential Papers, University Archives, University of Tennessee.

47. University of Tennessee *Daily Beacon,* February 10, March 29, 1966; *Knoxville News-Sentinel,* February 5, 1966; University of Tennessee *Context,* March 29, 1990, December 2, 1994; *Knoxville Journal,* February 5, 1966, May 22, 1989; *Nashville Tennessean,* September 14, 1967; Earl M. Ramer to Scholarship Committee, September 28, 1967, Earl M. Ramer Papers, University Archives, University of Tennessee.

48. Haywood was later responsible for a key federal court ruling in sports law, which struck down the NBA rule prohibiting teams from drafting college players until they had finished their college careers. *University of Tennessee Basketball Media Guide* (1969); *Knoxville Journal,* February 5, 1966; *Nashville News Sentinel,* February 5, 1966; University of Tennessee *Daily Beacon,* May 23, 1967; Arthur J. Bergstrom to Earl M. Ramer, March 25, 1967; George R. Woodruff to Ray Mears, July 6, 1967; Woodruff to A. M. Coleman, July 6, 1967; Coleman to Ramer, July 17, 1967; Coleman to Woodruff, September 11, 1967, Ramer Papers; Spencer Haywood, with Scott Ostler, *Spencer Haywood: The Rise, the Fall, the Recovery* (New York: Amistad, 1992), 94–97; http://www.sportslawnews. com/archive/history/-SpencerHaywoodcase.html.

49. *University of Tennessee Basketball Media Guide* (1969, 1970, 1971, 1972, 1973, 1974, 1975, 1976).

50. *Knoxville News-Sentinel,* April 5, 1989; *Nashville Tennessean,* April 4, 1989; *Nashville Banner,* April 5, 1989; *Chattanooga Times,* April 5, 1989; *Knoxville Journal,* April 6, 26, 27, May 26, 1989; *El Paso Times,* April 10, 11, 1989; Wade Houston, telephone interview by author, December 8, 2009. UT coaches worried that the country club incident might adversely affect their recruitment of black athletes.

51. Samuel Proctor and Wright Langley, *Gator History: A Pictorial History of the University of Florida* (Gainesville: South Star Publishing, 1986), 18–25, 39, 47–48; David T. Bruce, "The Desegregation of Intercollegiate Athletics in the State of Florida" (honors thesis, University of South Florida, 1996), 29–30, 34; Wallenstein, "Black Southerners and Non-black Universities," 137–39.

52. *University of Florida Football Media Guide* (1993); *New York Times,* April 13, 1963, 14; Norman Sloan, with Larry Guest, *Confessions of a Coach* (Nashville: Rutledge Hill, 1991), 143–44; Bruce, "Desegregation of Intercollegiate Athletics," 31–32.

53. After a game against LSU in Baton Rouge, a group of hostile white men forced Steve Williams and several white UF teammates to flee a local café without being served. Mandell Glicksberg to Willard F. Gray, October 1, 1969, David Mathews Papers, William Stanley Hoole Special Collections, University of Alabama Library; Bruce, "Desegregation of Intercollegiate Athletics," 39–43; Betty Stewart-Dowdell and Kevin M. McCarthy, *African Americans at the University of Florida* (Gainesville: B. J. Stewart-Dowdell, 2003), 63–65; Jacobs, *Across the Line,* 311–15.

54. Bruce, "Desegregation of Intercollegiate Athletics," 50–75.

55. Carroll Joseph Dugas, "The Dismantling of de jure Segregation in Louisiana, 1954–1974" (Ph.D. diss., Louisiana State University, 1989), 140–56; *Kansas City Call,* November 10, 1950; *Baton Rouge State Times,* June 9, 1964; Minutes, Board of Supervisors Meeting, April 7, 1956, Louisiana Collection; Adam Fairclough, *Race and Democracy: The Civil Rights Struggle in Louisiana, 1915–1972* (Athens: University of Georgia Press, 1995), 165–66, 219; Michael G. Wade, "Four Who Would: *Constantine*

v. Southwestern Louisiana Institute (1954) and the Desegregation of Louisiana's State Colleges," in *Higher Education and the Civil Rights Movement: White Supremacy, Black Southerners, and College Campuses,* edited by Peter Wallenstein (Gainesville: University Press of Florida, 2008), 60–91.

56. *Southeastern Conference Basketball Media Guide* (1991).

57. Louisiana State University *Daily Reveille,* February 16, 1971.

58. Ibid., February 10, 16, 17, 1971, February 22, 2005; *USA Today,* March 31, 2006; *Southeastern Conference Basketball Media Guide* (1991); Jacobs, *Across the Line,* 269–89.

59. *New York Times,* December 31, 1956, 13; *Jackson Clarion-Ledger,* December 31, 1956, January 1, 1957; *Atlanta Constitution,* December 31, 1956; *New York Post,* March 13, 2001.

60. *Atlanta Daily World,* March 6, 1957; *New Orleans Times-Picayune,* March 6, 1960.

61. University of Mississippi *Daily Mississippian,* September 9, November 18, 1970, September 20, 1991; *University of Mississippi Basketball Media Guide* (1971, 1972, 1973, 1974, 1975, 1976); *El Paso Times,* March 31, 1992.

62. CBS SportsLine.com, March 15, 2001; *Los Angeles Times,* March 16, 2001; *New York Post,* March 13, 2001.

63. In the fall of 1906 a small group of MSU undergraduates formed an unauthorized school basketball team. After they lost their first game to the nearby Columbus Athletic Club by 41–10, they became demoralized and disbanded. John K. Bettersworth, *People's University: The Centennial History of Mississippi State* (Jackson: University Press of Mississippi, 1980), 4–8, 113; Jacobs, *Across the Line,* 291–309; *Mississippi State University Basketball Media Guide* (2004); Henderson, "1963 Mississippi State University Basketball Controversy," 835; Robert Hartley, interview by author, Starkville, Miss., August 15, 1989.

64. *Jackson Daily News,* December 29, 31, 1956; *Jackson Clarion Ledger,* December 30, 1956, January 1, 1957; *Lexington Herald,* December 30, 1956, March 8, 1963; *Mississippi State University Basketball Media Guide* (2004); Hartley interview.

65. *Memphis Commercial Appeal,* March 1, 1959; *Mississippi State Alumnus,* March 1959; Henderson, "1963 Mississippi State University Basketball Controversy," 832, 837–38.

66. Mississippi State University *Reflector,* February 28, 1961, March 1, 8, 15, 1962; *Lexington Herald,* February 7, 1963; Henderson, "1963 Mississippi State University Basketball Controversy," 831.

67. Mississippi State University *Reflector,* February 28, March 9, 14, 1963; Colvard, *Mixed Emotions,* 58–65, 76–76; Hartley interview.

68. Colvard, *Mixed Emotions,* 73–81; Mississippi State University *Reflector,* March 7, 1963; *Jackson Clarion-Ledger,* March 6, 1963; *Meredian Star,* quoted in the University of Kentucky *Kentucky Kernel,* March 7, 1963; Henderson, "1963 Mississippi State University Basketball Controversy," 840–44; miscellaneous letters, postcards, and telegrams to President Dean W. Colvard, Colvard Presidential Papers, Department of Archives, Mitchell Memorial Library, Mississippi State University.

69. Colvard, *Mixed Emotions,* 82–87, 158–66; *New York Times,* March 11, 1963, 5; Hartley interview.

70. *Memphis Commercial Appeal,* March 15, 1963; Colvard, *Mixed Emotions,* 93, 178–79; *New York Times,* March 15, 1963, 15; *Jackson Clarion-Ledger,* March 13, 1988; Henderson, "1963 Mississippi State University Basketball Controversy," 850–51.

71. Wolff, "Ghosts of Mississippi," 70–71; Leland Mitchell, telephone interview by author, August 15, 1989.

72. *Rebel Underground,* undated clipping; *Memphis Commercial Appeal,* undated clippings, Department of Archives, Mitchell Memorial Library, Mississippi State University; *Jackson Clarion-Ledger,* March 23, 1963.

73. Colvard, *Mixed Emotions,* 109–27, 131, 137; Bettersworth, *People's University,* 350–51, 393.

74. *Mississippi State University Basketball Media Guide* (1973, 2004); *Southeastern Conference Basketball Media Guide* (1990–91); Colvard, *Mixed Emotions,* 135.

Chapter 9. The "Final Citadel of Segregation"

1. Despite the promises of a friendly welcome in Birmingham, several USC players prudently smuggled several knives and pistols into their suitcases for additional protection if needed. University of Alabama *Crimson-White,* September 14, October 19, 1970; *Atlanta Journal,* September 14, 1970; Alfred Van Hoose, telephone interview by author, September 15, 1990; *New York Times,* December 23, 1989; Keith Dunnavant, *Coach: The Life of Paul "Bear" Bryant* (New York: Simon and Schuster, 1996), 247–57, 305; Allen Barra, *The Last Coach: A Life of Paul "Bear" Bryant* (New York: W. W. Norton, 2005), 366–70; *Anniston Star,* December 22, 1991; "Run for Respect" (reprint), *Atlanta Constitution,* September 7–14, 1986. See also Dan Yaeger, with Sam Cunningham and John Papadakis, *The Turning of the Tide: How One Game Changed the South* (New York: Center Street, 2006).

2. Joan Paul, Richard V. McGhee, and Helen Fant, "The Arrival and Ascendance of Black Athletes in the Southeastern Conference, 1966–1980," *Phylon* 45 (1984): 290.

3. The phrase comes from an article by Sam Heys in the *Atlanta Constitution,* January 12, 1988.

4. University of Kentucky *Kentucky Kernel,* March 27, April 7, 1964; University of Texas *Daily Texan,* December 15, 1964, February 11, 1965; *New York Times,* April 9, 1965, 16; December 20, 1965, 56.

5. *Lexington Herald,* December 20, 23, 1965; *New York Times,* December 20, 1965, 56; Mrs. William Northington to Edward T. Breathitt, December 22, 27, 1965; Mrs. Edwin I. Baer to Breathitt, December 21, 1965, John W. Oswald Papers, King Library, University of Kentucky.

6. *University of Kentucky Football Media Guide* (1967, 1968); University of Kentucky *Kentucky Kernel,* September 5, 1967.

7. Two weeks after Page's accident, freshman football player Cecil New, who was white, also suffered a broken neck in a scrimmage, but his injury was not life threatening. University of Kentucky *Kentucky Kernel,* October 29, 1964, September 8, 11, 13,

1967; "Run for Respect," 2; A. M. Coleman to Robert A. Page, October 3, 1967, copy in Oswald Papers.

8. University of Kentucky *Kentucky Kernel,* October 2–4, 1967; "Run for Respect," 2.

9. University of Kentucky *Kentucky Kernel,* October 23, 24, 1967; "Run for Respect," 2; *Houston Informer,* June 15, 1968.

10. University of Kentucky *Kentucky Kernel,* February 18, 1971; "Run for Respect," 2.

11. University of Kentucky *Kentucky Kernel,* February 18, 1971.

12. Boston College brought one African American reserve player to Knoxville for an October 1964 game, but he did not see action in BC's 16–14 loss. *Memphis Commercial Appeal,* February 1, 1956; University of Tennessee *Daily Beacon,* September 29, 30, October 8, 26, 27, November 4, 1965, February 10, March 29, 1966; *Knoxville Journal,* February 5, 1966; *Knoxville News-Sentinel,* April 23, 1961, February 5, 1966; Minutes, Board of Athletics Meeting, April 28, 1961, May 4, 1963, and Tom Elam to Holt, March 19, 1962, Holt Presidential Papers; Richard Pennington, *Breaking the Ice: The Racial Integration of Southwest Conference Football* (Jefferson, N.C.: McFarland, 1987), 10; Chris Cameron, e-mail to author, July 13, 2004.

13. University of Tennessee *Daily Beacon,* May 12, 1965, January 31, February 1, April 15, May 10, 1967; *Nashville Tennessean,* April 15, 1967; James Riley Montgomery, Stanley J. Folmsbee, and Lee Seifert Green, *To Foster Knowledge: A History of the University of Tennessee, 1794–1970* (Knoxville: University of Tennessee Press, 1984), 269; Earl M. Ramer to Bob Woodruff, April 28, 1967, Earl M. Ramer Papers, University Archives, University of Tennessee.

14. Holloway was a popular player with Tennessee fans, but he understood that there were limits to this support. "As long as you had that orange jersey on, you were fine," he later recalled. "Of course, after that, you were just another black man in town." *Nashville Tennessean,* September 3, 14, 1967; *Knoxville Journal,* May 22, 1989; *Washington Post,* November 25, 1972; University of Tennessee *Daily Beacon,* October 16, 1968; *Jackson Clarion-Ledger,* July 25, 2004.

15. *Nashville Tennessean,* May 29, 1971; *Knoxville Journal,* May 22, 1989.

16. Malcolm McMillan and Allen Jones, *Through the Years: Auburn from 1856* (Auburn, Ala.: Auburn University, 1977), 1–3, 7–9, 29; L. Andrew Doyle, "'The Public Is All but Intoxicated on Football': Spright Dowell and the Politics of Football at Auburn, 1920–1927," paper presented at the annual meeting of the North American Society for Sport History, Auburn, Ala., May 1996.

17. Harry M. Philpott Oral History Transcripts, University Archives, Auburn University, 28–29, 243–45, 325–26, 333; George Kennedy to Philpott, March 15, 1968, Bettie M. King to Philpott, March 20, 1968, and Charles F. Simmons to Willard F. Gray, August 15, 1969, all in Harry M. Philpott Papers, University Archives, Ralph B. Draughon Library, Auburn University; Wilford S. Bailey, interview by author, Auburn, Ala., July 28, 1990; Auburn University *Plainsman,* March 28, 1968; confidential source (on Jordan's response).

18. Auburn University *Plainsman,* January 30, 1969; *Anniston Star,* December 24, 1991; *Auburn University Football Media Guide* (1969, 1970, 1971, 1972).

19. *Anniston Star,* December 24, 1961; *Birmingham News,* October 25, 1990; James Owens, telephone interview by author, August 3, 2005; *Auburn University Football Media Guide* (1972, 1973, 1974, 1975).

20. *Anniston Star,* December 24, 1991; Sam Heys, "It's a Whole New Ball Game," *Atlanta Weekly,* February 21, 1982.

21. Paul K. Conkin, *Gone with the Ivy: A Biography of Vanderbilt University* (Knoxville: University of Tennessee Press, 1985), 80–81, 136–41, 214–17, 307–11, 430–31, 540; Vanderbilt University *Hustler,* October 22, 29, 1948, November 2, 1962.

22. George Leonard, "The Jess Neely Story," *Nashville Magazine,* 1969; "Concerned Students" to Alexander Heard, April 23, 1968; and unidentified memo, 1968, all in Chancellor's Records, Alexander Heard Papers, Jean and Alexander Heard Library, Vanderbilt University; Vanderbilt University *Hustler,* April 28, October 13, December 6, 1967, April 5, 1968, February 5, 1971.

23. Statement by Jess Neely, April 25, 1968; Confidential Memorandum, Alexander Heard to Rob Roy Purdy, August 8, 1969; Heard to Purdy, December 7, 1969; Purdy to Heard, January 23, 1970; and Heard to Riggins R. Earl Jr. and Patrick J. Gilpin, August 8, 1969, all in Chancellor's Records, Heard Papers; Minutes, Executive Committee, Board of Trust, July 29, 1969, University Archives; Vanderbilt University *Hustler,* May 3, 1968, May 2, 16, 1969; Vanderbilt University *Commodore,* 1971.

24. Conkin, *Gone with the Ivy,* 698–700; Minutes, Executive Committee, Board of Trust, July 29, 1969, January 6, 1970, University Archives; Nashville *Tennessean,* September 1, 1967; Vanderbilt University *Hustler,* January 9, February 25, September 18, 1970, February 9, 1971, January 23, 1973; *Vanderbilt University Football Media Guide* (1969, 1970, 1971, 1972, 1973, 1974, 1975, 1993).

25. John K. Bettersworth, *People's University: The Centennial History of Mississippi State* (Jackson: University Press of Mississippi, 1980), 4–8, 113.

26. Paulette Martis, e-mail to author, August 1, 2003; John Matthew Smith, e-mail to author, August 27, 2006; *New York Times,* November 5, 1946, 36; January 19, 1956, 22; *Jackson Daily News,* December 29, 1956; *Lexington Herald,* December 30, 1956; Bettersworth, *People's University,* 343–51.

27. Pennington, *Breaking the Ice,* 34–40, 46.

28. Bettersworth, *People's University,* 342–43, 432–34; *Washington Post,* November 25, 1972; Mississippi State University *Reflector,* January 26, 1973.

29. Mississippi State University *Reflector,* October 20, November 17, 1972.

30. *Washington Post,* November 25, 1972; Rocky Felker, telephone interview by author, August 5, 2003; Bettersworth, *People's University,* 434–66; *New York Times,* December 2, 2003, C19; *Jackson Clarion-Ledger,* July 25, 2004.

31. *University of Florida Football Media Guide* (1993); *New York Times,* April 13, 1963, 14.

32. *Christian Science Monitor,* February 23, 1968; David T. Bruce, "The Desegregation of Intercollegiate Athletics in the State of Florida" (honors thesis, University of South Florida, 1996), 33–37.

33. Bruce, "Desegregation of Intercollegiate Athletics," 39–41; Mandell Glicksberg to Willard F. Gray, October 1, 1969, Mathews Papers, William Stanley Hoole Special Col-

lections (hereafter WSHSC), University of Alabama Library, Tuscaloosa; Norman Sloan, with Larry Guest, *Confessions of a Coach* (Nashville: Rutledge Hill, 1991), 143–44.

34. Heys, "It's a Whole New Ball Game"; Bruce, "Desegregation of Intercollegiate Athletics," 44–48.

35. Gaffney later recalled that at a Florida road game his grandmother once hit a white spectator over the head with her purse, after the male fan yelled racial insults at him. *Washington Post,* November 25, 1972; *Jackson Clarion-Ledger,* July 25, 2004.

36. E. Culpepper Clark, *The Schoolhouse Door: Segregation's Last Stand at the University of Alabama* (New York: Oxford University Press, 1993), 21.

37. Brent Wellborn, "Coach Paul Bryant and the Integration of the University of Alabama Football Team," *Southern Historian* 18 (Spring 1997): 70–71; James B. Laseter, telegram to Bear Bryant, December 7, 1959; B. G. Robison Jr. to Frank A. Rose, December 7, 1959; Gessner T. McCorvey to Rose, December 7, 1959; Rose to M. Alston Keith, December 16, 1959; Hill Ferguson to J. Y. Brame, December 23, 1959; Harry J. Greene to John M. Gallalee, December 14, 1959; and copy of NAACP Resolution, December 19, 1959, all in Frank A. Rose Papers, WSHSC; Paul W. Bryant and John Underwood, *Bear: The Hard Life and Good Times of Alabama's Coach Bryant* (Boston: Little, Brown, 1974), 300–302; Barra, *Last Coach,* 227–29.

38. Clark, *Schoolhouse Door,* 40–113; Kurt Edward Kemper, "The Smell of the Roses and the Color of the Players: College Football and the Expansion of the Civil Rights Movement in the West," *Journal of Sport History* 31 (Fall 2004): 317–39; *Los Angeles Times,* November 19, 20, 29, 1961, and miscellaneous clippings, in possession of author; Andrew Doyle, "An Atheist in Alabama Is Someone Who Doesn't Believe in Bear Bryant: A Symbol for an Embattled South," in *The Sporting World of the Modern South,* edited by Patrick Miller (Urbana: University of Illinois Press, 2002), 247–58. For an incisive cultural study of the 1961 Rose Bowl controversy, see Kurt Kemper, *College Football and American Culture in the Cold War Era* (Urbana: University of Illinois Press, 2009).

39. Doyle, "Atheist in Alabama," 247–48, 262–67; Bryant and Underwood, *Bear,* 300–301; Dunnavant, *Coach,* 249, 252–53.

40. J. Jefferson Bennett to Paul W. Bryant, November 12, 1965, Rose Papers; Timothy J. Bryant, "Fumble II: Coach Paul 'Bear' Bryant on Trial for a Second Time," paper presented at the annual meeting of the North American Society for Sport History, London, Ontario, May 2001; Dunnavant, *Coach,* 254–55.

41. Bryant, "Fumble II"; Willard F. Gray to David Mathews, August 19, 1968; Charles J. Thornton to Eddie Mullins, August 14, 1968, David Mathews Papers, WSHSC; University of Alabama *Crimson-White,* October 27, November 10, 1969; *Birmingham Post-Herald,* July 23, 1969; unidentified clipping in scrapbook, Office of Sports Information, University of Alabama; Yaeger, *Turning of the Tide,* 62–64; *Anniston Star,* December 22, 23, 1991.

42. Bryant and Underwood, *Bear,* 303; Dunnavant, *Coach,* 255; *Anniston Star,* December 22, 23, 1991; Bruce Graham, "Jackson Got 'Em with Thunder," *'Bama,* October 1983, 25; Bryant, "Fumble II."

43. *Des Moines Register,* September 13, 1970, *Arkansas Gazette* (Little Rock), September 15, 1970, undated clippings, all in scrapbook, Office of Sports Information, University of Alabama; Dunnavant, *Coach,* 256–57.

44. Bryant and Underwood, *Bear,* 303–4; Dunnavant, *Coach,* 257–58; *Anniston Star,* December 23, 1991; *Los Angeles Herald-Examiner,* September 7, 1971; *Alabama Journal* (Montgomery), n.d.; *Nashville Banner,* n.d.; and miscellaneous unidentified clippings, in scrapbook, Office of Sports Information, University of Alabama.

45. Bryant and Underwood, *Bear,* 303; Dunnavant, *Coach,* 257–58; *University of Alabama Football Media Guide* (1972, 1973, 1974). See also John David Briley, *Career in Crisis: Paul "Bear" Bryant and the 1971 Season of Change* (Macon: Mercer University Press, 2006).

46. Paul, McGhee, and Fant, "Arrival and Ascendance of Black Athletes," 287–89; Barra, *Last Coach,* 378–79.

47. *Southeastern Conference Football Media Guide* (1989).

48. Minutes, Board of Supervisors Meetings, February 18, April 7, May 28, 1956, Louisiana Collection, Hill Memorial Library, Louisiana State University. For a detailed account of LSU's struggle with segregationists over athletic policy, see Kemper, *College Football and American Culture,* 80–115.

49. Act no. 579, copy in possession of author; *Baton Rouge Morning Advocate,* July 6, 16, 1956; LSU *Daily Reveille,* September 13, 1956; *New Orleans Times-Picayune,* July 14, 1956; *Baton Rouge State Times,* December 28, 1964; Adam Fairclough, *Race and Democracy: The Civil Rights Struggle in Louisiana, 1915–1972* (Athens: University of Georgia Press, 1995), 205–6.

50. Ken Rappoport, *The Syracuse Football Story* (Huntsville, Ala.: Strode Publishers, 1975), 254–56; Pennington, *Breaking the Ice,* 72; University of Kentucky *Kentucky Kernel,* October 23, 1967; *New Orleans Times-Picayune,* January 1, 1984. In the late 1950s and early 1960s, LSU won SEC championships in baseball, golf, tennis, and track but declined to compete in NCAA playoffs in order to avoid any possible competition against black athletes.

51. LSU *Daily Reveille,* December 8, 1970, March 18, September 28, October 13, 1971; January 21, 1972; *Baton Rouge State Times,* April 27, 1968; miscellaneous clippings, vertical file, Louisiana Collection.

52. LSU *Daily Reveille,* February 16, 1971; Lora Hinton, interview by Mary Hebert, September 1, 1993, T. Harry Williams Center for Oral History, Louisiana State University.

53. LSU *Daily Reveille,* March 18, 1971; *New Orleans States-Item,* August 12, 1971; Hinton interview; *LSU Football Media Guide* (1975).

54. Kevin P. Thornton, "Symbolism at Ole Miss and *The Crisis* of Southern Identity," *South Atlantic Quarterly* 86 (Summer 1987): 254–59; Nadine Cohodas, *The Band Played Dixie: Race and the Liberal Conscience at Ole Miss* (New York: Free Press, 1997), 9–12, 20–21, 34, 41, 57–87; University of Mississippi *Mississippian,* November 23, 1929, November 17, 1967; *Oxford Eagle,* October 15, 1953; James W. Silver, *Mississippi: The Closed Society* (New York: Harcourt, Brace, and World), 119–20. On the Ole Miss riot, see William Doyle, *An American Insurrection: The Battle of Oxford, Mississippi, 1962* (New York: Doubleday, 2001).

55. John Vaught, *Rebel Coach: My Football Family* (Memphis: Memphis State University Press, 1971), 113–23; Cohodas, *Band Played Dixie,* 89–90.

56. In another possible violation of state policy, the University of Southern Mississippi was reportedly able to play a University of the Pacific team that included one black player by pretending that he was a native Hawaiian. Penelope Krosch, e-mail to author, October 5, 1998; *New York Times,* December 31, 1956, 13, January 19, 1956, 22; Russell J. Henderson, "The 1963 Mississippi State University Basketball Controversy and the Repeal of the Unwritten Law: 'Something More than the Game Will Be Lost,'" *Journal of Southern History* 63 (November 1997): 827–30; *Atlanta Daily World,* December 4, 7, 1955.

57. Nadine Cohodas incorrectly states that the 1964 Memphis State game was the first integrated contest held at Ole Miss. Minutes, Board of Trustees of State Institutions of Higher Learning, March 9, 21, April 18, 1963, September 17, December 17, 1964, University Archives, University of Mississippi Library, Oxford; Silver, *Mississippi: The Closed Society,* 318–19; Cohodas, *Band Played Dixie,* 114–15; David G. Sansing, *Making Haste Slowly: The Troubled History of Higher Education in Mississippi* (Jackson: University Press of Mississippi, 1990), 198–200.

58. *New York Times,* December 20, 1964, sec. 5, p. 1; Silver, *Mississippi: The Closed Society,* 321; Pennington, *Breaking the Ice,* 37–42.

59. Pennington, *Breaking the Ice,* 46–47; *Houston Informer,* September 17, 1966; University of Mississippi *Daily Mississippian,* October 24, 26, 30, 1967, May 6, 7, 1969, March 6, 1970; *Jackson Daily News,* September 17, 1970.

60. The BSU newsletter used a Confederate flag on its cover, but with a raised black fist superimposed on top of the flag. University of Mississippi *Daily Mississippian,* March 27, May 9, 1969, February 13, March 6, 9, 19, September 25, 1970; Cohodas, *Band Played Dixie,* 135, 146, 151, 154; Anthony W. James, "A Demand for Racial Equality: The 1970 Black Student Protest at the University of Mississippi," *Journal of Mississippi History* 57 (1995): 97–120.

61. In February 1970 the UM student newspaper pointed out that historically black Jackson State College reportedly had twenty-two former football players competing in the National Football League, more than either Ole Miss or Mississippi State. Cohodas, *Band Played Dixie,* 168–70; University of Southern Mississippi *Student Printz,* October 20, 1970; University of Mississippi *Daily Mississippian,* February 5, October 19, 20, 21, November 18, 1970, April 23, October 15, 1971; *El Paso Times,* December 11, 1988; John W. Cox and Gregg Bennett, *Rock Solid: Southern Miss Football* (Jackson: University Press of Mississippi, 2004), 129–46.

62. University of Mississippi *Daily Mississippian,* October 21, November 5, 1970, January 27, April 23, 1971, February 9, 1972; *Memphis Commercial Appeal,* October 26, 1972, November 12, 1975.

63. Warner Alford, interview by author, Oxford, Miss., March 24, 1994; Ben Williams and James Reed Files, Department of Intercollegiate Athletics, University of Mississippi; Cohodas, *Band Played Dixie,* 170–72; *Memphis Commercial Appeal,* October 26, 1972; University of Mississippi *Daily Mississippian,* September 19, 22, 25, 1972.

64. *Ole Miss 1976* (Oxford: University of Mississippi, 1976); Cohodas, *Band Played Dixie,* 185–86.

65. *University of Mississippi Football Media Guide* (1974, 1975, 1976, 1993); *Memphis Commercial Appeal,* February 11, 1975.

66. Cohodas, *Band Played Dixie*, 199–203, 213–20, 251–53; Thornton, "Symbolism at Ole Miss," 265–66; unidentified newspaper clipping, June 3, 1980, in "Athletics," vertical file, University of Mississippi Library; William Nack, "Look Away, Dixie Land," *Sports Illustrated*, November 3, 1997, 114; *Oxford Eagle*, April 26, 1993.

67. Thomas G. Dyer, *The University of Georgia: A Bicentennial History, 1785–1985* (Athens: University of Georgia Press, 1985), 165, 173, 185, 246, 285; Charles H. Martin, "Racial Change and 'Big-Time' College Football in Georgia: The Age of Segregation, 1892–1957," *Georgia Historical Quarterly* 80 (Fall 1996): 549–62.

68. *New Orleans Louisiana Weekly*, April 23, 1966; Dyer, *University of Georgia*, 334; University of Georgia *Red and Black*, January 20, 1966, February 4, 1969; *Athens Daily News*, October 3, 1991.

69. University of Georgia *Red and Black*, April 28, 1966, November 12, 1968, January 23, March 27, April 1, 1969.

70. University of Georgia *Red and Black*, June 24, 1969, February 24, 1970; *Athens Banner-Herald*, December 14, 1970; *Athens Daily News*, October 3, 1991; *University of Georgia Football Media Guide* (1971, 1972, 1973, 1974, 1975, 1976).

71. Jeff Prugh, *Herschel Walker: From the Georgia Backwoods and the Heisman Trophy to the Pros* (New York: Random House, 1983), 59–68, 76, 100–102; Loran Smith and Lewis Grizzard, *Glory! Glory! Georgia's 1980 Championship Season* (Atlanta: Peachtree Publishers, 1981), 69–75; "Run for Respect," 5; *University of Georgia Football Media Guide* (1993), 166.

72. Prugh, *Herschel Walker*, 114–26; Smith and Grizzard, *Glory! Glory!* ix.

73. Prugh, *Herschel Walker*, 106–22; "Run for Respect," 5.

Conclusion

1. *Atlanta Daily World*, January 1, 1957.

2. Herbert Blumer, "The Future of the Color Line," in *The South in Continuity and Change*, edited by John C. McKinney and Edgar T. Thompson (Durham: Duke University Press, 1965), 323.

3. *Meredian Star*, quoted in University of Kentucky *Kentucky Kernel*, March 7, 1963.

4. Texas Western College *Prospector*, April 16, 1955.

5. Nadine Cohodas, *The Band Played Dixie: Race and the Liberal Conscience at Ole Miss* (New York: Free Press, 1997), 217.

6. On the complex reaction of white southerners to racial integration, see Jason Sokol, *There Goes My Everything: White Southerners in the Age of Civil Rights, 1945–1975* (New York: Random House, 2006).

7. William Warren Rogers et al., *Alabama: The History of a Deep South State* (Tuscaloosa: University of Alabama Press, 1994), 539; *Oakland Tribune*, December 1941, included in Ralph Shaffer, e-mail to author, January 6, 2008; Norman Sloan, with Larry Guest, *Confessions of a Coach* (Nashville: Rutledge Hill, 1991), 137; James Webster, telephone interview by author, November 29, 1994.

8. Barry Jacobs, *Across the Line: Profiles in Basketball Courage—Tales of the First Black Players in the ACC and the SEC* (Guilford, Conn.: Lyons Press, 2008), 131–34, 277, 283.

9. In 1968 Grambling recruited its first white player, quarterback James Gregory, who was known as the "White Tiger" and became the subject of a 1981 movie. Tuskegee College suited up its first white football player in 1969. O. K. Davis, *Grambling's Gridiron Glory: Eddie Robinson and the Tigers' Success Story* (Ruston, La.: M & M Printing, 1983), 7–9, 22, 39, 59–61; "Run for Respect" (reprint), *Atlanta Constitution,* September 7–14, 1986, 6; John Matthew Smith, "'Breaking the Plane': Integration and Black Protest in Michigan State University Football during the 1960s," *Michigan Historical Review* 33 (Fall 2007): 101–30.

10. *New York Times,* April 21, 1963, 8; *Crisis* 46 (November 1939): 337; University of Texas *Daily Texan,* November 21, 1963.

11. John Egerton, *The Americanization of Dixie: The Southernization of America* (New York: Harpers Magazine Press, 1974), 176–78; Wilford S. Bailey, interview by author, Auburn, Ala., July 28, 1990.

12. Patrick B. Miller, "Muscular Assimilationism: Sport and the Paradoxes of Racial Reform," in *Race and Sport: The Struggle for Equality On and Off the Field,* edited by Charles K. Ross (Jackson: University Press of Mississippi, 2004), 174.

Sources

For the convenience of the reader, I have provided in each chapter's notes a full bibliographical citation at the first reference to each source used in that particular chapter. Some of the more important resources that I have relied on for this project merit further acknowledgment, however. Presidential and other administrative papers in university archives were extremely valuable to my research. Among those that proved especially fruitful were the various collections of the Frank P. Graham Papers in Wilson Library, University of North Carolina; the C. M. Snelling Papers in Hargrett Rare Book and Manuscript Library, University of Georgia; the Frank G. Dickey Papers and John W. Oswald Papers in King Library, University of Kentucky; the Alexander Heard Papers, Jean and Alexander Heard Library, Vanderbilt Library; and the Harry M. Philpott Papers and Harry M. Philpott Oral History Transcripts, University Archives, Ralph B. Draughon Library, Auburn University.

Student newspapers and black-oriented newspapers served as a rich and indispensable resource as well. Among those that I used extensively were the University of Kentucky *Kentucky Kernel,* the University of Georgia *Red and Black,* the University of Texas *Daily Texan,* the *Pittsburgh Courier,* the *Atlanta Daily World,* and the *Houston Informer.* The *New York Times* was, of course, an exceptionally useful aid in identifying obscure racial incidents in sports over the decades. Media guides produced annually by universities about their own athletic teams are a treasure trove of information about team and individual records, yearly schedules, players' and coaches' backgrounds, statistical data, and various bits of athletic lore. I have mostly used the older printed versions, but all Division I schools now post online the media guides for their most recent seasons, as a service to journalists, fans, and researchers.

Interviews with players, coaches, administrators, and journalists were essential to the research for this volume. I was fortunate enough to conduct formal interviews with the following individuals: Warner Alford, Wilford S. Bailey, Jack Bass, Charles T. Brown, Charles Davis, John Guthrie, Robert Hartley, Alfred Heartley, Wade Houston, Ronald W. Hyatt, C. M. Newton, Russell Rice, Nevil Shed, Roy Skinner, and D. Joe Williams. In addition, I conducted telephone interviews with: Joe Atkins, Charles T. Brown, James Cash, Clyde E. Chesney, Claudius B. Claiborne, Richard T. Culberson, Bill Dooley, Rocky Felker, Marvin Francis, Alvis Glidewell, Bobby Grier, Maurice Harris, Alexander Heard, Darryl Hill, Irwin R. Holmes, Wade Houston, Billy Jones, Howard Kleinberg, Lenny Lyles, Marcus Martin, Felix R. McKnight, Leland Mitchell, James Owens, Tommy Reaux, Alfred Van Hoose, Morrison Warren, James Webster, J. M. Whitaker, and Sam Williams. To supplement my own interviews I made frequent use of published and archived oral history interviews conducted by other researchers.

Institutional histories, especially those focusing on the desegregation of higher education, were another important type of source. Among the ones that I found especially useful are: Paul Conklin, *Gone with the Ivy: A Biography of Vanderbilt University* (Knoxville: University of Tennessee Press, 1985); Thomas G. Dyer, *The University of Georgia: A Bicentennial History, 1785–1985* (Athens: University of Georgia Press, 1985); Melissa Kean, *Desegregating Private Higher Education in the South: Duke, Emory, Rice, Tulane, and Vanderbilt* (Baton Rouge: Louisiana State University Press, 2008); and Amilcar Shabazz, *Advancing Democracy: African Americans and the Struggle for Access and Equity in Higher Education in Texas* (Chapel Hill: University of North Carolina Press, 2004). Also quite valuable were specialized studies that examine specific athletic programs or individual coaches, especially the following: Allen Barra, *The Last Coach: A Life of Paul "Bear" Bryant* (New York: W. W. Norton, 2005); Bill Beezley, *The Wolfpack: Intercollegiate Athletics at North Carolina State University* (Raleigh: North Carolina State University, 1976); John Behee, *Hail to the Victors!* (Ann Arbor: Ulrich's Books, 1974); Nadine Cohodas, *The Band Played Dixie: Race and the Liberal Conscience at Ole Miss* (New York: Free Press, 1997); Robin Lester, *Stagg's University: The Rise, Decline, and Fall of Big-Time Football at Chicago* (Urbana: University of Illinois Press, 1995); Katherine Lopez, *Cougars of Any Color: The Integration of University of Houston Athletics, 1964–1968* (Jefferson, N.C.: McFarland, 2008); and Bert Nelli and Steve Nelli, *The Winning Tradition: A History of Kentucky Wildcat Basketball*, 2nd ed. (Lexington: University Press of Kentucky, 1998).

General surveys and interpretive studies of sport history that informed my thinking (but for which their authors should be held blameless) include: Pamela Grundy, *Learning to Win: Sports, Education, and Social Change in Twentieth-Century North Carolina* (Chapel Hill: University of North Carolina Press, 2001);

Michael Oriard, *King Football: Sport and Spectacle in the Golden Age of Radio and Newsreels, Movies, and Magazines, the Weekly and the Daily Press* (Chapel Hill: University of North Carolina Press, 2001); Oriard, *Reading Football: How the Popular Press Created an American Spectacle* (Chapel Hill: University of North Carolina Press, 1993); Benjamin G. Rader, *American Sports: From the Age of Folk Games to the Age of Televised Sports,* 6th ed. (Upper Saddle River, N.J.: Pearson, 2009); Ronald A. Smith, *Sports and Freedom: The Rise of Big-Time College Athletics* (New York: Oxford University Press, 1988); and John Sayle Watterson, *College Football: History, Spectacle, Controversy* (Baltimore: Johns Hopkins University Press, 2000).

The historical literature on African Americans and sports continues to grow. I relied heavily on the following works: Bruce Adelson, *Brushing Back Jim Crow: The Integration of Minor-League Baseball in the American South* (Charlottesville: University Press of Virginia, 1999); Ocania Chalk, *Black College Sport* (New York: Dodd, Mead, 1976); Nelson George, *Elevating the Game: Black Men and Basketball* (New York: Harper Collins, 1992); Barry Jacobs, *Across the Line: Profiles in Basketball Courage—Tales of the First Black Players in the ACC and the SEC* (Guilford, Conn.: Lyons Press, 2008); Patrick B. Miller, "Muscular Assimilationism: Sport and the Paradoxes of Racial Reform," in *Race and Sport: The Struggle for Equality On and Off the Field,* edited by Charles K. Ross (Jackson: University Press of Mississippi, 2004); Richard Pennington, *Breaking the Ice: The Racial Integration of Southwest Conference Football* (Jefferson, N.C.: McFarland, 1987); Charles K. Ross, *Outside the Lines: African Americans and the Integration of the National Football League* (New York: New York University Press, 1999); and A. S. "Doc" Young, *Negro Firsts in Sports* (Chicago: Johnson Publishing, 1963). In addition, Arthur R. Ashe Jr., *A Hard Road to Glory: A History of the African-American Athlete,* 3 vols. (New York: Warner Books, 1988), still remains a valuable resource, but it must be used carefully since it contains many factual errors.

Index

Phillips, Mike, 236
Phillips, O. A. "Bum," 105
Philpott, Harry M., 226, 264
Pickens, Larry, 39–40
Pierce, Samuel Jr., 50–51, 316n45
Pittman, Jim, 200
Pitts, Orville, 85–86
Pittsburgh Courier, 24, 26, 33, 45
Plessy v. Ferguson, 12, 78
Pollard, Fritz, 12, 22, 80, 309n23
Pollard, John H., 17
Poole, Robert F., 145
Pope, Clarence, 290
Prairie View Interscholastic League, 188, 191–92
Princeton University, 3, 11, 59
private vs. public universities, 297–98
professional team sports, 57–58. *See also leagues and conferences*
Prospector, 100
public school desegregation, 88
public vs. private universities, 297–98

Rabenhorst, Harry, 244
racial exclusion. *See* gentleman's agreement; Jim Crow code
racial quotas on teams, 151–52, 163, 301
racial stereotypes, 302–3
Rader, Benjamin, 19, 70
radio, 19
Rainach, William, 84
Raney, Dallas P. "Pete," 213
Ransom, Samuel L., 68–69
Ray, John, 261
Ray, Joseph, 105, 110, 116, 117
Reaux, Tommy, 198
Rebel Underground, 252, 253
Red and Black, (University of Georgia), 26
Reed, Dwight, 28
Reed, James, 286–87
Reeves, Marion Francis, 145–46
regional colleges, 92–93
religious affiliation, 297–98
Rice, Grantland, 19–20
Rice, William Marsh, 202

Rice University, 202–4
Richardson, Jon, 213
Richardson, Nolan, 109, 110
Richmond Times-Dispatch, xvi, 1, 23–24
Riddle, John, 24–25
Rightmire, George A., 29
Rivers, Morris, 168
Roberts, Bobby, 171
Roberts, Cornelius, 335n8
Roberts, M. M., 251
Robertson, Oscar, 74, 154, 155, 156
Robeson, Paul, 10, 17–18, 22, 69
Robey, Rick, 236
Robinson, Eddie, 302
Robinson, Harold, 76
Robinson, Jackie, 13, 38, 58, 154
Robinson, Larry, 240
Robinson, Theotis Jr., 237
Robiskie, Terry, 281
Roche, John, 165, 173
Rockne, Knute, 19
Rodgers, Guy, 156
Rodney, Lester, 42
Rogers, George, 142, 300
Rollins, Wayne "Tree," 171–72
Roosevelt, Eleanor, 47
Roosevelt, Theodore, 3, 6
Rose, Frank, 228
Rose, Glen, 212–13
Rose Bowl, 20, 36, 274
Rosemond, Ken, 230
Rosenbluth, Lenny, 150
Rowe, Thad, 142
Royal, Darrell, 204, 206, 207–8, 209–10
Rupp, Adolph, 90, 114, 115, 218, 231–35
Russell, Bill, 79, 155–56
Rutgers University, 3, 17–18, 69

Sadler, M. E., 189, 200
Sam Houston State University, 188
Sampson, Ralph, 151, 177–78, 178, 300
San Angelo Junior College, 92–93
Sanford, G. Foster, 18
Santa Barbara State College, 39–40
Santa Fe New Mexican, 101

CHARLES H. MARTIN is an associate professor of history at the University of Texas at El Paso and the author of *The Angelo Herndon Case and Southern Justice*.

SPORT AND SOCIETY

Saying It's So: A Cultural History of the Black Sox Scandal   *Daniel A. Nathan*
The Nazi Olympics: Sport, Politics, and Appeasement in the 1930s   *Edited by*
   Arnd Krüger and William Murray
The Unlevel Playing Field: A Documentary History of the African American
   Experience in Sport   *David K. Wiggins and Patrick B. Miller*
Sports in Zion: Mormon Recreation, 1890–1940   *Richard Ian Kimball*
Sweet William: The Life of Billy Conn   *Andrew O'Toole*
Sports in Chicago   *Edited by Elliot J. Gorn*
The Chicago Sports Reader   *Edited by Steven A. Riess and Gerald R. Gems*
College Football and American Culture in the Cold War Era   *Kurt Edward Kemper*
The End of Amateurism in American Track and Field   *Joseph M. Turrini*
Benching Jim Crow: The Rise and Fall of the Color Line in Southern College Sports,
   1890–1980   *Charles H. Martin*

REPRINT EDITIONS

The Nazi Olympics   *Richard D. Mandell*
Sports in the Western World (2d ed.)   *William J. Baker*
Jesse Owens: An American Life   *William J. Baker*

The University of Illinois Press
is a founding member of the
Association of American University Presses.

University of Illinois Press
1325 South Oak Street
Champaign, IL 61820-6903
www.press.uillinois.edu